杨振之　罗宇华 / 主编

# The New Trend of the Tourism Industry Development in China and Spain

Proceedings of the 7th International Conference on Tourism and Hospitality between China and Spain (ICTCHS2017)

# 中国与西班牙旅游业发展新趋势

2017第七届中国—西班牙旅游与接待国际会议（ICTCHS2017）论文集

Sichuan University Press
四川大学出版社

责任编辑:余　芳
责任校对:周　洁
封面设计:阿　林
责任印制:王　炜

**图书在版编目(CIP)数据**

中国与西班牙旅游业发展新趋势：2017 第七届中国—西班牙旅游与接待国际会议（ICTCHS2017）论文集 / 杨振之，罗宇华主编. —成都：四川大学出版社，2017.12

ISBN 978-7-5690-1515-7

Ⅰ.①中…　Ⅱ.①杨…　②罗…　Ⅲ.①旅游业发展-中国-国际会议-文集②旅游业发展-西班牙-国际会议-文集　Ⅳ.①F592.3-53②F595.513-53

中国版本图书馆 CIP 数据核字（2017）第 319614 号

书名　**中国与西班牙旅游业发展新趋势**
——2017 第七届中国—西班牙旅游与接待国际会议(ICTCHS2017)论文集
**Zhongguo yu Xibanya Lüyouye Fazhan Xinqushi**
**—2017 Diqijie Zhongguo—Xibanya Lüyou yu Jiedai Guoji Huiyi(ICTCHS2017)Lunwenji**

主　　编　杨振之　罗宇华
出　　版　四川大学出版社
地　　址　成都市一环路南一段 24 号 (610065)
发　　行　四川大学出版社
书　　号　ISBN 978-7-5690-1515-7
印　　刷　四川盛图彩色印刷有限公司
成品尺寸　185 mm×260 mm
印　　张　26.25
字　　数　834 千字
版　　次　2017 年 12 月第 1 版
印　　次　2017 年 12 月第 1 次印刷
定　　价　125.00 元

◆读者邮购本书,请与本社发行科联系。
电话:(028)85408408/(028)85401670/
(028)85408023　邮政编码:610065
◆本社图书如有印装质量问题,请
寄回出版社调换。
◆网址:http://www.scupress.net

《中国与西班牙旅游业发展新趋势
——2017第七届中国—西班牙旅游与接待国际会议（ICTCHS2017）论文集》

# 编 委 会

# Conference Committee

**Founding Chair**

Luo Yuhua, University of Balearic Islands

**Advisory Board**

Bai Changhong, dean of the College of Tourism and Service Management, Nankai University

Bao Jigang, dean of the School of Tourism Management, Sun Yat-sen University

Bartolomé Deya, dean of the Faculty of Tourism, University of the Balearic Islands

Jafar Jafari, University of Balearic Islands and University do Algarve

**Conference Chairs**

Yang Zhenzhi, professor, Tourism School, Sichuan University

Maria Concepción Garcia, dean of the Faculty of Commerce and Tourism, University Complutense

**Academic Secretary of the Conference**

Wu Chuntao, Sichuan University

María García Hernández, Universidad Complutense de Madrid

Vicente Ramos, University of Balearic Islands

**Program Committee**

Xu Hong, Nankai University

Li Zhong, Nankai University

Salvador Anton Clavé, University Rovira i Virgili, Tarragona

Bai Kai, Shanxi Normal University

Chen Zengxiang, Nankai University

Gao Jun, Shanghai Normal University

Antonio Guevara Plaza, University of Malaga

Jaume Guia, University of Girona

Li Shumin, North West University

Li Zhiyong, Sichuan University

Liang Mingzhu, Jinan University

Enric López C., EU CETT-University of Barcelona

Ma Yong, Hubei University

Ma Lin, Kunming University of Science and Technology

Ma Bo, Qingdao University

Diego Medina Muñoz, Universidad de Las Palmas de Gran Canaria

Francesc Sastre Alberti, University of Balearic Islands

Song Haiyan, The Hong Kong Polytechnic University

Sun Jiuxia, Sun Yat-sen University

Maria Tugores, University of Balearic Islands

Xie Yanjun, Dongbei University of Finance and Economics

Ye Hong, South West University of Finance and Economics

Zeng Guojun, Sun Yat-sen University

Zhang Lingyun, Beijing Union University

Zhang Hui, Beijing Jiaotong University

Zhang Meng, South West University of Finance and Economics

Zheng Yaoxing, Fujian Normal University

Zou Tongxian, Beijing International Studies University

# Part I Tourism and Sense of Place



# Part II Tourism Industry and Regional Development

## Part III Destination Image and Tourist Behavior

# PART I

# Tourism and Sense of Place

# An Empirical Study on Local Architecture Heritage Attractions' Sustainable Development from the Perspective of Eco-efficiency: A Case Study of World Culture Heritage, Fujian Earth Building Attractions

Bao Lisi[1], Yang Zhenzhi[2*]

**Abstract:** The heritage of local rural architecture is the coagulation of human farming civilization and wisdom. The Chinese nation has 7,000 years' history of farming civilization, and it is abundant in local architectural heritage, which is the important carrier of culture connotation. Eco-efficiency theory offers the effective way to value the attraction's low carbon level and its sustainability, and the essence of tourism ecological efficiency lies in the balance between tourism economic growth and the influence of tourism environment, so as to improve the sustainable development ability of tourist destination. This paper evaluates tourism's impact on environment by measuring tourists' carbon footprint from transportation, accommodation, shopping, entertainment, etc. The number of carbon footprint from transportation is the highest, totaling 531,565.158 t, accounting for 96.52% of the total carbon footprint produced by tourists. Accommodation carbon footprint is 18,376.046 t, occupying the second highest position, 3.33% of the total. The carbon footprint of scenic spot management was 710.071 t, ranking the third, accounting for 0.129% of the total. Therefore, transportation and accommodation are the key points of saving energy and reducing the carbon emission. Combining the tourism revenue, the eco-efficiency of Fujian earth building attractions shows that per ton of carbon footprint just contributes 231.7 RMB economical value. Compared with other attractions, Fujian earth buildings attractions' ecological efficiency is very low. Based on empirical study, this paper proposes the countermeasures for improving ecological efficiency.

**Keywords:** sustainable development; eco-efficiency; carbon footprint; life cycle assessment; Fujian earth building attractions

1 Sichuan University, Chengdu, China; Sichuan Tourism University, Chengdu, China.

2* Sichuan University, Chengdu, China. yzz310@163.com. (In this book, the author with a "*"mark is the corresponding author.)

## Ⅰ. Introduction

Global warming is one of the most serious environmental problems human society is facing, and the greenhouse gas represented by carbon dioxide is considered to be the important cause of climate change. A large number of carbon dioxide emissions have taken place from human activities since the Industrial Revolution. Tourism industry, as an important industry around the world, should shoulder a major responsibility for it. Tourism involves numerous industry categories, and it should be the forefront of energy conservation and emissions reduction as well as the role-model. In this case, low carbon tourism must be the trend of the tourism development, for it can represent the sustainability of this industry in most terms. Based on the terminal consumer perspective, measuring tourists' carbon footprint is operable and can more accurately reflect the tourism industry carbon emissions. The authors do the measurement from the 4 tourism elements, i.e., transportation, accommodation, shopping and entertainment. Measuring visitors' carbon footprint is one of the effective ways to value the attraction's low carbon level and its sustainability.

The heritage of local rural architecture is the coagulation of human farming civilization and wisdom. A series of protection files about the local rural architecture heritage have been issued, including "The Vernacular Architecture Heritage Charter" approved by the International Vernacular Architecture Council in Mexico in 1999, which has improved protection for vernacular architecture heritage to a new height. The charter points out: "Vernacular architecture heritage occupies an important position in human emotion and pride, and it has been recognized as the characteristics and attractive products. It is the focal point of the life and the era, as well as the social historical record. It is human beings' products, and also the creation of the era. If not enough attention can be paid for protecting vernacular architecture to keep the core of human life, it will not be able to manifest the value of the heritage of humanity. "[1]

The Chinese nation has 7,000 years' history of farming civilization, and it is abundant in local architectural heritage, which is the important carrier of culture connotation. Scenic areas with the core attraction of local architecture heritage is developing rapidly in China, becoming one of the themes and important travelling destinations of modern mass tourism. The local constructions in China which have been selected in the world heritage list include "Fujian earth building", "Anhui ancient village" and "Kaiping tower and village". In addition, "Jiangnan water town", "Guizhou Miao and Dong minority nationalities' buildings", "Sichuan Tibetan and Qiang tower and villages", "Yunnan Hani terraced fields", "Shanxi local-style dwelling houses" and other historical and cultural towns, villages and vernacular architecture heritage projects have also been included in the "World Cultural Heritage Tentative List in China".

The world culture heritage, earth building in Fujian is the typical representative of this kind in China as well as in the world. With the native building materials and smart building structure design, as well as the ecological environment and vegetation, the earth buildings are real architectures of low energy consumption and carbon dioxide emissions, for the function of insulating thermal and wetness, of regulating indoor temperature, as well as the natural lighting. The earth building attractions in fact are the settlement of earth buildings, and they should have been low carbon and ecological attractions. But what is the fact?

This paper will have an empirical study on the visitors' carbon footprint of Fujian earth building attractions from transportation, accommodation, shopping and entertainment, and simultaneously have a statistic about the economic income obtained from the tourism, so as to calculate the eco-efficiency of the attractions, based on which the author tries to put forward the countermeasures to achieve the sustainable development of the world culture heritage, Fujian earth building attractions. By searching the relative research, the author hasn't found the achievements existed.

## Ⅱ. Methodology

Tourism eco-efficiency is the concept of eco-efficiency (EE), which is a measure of Efficiency in both ecology and economy. Ecological efficiency in economics refers to the efficiency of ecological resources to meet human needs. It is the ratio of output to input. The currently accepted formula for ecological efficiency is the computational model proposed by the world council on sustainable development of industry and commerce[2]:

$$\text{Ecological efficiency}=\frac{\text{the value of a product or service}}{\text{Environment effects}}=\frac{\text{increment of a product or service}}{\text{increment of environment}} \quad (1)$$

The essence of tourism ecological efficiency lies in the balance between tourism economic growth and the influence of tourism environment, so as to improve the sustainable development ability of tourist destination[3]. From the formula above, it can be found that the value of a product or service and environment effects are the decisive factors for calculating tourism eco-efficiency. The value of tourism products and service can be attained from the statistical data offered by the local tourism bureau. As for the environment effects, this paper will use carbon footprint to evaluate based on the life cycle analysis (LCA).

Carbon footprint originated from the concept of ecological footprint, is a kind of greenhouse gas quantitative methods. The concept of carbon footprint has been recognized around the world, providing uniform quantitative indicators and units, to cope with global warming by limiting greenhouse gas emissions which causes human existence serious problems of environmental degradation. According to the fifth assessment report released by Intergovernmental Panel on Climate Change (IPCC), greenhouse gas emissions will lead to climate system's further warming, causing the possibility of irreversible influence, high temperature and more extreme events. The longer we take action, the higher the cost we will spend[4].

Life cycle assessment (LCA) aims to calculate the carbon footprint of products or service, from the cradle to the grave, so each phase of the effects on the environment are taken into account. LCA breaks the bottleneck of direct calculation, which ignores the effects caused by a large number of intermediate links and indirect data. According to the technical framework defined by ISO 14040 standard, evaluation process includes purpose and scope of LCA, inventory analysis, impact assessment and results' interpretation, as shown in Figure 1. Totally, there are four steps: the determination of the target and the scope, the life cycle inventory analysis, the life-cycle impact assessment, and the lifecycle explanation. In addition, assumptions must be set, due to actual situation and the data obtained involved in all stages, which are always flawed.

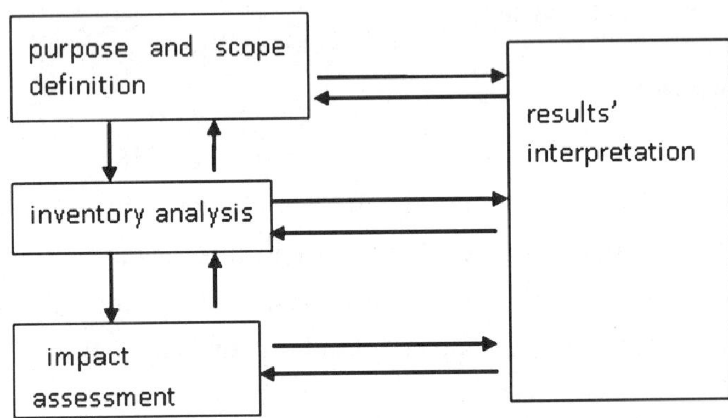


Figure 1 ISO14040 LCA Assessment Framework

Measuring the tourist destinations' carbon footprints based on LCA is the core of this paper. Sun Ruihong reconstructs the carbon dioxide emission list of tourism destinations through the hybrid life cycle assessment method in "A Study on the Innovation Design of Carbon Dioxide Emission Inventory in Tourist Destinations"[5]. And some other researchers such as Li Xiaoqin, Hou Wenliang, Yin Yuan and so on have had the relative studies. Based on all the researches above, the authors regard that the total visitors' carbon footprint can be estimated by the models below. In the formula (2), CF refers to the total amount of the carbon footprint, and it is composed of the carbon footprint produced in the phase of transportation, accommodation, sightseeing, catering, shopping, and entertainment.

$$CF=\sum (CF_{transportation}+CF_{accommodation}+CF_{sightseeing}+CF_{catering}+CF_{shopping}+CF_{entertainment}) \quad (2)$$

Aiming to the research target of this paper, Fujian earth building attractions, local and rural architectures' energy consumptions and carbon footprints should be the key, for the rural architectures are the main places where accommodation, sightseeing, catering, shopping and entertainment take place. G. P. Gerilla, K. Teknomo, and K. Hokao[6] made a comparative study on the greenhouse gases, among which carbon dioxide occupies the biggest proportion, between the traditional Japanese wood house and the modern house with the method of LCA. The domestic scholar, Qiao Yongfeng had a similar contrast research between Yaodong, Shanxi rural architecture, and modern buildings[7]. The results of the two empirical studies come to the similar conclusion: the local and rural architectures are much more energy saving and emit much less carbon dioxide than the modern buildings. On the basis of the researches above, the authors of this paper attempt to do the relative empirical study on the target of the well-known world culture heritage, Fujian earth buildings.

## Ⅲ. Data Resources and Collection of Carbon

Firstly, tourism transportation is an important part of the carbon footprint of the tourism industry, which is made up of external transportation, central transportation and internal transportation. In this study, the external traffic carbon footprint refers specifically to the carbon footprint produced by transportation from visitors' source region to the tourist destination, Xiamen. Central transportation carbon footprint refers to the carbon footprint produced from the destination, Xiamen to earth building attraction. The internal traffic carbon footprint is the carbon footprint produced by electric sightseeing vehicles for visitors in the scenic spot. Fujian earth building attractions belong to the world cultural heritage, and the cultural resources level is very high, but due to the geographical location, the earth building attractions haven't become a truly international or domestic tourist destination. Its development basically relies on the city of Xiamen. The main visitor source is from the Yangtze river delta and north China, accounting for 70% of the total population. In Xiamen, the visitors usually choose Gulang Island, South Putuo Temple, Xiamen University, Jiageng Park for sightseeing and vocation. Therefore, the problem of contribution coefficient must be taken into consideration while the external transport carbon footprint being estimated.

Secondly, visitors' accommodation carbon footprint is another important component. The attraction accommodation facilities include earth building homestay inn and the star hotels. This paper focuses on the comparison of the gap between the two accommodation facilities' carbon footprint on the phrase of operation. The carbon footprint produced in the phrase of operation mainly comes from energy consumption, such as lighting, air conditioning, elevators, and gas for cooking.

Thirdly, as for the catering service and shopping, the relative carbon footprint produced by restaurants and shopping mainly refers to the amount of energy and carbon footprints that a business owner produces by providing services. To make the data more accurate, the commercial electricity data have been provided by the local power statistics stations.

Fourthly, in terms of the carbon footprint of entertainment projects, entertainment activities are mainly composed of the performance of folk culture, including ten times music, hakka folk music and folk activities such as marriage customs show which are largely free of energy consumption, so they do not produce carbon footprint.

Fifthly, the carbon footprint from attractions' management is calculated from the data offered by the management company, mainly including the carbon footprint produced from office energy consumption, personnel commuter energy consumption, as well as the attractions' waste treatment.

## Ⅳ. Results and Interpretations

i. *Results and interpretations of visitors' carbon footprint based on LCA*

According the data of 2016, the empirical results are shown as below:

The number of carbon footprint from transportation is the highest, totaling 531,565.158 t, accounting for 96.52% of the total carbon footprint produced by tourists. Accommodation carbon footprint is 18,376.046 t, occupying the second highest position, 3.33% of the total. The carbon footprint of sightseeing was 710.071 t, ranking the third, accounting for 0.129% of the total. Catering, shopping, and entertainment produce a total of 56.406 t, or 0.01% of the total. Therefore, transportation and accommodation are the key points of low-carbon tourism.

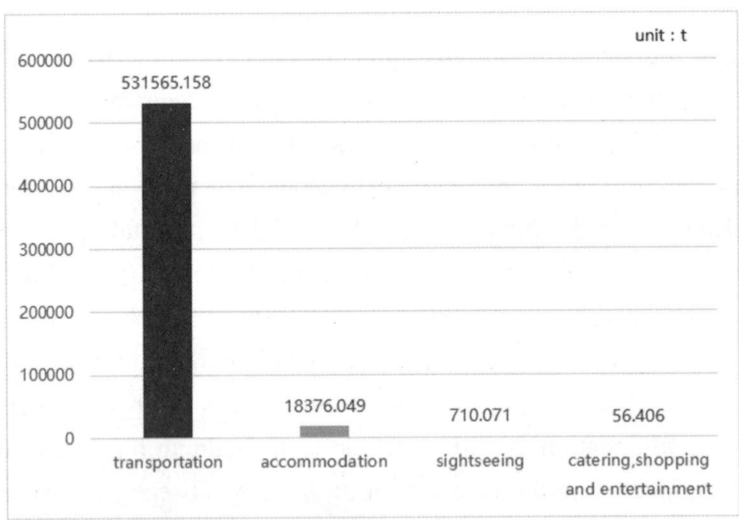


Figure 2　Distribution of Visitors' Carbon Footprints at Different Stages

In terms of the proportions of transportation carbon footprint, the one produced from the external transportation energy consumption accounts for 372,866.079 t; the carbon footprint produced from central transportation energy consumption occupies 158,697.308 t; the carbon footprint produced from internal transportation takes up 1.771 t. To dig the reason, it is not difficult to find high energy consumption transportation tool, planes contribute the biggest proportion, around 70% of the total transportation carbon footprint.

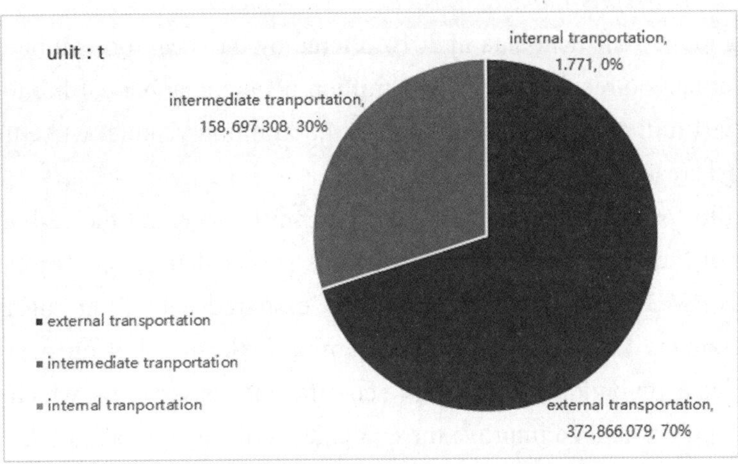


Figure 3 Distribution of Visitors' Transportation Carbon Footprints

In the aspect of accommodation, this paper not only accounts the number of visitors' carbon footprint, but also attempts to find the gap between the earth building homestay inns and star hotels. By investigating the energy consumption data from the earth building homestay inns and star hotels, it finds that the one room's carbon footprint in an earth building homestay is just 1/50 of the one in a star hotel.

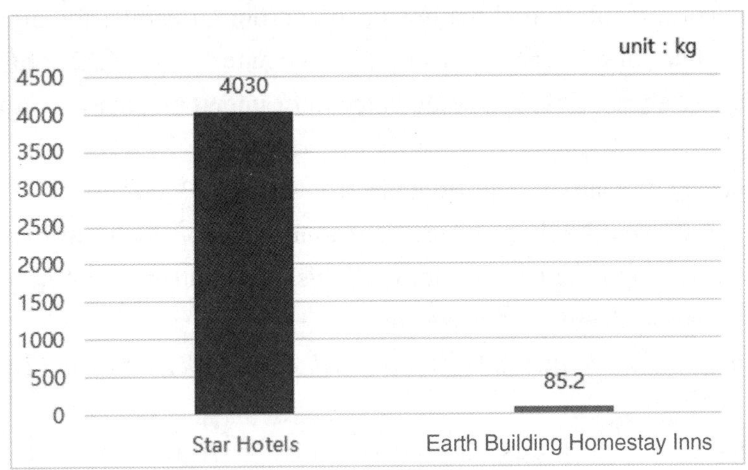


Figure 4 Contrast of Per Visitor's Carbon Footprint in Earth Building Homestay Inns and in the Star Hotels

The reason can be originated from the earth buildings' raw material, which helps the building with the function of thermal and wet insulation, so the buildings are warm in winter and cool in summer. And the earth buildings make clever and full use of the natural light by courtyards and open patio to achieve the effect of lighting and heat preservation. The ring corridors around the earth buildings have the function for air conditioning through air circulation. So electricity consumption is only used for night lighting and showers.

*ii. Results and interpretations of attractions' eco-efficiency*

According to the statistical data in 2016 offered by the local tourism bureau, Hongkeng earth building attraction received 2.361348 million people, Gaobei earth building attraction received 2.198994 million visitors, so in total of 4.56 million visitors, while tourism revenue in the two tourist areas is only 1.276 billion yuan.

According to formula (1), combining the tourism income and the carbon footprint, the eco-efficiency of Fujian earth building attractions shows that per ton of carbon footprint just contributes RMB 231.7 economical value. Compared with Kunming Expo Garden's ecological efficiency value, RMB 10,700 economical contribution per ton of carbon footprint[8], Fujian earth building attractions' eco-efficiency is very low, which is only 1/50 of the Kunming Expo Garden. To improve the ecological efficiency so as to achieve the purpose of sustainable development of Fujian earth building attractions, the countermeasures and suggestions are as follows.

## V. Improvement Countermeasures

*i. Strengthen low carbon advertising and encourage tourists to choose low-carbon travel mode*

From empirical study results of visitors' carbon footprint in Fujian earth building attractions, it is not difficult to find the highest proportion of carbon footprint comes from transportation, a total of 531,565.158 t in 2016, accounting for 96.52% of total visitors' carbon footprint. As a result, transportation is the most important path for carbon emissions' reduction.

Simultaneously, the survey questionnaire finds that 323 visitors, 51.3% of the total visitors interviewed, would like to reduce their tourist carbon footprint by choosing low-carbon transportation mode as the substitution. This questionnaire result is very consistent with western scholars such as Gossling's study.

*ii. Encourage visitors to accommodate in earth building homestay inn and reduce their carbon footprint*

According to the previous empirical study, visitors' carbon footprint from accommodation ranks the second, which is another important part to conserve the energy and reduce the carbon emissions. By investigating the energy consumption data from the earth building homestay inns and star hotels, it finds that one room's carbon footprint in an earth building homestay is just 1/50 of that in a star hotel. The low-carbon advantages of earth building homestay inns are fully demonstrated. At the same time, the questionnaire survey shows that visitors preferring earth building inns account for 70%, thus the local government should redistribute accommodation facilities by fully using existing earth buildings to meet the demand of tourists' accommodation, avoiding blind construction of modern star hotels of high energy consumption and high carbon emissions.

*iii. Increasing visitors' economic consumption and extending the stay time by excavating Hakka culture and creating tourism products of cultural experience*

Reducing visitors' carbon emission and increasing visitor's expense are the decisive factors to improve the ecologic efficiency. According to the survey, the author finds that 70% visitors choose one-day sightseeing trip, staying only 2-3 hours, with 200 yuan per capita. Except for the expense on admission tickets, consumptions on catering, shopping and entertainment are very low. The real reason for this situation can be originated from the homogeneity of tourism products, which can hardly make visitors to stay.

In fact, the earth building communities are very rich in local cultural resources which are suitable for visitors' experience, such as family culture, Confucian culture, rich Hakka folk activities, including dragon lantern dance, Hakka mountain songs, the big drum, the silk string, the trumpets, paper-cut, pottery and so on. Therefore, the cultural resources should be made full use of to increase the experience of tourists so as to make visitors to participate and experience.

*iv. Focus on eco-vacation tours based on a good ecological environment*

From the questionnaire, this paper also finds that the number of visitors who choose to avoid the smog and have ecological holiday is 129, accounting for 20.7% of the effective sample. The number of visitors who choose to avoid coldness and have ecological warm holiday is 67, taking up 10.7% of the effective sample. So 31.4% visitors choose earth build attractions for the purpose of the excellent ecological environment.

Under the background of serious smog and climate change in a large number of cities in China, Fujian earth building attractions should take good advantage of excellent climate condition and air quality to build ecological vocation tourism products, increasing the proportion of overnight tourists, extending visitors' stay time, increasing visitors' expense, so as to improve the ecological efficiency and achieve the sustainable development of the attractions.

*v. Encourage visitors to purchase the low-carbon tourism products*

According to the low carbon product preference survey, 157 visitors insist on purchasing low carbon tourism products, accounted for 24.7% of the sample. 440 visitors will choose to buy low carbon tourism products on the premise that the price difference between the ordinary products and low carbon products is not big, accounting for 69.3% of the whole sample. Overall, most visitors tend to prefer low-carbon travel products. Consequently, more low carbon tourism products should be designed for visitors to choose.

## Ⅵ. Concluding Remarks

Through this study, the author puts forward that the sustainability of tourist attractions or destinations can not only be evaluated by the impacts on environment produced by tourism, but also be evaluated by the economic contribution it brings. Consequently, the eco-efficiency theory, by balancing economic growth and tourism environment influence, is considered an effective way and method to promote the sustainable development of tourist attraction or destinations. Combining the tourism income, the eco-efficiency of Fujian earth building attractions shows that per ton of carbon footprint just contributes RMB 231.7 economical value. Compared with other attractions, Fujian earth buildings attractions' ecological efficiency is very low. Based on empirical study, this paper proposes the countermeasures for improving ecological efficiency.

Of course, this paper is not sufficient in some ways, which should be promoted in the following study. For instance, the carbon footprint data collection is so difficult, so this paper has to set up a large number of assumptions, which may affect the credibility of the findings to some extent. In the following study, LCA's each process should be more accurate to guarantee the finding accuracy, such as definition of the list, assumptions, data collections, and calculation methods.

## References

[1] Shan Jixiang. The concept and method of the preservation of local construction heritage [J]. *Urban Planning*, 2008 (12): 33-39.

[2] Zhao Liming. Research on the eco-efficiency of low carbon tourism [D]. Tianjing: Tianjing University, 2013.

[3] Gossling S, Peeters P, Ceron J-P, Dubois G, Patterson T, Richardson R B. The eco-efficiency of tourism [J]. *Ecological Economics*, 2005 (54): 417-434.

[4] The fifth IPCC report [R]. http://www.ipcc.ch/report/ar5/wg2/.

[5] Sun Ruihong. A study on the innovation design of carbon dioxide emission inventory in tourist destinations [J]. *China's Population, Resources and Environment*, 2016(5): 289-292.

[6] Gerilla G P, Tecnimo K, Hokao. An environmental assessment of wood and steel reinforce concrete housing construction[J]. *Building and Environment*, 2007(42): 2778-2784.

[7] Qiao Yongfeng. Analysis and evaluation between the traditional residential house based on the LCA[D]. Xi'an: Xi'an Architectural Science and Technology University, 2006.

[8] Li Peng. *Ecological Efficiency of Tourism*[M]. Beijing: Science Press, 2013: 147.

# A Research on the Sustainable Development of Rural Tourism Based on FPPSG: A Case Study of Chongdugou Scenic Spot of Henan Province

He Tao[1], Li Jiaxin[2], Li Jiao[3]

**Abstract:** In order to realize the sustainable development of rural tourism, this paper takes Chongdugou Scenic Spot in Luoyang City, Henan Province as an example, constructs the index system of sustainable development of rural tourism, and uses the Full Permutations Polygon Synthesis Graphic (FPPSG) Method to evaluate the sustainable development of tourism in Chongdugou from 2010-2016 and predict its potential development in 2020. The research results show that the sustainable development of tourism indicators system includes four categories of 26 indicators such as economic development, environmental protection, social progress and material recycling. In the past five years, the comprehensive index of sustainable development of tourism about Chongdugou tourism fluctuates between 0.28 and 0.48, meanwhile remains stable at 3-4 level, and still needs to be improved.

**Keywords:** rural tourism; sustainable development of tourism; index system; Full Permutations Polygon Synthesis Graphic (FPPSG) Method; Chongdugou

## Ⅰ. Introduction

Adriana Budeanu and others believe that sustainable development is the main direction of tourism's future development. [1] Since the concept of sustainable tourism development was formally proposed by the World Tourism Organization (WTO) in 1993, and "Sustainable Development of World Tourism" conference was successfully held in Spain in 1995, sustainable development model is gradually applied to the tourism industry. The quantitative evaluation of the sustainable development of tourism is an effective means to discover and solve the complex problems in the overall operation of tourism system.[2] Torres-Delgado and others believe that the sustainable development of tourism should be assessed by the index system;[3] to the sustainable development of tourism, the standard measurement of its capacity has become an important issue. And rural tourism is the carrier used by people in the post-modern society to

1 Sichuan University, Chengdu, China. thbt520@163.com.
2 Sichuan University, Chengdu, China.
3 Sichuan University, Chengdu, China.

return to nature and a new growth point of rural economic development. [4] The government regards developing rural tourism as an effective anti-poverty measure.[5] The author of this thesis will try to use the Full Permutations Polygon Synthesis Graphic (FPPSG) Method to analyze the sustainable development of Chongdugou Scenic Spot in Luoyang City, Henan Province, and to forecast the potential of its sustainable development, in order to enhance the sustainable development level of rural tourism in this place, and provide reference for decision-makers and practitioners of other rural tourism destination to make tourism policies.

## Ⅱ. Rural Tourism, the Sustainable Development of Tourism

The researches on rural tourism are mainly divided into the following aspects: influencing factors of rural tourism development which is studied by Wu Guanchen;[6] relevant stakeholders and communities involved in the study of Gu Hongmei[7] and Ba Duoxun;[8] the division of geographic and spatial structure of the rural tourism studied by Wu Bihu [9-10] and Cheng Zhe's[11] research on the driving mechanism of the rural tourism. The sustainable development of rural tourism has been studied from the perspective of property rights theory,[12] social network,[13] and some scholars have studied the development of rural tourism from the perspective of carbon emission.[14-15]

National Tourism Administration promoted the sustainable development of tourism from the government level, promulgated and implemented “the Basic Standards of National Green Tourism Demonstration” and “the Eco-Environmental Standards of Tourism Industry”. Wu Guoqin thinks that the researches on the sustainable development of tourism can mainly include the establishment of sustainable evaluation index of tourism destination development and the choice of evaluation methods.[16] Cenat & Gourdon, Li & Hou, Gao Ya and other scholars build the tourism sustainable development evaluation index system from the perspectives of social population, economic income, natural environment, tourism resources, etc.; [17-19] Wu Yiyen and other scholars try to build tourism sustainable development index system and use the fuzzy mathematics method, analytic hierarchy process and other methods to conduct an empirical analysis; [2,20] Zhang Jiekuan uses the system dynamics theory to build a model for the research on the sustainable development of tourism from the perspective of sustainable development of tourism systems and subsystems.[21] Tourism sustainable development evaluation index evaluation system is set, mainly focusing on the influences of the economic benefits, social culture, ecological environment and others. [22]

At present, many scholars are concerned about the importance of circular economy in the sustainable development of tourism. Circular economy, as an effective way of sustainable development, was proposed by the American economist K. Boulding in 1960s. It is a material recycling mode of production, which circularly uses the traditional production waste, in order to get more economic benefits based on the minimum investment costs, at the same time, reduce the waste as much as possible, improve the rate of resource utilization, and rationally use natural resources. Ming Qingzhong thinks that circular economy is an ecological economy and an effective way to develop sustainable tourism. [23] Lu Xue thinks that the circular economy is a theory that is essentially on the sustainable use of resources; the study of circular economy is on the maximization of resource efficiency and optimal allocation to meet the need of human survival and development, the core of which is to consider resource conservation under the influence of the social and environmental factors.[24] Geng and Allwood have improved the measurement of circular economy. [25-26] Data (Source: *China Statistical Yearbook 2001-2011*) shows that China's current development of circular economy improves obviously in view of the unit GDP energy consumption. But rural tourism is rarely developed from the perspective of circular economy to promote the sustainable development of rural tourism. It is a new field that researches on how to construct the sustainable development index system based on the theory of circular economy and measure the status and potential of sustainable development of rural tourism.

In general, the study of sustainable development of rural tourism still shows that it is more qualitative and less quantitative; the research does not pay enough attention to environmental benefits, instead, it emphasizes on economic benefits. The research on sustainable development of tourism is relatively mature, and the construction of index system includes related indicators such as economy, social culture, and environment, but there are also indicators that should not be used to collect information and measure. In view of this, it is of great significance to construct the index system of sustainable development of rural tourism which can reflect and measure the sustainable development level of rural tourism.

## Ⅲ. Research Design and Research Methods

*i. The Full Permutations Polygon Synthesis Graphic Method*

There are experts and scholars putting forward FPPSG in the evaluation of eco-city. [27] Through this method, scholars can determine whether the effect of different objects is good or not. For example, the higher the comprehensive evaluation index of environmental protection is, the lower the destruction of natural resources in the scenic area is; the higher the completeness of the ecosystem is, the higher the comprehensive evaluation index of material recycling is; the higher material recycling rate is, the higher the green development level is. Therefore, this study uses this method to assess the level and capacity of sustainable development of Chongdugou tourism.

The basic principle of this method is that there are $n$ index values that can be transformed into a scale that can be measured by a certain relationship. The distance from the maximum value of the scale range to the center point is fixed, and let's make a circle by the distance. The index values of each transformation can be reflected in the unique positive $n$-shapes of the circle. The order of the $n$-th transformation index can be connected to an irregular $n$-shape, and the different index order can be composed of different irregular $n$-shapes, all the irregular

$n$-shapes area of the average value of the area, and finally define the ratio of the average value and the area of the circle $n$ as the final comprehensive evaluation index.

The indicator transformation method uses the function $f(x)$ to convert the index value to −1 to 1:

$$f(x) = \frac{a(x+b)}{x+c}, a \neq 0, x \geq 0 \tag{1}$$

According to the requirements of the function conversion, $f(x)$ should be as follows:

$$f(L) = -1，f(T) = 0，f(U) = 1$$

In the formula, $L$ is the minimum value of the index value $x$, $U$ is the maximum value of the index value $x$, and $T$ is the critical value of the original index value $x$. According to the above three conditions, the result is as follows:

$$f(x) = \frac{(U-L)(x-T)}{(U+L-2T)x+UT+LT-2UL}, x \geq 0$$

Through the study of $f(x)$ , the quadratic derivative function $f(x)$ and the derivative function of $f(x)$, we find there is no breakpoint in the definition interval, $f(x)$ is a monotonically increasing function, and its growth rate is fast-slow-fast, that is, the normalization function changes the rate of change of the index value during the transformation process, but does not change the characteristic of the index value which is always increasing. It can be seen that the direction of the evaluation results of the transformation function and the original index value is the same, whether using the individual index or the comprehensive evaluation index to make the longitudinal comparison. Therefore, the larger the value of the normalized function $f(x)$ is, the better the evaluation result is. [28]

Thus, after the $i$-th index is standardized, the $f_i$ value is

$$f_i = \frac{(U_I-L_I)(x_i-T_I)}{(U_I-L_I-2T_I)x_i+U_IT_I+L_IT_I-2U_IL_I} \tag{2}$$

The normalization process of the $n$-th indicator can map all the index values one by one to the assemblage whose lower bound is −1 and the upper bound is 1. The graphics is to form the $n$-shapes with a radius of 2, its center points represent the points of respective indicators whose standardized value is −1, the placement of all the index value located on the connection line composed by the center of the circle of polygon circumcircle and the junction of the polygon and the circle, all the points which symbolize normalized value of 0 are in the middle of the connection line, the connection of each intermediate location constitutes the critical line of a comprehensive assessment. The critical line is the dividing line between the positive value and the negative value of the normalized value after the normalization of the indicators. The internal area is negative, while the external area is positive. [29]

Such a polygon can not only intuitively reflect the size of the indicators at different points in time and can reveal the relationship among the maximum and minimum value, the size of the threshold value of the index value and the maximum value of the sample data at different time points, and it can also calculate the comprehensive index value of the comprehensive evaluation system, according to the triangle composed by the indicators, two by two.

Then the comprehensive evaluation index of the Full Permutations Polygon is:

$$f = \frac{\sum_{i<j}^{i,j}(f_i + 1)(f_j + 1)}{2n(n-1)} \tag{3}$$

Finally, according to the calculated size of the comprehensive evaluation index and referring to a certain rating level, we determine the effect of different objects.

*ii. Research area*

Chongdugou Scenic Area was selected as the national eco-tourism demonstration area in 2015, and the current ecological environment protection there is better. The scenic area is located in Luanchuan County of Luoyang City, Henan Province, and it is a model village of China's rural tourism, and is one of the national 4A tourist attractions. There are three special characteristics in this scenic spots: water, bamboo and farmhouse hotel. The farmhouse hotel is a major feature of the area, the local villagers run farm hotels to develop the rural tourism, which is spoken highly by the Prime Minister Wang Yang and other national leaders and also rated as "the first village of Chinese farmhouse" by the national tourism director Wei Xiao'an. In 2015, annual tourist number reached 71.13 million, and the villagers created 57,305,500 yuan of total tourism revenue, an average of 43,000 yuan per person. Chongdugou tourism is a model of successful poverty alleviation.

*iii. Data sources*

In this paper, the data of the economic development, material recycling and gas, heating and environmental investment are mainly provided by the scenic area; in addition to environmental carrying capacity data from the scenic area planning, other environmental protection data comes from Luoyang Tourism Bureau and Statistics Bureau; some data come from the interviews of the relevant personnel in this spot, visitors and the survey of the local residents, as well as the comprehensive process of network information.

*iv. Data processing steps*

Based on the basic idea and thoughts of FPPSG, we can establish the following steps to study the sustainable development level of tourism:

The first step is to determine the critical value. Based on the sample data, the collected data from 2010 to 2015, 2016 and 2020, and the reference value of each index, the parameters in formula (2) are calculated, where $L_i$ is the minimum value of the sample data index $\boldsymbol{x}_i$, and $T_i$ is the mean value of the sample data, $\boldsymbol{x}_i$ and $U_i$ is the maximum value of the sample data index $\boldsymbol{x}_i$.

The second step is to converse the index value. Converse all the sample data into the same measurement, through putting the selected conversion function into formula (2), the author standardizes the data.

The third step is to calculate the single composite index. The converted index value data is substituted into formula (3) to calculate the values of each individual composite indicator. The development of each category in each period is evaluated by comparing the size of the comprehensive data and the index value of each level of the classification standard for sustainable tourism development.

The fourth step is to calculate the tourism sustainable development index. We analyze the comprehensive data of each category as the sample data, then repeat the third step, calculate the specific index value of the sustainable development level of Chongdugou tourism, and finally, refer to and contrast the grading standard of tourism sustainable development ability, to evaluate the sustainable development level and grade of Chongdugou's tourism in different period of time.

## Ⅳ. Construction of Rural Tourism Sustainable Development Index System

*i. Research on the tourism sustainable development index system*

Through studying the domestic and international researches on tourism sustainable development, the author finished the organization of existing index system (see Table 1). In the evaluation index system of sustainable development of tourism, the author has selected the specific indexes from subsystems such as the society, economy, culture, environment and resource of the tourism sustainable development system, in order to constitute the tourism sustainable development index system. The construction of tourism sustainable development index system mainly uses the principle selection and the Delphi method to determine the specific index. Then according to the selected comprehensive evaluation method, the index sample values are standardized, and the comprehensive evaluation index is calculated by the corresponding formula. And finally the quantitative evaluation of the sustainable development level of the target regional tourism is finished. In addition, with the deepening of the research, the tourism sustainable development index system is gradually mature, and many scholars begin to study the specific problems and embark on related empirical analysis on the basis of the index system constructed by the predecessors.

*ii. Principles for the construction of tourism sustainable index system*

The research on tourism sustainable development is aimed at a large research system. The information of this system is complex and complicated, and the fields involved are very extensive. Therefore, it is very difficult to determine the specific indexes when the system of tourism sustainable development research is established. Anderson believes that good system indicators are readily available, relatively easy to understand, and must be able to measure the important or meaningful content, can be compared vertically and relatively instant, can be used to compare different geographical areas, should be able to carry out international comparison, and other standards. [23]

This paper argues that the tourism sustainable development research index system should be able to reflect the real-time situation and future development potential of tourism sustainable development in the system, but also to reflect the economic development, environmental protection, social progress and material recycling of scenic areas. Specifically, the researchers should follow the principles of comprehensiveness, objectivity, simplicity, testability and dynamic principle.

Table 1 Summary of Domestic and Foreign Tourism Sustainable Development Index System

| Year | Author | Evaluation of the Comprehensive Layer | Number | Selection of Index | The Evaluation Method |
|---|---|---|---|---|---|
| 2001 | Wang Liangjian[30] | tourism resources and environmental protection capacity | 11 | principle selection | use analytical hierarchy process to determine the index weight multi-objective linear weighting function method comprehensive evaluation |
| | | tourism economic and social benefits | 9 | | |
| | | tourism hard and soft environment construction efforts | 9 | | |
| | | development ability of tourist market | 5 | | |
| 2008 | Wang Xin[31] | tourism resources and environment | 10 | principle primaries Delphi method | use Delphi method to determine the weight, expert assessment, weighted average comprehensive evaluation |
| | | tourism market impact | 9 | | |
| | | the support of development | 7 | | |
| | | social and economic coordination | 7 | | |
| | | auxiliary condition | 5 | | |
| 2011 | Gao Ya[19] | resource system | 8 | principle selection | use entropy weight method to determine the index weight,use comprehensive evaluation method to obtain the evaluation index |
| | | social system | 11 | | |
| | | economic system | 5 | | |
| | | environmental system | 5 | | |
| 2013 | Wu Jing[2] | tourism resources and environmental sustainability | 8 | principle selection | use total taxis of hierarchy to determine the index weight, multi-objective linear weight function method comprehensive evaluation |
| | | tourism economic sustainability | 6 | | |
| | | social sustainability of tourism | 5 | | |
| | | sustainable development potential of tourism destination | 4 | | |
| 2015 | Wu Guoqin[16] | sustainable of tourism resources | 4 | principle primaries Delphi method | use analytical hierarchy process to determine the weight, expert consultation method scoring, delete the maximum and minimum values and standardize, comprehensive evaluation of weighted sum |
| | | tourism environment carrying capacity | 4 | | |
| | | tourism economic development | 4 | | |
| | | protection of social culture | 4 | | |
| | | tourism development agency and management | 4 | | |

(To be continued)

(Continued Table 1)

| Year | Author | Evaluation of the Comprehensive Layer | Number | Selection of Index | The Evaluation Method |
|---|---|---|---|---|---|
| 2006 | Chris & Sirakaya[32] | human resources | 4 | Delphi method | experts's three rounds of evaluation on five aspects: politic, economy, culture, ecology, technique, and 125 factors, and finally come to the index system |
| | | policies and regulations | 9 | | |
| | | fund income | 3 | | |
| | | planning education | 10 | | |
| 2010 | Blancas[33] | social dimension | 8 | principle selection | a new two-level polymerization method |
| | | economic dimension | 8 | | |
| | | environmental dimension | 16 | | |
| 2016 | Tsung Hsieh[34] | stakeholders | - | Fuzzy Defer method | analytic Hierarchy Process for analysis of 141 Factors to determine Environmental and Stakeholder Rights |
| | | surroundings | - | | |

*iii. Construction of rural tourism sustainable tourism development index system*

In view of the above principles of construction of indicators, the author referred to the "eco-county, eco-city, ecological province construction indicators"[35] promulgated by the State Environmental Protection Administration indicators and tourism eco-economic evaluation index system framework in the research of Ming Qingzhong [23] (see Table 1), combining with the actual situation of rural tourism destination, and the sustainable development index system of Chongdugou tourism, including the economic development, environmental protection, social progress and material recycling. The economic development category includes the per capita tourism income, the per capita consumption level of the tourists, the per capita disposable income of the residents, the traffic income of the scenic spot, the ticket receipts and the number of tourists in the year. The environmental protection class includes the air quality (the number of days on which the air quality is equal to or better than Grade 2 standard), the water quality compliance rate of the scenic water function area, the capacity of the scenic area and the environmental compliance rate of the scenic area. The social progress category includes 6 indicators: the gas penetration rate, the rate of education, the per capita education level, the satisfaction rate of tourists and residents, the rate of environmental education, the proportion of environmental protection investment to total tourism income. The material recycling category includes seven indicators: tourism sewage disposal rate, garbage processing rate of tourists and local residents, the popularity proportion of water-saving equipment, the proportion of tourism clean energy accounted for the total energy, reduction in the use of plastic bags, the rate of the manufactory companies which should implement clean production, and eco-tourism toilet. There is a total of four categories of 26 indicators.

Then, combined with the local "12th Five-Year Plan" and "13th Five-Year Plan" and the local development of the scenic area, through the collection of relevant data of Chongdugou Scenic Spot in 2010-2015, on the basis of repeated understanding from the main principals of this scenic spot, the local government and other relevant departments, the authors come to the planning values and reference values of the year 2016 and 2020 and the different stages of development (see Table 2).

Table 2 Indicator System for Sustainable Development of Chongdugou Scenic Spot

| | Rating Integrated Layer Index | Evaluation Factor Layer Index | Reference Value |
|---|---|---|---|
| Comprehensive capacity of tourism sustainable development | Economic development | per capita of scenic area tourism income (yuan) | ⩾ 33000 |
| | | per capita consumption of tourists (yuan) | ⩾ 100 |
| | | resident per capita disposable income (yuan) | ⩾18000 |
| | | per unit area income of scenic area (yuan / ha) | 30000 |
| | | traffic income of scenic area (yuan) | 1500000 |
| | | ticket income (yuan) | 100000000 |
| | | the number of visitors received | 1000000 |
| | Environmental protection | air environmental quality (the number of days whose air quality is better than or equal to t 2 standard) | ⩾ 280 |
| | | water quality compliance rate of Scenic water function area (%) | 100, no more than four types of water |
| | | coverage rate of noise compliance area (%) | ⩾ 95 |
| | | scenic area forest coverage (%) | ⩾ 75 |
| | | environmental carrying capacity of scenic area | 15000 |
| | | scenic area environmental compliance rate (%) | 100 |
| | Social progress | gas penetration rate (%) | ⩾92 |
| | | heating rate (%) | ⩾ 80 |
| | | junior high school education penetration rate (%) | ⩾99 |
| | | visitors and residents satisfaction (%) | > 95 |
| | | environmental protection publicity and education penetration rate (%) | > 85 |
| | | the ratio of environmental investment to total tourism revenue (%) | 8 |
| | Recycling of substances | tourism sewage treatment rate (%) | 70 |
| | | visitors and local residents garbage disposal rate (%) | 100 |
| | | water - saving equipment popularity ratio (%) | 80 |
| | | the ratio of clean energy to total energy in tourism (%) | 80 |
| | | reduction in the use of plastic bags (%) | 20 |
| | | proportion of cleaner production enterprises (%) | 100 |
| | | eco - tourism toilet penetration rate (%) | 100 |

*iv. Classification of tourism sustainable development capability*

Based on the evaluation and rating methods of the comprehensive index at home and abroad, we design a five-level grading standard, the index range and the evaluation content of each grade, and give different grading reviews according to the evaluation index of different levels, so as to give the final comprehensive evaluation index a clear and definitive description (see Table 3).

Table 3 Classification of Tourism Sustainable Development Capacity

| Grade | Value | Evaluation |
|---|---|---|
| 1 | >0.80 | high level of development |
| 2 | 0.61-0.80 | higher level of development |
| 3 | 0.41-0.60 | level of development in general |
| 4 | 0.21-0.40 | lower level of development |
| 5 | <0.20 | low level of development |

## V. Empirical Results and Discussion

*i. An analysis on the sustainable development of tourism*

According to the research steps of sustainable development of tourism, the author analyzes the sustainable development ability of scenic tourism in four aspects, such as economic development, environmental protection, social progress and material recycling, using FPPSG, individual comprehensive evaluation index of 2016-2020, and finally calculates the comprehensive evaluation index through the individual comprehensive evaluation index, and finishes the comprehensive evaluation of the Chongdugou scenic tourism sustainable development capacity.

According to the research method for sustainable development of tourism and the second step, using formula (2), the relevant index data of the scenic area are standardized (the result keeps two decimal places). The results are shown in Table 4.

Table 4 Standardized Results of Indicator Data

| | | 2010 | 2011 | 2012 | 2013 | 2014 | 2015 | 2016 | 2020 |
|---|---|---|---|---|---|---|---|---|---|
| Economic development | per capita tourism revenue of scenic area | -1.00 | -0.52 | -0.36 | -0.22 | 0.05 | 0.22 | 0.56 | 1.00 |
| | per capita consumption of tourists | -0.89 | -0.72 | -1.00 | -0.80 | -0.54 | -0.06 | 0.30 | 0.77 |
| | per capita disposable income of residents | -1.00 | -0.79 | -0.60 | -0.47 | -0.39 | -0.26 | 0.24 | 1.00 |
| | per unit area income of Scenic area | -1.00 | -0.70 | -0.50 | -0.30 | -0.01 | 0.27 | 0.08 | 0.68 |
| | scenic small traffic income | -1.00 | -0.61 | -0.20 | -0.48 | -0.13 | 0.13 | 0.20 | 0.73 |
| | ticket income | -1.00 | -0.68 | -0.53 | -0.39 | -0.14 | 0.10 | 0.30 | 0.94 |
| | the number of visitors received | -1.00 | -0.71 | -0.45 | -0.25 | 0.06 | 0.20 | 0.38 | 1.00 |

(To be continued)

(Continued Table 4)

| | | 2010 | 2011 | 2012 | 2013 | 2014 | 2015 | 2016 | 2020 |
|---|---|---|---|---|---|---|---|---|---|
| Environmental protection | air environmental quality (the number of days whose quality is better than or equal to grade 2) | 0.31 | 0.01 | -0.60 | -1.00 | -0.20 | 0.04 | 0.14 | 1.00 |
| | water quality compliance rate of scenic water function area | 1.00 | -0.75 | -0.27 | -1.00 | 1.00 | 1.00 | 1.00 | 1.00 |
| | coverage rate of noise compliance area | -0.24 | -0.40 | -0.54 | -1.00 | -0.75 | -0.26 | 0.59 | 1.00 |
| | scenic forest coverage | 1.00 | 0.97 | 0.49 | 0.44 | 0.24 | 0.24 | 0.24 | -0.06 |
| | environmental carrying capacity of scenic area | -1.00 | -0.85 | -0.74 | -0.43 | -0.23 | 0.00 | 0.31 | 0.65 |
| | scenic environment compliance rate | 1.00 | 0.38 | -0.29 | -1.00 | -0.62 | -0.29 | 0.13 | 1.00 |
| Social progress | gas penetration rate | -1.00 | -0.64 | -0.39 | 0.00 | 0.27 | 0.41 | 0.70 | 1.00 |
| | heating penetration rate | -1.00 | -0.91 | -0.74 | -0.58 | -0.30 | -0.05 | 0.22 | 1.00 |
| | junior high school education penetration rate | -0.75 | -1.00 | -0.27 | -0.07 | 0.40 | 0.40 | 1.00 | 1.00 |
| | tourist and resident satisfaction | -0.68 | -1.00 | -0.84 | -0.38 | -0.08 | 0.61 | 0.61 | 1.00 |
| | environmental protection publicity and education penetration rate | -1.00 | -0.24 | -0.31 | -0.10 | 0.03 | 0.16 | 0.36 | 1.00 |
| | the ratio of environmental investment to total tourism revenue | -1.00 | -0.91 | -0.63 | -0.21 | -0.02 | 0.16 | 0.27 | 0.63 |
| Recycling of substances | tourism sewage treatment rate | -1.00 | -0.69 | -0.07 | 0.53 | 0.53 | 1.00 | 1.00 | 1.00 |
| | tourists and local residents garbage harmless treatment rate | -1.00 | -0.63 | -0.24 | -0.32 | 0.00 | 0.16 | 0.16 | 1.00 |
| | the popularity proposition of water-saving equipment | -1.00 | -0.92 | -0.61 | -0.40 | -0.12 | 0.19 | 0.34 | 0.63 |
| | tourism clean energy ratio to total energy | -1.00 | -0.86 | -0.55 | -0.21 | -0.09 | 0.45 | 0.61 | 1.00 |
| | reduction in the use of plastic bags | -0.78 | -1.00 | -0.56 | -0.11 | 0.11 | 0.35 | 0.55 | 1.00 |
| | proportion of enterprises should be implemented clean production | -1.00 | -0.61 | -0.19 | -0.03 | -0.03 | 0.24 | 0.43 | 1.00 |
| | eco-tourism toilet penetration rate | -1.00 | -0.69 | -0.54 | 0.21 | 0.75 | 1.00 | 1.00 | 1.00 |

*Note: This table is finished with the help of data which is provided by the Luoyang Tourism Bureau, Luoyang Statistics Bureau, Chongdugou scenic spot, network, local residents and tourists. Economic development and material recycling and gas, heating and environmental investment data is mainly from the scenic area directly; education and satisfaction data of the scenic area is from the questionnaire survey; most of the environmental protection data is from the Luoyang Tourism Bureau and the Statistics Bureau; while the environmental carrying capacity data comes from Scenic Planning.*

*ii. Economic development*

From the results of the comprehensive evaluation of economic development (see Table 5) we can see that the economic development evaluation index of Chongdugou Scenic Spot during 2010-2014 is lower than 0.2, the comprehensive evaluation is at level 5 and the development level is low. By 2015, it is up to 0.29 comprehensive evaluation at the level 4. The level of development has risen, but it is still low, mainly due to the lower level of per capita consumption of tourists, per capita disposable income level of residents in scenic areas and the ticket income of scenic areas accounted for too high a proportion. And then through further management, development and the specific implementation of the planning work, in 2016, the comprehensive evaluation index reaches 0.42, at the level 3, the level of development is in general; but by 2020, it will reach the peak of 0.88, at level 1, the development level is high. Generally speaking, the development level of the Chongdugou tourism economy is increasing, and it has strong economic development potential.

Table 5 Comprehensive Assessment of the Sustainable Development Ability of Each Stage of Chongdugou Scenic Area

| | 2010 | 2011 | 2012 | 2013 | 2014 | 2015 | 2016 | 2020 |
|---|---|---|---|---|---|---|---|---|
| Comprehensive Evaluation Index of Economic Development | 0.00 | 0.03 | 0.06 | 0.08 | 0.18 | 0.29 | 0.42 | 0.88 |
| Comprehensive Evaluation Index of Environmental Protection | 0.42 | 0.18 | 0.11 | 0.01 | 0.19 | 0.31 | 0.49 | 0.77 |
| Comprehensive Evaluation Index of Social Progress | 0.00 | 0.01 | 0.05 | 0.15 | 0.27 | 0.41 | 0.58 | 0.94 |
| Comprehensive Evaluation Index of Recycling of Substances | 0.00 | 0.01 | 0.09 | 0.22 | 0.34 | 0.55 | 0.62 | 0.95 |
| Comprehensive Evaluation Index of Sustainable Development | 0.30 | 0.28 | 0.29 | 0.31 | 0.39 | 0.48 | 0.58 | 0.89 |

*iii. Environmental protection*

According to the results of the individual comprehensive evaluation of environmental protection, it can be seen that the environmental protection index of the Chongdugou Scenic Spot in 2010 is at the level 3, and the development level is normal. During the period from 2011 to 2015, the air quality, environmental carrying capacity and the forest coverage rate present a U-shape structure, declining first and then rising, which may be related to the construction and planning of scenic spots, as well as tourism facilities such as peasant hotels for local residents. The latter's occupation of mountainous slopes has led to the reduction of forest cover. Later, as the tourism industry develops, people's awareness of environmental protection has been strengthened. In the later period, with the development of the tourism, people gradually strengthen their environmental protection awareness. The Environmental Protection Assessment Index is expected to reach 0.49 by the end of this year and will reach 0.77 by 2020, at a level 2, with a high level of development.

In general, the level of environmental protection has improved, but the forest coverage has declined, probably because the scenic area is located in mountain which is lack of free land, while further development and construction would take up more land resources, and the forest coverage rate will be further reduced. Although the standardized results show that the forest coverage rate in 2020 is in decline, it is only a relatively low value, which is lower than the average of the above years' data, and the forest coverage rate of the actual scenic area is still higher than 93%.

*iv. Social progress*

According to the results of the individual comprehensive evaluation of social progress (see Table 5), the current level of social progress index of Chongdugou tourism is not high. The social progress index in 2010-2014 is below level 4, and the level of development is between the low and the lower, mainly due to gas penetration, heating penetration, junior high school education and environmental protection investment which accounted for a relatively low ratio; in 2015, social progress evaluation index rose to 0.41, at level 3, which was classified as the general level of development. With the development of scenic spots and the improvement of living standards, social progress evaluation index reached 0.58 in 2016, by 2020, to 0.94, it will rise to level 1, at a high level of development.

In general, the Chongdugou Scenic Area has evolved from the initially typical poverty village into the model village of national rural tourism, known as the "the first village of Chinese farmhouses". Social progress has a certain development foundation, and it will have greater development potential in the future. In future development, with the improvement of the per capita education level and the strengthening of infrastructure construction in the scenic spot, the life at the scenic spot will be further improved.

*v. Recycling of substances*

According to the results of comprehensive evaluation of material recycling, the development level of Chongdugou is still low, but it is in an upward trend. The individual comprehensive index of material recycling for the Chongdugou in 2010 - 2012 is less than 0.2, at level 5 (see Table 5). The main reason is that the index of the penetration rate of eco-tourism toilets, the proportion of water-saving equipment used, and the proportion of the clean energy of tourism to the proportion of total energy and reduction rate in the use of plastic bags, are relatively low, which reached the general level in 2013 - 2015, rose to level 3; overall performance shows that the scope of application of circular economy rapidly expanses. Later, with the development and the strengthening of the awareness of local people and consumers' demand, Chongdugou scenic spot shall pay more attention to material recycling and reproduction reducing, using the least resources to obtain the maximum production and the highest efficiency. By the end of 2016, the index will reach 0.62, rise to level 2, and the development will rise to a higher level. By 2020, it will continue to grow, and will be at a high level of development.

In general, in the process of development of Chongdugou tourism, there will be more application of recycling, including resources recycling and material reproduction. And resource-saving consumption will also be on the rise.

*vi. Tourism sustainable development level*

The comprehensive index of sustainable development of Chongdugou scenic area between 2010 and 2015 is between 0.28 and 0.48 (see Table 5), and the overall level of development is at level 3-4. The comprehensive evaluation of development capability is between the low level and the general level. The capacity for sustainable development is still to be improved. Under the concept of increasing the utilization rate of material resources, such as increasing material recycling and waste recycling, the sustainable development index of the scenic spot in 2016 reached 0.58, and was at level 3. The sustainable development ability was 0.89, at level 1, so the scenic area had a higher capacity for sustainable development (Figure 1). Generally speaking, the level of sustainable development of tourism in Chongdugou is at the general level, the trend of overall development is gradually increasing, and the development prospect is better.

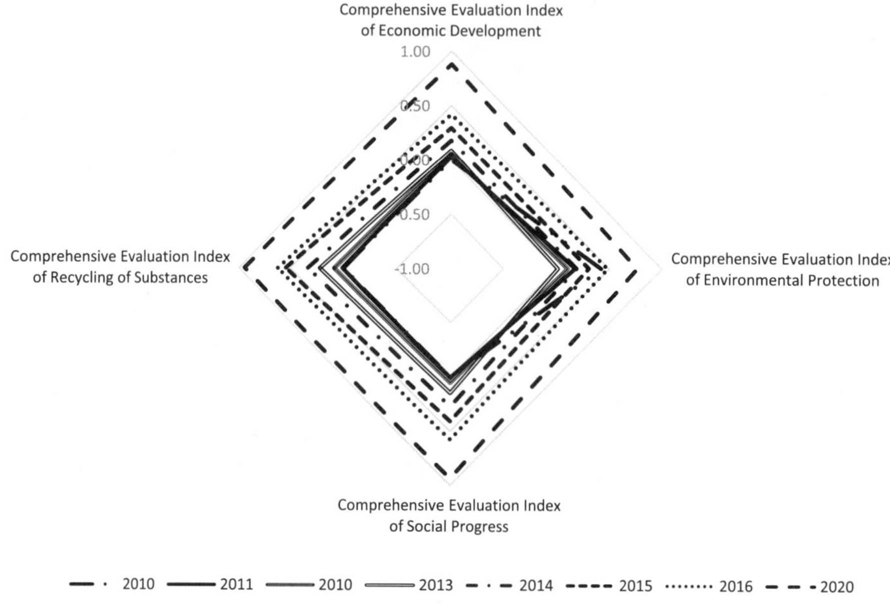


Figure 1 Comprehensive Ability of Chongdugou's Sustainable Development

## Ⅵ. Conclusion and Discussion

Based on the existing researches and the theory of circular economy, the authors construct the index system of sustainable development of Chongdugou Scenic Area from four aspects: economic development, environmental protection, social progress and material recycling, to assess the status of sustainable development of Chongdugou tourism, and put forward the corresponding development proposals to the sustainable development of rural tourism scenic areas.

The results show that: (1) The evaluation index system of sustainable development of rural tourism under the guidance of circular economy theory includes not only the subsystems such as traditional economic development, environmental protection and social progress, but also the subsystems of material recycling. The system consists of four categories of 26 indicators. (2) In the past five years, the comprehensive index of sustainable development of tourism in Chongdugou Scenic Area is between 0.28 and 0.48, and the sustainable development is at level 3-4, and there is still some distance from level 1. (3) Sustainable development of rural tourism develops towards a higher level. Economic development, social progress, material recycling and recycling of the individual comprehensive evaluation index are gradually increasing, although the comprehensive evaluation index of environmental protection has been reduced, it shows a steady trend of late growth. Overall, the sustainable development of tourism comprehensive evaluation index is on the rise, and the sustainable development of rural tourism capacity is in the steady increase.

The significance of this study is: (1) Apart from the application of circular economy to the sustainable development of rural tourism evaluation index system, and the comprehensive evaluation of rural tourism sustainable development potential in the theoretical level, this paper enriches the rural tourism and sustainable development research. (2) Based on FPPSG in the evaluation of eco-city, the authors finish the comprehensive assessment of the sustainable development of tourism in the period from 2010 to 2015 and the forecast of 2016 and 2020. It is more scientific and objective to use the area ratio to reflect comprehensive evaluation results, comparing with the traditional addition to do a comprehensive assessment of the weight, and it is not vulnerable to personal subjective factors. At the same time, the sustainable development of rural tourism research is complex and systematic, and it can reflect the principles of systematics and is suitable for the sustainable development of rural tourism. (3) This study also brings some enlightenment to government departments, scenic area managers, local residents as well as the tourism enterprises. The results of the empirical analysis of the Chongdugou Scenic Spot show that the sustainable development level is still at the level of Grade 3, therefore it is a relatively mature rural tourist area. In view of this, the rural tourist attractions need to continuously strengthen their sustainable development. To promote the sustainable development of rural tourism, the directors of scenic spots should improve the sustainable development level from four aspects respectively, namely, economic development, environmental protection, social progress and material recycling, according to the specific circumstances.

## References

[1] B Adriana, M Graham, M Gianna, Ooi C-S. Sustainable tourism: progress, challenges and opportunities[J]. *Journal of Cleaner Production*, 2016, 111(1): 285-294.

[2] Wu Jing. The construction and evaluation of the index system of tourism sustainable development[J]. *Inquiry into Economic Issues*, 2013, 10: 64-70.

[3] Torres-Delgado A, Saarinen J. Using indicators to assess sustainable tourism development: a review[J]. *Tourism Geographies*, 2014, 16(1): 31-47.

[4] Lu Xiaoli, Cheng Yuxing, Wang Liwei. A hot topic in rural tourism research at home and abroad: a review of literature in recent 20 years [J]. *Resources Science*, 2014, 36(1): 200-205.

[5] Li Ping, Ryan C, Cave J. Chinese rural tourism development: transition in the case of Qiyunshan, Anhui[J]. *Tourism Management*, 2016, 55 (2): 240-260.

[6] Wu Guangchen, Niu Xin, Xu Hengzhou. The mechanism and management tools of land circulation risk in rural tourism development [J]. *Issues in Agricultural Economy*, 2013(4): 63-68.

[7] Gu Hongmei. Study on the development of rural tourism and the construction of benefit sharing mechanism of rural residents: a case study of the tourism development in the northwest area of Haidian district, Beijing [J]. *Tourism Tribune*, 2012, 01: 26-30.

[8] Ba Duoxun, Xu Jinha. Study on rural tourism based on community participation: a case study of Wuyuan County in Jiangxi Province[J]. *Resource Development & Market*, 2013, 29(8): 867-869.

[9] Wu Bihu, Huang Zhuwei, Ma Xiaomeng. The spatial structure of rural tourism destination in Chinese cities[J]. *Scientia Geographica Sinica*, 2004, 24(6): 757-763.

[10] Xu Qing. Optimization of rural tourism spatial structure in Ningbo based on point-axis system theory [J]. *Economic Geography*, 2009, 29(6): 1042-1046.

[11] Cheng Zhe, Cai Jianmin, Cui Li, Li Yansui. The driving mechanism of industrial transformation in rural transformation: a case study of Panjin rural tourism [J]. *Research of Agricultural Modernization*, 2016, 01: 143-150.

[12] Zhang Ling, Wang Chaoen. Study on the sustainable development of rural tourism based on property right theory[J]. *Commercial Research*, 2011, 04: 192-196.

[13] Wang Sujie. Li Xiang. A study on sustainable rural tourism decision-making based on social network perspective: a case study of Yangjiabu Village, Weifang City, Shandong Province[J]. *Chinese Rural Economy*, 2011, 03: 59-69, 90.

[14] Deng Aiming, Huang Xin. Discussion on the construction of rural tourism function in the background of low carbon[J]. *Issues in Agricultural Economy*, 2013, 02: 105-109.

[15] Liu Xiao. Low-carbon tourism: a new model for future development of Beijing suburb[J]. *Social Sciences of Beijing*, 2010, 01: 42-46.

[16] Wu Guoqing. Evaluation of tourism sustainable development ability in Dabie mountain area of south[J]. *Areal Research and Development*, 2015, 34(4): 95-98.

[17] Cernat L, Gourdon J. Paths to success: benchmarking cross-country sustainable tourism[J]. *Tourism Management*, 2012,33(4): 1044-1056.

[18] Li H Q, Hou L C. Evaluation on sustainable development of scenic zone based on tourism ecological footprint: case study of Yellow Crane Tower in Hubei Province, China[J]. *Energy Procedia*, 2011, 26 (5): 145-151.

[19] Gao Ya. From the perspective of entropy weight to explore the sustainable development of tourism[A]. China Natural Resources Society, Xinjiang Natural Resources Society, 2011, 5.

[20] Wu Y Y, Wang H L, Ho Y F. Urban ecotourism: defining and assessing dimensions using fuzzy number construction[J]. *Tourism Management*, 2010, 31(3): 739-743.

[21] Zhang Jiekuan. Dynamic simulation of regional tourism sustainable development system[J]. *Systems Engineering: Theory & Practice*, 2011, 31(11): 101-107.

[22] Fen Qinliang, Qin Fanding, Li Weibing. A study on the sustainable development of rural tourism in the Pan- li River Valley [J]. *Journal of Anhui Agricultural Sciences*, 2012, 40(2): 882-884, 916.

[23] Ming Qingzhong, Li Qinglei. *Study on the Development of Tourism Circular Economy*[M]. Beijing: People's Publishing House, 2007, 11: 5-14, 210-211, 214-217.

[24] Lu Xue, Cheng Xinxue. A summary of the research on circular economy theory[J]. China Population, *Resources and Environment*, 2014, 24(5): 204-208.

[25] Geng Y, Sarkis J, Ulgiati S, et al. Measuring China's circular economy[J]. *Science*, 2013: 1526-1527.

[26] Allwood J M, Ashby M F, Gutowski T G, et al. Material efficiency: providing material services with less material production[J]. *Philosophical Transactions*, 2013, 371(1986): 201-204, 96.

[27] Gong Yanbing, Zhang Jiguo, Liang Xuechun. Water quality evaluation based on full permutation polygon comprehensive graphic method [J]. *China Population, Resources and Environment*, 2011, 21(9): 26-31.

[28] Zhang Lei, Li Nana, Zhao Huiru, Yang Kun. Comprehensive evaluation of energy conservation and emission reduction performance of thermal power enterprises based on all-array polygon graph index method[J]. *Electric Power*, 2014, 47(6): 145-150.

[29] Zhou Wei, Cao Yinggui, Qiao Luyin. Evaluation of intensive use of land in Xining city based on all-array polygon graph index method[J]. *China Land Sciences*, 2012, 26(4): 84-90.

[30] Wang Liangjian. Study on evaluation index system and evaluation method of tourism sustainable development[J]. *Tourism Tribune*, 2001(1): 67-70.

[31] Wang Xin, Gao Yancun. An empirical study on the construction and evaluation of evaluation index system of regional tourism sustainable development[J]. *Inquiry into Economic Issues*, 2008, 01: 137-140.

[32] Choia H C, Sirakaya E. Sustainability indicators for managing community tourism[J]. *Tourism Management*, 2006, 27(6): 1274-1289.

[33] Blancas F J, Gonzalez M, Lozano-Oyola M, Perez F. The assessment of sustainable tourism: application to Spanish coastal destinations[J]. *Ecological Indicators*, 2010, 10: 484-492.

[34] Tsung Hung Lee, Hsin-Pei Hsieh. Indicators of sustainable tourism: a case study from a Taiwan's wetland[J]. *Ecological Indicators*, 2016, 67(3): 779-787.

[35] State Environmental Protection Administration. Eco-county, eco-city, ecological province construction indicators [J]. *Environmental Protection*, 2003.

# A Research on the Spatial Distribution and Protection of Chongqing Traditional Village Based on GIS

Li Yuzhen[1], Liu Lu[2*], Xu Ningwei[3]

**Abstract:** The protection and utilization of traditional villages is a multi-disciplinary research focus at the moment. Based on the GIS spatial analysis tool, this article analyzes spatial distribution characteristics of traditional villages in Chongqing. The research shows that the structural types of traditional villages in Chongqing were identified agglomerate. The distribution of the traditional villages is comparatively centralized but the centralized area is overwhelmingly uneven among Chongqing. There are three centralized areas, which are ethnic minority villages. Based on the above spatial characteristics, we put forward that the collective memory, time and space, and national traditional culture are the main dimensions of the protection of traditional villages in Chongqing. The conclusion provides a new perspective for the protection of traditional villages in Chongqing.

**Keywords:** traditional villages; GIS; collective memory; time and space; national traditional culture

## Ⅰ. Introduction

The traditional village refers to the cultural heritage which formed earlier, condensed historical memory, reflecting the development process of civilization and having historical, cultural, scientific, artistic, social and economic value. In addition, it carries the changes of farming civilization, in the long history of precipitation into the traditional culture cohesion space, becomes the cultural heritage of the carrier, gene pool and heritage field. Traditional villages in the moment are the brightest pearl in the tourist circle and constructed as a nostalgia for people to find spiritual home. Meanwhile, because of the scarcity and non renewable nature of traditional villages, its protection has risen to the level of national policy. [1] The central work conference of urbanization held in Beijing in 2013 put forward: Mountains in sight and waters in view remind one of nostalgia.

1 Chongqing University of Technology, Chongqing, China.

2* Chongqing University of Technology, Chongqing, China. 792929823@qq.com.

3 Wuhan Maritime Vocational College, Wu Han, China.

In 2002, China first proposed the concept of historical and cultural villages and towns, and determined to protect them in legal form. In 2001, Ministry of Housing and Urban-Rural Development, Ministry of Culture, Ministry of Finance and State Administration of Cultural Heritage changed the customary term "ancient villages" to "traditional villages" and defined traditional villages as "the villages with a long history, rich traditional resources, considerable historical, cultural, scientific, artistic, social and economic value, thus deserving due protection". [2] The word "traditional" better reflects the traditional culture, national culture, regional culture typical, representative and inheritance. [3] So far, four groups of villages have been selected in the list of Chinese traditional villages.

Accompanied by large-scale migration of rural population, the loss of rural land and serious situation of the rural cultural fracture, retaining memories and nostalgia has become a hot issue. In the use of the traditional village at present, we generally will face three situations: cultural relics are protected, the scenic spots are developed and a symbolic resource for local governments to develop economy. [4] Correspondingly, it is facing multiple problems, first of all, the malignant competition and duplicated construction caused by the homogeneous development of traditional villages tourism resources. Secondly, the village space is overloaded, the tourism commercialization development is out of control and the village fabric and landscape fade away after its development. In the end, it is the materialization of active traditional villages, the rapid disappearance of national life style and modes of production that resulted in the hollow villages.

Chongqing is a gathering area for traditional villages, the survival and future of its traditional villages are facing many problems. Many villages are declining, only a few will become security units and get some protection while the majority of traditional villages, especially the remote and closed ones are basically in the state of self-destruction. With the accelerating process of urbanization in Chongqing, the production lifestyle and family structures of traditional village have changed, the aging of population is now a universal trend, and local cultural inheritance has not been passed on. The development and utilization of traditional villages are not satisfactory, the Commodity Market model of tourism exploitation in ethnic villages broke the original relatively closed natural economy structure and made a devastating impact on the village's original life style and culture ecology. The disappearance of a village means the lost of historical details, not only the disappearance of ancient architecture, but centuries of history and nostalgia.

This paper applied GIS technique to analyze the spatial distribution and patterns of traditional villages in Chongqing that were identified by the four ministries and commissions, which is of great significance to interpret and analyze the spatial distribution features of traditional villages in Chongqing under the background of tourism development.

## Ⅱ. Literature Review, Research Methods, Data Sources and Research Area Profiles

With a deep research on the protection of cultural heritage, the protection of traditional village is owning increasing attention in many fields. From the results of the full-text database of Chinese academic journals and science direct database, the academia attaches more importance to the research on traditional villages from the following aspects:

*i. Literature review*

*A. Status of domestic research on traditional villages*

The study of traditional villages involves multiple disciplines and research areas, in the academic results of the performance of innovative research methods and cutting-edge basic theory into the traditional village research. Sun Jiuxia (2017) pointed out that the traditional village studies show a multi-disciplinary perspective and interdisciplinary perspective. [5] Yu Ruyi (2013) used the theory of niche and species intrusion to study the reorganization of space social order caused by the invasion of tourism in traditional village communities. [6] Feng Shuhua (2013) used the symbiosis theory to establish the symbiosis unit of the ancient village and its main parameters and symbiotic interface, construct the symbiosis system of the ancient village, and optimize its symbiotic direction. [7] Sun Ying discusses the correlation between the spatial structure of the traditional village and the social and cultural activities on the traditional village space by space Syntax. Through the spatial structure diagram of spatial domain, social structure, activity and public space, Explain the social influencing factors of spatial construction. [8] The application of geographic information system (GIS) method in traditional village research is also a new feature recently. This method is mainly applied in the study of spatial differentiation characteristics[9] and spatial distribution pattern[10] of villages.

In addition, the study of tourists' perspective and Aboriginal perspective has made the study of traditional villages show diversity and comprehensiveness. Sun Jiuxia (2015) explored the change of residents local self-identity from the perspective of heritage production. [11] Li Wenbin (2011) built a tourist-aware loyalty correction model to explore the perception and perception of village tourists' perception. [12] Tang Wenyue(2014), based on the emotional attachment and functional attachment perspectives of the aborigines to the ancient villages, the paper studies the influence of the relocation wishes of the indigenous people in the ancient villages and its mechanism. [13] Weng Shixiu (2011) explored the rights of the community in the ancient village, clarifying the psychological power of the type of empowerment and institutional supply-type power of the dispute. [14]

*B. Status of foreign research on traditional villages*

Foreign traditional village research started in the 1960s. The study focuses on the sustainable development of traditional villages, the traditional village tourism, village landscape planning and the protection of traditional villages, such as legislation. [15] In the traditional sustainable development of villages, the main idea is to support the sustainable development of traditional villages, and usually with material and cultural heritage protection, village tourism, to improve the village environment and promote the modernization of the village phase combined with. [16] In the traditional village tourism research, developed countries and developing countries show very different research situation. The developed countries are concerned with the resource value of the traditional villages in the process of long-term evolution of nature and society, and advocate the development of traditional village tourism under the premise of ecological protection, [17] while developing countries are more concerned about the impact of tourism on traditional villages. [18] In the aspect of landscape planning, the study is on the principles and concepts of village landscape planning. [19] The protection of the traditional villages and towns, and the process of building heritage protection are closely related to the process of the village to enter, the heritage protection field has undergone a gradual understanding and deepening process. [20]

*ii. Research methods and data sources*

The paper applies Arcgis 10.1 spatial analysis tool and Excel as the data analysis platform, selects the nearest neighbor index, geographical concentration index and unbalanced index, the quantitative analysis of traditional villages in Chongqing, the nuclear density measurement. And then use Google Earth to determine the geographical coordinates of traditional villages, the Arcgis technology platform for vector mapping, the traditional village of geographical location, spatial pattern and other characteristics of the visual expression of the traditional villages in Chongqing, the spatial distribution characteristics.

The traditional village data collected in this paper mainly comes from the list of the first, second, third and fourth batch of Chinese traditional villages published by the Ministry of Housing and Urban-Rural Development, the Ministry of Culture and the Ministry of Finance. Based on the geography basic data of Chongqing, the spatial distribution of traditional villages in Chongqing was obtained by vectorization of map.

*iii. General situation of the study area*

Chongqing is located in the southwest of our country, with Han, Hui, Miao, Tujia ethnic groups. The traditional village mainly refers to the former country to build the village, and the village structure and location did not make a big change, with a long history, better preservation of the traditional culture of the village. These villages are the birthplace of Bayu culture, after thousands of years of civilization heritage and development, the villagers live together and multiply, breed a variety of traditional villages. From 2012 to present, four batches of 74 villages in Chongqing were included in the traditional Chinese village directory, located in various districts and counties. These traditional villages contain a lot of historical information and rich cultural landscape, which is an important legacy of Chongqing Bayu culture and farming civilization.

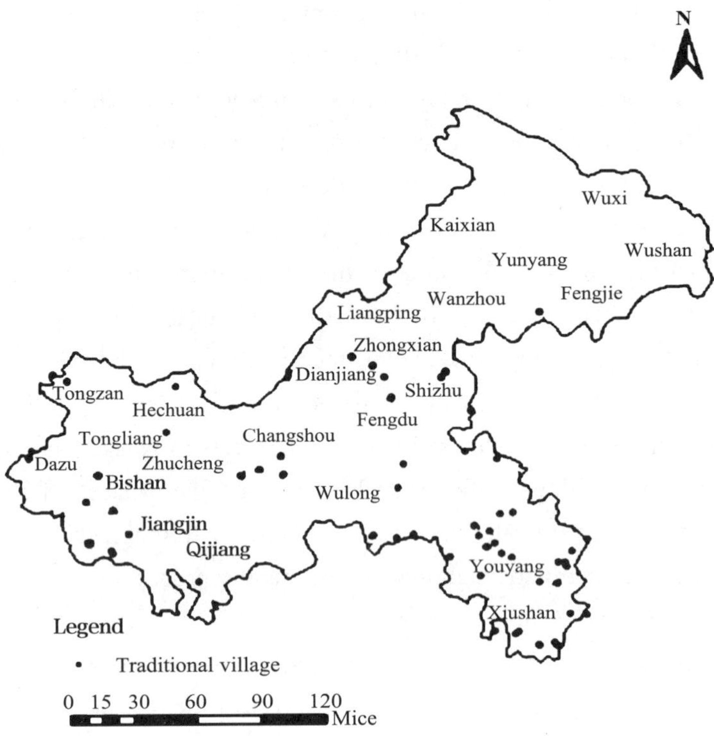


Figure 1 Spatial Distribution of Traditional Villages in Chongqing

## Ⅲ. Spatial Distribution Features Traditional Villages in Chongqing

*i. Spatial distribution type*

ArcGIS10.1 was applied for the vectorization of maps to obtain the spatial distribution of 74 traditional villages in Chongqing. Because the spatial distribution of traditional villages is affected by many factors, the exploration of its spatial distribution type is the first step to study the spatial distribution characteristics of traditional villages. Generally, traditional villages are point elements from the micro perspective. Spatial distribution of point elements includes even type, random type and agglomerate type. The three types can be identified using the nearest neighbor index.[22] The nearest neighbor index R is defined as the ratio of the real nearest neighbor to the theoretical nearest neighbor [See Formula (1)].

$$R = \frac{\bar{r_1}}{\bar{r_E}} = 2\sqrt{D} \tag{1}$$

$\bar{r}_1$ is the real nearest distance, $\bar{r}_E$ is the theoretic nearest distance, and $D$ is the point density. As $R = 1$, the point distribution is random; as $R>1$, distribution of point elements tends to be even; as $R<1$, distribution of point elements tends to be agglomerate.

Average Nearest Neighbor in Spatial Statistics Tools in ArcGIS10.1 was used for the calculation: $\bar{r}_1$ =0.256, $\bar{r}_E$ =0.386, $R = \bar{r}_1 / \bar{r}_E$ =0.663. The ratio of the real average nearest neighbor to the theoretical average nearest neighbor $R$ =0.663<1, distribution of traditional villages in Chongqing tends to be agglomerate.

This characteristic will have an important inspiration for the protection of traditional villages in Chongqing. First of all, the agglomerate spatial distribution claimed transition from the original single, point-like protection mode to the linear, over-surface one, from protection mode based on individual to space. Secondly, traditional villages are the filed of cultural heritage, condensed villages bring together similar or identical cultural heritage and provide space for the protection, survival and development of complex cultural heritage. Cultural heritage is a strong support for the value of villages, so the two can formed superposition force.

Further research found that the agglomerate spatial distribution of traditional villages is related to the memory of village residents and the villages with the same memory are more likely to agglomerate in space. The formation of memory is due to environmental stimuli or external stimulation to promote and stimulate the external power to construct memory, [23] on the contrary, memory also maps the environment and external forces. External forces acting on groups and forming of collective memory, which is a way of group identity and also a cultural construction. Groups within a certain range of space choose valuable things and store them as a collective memory according to their self-values.

The collective memory of the village is an important form of village memory, which is constructed by external force. The above external force includes history, war, folklore, values and so on, the same one will form a same collective memory while the same memories will react to village space. Thus the abstract collective memory of villages is associated with the agglomerate spatial distribution, even reflects the agglomerate spatial distribution creating similar collective memory. Therefore, we believe that collective memory attaches great importance to the formation of village spatial pattern.

Meanwhile, collective memory also has effect on the connection between each person in villages. Therefore, in the use of traditional villages, the stray memory of villages should get more attention, construction and strengthening to make the aborigines, managers and developers of villages recognize that the core values of traditional villages lie in its collective memory, and how to inherit it. When collective memory can be inherited and sustained effectively, it will be transformed into the identity of each person, thus forming a stronger dominant sense of ethic identity based on the collective memory. The fundamental reason that traditional ethnic villages can not be protected and inherited effectively is the lack of such identity awareness.

The agglomerate spatial distribution pattern of traditional villages in Chongqing is conducive to the formation of differential image design, development path and superposition force on the basis of the same collective memory. Tourism development of villages should base on collective memory of the aborigines, its development, protection and inheritance which is the continuation of memory. This process can be expressed in Figure 2, that is, protection and utilization of the Chongqing traditional villages should follow five steps: identify agglomerate area, determine theme, set cultural space, establish protected gathering area, form new agglomerate area. This model is also applicable to other traditional villages protection with agglomerate spatial features.

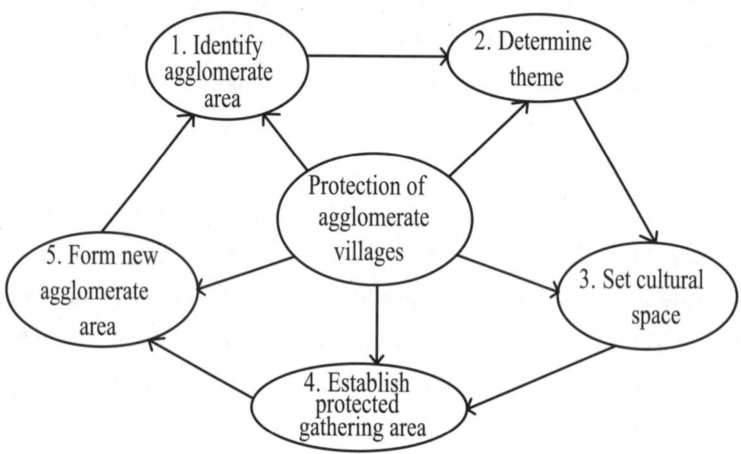


Figure 2 Protected Route of Agglomerate Villages

*ii. Spatial distribution equilibrium*

In the study of spatial distribution of traditional villages, we generally analyse traditional villages' traditional villages and equilibrium by Geographic concentration index and disequilibrium index. Geographic concentration index is an important index that it can reflect the degree of traditional villages concentration [See Formula (2)].

$$G = 100 \times \sqrt{\sum_{i=1}^{n}\left(\frac{X_i}{T}\right)^2} \tag{2}$$

In the formula: $G$ is Geographical concentration index of traditional villages in Chongqing; $X_i$ is the quantity of scenic area in the $i^{th}$ city, $T$ is the total number in traditional villages; $n$ is total number of districts and counties. The values of $G$ range from 0 to 100, the higher value is, the more concentrated traditional villages are. This paper counts up the distribution and ratio of traditional villages in Chongqing by sorting the List of Traditional Villages of China.

Table 1 Statistics of Spatial Distribution of Traditional Villages in Chongqing

| | Region and Country | Quantity | ratio (%) | Accumulation (%) |
|---|---|---|---|---|
| Northeast Chongqing | Chengkou | 1 | 1.32 | 1.32 |
| | Wuxi | 0 | 0 | 1.32 |
| | Wushan | 1 | 1.32 | 2.64 |
| | Kaixian | 0 | 0 | 2.64 |
| | Yunyang | 1 | 1.32 | 3.96 |
| | Fengjie | 0 | 0 | 3.96 |
| | Wanzhou | 2 | 2.63 | 6.59 |
| | Liangping | 1 | 1.32 | 7.91 |
| | Zhongxian | 4 | 5.26 | 13.17 |
| Yuzhong District | Shizhu | 3 | 3.95 | 17.12 |
| | Dianjiang | 0 | 0 | 17.12 |
| | Fengdu | 0 | 0 | 17.12 |
| | Changshou | 0 | 0 | 17.12 |
| | Fulin | 4 | 5.26 | 22.38 |
| Southeast Chongqing | Youyang | 22 | 28.95 | 51.33 |
| | Xiushan | 8 | 10.53 | 61.86 |
| | Pengshui | 4 | 5.26 | 67.12 |
| | Qianjiang | 4 | 5.26 | 72.38 |
| | Wulong | 5 | 6.58 | 78.95 |
| Southern Chongqing | Nanchuan | 0 | 0 | 78.95 |
| | Zhucheng | 2 | 2.63 | 81.58 |
| | Qijiang | 1 | 1.32 | 84.22 |
| Western Chongqing | Hechuan | 1 | 1.32 | 85.54 |
| | Tongnan | 3 | 3.95 | 88.17 |
| | Dazu | 2 | 2.63 | 90.8 |
| | Jiangjin | 5 | 6.58 | 97.38 |
| | Bishan | 0 | 0 | 97.38 |
| | Yongchuan | 2 | 2.63 | 100 |
| | Tongliang | 0 | 0 | 100 |
| | Rongchang | 0 | 0 | 100 |
| | Total | 76 | 100 | 100 |

As Table 1 shows: $T$=76, $n$=30, then we can calculate the geographical concentration index of traditional villages in Chongqing $G$=34.86. It is assumed that the 76 traditional villages in Chongqing are averagely distributed in each county. In other words, quantity in each city/prefecture is 76/30=2.53, so the index of geographical concentration is 2.53, 34.86 is much higher than 2.53, and therefore the distribution of traditional villages in Chongqing is relatively concentrated.

According to the geographical conditions, natural factors and economic development of Chongqing, it can be divided in five major geographic regions the northeast, the southeast, the center, the south, the west and the northeast. The northeast includes the follow counties: Wanzhou, Wushan, Wuxi, Chengkou, Kaixian, Fengjie, Yunyang, Liangping, Zhongxian. The southeast includes Qianjiang, Xiushan, Youyang, Pengshui and Wulong. The center of Chongqing includes Changshou, Dianjiang, Fengdu, Shizhu. The south of Chongqing includes Nanchuang and Qijiang. And the west of Chongqing includes Jiangjin, Yongchuan, Shuangqiao, Hechuan, Tongliang, Dazu, Rongchang, Bishan, Tongnan. According to Table 1, there are obvious differences in the spatial distribution of traditional villages in Chongqing, mainly distribute in the southeast and western.

The unbalance index reflects the equilibrium degree of the traditional villages in different regions [See Formula (3)].

$$S=\frac{\sum_{i=1}^{n}Y_i-50(n+1)}{100n-50(n+1)} \tag{3}$$

In this formula, $n$ refers the number of city/prefecture, $Y_i$ is the accumulated percentage of the $i^{th}$ one after ordering the ratio of a certain study object to the regional total within each region from high to low. The disequilibrium index $S$ ranges from 0 to 1, if the research objects are averagely distributed in each region, $S$=0; if all the subjects were concentrated in one area, the index $S$=1.

We can figure out that the unbalanced index $S$ =0.4476. It shows that the spatial distribution of traditional villages in Chongqing is not balanced. The most concentrated area is the southeast of Chongqing, which accounts for 56.58% of the total area, the second is the west of Chongqing which accounts for 17.11%, the third is the northeast of Chongqing which accounts for 13.17%, the least one is the center and south which accounts for 9.21% and 3.95%.

Based on the above data, the distribution of traditional villages in Chongqing is concentrated but the area is unbalanced, which originates from the development of traditional villages.Traditional villages have experienced hundreds of years or even thousands of years history and cultural changes, then bred diversity villages during dynasty change in the war and peace, farming and civilization, the environment and climate change. Among the villages, the outstanding ones have been selected into the List of Traditional Village in China because of the high value of tangible and intangible heritage. It is worth thinking that what force is related to the formation of traditional village value and which dimensions can be used to discuss the present value of villages that have undergone changes.We think that time and space are the coordinate axes of traditional village value, the two dimensions constitute the value of traditional villages.

There is a positive correlation between time dimension and village value. The value for time, and then determine the value, the longer the time, the more obvious the value. At the same time, villages can store time, which can be the storage of time and space. If the past time loses the space, the value of time cannot be reflected. Corresponding to the change of time is space change, the change of village on the axis of time represents the change of village space. The space of the village carries the information of the past. Let the others find what is relevant and useful to us in the past. On this basis, the village can retain the history, reproduce the time and space of history. So space supports time, time is dependent of space. In this sense, the existence of all cultural economy is the existence of time and space. The traditional village becomes the dialectical unity of time and space reproduction. [24]

But at present, time and space of many traditional villages have not been reproduced, moreover, these two dimensions are decreasing. Firstly, we can see the performance in the space heritage, that cannot absorb local labor force due to the lack of industry support. The problem of loss of indigenous villages is serious, numerous people move to cities and towns, the population and economy of the village is shrinking day by day, and many villages are facing with the problem of rural hollowing. However, the villages whose cultural value and tourism value have been exhausted and rapidly changed by rapid urbanization. [25]

On the other hand, most of traditional villages are scattered in remote areas, whose economic development is relatively backward, the essential infrastructure and public services is relatively poor and partial function is unavailable. These above cannot meet the needs of modern people's production and life style, so it is inevitable that traditional villages can not keep the aborigines and will lose the inheritance, which is an important reason for the disappearance of the village. The deep reason is the lack of inheritance that results in the loss of spatial value of villages.

Secondly is the problem of time dimension. A complete village is the memory of time, carrying history and culture of a nation. However, the utilization and development of preserving traditional villages, which basically reflect in its tourism survival. The assimilation of traditional culture and the marginalization of indigenous people in the process of tourism make the value of time dimension of traditional villages almost disappear. A village is a small community unit and its natural carrying capacity is limited so its traditional culture is rapidly assimilated during the process of the development. Consequently, the aboriginal people in the village are on the edge and have no rights to speak, and even their interest demands are marginalized. Thus another deep-seated reason for the vanish of traditional villages is the lost value on the time dimension.

For the utilization and development of traditional villages, tourism is just recognized as a medium or a way, while the essence is to improve the quality of aboriginal villages life. In the utilization of the villages, the benefits of aborigines should be put in the first place. Secondly, traditional houses should be transformed and their living quality should be improved. Finally, we should carry out the construction of the endogenous organization, which can form a diversified participation mechanism and interest coordination mechanism. The trend of utilization and development of traditional villages tend to make rural and city return back to nature.

*iii. Kernel density analysis*

Kernel density analysis tool within ArcGIS10.1 is applied to analyze the density distribution of 76 traditional villages in Chongqing and generate the density distribution of the traditional villages in Chongqing (see Figure 3).

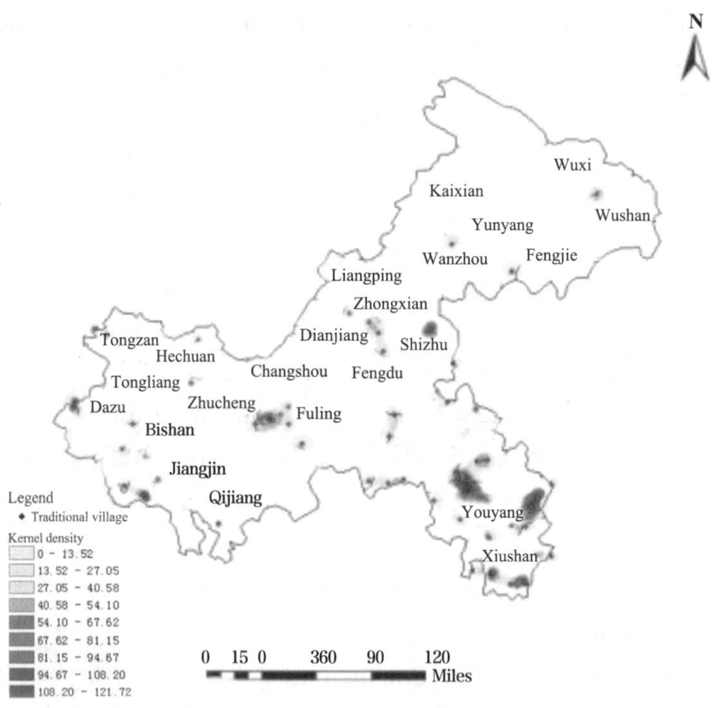


Figure 3 Density Distribution of the Traditional Villages in Chongqing

The spatial distribution of the traditional villages in Chongqing has three high density areas, which is Youyang, Xiushan and Shizhu. Youyang Tujia and Miao Autonomous County and Xiushan Tujia and Miao Autonomous County are located in the hinterland of Wuling mountain, that are the two most remote counties in Chongqing. Shizhu Tujia Autonomous County is part of Wushan and Daloushan district of Zhongshan. The three high density areas are located in the minority autonomous county, which reflects that ethnic villages have been recognized for their better retention of nationality in the condition that many villages become bleak generally, and the ethnic villages are brought into the List of Traditional Villages. So we can find that ethnic characteristics play an important role in the protection and identification of traditional villages.

In this process, we can find that the importance of ethnic traditional culture has been highlighted because it constitutes the internal motive force for the survival and continuation of national villages, which is a guarantee to be preserved and stands out in many villages. Ethnic traditional culture is the symbol of a nation which is different from other nationalities, especially the ethnic consciousness and relatively stable ethnic relations among the ethnic groups.When we improve the stability of the national cultural heritage, villages in historical changes keep the national characteristics. [26] The consciousness of ethnic groups and the consistency of national cultural and identity form a distinctive national identity. The original villages show their own national culture and national identity by life style, sense of worth and world views, which can help them to distinguish themselves from others, in this way, national characteristics are prominent and local characteristics get clear.

The nationality of the village can enhance the cohesion of the village, the national memory of the aboriginal people is an important tie to link the relationship among the people in the village, that is part of the spirit of traditional culture. The spirit of traditional culture has become a tool to resist foreign culture because of its obvious identification, however, the material level and system level of traditional culture are easy to be assimilated because of the pursuit of application and rationality. That is why some of the traditional ethnic villages in the rapid development of tourism lost the characteristics of the village and the root causes of ethnicity. Studies on protection and utilization of traditional villages are to establish an ecological environment of national traditional culture, which can help villages find a balance point between the spiritual and the material, the traditional and the modern when be used, then it can make the village being consistent with modern society to achieve the transition from a traditional village to a modern one.

## Ⅳ. Conclusions

Through the above analysis, we can get the following three basic conclusions.

Firstly, the value of traditional village lies in its collective memory. Collective memory is the collective crystallization of aborigines, there is no collective memory without aborigines, and protection of indigenous people means protecting traditional villages. The aborigines give the village collective cultural significance, which presents a diachronic process of subjective existence and collective identity. They carry the collective memory and cultural identity of the village. The collective memory of the aborigines is the source of the revival of traditional villages to help us find out what the village used to be.

Secondly, place is influenced by culture for a long time. [27] The traditional village is a multi-level diachronic cultural accumulation while culture is a powerful means to control the village space. There is a relative relationship between the spatial distribution and memory, time and space, village protection is closely related to these factors of time and space.

Thirdly, nationality is a key driving force for the development of traditional villages, which is an important feature that distinguishes it from other villages. Nationality has achieved the national culture and economy effectively fitting in the development of rural tourism, that is a transit of national resources to tourism capital. On the premise of the subjectivity of national cultural heritage and the authenticity of the village tourism performance, the positive interaction between ethnic cultural heritage and village tourism is an important advantage of the national culture and the inheritance of ethnic villages. It is an significant advantage of national culture and national heritage. The integration of national characteristics and national living space, the existence of the national space will constitute one of the further research of traditional villages.

Traditional villages embody the cultural nutrients left in different historical periods, which can filter the impurities and precipitation essence and finally become the present style villages. The value of village lies not in the existence of the village itself, but in that the village is regarded as a cultural carrier and what it used to be. Village protection is not only to protect the old houses, temples, ancestral halls and other material carriers, but to protect history, space, and the value of protecting the village's past.

## ACKNOWLEDGMENT

The authors gratefully acknowledge financial support from the National Social Science Foundation of China, project of "Research of the Protection and Inheritance of Cultural Heritage Corridor in the Three Gorges Reservoir Area"( 13CGL156).

## References

[1] Huang Haifeng. Xi Jinping's traditional culture and its value of the times[J]. *Journal of Chongqing University of Technology (Social Science)*, 2017(31): 120-127.

[2] Hu Yan, Chen Sheng. The concept and cultural connotation of traditional villages [J]. U*rban Development*, 2017(21): 10-12.

[3] Sun Jiuying. The traditional village: theoretical connotation and development path of tourism [J]. *Tourism Tribune*, 2017(32): 1-3.

[4] Li Zhixiu. Study on the protection mode of ancient villages: taking Jiangxi Province as an example [J]. *Jiangxi Social Sciences*, 2012(1): 238-240.

[5] Sun Jiuying. The traditional village: theoretical connotation and development path of tourism [J]. *Tourism Tribune*, 2017(32): 1-3.

[6] Yu Ruyi, Liang Liuke. The invasion and succession of tourism population and the reorganization of spatial order in ancient villages: a case study of the ancient village of Huizhou in Hongcun [J]. *Economic Geography*, 2013(33): 165-170.

[7] Feng Shuhua. Discussion on symbiosis evolution model of ancient village based on symbiosis theory[J]. *Economic Geography*, 2013(33): 155-162.

[8] Sun Ying, Xiao Dawei, Wang Yushun. A syntactic analysis of the space of traditional villages: taking meizhou as an example [J]. *Urban Development Research*, 2015(22): 63-70.

[9] Gu Kang, Chu Jinglong, Wang Yongzhen. Spatial differentiation of comprehensive quality of ancient villages in Huangshan City: an empirical study based on 101 ancient villages[J]. *Geographical Research*, 2014(33): 2034-2042.

[10] Liu Dajun, Hu Jing. A study on the spatial distribution pattern of chinese traditional villages[J]. *China Population Resources and Environment*, 2014(24): 157-162.

[11] Sun Jiuying, Zhou Yi. Local recognition of residents in heritage tourism diao xiao symbols, memory and space [J]. *Geographical Research*, 2015(34): 2381-2394.

[12] Li Wenbin. A study on the tourist loyalty model of ancient villages: based on the visible perceptual value and its dimension [J]. *Geographical Research*, 2011(30): 37-48.

[13] Tang Wenyue. The influence of local attachment of ancient villagers on their moving intention in the background of tourism development: taking Wuyuan Ancient Village as an example [J]. *Economic Management*, 2014(20): 124-132.

[14] Weng Shixiu, Peng Hua. A study on the empowerment of the villages in the primary stage of the development of the weak rights in the early stage of tourism development: a case study of the Furong Village in Nanxi River, Zhejiang Province [J]. *Journal of Tourism*, 2017(26): 53-59.

[15] Liu Long. Analysis of journal papers about studies of ancient Chinese villages [J]. *Canadian Social Science*, 2015(11): 133-137.

[16] Sharpley R. Rural tourism and the challenge of tourism diversification: the case of Cyprus [J]. *Tourism Management*, 2002(23): 233-244.

[17] Hashemi H, Ghaffary G. A proposed sustainable rural development index (SRDI): lessons from Hajij Village [J]. *Tourism Management,* 2016(59): 130-138.

[18] Huang Qiuyun. Vernacular landscape leading the way: the holistic protection and revival of Hani ancient village under the background of Yuanyang terraced fields register on the world heritage [J]. *Advanced Materials Research*, 2014(1030): 2468-2488.

[19] Nakama Y. Traditional village forest landscapes: tourists' attitudes and preferences for conservation [J]. *Tourism Management*, 2017(59): 652-662.

[20] Levine S R, Hughes T M, Ryan M C. Generating sustainable towns from Chinese villages: a system modelling approach [J]. *Journal of Environmental Management,* 2008(87): 305-316.

[21] Tong Yuquan. Study on spatial differentiation of Chinese traditional villages based on GIS [J]. *Human Geography*, 2014(4): 44-51.

[22] Tao Dongfeng. Memory is a kind of cultural construction: on collective memory [J]. *Chinese Book Review*, 2010(9): 69-74.

[23] Hu Huilin. An outline of time and space culture economics [J]. *Explore and Contend*, 2013(5): 10-16.

[24] Xu Chuncheng, Wan Zhiqin. On the basic thinking of traditional village protection [J]. *Journal of Huazhong Agricultural University (Social Science Edition)*, 2015(6): 58-64.

[25] Qi Ji. Research on the development of community cultural heritage from the perspective of urbanization [J]. *Chinese Culture Forum*, 2016(122): 26-29.

[26] Yi Futuan. *Space and Place in the Perspective of Experience* [M]. Taipei: Taipei Institute for Compilation and Translation, 1998: 53.

[27] Wu Yueping, Zhang Xiaoping. Multidimensional perspectives on "cultural space" research at home and abroad [J]. *Journal of Southwest University for Nationalities (Humanities and Social Sciences)*, 2016(37): 7-12.

# The Development of "Chuangke" in Rural Tourism: A Case Study of Rural Scenic Spot in Chengdu Sansheng Township

Liu Tingting[1*]

**Abstract:** Based on the analysis of the development of rural tourism in China, this paper discusses the concept and development model of "Chuangke" in rural tourism. Taking the rural tourism scenic spot of Sansheng Township in Chengdu as an example, this paper analyzes its development stage and characteristics, puts forward the existing problems in the development, and makes proposals for further development, with a view to effectively achieving integrative development of "Chuangke" and tourism in future rural tourism.

**Keywords:** rural tourism; Chuangke; development; study; development mode; problem; suggestions

From the 1990s, Chinese rural scenic spots had attracted lots of urban tourists by the unique "Original Home" tourism resources. Country tourism originated from the initial stage of eating farm meals, playing farm cards, and living in the farm house, transited to the developing stage of planting vegetables and picking fruits, and then developed to the leisure stage of constructing country lodge resort. [1] Country tourist scenic spots have been continuously improving their service level and developing new projects. Currently, with the enrichment of tourists' experience and the continuous change of travel demands, country tourism has entered from the era of leisure sightseeing into the era of experiencing life, which offers a new challenge for the development of country tourism.

In 2015, the General Office of the State Council of China printed and distributed "Opinions on Further Developing Tourism Investment and Consumption", which clearly proposed for the first time the project to develop "Chuangke" program in the country. A series of country tourism Chuangke demonstration bases are going to be settled. [2] In August 2016, China National Tourism Administration confirmed and qualified 60 "Country Tourism Chuangke Demonstration Bases".

1* Chengdu College of University of Electronic Science and Technology of China, Chengdu, China. 106881393@qq.com.

## Ⅰ. A Brief Introduction to "Chuangke" in Rural Tourism

*i. The concept of "Chuangke"*

The Chinese term "Chuangke" comes from the English word "Maker", which originated from the founder of Silicon Valley or FabLab ("personal manufacturing laboratory") of Massachusetts Institute of Technology in the United States of America. Generally speaking, "Chuangke" refers to the "self-made innovator" from the perspective of historical development. [3] In December 2012, Chris Anderson proposed that the next decade will be the era of "Maker" in his book *Crew: New Industrial Revolution*, and declared the arrival of the individual manufacturing era.

In 2011, the term "Chuangke" appeared in China. It was introduced from the corresponding foreign expression and was translated into Chinese. Different from its corresponding foreign expression, "Chuangke" in China is more combined with innovation, which weakens the characteristics in manufacturing and technology industries and has been widely applied to major areas like science, technology, education, culture, business, etc. In China, "Chuangke" not only needs independent innovation ideas and capabilities, but also their own resources related to entrepreneurship. At present, as long as the person who is able to apply the individual's innovative ideas to the process of self-entrepreneurship, he will be generally referred to as a "Chuangke".

In recent years, the personalized business opportunities continue to emerge in tourism industry. On the one hand, the tourism needs "Chuangke", and on the other hand, "Chuangke" needs tourism resources. In this case, tourism "Chuangke" gradually develops. Based on science and technology, culture, country and other resources, by building tourist centers (like Guizhou Chishui Yun Travel Inn Center), setting up travel maker spaces (like Tourism Innovation and Creative Business Platform of Hunan University Students), building Rural Travel Internet APP (like "Xiaxiangke" APP), [4] and creating demonstration bases of "Chuangke" in China's rural tourism, etc., tourism "Chuangke" has become a new force in the development of China's tourism.

*ii. The model of "Chuangke" in the development of rural tourism in China*

In China, the earliest "Chuangke" in rural tourism came from abroad. From the history and characteristics of development, "Chuangkes" use rural resources to start their own businesses mainly in the following three models:

*A. Country hotel + "Chuangke"*

At the very beginning, some foreigners from developed countries came to work, study, live or travel in China. They had experienced the industrial age, so they were attracted by the natural ecological environment of China's villages. Then they lived in the country, engaged in accommodation and hospitality activities, and gradually built some rural leisure resort hotels, thus opening their business trip. "Yangjiale" in Mount Mogan of Zhejiang Moganshan, Gege

Tree Hotel in Yangshuo, Guilin are typical representatives.

Rural leisure resort hotels run by foreign "Chuangke" attracted a large number of tourists to the country they are in. Then, many villages in China were inspired to introduce in "Chuangke" (including foreigners and Chinese people). They began to use the old houses to build featured country inn or homestay, rural intelligent hotels, etc., and constantly enriched and improved the hotels' leisure products, hoping that the rural tourists will change their plans from sightseeing to accommodation. These rural hotels has greatly enriched the experience of rural leisure and enhanced the attractiveness of rural tourism.

*B. Agricultural and sideline products+ "Chuangke"*

As a result of the village's unique resources, environment and the current public demand for the green farm products, a group of graduates of agriculture-related majors and other urban workers went to the country to start businesses. Some of these village "Chuangkes" cultivated cash crops themselves, raised poultry, and constructed small farms, to attract urban residents leisurely travel to the farms on weekends. At the same time, they provided customized agricultural and sideline products to urban residents. Some of them cooperated with the villagers, carried out centralized purchasing, unified packaging on the agricultural and sideline products and handicrafts and formed their own brand, using online and offline multi-channel sales, like "Bancang people" in Changsha, Hunan.

*C. Cultural innovation+ "Chuangke"*

This kind of village "Chuangke" has promoted the development of rural tourism mainly through cultural innovation. It can be divided into the following two types.

One is the art-studio which is established by the foreign artists. Famous artists created new rural tourist attractions through such ways as investing to build a studio in the village, operating the inn, showing the process of artistic creation, and the displaying, exchanging and selling of art products. A large number of tourists are attracted and travel to the countries where the studio is in. From the late 1990s, many foreign investors went into the country, invested in leisure industry and constructed art studios in rural area. For example, in 2001, a Taiwan investor Adan rented a plot of land in Lashihai of Lijiang to establish "Pangu" creative commune—"Wagangzhai" studio. As a well-known tourist souvenir designer and producer, he used his unique artistic creativity to make furniture from waste wood, and then sell the furniture in the ancient city of Lijiang. Also, in the Shuanglang of Dali, Yang Liping and Zhao Qing, as the representatives of the artists, built art studios and inns, so that the small village of Erhai was full of ambience of literature and art, and also became a well-known tourist destination because of the celebrity effect.

Another type is the arts district where village "Chuangkes" gather. The local government supports the construction and remodelling of workshops, and offers preferential policies to attract artists and investors to start their own businesses in the countryside, which has formed the cluster effect. Take Songzhuang in Tongzhou of Beijing for example. Painters kept arriving and stayed there since 1994, and gradually formed an artist community. In 2008, China's Songzhuang Art Circle District was constructed. And now the creative culture industrial park is vigorously being built. The entrance of the village "Chuangke" has turned a little-known village into the largest and most popular cultural and creative industry cluster in Beijing and even China, which attracts many tourists. This kind of area, which is developed by art village and painting village, is mostly located around the city. And the village "Chuangke" in the rural tourist attraction of Chengdu Sansheng Township belongs to this type.

## Ⅱ. An Analysis on the Development of "Chuangke" in the Rural Tourist Attraction of Sansheng Township in Chengdu

The rural tourist scenic spots in the suburbs of big cities are different from the rural areas of the cities because of their special geographical location. This determines that the rural tourist scenic spots in the suburbs of big cities can not only rely on the original countryside, but also need to take account of the urban recreation function, develop innovative projects and keep pace with the times. Chengdu Sansheng Township rural tourist scenic area is a national 4A level scenic spot. "Chuangke" was introduced on the basis of the famous scenic spot. At the time, the mode—a famous scenic spot + "Chuangke" is also an innovation.

*i. Development stage*

"Chuangkes" in Chengdu Sansheng Township rural tourist scenic area mainly concentrate in the Lotus Pond Moonlight scenic area, including Blue Top Art Gallery, Blue Top Contemporary Art Base, Blue Top Youth Art Village, Blue Top Club, and Wanfu Scenery Painting Village. So far, the development has gone through two stages:

The first stage is the starting phase of the studio. In 2004, artists led by Zhou Chunya took advantage of a simple factory near Chuqiao of Chengdu, and formed an early blue top art zone. This is an open studio phase of the community. A group of artists came together to create a community of artists because of their common beliefs. The working conditions of the old blue top art zone were especially poor. There were serious air, noise and groundwater pollution, which affected artists' creation to a certain extent. With the increasing popularity of the old blue art district in the society, the environmental problems in the art district have attracted the attention of the local government in Chengdu.

The second stage is the creating stage of the art zone. In 2009, Chengdu Sansheng Township government provided land, capitals and some other preferential policies to attract artists to move the old blue top art zone to Sansheng Township Lotus Pond Moonlight scenic area, and gradually completed the blue top phase Ⅰ, phase Ⅱ, phase Ⅲ projects. In 2010, the Blue Top Company rented the whole new resettlement area built by the government and then sublet workshops to young artists. The good creation environment attracted a large number of young artists at home and abroad. Most of the time there were almost 50 young artists in youth arts village. At the same time, Chengdu Sansheng Township has attracted another group of national painting artists, which formed the present Wanfu Scenery Painting Village. Through various efforts, "Chuangkes" in Chengdu Sansheng Township finally realized the transformation from a spontaneous community to an organized art district in the development mode.

In general, the "Chuangke" community of Chengdu Sansheng Township rural tourism area is still in its development stage.

*ii. Development features*

The development of the "Chuangke" community in Chengdu Sansheng Township rural tourism area mainly shows the following three characteristics.

*A. The "Chuangke" group based on the artists*

Chengdu Sansheng Township belongs to the tourist areas on the outskirts of the city or the country, which has a convenient location and beautiful natural environment. It enables the famous city artists to find a quiet environment, create art and enjoy the convenience of city life and work. The "Chuangke" community in Chengdu Sansheng Township rural tourism scenic area is a place where artist studios led by well-known painters spontaneously gather together. The cultural creativity mainly embodied in painting art, and the current main work includes making art, painting education, displaying, selling works of art, etc.

*B. Cooperation on two-way attraction in development mode*

The formation of the region benefited from the two-way attraction cooperation between the government and the artists. Due to the need of a good environment attraction of "Chuangke" artists and the demand of new production factors in Sansheng Township rural tourism scenic area, the government promoted cooperation on two-way attraction through preferential policy level.

*C. Open and private sharing of community construction*

"Chuangke" community in Chengdu Sansheng Township rural tourist scenic area has both private close space and open space. The blue top studio takes the old spirit and holds open activities. There is open community management in blue youth art village, which opens to both the international art creators and families. Both the individual painter and the artist family from the other countries can rent an independent house to stay for a long time to compose, and enjoy the exclusive close space. Even if the rent for a month rises from 9 yuan to 18 yuan per square meter now, the houses are still in short supply. Wanfu Scenery Painting Village adopts a strict appointment system for community management. The outsiders should make an appointment first with the owner in order to enter the art district, in which the "Chuangke" enjoys a high degree of privacy.

*iii. Major problems in development*

The development of Chengdu Sansheng Township rural tourist scenic area has led to a new round of planning and construction, which has promoted the comprehensive development of the region and increased the overall value of the region. From the tourism's point of view, "Chuangke" injected new cultural connotations for the rural tourism scenic area, enriched tourism resources to a certain extent; however, the current poor experience of tourists is a major problem.

At present, the area where the Chuangke is located has not been able to integrate well with the Lotus Pond Moonlight scenic spot. In the "Chuangke" community, it is difficult to find consumable products. Because of the inconvenient traffic and serious lack of tourist infrastructure, visitors can't experience innovative tourism products brought by "Chuangke".

## Ⅲ. Suggestions on the Development of "Chuangke" Base in Chengdu Sansheng Township Rural Tourist Attraction

*i. To improve the community management*

Urban, suburban and rural areas have their unique location advantages, while retaining the rural original landscape. They can quickly integrate with the urban fast-paced work life at the same time. The "Chuangke" base of Chengdu Sansheng Township rural tourist scenic spot should strengthen the construction and management of the living, working and leisure integration community to find a balance. Supporting the leisure facilities in the community and creating a communication platform aim to build harmonious "Chuangke" community, let the artists achieve new heights of innovation in a comfortable, convenient and relaxed environment and attract more "Chuangkes" to join the country life. [5]

*ii. To improve the sharing mechanism of interests*

Rural "Chuangke" injected a new creative capital for the development of the entire region and brought new factors of production. Government supports "Chuangke" in such aspects as increasing economy, manpower, and market credit to meet the demand of the basic interests of "Chuangke". At the same time, the government also takes into account the interests of local residents and tourists, and respects the local residents' living environment and the traditional lives. This can help form the effective mechanism of sharing local employment, innovation of residents travel business mode and experience on product upgrading. [6]

*iii. To innovate characteristics of products and improve the relevant industry chain*

As a rural tourist attraction in the suburb of the city, Chengdu Sansheng Township rural tourist scenic spot should meet the needs of urban leisure. On the other hand, as a national 4A scenic spot, Sansheng Township needs to improve the tourist products so as to make people stay on vacation and make rural tourism a way of life. Sansheng Township scenic spot should reasonably use resources, examine the resource advantages, distinguish from the original natural amorous feelings of remote mountainous area and create for city tourists a fine country life. We should find for tourists new ways of life in the new lifestyles created by “Chuangke”. If we want to develop innovative featured products, we should make full use of the creative spirit, which can take the culture into the original Sansheng Township characteristic resources and form unique creative products. We should make the creative culture easy to digest and integrate creative products into the tourists’ lifestyles, enhance the development of entertainment products, meet the needs of tourism market and form a rural tourism holiday destination.

Taking artistic creation, display, communication, derivatives trading and “creative + rural tourism resources” development as the main line, we strengthen the innovation of the agricultural and sideline products, handicrafts, and the development of “Chuangke” hotels and characteristics of derivative products. This can make it having both the pure nature of rural agricultural and sideline products and the pursuit of the art of life, which can help create their own brands, gradually improve rural tourism emerging industry chains, form a creative industry park and creative tourism life park. It can develop in a multidimensional direction.

*iv. To optimize the tourism environment and enhance the tourism experience*

In order to strengthen the construction of scenic infrastructure, we need to improve the transportation system first. For example, there are only tourist rickshaws, Mobike, OFO in the area, which challenges tourists who can’t ride and haven’t cars and reduce the “Chuangke” community’s accessibility. Secondly we should perfect the scenic identification system. The “Chuangke” gathering area is clearly lack of identification system settings. At last we should enhance the sense of tourism services. To improve the level of scenic service, whether it is the original scenic area or “Chuangke”, it is the key to improve the service awareness of local residents. We should construct tourist advisory center in major nodes to achieve scenic area service without dead ends. Meanwhile, we need to strengthen the construction of intelligent areas, and to enhance the guidance of the navigation, interpretation, characteristic agricultural products purchase, cultural creative activities and other aspects so as to promote the tourism experience of tourists through information technology.

*v. To promote the integration of development and increase marketing*

The development of “Chuangke” base in rural tourist scenic area not only takes the tourist market as a guide, the ecological environment as the basis and the cultural creativity as a breakthrough, but integrates the common development of the Internet and the financial industry, which lets it become the effective thrust of scenic area development. In particular, we should make full use of the advantages of the Internet to enhance the visibility of the scenic spots, establish brand, create Internet +“Chuangke” tourism products, and further strengthen marketing of scenic spots.

## Ⅳ. Conclusions

Chengdu Sansheng Township rural tourist scenic area is a typical urban, suburban and rural tourist attraction. There are obvious differences in the tourism resources owned by villages in different regions of China. There are also specific situations in the development of "Chuangke" in different rural tourism. In general, the emergence of "Chuangke" in China's rural tourism is actually a concrete practice of the reform and innovation of rural tourism development. At present, it is still in the development stage. In the future, China's rural tourism "Chuangke" should focus on solving the following problems:

*i. Clear their own demands & enhance the regional value*

The ultimate goal of the development of rural tourism "Chuangke" is to enhance the overall value of the original rural tourism resources. The value of the resources owned by the operators, residents and governments of the rural tourism destination will be improved, and the core competitiveness of the region as a whole will be enhanced. In the development, the rural tourist scenic areas need to deal with the relationship between the new factors of production—"Chuangke" and the original rural resources. The development of rural tourism "Chuangke" should be based on respecting the original rural resources, and should be coordinated with the characteristics of the original rural tourism resources, and the development model suitable for the characteristics of rural tourism resources in the region should be developed to achieve the new innovation in China's original rural tourism "Chuangke" model. The development of the focus should also be different. Remote mountainous areas should pay more attention to rural tourism "Chuangke" on the rural poverty alleviation project; Cities and suburbs should keep the "original rural" style at the same time, and should pay more attention to enhance leisure and entertainment functions as a supporting area of the city. Rural tourism scenic areas need to develop the "Chuangke" through a scientific planning, clear their own demands, and a reasonable position. Not all rural tourism scenic areas are suitable for the development of "Chuangke".

*ii. Strengthen the interaction of resources & innovate product design*

In the development of rural tourism scenic areas, "Chuangke" resources need to interact with the rural tourism resources, to avoid being fragmented. In all kinds of tourism activities, the design of tourism products is related to rural "Chuangke", from leisure experience, shopping and entertainment products to scenic landscape items, public infrastructure, tourist reception facilities, etc., reflecting the combination of "Chuangke" culture and rural culture. Rural tourism scenic areas need to strengthen the development of boutique tourism commodity, develop more attractive innovative tourism products, and establish their own brands.

*iii. Expand the emerging markets & strengthen publicity and promotion*

In most Chinese rural tourism scenic areas, the traditional rural tourism products are more favored by the elderly. In the development of rural tourism "Chuangke", we should actively expand the rural tourism market such as young tourists and parent-child tourists, [7] pay attention to marketing, especially network marketing; strengthen promotional activities, stimulate the motive of travel of tourists, and let them want to come again.

*iv. Improve service quality & improve the management*

Most Chinese rural tourism scenic areas need to be further improved in tourism service functions of the rural "Chuangke", and the quality of service. In the management, rural tourism scenic areas need to strengthen the professional training of service and management, cultivate professional scenic management personnel. At the same time, the government should increase policy support. Government and business entities need to take into account the interests of all parties in the management process. Rural tourism scenic areas need to partition function in space, share the benefits of resources, and ultimately to achieve the efficient management in the process of development in rural tourism.

## References

[1] Zou Tongqian. A study on the development model of rural tourism in China: a comparison between Chengdu farmhouse and Beijing folk village and the countermeasures[J]. *Tourism Tribune*, 2005(3): 63-68.

[2] Several opinions of the general office of the State Council on further promoting tourism investment and consumption[J]. *State Council issued*, 2015.

[3] Xiang Shiqing. The concept and connotation of the Chuangke [J].*China Science and Technology Education*, 2016(5):70-71.

[4] http://www.xiaxiangke.com.

[5] Simmons D G. Community participation in tourism planning[J]. *Tourism Management*, 1994(2):15.

[6] Trakolis D. Local people's perception of planning and management issues in Prespes Lakes National Park, Greece[J]. *Journal of Environmental Management*, 2001(3): 61.

[7] Gartner W C. Rural tourism development in the USA[J]. *International Journal of Tourism Research*, 2016(6): 151-164.

# A Study on the Development of Interactive Relations Between Scenic Areas and Local Communities Based on Social Interaction Theory: Taking Guangzhou Baishuizhai Scenic Area as an Example

Zhang Xilin[1*]

**Abstract:** Based on social interaction theory, taking Guangzhou Baishuizhai Scenic Area as an example, this paper studies the development of interactive relations between scenic areas and local communities with six types of social interaction such as exchange, cooperation, competition, conflict, coercion and compliance. Through the survey, it is concluded that the present social interaction type of the Baishuizhai Scenic Area is cooperative interaction. The relation between the two sides is in a conflict stage. In view of the existing problems, this paper puts forward five countermeasures, including the enrichment of industrial structure, the improvement of the system of laws and regulations and the coordination of the communication mechanism, the fulfillment of the social responsibility by scenic areas, the change of the administrative system by the government and the enhancement of the autonomous consciousness of community residents.

**Keywords:** social interaction; scenic areas; community; Guangzhou Baishuizhai Scenic Area

## Ⅰ. Introduction

On one hand, the development of scenic areas influences the daily life of the residents of local communities; on the other hand, the healthy development of local communities influences the steady development of scenic areas. However, traditionally, the community was seldom deemed as the predominant subject of interest in the management of scenic areas and there still exists a host of problems in the interaction between scenic areas and local communities. On the basis of different earnings from the scenic spots, communities take different positions towards the development of the local tourist attractions, i.e. supportive, marginal and opposing; considering different positions, they take corresponding actions, such

1* Zhaoqing University, Zhaoqing, China. Sydeny181212@163. com.

as integration, monitoring, defense and uniting respectively. [1] These actions form various social interactions between tourist attractions and local communities, which will directly affect the sustainable development of tourist attractions.

This study takes Guangzhou Baishuizhai Scenic Area as the research object. Through the study of the development of the interaction between scenic areas and local communities and the analysis of the types of interaction, and forms of manifestation as well as their characteristics, the study aims to discover the relevant problems and provide corresponding solutions, in the hope of promoting the harmonious development of the interaction between scenic areas and local communities. Surely, on the one hand, it is also hoped that these solutions can be conducive to the interaction between the Baishuizhai Scenic Area and the local community, thus winning the support of the residents of local community for the steady development of the Baishuizhai Scenic Area; on the other hand, it is expected that these solutions can make the local community to actively participate in the interaction with the Baishuizhai Scenic Area, thus safeguarding the status of the local community as the subject of development and the pertinent interests.

## Ⅱ. Related Research Review

*i. Research theory and relevant concepts*

*A. Social interaction*

Social interaction refers to the interaction and mutual connection between individuals. This term was first put forward by German sociologist Georg Simmel in his book *Sociology* in 1908. Social interaction between individuals is caused by common purposes and common interests, or by different purposes and different interests. The former can be called cooperative social interaction. The interests of both sides involving in such interaction is not subject to a direct contradiction, including the forms like cooperation, adaptation, assimilation and so on. The latter can be called antagonistic social interaction. The interests of both sides involving in such interaction is subject to a direct or indirect contradiction, including the forms like competition, conflict, obedience, etc. In the process of pursuing self-interest, individuals and organizations will inevitably be involved in social interactions. Cooperation, coercion, conflict, competition, compliance and other behaviors actively or passively with the dissemination of information as the basis will ultimately have a certain impact on the two sides in interaction and the relationship between the two. At present, the researches on social interaction theory mainly focus on conflict and interactive behaviors. In the process of reaching consensus on interest between tourist attractions and the local communities, the two sides need to carry out various types of multiple social interactions in order to ultimately ensure the smooth development of tourist attractions and local communities.

*B. Community*

The term "community" was first originated in the work of *Gemeinschaft and Gesellschaft* by German sociologist Ferdinand in 1887, while its definition was first made by American sociologist Rorber E. Park in 1936. He believed that the community should have the following characteristics: (1) it has a group of people organized by region; (2) these people are deeply rooted in the land they live on; (3) everyone in the community is living in an interdependent relationship. [2] The community studied in this paper mainly refers to the villages within the scope of the administrative management of the Baishuizhai Scenic Area.

*ii. Research about the interactive relationship between scenic areas and communities*

Liu Ping and Si Wei (2009) advocated that the scenic areas and residents should be viewed as two primary subjects of development on the basis of synergetics, system theory and cybernetics, in order to achieve the sustainable development of scenic areas and the harmonious development of local communities; [3] Chen Yaohua and Jin Xiaofeng (2009) discussed the requirements for the planning and building of residential areas against the backdrop of the planning of the scenic areas and the construction of new countryside, and explored the interactive relations between the scenic areas and the residential areas in the context of the construction new rural areas. The authors believe that it is essential to insist on the joint development of both the scenic areas and villages. [4]

Marphy (1985) mentions the concept of "community participation" in *Tourism: Community Approaches*, which combines community and tourism for the first time. With the deepening of research, the concept "tourism community" gradually takes shape with its research focusing on the impact range and intensity of tourism. [2-5] Since the beginning of the interactive development of urban and rural areas, [6-8] the existing researches mainly focus on the interaction factors among the market, community residents and non-governmental organizations in the development of tourism, as well as the interaction researches on environment, culture, society impact in tourism development and the interaction researches on tourism development and local landscape changes. [9-11] From the perspective of stakeholders, many scholars conduct researches on the coordinated development of stakeholders in tourist attractions. Jamal (2005) commented the sustainable development strategies for national parks in France based on Delphi method, [13] Garcia (2013) introduced a theoretical and methodological framework for promoting the cooperation between tourism organizations and stakeholders in tourism sustainability assessment. [14] In addition, community support and community empowerment in the development of tourist attractions have become a new trend in recent years in the application of social interaction theory. [15-16] In reality, the development of the vast majority of tourist attractions is operated by the developers, governments or non-governmental organizations. However, the development of tourist attractions must rely on the socio-economic environment of local communities. Therefore, it is necessary for tourist attractions to establish cooperative relationship with the local communities and actively promote the normative participation and cooperation between the two behavioral agents, i.e. local communities and tourist attractions, in the tourism development.

This paper, on the basis of previous studies, taking the suburban scenic areas as the research object, studies the development of scenic areas and local communities in the light of social interaction theory.

## Ⅲ. The Development of the Scenic Areas and the Local Communities in the Light of Social Interaction Theory

Social interaction is divided into exchange, cooperation, competition, conflict, coercion and compliance according to the interests, the power relationship and the nature of the subjects of the social interaction.

*i. Exchange*

When social interaction occurs among individuals or groups in some manner, its aim is to obtain remuneration or return, thus forming the relationship of exchange. The return may not be tangible material. It may not have a clear purpose. But most social exchanges follow the principle of reciprocity. [5]

Whether it is due to the spatial relationship between the two sides, or it is because of the need for support and assistance from the other side for facilitating the better development of both sides, the interaction occurs between scenic areas and local communities, thus forming a multi-level complex system.

The scenic area-community is a complex system of “nature-society”. Its naturality is embodied in the tangible resources, involving various types of “things”, such as the connection between natural resources or human resources and between things in scenic areas. Its sociality is reflected in the “people”, such as the relationships among scenic areas, communities, tourists and other diversified subjects of interests. Therefore, the most important elements are “people” and “things”in the process of the formation of the scenic area-community system. Actually, such process is a “people-things” exchange. That is to say, it is a process of the flow, exchange and value recreation of money, manpower, culture, environment, resources, information and other elements.

*ii. Cooperation*

The reason why the scenic area-community can be synthesized into a system is that there are common interests and goals between the two sides, which can be greater economic benefits that the scenic area and community need, or be the goal of boosting the faster and better development of local tourism industry. As a result of common interests and goals, there occurs a mutually cooperative relation between scenic areas and local communities. On the one hand, the development of scenic areas drives the economic development of the communities, improves the construction of local infrastructure, and enhances the employment rate of some people, which are conducive to the harmonious development of local communities; on the other hand, the improvement of infrastructure in the local communities creates a good community environment and lays a solid foundation for attracting more tourists, which is favorable to the development of tourism in scenic areas. Therefore, in order to achieve the the common interests and goals of both sides, a cooperative relationship is formed between scenic areas and local communities.

*iii. Competition*

Competition is a cooperative conflict. Traditionally, cooperation and competition are a pair of antonyms. However, in modern society, the integration of competition and competition in the new business strategy is likely to achieve a win-win situation. [5] The development of scenic areas may make the tourism industry an important part of the economic development of local communities. However, the development of the tourism industry does not bring considerable benefits for the residents of local community. For instance, if the residents do not feel that the development of tourism industry creates benefits for them, they may feel so depressed for the tourism industry that reject its development, thus forming an indirect objection. As a result, there is a competitive relationship between scenic areas and local communities. If scenic areas ignore the community factors and community residents' requirements, there may be environmental pollution, economic chaos and other negative consequences. If the vicious competition is caused because scenic areas fail to coordinate the organization of the operation of tourism products of local communities, there will be some impact on the development of scenic areas and local communities. This competition is a kind of attendant phenomenon, or it can be said to be an inevitable phenomenon.

*iv. Conflict*

Conflict can also have a positive effect and can become a force to promote close unity within both sides. It can also force the two sides to face the problem to deepen understanding and can also lead to the necessary social changes. Although society can, to some extent, succeed in eliminating conflicts, a society without conflict will be a lifeless and boring society. [5] The conflict between scenic areas and local communities mainly happens in the process of capital and interest games of the stakeholders. The communities should be the subjects of the development of scenic areas and local communities, but the communities have little power in the development process. The communities are at the bottom of the power structure, that is, in a weak position. Sometimes, the power gap will lead to imbalance in the distribution of benefits. The expectations of the communities for the development of scenic areas could have been mutual-benefit and win-win results. Nevertheless, when the results are detrimental to their own interests, they may take all kinds of boycotts or sabotage.

*v. Coercion*

Like conflict, coercion is often seen as a form of negative social interaction, but it also has a positive social function. [6] The adverse competition and conflict occur between scenic areas and local communities is bound to affect the respective development of scenic areas and local communities. However, in order to safeguard their own interests, scenic areas and local communities will take relevant means to solve the adverse effects. These means may be the relevant provisions made by scenic areas or the participation of local communities in the pertinent planning of scenic areas. Yet it also may be the will that is imposed on the other side by one side. However, the means of coercion can sometimes alleviate the adverse competition or conflict between the two sides.

*vi. Compliance*

Compliance means that both sides or various sides adjust their behaviors in order to achieve mutual adaptation. Compliance includes three types, namely, reconciliation, compromise, tolerance. [5] The interaction between scenic areas and local communities will be bound to exert a profound influence on both sides. The value standards, morality, and lifestyle will penetrate each other, forming a subtle influence. The scenic areas can give a full play to the multiplier effect of tourism, utilizing the development of scenic areas to promote community employment and drive the revitalization of related industries within the local communities, extending the tourism product industry chain to local communities, and attracting local communities to actively involve in the economic development. The local communities can provide primary tourism consumer goods and a variety of raw materials; participate in the construction of the infrastructure in scenic areas; contract or run tourism enterprises and conduct business operations in catering, family hotels, transportation, tourism artifacts etc. Thus, it can be concluded that the scenic areas and local communities adjust their behaviors in the process of interaction to achieve mutual adaptation.

## Ⅳ. Survey and Evaluation on the Development of the Interaction between Baishuizhai Scenic Area and the Local Community

*i. Existing types of interaction*

According to the interests relationship, social interaction is divided into cooperative interaction, competitive interaction and conflict interaction. The survey was conducted in the local communities around the Scenic Area by adopting the questionnaires and semi-structured interviews. The interviewees expressed their feelings in an objective way. At last, 113 valid questionnaires were taken back. The results of the questionnaires and the interviews were analyzed statistically. In combination with these results, a study is conducted to analyze the existing interactive relationship between the Baishuizhai Scenic Area and the local community.

*A. An analysis of the local communities' demand for the Baishuizhai Scenic Area and their status quo*

a. Providing jobs

According to the survey statistics, 69.23% of the respondents believed that the development of the Baishuizhai Scenic Area increases employment opportunities. However, after interviews, it is found that the residents of the local communities are mostly employed as cooks, sanitation workers, security staff, garden workers etc. who mainly do the physical labor and that other types of jobs are created by the development of other industries driven by the Scenic Area.

b. Providing new momentum for economic growth

The development of the Baishuizhai Scenic Area has led to the development of local eco-tourism and other related industries. The local community has started to develop large-scale urban agriculture projects such as fruits and vegetables, flowers and nursery stock, facilitating the transformation of agricultural products to tourism products. In 2013, Paitan Town established 15 large-scale eco-agriculture bases. The farm hotels, sightseeing agriculture, as well as the tourist shopping street around and near the Scenic Area boost the local community to participate in the tourism industry chain, bringing new momentum for economic growth of the local community.

*B. An analysis of the Baishuizhai Scenic Area's demand for the local community and its status quo*

a. Buffering and protection

A good landscape interface is formed thanks to the unified landscape arrangement for the land within the Scenic Area and surrounding the local communities, the upgrading of the entrance road of Baishuizhai Scenic Area and the building of green-land along the roads. Such landscape interface can buffer and protect the environment of the Scenic Area.

b. Supply and service

After the establishment of the Scenic Area, the residents of the local community set up farm hotels, a variety of star hotels, travel products shops and other tourist service points around the Scenic Area which provide a variety of tourism supplies and services.

c. Creating the humanistic environment

The humanistic environment of the local community includes the community's economic environment, cultural environment, infrastructure environment, policy environment, human resources and environment. The Baishuizhai Scenic Area has three categories of humanistic landscape resources such as residential ancestral halls, religious buildings, and engineering constructions. There are many historical buildings in the villages of the local community which were built during the Ming and Qing Dynasties, boasting a strong historical and cultural atmosphere which creates a better humanistic environment for the development of the tourism in the Scenic Area.

From the above analysis of the mutual demand between the Baishuizhai Scenic Area and the local community and their status quo, it can be concluded that the Baishuizhai Scenic Area and the local community conduct cooperation to facilitate mutual development. Therefore, at present, the interactive relation between the Scenic Area and the local community is cooperative interaction.

*ii. The current stage of the relation between the Scenic Area and the local communities*

In order to study the current stage between the Baishuizhai Scenic Area and the local community, the author made a questionnaire and an interview on the opinions of the residents of the local community regarding the development of the Baishuizhai Scenic Area. The survey found that there was a series of problems in the interactive development of the Baishuizhai Scenic Area and the local community.

*A. Problems in industry economy*

Due to the relatively remote geographical location of the Baishuizhai Scenic Area and low level of economic development of the local community, most of the residents rely mainly on agriculture, planting and temporary jobs to obtain household income under the original economic conditions. After the introduction of the tourism into the local community, its development drives the development of other industries dramatically. Under such circumstance, the residents of the local community turn their eyes on the tourism one after another to seek greater commercial opportunities. Among the respondents, 69.2% of the residents still rely mainly on agriculture and planting to gain the income, 61.5% of the residents earn the money by doing temporary jobs in cities, 46.2% of the residents rely on happy farmhouse and rural tourism to get the income, and the other few make money through other means. However, owing to the constraints of land tenure, industrial type etc., the progress of industrial innovation is slow, and industrial transfer fails go deep into the local communities, restricting the growth of overall economic strength of the local community.

*B. Problems in management mechanism*

a. Uneven distribution of benefits of the Scenic Area

The development of the Baishuizhai Scenic Area has led to the development of the economy of the local community. The income of the local tourism industry has increased year by year. The living standard of the residents of the local community have been greatly improved by involving in the tourism industry. However, there is a great gap among the villages of the local community in terms of the job opportunities and economic benefits created by the development of the Scenic Area. The villages, which are near the Scenic Area or have resource advantages to develop the tourism industry, gain more job opportunities. Besides, the development of happy farmhouse and other related industries have also get substantial financial and technical support from the government, and the management agencies of the Scenic Area can also gain relevant compensation. On the contrary, the villages in the town get less share of benefits of the Scenic Area and cannot get the targeted support from the government. According to the survey results, if the interests of the Scenic Area are distributed to the local communities in a certain proportion, the exact figure between the above-mentioned two sides is about 6.24:3.76. Uneven distribution of benefits will lead to a greater gap between the rich and the poor in the local community and will be likely to cause psychological imbalance of the residents of other villages, thus forming the social problems obstructing the harmonious development of the local community.

b. Deficiency in system of laws and regulations and lack of related interests coordination and supervision mechanism

In addition to maintaining the market order of the local community, the relevant laws and regulations impose restrictions on the development and operation of tourism developers and operators, forming a healthy competition in the market order and safeguarding the legitimate interests of the residents of the local community. In the survey, 84.62% of the residents said that there were no related interest coordination organizations in the local community, 76.95% of the residents thought that there was imperfectness in interests distribution and supervision mechanism of the Baishuizhai Scenic Area and that the information was not transparent, and 76.92% of the respondents believed that there was still much to do to improve the policies and regulations in relation to the development and operation of the Scenic Area and that the management and operation of the Scenic Area have not yet formed a system.

c. The lack of the awareness of responsibilities of the managers and operators of the Scenic Area

In the daily management and operation of the Baishuizhai Scenic Area, the managers mainly focus on maintaining the normal work of the Scenic Area, while the operators pay more attention to the pursuit of economic interests. According to the survey results, the managers accused the residents of local communities of destroying the resources and the environment in the Scenic Area, but they did not make recommendations on how to improve the environmental protection awareness of the residents of the local community. The operators believed that the residents of the local community lacked the awareness of environmental protection and sanitation maintenance. The managers of the Scenic Area failed to communicate with the residents of the local community in the daily management of the Scenic Area in a direct way and there were difficulties in communication between them.

## V. Countermeasures for the Development of Interactive Relations between the Baishuizhai Scenic Area and the Local Community Based on Social Interaction Theory

According to the survey results, the interaction between the Baishuizhai Scenic Area and the local community is still in the stage of conflict. In order to solve the conflict problems in the development of the interaction between the two sides and make improvements in their interactive relation, the following countermeasures are put forward:

*i. Enriching industrial structure and promoting the development of diversified industries*

According to the resource and development conditions of the local community, there is a great need to formulate the targeted industrial development, enrich the existing industrial structure, and promote the development of diversified industries in the local community. For the villages with the natural and cultural resources and convenient traffic conditions for the development of tourism, the advantages of the tertiary industry should be given a full play to focus on the development of sightseeing tourism. For the villages located in the Scenic Area or in the vicinity of the Scenic Area, the priority should be given over the development of tourism-related supporting services reception.

*ii. Improving the system of laws and regulations as well as the communication and coordination mechanisms*

From the win-win perspectives of the Scenic Area, the government and the local community, the efforts should be made to establish and improve relevant laws and regulations and management policies, in order to safeguard legitimate interests of the above-mentioned three sides.

Patsy Healey argues that the result of justice is derived from a just process, not only considering the fairness of the results, but also taking into account the material resource allocation, policy statement and implementation process. Collaboration and interaction between stakeholder groups should be carried out in the process of policy formulation and implementation. In addition, the joint participation of stakeholder groups should be expanded beyond the traditional authority elite. Improving the communication and coordination mechanism can help alleviate the interests disputes arising from stakeholder groups, serving as an effective way to ensure the maximization of overall interests and long-term interests. [7] Therefore, the relevant institutions and organizations for interests adjustment should be established to coordinate the interests of the stakeholders in the development of the Scenic Area and solve the communication problems between the managers of the Scenic Area and the residents of the local community.

*iii. Assuming certain social responsibilities by the Scenic Area, as the tourism enterprise*

A scenic area is not only an individual engaging in the tourism development as well as the management and operation of the scenic area, but also is an indispensable component of the local community, with a certain responsibility for the community services. The Baishuizhai Scenic Area, as a tourism enterprise, should bear corresponding social responsibility to help the local community to develop in a better way. Only by integrating itself into the local community's normal activities can a scenic area create a high-quality environment and a harmonious scenic area-community environment, so that scenic areas in this good environment to get better development. As a result, the scenic area can ultimately achieve better development in such a sound environment.

*iv. Transforming the administrative system and establishing a management model by the government under the cooperation of both the government and the residents*

In view of the interaction between the Scenic Area and the local community, many of the interaction activities of the local community are driven by the government's guidance and promotion. As the government implements the centralized control management methods, the residents of the local community have no real power or financial power in the management of the scenic area or the community. Therefore, the interaction between the Baishuizhai Scenic Area and the local community can be only achieved through the government. For this reason, the government should change the management model, and decentralize appropriate power to the residents of the local community, thus creating a management model under the cooperation between the government and residents to achieve democratization and diversification of decision-making. In doing so, the interests of local community can be guaranteed, so that they will participate in the interaction with the scenic area.

## Ⅵ. Conclusion

This paper takes the social interaction theory as a perspective to examine the interaction between the Baishuizhai Scenic Area and the local community. Through the field survey and related analysis, it is concluded that there exists the cooperative interaction between the Baishuizhai Scenic Area and the local community and the relationship of both sides is in the stage of conflict. In addition, the relevant countermeasures are proposed in a response to the current problems.

## References

[1] Sheehan L R, Ritchie J R. Destination stakeholders exploring identity and salience[J]. *Annals of Tourism Research*, 2005, 32(3): 711-734.

[2] Falaka S, Chiunb L M, Wee A Y. A repositioning strategy for rural tourism in Malaysia community's perspective[J]. *Social and Behavioral Sciences*, 2014 (144): 412-415.

[3] Sloan P, Legrand W, Kaufmann C S. A survey of social entrepreneurial community-based hospitality and tourism initiatives in developing economies[J]. *Worldwide Hospitality & Tourism Themes*, 2014, 6 (6): 51-61.

[4] Abdollahzadeh G, Sharifzadeh A. Rural residents' perceptions toward tourism development: a study from Iran[J]. *International Journal of Tourism Research*, 2014(16): 126-136.

[5] Androniki K. The importance of social media on holiday visitors' choices: the case of Athens, Greece[J]. *Euro Med Journal of Business*, 2015, 10(3): 360-374.

[6] Preston D. Rural-urban and inter-settlement interaction: theory and analytical structure[J]. *Area*, 1975, 7(3) :171-174.

[7] Gould W T S. Rural-urban interaction in the third world[J]. *Area*, 1982, 14(4): 334-334.

[8] Rondinelli D A. Applied methods of regional analysis: the spatial dimensions of development policy[J]. *Economic Geography*, 1985, 61(4): 376-379.

[9] Kayat K. Power, social exchanges and tourism in Langkawi: rethinking resident perceptions[J]. *International Journal of Tourism Research*, 2002, 4(3): 171-191.

[10] Gtrner D, Rybar P, Engel J, Domaracka L. Geotourism marketing in lake constance region[J]. *Acta Montanistica Slovaca*, 2009, 14(2): 197-204.

[11] Moyle B, Croy G, Weiler B. Tourism interaction on islands: the community and visitor social exchange[J]. *International Journal of Culture Tourism and Hospitality Research*, 2010, 4(2): 96-107.

[12] Jamal T, Tanase A. Impacts and conflicts surrounding Dracula Park, Romania: the role of sustainable tourism principles[J]. *Journal of Sustainable Tourism*, 2005, 13(5): 440-455.

[13] García-Melón M, Gómez-Navarro T, Acuña-Dutra S. A combined ANP-Delphi approach to evaluate sustainable tourism[J]. *Environmental Impact Assessment Review*, 2012(34): 41-50.

[14] Garcíarosell J C, Mäkinen J. An integrative framework for sustainability evaluation in tourism: applying the framework to tourism product development in Finnish Lapland[J]. *Journal of Sustainable Tourism*, 2013, 21(3): 396-416.

[15] Boley B B, McGehee N G, Perdue R R, Long P. Empowerment and resident attitudes toward tourism: strengthening the theoretical foundation through a Weberian lens[J]. *Annals of Tourism Research*, 2014 (49): 33-50.

[16] Han G S, Wu P L, Huang Y W, Yang Z. Tourism development and the disempowerment of host residents: types and formative mechanisms[J]. *Tourism Geographies*, 2014, 16(5): 717-740.

# A Construction and Empirical Analysis of Community Satisfaction and Tourism Support: A Case Study of Sansheng Flower Village in Chengdu

Cai Yinchun[1*], Yang Zhenzhi[2], Chen Kaijian[3]

**Abstract:** By adopting the non-recursion model, which matches more with the law of real tourism development, this study built a model of the structural relation of the seven latent variables—sense of community, community involvement, resident expectations, perceived benefits of tourism, perceived costs of tourism community satisfaction and tourism support, and conducted a field research on a famous rural tourism destination in China—Sansheng Flower Village. The results of this study indicate: Sense of community and community involvement have significantly positive influence on perceived benefits of tourism and have significantly negative influence on perceived costs of tourism; the negative influence of resident expectations on perceived costs of tourism is not significant; perceived benefits of tourism has significantly positive influence on both community satisfaction and tourism support; perceived costs of tourism has significantly negative influence on community satisfaction; community satisfaction and tourism support influence each other, and the influence is significant and positive.

**Keywords:** rural tourism; community satisfaction; tourism support; structural equation model

## Ⅰ. Introduction

Human beings, living in this universe, walk the resident life to faraway places to quest for selves and gain self-revealed poetic flavor; thus, traveling itself is "dwelling of poetic flavor" [1]. With the rapid development of cities, individuals, who are living in a fast-paced and competitive society, are motivated by an ever-increasing desire to return to a natural and simple state of life. However, it is hard for them to find some idyllic habitats for their mind due to the congestion and bustle of the city life. As a result, with its simple and true atmosphere, pastoral scenery and leisurely lifestyle, the countryside is becoming popular

1* Sichuan Academy of Sciences, Chengdu, China; Sichuan University, Chengdu, China. caiyinchun_666@163.com.

2 Sichuan University, Chengdu, China.

3 Sichuan University, Chengdu, China.

among urban residents. And because of this, the fast development of rural tourism has been increasingly undermining the economy, society and environment of rural areas. [2] However, it is the community residents who are mostly susceptible to both the positive and negative results brought by the tourism. To achieve sustainable growth of the local tourism, it is necessary for us to explore deeply community residents' attitude and behavior tendency towards the local tourism.

Researches on community satisfaction and tourism support have experienced a process from "irrational" to "rational". [3] Originally, the qualitative method was adopted as a major method for studying community satisfaction and tourism support, which is realized by means of field investigation, in-depth interview and others. As the study proceeds further, more researchers began to borrow theoretical models from other fields, including the place attachment theory, [5][6][7] tourism life cycle theory[8][9] and social exchange theory, [13][14][15] etc. Community satisfaction and tourism support are mainly influenced by tourism perception which includes perceived benefits of tourism and perceived costs of tourism. [9][12] Through document sorting, it is found that scholars have done much researches on perceived benefits of tourism and perceived costs of tourism. They hold the view that the main factors influencing perceived benefits of tourism and perceived costs of tourism are: sense of community, community involvement, environmental attitude and so on. [13][16] As for domestic tourism studies, tourism geography scholars took the initiative to apply structural equation model to verify factors influencing community satisfaction and tourism support. And they've gained major breakthrough in this field. However, there are still problems such as confounding indirect acting factors and inconspicuous discriminability in terms of existing literature. Furthermore, the application of structural equation model takes the form of recursive model while non-recursive model has not yet been found. Thus, the research takes community satisfaction and tourism support as its object again, hoping to promote studies in this field and make a contribution to the actual development of tourism.

Rural residents in "Five Golden Flowers" of Sansheng Flower Village in Chengdu City are the objects of this research. Sense of community, community involvement, resident expectation, perceived benefits of tourism, perceived costs of tourism, community satisfaction, and tourism support are selected as the seven latent variables. The paper proposes an assumption based on the knowledge of theoretical relationship between the latent variables; and it also takes perceived benefits of tourism and perceived costs of tourism as mediator variables, so as to develop a structural relationship model of sense of community, community involvement, resident expectation—community satisfaction, and tourism support; moreover, this paper makes an empirical analysis on the influencing factors of community satisfaction and tourism support, in the hope of providing a relatively complete academic explanation for structural relationship between residents' community satisfaction and tourism support in rural tourist destinations.

*i. Literature review and research hypothesis*

*A. Community satisfaction and tourism support*

Community satisfaction, accounting for an important part in community planning and development, is an important manifestation of residents' tourism perception. [17] Residents with high community satisfaction are more willing to engage in tourism development. By contrast, residents with low community satisfaction have a relatively inconsistent attitude towards the development of local tourism. Presently, as community satisfaction is generally regarded as a single variable, studies about relationship between community satisfaction and tourism support are relatively few. Nunkoo[10] developed a community support model based on social exchange theory. Nunkoo's research indicates that community support is influenced by perceived benefits of tourism, perceived costs of tourism and community satisfaction, and it has also confirmed that community satisfaction has a significant positive impact on tourism support. When they studied the influence of community attachment and attitudes on tourism development, McCool et al. [31] found that tourism support has a conspicuously positive effect on community satisfaction. Hence, based on the above studies, this research proposes the following hypotheses:

$H_{3d}$: *community satisfaction has a notably positive influence on tourism support;*

$H_{3c}$: *tourism support has a notably positive influence on community satisfaction.*

*B. Perception of tourism impact*

Perception of tourism impact has always been a focus of tourism study. At present, residents' perception of tourism impact is mainly manifested in three dimensions, namely, economy, socioculture and environment, but all of them incorporate a positive perception and a negative perception at the same time. [3][17][27] The positive perception toward tourism impact by residents is called perceived benefits of tourism, and the negative perception is called perceived costs of tourism. [2] Studies have shown that residents' perception toward tourism impact is closely associated with community satisfaction and tourism support. To be more specific, if residents could perceive that benefits obtained from tourism development, and the costs are also acceptable at the same time, the more they perceive, then they will be more satisfied with the community, and will be more willing to participate in the development of tourism; However, if the cost perception of community residents is greater, they are more likely to oppose the development of local tourism. Therefore, perception of tourism impact is an important content of researches on community satisfaction and tourism support.

Since 1960s, there have been many studies about residents' perception of tourism impact, which mainly focus on the dimensions of residents' perception, relevant interpretation models, relationships between residents' perception and tourism support, and others. Ko et al. [17] discussed relationships between positive perception of tourism impact and community satisfaction, negative perception of tourism impact and community satisfaction respectively. Results have shown that positive impact perception has a positive influence on community satisfaction while the negative one has a negative influence. Both the studies conducted by Cursoy and Dyer[16] have indicated that the perceived benefits of tourism has a positive impact on residents' support for tourism development. Thus, based on the above studies, this research proposes hypotheses as follows:

*$H_{1c}$: the perceived benefits of tourism has a prominently positive impact on community satisfaction;*

*$H_{1d}$: the perceived benefits of tourism has a significantly positive influence on tourism support;*

*$H_{2c}$: the perceived benefits of tourism has a significantly negative influence on community satisfaction;*

*$H_{2d}$: the perceived costs of tourism has a significantly negative influence on community satisfaction.*

*C. Sense of community*

Sense of community which is an important content of studying the sustainable development of community at tourist site refers to a psychological state that residents classify themselves into some groups in a region; such kind of psychological state reflects both the confirmation of the identity of the community, and personal feelings that mainly contain the feelings of engagement, attachment, dependence and so on. [18] Some scholars have also indicated that there are obvious differences at home and abroad in the study of the sense of community. Western researchers believe that residents' sense of community will be stronger, if they can share a better social relationship, live longer in the community, feel more satisfied with the community, and participate in more community activities. While in China, studies have found that the most essential factor influencing residents' sense of community is the social relationship of community residents, following are the quality of community environment and the degree of participation in community activities.

Existing studies have shown that the stronger the residents' sense of community, the higher the satisfaction of their community, the more they can perceive the positive impact of tourism on the community, thus they will neglect the negative impact and further support the development of community tourism. Goudy [20] believes that sense of community has an outstandingly positive impact on tourism perception, and residents with stronger sense of community will be more likely to perceive the positive impact of tourism on the community, and underestimate the negative impact of tourism on the community. J. Ap thinks that the sense of community is beneficial to the formation of residents' positive tourism impact perception, and it can make residents pay attention to the negative impact of tourism perception; and residents with stronger sense of community may be more concerned about the negative impact of tourism. Through field investigations, researches and demonstrations, the majority of domestic scholars think that sense of community is positively associated with tourism perception. Thus, in accordance with the above studies, this research proposes hypotheses as follows:

*$H_{1a}$: the sense of community has a significantly positive influence on perceived benefits of tourism;*

*$H_{1b}$: the sense of community has a significantly negative influence on perceived costs of tourism.*

*D. Community involvement*

With the development of tourism, scholars began to realize the important role that community plays in the development of tourism, and began to combine it with tourism theories of sustainable development. In line with the stakeholder theory, the development of tourism can lead to interest games between various interest groups, and residents are gradually marginalized as a result of "lack of right" and "lack of capability", which will eventually harm the sustainable development of local tourism. [20] In recent years, community involvement, has been integrated into tourism planning, which is regarded as an important approach to reduce the negative impact of tourism, creat a favorable environment for tourism development, and achieve sustainable development of tourism. Community residents' satisfaction with the community and the degree of tourism support are largely determined by their participation, that is, with higher participation, residents could gain more benefits from tourism development and then their community satisfaction will be higher and they will support the development of local community tourism more. [21] Therefore, community involvement is the premise of improving residents' community satisfaction and tourism support.

In 1985, Murphy first brought about the concept of community involvement in his book *Tourism: A Community Approach*. Then this concept was gradually applied into some researches by other scholars. Present domestic and international studies on community involvement in tourism development are not few and mainly aim to emphasize the importance of community involvement to sustainable tourism development. However, there are few studies about the impact of community involvement on tourism conception from the empirical view. Gursoy[23] divided tourism impact perception of residents into perceived benefits of tourism and perceived costs of tourism by applying social exchange theory, based on which Gursoy established community support for tourism development. Lepp[24] conducted a research on Bigoodi Village in Uganda and found that residents' perception of tourism will be more positive as the more they engage in local tourism. In this way, tourism can drive the development of agriculture, so as to increase local residents' income and eventually promote community development. In addition, he proposed an assumption that the positive attitude could be turned into behavior supporting tourism development based on behavioral reasonableness. Wang and Qu[2] verified that community involvement has an arrestingly positive correlation with tourism impact perception by building structural relationship models of community residents' attitude towards tourism development. Thus, in accordance with the above studies, this research proposes hypotheses as follows:

*$H_{2a}$: community involvement has a significantly positive influence on perceived benefits of tourism;*

*$H_{2b}$: community involvement has a significantly negative influence on perceived costs of tourism.*

*E. Resident expectations*

Expectation, which is a kind of psychological activity, means that people have the wish to achieve certain goals or meet some needs within certain period of time in line with their own existing capability and experience. [24] Early in 1964, Vroom first proposed the "Expectancy Theory", which combines the expectancy for future events with behavior of individuals. It has a basic assumption that the behavior of individuals is the result of individual expectancy, and such behavior will be reinforced as expectancy is intensified. The "Expectancy Theory" has been widely applied in psychology, behavioristics and other fields since it was presented.

In accordance with previous literature, the "Expectancy Theory" in studies on tourism is mainly focused on tourist satisfaction and studies taking residents as the objective is relatively few. In other words, "resident expectancy" has not received enough attention and support. Marsh and Henshall [26] realized that economic and social expectancy of local residents mean a lot to the development of local tourism and their favorable impression of tourists. Teye et al. had found that the large gap between local residents' economic expectancy and actual income caused the residents' and tourism workers' negative attitude towards tourism development, when they studied residents' attitude to tourism development of two villages in Ghana. Xu Zhenxiao, a domestic scholar, based on the two basic theories of "community attachment" and "expectancy theory", takes residents' tourism development expectancy as a mediator variable, and built a theoretical model of residents' community attachment to tourism support, and his study has shown that residents' expectancy has a significant positive influence on the perceived benefits of tourism and has a significant negative influence on perceived costs of tourism. Thus, in accordance with the above studies, this research proposes hypotheses as follows:

*$H_{3a}$: residents' expectancy has a significantly positive influence on perceived benefits of tourism;*

*$H_{2b}$: residents' expectancy has a significantly negative influence on perceived costs of tourism.*

Hereby, based on the above hypotheses, a conceptual model of community satisfaction and tourism support is built as in Figure 1.

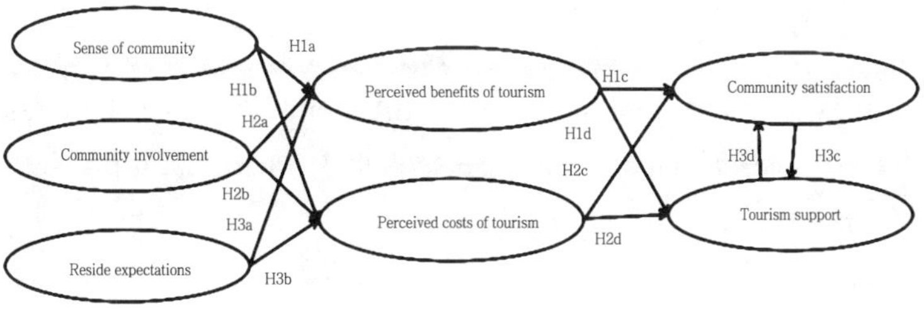

Figure 1 Conceptual Model

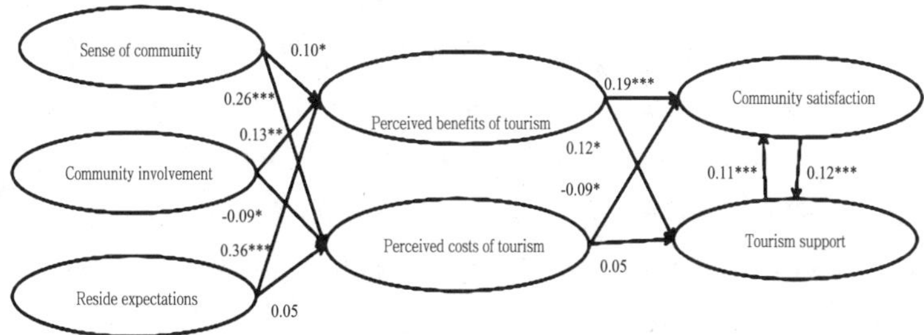


Figure 2 Path Coefficient of Structural Equation Model

Note: * represents $P<0.05$, ** represents $P<0.01$, and *** $P<0.001$. The dotted line indicts that the path is not significant.

## Ⅱ. Research Design

*i. Research area*

Sansheng Flower Village is located in Jinjiang District, Chengdu, which is the birthplace of China's rural tourism with a total area of 15,000 *mu*. Today, Sansheng Flower Village, featuring rural tourism and sightseeing leisure agriculture, is mainly divided into five scenic spots: Xingfu Meilin, Jiangjia Caidi, Hetang Yuese, Dongli Juyuan, and Huaxiang Nongju, also known as "Five Golden Flowers".

It has been granted the honor of "tourist scenic spot of AAAA class of the state", and awarded "the National Model Prize for Residential Environment" and so on. In recent years, Sansheng Flower Village annually accommodates about 13 million tourists, and the annual output value is as high as 260 million yuan and the collective income of the village reaches 46.55 million yuan, of which "Five Golden Flowers" tourism district contributes nearly 10 million yuan to local fiscal revenue every year. With the development of rural tourism, the level of community development is increasing day by day. Therefore, the case study in this research is very representative.

*ii. Questionnaire design and variable measurement*

According to the concept model of community satisfaction and tourism support in Figure 1, the measurement of each latent variable is based on the existing researches, and by combining with the actual situation of the case, it synthesizes or draws on the existing questionnaire to conduct a preliminary design questionnaire. Then, opinions of experts who have in-depth studies on the case are considered to improve the rationality and clarity of the items in the questionnaire, and supplement the items that may be missed. Finally, 52 graduate students of tourism management are selected to conduct a pre-survey, and further improvement of the questionnaire is made based on the results. The final questionnaire is composed of eight parts: sense of community, community involvement, resident expectations, perceived benefits of tourism, perceived costs of tourism, community satisfaction, tourism support, and demographic characteristics.

Referring to the research results of Wang, [2] McCoo, [31] Du, [32] and Williams, [33] the measurement of sense of community includes 3 options, such as “I have a strong sense of belonging to my village”, “Compared with other places, I like my village more” and “I will be very sad if moving out of the village”. The measurement of community involvement, referring to studies presented by Feng, [34] Wang, [2] Yang , [35] includes 4 items as “participate in decision-making and management of tourism”, “achieve shared interests with investors”, “participate in tourism project management” and “participate in tourism education and training”. Resident expectations, referring to studies of Wang et al. (2011), is mainly measured from three aspects, including “expectations for economic impact”, “expectations for social impact” and “expectations for environmental impact”. Perceived benefits of tourism, referring to research results presented by Wang, [2] Lankford [36]and Du, [32] is primarily measured from three aspects, including “perceived economic benefits”, “perceived social and cultural benefits”, and “perceived environmental benefits”, among which perceived economic benefits contain 3 items, namely, the “increased job opportunities for villagers”, “raised villagers’ incomes” and “improved local economic development”; perceived social and cultural benefits contain 2 items, namely, the “enhanced knowledge and understanding of local culture” and “increased residents hospitality”; perceived environmental benefits contain 2 items as “improved infrastructure” and “enhanced environmental awareness of residents”. The measurement of perceived costs of tourism, similarly referring to research results of Wang, [2] Lankfork[36] and Du, [32] mainly includes 7 items, namely, “causing unfair distribution of interests”, “increasing the cost of living for villagers”, “affecting local cultural traditions and customs”, “decreasing trust between villagers”, “destroying the local natural environment”, “increasing the local environmental pollution” and “causing traffic congestion and parking difficulty”. The measurement of community satisfaction, in reference to research results of Wang & Lu, [9] Nunkoo (2011) and Grzeskowiak, [37] includes 3 items, namely, “satisfying with the overall situation of the village”, “considering the village as the ideal place for inhabitation” and “satisfying with the life quality in the village”. The measurement of tourism support, in reference to the study results of Nunkoo (2011), Wang[2] and Lu, [38] includes 4 items, namely, “actively supporting the the development of local tourism ”, “welcoming tourists to the village”, “continuing to participate in tourism development” and "considering tourism as the future of the village".

5-point Likert scale is adopted in the above measurements, which includes "strongly disagree, disagree, general agree, agree, and strongly agree" and "very low, low, general, high, very high", and then assign 1-5 points from low to high according to perception. The last part of the questionnaire is the demographic characteristics, which mainly includes the respondent's gender, age, degree of education, family income, and so on.

*iii. Data analysis and collection*

This paper mainly uses AMOS21.0 and SPSS21.0 software to analyze data. Firstly, the confirmation factor analysis of the measurement model is conducted. The reliability and validity of the questionnaire are analyzed to examine if the internal consistency, convergent validity and discriminant validity of the observed variables of each latent variable is good and if the adjustment or modification are needed. Then, if the measurement model fulfills the requirement, the structural model analysis will be carried out to verify the research hypotheses presented in this paper.

The study mainly uses on-site one-to-one filling-in and answering method. In order to ensure the validity and objectivity of the data, the research group members especially asked a local primary school teacher to lead the household survey and data collection. Besides, in view of low education, poor reading and comprehension ability of some residents, the teachers and researchers will make a popular explanation on the site to help them complete the questionnaires. Then, a total of 600 questionnaires are distributed and 565 were recovered, of which 542 are valid questionnaires, the recovery and effective questionnaire rates reach to 94.2% and 90% respectively.

*iv. Sample structure*

As shown in the survey data of "Five Golden Flowers" in Sansheng Flower Village, the sample characteristics of the respondents as follows: (1) in the gender structure, the proportion of male and female is close, 48.2% males and 51.8% females; (2) in the age structure, most of the respondents are in the range from 31 to 60, accounting for 75.6%; (3) the education level is mainly middle and low, of which the proportion of residents with junior high school and below degree is 32.7%, high school education 36.3%, junior college 20.3%, bachelor's degree 8.7%, master degree and above 2%; (4) regarding household income source, 86.7% of them are directly or indirectly related to the tourism industry, and only 13.3% are not from the tourism sector; (5) in terms of the average monthly income, the proportion of the residents with less than 2,000 yuan is 15.3%, 2,001-4,000 yuan 60.9%, 4,001-8,000 yuan 20.5%, and more than 8,000 yuan 3.3%.

## Ⅲ. Test and Analysis

*i. Confirmation factor analysis*

In order to test whether the theoretical model works, the study firstly analyzes the reliability of the overall sample data. First, the overall scale reliability and the reliability of the scale for each latent variable are checked by using Cronbach's α reliability. Second, the measurement reliability of each observed variable to its latent variable is examined through composite reliability. In general, it can be inferred that the scale is well consistent only when Cronbach's α reliability coefficient and composite reliability value are greater than 0.7. As shown in Table 1, using the SPSS21.0 to test the scale, the Cronbach's α value of each latent variable ranges from 0.8178 to 0.9840 and the α value for the scale is 0.8434, both greater than the minimum critical value 0.7. Based on Fornell's composite reliability formula and through the standardized factor loading, the composite reliability of each latent variable is calculated and the results range from 0.8587 to 0.9840, greater than the critical value 0.7, indicating that the observed variable of each latent variable has a relatively good internal consistency and the questionnaire has good reliability and stability.

Table 1 Results for Confirmation Factor Analysis

| Latent Variables | Observed Variables | Standardized Load | S. E | *t* Value C. R | Composite Reliability | Cronbach's Alpha Value | AVE |
|---|---|---|---|---|---|---|---|
| Sense of Community | SC1: | 0.890*** | 0.032 | 31.070 | 0.9328 | 0.9326 | 0.8222 |
| | SC2 | 0.923*** | 0.030 | 33.401 | | | |
| | SC3 | 0.907*** | NA | NA | | | |
| Community participation | CI1 | 0.922*** | 0.020 | 47.572 | 0.9727 | 0.9755 | 0.9095 |
| | CI2 | 0.961*** | 0.016 | 60.770 | | | |
| | CI3 | 0.974*** | NA | NA | | | |
| | CI4 | 0.957*** | 0.070 | 59.248 | | | |
| Resident Expectations | RE1 | 0.767*** | 0.063 | 15.701 | 0.8187 | 0.8178 | 0.6008 |
| | RE2 | 0.796*** | 0.062 | 16.413 | | | |
| | RE3 | 0.762*** | NA | NA | | | |
| Perceived Benefits of Tourism | PBT1 | 0.945*** | 0.022 | 46.427 | 0.9840 | 0.9840 | 0.8979 |
| | PBT2 | 0.958*** | 0.020 | 49.873 | | | |
| | PBT3 | 0.944*** | NA | NA | | | |
| | PBT4 | 0.944*** | 0.022 | 46.543 | | | |
| | PBT5 | 0.946*** | 0.021 | 46.798 | | | |
| | PBT6 | 0.950*** | 0.021 | 47.913 | | | |
| | PBT7 | 0.946*** | 0.021 | 46.865 | | | |

(To be continued)

(Continued Table 1)

| Latent Variables | Observed Variables | Standardized Load | S. E | *t* Value C. R | Composite Reliability | Cronbach's Alpha Value | AVE |
|---|---|---|---|---|---|---|---|
| Perceived Costs of Tourism | PCT1 | 0.827*** | 0.043 | 23.038 | 0.9372 | 0.9371 | 0.6807 |
| | PCT2 | 0.807*** | 0.044 | 21.955 | | | |
| | PCT3 | 0.823*** | NA | NA | | | |
| | PCT4 | 0.826*** | 0.430 | 23.061 | | | |
| | PCT5 | 0.843*** | 0.044 | 23.584 | | | |
| | PCT6 | 0.823*** | 0.044 | 22.661 | | | |
| | PCT7 | 0.826*** | 0.430 | 22.999 | | | |
| Community Satisfaction | CS1 | 0.932*** | 0.021 | 47.757 | 0.9603 | 0.9598 | 0.8898 |
| | CS2 | 0.922*** | 0.021 | 45.743 | | | |
| | CS3 | 0.975*** | NA | NA | | | |
| Tourism Support | TS1 | 0.735*** | 0.056 | 16.836 | 0.8581 | 0.8576 | 0.6022 |
| | TS2 | 0.813*** | 0.056 | 18.536 | | | |
| | TS3 | 0.781*** | NA | NA | | | |
| | TS4 | 0.773*** | 0.055 | 17.622 | | | |

Note: NA indicates that the regression coefficient is fixed to 1 and the *t* value is not available; *** represents $P<0.001$.

Before the structural equation model is analyzed, a validity test is required. The validity test mainly includes the convergent validity and discriminant validity. The convergent validity is used to check whether there is correlation and convergence between different observed variables of the same latent variable, which is conducted through examining whether the standardized path coefficient *t* is significant at a certain level. As shown in Table 1 that each observed variable of the standardized path coefficient *t* is in the range from 15.701 to 60.770, all of which significant at the level of 0.001. Therefore, the latent variables in this paper have good convergent validity. The discriminant validity is used to test whether there is a significant difference between the latent variables through comparing the square of the correlation coefficient between any two latent variables and their AVE. When the latter is greater than the former, it indicates that there is a significant difference between latent variables. As shown in Table 1 and Table 2, there is a significant difference between latent variables.

Table 2 Correlation Matrix for Overall Measurement Model

| Latent Variable | 1 | 2 | 3 | 4 | 5 | 6 | 7 |
|---|---|---|---|---|---|---|---|
| 1. Sense of Community | 1 | | | | | | |
| 2. Community involvement | 0.141 | 1 | | | | | |

(To be continued)

(Continued Table 2)

| 3. Resident Expectations | 0.115 | 0.243 | 1 | | | | |
|---|---|---|---|---|---|---|---|
| 4. Perceived Benefits of Tourism | 0.159 | 0.235 | 0.403 | 1 | | | |
| 5. Perceived Costs of Tourism | -0.281 | -0.142 | -0.094 | -0.134 | 1 | | |
| 6. Community Satisfaction | 0.155 | 0.141 | 0.314 | 0.218 | -0.113 | 1 | |
| 7. Tourism support | 0.053 | 0.118 | 0.069 | 0.134 | 0.019 | 0.249 | 1 |

The main reference of the comprehensive measurement model is the fitting index of all potential variables. As can be seen from the main indexes in this paper, the absolute fit index $\chi^2$/df = 2.071, and less than 3; GFI = 0.911, AGFI = 0.894, reaching or approaching 0.9; RMSEA = 0.044, RMR = 0.041, both less than 0.05. The incremental fit index NFI = 0.953, RFI = 0.948, IFI = 0.975, TLI = 0.972, and CFI = 0.975, all of which are greater than 0.9. The parsimonious fit index PGFI = 0.759, PNFI = 0.847 and PCFI = 0.866, all of which are greater than the critical value 0.5. Therefore, the reliability and validity of the overall measurement model can meet the standard and no further modification is needed. Then the next structural equation model analysis can be carried out.

*ii. The building and hypothesis test of the structural equation model*

According to the results of confirmation factor analysis, further structure equation analysis can be conducted since the model has ideal reliability and validity. The model built in this paper is a non-recursive model where two latent variables, community satisfaction and tourism support, have positive influence on each other. Firstly, imposing no parameter limitation was imposed the model and latent variables and observed variables of overall the measurement model was imported into the conceptual model, after conducting parameter estimation toward data by maximum likelihood method, it turns out that the model cannot be identified because the non-recursive model drops into endless loop. As a result, restrictions need to be added to certain parameters of the model. Here we further set that community satisfaction has the same influence as tourism support in order to explain that these two variables have significantly positive influence on each other. According to the results, except for AGFI=0.891 is lower than 0.9, other indicators of the equation model reach the fit criteria. Among these criteria, absolute fit measures $\chi^2$/df=2.127, GFI=0.908, RMSEA=0.046, RMR=0.069, all of them up to the fit criteria; incremental fit measures, NFI=0.951, RFI=0.946, IFI=0.974, TLI=0.971, CFI=0.974, all higher than 0.9; parsimonious fit measures, PGFI=0.769, PNFI=0.859, PCFI=0.879, meet the fit that is larger than critical value of 0.5. Generally, the theoretical model built in this paper has a relatively ideal fitting capability towards the studied data.

Based on the test results of the model, 10 of 12 hypotheses have been confirmed while $H_{3b}$ and $H_{2d}$ failed to be supported (see Table 3). Results of hypotheses test can be analyzed and concluded from the following aspects:

Table 3 Path Testing Table of Structural Equation Model

| Hypothesis | Path Name | Standardized Path Coefficient | *t* C.R | *P* value | Testing Results |
|---|---|---|---|---|---|
| $H_{1a}$: Sense of community has significantly positive influence on perceived benefits of tourism. | W25 | 0.100 | 2.396 | 0.017 | support |
| $H_{1b}$: Sense of community has significantly negative influence on perceived costs of tourism. | W26 | -0.263 | -5.768 | *** | support |
| $H_{2a}$: community involvement has significantly positive influence on perceived benefits of tourism. | W27 | 0.134 | 3.183 | 0.001 | support |
| $H_{2b}$: community involvement has significantly negative influence on perceived costs of tourism. | W28 | -0.094 | -2.087 | 0.037 | support |
| $H_{3a}$: Resident expectations have significantly positive influence on perceived benefits of tourism. | W29 | 0.360 | 7.507 | *** | support |
| $H_{3b}$: Resident expectations have significantly negative influence on perceived costs of tourism. | W30 | -0.048 | -0.976 | 0.329 | support |
| $H_{1c}$: Perceived benefits have significantly positive influence on community satisfaction. | W33 | 0.192 | 4.493 | *** | support |
| $H_{1d}$: Perceived benefits of tourism have significantly positive influence on tourism support. | W31 | 0.115 | 2.476 | 0.013 | support |
| $H_{2c}$: Perceived costs of tourism have significantly negative influence on community satisfaction. | W32 | -0.092 | -2.120 | 0.034 | support |
| $H_{2d}$: Perceived costs of tourism have significantly negative influence on tourism support. | W34 | 0.046 | 0.972 | 0.331 | support |
| $H_{3d}$: Community satisfaction has significantly positive influence on tourism support. | W36 | 0.115 | 4.995 | *** | support |
| $H_{3c}$: Tourism support has significantly positive influence on community satisfaction. | W35 | 0.119 | 4.995 | *** | support |

Note: *** represents $P<0.001$.

(1) Sense of community has significantly positive influence on perceived benefits of tourism, i.e. $H_{1a}$ is supported. For residents with stronger sense of community, they are more likely to perceive the benefits brought by tourism development to the community and hence underestimate the negative influence of tourism. Thus, strengthening sense of community of residents helps intensify the perception of residents toward the positive influence of tourism.

(2) Sense of community has significantly negative influence on perceived costs of tourism. Let's say $H_{1b}$ is supported. That is in line with research results of Goudy: residents with strong community sense are usually tend to pay much attention to tourism's positive influence on community, thus underestimating or even omitting its negative impact.

(3) Community involvement exerts significant effect on perceived benefits of tourism, so $H_{2a}$ is valid. The higher the community involvement is, the more positive the attitudes of residents toward tourism are, hereby the more obvious the perceived benefits of tourism. In

modern tourism development, community involvement attracts more and more attention of local government and tourism are planning companies. Therefore, community involvement is crucial no matter for tourism development planning or tourism development policies.

(4) Community involvement imposes significant and negative influence on perceived costs of tourism, which means hypothesis $H_{2b}$ is supported. Enhancing community involvement of residents can effectively lower the perception of residents toward the downside of tourism, which is inconsistent with research results of J. Ap. Residents of Sansheng Flower Village all emphasize tourism development with a positive attitude and a high participation, so perceived costs of tourism are relatively low.

(5) Resident expectations affect perceived costs of tourism significantly and positively, and hypothesis $H_{3a}$ is valid. Expectation is a type of mental state. Higher expectations of residents to local tourism can inspire these residents to participate in tourism more actively, thus obtaining stronger tourism costs perception. Our research team found that the local villagers with strong sense of tourism benefits are tended to have higher expectations.

(6) Perceived benefits of tourism have a significantly positive influence on community satisfaction, which confirms hypothesis $H_{1c}$. There is a close relation between perceived influence of tourism and community satisfaction. If community members can perceive benefits from tourism development, they will be more proud of their community and be more satisfied with their community. In Sansheng Flower Village, most residents can benefit from tourism development, so they can evidently feel the welfare led by tourism development of local area.

(7) Perceived benefits of tourism have significant positive impact on tourism support, here assuming $H_{1d}$ is true. According to social exchange theory, if expected return is greater than costs, residents are inclined to support tourism development. Residents who perceive more benefits of tourism will be more willing to be supporters of tourism development, to receive foreign investment and to welcome tourists.

(8) Perceived costs of tourism exert a significantly negative impact on community satisfaction, here assuming $H_{2c}$ is valid. Due to stronger perception of tourism's negative impact on the community, residents may be more sensitive to changes in the community, and be more dissatisfied with the community itself.

(9) Community satisfaction has a significant positive impact on tourism support, here assuming $H_{3d}$ is supported. As is confirmed by Nukoo, [26] residents with higher community satisfaction are apt to be involved in tourism development.

(10) Tourism support has a significant positive impact on community satisfaction, here assuming $H_{3c}$ is supported. With the development of tourism, the more residents benefit, the higher the tourism support is, the stronger the pride of residents will be satisfied by their community. Community residents of Sansheng Flower Village have shown higher satisfaction to their community when their support to tourism is strengthened.

There are two hypotheses that are denied, both of which are related to perceived costs of tourism. At present, Sansheng Flower Village is in the phase of high-speed tourism development, so participation is relatively more active, making it easy for residents to omit the negative influence of tourism development. So the strong perception of benefits of tourism is accompanied by the weak perception of costs.

(1) Resident expectations exert no significant negative influence on perceived costs of tourism, so hypothesis $H_{3b}$ is not supported. The degree of resident expectations is varied, thus perception of costs of tourism is also different. As a result, for the overall studied data, there is no sufficient ground to prove that resident expectations have significant negative influence on perceived costs of tourism.

(2) Perceived costs of tourism have no significant influence on tourism support, which means hypothesis $H_{2d}$ is not valid. Standardized path coefficient is 0.046 ($P$=0.331), which is incompatible with the hypothesis. The tourism industry level of Sansheng Flower Village is high. Though costs are perceived by residents, perceived costs of tourism do not significantly influence tourism support owing to related people-benefiting policies introduced by scenic area management department and village committee.

## Ⅳ. Research Conclusions and Discussion

Residents in scenic spots are one of the main stakeholders of tourism development, and the main parts of tourism products as well(2008). Based on the present research results, this paper studied residents' community sense and tourism support by constructing structural equation model. Then, the following conclusions are reached:

(1) Sense of community, community involvement and resident expectations have a significantly positive influence on perceived benefits of tourism. Among these three, resident expectations has the greatest impact on perceived benefits of tourism with a path coefficient of 0.360, which means that expectations of residents themselves on the development of local tourism directly propel their perception of benefits of tourism, a point usually neglected by most domestic scholars. Compared with sense of community and community involvement, resident expectations are more direct and more realistic, a mental state easily to be formed in a relatively short time period while the enhancement of sense of community and community involvement is a deepening and relatively time-consuming process.

(2) Sense of community and community involvement have a significantly negative influence on perceived costs of tourism. It is manifested that the stronger sense of community is, the weaker the perception of tourism costs. For this reason, strengthening sense of community of residents can lower their perception of tourism costs. The higher the tourism participation of those residents, the lower the perceived costs of tourism, so tourism management departments should lay more emphasis on "community involvement".

(3) Perceived benefits significantly affect community satisfaction and tourism support

in a positive direction. Therefore, promoting perception of positive influence for residents in rural scenic spots can evidently lift their satisfaction toward their community, and at the same time can lift their support to the development of local tourism. Here, standardized path coefficient of perceived benefits of tourism to community satisfaction is 0.192, while that of perceived benefits of tourism to tourism support is 0.115, revealing that perceived benefits of tourism exert larger influence on community satisfaction.

(4) Perceived costs of tourism have a significantly negative influence on community satisfaction. Obviously, with the increase of residents' tourism costs perception, their satisfaction with the community will gradually decrease.

(5) Community satisfaction and tourism support significantly and positively affect each other. The usage of the non-recursion model is aimed to illustrate that some closely related variables do not simply have unidirectional influence on each other, but impose causal relations. Our research shows that the increasing of community satisfaction can obviously lift residential support to the development of local tourism. Meanwhile, residents are more satisfied about their own community with the increase of their support for tourism.

(6) Resident expectations have no significantly negative influence on perceived costs of tourism, which violates the opinion of certain researchers. This could possibly come from the fact that they take no consideration into the varied resident expectations which bring different perception of costs of tourism, especially when local tourism is prosperously developing. At this moment, the focus of residents is usually placed on tourism benefits, thus neglecting the negative influence of tourism development on local area.

(7) Perceived costs of tourism has no significantly direct influence on tourism support. Although tourism development more or less brings negative influence on local area, a series of people-benefiting policies formulated by scenic spots management departments and village committee ensure the benefits of villagers and hence strengthen their support to tourism. Consequently, perceived costs of tourism has no direct impact on residents' support for tourism.

## Ⅴ. Research Limitations and Future Directions

Although most of the hypotheses presented in this paper have been confirmed, there are still some limitations. To start with, sampling survey has its shortcomings. The rationality of scales can be improved to research on situations at different time in different rural communities. Therefore, future research can be carried out in other rural tourism destinations to test the effectiveness of the research results. Secondly, even though in the same rural scenic spot, in different life stages, residents may show different attitudes toward tourism. This paper does not follow up in a long term, so future research can adopt the method of tracking survey to get vertical data of residents in scenic spots to compare and analyze. Thirdly, this paper boldly utilizes the non-recursive structural equation model. On the condition that no restrictions are imposed on parameters, since the model fails to be identified, the influential power of community satisfaction on tourism support is set to be equal to that of tourism support on community satisfaction, which is merely used to explain that these two latent variables, community satisfaction and tourism support positively affect each other. At this moment, path coefficients of them cannot be compared and measured quantitatively, and thus the influential degree of these two latent variables are not able to be judged. Consequently, in the future, the application of the non-recursive structural equation model in tourism research can be explored, which will be more in line with the reality of tourism development. In general, the above-mentioned limitations not only reveal the deficiencies of this paper, but also point out direction for the follow-up study. In-depth research on the community satisfaction and tourism support of residents in rural tourism areas require the author to make a comprehensive study from the aspects of technology, thinking and method in the future research.

## References

[1] Yang Zhenzhi. On the nature of tourism destination[J]. *Tourism Tribune*, 2014, 29: 13-21.

[2] Wang Chunyang, Qu Hailin. The influence factors of community residents' attitude toward tourism development in the village heritage[J]. *Journal of Geography*, 2014, 69: 278-288.

[3] Gursoy D, Rutherford D G. Host attitudes toward tourism: an improved structural model[J]. *Annals of Tourism Research*, 2004, 31: 495-516.

[4] Woo E, Kim H, Uysal M. Life satisfaction and support for tourism development[J]. *Annals of Tourism Research*, 2015, 50: 84-97.

[5] Xu Zhenxiao, Zhang Jie, Geoffrey Wall, et al. The influence of residents' sense of place on the support of regional tourism development: a case study of Jiuzhaigou tourism core community[J]. *Journal of Geography*, 2009, 64: 736-744.

[6] Wang Suosheng, Xu Honggang. Influence of place-based senses of distinctiveness, continuity, self-esteem and self-efficacy on residents' attitudes toward tourism[J]. *Tourism Management*, 2015, 47: 241-250.

[7] Veasna S, Wu Wann Yih, Huang Chu Hsin. The impact of destination source credibility on destination satisfaction: the mediating effects of destination attachment and destination image[J]. *Tourism Management*, 2013, 36: 511-526.

[8] Cui X, Ryan C. Perceptions of place, modernity and the impacts of tourism: differences among rural and urban residents of Ankang, China: a likelihood ratio analysis[J]. *Tourism Management*, 2011, 32: 604-615.

[9] Wang Yong, Lu Lin. Community tourism support model based on social exchange theory and its application: a case study of Mount Huangshan Scenic Area gateway community[J]. *Journal of Geography*, 2014, 69: 1557-1574.

[10] Nunkoo R, Ramkissoon H. Developing a community support model for tourism[J]. *Annals of Tourism Research*, 2011, 38: 964-988.

[11] Sabatelli R M. Exploring relationship satisfaction: a social exchange perspective on the interdependence between theory, research, and practice[J]. *Family Relations*, 1988, 37: 217-222.

[12] Wang Xia, Zhen Feng, Wu Xiaogen, et al. Driving factors of residents' satisfaction in tourism development: a case study of Yangshuo County[J]. *Geographical Research*, 2010, 29: 841-851.

[13] Park D B, Nunkoo R, Yoon Y S. Rural residents' attitudes to tourism and the moderating effects of social capital[J]. *Tourism Geographies: An International Journal of Tourism Space Place & Environment*, 2015, 17: 112-133.

[14] Yoon Y, Gursoy D, Chen J S. Validating a tourism development theory with structural equation modeling[J]. *Tourism Management*, 2001, 22: 363-372.

[15] Cengiz E, Kirkbir F. A structural model suggestion about relationship between total tourism affect perceived by local residents and tourism support[J]. *Anadolu University Journal of Social Sciences*, 2007, 7: 19-38.

[16] Dyer P, Gursoy D, Sharma B, et al. Structural modeling of resident perceptions of tourism and associated development on the Sunshine Coast, Australia[J]. *Steel in Translation*, 2007, 28: 409-422.

[17] Ko D W, Stewart W P. A structural equation model of residents' attitudes for tourism development[J]. *Tourism Management*, 2002, 23: 521-530.

[18] Nunkoo R, Ramkissoo H. Developing a community support model for tourism[J]. *Annals of Tourism Research*, 2011, 38: 964-988.

[19] Single Jingjing. A sense of community and community satisfaction in city[J]. 2008: 58-64.

[20] Goudy W J. Community attachment in a rural region[J]. *Rural Sociology*, 1990, 55: 178-198.

[21] Yang Zhenzhi, Shi Hong, Yang Dan, et al. Analysis of core stakeholder behaviour in the tourism community using economic game theory[J]. *Tourism Economics*, 2015, 21: 1169-1187.

[22] Ragheb M G, Griffith C A. The contribution of leisure participation and leisure satisfaction to life satisfaction of older persons[J]. *Journal of Leisure Research*, 1982, 14: 295-306..

[23] Gursoy D, Jurowski C, Uysal M. Resident attitudes: a structural modeling approach[J]. *Annals of Tourism Research*, 2002, 29: 79-105.

[24] Lepp A. Residents' attitudes towards tourism in Bigodi Village, Uganda[J]. *Tourism Management*, 2007, 28: 876-885.

[25] Oliver R L. A cognitive model of the antecedents and consequences of satisfaction decisions[J]. *Journal of Marketing Research*, 1980, 17: 460-469.

[26] Marsh N R, Henshall B D. Planning better tourism: the strategic importance of tourist-resident expectations and interactions[J]. *Tourism Recreation Research*, 1987, 12: 47-54.

[27] Madrigal R. Residents' perceptions and the role of government[J]. *Annals of Tourism Research*, 1995, 22: 86-102.

[28] Lindberg K, Johnson R L. Modeling resident attitudes toward tourism[J]. *Annals of Tourism Research*, 1997, 24: 402-424.

[29] Haralambopoulos N, Pizam A. Perceived impacts of tourism: the case of samos[J]. *Annals of Tourism Research*, 1996, 23: 503-526.

[30] Yang Kaikai. Study on the impact of rural tourism on the satisfaction of the residents in the destination[D]. Hangzhou: Zhejiang University, 2008.

[31] Mccool S F, S. R. Martin S R. Community attachment and attitudes toward tourism development[J]. *Journal of Travel Research*, 1994, 32: 29-34.

[32] Du Zongbin, Su Qin, Jiang Liao. Rural tourism destination resident community attachment model and its application: taking Anji, Zhejiang as an example[J]. *Tourism Tribune*, 2013, 28: 65-74.

[33] Haggard L M, Williams D R. Identify affirmation through leisure activities: leisure symbols of the self[J]. *Journal of Leisure Research*, 1992.

[34] Feng Shuhua, Sha Run. Rural tourism evaluation model: a case study of Wuyuan in Jiangxi Province[J]. *Geographical Research*, 2007, 26: 616-624.

[35] Yang Xingzhu, Lu Lin, Wang Qun. Structural model of farmers' participation in tourism decision making and its application[J]. *Journal of Geography*, 2005, 60: 928-940.

[36] Lankford S V, Howard D R. Developing a tourism impact attitude scale[J]. *Annals of Tourism Research*, 1994, 21: 121-139.

[37] Grzeskowiak S, Sirgy M J, Widgery R. Residents' satisfaction with community services: predictors and outcomes[J]. *Journal of Regional Analysis & Policy*, 2003, 33.

[38] Lu Song, Zhang Jie, Li Donghe, et al. Residents' perceptions and attitudes towards tourism impacts: a comparison of Xidi and Jiuzhaigou scenic area as an example[J]. *Journal of Geography*, 2008, 63: 646-656.

[39] Jiang Yiyi, Wang Yanglin, Cheng Shengkui, et al. Tourism landscape ecological system theory[J]. *Journal of Ecology*, 2008, 28: 1786-1793.

# A Tripartite Game Analysis of Low-carbon Tourism

Ma Zuozhenmo[1*], Cai Kexin[2], Pan Jinyu[3]

**Abstract:** Governmental sector and tourism enterprises are recognized as two principal responsible entities for the development of the low-carbon tourism. However, such enterprises can evade government's supervision for its profits maximization due to the local government's insufficient monitoring ability and asymmetric information. Consequently, by introducing an independent third party and basing on a conceptual model, this paper has examined the internal mechanism of their interactions between those three sectors. Besides, based on the game theory, a game tripartite model in relation to the local government, the third-party and tourism enterprise has been constructed. Also, the recommendation effect of government regulation on the low-carbon development of tourism enterprises is considered. Based on the research of tripartite supervision game, the rent-seeking behavior is related to three factors: the coefficient of local government's supervision ability, the regulation cost, and levels of punishment for third-parties and enterprises. Finally, this paper has provided a mixed strategy Nash equilibrium solution and its decision-making analysis along with determinants of these decisions.

**Keywords:** low-carbon tourism; the tripartite game; Nash equilibrium; sustainable development

## Ⅰ. Introduction

Nowadays, global warming becomes a big economic and environmental challenge for the whole world, and the human activity is the main cause of this challenge. [1] In recent years, a series of severe natural disasters, such as droughts, floods and rainstorms, have made humans be aware of the global climate anomalies. The ultimate measure to solve the climate change is to weak the relationship between economic growth and greenhouse gas emissions, and establish a low-carbon development pattern. [2] As a result, the low-carbon economy, which protects the global climate, has risen rapidly around the world and has received

1* Sichuan University, Chengdu, China. mzzm1026@163.com.

2 Sichuan University, Chengdu, China.

3 Sichuan University, Chengdu, China.

positive responses from various countries. Low-carbon economy aims to reduce greenhouse gas emissions and to establish an economic development model based on low-power, low pollution, low emission, which is another major progress of the human society after the agricultural and industrial civilization. As one of the world's largest and fastest growing industries, tourism plays a significant role in the development of low-carbon economy, and gets wide attentions all over the world. *The Tourism and Climate Change Gilbert Declaration*, which is released by the World Tourism Organization at the first international conference on climate change and tourism has pointed out that climate change has substantial effect on the sustainable development of tourism. Also, there is a mutual influence between them. On the one hand, tourism economy is sensitive to climate change. On the other hand, tourism and its related activities are responsible for nearly 5% of the carbon dioxide emissions in the world, which is the main cause of the climate change. [3] Therefore, the tourism should vigorously promote low-carbon tourism. However, the research, such as how to effectively implement low-carbon tourism, and how the local government strictly monitor the enterprise on the carbon emissions control, is clearly lagging behind the need of reality. Thus, a corresponding theory is desired. Based on this background, this paper sorts out the related theory upon the low-carbon tourism both at home and abroad. Then, it builds a decision model between the interdependent and interrelated stakeholders in the use of the game theory, and to analyze the equilibrium result. Hope to make certain contribution to the theory and practice of low-carbon tourism.

## Ⅱ. Literature Review

The concept of low-carbon tourism was first proposed in the report of the *Towards a Low Carbon Travel and Tourism Sector*, presented at the Copenhagen Conference in May 2009, at the World Economic Forum in May. [4] Academics have carried out extensive research around low-carbon tourism, foreign scholars mainly adopt empirical analysis method to investigate the public attitude towards low-carbon tourism, tourist problems such as carbon emissions measurement, energy conservation and emissions reduction measures. [5] Domestic research focuses on the definition, evaluation system, implementation path and development mode.

Dickinson, Robbins and Lumsdon believe that tourism will cause large amounts of carbon emissions, so we can apply "slow travel" which can effectively reduce the carbon footprint of tourism. [7] Some scholars have exposed the shortcomings of the national climate change strategy on the basis of analyzing the existing policy system, such as not coordinating with the tourism development strategy and insufficient communication among relevant government departments. The corporate strategy used by tourism companies to deal with climate problems has also attracted the attention of limited number of academics. [8] There are more empirical studies on energy consumption, carbon emission levels and mitigation measures of tourism enterprises especially hotels. By contrast, the domestic research on low-carbon tourism stakeholders and their relationship is more abundant. Shi Peihua and Wu Pu have provided some effective policy recommendations for government departments to promote low-carbon tourism, and conclude with six key measures. [9] Cai Meng, Wang Yuming have put forward that the basic level of low-carbon tourism development is that the local government manages the promotion of the tourism carbon transfer mechanism, formulates the relevant evaluation system and supervisory agency, and works together with the relevant stakeholders to foster a harmonious and high-quality carbon sink travel experience environment. [10]

As two main stakeholders of low carbon tourism, the game analysis of government and tourism enterprises is still very deficient, only three relevant documents have been collected. Xie Yu, Bi Weiqiang analyzed the behavior decision of the local government and the tourism enterprises in the low-carbon development through the evolutionary game model, besides they get the win-win situation of the local government taking environmental protection supervision and tourism enterprises implementing low-carbon measures based on the advantage strategy analysis. [11] Su Xingguo and Hu Yue introduced Leontief model to investigate the complete information dynamic repeated game process between tourism management department and the investments and operators of scenic area, and presented some suggestions on low carbon development[12]. Wu Yan built a complete information static model on whether the local government takes measures as well as whether the tourist area takes low-carbon measures to discuss the impact of the low-carbon tourism costs, penalties for deregulation and other factors on the decision-making of both sides. [13]

## Ⅲ. Research Design

*i. The conceptual model*

In the process of low-carbon tourism supervision, due to the different participants in the pursuit of different objectives, it is difficult to achieve the unity of the supervisor and the implementation of the party. [14] In order to analyze the relationship among the local government, the third-parties (Party Certification Institution) and the tourism enterprises, this paper presents a conceptual model of its relationship, as shown in Figure 1, to explore the internal mechanisms of interaction between the stakeholders.

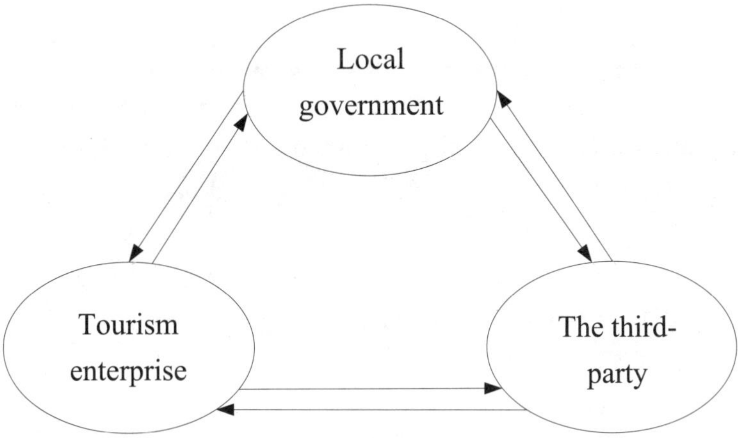

Figure 1 Conceptual Model

The local government provides a legal basis for the protection of low-carbon tourism development, clear environmental regulations and low-carbon production rules. Through policy support, environmental protection and other measures, the local government provides appropriate subsidies and support for low-carbon production of tourism enterprises which can effectively stimulate the enthusiasm of enterprises to carry out low-carbon production. But the insufficiency of government has become more and more obvious such as its insufficient of the supervision capacity in the process of supervising low-carbon tourism, limited scope of supervision, and low oversight efficiency of supervision. Nationality has achieved the national culture and economy effectively fitting in the development of rural tourism, that is a transit of national resources to tourism capital. On the premise of the subjectivity of national cultural heritage and the authenticity of the village tourism performance, the positive interaction between ethnic cultural heritage and village tourism is an important advantage of the national culture and the inheritance of ethnic villages.

The third-party refers to the product inspection institutions with specific testing abilities and conditions which has CNAS accreditation issued by China National Certification and Accreditation Administration and passes the CMA certification issued by the national quality supervision and quarantine. The entrusted third-party can supervise the tourism enterprises with low-carbon production within the scope of their duties, and ensure the legality and standardization of the qualifications and behaviors of enterprises.

As the key subject of low-carbon tourism development, tourism enterprises should meet the requirements of low pollution and low-carbon emissions in product positioning, design, selection and production process. Although enterprises have realized the returns, market opportunities and great potential of green products, due to the production of green products and promotion require a large number of funds and technical support, in the market economy, tourism enterprises tend to pursue their own economic interests and neglect the environmental problems, in order to obtain the maximum profit, power rent-seeking with third-parties will occur.

Comprehensive analysis shows that the local government, the third-parties and tourism enterprises are closely related in the low-carbon tourism supervision. The tourism enterprises produce green products, and the local government and the third-parties supervise their actions. In certain cases, tourism enterprises and the third-party would have rent-seeking behavior, then the local government should clarify the interactive relationship between tourism enterprises and the third-party, and properly solving the rent-seeking problem is essential to regulate low-carbon tourism market and improve the quality of green products.

*ii. Model hypothesis*

The model can inspect the game model selection of a certain tourism enterprises (such as hotel industry), and the game between the management departments (local government and the third-party) to supervise their carbon emissions. To simplify the game model, the following assumptions are made:

(1) Under the condition of incomplete information, and the game subject is bounded rationality.

(2) The local government is to maximize the interests of the community as a whole, tourism enterprises and third-parties to maximize the pursuit of profit as the goal of choice strategy. Each participant has two strategic choices, the tourism enterprise strategy set $A(A_1, A_2)$=(rent-seeking, no rent-seeking); Third-party strategy set $B(B_1, B_2)$=(accepting rent-seeking, refusing rent-seeking); Government strategy set $C(C_1, C_2)$=(supervised, unsupervised).

(3) When the local government directly monitors the tourism enterprise, the input cost of the tourism enterprise is $C_1$. When the third-party is entrusted to supervise the tourism enterprise, the cost of the tourism enterprise input is $C_2$. If the $C_1= C_2$ shows that the third-parties perform their duties in place, there is no power rent-seeking phenomenon; if the $C_1<C_2$ indicates that the third-party and the tourism enterprise exist right rent-seeking activities, at this point, third-parties gain additional profits from corporate bribery of Vs, then the local government's loss of $C_1- C_2$.

(4) Because of the concealment of rent-seeking activities between the third-parties and the tourism enterprises, there are two cases when the local government monitors the behaviors of the two parties, $P = (P_1, P_2)$ = (confirmed violations, violations not found). The ability coefficient of local government finds out rent-seeking exists between two parties is $\varphi$ ($0\leqslant\varphi\leqslant 1$), the cost of supervision is Cg. If rent-seeking phenomenon is found between the third-parties and the tourism enterprises, the local government's economic penalties for the third-parties and enterprises were $Q_s$ *and* $Q_e$.

(5) Assuming that the probability of government supervision is $\chi$, the probability of no supervision is $1X_\chi$; the probability of rent-seeking activity is $Y$, the probability of no rent-seeking is $1\text{-}Y$.

According to the above hypothesis and the parameter settings, we can get the strategy combination and payment matrix of the local government, the tourism enterprise and the third-party, and the game model of the mixed strategy is shown in Table 1.

Table 1 Tripartite Game among Local Government, Tourism Enterprise and the Third Partyies

| Tourism Enterprises<br>The Third Parties | | Local Government | | |
|---|---|---|---|---|
| | | supervision($\chi$) | | not supervised ($1-\chi$) |
| | | detect violations ($P$) | no violation detected ($1-P$) | |
| | Rent-seeking | $V_s$-$Q_s$<br>$C_1$-$C_2$ -$V_s$-$Q_s$<br>$Q_s$+$Q_e$-($C_1$-$C_2$)-$C_g$ | $Vs$<br>$C_1$-$C_2$-$V_s$<br>$-$($C_1$-$C_2$) -$C_g$ | $V_s$<br>$C_1$-$C_2$ -$V_s$<br>-($C_1$-$C_2$) |
| | No rent-seeking | 0<br>0<br>$-C_g$ | 0<br>0<br>$-C_g$ | 0<br>0<br>0 |

## Ⅳ. Model Solving and Analysis

*i. Model solving*

(1) According to the mixed strategy game matrix that has been established, the expected profit of the local government's supervision strategy selection is $U_1$ when "$y$" which is the probability of rent-seeking by enterprises and the third-parties is preset, so:

$$\begin{aligned} U_1 &= py[Q_s+Q_e-(C_1-C_2)-C_g]-p(1-y)C_g \\ &= py[Q_s+Q_e-(C_1-C_2)]-pyC_g-pC_g+pyC_g \\ &= py[Q_s+Q_e-(C_1-C_2)]-pC_g \end{aligned}$$

Similarly, for a given "$y$", the expected profit of the local government's unsupervised strategy selection is $U_2$, so:

$$\begin{aligned} U_2 &= -y(C_1-C_2)+0\times(1-y) \\ &= -y(C_1-C_2) \end{aligned}$$

If $U_1=U_2$, The game achieves equilibrium, so:

$$\begin{aligned} & py[Q_s-Q_e-(C_1-C_2)]-PC_g=-y(C_1-C_2) \\ & \Rightarrow p[Q_s+Q_e-(C_1-C_2)]y+(C_1-C_2)y=pC_g \\ & \Rightarrow y^* = \frac{p\cdot C_g}{p\cdot[Q_s+Q_e-(C_1-C_2)]+(C_1-C_2)} \end{aligned}$$

So the Nash equilibrium of the rent-seeking between the third-party and enterprise is $y^*$

$$y^* = \frac{p\cdot C_g}{p\cdot[Q_s+Q_e-(C_1-C_2)]+(C_1-C_2)} \quad (1)$$

As shown by Equation(1), the analysis results are as follows:

1) When the "$y$" which is the probability of the tourism enterprises and the third-parties

choose to rent meets "$y$"= $y$*, then the local government can randomly choose to supervise or not supervise, because at this time whether to supervise or not, the local government's incomes equal, and if to supervise, the local government will bear a cost of " $C_g$ ".

2) When the "$y$" which is the probability of tourism enterprises and the third-parties choose to rent meets "$y$">$y$*, then the local government should choose the strategy of supervision, supervision will carry out low-carbon business for the tourism enterprises.

3) When the "$y$" which is the probability of tourism enterprises and the third-parties choose to rent meets "$y$"<$y$*, then the local government should choose the strategy of no supervision.

(2) According to the mixed strategy game matrix that has been established, the expected profit of the third-party participating rent-seeking behavior of enterprises is $U_3$ when "$x$" is the probability of choosing supervisory strategy, so:

$$\begin{aligned} U_3 &= px(V_s - Q_s) + x(1-p)V_s + (1-x)V_s \\ &= pxV_s - pxQ_s + xV_s - xpV_s + V_s - xV_s \\ &= V_s - pxQ_s \end{aligned}$$

For a given $x$, the expected revenue value of the third party's policy choose not accept enterprise's rent-seeking is $U_4$, so:

$$U_4 = 0$$

If $U_3 = U_4$, the game achieves equilibrium, so:

$$\begin{aligned} &V_s - pxQ_s = 0 \\ &\Rightarrow x_1^* = \frac{V_s}{p \cdot Q_s} \end{aligned}$$

Therefore, the Nash equilibrium of supervision and no supervision of the local government is $x_1$*

$$x_1^* = \frac{V_s}{p \cdot Q_s} \tag{2}$$

As shown by Equation(2), the analysis results are as follows:

1) When the probability of the local government to choose supervision meets $x=x_1$*, the third-party can choose the behavior strategy at random;

2) When the probability of the local government to choose the supervision is $x<x_1^*$, the third-party optimal strategy is to seek the rent-seeking behavior as accepting the bribe of the tourism enterprise.

3) When the probability of local government chooses the supervision $x>x_1^*$, at this time the third-party optimal strategy is to seek the rent-seeking behavior that does not accept the bribe of the tourism enterprise.

(3) According to the game matrix of mixed strategy established, the expected return value of the rent-seeking strategy for enterprise is $U_5$ when the probability of government

chooses the monitoring strategy "*x*" is given.

$$U_5=px(C_1-C_2-V_s-Q_s)+x(1-p)(C_1-C_2-V_s)+(1-x)(C_1-C_2-V_s)$$
$$=px(C_1-C_2-V_s)-xpQ_s+x(1-p)+x(C_1-C_2-V_s)-xp(C_1-C_2-V_s)+(C_1-C_2-V_s)-x(C_1-C_2-V_s)$$
$$=(C_1-C_2-V_s)-xpQ_s$$

For a given *x*, the expected revenue value of no rent-seeking for the tourism enterprise is $U_6$, so:

$$U_6=0$$

If $U_5=U_6$, The game achieves equilibrium, so:

$$(C_1-C_2-V_s)-xpQ_s=0$$
$$\Rightarrow x_2^*=\frac{C_1-C_2-V_s}{p\cdot Q_s}$$

Therefore, the Nash equilibrium of supervision and no supervision of the local government is $x_2$*

$$x_2^*=\frac{C_1-C_2-V_s}{p\cdot Q_s} \tag{3}$$

As shown by Equation(3), the analysis results are as follows:

1) When the probability of local government chooses supervision is $x=x_2$*, the tourism enterprise chooses its own behavior strategy at random because there is no difference in earnings at this time;

2) When the probability of local government chooses supervision $x<x_1^*$, at this time, the local government's supervision is small, the tourism enterprise has a fluke mentality, in order to gain greater benefits, chooses to bribe the third parties, rent-seeking behavior occurs;

3) When the probability of local government chooses supervision $x>x_1$*, at this time, the local government supervision is great, the probability of rent-seeking is too large, the tourism enterprise should choose the strategy which is "no rent-seeking".

In summary, the Nash equilibrium of the mixed strategy game model is $y^*=\frac{p\cdot C_g}{p\cdot[Q_s+Q_e-(C_1-C_2)]+(C_1-C_2)}$, $x_1^*=\frac{V_s}{p\cdot Q_s}$, namely the third-party and the tourism enterprise $y^*=\frac{p\cdot C_g}{p\cdot[Q_s+Q_e-(C_1-C_2)]+(C_1-C_2)}$ takes as the probability of rent-seeking behavior, the local government takes $x_1^*=\frac{V_s}{p\cdot Q_s}$ as the probability of supervision; or $y^*=\frac{p\cdot C_g}{p\cdot[Q_s+Q_e-(C_1-C_2)]+(C_1-C_2)}$, $x_2^*=\frac{C_1-C_2-V_s}{p\cdot Q_s}$, namely the third-party and the tourism enterprise take $y^*=\frac{p\cdot C_g}{p\cdot[Q_s+Q_e-(C_1-C_2)]+(C_1-C_2)}$

as the probability of rent-seeking behavior, the local government takes $x_2^* = \frac{C_1 - C_2 - V_s}{p \cdot Q_s}$ as the probability of supervision.

*ii. Game model analysis*

In order to strictly control the tourism enterprises to carry out low-carbon development, and avoid the rent-seeking behaviors between third-party and the tourism enterprise in the supervision of low-carbon development process, and improve the efficiency of governmental supervision, it needs to design some of the best strategy mechanisms.Through the above analysis, we obtained:

$$\begin{cases} y^* = \frac{p \cdot C_g}{p \cdot [Q_s + Q_e - (C_1 - C_2)] + (C_1 - C_2)} & (4) \\ x_1^* = \frac{V_s}{p \cdot Q_s} & (5) \\ x_2^* = \frac{C_1 - C_2 - V_s}{p \cdot Q_s} & (6) \end{cases}$$

According to the analysis of the above three types, we can draw the following conclusions:

(1) The factors that influence the rent-seeking power between the third-parties and the tourism enterprises.

According to Equation(4) we can see the equilibrium probability of the rent-seeking of the third-party and the tourism enterprise is "$y^*$", and the size of the $y^*$is related to $p$, $C_g$, $Q_s$, $Q_e$, and $(C_1-C_2)$, $y^*$ is directly proportional to $C_g$, inversely proportional to $p$, $Q_s$, $Q_e$, and $(C_1-C_2)$.

In order to stop the power rent-seeking between enterprises and the third parties, which affects the low-carbon development level of tourism, try to minimizes the probability of rent-seeking $y^*$ by increasing the values of $p$, $Q_s$, $Q_e$, and $Cg$. That is to raise $p$ which is the capability coefficient of the local government's ability of successful supervision, and to increase the size of government oversight costs $Cg$. When the third party and the tourism enterprise are found to have rent-seeking behaviors, increasing the local government's economic penalty for the third parties and the tourism enterprise $Q_s$, $Q_e$, thus it has a certain deterrent effect to the third party and enterprise, and effectively reduce the probability of rent-seeking.

(2) The factors that influence the local government to supervise the rent-seeking of the third-party and the tourism enterprise.

Analysis of the "$x$" that is the probability of governmental supervision on rent-seeking behavior of third-parties and enterprises is divided into two cases:

1) When the interests of the third-parties are in the first place, it is known by $x_1^* = \frac{V_s}{p \cdot Q_s}$,

$x_1^*$ is related to $V_s$, $p$, and $Q_s$, is directly proportional to $V_s$, inversely proportional to $p$ and $Q_s$.

In order to improve the efficiency of the local government's supervision, it must reduce the probability of governmental supervision, it should reduce the additional income of the third-parties from corporate bribery as $V_s$, increase the capacity coefficient $p$of government's successful supervision, and increase the economic penalty for rent-seeking behaviors of the third parties.

2) when the interests of the tourism enterprise are in the first place, it is known by $x_2^* = \frac{C_1-C_2-V_s}{p \cdot Q_s}$, the value of is related to $C_1$, $C_2$, $V_s$, $p$ and $Q_s$ is inversely proportional to $V_s$, and is proportional to $p$, $Q_s$, and $(C_1-C_2)$.

In order to reduce the probability of governmental supervision, we can increase the cost of enterprise and the third-party's rent-seeking $V_s$, and increase economic penalties $Q_s$ for companies who take rent-seeking, and improve the capacity coefficient $p$ of government's successful supervision.

## V. Conclusion and Discussion

In this paper, a three-party game model related to the local government, the third-party and tourism enterprises during the low-carbon tourism promotion is constructed. Also, the recommendation effect of government regulation on the low-carbon development of tourism enterprises is considered. Based on the research of tripartite supervision game, the rent-seeking behavior is related to three factors: the coefficient of local government's supervision ability, the regulation cost, and levels of punishment for third-parties and enterprises.

Therefore, in the local government's point of view, measures to avoid the rent-seeking activities from third parties and the tourism enterprises, and give full play to the independent regulation are as follows:

The third-party in the paper is the low-carbon certification body, so there is a need to accelerate the process of such institution's establishment, enact laws for authorization bodies, and further improve the qualification management of national inspection. The social intermediary institutions involved in goods inspection and accreditation should be legally established and independent with state administrative organs.When there are loopholes in levels and measures of punishment for rent-seeking activities, we should improve the relevant legal system in relation to the third-party certification.The local government should strengthen the supervision, and raise the access threshold for the certification organizations through horizontal comparison in aspect of capital investment, infrastructure and staffing, etc. As for the third-party that has been approved, it is more effective to check out rent-seeking behaviors between the third parties and enterprises by enhancing regulation, increasing checking frequency, along with certain random/regular/specific inspection etc.

This paper has set up a game model of rent-seeking among government, the third-party and enterprise under the complete information static condition.The paper also analyzes these three stake holders' strategy choices respectively.

Further research is needed to investigate the incomplete information game with multi-participant, and the research on the low-carbon tourism specialized problems shall be deeper.

## References


[1] Solomon S, Qin D, Manning M, et al. *Climate Change 2007: The Physical Science Basis. Contribution of Working Group I to the Fourth Assessment Report of the Intergovernmental Panel on Climate Change*[M]. Cambridge: Cambridge University Press, 2007.

[2] Zhuang Guiyang. *How Will China Move towards a Low Carbon Economy*[M]. *Beijing: China Meteorological Press*, 2007.

[3] Scott D, Hall C M, Gössling S. *Tourism and Climate Change: Impacts, Adaptation and Mitigation*[M]. *London: Routledge*, 2012.

[4] Chiesa T, Gantan A. Towards a low-carbon travel and tourism sector[J]. *World Economic Forum, Rep.*, 2009.

[5] Higham J E S, Cohen S A. Canary in the coalmine: Norwegian attitudes towards climate change and extreme long-haul air travel to Aotearoa/New Zealand[J]. *Tourism Management*, 2011(32): 98-105.

[6] Gössling S. *Carbon Management in Tourism: Mitigating the Impacts on Climate Change*[M]. Oxford: Routledge, 2010.

[7] Janet E D, Derek R, Les L D. Holiday travel discourses and climate change[J]. *Journal of Transport Geography*, 2010(18): 482-489.

[8] Smith A, Grosbois D. The adoption of corporate social responsibility practices in the airline industry[J]. *Journal of Sustainable Tourism*, 2011(19): 59-78.

[9] Shi Peihua, Wu Pu. Thought and measure of developing low-carbon tourism[N]. *China Tourism News*, 2010-01-08:10.

[10] Cai Meng, Wang Yuming. Low-carbon tourism: a new type of development pattern[J]. *Tourism Tribune*, 2010(25): 13-17.

[11] Xie Yu, Bi Weiqiang. Evolutionary game between local government and tourism enterprise in the process of low-carbon tourism promotion[J]. *Special Zone Economy*, 2013(2): 100-102.

[12] Su Xingguo, Hu Yue. Game analysis among players in the process of low-carbon tourism promotion[J]. *China Collective Economy*, 2011(27):33-134.

[13] Wu Yan. Game between local government and scenic attraction in the development of low-carbon[J]. *Tourism Manager Journal*, 2010(24): 204.

[14] Liu Changyu, Yu Tao. Study on the tripartite game in quality regulation of green products[J]. *China Population Resources and Environment*, 2015(25):10-13.

[15] Wang Jingyu, Shi Anna. Analysis of central and local government behavior game in low-carbon technology diffusion [J]. *Science & Technology Progress and Policy*, 2011(28):12-15.

[16] Yang Zhenzhi, Shi Hong, Yang Dan, et al. Analysis of core stakeholder behaviour in the tourism community using economic game theory[J]. *Tourism Economics*, 2015(21):1169-1187.

[17] Wang Chunyang, Qu Hailin. The influence factors of community residents' attitude toward tourism development in the village heritage[J]. *Journal of Geography*, 2014(69): 278-288.

[18] Yang Zhenzhi. On the nature of tourism destination[J].*Tourism Tribune*, 2014(29):13-21.

[19] Gursoy D, Rutherford D G. Host attitudes toward tourism: an improved structural model[J]. *Annals of Tourism Research*, 2004(31):495-516.

[20] Yan Yu, Yu Jian. The role of consumer organizations in the prevention of adverse selection of green products market[J]. *Consumer Economics*, 2013(3): 43-45.

[21] Gao Honggui. The multi-game research on green economic development in China[J]. *China Population, Resources and Environment*, 2012(4): 13-18.

[22] Wang Wenjing, Du Huiying, Lu Tingjie. Cloud service trust models based on the third-party certification[J]. *Systems Engineering: Theory & Practice*, 2012(12): 2774-2775.

[23] Peter D M, Hooman E. Consumer perceptions of third party product quality ratings[J]. *Journal of Business Research*, 2011(64):1067-1073.

[24] Zhu Qinghua, Wang Ming. Study on responsibility of governments in the process of supply and demand of green products based on economic analysis[J]. *China Population, Resources and Environment*, 2010(2):173-176.

# A Research on the Importance of Community Empowerment in the Context of Game Analysis

Xia Wenjing[1], Zhu Qiongqiong[2*], He Tao[3]

**Abstract:** Community participation is the most effective way to absorb pro-poor tourism. And the game behavior among community residents, developers and government who are the core stakeholders of pro-poor tourism, has a great impact on the effectiveness of pro-poor tourism. However, the community residents who are both the recipients and the ultimate target of pro-poor tourism, are often in a passive position, making the achievement of tourism poverty alleviation less effective. Based on the theory of community empowerment, this paper emphasizes the importance of community empowerment through analyzing the game between community residents and developers.

**Keywords:** pro-poor tourism; stakeholder; community empowerment; game

## Ⅰ. Introduction

Poverty is a worldwide problem which has been considered one of the most serious problems in the world by the United Nations. The poverty, a widespread social phenomenon, is not only a matter of material life relative to wealth, but also a comprehensive and complex social problem involving many aspects such as society, culture and politics and so on. Thus, helping the poor to develop the economy and increase their income is just one aspect of changing the state of poverty. The only way is to make the poor people get the ability to create income and opportunities, which are the foundation for poverty alleviation. Different from the previous "blood transfusion" poverty alleviation model, tourism poverty alleviation as a "hematopoietic" poverty alleviation model has become one of the most preferential policies for underdeveloped economy but well-diversified tourism resources region.

Community participation in tourism poverty alleviation is also considered as an effective way to achieve the goal of tourism poverty alleviation. Community participation theory is helpful to solve the conflict between communities and developers in tourism poverty alleviation, and has been widely used in tourism research and tourism planning both at home

1 Chongqing Business Vocational College, Chongqing, China.
2* Sichuan University, Chengdu, China. 1240866271@qq.com.
3 Sichuan University, Chengdu, China.

and abroad. Community participation in tourism development is to take the community as the main body of tourism development to participate in the decision-making and implementation system of major issues concerning tourism development, such as tourism planning and tourism development, so as to achieve the goal of protecting the interests of the community. Community participation in tourism poverty alleviation plays a role in providing tourism product quality, protecting tourism resources and environment, promoting sustainable development of tourism, establishing community participation safeguard mechanism and profit distribution mechanism.

However, from the practice of all countries, especially in developing countries, "community participation is only symbolic, tourism continues to be controlled by developers and governments, rather than community interests". "This kind of participation is nothing more than a cover-up to public relations. It merely allows the local community to respond to the forthcoming program, plan, advice and development within a very small range (Macbeth, 1996)." [1] According to the theory of tourism stakeholders, most of the benefits of tourism poverty alleviation are occupied by developers, while the interests of the community residents who are the subjects of tourism development and the main undertakers of tourism development costs in pro-poor tourism are often excluded.

Currently, the participation of the community is just regarded as an economic and technological instead of a participatory process of political rights, which is the reason why tourism poverty cannot make real progress in practice.[2] Based on the political attributes of tourism development and the deep understanding of the shortcomings of the current community participation theory, the theory of Western tourism empowerment came into being.

This paper is to analyze the relationship of pro-poor tourism stakeholders through the use of game theory. It aims to balance the rights of the government, developers, and community residents in the process of pro-poor tourism, thereby achieving the balance of the interests of multiple parties.

## Ⅱ. Literature Review

*i. Stakeholder theory*

In the 1960s, researchers at the Stanford Institute of the United States first proposed the concept of stakeholders, referring to those who support the existence of the relevant entities. Subsequently, the stakeholder theory has received wide attention. Until 1984, Freeman first systematically proposed the stakeholder theory in his book, *Strategic Management: A Stakeholder Approach*, which also symbolizes the theory was formally formed. Freeman argues that "stakeholder are individuals and groups that can influence the fulfillment of the goals of an organization or can be affected by organization in the process of achieving its goals"[3]. Huang Dayong, Du Yiran (2015) argued that " due to paying close attention to the same thing, there will be contradiction of interests, power, and so on among the different stakeholders. Therefore, they put forward the corresponding solution" [4].

In the 1980s, the concept of stakeholder theory was introduced in the field of tourism research. On October 1, 1999, at the thirteenth session of the World Tourism Organization, the word "stakeholder" was explicitly adopted in the *Global Code of Ethics for Tourism* to provide a reference standards for the behavior of different stakeholders in the development of tourism. That marked that the concept "tourism stakeholders" had been officially recognized.

In China, Zhang Guangrui (2000) first proposed the stakeholder theory.[5] Zhang Wei, Wu Bihu (2002) applied theory of stakeholder interests to the tourism planning in Leshan City, Sichuan Province, and used the qualitative and quantitative methods to analyze the tourism consciousness and interest expression of different stakeholders. They finally discussed and put forward the application channels of "stakeholder" theory in China's regional tourism development and planning.[6]

Based on the three aspects of the relation among the degree of relation, the influence, the nature of interests, Xia Zancai (2003) established a stakeholder map of the travel agency, and divided the map into two levels: core layer, and strategic layer and periphery layer. According to the degree of interest's relation, [7] Yan Youbing, Xiao Yao (2007) divided the stakeholders of the tourist attractions into two categories: direct stakeholders and indirect stakeholders. [8]

Based on the analysis of the ancient villages, Wu Xianfu (2007), in the views of the nature of stakeholders and the extent of the impact, classified the stakeholders in the ancient village into core stakeholder and dormant stakeholder, and the two kinds can be transformed from each other. Furthermore, the conversion depends on one or several factors including the evolution of the tourism life cycle and the policy, the changes in the system and so on. [9] Liu Shanshan (2016) who had a similar classification, divided stakeholders into core and non-core types. [10]

The research of stakeholder theory is of great significance to the study of pro-poor tourism in China. Stakeholder theory also plays an important guiding role in community participation in pro-poor tourism and tourism development strategy.

There are different stakeholders in tourism development process. Clare Gunn, Tegert Val (2005) proposed that we should take into account the interests of tourists, local residents, government, tourism enterprises and other parties in the tourism development. [11] According to the work of pro-poor tourism, the stakeholders are divided into core stakeholders and key stakeholders in this paper. Among them, the core stakeholders are mainly government, developers and community residents; In addition to the core stakeholders, the main stakeholders include tourists, tourism enterprises, banks and financial institutions, etc.

*ii. Community empowerment theory*

The research community, community tourism, and community participation have fully developed in foreign countries. In recent years, these concepts and related theories have been continuously studied by domestic scholars. However, there is a lack of analysis of the relationship between politics and rights in our country. It merely considers community participation as an economic and technological process rather than taking community participation as a political right process, which is the reason why community participation in tourism poverty alleviation and tourism development can not make progress. Thus, community empowerment is proposed as a concept and will be further studied.

American scholar Barbara Solomon (1976) published the *Black Empowerment: Social Work in Oppressed Communities,* who firstly raised the concept "empowerment" from the perspective of race. [12] Akama J (1996) first proposed the necessity of empowering community residents in the study of eco-tourism in Kenya.[13] Scheyvens (1999) formally introduced the empowerment theory into ecotourism research. [14]

Wang Ning (2006), a Chinese scholar, took the lead in the study of theory of empowerment.[15] At present, the related research mainly focuses on the analysis and research of foreign related theories, and the application of the theory of empowerment to specific fields. Zuo Bing, Bao Jigang (2008) proposed that empowerment is composed of the right, no right, to the right, increasing the right, as well as the core concept.[16] The rights or powers are the basic concepts of the theory of empowerment, and the empowerment is the most central concept in the whole theory of empowerment and its work practice. It refers to enhancing the individual's ability and the awareness through the use of external interventions and aids to reduce or eliminate the sense of powerlessness, with the ultimate goal of gaining access to action for society and its achievement of social change. Specifically, they analyzed the concrete theory of western tourism empowerment. They also believed that theoretical research of stakeholders and community participation is flawed, and the theory of western tourism empowerment is put forward on the basis of the first two, pointing out that the empowerment must be realized simultaneously through the three forms of personal empowerment, administrative empowerment and policy empowerment.They thought that in the order of empowerment, the personal empowerment should take precedence over the community empowerment, namely the tourism empowerment should first focus on the development of individual rights and self-efficacy. Only in the premise of protecting human rights, poor residents can really benefit from the development of tourism. Bao Jigang, Sun Jiuxia (2008), through empirical analysis and discussion of the community participation in tourism development of Yubeng village in Yunling Township, Diqing Prefecture, Yunnan Province, considered that the community has basically achieved the economic empowerment, psychological empowerment and some political empowerment, but the community has not yet really implemented empowerment. [17] Chen Yun(2015) established an evaluation index system for the empowerment of tourism communities, and took Yangjiang Hailing Island as an example to carry out the empirical analysis. [18]

Based on the community participation in pro-poor tourism work, this paper, taking the community residents as the core, establishes a game model between the community residents and developers to study the importance of community empowerment, especially in the context of community empowerment.

## Ⅲ. Game Model Construction

The government is the leader of pro-poor tourism and plays the most important role in the work. The main purpose of government action is first of all to improve the economic situation in poor areas and help the poor residents to get rid of poverty. With the progress of pro-poor tourism work, the "poor" supported by the pro-poor tourism is not only material poverty, but also spiritual poverty. By giving the rights to residents in poverty-stricken areas and cultivating their own capacity, poverty alleviation in a real sense can be achieved and the phenomenon of "returning to poverty" can be avoided.

Developers, whose main purpose is to obtain economic benefits and maximize profits, are the main participants in tourism poverty alleviation.

They not only provide good tourism-related services for tourists and local residents to better enjoy and utilize the natural resources of the tourist areas, but also bring benefits to the poor areas and the poor. But the reality is that out of the developers' own interests and with the purpose of safeguarding their own interests, they will be against the interests of local residents to a certain extent, making contradictions between the two.

The community residents are the most crucial group among the stakeholders in pro-poor tourism. They are the core stakeholders, playing important roles of manager and operator. Also, they are the vital factor to realize their own poverty alleviation and for the healthy development of pro-poor tourism. Therefore, the poor residents need to take the initiative to participate in pro-poor tourism work, and defend their own rights in the interests conflict with developers.

Sofield (2003) pointed out that only community empowerment can highlight the dominant position of the community in tourism development. So, empowerment is an important prerequisite for the realization of sustainable development, and the awareness of empowerment must penetrate the entire tourism system. He viewed the results of community development as the structure of the power relations between actors and draws lesson from the Ap's (1992) social exchange diagram to analyze the three outcomes that communities and developers may have in the exchange of rights. [19]

As shown in Table 1, there are four kinds of situations, only when the rights of community residents and developers are strong, will there be a balanced win-win situation between the two, such as the first case. The balance in the fourth case makes both sides have no initiative to participate in tourism and tourism cannot develop. In the second and third cases, when either party has a strong right, it will fail to reach a balance, causing the other party to lose. Under such circumstances, the losing party is not satisfied with the result of the exchange, which may damage or suspend both parties interest exchange, resulting in tourism development being not sustainable.

On this basis, Sofitel sums up five points. First, the sustainable development of community tourism is inseparable from the factor of community empowerment; Second, in the past community tourism development model, the community is excluded from the sharing of rights, and the traditional community participation mechanism and empowerment method can't make the development of tourism sustainable. Third, tourism is sustainable only when the traditional way of empowerment is improved to a legitimate empowerment. Fourth, the community empowerment is often constrained by the environment and the system. Thus, the legitimate empowerment must reallocate the unbalanced power relations between communities and external societies. Fifth, community empowerment requires long-term support and cooperation from the local government, but can't be achieved by its own strength.

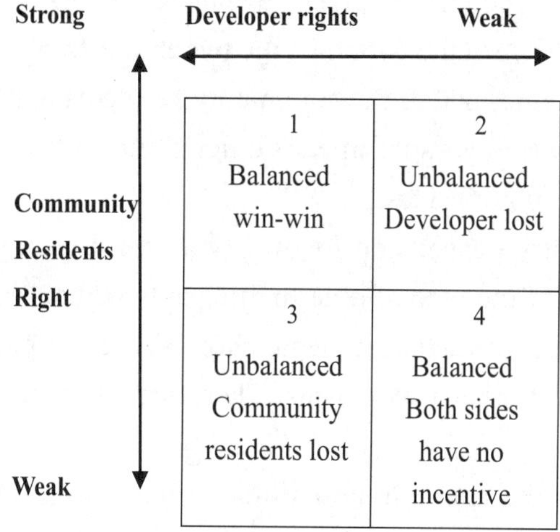


Figure 1 Exchange Results Between Community and Developer Social (Power)

Source: Sofield T H B. *Empowerment for sustainable tourism development*, Pergamon, 2003: 245. Slightly changed.

During the work of pro-poor tourism, the relationships among the government, community residents in poor areas, and developers are actually a process of game, balancing the allocation of resources and interests, as well as social formation among stakeholders through transaction, negotiation, transfer of benefits and responsibility sharing. Therefore, in the context of government empowerment namely community empowerment, this paper mainly studies the game between the community residents and developers.

*i. Hypothesis of game model*

(1) Participants in the game: community residents and tourists. Both of them understand

the structure of the game and their own gains or payments.

(2) There are two types of community residents: rights and no rights. The income of the community residents under normal conditions is A. If the community residents are in the conflict of developers, the cost of choosing the complaint is F.

(3) There are two kinds of interests for the residents of the local community in the process of developers participating in pro-poor tourism: infringement of interests and non-infringement of interests. That developers' benefits in the case of encroaching on the interests of poor residents is recorded as "B". The loss of the interests of community residents is "C". Getting benefits without infringing upon the interests of poor residents benefit is "0". If the developer violates the interests of the residents, and the community residents use the right to adjust with the developer or complain to the government, then the developer is fined, which is denoted by "D".

(4) Under the circumstance that community residents do not complain when their interests are violated, they often conflict with the developer. Although both of them will be influenced, this time assuming no impact on the developer, the loss of community residents is "E". If there is no conflict between the two, then the two interests do not change.

(5) In this two-party game model, the community residents and developers take action at the same time, they are not fully aware of each other's information. Meanwhile, they can't fully understand the benefit of both sides.

The choice of each party depends on its own type, since each participant only knows the probability distribution of the type of other participants without knowing their true type, so they can't accurately know the actual strategic choices of other participants. But they can predict the type of choice of other participants. Therefore, it is an incomplete static game type.

Thus, on the basis of the above assumptions, a matrix of community residents and developers' game is obtained, as shown in Table 1.

Table 1 Incomplete Information Static Game Strategy

| Type | Community Residents | | | |
|---|---|---|---|---|
| | Complain | | No Complain | |
| Developer | Availability | Invalid | Conflict | Compromise |
| Infringement of interest | (-D, A+D-F) | (B, A-C-F) | (B, A-C-E) | (B, A-C) |
| Non-infringement interests | (0, A-F) | (0, A-F) | (0, A) | (0, A) |

*ii. Harsanyi conversion*

Harsanyi (1967) proposed the type classification based on insufficient understanding of the state of benefit in the game model, and then put forward a complete but imperfect information dynamic model after the incomplete information static model, that is, the so-called Harsanyi transformation.[20] Therefore, on this basis, this paper conducts the Heisenly transformation of the above information and constructs a unified probability model to describe the participants' incomplete information processing in the game, so as to transform the incomplete information game into complete but imperfect information game.

Accordingly, it is assumed that the probability of community residents complaining is "p", the probability of not complaining is "1-p", the probability of developers violating the interests of the residents is "q", and the probability of non-infringement is "1-q". The rights the community residents own will have influence on the effectiveness of complaints. When community residents resort to complaining, the greater the rights of residents, the greater the effect of complaints when their interests are violated. The probability of valid complaints is "r", while invalid is "1-r". The probability of community residents and developers conflict with each other is "m", and no conflict is "1-m". So, the original incomplete information game is transformed into completely imperfect information game. As shown in Figure 2.

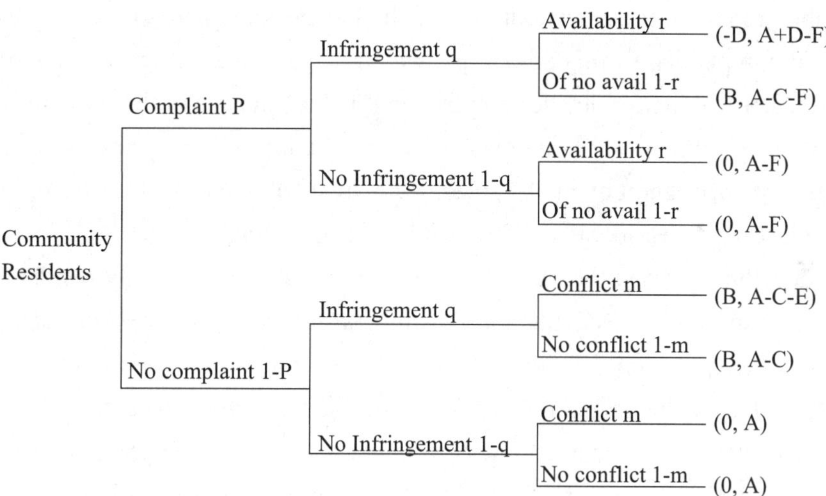


Figure 2 The Harsanyi Transformation of Community Residents and Developers Game

*iii. Equilibrium solution and result analysis of game model*

*A. Game model solving*

According to the game model after the transformation of Harsanyi, the model is solved. The expected benefits of community residents are as follows.

$$W1=p\{r[q(A+D-F)+(1-q)(A-F)]+(1-r)[q(A-C-F)+(1-q)(A-F)]\}+(1-P)\{m[q(A-C-E)+(1-q)*A]+(1-m)[q(A-C)+(1-q)*A]\}=P(rqD+qCr+qEm-F)+A-qEm-qC$$

The developer's expected benefits are as follows.

W2=q{p[r(-D)+(1-r)*B]+(1-p)[m*B+(1-m)*B]}+(1-q){p[r*0+(1-r)*0]+(1-p)[m*0+(1-m)*0]=-q(pr[D+B]+B)

Through the above formula, the biggest gains of the community residents and developers will be solved, that is, to find the partial derivative of p for W1 and the partial derivative of q for W2, then make the partial derivative zero, and finally get the Nash equilibrium solution as follows.

q=F/(Dr+Cr+Em)

P=B/r(D+B)

*B. Conclusion from the above formula*

(1) If the community residents want to maximize their benefits in pro-poor tourism, they must guarantee that the probability of having right is P = B/r (D + B). However, to maximize the benefits of developers, it is necessary to infringe the interests of community residents with the probability of q = F/(Dr + Cr + Em).

(2) For community residents, if "r" increases, it means that the rights of community residents in the process of pro-poor tourism will be increased, which will have greater effect on the result of complaints. At this point, "p", which is the probability of complaints, will be reduced. And the probability of developer infringing on the interests of the residents that is "q" also will be reduced. When "D" is increased, the probability of complaints will be reduced, the probability of infringement of the interests of residents should also be reduced, as a result, the interests of the residents will be guaranteed accordingly.

(3) For developers, when the "D", the complaints cost of community residents, and the "E", the loss of community residents and developers in the conflict are increased, this will not only makes the community residents often choose not to complain because of a huge cost, but also increases the probability of developer infringe their interests. When the "C", interests of the residents are infringed, they will always choose to complain, so the developer may be punished. And if the community residents have greater power, its impact on the result of complaint "r"will be greater. Developers are bound to suffer greater penalties for their violations, thus, the probability of infringement of interest"Q", will be lowered.

(4) Based on the above two formulas, as soon as the community residents or the poor people in the pro-poor tourism can have greater power, more right to speak and decide, their complaints will have greater effect, promoting their better participation in pro-poor tourism. In this case, not only it will reduce the probability of developers participating in pro-poor tourism infringement on the interests of community residents, and allow the residents independently to choose some reputable developers, but also lower the complaints rate, establish good social relations, and build a harmonious society, achieving poverty alleviation in the true sense.

## Ⅳ. Conclusion

In the work of pro-poor tourism, most of the poverty-stricken areas are remote and backward. Community residents are in the obviously weak and passive position, and it is far from enough for the community participation involving in pro-poor tourism. There are two reasons. On the one hand, it is that the community residents of the sense of identity, sense of belonging, sense of responsibility and participation is not enough. On the other hand, it is that the community residents do not fully understand their own rights, and the empowerment in the community has not been truly implemented. As a result, what have been done in the pro-poor tourism still leave much to be desired, although great achievements have been made.

Therefore, community empowerment is imminent, changing the community residents from passive participation into active action, breaking the unbalanced power relations, and gaining access to decision-making in tourism development. It will ensure that local residents can maximize their interests and control the development of tourism in the local government, so as to achieve "letting the tourism for residents' use rather than residents are used for tourism". [21]

## References

[1] Macbeth J. Dissonance and paradox in tourism planning: people first? [J]. *Analysis Research Series*, 1994, 3: 2-18.

[2] Chen Hongbing, Hu Xiao. China's community empowerment context analysis [J]. *Academic Discussion*, 2011: 82-83.

[3] Freeman R E. *Strategic Management: A Stakeholder Approach* [M]. Boston: Pitman, 1984.

[4] Huang Dayong, Du Yiran. Literature review of theory on stakeholder in tourism development area [J]. *Chongqing Technological Business University*, 2015, 32(2): 71-75.

[5] Zhang Guangrui. Global tourism ethics[J]. *Journal of Tourism*, 2000 (3): 71-74.

[6] Zhang Wei, Wu Bihu. The application of the theory of interest substance in regional tourism planning: a case study of Leshan City, Sichuan Province[J]. *Journal of Tourism*, 2002 (4): 63-68.

[7] Xia Zancai. Stakeholder theory and travel agency stakeholders basic chart [J]. *Spectrum Hunan Normal University Social Sciences*, 2003 (3): 72-77.

[8] Yan Youbing, Xiao Yao. Study on economic governance model of stakeholders' joint governance in tourism scenic sites[J]. *Social Sciences*, 2007 (3): 108-112.

[9] Wu Xianfu. Based on the theory of the main interests of the ancient village tourism development research[D]. Xiangtan: Xiangtan University, 2007.

[10] Liu Shanshan. Research on the differences of rural tourism environmental impact perception of tourism stakeholders[D]. Hangzhou: Zhejiang Gongshang University, 2016: 22-25.

[11] Claire Gunn, Tegot Val. *Tourism Planning: Theory and Case*[M]. Wu Bihu, Wu Dongqin trans. Dalian: Northeast University of Finance and Economics Press, 2005.

[12] Zhou Lingang. The theory of exciting power: a literature review [J]. *Journal of Shenzhen University (Humanities and Social Sciences)*, 2005 (11): 45-50.

[13] Akama J. Western environmental values and nature-based tourism in Kenya[J]. *Tourism Management*, 1996, 17(8): 567-574.

[14] Scheyvens R. Ecotourism and the empowerment of local communities[J]. *Tourism Management*, 1999(20): 245-249.

[15] Wang Ning. Consumer empowerment or consumer empowerment: are examination of the transformation of urban consumption patterns in China[J]. *Journal of Zhongshan University (Social Science Edition)*, 2006 (6): 100-106.

[16] Zuo Bing, Bao Jigang. From "community participation" to "community empowerment": a review of western "tourism empowerment" theory [J]. *Journal of Tourism*, 2008 (4): 58-63.

[17] Bao Jigang, Sun Jiuxia. Yubun village community tourism: community participation and its significance [J]. *Tourism Forum*, 2008 (1): 58-65.

[18] Chen Yun. Research on the right predicament of Guangdong coastal tourism development and community empowerment[D]. Guangzhou: Guangzhou University, 2015: 31-35.

[19] Sofield T H B. *The Empowerment for Sustainable Tourism Development* [M]. London: Pergamon, 2003.

[20] Eric Rasmusen. *Games and Information: An Introduction to Game Theory*[M]. Han Song, Zhang Qingwei, et al., trans. Beijing: China Renmin University Press, 2009.

[21] Zhang Weiying. *Game Theory and Information Economics*[M]. Shanghai: Shanghai Sanlian Bookstore, Shanghai People's Publishing House, 1996.

# A Research on the Tourism Innovation and Development of Historic Towns Based on the Analysis of Spatial Competitive Characteristics: A Case Study of Phoenix Historic City and Zhenyuan Historic Town

Teng Mengqin[1*]

**Abstract:** There are more and more tourism types with the development of "big tourism", and historic town tourism has become a new approach showing the characteristics of the town. In recent years, the historic town tourism has been growing vigorously, but the inevitable tourism space competition restricts the market influence of some adjacent tourism. The article takes West Hunan Phoenix Historic City and Zhenyuan Historic Town as an example to complete the empirical research. Based on the analysis of the equivalence of tourism resources endowment between two regions, this paper constructs the index system of tourism competitiveness of historic towns. The spatial competition characteristics of the tourism development between the two regions which include the similarity of spatial cognition, the convergence of target market, the accessibility of traffic and the similarity of radiation in surrounding cities are summarized. At the same time, combining with the existing effect evaluation of the historic town tourism, this paper analyzes the dilemma faced by the two places in the space substitution, and puts forward the countermeasures of tourism development. The study aims to promote the innovation of the tourism development mechanism and the sustainable development of the two historic towns under the background of comprehensive tourism development.

**Keywords:** historic town tourism; spatial competition; innovation and development

## Ⅰ. Introduction

"The spatial competition of the tourist destination is caused by the emergence of multiple tourist sites in the same area. When multiple tourist sites appear in the same area,

1* Northwest Minzu University, Lan Zhou, China. 260655813@qq.com.

their respective attraction tends to show the dynamic change of trade-off or synchronous growth and the reorganization of the regional tourism market structure." [1] It reveals the external characteristics of space competition and the varied features of source market structure, and the spatial change of the market structure is the result of the alternative competition. [2] According to the relationship between the tourist destination, space competition can be divided into two types. One is the exclusive competition, which mainly occurs in the tourist destination possessing the same or similar types of tourism resources. The other is the symbiotic competition, occurring in the tourist destination which has a large difference between them. In general, the spatial competition mainly occurs between the same type of tourism destinations, as well as the adjacent historic town tourism.

The new development mechanism has been created depending on tourism elements and regional industrial basis. Phoenix Historic City and Zhenyuan Historic Town both uphold the "protection + culture" principle and promote the integration of agricultural, cultural and tourism development vigorously. However, by the influence of space competition the two places show the characteristics of alternative competition and the shelter effect of space development in tourism market influence and developing space, which makes the two destinations in a dilemma. It restricts the influence of tourism market in the two regions and the further development of tourism development space.

## Ⅱ. The Analysis of Tourism Resources Endowment

Phoenix Historic City has plenty tourism resources, like beautiful natural scenery and cultural background, which form a unique advantage. It has the largest number of cultural relics and historic sites in the southwest, with 116 historic sites and more than 120 residential buildings.

Zhenyuan Historic Town also has a wealth of tourism resources. There are 50 blocks of historic buildings, 33 historic houses, 12 historic tiers, 8 historic roads and 5 historic post roads in the city, which have a certain geographical reputation.

There are many same characteristics in terms of quantity, distribution range and distribution intensity in tourism resource endowment. As for the structure of the resource, there are many old historic buildings in the town. The value and function of tourism resources also show the homogeneity of tourism resources in historic towns. To sum up, two regions are equal in tourism resources endowment, and the core attractions of tourism development are similar in the quality, form and structure convergence. Therefore, the spatial competition under the same resource endowment is the alternative competition. Taking Phoenix Historic City as an example, its tourist attractions increase because of the decrease of the tourism attractiveness of Zhenyuan Historic Town. Under the existing development conditions, alternative competition is mainly manifested as an alternative choice for tourists. Phoenix Historic City (2016) received a total of 12.5 million domestic and foreign tourists, and in the same year, the amount of tourists who have a trip in Zhenyuan Historic Town is merely 7.24 million, showing the source market structure in the flow of space changes.

## Ⅲ. Research Methods

*i. Method selection*

This paper uses the analytic hierarchy process (AHP) to construct the spatial competitiveness index system based on the four elements and evaluates the effect of tourism development, as the "breakthrough" of tourism development dilemma between the two historic towns. Analytic Hierarchy Process (AHP) is a decision-making method that decomposes the elements related to decision-making into the objectives, criteria and schemes, and conducts qualitative and quantitative analysis. At the same time, factor analysis is used to evaluate the spatial competitiveness of the two regions. Factor analysis is a research method that sums up several variables into several important influencing factors to describe most of the information of the original data through the classification and summary of variables. [3] Therefore, we use factor analysis to find out the key indicators of tourism market and tourism development space, as the basis for the reform of tourism development mechanism between the two places.

*ii. Data sources*

The data for the two indicators are mainly derived from the statistical bulletin of the national economic and social development (2010-2016) issued by the State Bureau of Statistics and the Provincial Bureau of Statistics, the provincial government portal, industry research report and related periodicals.

*iii. The establishment of indicators*

The spatial competitiveness of the tourism space is based on the theory of spatial competition of the tourist destination. It can be reflected in four aspects: the theory of tourism distance decay, resource endowment and function, competitive advantage and space-time evolution. [4] Therefore, the article selects indicators from the tourist source and destination system in terms of applicability, operability, quantifiability. At the same time, we consider the establishment of some regional tourism development indicators. That is, the paper constructs the index system of urban tourism spatial competitiveness, including four categories, a total of 12 indicators. Using the questionnaire survey, we determine the weight of the index according to the tourist awareness and AHP software (see Table 1).

Table 1 Tourism Space Competitiveness Index System

| Target Level | Criteria Level | Index Level | Weights |
|---|---|---|---|
| Space competitiveness(A) | Visitors' cognition(B1) | Number of tourist reception(C1) | 0.0775 |
| | | Tourist resort rate(C2) | 0.0388 |
| | The composition of tourists(B2) | Primary source market share(C3) | 0.0617 |
| | | Entry market share(C4) | 0.1234 |
| | Tourism traffic situation(B3) | Traffic trips(C5) | 0.0246 |
| | | Number of tourist lines(C6) | 0.0631 |
| | | Number of parking spaces(C7) | 0.1956 |
| | | Visitors turnover(C8) | 0.1750 |
| | Surrounding city status(B4) | Number of urban groups(C9) | 0.0254 |
| | | Number of Large and medium cities(C10) | 0.0314 |
| | | Urban space carrying capacity(C11) | 0.0346 |
| | | Tourism revenue rate(C12) | 0.1489 |

## Ⅳ. Data Analysis

*i. Factor analysis*

Using the SPSS19.0 statistical software for factor analysis, first, we use KMO and Bartlett spherical test to determine whether the data is suitable for factor analysis. Then, the test results are as follows.

Table 2 Space Competitiveness KMO and Bartlett's Test Value

| Kaiser-Meyer-Olkin Measure of Sampling Adequacy | | .642 |
|---|---|---|
| Bartlett's Test of Sphericity | Approx. Chi-Square | 548.897 |
| | df | 66 |
| | sig | .000 |

The data in Table 2 shows that the value of KMO is 0.642. Since the value of KMO is between 0.5 and 1, the data is suitable for factor analysis. At the same time, the Bartlett spherical test value is 0.000, passing the Bartlett spherical test with a significance of 0.05, and indicates a strong correlation between the original data. The main factor cumulative variance table (Table 3) and the factor load matrix after rotation are obtained (Table 4).

Table 3 shows the cumulative variance table for the analysis of tourism spatial competitiveness data. According to the principle that the extraction factor must be greater than the eigenvalue 1, two common factors are obtained, and the characteristic values are

7.482 and 3.226 respectively. And the contribution rate of the extracted principal component is 89.236%, which satisfies the requirement of cumulative variance contribution rate greater than or equal to 85%, and the loss of data information is 10.764%.

In the initial analysis, the load of the principal factor in each variable is similar, so the maximum variance method is used to rotate the matrix to make the factor load decentralized. Then the factor load matrix after the tourism competitiveness of the town is obtained. As can be seen from Table 4, since the validity of the 12 original variables in each component is greater than 0.5, they are effective. However, the validity of C6 (Number of tourist lines) is greater than 0.5 in the two components, indicating that the validity is not concentrated, so it can be omitted. According to the factor load matrix after rotation and the actual factors influencing the tourism market and tourism development space of the historic town, Seven indicators with larger loads are summarized as a regional internal factors, including C7 (number of parking spaces), C11 (urban space carrying capacity), C3 (primary source market share), C1 (number of tourist reception), C2 (tourism re-rate), C4 (entry market share) and C9 (Number of urban groups), which contain 59.548% of the original data. The remaining four indicators have a larger load in the main factor 2, so it is summarized as a regional external factor, which contain 29.688% of the original data. [5]

Table 3 Space Competitiveness Principal Factor Cumulative Variance Explained

| Component | Rotation Sums of Squared Loadings | | |
|---|---|---|---|
| | Total | % of Variance | Cumulative % |
| F1 | 7.146 | 59.548 | 59.548 |
| F2 | 3.563 | 29.688 | 89.236 |

Table 4 Space Competitiveness Rotated Component Matrix

| index | F1 | F2 |
|---|---|---|
| C7 | .986 | |
| C11 | .986 | |
| C3 | -.971 | |
| C1 | .957 | |
| C2 | .877 | |
| C4 | .822 | |
| C9 | .787 | |
| C6 | .737 | .642 |
| C5 | | .915 |
| C12 | | .885 |

(To be continued)

(Continued Table 4)

| index | F1 | F2 |
|---|---|---|
| C10 | | .816 |
| C8 | | -.700 |

According to the factor score coefficient matrix (see Table 5 ), the principal factor score model is constructed according to the original variable coefficient, Fi = a1c1 + a2c2 +... + a12c12, where Fi is the main factor score; a1, a2,... a12 for the variable coefficient; c1, c2,... c12 for each factor score. On the basis of the main factor score, we construct an annual tourism spatial competitiveness score model with the main factor cumulative variance table (Table 3), F = b1F1 + b2F2, where F1 and F2 are the two principal factor scores; b1, b2 is the contribution rate of the factor in the total variance. [3]

Table 5 Factor Score Coefficient Matrix

| | Component | |
|---|---|---|
| | F1 | F2 |
| C1 | .131 | .018 |
| C2 | .108 | .091 |
| C3 | -.143 | .047 |
| C4 | .114 | .004 |
| C5 | -.080 | .283 |
| C6 | .078 | .155 |
| C7 | .147 | -.059 |
| C8 | .100 | -.229 |
| C9 | .131 | -.132 |
| C10 | .043 | .215 |
| C11 | .146 | -.051 |
| C12 | .017 | .243 |

*ii. Factor analysis of the results*

According to the SPSS19.0 software factor score coefficient matrix, the 2014-2016 Phoenix Historic City and Zhenyuan Historic Town are selected as the analysis objects, and the spatial competitiveness of each year is obtained as follows:

Table 6 Tourism Space Competitiveness Score

| Destination (year) | F1 | F2 | Comprehensive Scores | competitiveness Rank |
|---|---|---|---|---|
| Phoenix Historic City (2016) | 2.7248 | .2245 | 1.6893 | 1 |
| Phoenix Historic City (2015) | 1.9070 | .2107 | 1.1979 | 2 |
| Phoenix Historic City (2014) | .9346 | .4683 | .6953 | 3 |
| Zhenyuan Historic Town(2016) | 1.2387 | -1.6258 | .2549 | 4 |
| Zhenyuan Historic Town(2015) | .5970 | -1.6230 | -.1264 | 5 |
| Zhenyuan Historic Town(2014) | .0143 | -1.2971 | -.2998 | 6 |

The samples selected the index data in the two different years of the two destinations. The paper compares the data using horizontal and vertical method. According to the data, the tourism space competitiveness of Phoenix Historic City is obviously higher than that of Zhenyuan Historic Town. Therefore, the space competitiveness of Phoenix Historic City is stronger than that of Zhenyuan, which is the result of the two main factors. But on the whole, the two places have its own development characteristics and dilemmas under the effect of space competitiveness. It is also possible to conclude that the score of external influence factors in two regions are lower than those of the regional internal factors. Therefore, for Phoenix Historic City, the historic town of tourism innovation should focus on regional external factors' transformation and upgrading. And the innovation of Zhenyuan tourism should take the external factors as a key indicator of its tourism market and tourism development space, supplemented by the steady development of various factors within the region.

## V. Analysis on the Characteristics of Tourism Competition in Historic Towns

*i. The similar substitution of spatial awareness*

There are "law of contiguity" and "substitution of approximation", "law of similarity" and "substitution and similarity" in the process of cognition of tourism space. If one destination is adjacent to the geographical competitor, it is not easy for tourist to distinguish their images. The reason for the similar substitution comes from the geographical proximity of the tourist destination and the proximity of the cognitive element. [6]

From the geographic spatial distribution, Phoenix Historic City is located in the western region of Hunan Province, and Zhenyuan Town is located in the eastern part of Guizhou Province, both in the junction of Hunan and Guizhou, about 200 km away. Because of the close geographical location, it is easy to use the image of the known destination to replace the unknown destination when people choose some tourist destinations, resulting in the same level of alternative between the tourist destinations. [6]

From the cognitive factors, people often know the similarity of ancient architectural style and cultural style, but ignoring the differences in the regional cultural between them. The similarity of cognition enlarges the characteristics of the "common characteristics" of the historic town tourism. In the sightseeing-type tourist and low revisit rates of the common role, long distance tourists tend to choose a well-known historic town as their tourism destination.

*ii. Spatial adjacency effect of target market*

The statistics show that the main customer market of Phoenix Historic City and Zhenyuan Town is from the surrounding area. In 2016, the primary customer market of Phoenix Historic City accounted for 43.2%, mainly from Hunan Province and Guangzhou, Hubei, Sichuan Provinces. In the same year, the tourists of Zhenyuan Historic Town are mostly from the surrounding provinces, like Chongqing, Hunan, Sichuan Provinces and so on.

In the distribution of primary source market, the geographical location of the two regions are similar, and are not in the main transport hub, so both of them are dependent on external traffic and influenced by the distance decay law. In general, there is a strong core concentration and peripheral dispersion. Therefore, the target markets of two towns inevitably produce the neighbourhood effect, which exacerbates the influence of the destination confusion choice. At the same time, under the influence of the tourism space competition, the two towns exist the opportunity cost of the tourist market.

*iii. The convergence of traffic conditions*

Traffic accessibility is the key factor for tourists entering the historic town, which is one of the objective conditions to ensure the tourists complete the tourism activities. As the two towns belong to the autonomous prefecture of the county, the traffic is dependent on the city they belong to and traffic connection. The tourists have to arrive at Zhang Jiajie Lotus Airport, Tongren Phoenix Airport, Changsha Railway Station and Jishou Train Station at first and take the car to Phoenix Historic City, as well as Zhenyuan. Therefore, the traffic accessibility of two regions shows a strong convergence.

On account of the effect of the convergence of traffic conditions, the characteristics of tourism competition in the two places show the alternative competition of spatial according to the theory of competitive advantage. The historic tourism town relying on its cognition to its own competitive advantage obtains a higher market share by more competitive production factors and production environment, and it is the same with Phoenix Historic City. Therefore, the convergence of traffic conditions limits the choice of tourists, and has enlarged the advantages of the tourist attraction. [2]

*iv. Similarity of radiation in urban area*

The adsorption capacity and bearing capacity of the external cities in the region have obvious auxiliary effect on the growth of the passenger market and the development of the new market. The number of large and medium cities in the tourist destination and the number of urban agglomerations are the key indicators to measure the influence of the external urban radiation. For Phoenix Historic City and Zhenyuan Historic Town, the proximity of its geographical location determines the similarity of its periphery urban agglomeration. Therefore, it also shows the characteristics of the same type of competition under the characteristics of space competition. The similarity of the regional periphery has further enhanced the spatial competitiveness of the dominant tourist destination, which forms a shadow area of town tourism of Zhenyuan.

## Ⅵ. An Analysis of the Existing Predicament of Historic Town Tourism

*i. Image problem of historic town tourist*

Historic town tourism image embodies the image of the tourist destination and tourists' direct perception of the image. However, under the characteristics of tourism competition, the problem of tourism image has become the most important factor restricting the development of disadvantaged tourism in space competition. Phoenix Historic City, which is a higher level of tourism image and attracts many large-scale tourists, has produced alternative competition to Zhenyuan Historic Town facing the dilemma of tourism image. Similarly, for the historic city of Phoenix, the homogenization of historic town tourism makes no difference between the two places. Therefore, some tourists who go to Zhenyuan Historic Town will no longer go to the same type of sightseeing place, like Phoenix Historic City, [5] which caused the loss of some potential tourists. On the one hand, it reflects the problem that source market limited by the regional structure. On the other hand, it also reflects that the connotation of mining and positioning is not accurate. The future development of tourism in the two places should be aimed at reducing the confusion of geometric spatial identification and ambiguous tourist awareness to achieve a win-win situation between the two towns.

*ii. Market problem of historic town tourism*

The similarity of the tourism development model in the historic town and the characteristics of the alternative landlord selection determine the influence of the distance market in the two places. At present, the marketing of historic town is too much but lacks vitality. The main market is very broad but with poor access. On the contrary, potential market is weak but with strong alternative. Specifically, there is the same problem of low revisit rates in two towns. More visitors will go to Phoenix Historic City because of its fame, instead of Zhenyuan Historic Town, which is intensified by the neighbourhood effect of the two towns. Therefore, the effective turnover of the basic market and the development of the external market will become one of the key points of the historic town tourism mechanism's innovation. [7]

*iii. Traffic problem of historic town tourism*

The main factors restricting the development of Phoenix Historic City and Zhenyuan

Historic Town are the accessibility of the external traffic between the two places and the maturity of the internal transportation facilities. The internal and external transportation networks are the most basic factors to ensure the turnover of tourists and complete the tourism activities. On the current situation of tourism transportation of the two places, the key issue is the insufficient external traffic and the weak carrying capacity of internal facilities. Specifically, the historic city of Phoenix is limited by the rail traffic and relies on a single road solely. Zhenyuan Town has a strong external transport capacity, but also shows a problem that there is a single way of access. There are also some dilemmas about the facilities reception capacity and high level traffic reception facilities.

*iv. Industry problem of historic town tourism*

Historic town tourism development not only relies on the fully drive of domain tourism functional area, but also needs the composite drive of industry and extraterritorial city. Phoenix Historic City considers the tourism industry as a pillar industry, and the secondary industry also occupies an important position in the industrial structure, but the proportion of the primary industry is low. Zhenyuan Historic Town puts the secondary industry as the pillar, and vigorously promotes the steady development of the tertiary industry, but the primary industry also accounts for minimum. Although the three main industries account for a certain proportion, but the two regions do not achieve the integration of inter-industry trade development and don't have the cluster effect on integrated function area.

At the same time, in the extraterritorial city's adsorption and capacity, the agglomeration attached by the two towns has similar characteristics. Limited urban capacity has exacerbated space competition between the two towns, Phoenix Historic City's traffic and tourist turnover problem has been amplified, and the tourism shadow area which makes up of the space competition also has been gradually expanded.

## Ⅶ. The Countermeasure of Tourism Development and Innovation in Historic town

*i. Phoenix Historic City*

*A. Highlighting the characteristics of regional products, and strengthening the historic city image of identification*

In order to shift its focus, Phoenix Historic City should change the "marketing brand" to "marketing products", and continue to expand the support image of the historic city. At the same time, the city should play the special role of tourism products' characteristics in the destination image, to reduce the loss of potential tourists caused by the same type of tourism space competition. Based on the existing tourism brand advantage, it should develop a series of tourism products and projects, which would highlight the geographical and cultural characteristics of the city, and promote the regional characteristics of tourist products to guide visitors' spatial cognition. All of those would indirectly strengthen the identification of the "World Phoenix" image. It is designed to change the current situation of low revisit rates, and reduce the blur of tourism image in spatial identification.

*B. Seeking the cooperation between urban groups, and jointly promoting the tourism market*

The development of the historic city tourism market should actively seek the cooperation among the urban agglomeration and jointly build the "bridging mechanism" of the tourist market. The "bridging mechanism" could transport many far-distance tourists who are mainly from Jingjinji, Yangtze River Delta Urban Agglomerations, Liaozhongnan City Groups, Harbin-Changchun megalopolis to Phoenix Historic City. At the same time, so as to achieve the joint development of tourism market long-term mechanism, the historic city should further consolidate the tourism cooperation with the western Hubei, Qiandong, Qiandongnan, northern Guangxi region and Chengdu-Chongqing city group.

*C. Strengthening the regional traffic connection, promoting the contiguous construction of tourism transportation*

In order to change the lack of external traffic in the historic city, the innovation should focus on upgrading the external transportation, and building a "rail", "road" and "airline" contiguous transport system around Phoenix Historic City. On the one hand, for achieving the traffic connection between historic city and surrounding area, the town should open up fly-drive traffic links, increasing the construction of high-speed airport green line, the town high-speed rail station and tourist bus lines, and reduce the number of traffic trips to improve the efficiency of tourist turnover. On the other hand, the town should strengthen the upgrading of internal traffic within the regions, improving the construction of internal transport facilities. Promoting the construction of ecological parking, self-driving camps and rural tourism roads to enhance the carrying capacity of internal transport facilities is essential. Last but not least, it is also necessary that the town should establish an internal and external linkage traffic network in order to enhance the traffic accessibility of historic town.

*D. Accelerating the integration of internal industries, and building a new tourism industry circle*

The town should fully integrate the relevant industrial resources and assess the comprehensive contribution rate of the industry, seeking the integration development among the three major industries. Phoenix Historic Town should play the "tourism +" function actively, and vigorously promote the "tourism + agriculture", "tourism + industry", "tourism + Internet" joint development. It is also important to tap the potential of modern agriculture to develop leisure rural tourism, relying on new industrial technology to develop special industrial tourism. The town gradually emerges a global tourism industry circle which regards tourism as a core and achieves the development of other industries. Meanwhile, historic city should also strengthen cooperation with large and medium-sized cities in the region to improve the space utilization capacity of limited bearing capacity, and jointly promote the transformation of historic city products, management upgrades and industrial efficiency.

*ii. Zhenyuan Historic Town*

*A. Creating a creative tourist destination images, and cultivating a famous tourist destination trademark*

Zhenyuan Historic Town should fully integrate the elements of resource, tap the connotation of historic town, and make an accurate positioning. [8] In the construction of wisdom tourism, it could do a good job in VI, UI design of new town tourism image and guide the creative image into the tourism information sharing platform of Zhenyuan to realize the digital media of historic town image. At the same time, the local government and enterprises should actively implement the image marketing strategy, guiding tourists to identify, remember and spread. And it also should expand the market influence of new town tourism image, and dilute the effect of the space substitution.

In addition, it also should transform its tourism brand into the tourist trademark. The local government should cultivate Zhenyuan Town tourism trademark, as a well-known trademarks in Guizhou Province and China's well-known trademarks focus on nurturing. To improve the visibility and reputation, Zhenyuan Historic Town can do the marketing and brand building by some creative tourism cultural events, and it would enhance the comprehensive competitiveness of the image promotion of Zhenyuan Historic Town.

*B. Seeking regional cooperation, and achieving the sharing of tourists*

Zhenyuan Historic Town should seek cooperation with Phoenix Historic City on the basis of a reshape of tourist destination image. The local should achieve mutual supply of resources and tourists through the combination of barrier-free travel routes with development of regional differences in tourism products. At the same time, Zhenyuan Historic Town can also establish cooperation with the surrounding city and strengthen the effective turnover of the basic market to reduce the existing tourist market structure. Beyond that, we should actively explore the western market, so as to develop a good interactive sharing system and achieve the effective docking with target market. Not only it is good for the excavation of tourists market but also it benefits for effectively avoiding the positive competition with the dominant tourist destination. [9]

*C. Strengthening the construction of transport facilities, and enhancing the turnover rate of tourists*

Zhenyuan Historic Town should further build a tourist system with some more clear functions, which connect external urban traffic network to the core scenic spots so as to increase the turnover rate of tourists. At the same time, the local are supposed to speed up the construction of internal transport facilities, creating a high level of 3d parking lot, scenic parking, public parking and other traffic parking service system to improve the town's internal traffic facilities reception capacity and achieve the seamless docking of internal and external traffic.

*D. Constructing multiple industry clusters, and developing a regional joint tourism*

Gradually, breaking the one-way linear development model of town tourism, the local should build multiple functional industry clusters actively in order to play the role of radiation in the tourism industry. On this basis, Zhenyuan Historic Town could promote the construction of areas with different functions, like leisure area, rural tourism area, high technology industrial area, digital tourism area, fused with the characteristics of the first and second industries. At the same time, the local should promote the exchange of special tourism projects, seeking cooperation with the regional tourism city and developing the regional joint tourism.

## Ⅷ. Conclusions

Tourism space competition is a state of the spatial relations of tourist destination, which is actually a manifestation of the imbalance of tourism spatial structure. Therefore, a better development of historic town tourism needs to adjust this imbalance through innovation of development mechanism. Based on the analysis of the characteristics of the spatial competition of the tourist destination and the relevant theories, this paper explores the tourism innovation of the two historic towns. Finally, the conclusions are listed as follows: reforming the tourism development mechanism of the historic town is the indispensable way to expand the influence of the local tourism market and to stimulate the greatest vitality of the town tourism. Through multiplier effect of all-for-one tourism, the sustainable development of the town tourism can be promoted by the comprehensive tourism.

## References

[1] Bao Jigang, Peng Hua. A study of spatial competition between the famous mountain tourist resorts: with the three famous mountains in southern Anhui as an example [J]. *Human Geography*, 1994, 9(2): 4-8.

[2] Li Hui. Development research of the disadvantaged tourism areas under the spatial competition: a case study of Tianzhu Mountain [D]. Anhui: Anhui University, 2012.

[3] Chen Cheng. A study on the evaluation of tourism competitiveness in five provinces in northwest China [D]. Lanzhou: Northwest Minzu University, 2015.

[4] Xu Chunxiao, Wang Fuyuan, Wang Kaiyong, Li Ping. Exploring destination spatial competition rules: a case study of Hunan Province[J]. *Geographical Research*, 2017, 36(2): 321-335.

[5] Yu Shizhong. Research on the development of tourist town in Sichuan based on Huanglongxi Town [D]. Sichuan: Sichuan Normal University, 2014.

[6] Lu Jia, Zhang Jie, Gu Chaolin. A study of spatial competition and regional cooperation involving tourism planning: a case study of the six historic towns in Jiangsu and Zhejiang[J]. *Human Geography*, 2005, 20(3):79-83.

[7] Di Juanjuan. A study on tourism competitiveness of historical and cultural cities: taking Kaifeng as an example[D]. Guilin: Guangxi Normal University, 2008.

[8] Su Xu. On the promotion and maintenance strategies of tourism image in historic towns: taking Zhejiang

Province as an example[J]. *Journal of Yangtze University (Social Science)*, 2015, 38(8): 66-70.

[9] Chen Zhigang. Study on spatial competition of tourist cities based on comprehensive tourism competitiveness: a case study of excellent cities in Jiangsu Province[D]. Nanjing: Nanjing Normal University, 2004.

[10] Yin Yimei. To construct the tourism spatial cooperation: competition analyzing model[J]. *Journal of Jiangxi University of Finance and Economics*, 2003, 2: 66-71.

[11] Xie Mingli. The spatial competition of hakka traditional dwelling tourism in west of Fujian: a case study of earth building in Yongding and traditional dwelling in Peitian[J]. *Fujian Geograph*y, 2003, 18(2):34-37.

# The Influence Structure of the Experience Factors in Literary Places: A Case Study of Dufu Thatched Cottage in Chengdu

Cui Lihua[1], Cheng Li[2*]

**Abstract:** In recent years, the literary tourism is booming around the world. Literary place of interest is regarded as a kind of low cost and high yield tourism resource, which has been widely developed. Taking Dufu Thatched Cottage in Chengdu as a typical example, this paper focuses on the structure and the relationship of the perception about authenticity, literariness, affectivity, aesthetics and service. Using the data collected from Dufu Thatched Cottage through questionnaire survey, we build the path of relationship among the five dimensions and tourism satisfaction and loyalty by factor analysis and structural equation model. We found that the authenticity, literariness, affectivity, aesthetics and service of literary places have positive influences on tourist' satisfaction and loyalty, which illustrates the significance of experience factors to establishment of the literary place. The exploration and analysis about tourists' satisfaction of and loyalty to the literary places of interest will provide valuable reference in planning and designing of literary place in the future.

**Keywords:** literary places; experience factor; satisfaction; loyalty; Dufu Thatched Cottage; structural equation model

## Ⅰ. Introduction

In recent years, literary tourism around the world is in the ascendant[1]. Literature and tourism have a natural connection. Since ancient times, tourism activities has given birth to countless wonderful literature, and literary works of specific space description or the author's own space experience also has a strong attraction to tourists, [2] becoming the main part of literary tourist resources. As Shen Zuxiang said, since the beginning of the literature, there has been a good relationship between the tourism and literature. [3] When the literature is fashionable, the literary tourism will become popular. [4]

1 Sichuan University, Chengdu, China.
2* Sichuan University, Chengdu, China. chengli@scu.edu.cn.

In terms of our country, from the beginning of Sui Dynasty and Tang Dynasty, the imperial examination system has closely connected the political career with academic life, stimulating the existence of many writers and scholars and their influential literary works. Since the beginning of the reform and opening up policy, China has launched Lu Town Shaoxing, the former residence of Guo Moruo, the former residence of Shen Congwen and other tourist attractions. In the various cultural tourism, the theme of the literary tourism is to experience the scenes in literary works and visit places where the writers once travelled, which is gradually drawing the attention. [4] Literary tourism has also become a hot spot in tourism research.

The development of the experience economy has brought tourism into a new era. Tourists' attention to the tourism experience is increasing, the experience factors in the tour of the tourists bear an increasingly important role. The domestic scholar Xie Yanjun said bluntly: Tourism experience is the core content of tourism research. There are similarities and differences in the experiential factors between literary tourism and other tourist destinations.

This paper attempts to explore the experience factors of literary tourism, from the perspective of tourists to micro-analyze the literary tourism, including authenticity, affectivity, aesthetic, service and unique literariness in literary tourism. It determines the different factors on the tourists satisfaction and loyalty. Through the researches of the experience factors of literary tourism at home and abroad, the destinations of literary tourism and other tourist areas are mostly regarded as the same type of resources, and literariness is rarely researched. It is hoped that this paper can make up the gap of this research and contribute to the cultural tourism for better integration into the environment of the experience economy.

## Ⅱ. Literature Review

Cultural tourism is different from literary tourism: Literary tourism is a sub-section of cultural tourism. Scholars at home and abroad don't have a unified definition of cultural tourism. However, it is generally believed that cultural tourism has two important elements. The first element emphasizes product attributes. Many scholars insist that cultural tourism is based on tourism cultural resources, and it is a kind of tourism product which aims at making tourists gain cultural experience and increasing wisdom; The second element emphasizes the tourist experience. Cultural tourism refers to tourists in order to gain special cultures to have deep experience about the tourism resources connotation, and obtain a full range of spiritual and cultural enjoyment. [5] Zhao Kang et al. (1993)[6] believe that literary tourism is an activity which refers to the use of various genres of literary works as the basis, the use of its visibility and various identity to the literary works and the aesthetic taste of people from different regions and social class. With a certain physical mean, it reproduces the characters, scenes, plots and so on, which are created in the original language and make the visitors become the part of it. By using the aesthetic role, a full range of material and cultural enjoyment of a tourism activities will be obtained. Herbert believes that the sites of literary tourism are not only the places where the history events happened, whether the writers were born or dead, they are also part of society, which are developed and enlarged in order to attract tourists for sightseeing. He divides literary tourism into three categories: One related to the writers, one related to literary works scenes, and one related to emotional value, nostalgia, memory, symbol and so on. The connotation of the latter is more broad and more profound than a particular writer or works. [7-8] Corresponding literary tourists often have three kinds of travel motives: To find the place in the description of literary works, [9] to find the writer's life trajectory, [10] to visit the author and the relevant places with the special feelings for literary works and authors. [11][12] Different motives cause different tourism experience. [13] In this paper, literary places mean that tourist attractions appear due to literary works and writers.

The research of literary tourism on domestic is independent, but it is only a sub-section of heritage tourism on overseas. Poria et al. (2001) had clearly pointed out that literary tourism is a cultural heritage whose value is based on the literary value, and tourist activities are also consistent; [14] Squire (1994) and Herbert (2001) believed that no matter how the literary tourism is defined, the important theory of the heritage also applies to the literary places, [15][16] and they proposed a specific operational model. [17]

As an important part of tourism, literary tourism can meet the tourism spirit demand of tourists with high cultural awareness, add cultural color to tourism resources, promote the development of resources, [18] and bring an unexpected positive effect on the protection and publicity of local cultural and cultural heritage. [19][20] In addition, literary works can help tourists adapt to unfamiliar cultural environment, as the role of alternative tour guides. [21]-[23] Other than the common nature of tourism resources, there are some unique characteristics of their own: times, art, knowledge, association and culture. [24] Additionally, since many literary tourist attractions are the prototypes of some literary works, it also has reproducibility. [25]

The travel experience was first proposed by Boorsitin (1964), who thought that the tourism experience is a popular consumer behavior, and that the traveler has a distorted tourism experience. Yanjun's (1999) idea is widely accepted in China. He insisted that the tourism experience refers to the physical and mental satisfaction of tourists when they are in the deep integration with the current situation, it is the results of mutual communication and interaction between the inherent psychological activities and the surface presented by tourism objects, through activities such as viewing, communication, imitation and consumption.

According to the content of the tourism experience, Joseph Pine and James Gilmore (2002) divided the experience into four categories: entertainment, education, escape and estheticism, simplified as "4E". [26] Entertainment experience is the experience method mainly about absorption, which makes the customer focus and acquire pleasure through the senses during an activity; Education experience is the initiative of consumers to experience, to learn knowledge and skills; The experience of escaping the real world is that the recipients take the initiative to participate and completely immerse in the environment caused by experience to achieve "ecstasy" state; Estheticism experience is to create the environment with the charm and comfortable atmosphere for customers, and let people immerse in the environment. The classification of "4E" experience is most influential.The types of experience proposed by other scholars are mostly evolved from its classification. Vitters et al. (2000)based on the degree of experience, put forward the use of " flow-simplex" to measure the experience of tourism, whose measurement includes: tiring-interesting, relaxing-nervous, happy-unpleasant, interesting-boring and challenging-dull. [27]

In general, the study of literary tourism is still at the primary stage. Its definition, characteristics, or related theories and case studies are not many, and there is still a lot of developing space for literary tourism research. In the specific research, very few people distinguish between literary tourism and other tourist areas to research their experience factors, most of them use the existing experience classification, and ignore the characteristics of literary tourism itself.

## Ⅲ. Research Hypothesis and Model Construction

Scholars divide tourism experience into different categories, which cover a wide range, including entertaining experience, educational experience, recluse experience, aesthetic experience, expectation experience, social experience, physical experience, psychological experience, intellectual experience, etc. [28]-[31] This paper, based on previous studies, has extracted the authenticity, literariness, affectivity, aesthetics and service of literary places, and tested its effects on tourists' satisfaction and loyalty.

Authenticity is a hotspot in the study of literary tourism, and the authenticity of tourists to cultural heritage is an important reason for their satisfaction and loyalty(Swanson, Horridge, 2004; 2006). Zhou Yaqing and Wu Maoying et al. (2007) further pointed out that the perception of tourists' "authenticity" during the tour is often proportional to their satisfaction and loyalty. [32] Accordingly, the following research hypotheses are proposed:

*H1: The tourists' perception on authenticity has positive influence on tourists' satisfaction.*

*H2: The tourists' perception on authenticity has positive influence on tourists' loyalty.*

Literariness is the most prominent and important experience factor of literary tourism. The process of the tourists' tour is a cultural pilgrimage. By restoring the literary scene, or showing the writer's living environment, the visitors will feel the cultural atmosphere, which is the original intention of literary tourists. Therefore, the tourists' perceptions on literariness have a significant impact on their satisfaction and loyalty. Accordingly, the following assumptions are made:

*H3: The tourists' perception on literariness has positive influence on tourists' satisfaction.*

*H4: The tourists' perception on literariness has positive influence on tourists' loyalty.*

Affectivity is the tourists' experience of the emotional levels. [33] The emotional experience during the interaction between tourists and tourist attractions is an important part of the tourism experience. [34]-[36] The core of emotion is the tone of happiness, [37] which is the most important feature of emotion. The acquisition of tourists' satisfaction during the affectivity experience can improve the satisfaction and loyalty of tourists. [38] Accordingly, the following research hypotheses are proposed:

*H5: The tourists' perception on affectivity has positive influence on tourists' satisfaction.*

*H6: The tourists' perception on affectivity has positive influence on tourists' loyalty.*

Aesthetics is one of the most important factors in the tourism experience. [39][40] It is the most important form of experience in tourism.Through the sensory experience, tourists can feel relaxed and energetic, and then have other types of experiences to enhance the tourism satisfaction and loyalty. Moreover, the tourism experience of most tourists may be lingering in the aesthetic senses. Therefore, Aesthetics is vital to the tourists' satisfaction and loyalty. [41] Accordingly, the following hypotheses are proposed:

*H7: The tourists' perception on aesthetics has positive influence on tourists' satisfaction.*

*H8: The tourists' perception on aesthetics has positive influence on tourists' loyalty.*

Service is focusing on food, traveling, shopping and entertainment. Taplin et al. (2015) [42] and Zhou Yang et al. (2016) [43] conducted a survey of tourists' satisfaction and the willingness to re-visit, and they believed that the service of tourism places is the key factor to tourist' satisfaction, by improving the service experience of tourists to get tourists' loyalty. Accordingly, the following hypotheses are made:

*H9: The tourists' perception on service has positive influence on tourists' satisfaction.*

*H10: The tourists' perception on service has positive influence on tourists' loyalty.*

The satisfaction of tourists to the tourist attractions will make them feel pleasant, and then have the desire to re-visit the scenic spots and maintain certain loyalty. The positive effects of satisfaction on loyalty have been widely recognized by academia. Yoon, Uysal (2005), [44] Sun et al. (2013) [45] and Chen, Tsai (2007) [46] all proved that loyalty has a positive impact on satisfaction. Accordingly, the following hypothesis is proposed:

*H11: The tourists' satisfaction has positive influence on tourists' loyalty.*

Based on the above hypotheses, we can get the conceptual model of tourists' satisfaction of and loyalty to the literary places of interest (see Figure 1).

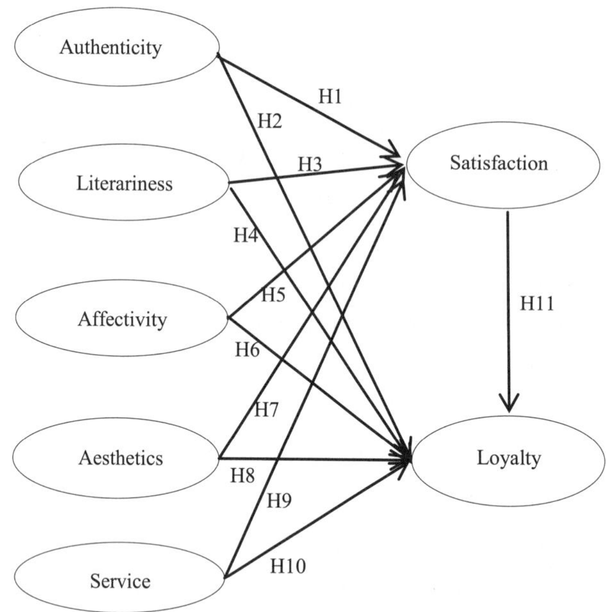


Figure 1 Conceptual Model of Tourists' Satisfaction of and Loyalty to the Literary Places of Interest

## Ⅳ. Empirical Analysis

*i. Data Collection*

On March 17, 2017, the questionnaires were distributed in Chengdu Dufu Thatched Cottage, and the pre-survey was carried out. The questionnaire was modified according to the problems during pre-survey. In the way of non-probability sampling survey, we conducted a formal investigation from March 25th-28th in 2017 in Dufu Thatched Cottage. During this, 525 questionnaires were distributed, 502 valid questionnaires were retrieved, and the rate of effective questionnaire was 95.6%.

The proportion of men and women in the survey accounts for 47.8% and 52.2% respectively. The subjects are mainly young and the proportion of the people from 18 to 35 years old accounts for 80.9%. The undergraduate surveyed subjects account for 58.4%. The proportion of junior college and master follow as second, which is 17.5% and 16.7% respectively. The highest proportion of career is students, which takes up 32.5%, then followed by company staff, accounting for 23.9%; The people with average monthly income below 2000 yuan accounts for 31.3%. The proportion of those with 2000-6000 yuan monthly salary is relatively high, each accounts for about 20%; 80.7% of the tourists have visited other literary places.

*ii. Data analysis*

In order to explore the influence of experience factors on tourists, 24 variables of tourists' experience factors were analysed by SPSS23.0 software for exploratory factor analysis. The principal component analysis was used to conduct varimax-rotation 7 common factors are forced to be extracted, the items greater than 0.5 are retained, among which the load of B3 and F6 are less than 0.5, which have been removed.

The overall Cronbach's alpha of the 24 variables is 0.931, which is greater than 0.7, indicating that the internal consistency of the data is credible. KMO value is 0.936. According to KMO value decision criteria proposed by Kaiser, the effect on common factor extraction of the data achieves "excellent" standard (Wang Baojin, 2007); the Chi-Square of KMO and Bartlett's Test is 5820.261, the degree of freedom is 276, $p<0.001$, indicating that the partial correlation coefficient matrix is not the identity matrix, and the data is suitable for factor analysis; the five common factors of Cronbach's alpha are more than 0.7, which is acceptable. [48] It can explain the 62.967% information of original 27 variables. Combined the division of Pine et al. (2002), [49] Revilla, Dodd (2003), [9] Xie, Wu (2012), [22] Zou Tongqian (2003), [50] Li Xiaoqin (2006), [51] Long Jiangzhi (2009) [52] and other scholars, their partitioning of the experience factors are named as authenticity, literariness, affectivity, aesthetic and service.

Secondly, this paper uses SmartPLS software based on the partial least squares algorithm to carry out the structural equation modelling, which has no requirement on the normality of the data, and is especially suitable for the prediction of the smaller sample. [53][54] The research possesses both the theory development and verification as a whole.

Evaluation of the model is based on the two-stage evaluation method recommended by Anderson et al. (1988). [55] First of all, the measurement model is evaluated, and then the structural model is evaluated. The path coefficients and the significance of the external load are calculated to determine whether the path assumption is passed and the predictive validity of the structural model is calculated by blindfolding.

Table 1 Convergent Validity and Reliability Evaluation

| Construct | Indicators | Outer Loadings | Composite Reliability | Cronbach's α | AVE |
|---|---|---|---|---|---|
| Authenticity | A1 Architecture authenticity | 0.874 | 0.882 | 0.821 | 0.652 |
| | A2 Antique authenticity | 0.781 | | | |
| | A3 Landscape authenticity | 0.807 | | | |
| | A4 Road authenticity | 0.764 | | | |
| Literariness | B1 Introduction of Dufu | 0.862 | 0.906 | 0.746 | 0.616 |
| | B2 Understanding of Dufu | 0.920 | | | |
| Affectivity | C1 Memory | 0.766 | 0.886 | 0.874 | 0.795 |
| | C2 Nostalgia | 0.764 | | | |
| | C3 Patriotic emotion | 0.786 | | | |
| | C4 Reading Dufu's poems | 0.789 | | | |
| | C5 Respecting Dufu | 0.813 | | | |
| | C6 Stimulating interest | 0.789 | | | |

(To be continued)

(Continued Table 1)

| Construct | Indicators | Outer Loadings | Composite Reliability | Cronbach's α | AVE |
|---|---|---|---|---|---|
| Aesthetics | D1 Visual Enjoyment | 0.807 | 0.885 | 0.837 | 0.607 |
| | D2 Acoustic Enjoyment | 0.744 | | | |
| | D3 Olfactory Enjoyment | 0.775 | | | |
| | D4 Man-earth Harmony | 0.805 | | | |
| | D5 Following Aesthetic | 0.763 | | | |
| Service | E2 Souvenir Features | 0.739 | 0.879 | 0.828 | 0.594 |
| | E3 Reasonable Ticket Price | 0.740 | | | |
| | E4 Charm of Activities | 0.791 | | | |
| | E5 Courteous Service | 0.866 | | | |
| Satisfaction | F1 Tourism Satisfaction | 0.903 | 0.935 | 0.904 | 0.781 |
| | F2 Expectation Realization | 0.876 | | | |
| | F3 Pleasant Journey. | 0.882 | | | |
| | F4 Reasonable Costs | 0.875 | | | |
| Loyalty | G1 Willingness to Re-visit | 0.855 | 0.939 | 0.924 | 0.755 |
| | G3 Willingness to Recommend | 0.909 | | | |
| | G4 Willingness to Compliment | 0.907 | | | |
| | G5 Willingness for Publicity | 0.806 | | | |
| | G6 Behavior to Re-travel | 0.863 | | | |

Table 2 The Relevance of the Construct and the Square Root of AVE

| | Authenticity | Literariness | Affectivity | Aesthetics | Service | Satisfaction | Loyalty |
|---|---|---|---|---|---|---|---|
| Authenticity | 0.808 | | | | | | |
| Literariness | 0.434 | 0.892 | | | | | |
| Affectivity | 0.458 | 0.624 | 0.785 | | | | |
| Aesthetics | 0.390 | 0.524 | 0.606 | 0.779 | | | |
| Service | 0.506 | 0.458 | 0.564 | 0.534 | 0.771 | | |
| Satisfaction | 0.495 | 0.544 | 0.576 | 0.614 | 0.658 | 0.884 | |
| Loyalty | 0.498 | 0.528 | 0.562 | 0.551 | 0.629 | 0.780 | 0.869 |
| Note: The figure on the diagonal indicates the square of the corresponding AVE value. | | | | | | | |

Table 3 Test Results of Hypotheses

| Hypotheses | Path Relationship | Path Coefficient | T Value | True or False |
|---|---|---|---|---|
| H1 | Authenticity -Satisfaction | 0.118 | 2.658*** | True |
| H2 | Authenticity -Loyalty | 0.080 | 3.437*** | True |
| H3 | Literariness-Satisfaction | 0.152 | 3.979*** | True |

(To be continued)

(Continued Table 3)

| Hypotheses | Path Relationship | Path Coefficient | T Value | True or False |
|---|---|---|---|---|
| H4 | Literariness-Loyalty | 0.072 | 3.539*** | True |
| H5 | Affectivity-Satisfaction | 0.073 | 1.602 | False |
| H6 | Affectivity-Loyalty | 0.067 | 2.107** | True |
| H7 | Aesthetics-Satisfaction | 0.257 | 5.777*** | True |
| H8 | Aesthetics-Loyalty | 0.026 | 3.811*** | True |
| H9 | Service-Satisfaction | 0.350 | 8.098*** | True |
| H10 | Service-Loyalty | 0.139 | 7.103*** | True |
| H11 | Satisfaction-Loyalty | 0.555 | 12.579*** | True |
| Note: *:$P<0.1$;**:$P<0.05$;***:$P<0.01$ | | | | |

Table 4 The Discriminant Coefficient $R^2$ of the Endogenous Construct and the Predictive Correlation $Q^2$

| Construct | Communality | $Q^2$ | Redundancy | $R^2$ |
|---|---|---|---|---|
| Authenticity | 0.652 | | | |
| Literariness | 0.795 | | | |
| Affectivity | 0.615 | | | |
| Aesthetics | 0.607 | | | |
| Service | 0.594 | | | |
| Satisfaction | 0.781 | 0.440 | 0.195 | 0.572 |
| Loyalty | 0.755 | 0.483 | 0.020 | 0.650 |

It can be seen from Table 1 that the minimum composite reliability of the latent variable is 0.882, which is better than 0.7, indicating that the data reliability is better; The minimum AVE value is 0.607, more than 0.5, [56] and the open square root of the AVE value is larger than the corresponding correlation coefficient of the latent variable (see Table 2), indicating that the discriminant validity is good. [57] In the external load of the reflective indicator, the external load of H2 is less than 0.4, which has been removed directly. The external load of E1 is less than 0.7, and the AVE values of the service dimension and the common degree are improved after the deletion. Therefore, E1 is deleted, the external loads of other items do not exceed 0.7. The parameter evaluation of the measurement model shows that the reliability and validity of the latent variables are very strong.

After the validity of the measurement model is verified, the hypothesis model is validated and evaluated.

After evaluating the measurement model, the study also needs to evaluate the structure model. In the 11 hypotheses of this study, only the path relationship between affectivity and satisfaction is not passed, and the other hypotheses are true, as shown in Table 3.

The coefficient of determination $R^2$ has the explanatory ability of the variation (variance) of the endogenous latent variable done by the exogenous latent variable. The endogenous latent variable of this study are satisfaction and loyalty $R^2$ is 0.572 and 0.650 respectively, indicating the explained percentage of these endogenous latent variables. In addition, PLS-SEM used Stom-Gasser $Q^2$ test model to verify the predictive relevance (Wetzels, 2009). [58] $Q^2>0$ indicates that the model has predictive correlation with the endogenous potential variables, taking D=7, and the $Q^2$ of the endogenous latent variable is greater than 0, and the prediction correlation of the model is significant.

The overall predictive ability of the structural model is measured by goodness-of-fit, [59] which is the geometric mean of the mean of the communality and the mean of the discriminant coefficients. [60] And the commonality is equal to the AVE value. The overall goodness-of-fit of the study is GoF = 0.647, which is greater than the strong critical value of 0.360 defined by Wetzels et al. (2009), [61] indicating that the overall fitting effect of the model is good.

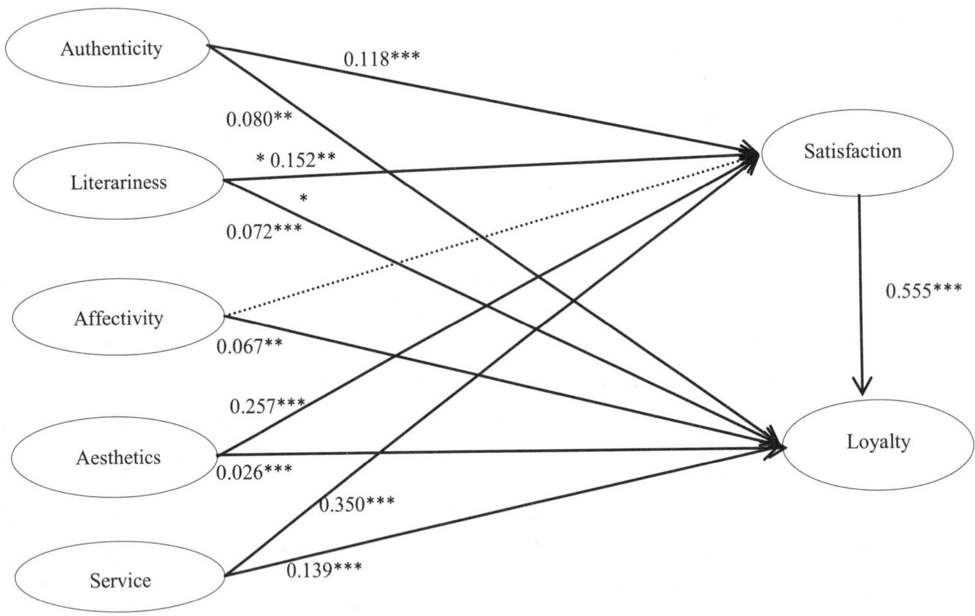


Figure 2 The Path Coefficient of Structural Model

## V. Conclusion and Results

Based on the analysis of the first-hand data collected from field researches, this paper examines the relationship among tourists' authenticity, literariness, affectivity, aesthetic, service and tourism loyalty and satisfaction in the literary tourism places through partial least squares model. The main conclusions and results are as follows:

Firstly, the tourist's experience of authenticity, literariness, affectivity, aesthetic and service in the literary tourism places have a significant impact on satisfaction and loyalty. But the tourists' satisfaction based on experience factors is higher than loyalty, the tourist's perception of experience factors has a more direct and powerful effect on satisfaction, while the tourist's perception of loyalty is lagging behind and satisfaction has a considerable influence on loyalty.

Secondly, in the relationships between satisfaction and the experience factors in the literary tourism, service has the closest relationship with satisfaction (β= 0.350), followed by aesthetics (β= 0.257), and the last ones are the literariness (β= 0.152) and authenticity (β= 0.118), but there is no positive impact between affectivity and tourist's satisfaction. It illustrates that service and aesthetics experience as the most direct experience during travelling, and they have more profound impact on satisfaction; While authenticity and literariness are indirect experiences of tourists, they have less profound impact on satisfaction; As a deep experience, affectivity experience can not be acquired by all the tourist, which has no impact on satisfaction. Therefore, the aesthetics of scenic landscape, the layout of auditory landscape and literariness, as well as the scenic service content, service quality are very important to tourist's satisfaction.

Thirdly, the relationships between the experience factors of tourists in the literary places and loyalty are weak. Among them, service is the most closely related to loyalty (β= 0.139), followed by authenticity (β=0.080), and last ones are literariness (β= 0.072) and affectivity (β=0.067).The relationship between aesthetics and loyalty is very weak (β=0.026). It suggests that the tourist's loyalty is closely related to service and authenticity experience. As deeper experience, literariness and affectivity also have a certain degree of influence on tourists' loyalty. If you want to attract the tourists for a long time and improve the visitor's re-travel rate, the scenic service system, landscape authenticity, literariness and affectivity should be considered more than before, and the landscape and the writer, literary works should be more integrated; Although aesthetic is closely related to tourist's satisfaction, no matter how beautiful the scenic spots are, it cannot attract tourists to visit the literary tourism places for many times.

Finally, due to the insufficient summarization of the experience factors in the literary tourism, the experience factors in the construction of the whole model are not complete. In the follow-up research, we should fully explore the various factors of the literary tourism places and complete the model.

This paper has theoretical and practical significance. In the theoretical aspect, this paper has supplemented the gaps of literariness and affectivity in the literary tourism research and also expanded the empirical study of literary tourism. In the practical aspect, at the present time when literary tourism is increasingly flourishing, this paper provides certain reference value for the landscape layout and cultural excavation of literary places. Except focusing on authenticity, literariness, affectivity, aesthetics, and the service quality of scenic spots should be paid attention to in particular.

## ACKNOWLEDGMENT

I would like to extend my sincere gratitude to my supervisor, Cheng Li, for his instructive advice and useful suggestions on my thesis. I am deeply grateful of his help in the completion of this thesis. And special thanks should go to my friends who have put considerable time and effort into their comments on the draft.

## References

[1] Hoppen A, Brown L, Fyall A. Literary tourism: opportunities and challenges for the marketing and branding of destinations[J]. *Journal of Destination Marketing & Management*, 2014(3): 37-47.

[2] Robinson M, Andersen H C. *Literature and Tourism: Essays in the Reading and Writing of Tourism*[M]. 2nd ed. London: Continuum, 2002: 34-42.

[3] Shen Zuxiang. *Tourism & Chinese Culture*[M]. 3rd ed. Beijing: Tourism Education Press, 2002: 145-156.

[4] Busby G, Klug J. Movie-induced tourism: the challenge of measurement and other issues[J]. *Journal of Vacation Marketing*, 2001(7): 316-332.

[5] Jing Bo, Luo Gaoyuan, Li Dan, Wang Lihua, Huan Yanling, Sun Yingqian. The protection and development of literary heritage tourist destinations: take Dongping Town, Shandong Province as an example[J]. *Journal of Shandong Administration Institute and Shandong Economic Management Personnel Institute*, 2010(6): 71-73.

[6] Hou Bing, Huang Zhenfang, Xu Haijun. On spatial form of cultural tourism: based on the summary of cultural space and enlightenment[J]. *Tourism Tribune*, 2011(26): 70-77.

[7] Zhao Kang, Liu Deyan. On literary tourism[J].*Tourism Tribune*, 1993(6): 43-46.

[8] Herbert D. Literary places, tourism and the heritage experience[J]. *Annals of Tourism Research*, 2001(8): 312-333.

[9] Herbert D. Artistic and literary places in France as tourist attraction[J]. *Tourism Management*, 1996(2): 77-85.

[10] Pocock D C, Mallory W E, Housley P S. *Haworth: The Experience of a Literary Place*[M]. Syracuse: Syracuse University Press, 1987: 179-186.

[11] Marsh K. *Writers and Their Houses*[M]. 1st ed. London: Hamish Hamilton, 1993: 89-99.

[12] Squire S J. Valuing countryside: reflections on Beatrix Potter tourism[J]. *Area*, 1993(25): 5-10.

[13] Squire S J. Gender and tourist experiences: assessing women's shared meanings for Beatrix Potter[J]. *Leisure Studies*, 1994(13): 195-209.

[14] Zhong Tingting. Study on development of high density literature tourism from the perspective of experience economy [D]. Qingdao: Ocean University of China, 2014.

[15] Poria Y, Butler R, Airey D. The core of heritage tourism[J]. *Annals of Tourism Research*, 2003(30): 238-254.

[16] Squire S J. The culture values of literary tourism[J]. *Annals of tourism research*, 1994(21): 103-120.

[17] Herbert D. Literary places, tourism and the heritage experiences [J]. *Annals of Tourism Research*, 2001(28): 312-333.

[18] Wang Yang. A study review on literature tourism[J]. *Gree Science and Technology*, 2010(10):156-157.

[19] Pan Dandan. Research on the Development of cultural tourism products based on literary background[J].

Hangzhou: Zhejiang Normal University, 2012.

[20] Li Gang. The spatialization of literature and literary space: a research on tourism space culture placement with literature resource[J]. *Tourism Forum*, 2016(1): 50-54.

[21] Wang Ruizhu. Several problems in the master plan of foreign historic cities: organization of urban spatial network and composition axis[J]. *City Planning*, 1993(3): 56-60.

[22] Pan Dandan. *Research on the Development of Cultural Tourism Products Based on Literary Background*[M]. Hangzhou: Zhejiang Normal University, 2012: 133-156.

[23] Li Gang. The spatialization of literature and literary space:a research on tourism space culture placement with literature resource[J]. *Tourism Forum*, 2016(1): 50-54.

[24] Yu Xiaojuan. Ancient poetry in contemporary Chinese tourism [J]. *Tourism Management*, 2016(54): 393-403.

[25] Xu Xuehua. Research on the development of literature tourism resources based on tourists' experience[J]. Jinan: Jinan University, 2011.

[26] Shen Liyan. Analysis on the exploitation of literary tourism resources[J]. *Tourism Management Research*, 2014(5): 24.

[27] Pine B J, James H G. *Experience the Economy*[M]. 2nd ed. Beijing: Mechanical Industry Press, 2002: 46-57.

[28] Vitters J, Vorkinn M, Vistal O I, Vaaghnd J. Tourist experience and attractions[J]. *Annals of Tourism Research*, 2000(2): 432-450.

[29] Pine B J, James H G. *The Experience Economy: Work Is Theatre & Every Business a Stage*[M]. 3rd ed. Boston: Harvard Business Press, 1999: 134-145.

[30] Chhetria P, Arrowsmitha C, Jackson M. Determining hiking experiences in nature-based tourist destinations[J]. *Tourism Management*, 2004(25): 31-43.

[31] Zou Tongqian, Wu Liyun. The nature and categories of tourism experiences and developing principles[J]. *Tourism Science,* 2003(4): 7-10.

[32] Xie Yanjun. *A study of tourism experience: a phenomenological perspective*[M]. 4th ed. Tianjing: Nankai University Press, 2005: 103-121.

[33] Zhou Yaqing, Wu Maoying, Zhou Yongguang, Zhu Yanhong. Theory of "authenticity" and its comparison in tourism study[J]. *Tourism Tribune*, 2007(6): 42-47.

[34] Li Xiaoqin. Tourism experience factors and foundation of dynamic model[J]. *Journal of Guilin Institute of Tourism*, 2006(5): 609-611.

[35] Zou Tongqian, Wu Liyun. The nature and categories of tourism experiences and developing principles[J]. *Tourism Science*, 2003(4): 7-10.

[36] Dou Qing. Tourism experience[D]. Nanning: Guangxi University, 2003.

[37] Xie Yanjun, Wu Kai. From expectations to feelings: an interactive model for quality tourist experience[J]. *Tourism Science*, 2000(2): 1-4.

[38] Victor S, Johnston W E. *The Source of Emotion: Science on Human Emotion*[M]. 4th ed. Shanghai: Shanghai Science and Technology Press, 2002: 86-98.

[39] Zhang Jun. Modelling repeat visitation[C]. 40th European Congress, Barcelona European Regional Science Association, 2000: 78-85.

[40] Pine B J, James H G. *Experience the Economy*[M]. 2nd ed. Beijing: Mechanical Industry Press, 2002: 210-219.

[41] Wu Hongjin, Long Jiangzhi. The theoretical model of tourism experience generation[J]. *Social Science Journal*, 2009(3): 46-49.

[42] Long Jiangzhi. The hierarchy model of tourism experience: based on the spectrum of consciousness[J]. *Journal Beijing International Studies University*, 2009(12): 9-19.

[43] Taplin R H, Rodger K, Moore S A. A method for testing the effect of management interventions on the satisfaction and loyalty of national park visitors[J]. *Leisure Sciences*, 2016(38): 140-160.

[44] Zhou Yang, He Junhong, Rong Hao. The evaluation of tourist satisfaction and its influencing factors in rural tourism in China[J]. *Management of the Economy*, 2016(7): 156-166.

[45] Yoon Y, Uysal M. An examination of the effects of motivation and satisfaction on destination loyalty: a structural model[J]. *Tourism management*, 2016(5): 167-173.

[46] Sun Xue, Chi Chenggui, Xu He. Developing destination loyalty: the case of Hainan Island[J]. *Annals of Tourism Research*, 2013(43): 547-577.

[47] Chen C F, Tsai D C. How destination image and evaluative factors affect behavioral intentions?[J]. *Tourism Management*, 2007(28): 1115-1122.

[48] Hair J F, Black W C, Babin B J, Anderson R E. *Multivariate Data Analysis* [M]. 7th ed. Beijing: China Machine Press, 2011: 78-86.

[49] Pine B J, James H G. *Experience the Economy*[M]. 4th ed. Beijing: Mechanical Industry Press, 2002.

[50] Zou Tongqian, Wu Liyun. The nature and categories of tourism experiences and developing principles[J]. *Tourism Science*, 2003(4): 7-10.

[51] Li Xiaoqin. Tourism experience factors and foundation of dynamic model[J]. *Journal of Guilin Institute of Tourism*, 2006(5): 609-611.

[52] Long Jiangzhi. The hierarchy model of tourism experience: based on the spectrum of consciousness[J]. *Journal Beijing International Studies University*, 2009(11): 9-19.

[53] Reinartz W, Haenlein M, Henseler J. An empirical comparison of the efficacy of covariance-based and variance-based SEM[J]. *International Journal of Market Research*, 2009(26): 332-344.

[54] Hair J F, Sarstedt M, Ringle C M, Mena J A. An assessment of the use of partial least squares structural equation modeling in marketing research[J]. *Journal of the Academy of Marketing Science*, 2012(40): 414-433.

[55] Anderson J C, Gerbing D W. Structural equation modelling in practice: a review and recommended two-step approach[J]. *Psychology Bulletin*, 2013(103): 411-423.

[56] Bagozzi R P, Yi Y. Evaluation of structural equation models[J]. *Journal of the Academy of Marketing Science*, 1988(16): 74-94.

[57] Fornell C, Larcker D F. Structural equation models with unobservable variables and measurement error: algebra and statistics[J]. *Journal of Marketing Research*, 1981(18): 382-388.

[58] Wetzels W, Schröder G O, Oppen C. Using PLS path modelling for assessing hierarchical construct models: guidelines and empirical illustration[J]. *MIS Quarterly*, 2009(33): 177-195.

[59] Chin W W. *How to Write up and Report PLS Analyses*[M]. Berlin: Springer Press, 2011: 655-689.

[60] Tenenhaus M, Vinzi V E, Chatelin Y M, Lauro C. PLS path modeling[J].*Computational Statistics & Data Analysis*, 2005(48): 159-205.

[61] Wetzels M, Schröder G O, Oppen C. Using PLS path modelling for assessing hierarchical construct models: guidelines and empirical illustration[J]. *MIS Quarterly*, 2009(33): 177-195.

# Tourism Placemaking: The Story of Kuanzhai Alley in Chengdu, China

Shen Xingju[1*]

**Abstract:** Placemaking refers to a deliberate and purposeful approach to place creation. Tourism placemaking is a specific type of placemaking that emphasizes tourism use. Today, planned placemaking is widely seen in the form of themed pedestrian-oriented shopping streets and town shop entertainment and entertainment venues, which are major attractions for both residents and tourists in many cities. Kuanzhai Alley is one of the three Key Conservation Areas in Chengdu City, Sichuan Province. It is also the only area with rich architectural and social characteristic features of residential buildings dating back to the Qing Dynasty. The renovation and placemaking of Kuanzhai Alley was based on the culture and history of the local community, and accomplished by a collaborative effort among agencies from tourism, business, and the government. The renovation improved infrastructure, restored and preserved historical buildings, and the upgraded level and quality of advertisements. Tourists played a role in placemaking by sharing images and stories through social media. As tourists consume the place, they become co-producers and co-performers in placemaking.

**Keywords:** tourism, placemaking, Kuanzhai Alley, heritage, Chengdu

## Ⅰ. Introduction

Placemaking is a multi-faceted approach to the planning, design and management of public space. It means how a particular social group imprints its culture on a landscape and gives meaning to a geographic space. [1][2] Place-making is an ongoing process that never ends. In the history, many of the capital cities of Europe re-made into symbols of the nation-state was placemaking. Today, urban and community design is also considered placemaking. Placemaking has been a part of the urban planning, architecture and landscape architecture fields. [3] In recent years, placemaking has become popular in tourist destination planning, especially in ethnic neighbourhood such as the Chinatowns, Korea towns, Japan towns, Little Italy's, and Scandinavian and German theme towns that are often found in US cities. [4] Place

1* Southwest Minzu University, Sichuan, China. sxju@163.com.

making is an activity that humans naturally do as individuals and in social groups in the places that they inhabit. In tourism, placemaking is regarded as the foundation of most tourist attractions. [5][6]

Today, placemaking is widely seen in the form of themed pedestrian-oriented shopping streets and downtown shoppertainment and entertainment venues, which are major attractions for both local residents and visiting tourists in many cities.[7][8] Tourism destination planning and marketing are fundamentally placemaking actions intended to shape the image and image ability of a place. [9][10] The most popular places to visit are those that mix a large variety of ingredients into great experiences. Many towns and cities have been considering, or have created such places. To create attractive places needs to combine many factors. While it is easy to express the importance of place shaping, it is more difficult to know what and how people, including the government, tourism organizations, local residents, and tourists, can do about it.

Planners pay a vast amount of attention to placemaking as they prepare their local development frameworks and action plans. Research shows that people like to seek a range of experiences including browsing, exploring, dipping into cultural experiences, enjoying the atmosphere, shopping, and eating out. All these are considerations of placemaking.

Placemaking is a normal human behaviour. In tourism placemaking, it is the intentional, planned and globalizing effort to brand and theme places, which are often conducted by governments and tourism authorities. An understanding of placemaking gives insight into research questions on the economy of tourism and the roles of hosts and guests in co-producing tourism places . [11][12] Take Kuanzhai Alley as a case, this paper aims to provide ideas and answer the following questions: (1) How do cities make their historical area more attractive for local residents and tourists? (2) What roles do government and enterprises play in tourism placemaking? (3) What role do tourists play in making the place?

## Ⅱ. Kuanzhai Alley and Placemaking

Kuan (Wide) Zhai (Narrow) Xiangzi (Alley) is part of a historical section of Chengdu known as “Thousand-Year Lesser City” which preserves a large number of hundreds of years’ old historical architectural structures. It is one of the three Key Conservation Areas in Chengdu City, Sichuan Province. It is the only one that retains rich architectural and social characteristic features of residential buildings dating back to the Qing Dynasty (about 200-300 years ago). The China Lane Cultural Protection Program has listed Chengdu City in its “Famous Historical and Cultural Cities Conservation Plan” in the 1980s. Kuanzhai Alley is also the only existing northern alley cultural and architectural style historical neighbourhood found in the south.

*i. Tourism functions*

The Kuan Alley was known as Xingren Hutong in the Qing Dynasty and renamed Wide

Alley later. The alley has the largest number of very well preserved ancient architectural structures in the entire section. More than 20 characteristic compounds in the alley have maintained the facades from the old times, which brings about a nostalgic touch and make the place the most popular in the area (Figure 1).

Figure 1 The Old Brick Wall in the Kuan Alley

The Kuan Alley presents a more reminiscent pattern compared to the other two alleys in appearance, and it well preserves the leisurely life prototype of traditional Chengdu. In contrast, the Narrow Alley today gathers western food restaurants and cafes, clubs, and theme culture businesses that together create a destination for leisurely life anchored on western cuisines, art recreation, and wellness life (Figure 2).

Figure 2 Tea Ceremony Show at a Tea House

*ii. Tourism placemaking*

One side of the Kuanzhai Alley are original façades, and the other side are the cultural brick walls from past generations and snapshot walls of folk customs. If we think the Kuan Alley and Zhai Alley to have perfectly captured the leisure and idleness of Chengdu people, the Jing Alley stands out as a classic epitome of the folk culture of Chengdu. Apart from the intriguing cultural brick walls, the Jing Alley retains the state of folk life of the older Chengdu. It also provides feature delicacies and folk cultural performances that characterize the city, making the stay at Jing Alley an interactive experience of past life of Chengdu.

Kuanzhai Alley has different glamour and fun activities at different times. During the day, the sense of relaxation is embodied at every corner: old folks lying in bamboo chairs, drinking tea and chatting; children singing and playing while on their way home from school. Adding to the special feeling of the place are the abundances of vines and flowers decorating the walls. All these represent Kuaizhai Alley's tourist attraction.

As night falls, Kuanzhai Alley changes its appearance when music, wine and delicious food are served, which represents the other side of Chengdu and reflects adaptation to modern tastes of living. As a symbol of traditional Chengdu, Kuanzhai Alley is best described by a tourism advertisement slogan which says "Kuanzhai Alley, Chengdu's face, Chengdu's pace and Chengdu's flavour".

## Ⅲ. Tourism Placemaking of Kuanzhai Alley

*i. Tourism placemaking features of Kuanzhai Alley*

Urban designs has been regarded as the art of placemaking because it is the process of creating quality places where people want to live, work, play, shop, learn, and visit.[13][14][15] For many urban dwellers, a city's heart lies in its downtown core. This perception is often coupled with romantic images of vibrant public squares, bustling main streets, and quaint storefronts juxtaposed with scenes of neighbourliness, civic pride, and shared identity. Although placemaking is often considered to be a purposefully planned activity, there are two key points that need to be noted. First, all places undergo some form of placemaking. Placemaking is an inherent process in the creation, definition and evolution of places. In tourism, placemaking is also fundamental to the tourist attractiveness of a place. Understanding placemaking from both its organic and planned perspectives is an essential part of tourism destination development and marketing study. [1] Second, tourism is primarily an economic activity that encourages placemaking. The best tourism places are most likely those that exhibit both strong placemaking processes. [16]

Placemaking of Kuanzhai Alley was an essential part of a master planned Historical Area Renovation Project of Chengdu City. Led by the city government, a state-owned company, the Chengdu Culture & Tourism Development Co., Ltd., was founded in March of 2007 to take charge of the project that aimed to deepen cultural and tourism system renovation, optimize cultural and tourism resources allocation, as well as promote the tourism industry. It was expected that the project would build a main platform for investment, financing and operation to promote the brand-oriented and internationalized Chengdu's culture and tourism through modern cosmopolitan elements, professional designs, and marketing influence. Kuanzhai Alley was privileged in placemaking environments including both physical design and image branding, and for domestic and international tourist consumption. Table 1 lists considerations in tourism placemaking of Kuanzhai Alley.

Table 1 Considerations in Tourism Placemaking

| | General Placemaking | Tourism Placemaking of Kuanzhai Alley |
|---|---|---|
| Driver of change | Government, developers, socio-political Structure | Chengdu Municipal Government, Chengdu Culture & Tourism Development Company |
| Process of change | Top-down, master planned, hyper-neoliberal placemaking, intentional worldmaking | Top-down, intentional worldmaking |
| Tourists | Mass tourists | Mass tourists |
| Ownership & accessibility | Outsider owners, easy to visit, accessible | Outsider owners, easy to visit, accessible |
| Security | Safe, known, predictable, familiar | Safe, known |
| Sought experiences | Recreation, leisure, common, mass | Recreation, leisure |
| Social space | Front region | Front region |
| Authenticity | Inauthentic, contrived, fantasy, Disneyfication, simulacra, placelessness | Authentic, historical, reminiscence, fantasy |
| Transformation | Rapid change, high efficiency, path creation | Restoration, rapid change, high efficiency |
| Development stage (TALC) | Consolidation | Consolidation |
| Capacity | Large/high capacity | High capacity |
| Guiding | Guided, tourism cognita | Guided |
| Market orientation | International directed, industrial tourism | Industrial tourism |
| Experience | Recreational, diversionary | Recreational |
| Semiotics | Marker involvement, brand or theme oriented, sight sacralization, socially constructed, metanarratives | Marker involvement, brand or theme oriented, sight sacralization, socially constructed, |
| Fame | Famous, important | Famous |

Note: Adapted from Alan A. Lew.[3]

Two conflicting objectives of the historical area renovation project had emerged: conservation and commercial success. The city government emphasized protection and conservation of the cultural heritages of the area, but it was not willing to undertake all the costs. Investors were more interested in investment effect, but protection and conservation could be concerned. The focus of the argument fell on the balance between the residential and business areas. Finally, an agreement was reached that the layout and style of buildings would be preserved and all the construction material to use would have to be traditional. However, a considerable number of residents would have to be evacuated from the historical area. Upon completion of the project in June 2008, only one hundred (out of nine hundred) households were retained. Those who stayed in the renovated historical section fell in three categories: the wealthier, government offices, and those who had really strong feelings about the alley. The project has successfully made Kuanzhai Alley a symbolic site of the old Chengdu.

*ii. Tourism placemaking*

Physical characteristics and uses of the built environment also contribute to placemaking. Research has demonstrated that characteristics of the built environment support social interaction in urban areas. Such characteristics include sitting space and street furniture, green space and landscaping, and a variety of commercial and public activities. In Kuanzhai Alley, the following built environment is considered to contribute to tourism placemaking.

1) Landscape creation by storytelling. By telling stories, the Kuanzhai Alley links the landscape to Chengdu's history and culture. Meanwhile, storytelling creates a cozy atmosphere to deliver lively historical memories to visitors.

2) Scene creation. The Brick Culture Wall is a 400 meter long wall in the Jing Alley built with historical bricks and sculpted to display historical sites such as the post office, barracks, as well as daily life of the past. As a theme of the alley, it reflects the lifestyle of Kuanzhai Alley residents. It takes tourists back to the old times of Chengdu.

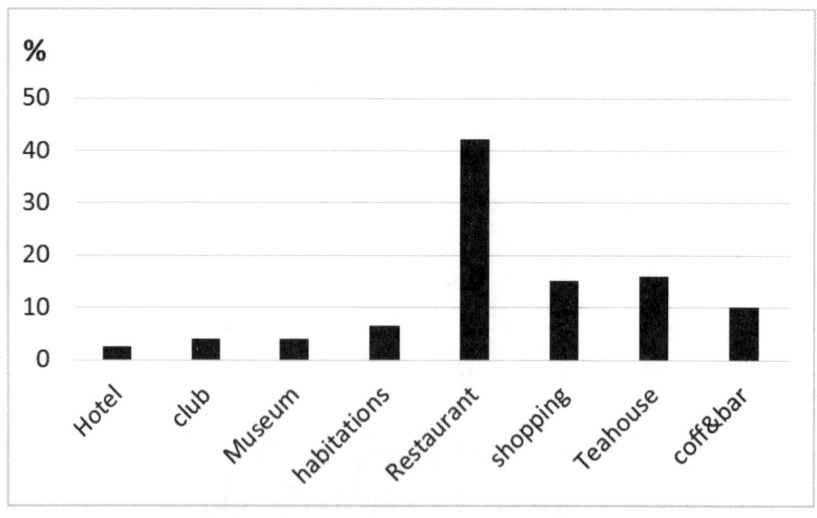


Figure 3 Recreation Space Created by Different Users of the Kuanzhai Alley

3) Recreation space design. There is a set of tools used by design professionals and governments to guide infrastructure growth. The design of Kuanzhai Alley focused on

placemaking of public spaces in a community, which includes streets, parks, as well as other recreational and open spaces. Besides the design of public space, users (business owners) of the alley also created different recreational spaces (Figure 3).

## Ⅳ. Analysis

*i. Patterns of tourism placemaking of Kuanzhai Alley*

The tourism placemaking process, which integrates business and conservation, has made Kuanzhai Alley a leisurely, fashionable, and unique courtyard consumption experiencing area. It has successfully created a comprehensive tourism attraction for the City of Chengdu. Table 2 shows themes, functions, and life styles of each alley in Kuanzhai Alley historical area after placemaking.

Table 2 Themes, Functions, and Life Styles after Placemaking

| Alley | Theme | Function | Life Style |
|---|---|---|---|
| Kuan Alley | Tourism and leisure theme recreation area | Hotel, teahouse, club, folk, restaurant, spa | Leisure, traditional |
| Zhai Alley | Brand business theme, shopping | Western food, art, cultural centres, museums | Slow, modern |
| Jing Alley | Fashion entertainment area | Bar, retail, Idea Stores, dessert | Modern |

*ii. The success of tourism placemaking*

The Tourism Office of Chengdu played an important role in promoting placemaking and the renovating of a community rich in culture and full of life. To make a place, interaction between people in a social and cultural environment is essential.

According to the Tourism Office of Chengdu, the Kuan Alley and Zhai Alley attracted about 170 thousand tourists on the New Year's Day of 2017. From 2008 to the present, Kuan Alley and Zhai Alley, the core section of the historical and cultural conservation area, has received a total of 72 million domestic and foreign tourists.

According to statistics, more than 70 major tourism attractions in Sichuan Province received a total of 6 million tourists during the National Day holiday season of 2015, among which the top seven scenic spots were located in Chengdu City. With 600 thousands tourists received during the holiday season, Kuan Zhai Alley was ranked topmost and became the most popular tourist attraction. Figure 4 shows annual visitors of a few major tourism attractions in Sichuan in 2015.

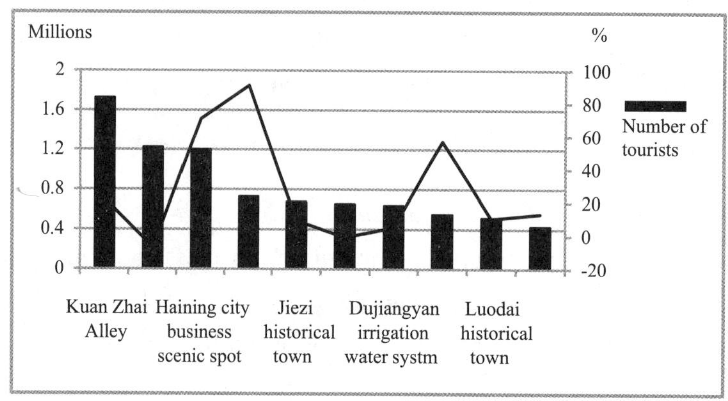


Figure 4 Tourists and Year-on-year Growth Rate in 2015

*iii. Tourists help shape image*

Tourists are involved in creating place stories and sharing images and stories through social media. [17][18] Many visitors share their travel experiences on various social media sites. They perceive the history of the old town and write reviews of the old Chengdu on social media based on their real life experience, which in a sense help build the image of Kuanzhai Alley and spread it to more people. Table 3 shows reviews of Kuanzhai Alley on a few influential travel websites in China.

Table 3 Public Reviews of Kuanzhai Alley

| Website | Reviews | Score | Ranking |
|---|---|---|---|
| qunar.com | 1,352 | 4.4/5 | 1 |
| Ctrip.com | 8,345 | 4.4/5 | |
| mafengwo.cn | 7,946 | NA | 1 |
| dianping.com | 3,736 | NA | 1 |
| lvmama.com | 30 | 95.30% | 3 |

## V. Conclusion

Placemaking is the process of creating public spaces that promote people's health, happiness, and well-being. It is a multi-faceted process including planning, design and management of public spaces. Tourism placemaking is special type that also has the intention to promote recreational use of the place by tourists. Factors contributing to a successful placemaking include the historical and cultural background of the place, the support of the government and participation of local people, a good planning and quality designs, etc. Kuanzhai Alley satisfies all the conditions needed for a success for a place making, and it succeeded.

First, Kuanzhai Alley is a historical section in Chengdu City. It has a large number of well-preserved historical architectural structures and a deep culture. The neighbourhood preserves a leisurely life prototype of the traditional Chengdu. Moreover, the renovation of the historical area was strongly supported by the city government. A state-owned company was established to take charge of the renovation project in order to assure the preservation and conservation of historical and cultural heritages and protect investor's interests. The renovation project has successfully made the place for tourism, preserved historical and cultural heritages, and boosted the tourism industry of Chengdu. Furthermore, local people and business owners are active players in placemaking. They not only create public recreation spaces such as restaurants, teahouses, and shops, but also present culture through performing and practising the traditional life style. Finally, the success of tourism placemaking has brought in large number of tourists, who in turn help build the image of the place by sharing their travel experiences to wider audience. As tourists consume place, they become co-producers and co-performers of the continuing placemaking. [19][20]

## ACKNOWLEDGMENT

This paper is supported by the National Nature Science Foundation of China and the Central Universities Fund Project of Southwest Minzu University.(Grant No. 41401604 & 2017SYB04).

## References

[1] Tuan Y F. *Space and Place: The Perspective of Experience* [M]. Minneapolis: University of Minnesota Press, 1977.

[2] Cilliers E J, Timmermans W. The importance of creative participatory planning in the public place-making process [J]. *Environment and Planning B: Planning and Design*, 2014(41): 413-429.

[3] Lew A A. Tourism planning and place making: place making or placemaking? [J]. T*ourism Geographies*, 2017(2): 1-19.

[4] Vale L J. *Architecture, Power and National Identity* [M]. 2nd ed. London: Routledge, 1992.

[5] Gottdiener M. *The Theming of America: American Dreams, Media Fantasies, and Themed Environments*[M]. 2nd ed. Boulder: Westview Press, 2001.

[6] Paradis T W. Theming, Tourism, and Fantasy city [M]// A A Lew, C M Hall, A M Williams, ed. *A Companion to Tourism*. London: Blackwell, 2004.

[7] Wyckoff W A, Neumann B, Pape G, Schindler K. Placemaking as and economic development tool: a placemaking guide[D]. East Lansing, MI: Michigan State University, 2015.

[8] Rickly-Boyd J M. The tourist narrative[J]. *Tourist Studies*, 2010(3): 259-280.

[9] Lew A A. Authenticity and sense of place in the tourism development experience of older retail districts[J]. *Journal of Travel Research*, 1989(4): 15-22.

[10] Paradis T W. Theming, tourism, and fantasy city[M]// A A Lew, C M Hall, A M Williams, ed. *A Companion to Tourism*. London: Blackwell, 2004.

[11] Ritzer G, Liska A. "McDisneyization" and "post-tourism"[M]// C Rojek, J Urry, eds. *Touring Cultures: Transformations of Travel and Theory*, London: Routledge, 1997: 96-109.

[12] Su X. The imagination of place and tourism consumption: a case study of Lijiang Ancient Town, China[J]. *Tourism Geographies*, 2010(3): 412-434.

[13] Wyckoff M A, Neumann B, Pape G, Schindler K. *Placemaking as an Economic Development Tool: A Placemaking Guide* [M]. East Lansing, MI: Land Policy Institute, Michigan State University, 2015.

[14] Lew A A, McKercher B. Modeling the movement of tourists in a local destination[J]. *Annals of Tourism Research*, 2006(3): 403-423.

[15] Hoelscher S. *Heritage on Stage: The Invention of Ethnic Place in America's Little Switzerland*[M]. Madison: The University of Wisconsin Press, 1998.

[16] Bosker B. Why China's homeowners want to live in fake Paris[J/OL]. *The World Post*. http://www.huffingtonpost.com/bianca-bosker/china-fake-towns_b_4610715.html, 2014.

[17] Dredge D, Jenkins J D. Destination place identity and regional tourism policy[J]. *Tourism Geographies*, 2003(4): 383-407.

[18] Project for Public Spaces (PPS). The Power of 10+: Applying Placemaking at Every Scale[EB/OL]. Project for Public Spaces website. http://www.pps.org/reference/the-power-of-10/, 2015.

[19] McCann J. The cultural politics of local economic development: meaning-making, place-making and the urban policy process[J]. *Geoforum*, 2002(33): 385-398.

[20] Zhang S, Zhu C, Sin J K O, Mok O K T. A novel ultrathin elevated channel low-temperature poly-Si TFT[J]. *ICTCHS Electron Device Lett*, 1999(20): 569-571.

# Leisure Activity Shortage of Left-behind Children in China's Rural Areas: A Case Study of X Township, P County, S Province, China

Zhang Xilin[1*]

**Abstract:** Daily leisure activities of preschool children in China's rural areas are usually neglected to varying degrees. This paper studies the status of leisure activities of left-behind children in the rural areas of X Village, P County, S Province, China and analyzes the causes of leisure activity shortage among left-behind children in rural areas by way of interview and field survey. The study then makes suggestions to improve the leisure situation of left-behind children in rural areas: to conduct education about and practice of leisure activities for rural children, provide and maintain leisure facilities and promote participation in leisure activities.

**Keywords:** left-behind children; leisure; education; Chinese rural areas

## Ⅰ. Introduction

Leisure activities are of vital significance to children's growth, promoting their development in emotion, imagination, creativity and formation of self awareness. American scholar Larsen holds that meaningful leisure activities which children like are humanistic teachings. [1] Article 31 of the Convention on the Rights of the Child requires contracting states to "recognize the right of the child to rest and leisure, to engage in play and recreational activities appropriate to the age of the child and to participate freely in cultural life and the arts. States Parties shall respect and promote the relevant rights of the child to participate and shall encourage the provision of appropriate and equal opportunities for leisure activity". Article 21 of the Law of PRC on the Protection of Minors formulated in 1992 requires that "people's governments at all levels shall create conditions to establish and improve the leisure activity facilities suitable for the cultural life of minors". Although leisure plays a valuable role in promoting child's physical and mental health development, the rights to recreation of children in rural areas have not been recognized and supported by some adults.

1* Zhaoqing University, Zhaoqing, China. sydeny181212@163.com.

After going through literatures on leisure and recreational activities of children, the author finds that Swanson (1993) first conducted relevant researches and found that the education on left-behind children calls for guidance and support from the whole social system including schools, family, community and enterprises to shape the future of children. [2] Pottinger (2005)[3], Baucr & Thompson (2006), Givaudan (2013) [4] and other scholars mainly focused on issues of left-behind children in China and Southeast Asia countries such as children's growth and education, physical and psychological health, behaviors and personalities formation in lack of parental care, exploring the impact of left-behind life on children in terms of life, education, medical health, behaviors and psychology. Their results and findings are also different from each other. Existing studies of child leisure focus on those over 12 years old and very few of them are about preschoolers less than 7 years old. Krzysztof Sas-Nowosielski (2006) used planning behavior theory and development modal to study children's labor activities in leisure time. Garcia and Ruiz (2013) [5] studied labor involved in leisure activities of Spanish children between 12 and 17. Sharp et al. (2015) [6] explored the organized leisure activity of children in rural areas.

Given the inadequacy of study on leisure activities of left-behind children in rural areas and the fact that existing domestic academic researches mainly focus on related areas of child's leisure as a whole, this paper attempts to study the daily leisure activities of left-behind children in rural areas, in a bid to put forward solutions to improve the recreational life of the left-behind children in rural areas and promote the healthy growth of this special group.

## Ⅱ. Survey on the Status Quo of Leisure Activities of Left-behind Children in Rural Areas

### *i. Definition of left-behind children*

In China, the left-behind children refers to children who live in their hometown or board with their relatives as both or either one of their parents are migrate workers in other places. Children's age is defined as the young people over 4 years old and who have not yet experienced adolescence. This paper mainly studies the preschool children of 4 to 7 years old.

### *ii. Profile of the study case area*

The area of this study is located in X Township, P County, S Province in southern China, 12 kilometers away from the county. The place covers an area of 38 square kilometers, with a population of 85, 500 from 33 villages under the jurisdiction. Since 1980s, a large number of young and middle-aged rural labors in this village have moved to the economically developed cities in Pearl River Delta in Guangdong Province to make a living, in an attempt to improve the family living conditions. With the outflow of young and middle-aged rural labors, the number of left-behind children also gradually increased. Statistics show that left-behind preschool children accounted for 65% of the total. There are eight public basketball courts and three simple sports equipment spots for leisure activities in this township. The methods of interview and observation were adopted to survey the status quo of leisure activities of left-behind preschool children here.

*iii. The leisure status of left-behind preschool children*

*A. Characteristics of preschool children leisure*

According to the general situation of preschool children, leisure activities of this group feature the following characteristics: ① Adequate leisure time. ② Leisure activities close to nature; simple activities such as playing the sand, playing with brothers and sisters, playing games with neighboring partners, playing in the places where their guardians do farm work, or playing gadgets at home. ③ Limited kinds of leisure activities with watching TV and spontaneous games as the main forms. Most of TV programs they watch are children programs and animation. The choices of leisure for preschool children are limited because the guardians restrict the children for security reasons, and leisure props and recreational venues are limited. ④Details not taken care of during leisure activities due to limited energy of the guardian.

*B. Cases of interview for preschool children leisure activities*

After observations of and interviews for the preschool children in the township, four children were selected as typical cases for the research. Detailed information of the specific cases are as follows:

Table 1 Comparison of Preschool Children Leisure in Rural Areas Under Different Family Life Conditions

| Case number | Family life status | Major leisure activities | Advantages | Disadvantages |
|---|---|---|---|---|
| 1. Yuanyuan (female, 5-year-old) | Parents migrate out for work; Live with sister and grandparents; Not received preschool education yet. | Watching TV, playing in the yard, playing games with her sister, playing at neighbor's house. | Enough Leisure time; Free choices of leisure activities; More opportunities to be close to nature, which is conducive to the formation of independent personality. | Lack of playmates when the sister is at school; Too much time spent watching TV alone. |

(To be continued)

(Continued Table 1)

| Case number | Family life status | Major leisure activities | Advantages | Disadvantages |
|---|---|---|---|---|
| 2. Chaochao (male, 6-year-old) | Parents migrate out for work; Live with grandparents; Under kindergarten education. | Playing toys, watching TV when staying at home; Following grandparents to the vegetable garden to play; Playing at neighbor's home; Playing children games with classmates and learning children folk rhymes at school. | More freedom for leisure when staying at home, a small number of toys, more contact with nature; Enough playmates and rich types of leisure at school. | Lack playmates of the same age when stay at home, less leisure activities types, too much time spent in watching TV; Relatively naughty and unable to absorb in leisure knowledge imparted by teacher at school. |
| 3. Xiaoyu (female, 6-year-old) | Parents migrate out for work. Live with the grandparents and elder brother in a poor family. Under kindergarten education. | Watching TV, playing with neighboring children, or in a daze when at home; Learning children folk rhymes and playing games when in school. | Much leisure time at home; With leisure games to learn at school. | Lag behind other children in ability to enjoy recreational activities, vulnerable to be isolated by classmates. |
| 4. Wanyue (female, 6-year-old) | Parents teaching in the school in the township on weekdays; and coming back home on weekends; Living with her elder sister and younger brother and grandmother; Under kindergarten education. | Watching TV and listening to music discs, reading picture books, playing small toys, and playing with her sister and brother when at home; Active in learning children folk rhymes and playing games at school. | With playmates no matter at home or in school; rich types of leisure activities. | Relatively less sports leisure activities. |

Case 1, Case 2 and Case 3 share a problem: Though there is sufficient leisure time and free choices of leisure activities for left-behind preschool children, there is a lack of guidance and leisure activity materials as the guardians pay less attention to children leisure. With limited varieties of leisure choices, watching TV and free playing constitute the major forms of leisure. From the home visit of Case 2, it can be found that the most important "toy" is the TV. And the grandmother said the children would watch TV once they have spare time at home. The reasons why children spend too much time in watching TV lie in the following two factors: the limited types of leisure activities at home and the attraction of TV leisure to children. When children spend too much time watching TV, the time spent on outdoor activities will decrease accordingly. In the above cases, Xiaoyu has the most serious problems because her parents have no time or awareness to take care of her leisure activities, which results in her leisure ability weaker than the other classmates. She is slower than other students in learning new leisure skills, which affects her physical development. In addition, she is unable to keep up with the progress of teaching, which draws more special attention from teachers and classmates, thus affecting her mental health. Former Soviet psychologist Vygotsky argued that the knowledge construction of children can be promoted or influenced by the rest of people around. [2] 21 Children like Xiaoyu in this backward group need more guidance and help from schools and parents. The leisure status of Wanyue in Case 4 is ideal with a variety of leisure props and enough leisure partners making her childhood full of fun and interest. When participating in leisure activities, she has a pleasant experience and the joyfulness brought by the development of personal ability will serve as an internal motivation driving her to keep on learning. Wanyue's leisure situation is better than the other three children because her parents are teachers, who have certain knowledge about children leisure and can come back home once a week, providing her with leisure materials and leisure guidance. Sufficient companionship and participation of parents will improve the children's enthusiasm for leisure and is conducive to achieving better leisure effect.

## Ⅲ. Analysis on Causes of Shortage of Leisure Activities among Left-behind Children in Rural Areas

*i. Existing problems*

*A. Lack of variety in leisure activities*

It can be found from studies and visits that leisure activities of the majority of left-behind children are spontaneous, lacking correct guidance. Children leisure activities mainly include watching TV, playing games with other children. Elder children's leisure activities are mainly watching TV and bike-riding outdoors. In general, these leisure activities of left-behind children are relatively simple, with TV-watching and casual play as major activities. They have little or even no involvement in leisure activities conducive to learning.

*B. Imbalanced leisure structure*

The survey found that most leisure activities of children in rural area are recreational and close-to-natural ones, while those helpful to improve fitness, beauty appreciation, learning ability and interpersonal skills are seriously inadequate. The leisure status of these children is unable to meet the needs for their physical, intellectual and emotional development.

*C. Certain security risks*

In the leisure activities of these left-behind children, leisure with parents is usually only watching TV and occasionally chatting. The inadequate direct leisure communication between the two generations is not conducive to children emotional development. "Parents are the best teachers of the children", the guardian can exert a huge and far-reaching impact on helping the child to form a correct concept of leisure and develop certain leisure skills. As children often take part in activities alone, parents need to provide enough guidance on safety in leisure. However, most of the left-behind children do not have enough knowledge of safety and there are some hidden dangers in their leisure activities.

*ii. Causes analysis of the problem*

*A. Lack of leisure concept and inadequate attention paid to children leisure*

The concept of leisure guides people's leisure life. Most of the people living in the village are middle-aged farmers, left-behind elderly people and children. The adults of these people attach no importance to children leisure for poor economic capacity, low level of education and limited time. They think that the children have lived a better life so long as they have food to eat, cloth to keep warm and schools to go for education. Toys are regarded as not so necessary. They do not know the importance of leisure. Their limited financial capacity also makes them unable to bear expenses for leisure activities.

*B. More constraints of leisure activities*

First of all, the lack of leisure environment is one of the basic factors that hinder the leisure development of left-behind children. In rural areas, the low economic development level and inadequate investment in leisure result in the lack of leisure facilities and places, which limits the types of children's leisure activities and leads to children's lack of leisure skills and fails to meet the needs of physical and mental development of local children. There is hardly any place that specifically brings rich leisure experience for the children.

Second, a serious shortage of leisure consumption is one of the important reasons. Guardians mainly spend money on food, clothing and necessary education of left-behind children. Little money is spent on meeting children's leisure needs except expenditure on a TV that is regarded as necessary.

Finally, interpersonal constraints also affect children' leisure activities. Without appropriate instructors or suitable partners for leisure activities, left-behind children are unable to enjoy collective leisure.

## Ⅳ. Solutions and Findings of Improvement for Leisure of Left-behind Children

The research shows that limited financial ability, backward concept of leisure and other reasons lead to problems including limited variety, imbalanced structure and hidden risks in the leisure of children in this area, which are not good for the healthy development of children. After analysis of the reasons of problems, the author proposes the following suggestions:

*i. Learn from the experience of children leisure in the U.S.A.*

*A. Promoteing the children's participation in comprehensive and rich leisure activities*

In the developed western countries, children have comprehensive and rich choices for leisure, which are beneficial to their growth and development needs. They can acquire knowledge in the library, broaden horizon in the museum, enhance physical fitness in various sports field, make friends and enrich experience in the club, develop skills in summer camp and listen to lectures in college campus. The way to spend spare time often shows a child's true personality and affects his future development. This inspires families, schools and society to strive to provide children with good leisure conditions so that they can participate in various leisure activities for balanced and full development.

*B. Expanding participation in leisure activities and promoting rural leisure*

The diversity of leisure activities and expansion of participation is an important policy to expand leisure in the United States. In terms of leisure activities design, mutual cooperation and communication among different ages are of vital importance. In addition, to promote community leisure activity forms represents one of the trends. Professional recreational instructors can go to communities to provide services and encourage participation in activities to relax and improve physical health. [3] In terms of leisure, parents of left-behind children urgently need proper guidance of professionals to enhance leisure awareness and improve leisure skills to meet needs of both themselves and their children. The environment of guidance from the top and participation of residents needs to be established so as to improve the enthusiasm of the villagers for leisure activities and promote the development of leisure for rural left-behind children.

*ii. Specific measures*

Education of leisure is rarely conducted in school and at home in rural areas of China. The left-behind children in the township mainly live with their mother or grandparents. Under these two circumstances, the children guardians are unable to take children leisure education into account due to their limited time and energy. Besides, even if the guardians have free time and financial capacity to do this, they still cannot provide good leisure education and leisure conditions because they still lack the concept for leisure. To improve the leisure conditions of children left behind, endeavors should be made from the following three aspects:

*A. To carry out education on the concept of leisure*

The earliest study on how to acquire leisure interests and goals mainly focused on two aspects: outdoor entertainment and the perdurability of the influences of childhood learning on future life. In general, the familiarity of the natural resources and the activities of the leisure venue in the formative years makes the children more likely to participate in adult activities. [1] The leisure activities in one's childhood will have a lifelong impact on their development. The time guardians and children spend together, their leisure ideas, methods and leisure activities types will exert a direct and huge impact on the formation of habits for leisure activities in children. Before school education, children can learn some simple leisure and entertainment methods with instinct and parental guidance. This will be the basis of the child's leisure ability, affecting their future learning of leisure skills. When the child goes to school, family leisure education still plays an important role and will continue to affect the children's growth, even their whole life. The primary school in the township sets up no other education courses except the basic physical education, art classes and music classes, resulting in a shortage of leisure skills and imbalance of the development of leisure capacity. Therefore, schools at all levels should carry out necessary leisure education to teach staff reserve qualified talents. The teachers can put the principle of "learning through play" into practice and children can acquire necessary qualities and life skills in game playing. The villages should give full play to its role in leisure education by using blackboard, notice board and lectures to make the villagers better understand knowledge and methods related to leisure, thus improving the quality of children's leisure activities.

*B. Carry out education of leisure activity practice*

Certain atmosphere is needed to turn the leisure concept into practice. For the healthy and comprehensive growth of the next generation, schools, families and villages should create practice opportunities for children to have leisure activities and provide correct guidance. Aristotle pointed out that games are an essential method for learning and development of reason, especially for children less than 7 years old. Dewey held that children education in any times depends largely on game and entertainment. Li Haiyan et al. (2011) [7] found that games originating from rural activities are amusing and can improve countryside children's leisure and interpersonal and social skills. Kay and Moxham (1996) believed that rural games and rural leisure take nature as the venue and can bring children a sense of liberation and freedom, so they can be a perfect choice for children in rural areas as leisure activities. [8] As Thoreau once said, the inspiration of the world lies in the wild. Life close to nature can bring a different experience to children. Plants and animals are good friends of children while sunshine, air and earth are the basic conditions for children's leisure and rest. Life in the natural world can help to rapidly relieve the nervousness in life. Pleasant leisure activities and games can bring more inspiration.

Koka (2013), [9] Klinker et al. (2014) [10] and other researchers proved the promoting effect that school physical education can exert on children leisure. Teachers in rural kindergartens can combine sports and leisure in their teachings to guide students' learning of leisure in the process of doing sports.

One advantage of education of leisure activity practice at school is the large number of partners of the same age. As long as leisure activities are conducted in classes, the spread effect will be very strong. The moderate amount of leisure practice activities can make the relationship between teachers and students more harmonious. The integration of leisure activities and academic learning can further promote students' comprehensive ability.

At home, the guardian should use their spare time to guide children to participate in a variety of leisure activities, including activities of relaxation and recreation, fitness enhancing, learning and beauty appreciation to facilitate physical and emotional development of the children.

*C. Providing and maintaining supporting facilities*

The implementation of leisure activities calls for corresponding venues and props. For example, ball games need corresponding sites and the balls, while reading leisure activity needs excellent books. The sad fact is that left-behind children in the investigated areas are lack of these venues and props. To solve this problem of structural constraints, funds and efforts from schools, families, government and society are necessary to obtain the funds support as well as other material assistance of the public and governments at various levels and to improve supporting facilities, filling the library with more books, building more sports venues and purchasing sport equipment. Parents should cooperate with the school and villages to maintain the supporting leisure facilities, and provide children with basic leisure materials.

## V. Conclusion

Through the survey, the study finds that factors including limited financial conditions and the backward awareness of concept of leisure in the residents in X Township have led to problems such as a lack of variety of leisure activities, imbalanced leisure structure and the existence of certain security risks, which are not good for the comprehensive and healthy development of these children. Based on analysis of the causes of these problems, the following countermeasures are put forward to improve the situation, namely, to carry out education on concept of leisure, to start education of leisure activity practice and to provide and maintain supporting leisure facilities. In addition, efforts should be made to promote children's participation in comprehensive and rich leisure activities, expand leisure participation and improve leisure status of the rural left-behind children.

## References

[1] Lerner R M, Mckinney M H. It takes an entire village to raise a child[J]. *Psyccritiques*, 1993, 38(8).

[2] Miller D. Jamaican hands across the Atlantic: by Elaine Bauer & Paul Thompson[J]. *Journal of the Royal Anthropological Institute*, 2007, 13(3): 744-745.

[3] Pottinger A M. Children's experience of loss by parental migration in inner-city Jamaica[J]. *American Journal of Orthopsychiatry*, 2005, 75(4): 485-496.

[4] Givaudan M, Pick S. Children left behind: how to mitigate the effects and facilitate emotional and psychosocial development: supportive community networks can diminish the negative effects of parental migration[J]. *Child Abuse & Neglect*, 2013, 37(12): 1080.

[5] Garcia B E, Ruiz J F, Bush P L. Delving into the social ecology of leisure-time physical activity among adolescents from south eastern Spain[J]. *Journal of Physical Activity & Health*, 2013, 10(8): 1136-1144.

[6] Sharp E H, Tucker C J, Baril M E, et al. Breadth of participation in organized and unstructured leisure activities over time and rural adolescents' functioning[J]. Journal of youth & adolescence, 2015, 44(1): 62-76.

[7] Li Haiyan, Chen Peijie, Zhuang Jie. Revision and reliability validity assessment of children's leisure activities survey[J]. *Chinese Journal of School Health*, 2011.

[8] Kay G, Moxham N. Paths for whom? Countryside access for recreational walking[J]. *Leisure Studies*, 1996, 15(3): 171-183.

[9] Koka A. The effect of teacher and peers need support on students' motivation in physical education and its relationship to leisure time physical activity[J]. *Acta Kinesiologiae Universitatis Tartuensis*, 2013, 19: 48-62.

[10] Klinker C D, Schipperijn J, Christian H, et al. Using accelerometers and global positioning system devices to assess gender and age differences in children's school, transport, leisure and home based physical activity[J]. *International Journal of Behavioral Nutrition and Physical Activity*, 2014, 11(1): 8.

# PART II

# Tourism Industry and Regional Development

# An Analysis of Rural Tourism Development in China: Drawing Lessons from the Experience of the Development of Spanish Village Brigade

Luo Pengfei[1], Zhang Yingying[2], Ma Liqing[3*]

**Abstract:** In the last two decades, rural tourism has played a huge role in promoting social and economic development. Especially in recent years, it became a hot topic for scholars and concerned government departments. In Spain, rural tourism is at top level among Europe countries. We here focus on the specific problems existing in the development of rural tourism in China, choose Spain as a sample to learn from its successful experience and excavate the unique advantages of rural tourism development in China. The rich culture which is the soul of tourism widely exists in Chinese rural areas. Such feature is a huge source of tourist attraction if they can be properly promoted. Apart from drawing lessons from Spain, China should take advantage of its unique conditions to develop rural tourism products with Chinese special characteristics.

**Keywords:** rural tourism; Spain; China; development; culture

## Ⅰ. Introduction

The development of rural tourism in China began in the late 1980s. In the process of promoting urbanization and new rural development in China, rural tourism plays an important role.[1] However, the rural tourism in China has some problem such as lacking government support in policy, low knowledge level of farmers and lacking motivation to explore local features due to assimilation of urban cultures. In order to promote the development of rural tourism, it is necessary to study how to effectively promote rural tourism. Most of previous researchers made separate study of the development of Chinese rural tourism or rural tourism development in Spain. But few researches integrating rural tourism development in Spain and the current situation of China were made. Based on the analysis of the development of rural tourism in Spain and the problems existing in the rural tourism development in China, this paper makes some suggestions on the development of rural tourism in China to promote

1 Zhejiang Ocean University, Zhoushan, China.
2 Zhejiang Ocean University, Zhoushan, China.
3* Zhejiang Ocean University, Zhoushan, China. 1059251269@qq.com.

its development.

## Ⅱ. Concept of Rural Tourism

The concept of rural tourism has not been unified in the academic community. In English speaking countries, “rural tourism” has two alternative names, agritourism (tourism) and rural (rural tourism). In East Asia and Southeast Asia, countries and regions traditionally call tourism “agricultural tourism”. The European Union (EU) and the World Organization for Economic Cooperation and Development (OECD, 1994) define rural tourism as tourism activities that take place in the rural areas.[2] We here define rural tourism as activities which take place in the rural areas, based on the rural environment, making full use of all kinds of rural natural and cultural conditions and combining rural culture to meet the needs of tourists. The village, nature and humanity are the main characteristics of rural tourism promotion. It fully realizes the integration of the first industry and the tertiary industry in the new period. As a means of poverty alleviation, rural tourism plays an important role in increasing the local fiscal revenue, providing new jobs for local people to solve the problem of transfer surplus labor, adjusting the rural industry structure and strengthening the vitality local economy based on changing the traditional rural industry and promoting the development of local economy.

In the process of China’s urbanization and new rural development, rural tourism is an important step to promote rural development and drive the development of modern agriculture. It is an important means to increase the income and improve the living standard of farmers. It is also an important starting point for promoting the construction of beautiful countryside. Spain’s rural tourism has been fully developed after several decades, which provides a lot of experience for the development of rural tourism in China. However, in the process of the sustainable rural tourism development in China, there are some problems, such as inadequate development and environmental problems. We can learn experience from Spain to solve these problems.

## Ⅲ. The Development of Rural Tourism in Spain

At the beginning of the 1960s, Spain that is called “the kingdom of tourism” created the world’s first rural tourism. The hotel which is reconstructed from the castle is known as the “Palaiduo State Inn”[3]. At the same time, government planed and constructed large farms where some projects such as hiking, horseback riding, gliding, mountain climbing, rafting and other projects can held. In the 1990s, there were new forms of rural tourism in Spain in which the main purpose of the tourists is to go on vacation in the countryside, which is markedly different from the traditional village tourists whose main motivation is to meet family or friends. This new structure has created a new “modern village tourism” in the tourism academic circles. Through continuous development, the rural tourism in Spain has made greater progress, owing to the support of developed agriculture and also benefited from the following aspects:

*A. Government's support*

Spanish government provided many supports like manpower, financial resources, material resources, policy and technology in order to promote the development of rural tourism. A set of legislation and standards were established to ensure the status of rural tourism and the quality of products. According to these standards, buildings should be consistent with traditional architectural style and environment; building materials should match local characteristics; the accommodation can accommodate visitors with a capacity of 10 to 15 rooms and each room can get accommodation up to 4 tourists. These measures improved the quality of service, indirectly created a business card of rural tourism and promoted the standardized development of rural tourism.[4]Through technical assistance or training, Spanish government improved the technical level of farmers management and resource utilization efficiency. At the same time, the training guided farmers to know how to protect their own culture, how to enhance their cultural pride and how to protect resources and environment in rural areas. The training also taught people how to make full use of the cultural value of rural tourism. In terms of financial resources, the government gave special support and helped rural tourism providers through tax breaks, subsidies, low interest loans and investment. In addition, foreign investment was welcomed and injected new vitality into the development of rural tourism. On the policy resources, the government made reasonable and valuable project for the development of rural tourism. A series of relevant laws and regulations to regulate the development of rural tourism were also enacted; on technical resources, special technical personnel were arranged to train people who were engaged in rural tourism.

*B. Sublimation of traditional culture*

In the past 35 years, the number of tourists has increased by 8 million. In general, the integration of culture promotes the image of rural tourism and injects new vitality into tourism. They specially enhanced the tourist experience by making full use of ancient buildings, rural cultural relics, historical culture, folk festivals and folk art to develop new tourism. These items were closely combined with the traditional culture of Spain in the process of developing rural tourism. For example, Don Quixote Road and the windmill group which Quixote fought with are still open to the public for free; cultural heritage that is distributed in rural areas all over the country is also free of charge. [1] Instead of putting culture at the spiritual level, it combined culture and product to develop a new tourism product, ultimately to improve visitors' experience degree. Spain also fully created the diet culture. Don Quixote windmill, the medieval castle and characteristic food form an important tour line. The Ministry of Agriculture collects traditional recipes and traditional handicrafts which education and tourism departments also cooperate to develop. The road to Santiago which incorporates the cultural connotations of pilgrimage attracts many tourists.

*C. Environmental protection*

Spanish government focused on environmental protection. This initiative is also the main driving force for sustainable development of rural tourism development in Spain. It implements the EU environmental management and certification system (E-MAS) in several tourist destinations. People are required to protect the environment and integrate the theory of ecology and sustainable development into the development and utilization of rural tourism. [4] Before the development, the planning departments adhered to the concept of environmental protection, made some environmental protection research for the development object and analyzed and predicted possible influence of development; during the development, the relevant departments strengthened the inspection and supervision and the participants persisted in the rational development to protect the environment.

*D. Vigorous promote of publicity*

The Spanish government attaches great importance to publicity and promotion, setting up special promotional agencies and providing a large sum of financial support. On propaganda, Spain attaches great importance to the application of network technology in the promotion of sales, promotion means diversification through the network media, off-line information, exhibition, inviting foreign media and other forms of publicity and promotion. At the same time, the implementation of the "Spanish experts plan" invites the industry hands to go to Spain to do training and investigation. [6] The tourism management departments also set up a platform to support marketing to the media and advertising propaganda to announce the tourism destination image of Spain.

In the promotional strategy, since 1980s, a strategy that combined the unified and personal characters was adopted (specifically, taking a total advertising practices with a unified theme or format design to establish a unified image of the Spanish and then making the unique products according to the characteristics of each market). The slogan of Spanish tourism is often explained with emotion, such as "enthusiasm of life, everything bathing in sunshine". Under the stimulus of the propaganda, the people attach more importance to rural tourism and 36% of Spaniards spend their vacation in more than 1,000 rural tourist spots! 85% of the rural tourists drive to the farms within 100-150 kilometers at weekends.

*E. Association drive*

The Spanish Rural Tourism Association (ASETUR) is a non-governmental association, which has a good cooperative relationship with the government and plays a very important role in promoting the development of rural tourism in Spain. Owners getting together spontaneously, more than 60% owners of rural tourism operators have joined the association. [1]

*F. Independent management*

The origins of travel agency in Spain are individuals which adopt the way of family management. So the vitality of the enterprise is greatly aroused. In order to get long-term interests, enterprises will ensure the quality of products and services that can be seen from the customer satisfaction and loyalty (a total of 100 points, reaching an average of 84 points, the tourists visit same site in 40% more than ten times) which provide strong support for the further development of tourism market. The rural tourists in Spain have great autonomy, and operators pay great attention to the visitors' experience to participate in the activity. Tourists can walk into the farmhouse and live together with the farm owners. They can also stay away from the farm owners to take care of the affairs of life by themselves.

## Ⅳ. China's Rural Tourism Development Problems

Predicts from World Tourism Organization show that by 2020, China will become the world's largest tourist destination country. The number of tourists will reach 13,710 million people in time, accounting for 8.6% of the world market share. China's rural tourism is an important part of tourism development. [4] A series of problems arose in the development of rural economy, society, culture and the development of the environment.

*A. Lack of government support*

Some short boards exist in the process of the development such as lack of unified guidance for rural tourism, lack of related law to protect rural tourism operators' interests, lack of the perfect infrastructure, less perfect financial security system support and lack of awareness and action to explore the new world of township village tourism.[5] Meanwhile, most of the new construction of tourism investment are concentrated in the scenic spots and cultural relics.[2] Such common phenomenon that blocked roads, water and power supply shortage can be seen in many places. At the same time, the concerned regulations and the protection of rural traditional culture should be strengthened. Because of the lack of publicity, strategy and management, the characteristics of rural areas are rarely known. In addition, because the lack of effective management standards for rural tourism industry, crossing-management and blanking-management phenomenon also exist, resulting in market disorder, poor quality of products and vicious competition .

*B. Low overall quality of farmers and the sense of rural culture*

Unfortunately, our main operators of rural tourism also have short boards. Lack of professional knowledge, and unawareness of market competition and innovation, make a lot of rural tourism attractions lose the opportunity of publicity and promotion and result in low management level. Most farmers did not engage in rural tourism but left their own hometown to work in other places to get a higher income. Farmers' poor awareness of the environmental protection caused the environment and the sustainable development of rural tourism destroyed. Their management level is also low and not standardized. It directly results in poor quality rural tourism products. The urban dual-structure impact has long-term effects on the development of rural tourism. Farmers have lost the sense of pride and rural culture identity. The traditional culture in rural areas has been destroyed and assimilated by the urban culture. This has caused the farmers to emulate the urban culture and not to dig the essence or the true interpretation of the connotation of rural culture. At the same time, the operators do not pay full attention to protect the environment when they develop the rural tourism. The rural environment is destroyed and the resources are utilized unreasonably in the process of tourism industry development.

*C. Less social support*

Few corporations would like to put investment on rural tourism because it is an industry with long development cycle but slow effects. The development of rural tourism has a series of difficulties in China such as lack of financial support, poor technology and low management. It is difficult to scale the development of rural tourism industry. Moreover, it can't exert its linkage effect on other industries. At the same time, the lack of organization and institution of rural tourism development in China's rural areas is affecting this industry, resulting in the development of rural tourism to be relatively loose and without unified standard.

## V. Suggestion for Chinese Rural Tourism Development

After a systematic summary of the experience of the development of rural tourism in Spain and the analysis of the problems in China, the enlightenment of the development of rural tourism in Spain to the development of rural tourism in China is manifested in the following aspects:

*A. Increasing government support*

Government should play the role of regulation in the development of rural tourism in China, giving the unified plan of rural tourism development combined with local characteristics, highlighting the local rural culture, rural tourism laws and regulations, regulating market order after the implementation of the planning process during the improving and increasing of financial investment, and strengthening technical guidance to farmers to improve the modernization level and efficiency of rural tourism development and utilization of rural resources. The government should help farmers enhance their rural culture identity. At the same time, the government should play the leading role in the propaganda to make more people know well about the rural tourism. The government should also increase investment in rural areas and make lower threshold for farmers' loans to enhance the vitality of sustainable development.

*B. Giving full play to farmers' learning ability*

Farmers and operators should strengthen their own learning ability of innovation and development in the process of the development of rural tourism, in order to make the local rural tourism develop rapidly and effectively. The process of learning about development and management knowledge is not just a copy, but innovation-driven development based on local resources. We should pay attention to the local resources and cultural characteristics, mine resource advantages to develop their own unique tourism and find personalized development method. The development of rural tourism in Spain combines the local history, culture and folk traditions closely. China has a vast territory and owns different customs and abundant local culture all around the world. The living fossils of the local culture include music, architecture, drama, life style and utensils, which provide the impetus for the development of rural tourism. So farmers can develop diversified products with local characteristics and show local rural life to tourists. In the process of developing rural tourism, a large number of rural farmers can be turned into superior talents. Associations, governments and enterprises also need to follow the development of the rural tourism to serve farmers.

*C. Combine social resources advantages*

The advantages of all social resources should be combined to develop rural tourism by concerned government departments. For example, by integrating human resource, natural resource, technical and financial advantages resources through the establishment of the development of rural tourism association, the foundation of agricultural development fund and other forms of support finally bring together talented people to rural development and rural tourism. Entrepreneurs should be an important impetus of economic development in a region. Entrepreneurs will gathered here and bring advanced ideas and capital to promote the development of rural tourism and make it an industry integrating agriculture, industry and business. Through the mega-merger between governments and entrepreneurs, the weakness of the infrastructure can be solved, which is the core of all difficulties. The government guides to build a unified standard which can solve the problem of farmers' financial difficulties and reduce waste, increase the rural resources utilization level of resources and promote the industrialization development of rural tourism, once it is implemented.

*D. Building unique brands*

In China, various natural and human conditions exist in different rural areas. So each rural area can build a respective unique brand based on local characteristics and learn the experience of those successful cases when planning and building rural tourism in rural areas. [4] We will be able to make full use of the ocean resources to develop its products in developing rural tourism on the eastern seaboard to create a brand with the core of the ocean. Generally, because far west of the rural area has good natural conditions, it can utilize the advantages of pollution-free natural resources to create a unique piece of pure land. The geographical position of the central region is superior to others, which is the important place of the military in history, so it can make the best of the rich historical tradition to build ancient culture brands in developing rural tourism. In short, every rural area should fully exploit its cultural connotation in the process of developing rural tourism.

*E. Protecting the rural environment*

As we all know, if the environment is damaged, rural tourism can't be carried out smoothly, because the country's quiet and beautiful environment is an important factor attracting tourists. In order to achieve the aim to protect the environment, firstly, we need to emphasize the importance of the awareness of protecting environment and a scientific and reasonable plan which combines the advantages of the local infrastructures such as roads, water and attractions and the cooperation with the pollution. Secondly, we should strengthen the training of the operators, improve the management mode of the operators and reduce the pollution. Lastly but not least, we can also set up warning signs or protection promoting videos in the country to enhance people's awareness of environmental protection. Certainly, the local government can also introduce relevant regulations on environmental protection and standardize management of the environment to maintain long-term sustainability.

*F. Excavating the essence of rural tourism "culture"*

On 19th CPC National Congress, the Central Committee of the Communist Party of China pointed out that the revival of traditional culture should be fully carried out, which provides good policy opportunities for the development of traditional culture in rural areas. Along with the improvement of living standard and consuming ability, people transfer the tourism consumption demand from sightseeing to leisure and pay more attention to the spiritual enjoyment, which is a great market condition of the development of rural tourism. Compared with the prosperity of the city, the rural area has a great attraction to the tourist with the strong nostalgia which includes "nostalgia in labor", "nostalgia on the tip of the tongue", "quiet nostalgia" and so on. It meets with the taste of tracing back to the homesickness for people who live in a busy city for a long time. The special snack, farming devices, native language, and environment are the media through which people can get a sense of satisfaction. In the process of development of rural tourism, focusing on the excavation of the "local culture",[5] the village can build the external base of rural tourism according to the local characteristics of the housing construction, such as Minshuku and town with characteristics. The village can also make full use of the ancient celebrities, the history stories, allusions, cultural village legends and other materials to excavate their deep meaning to let people feel the soul of rural tourism from their experience and create the country's unique brand and name card. They can vigorously develop tourism products through cultural festivals to maintain the vitality of rural tourism, enhance the visibility of tourism destinations and improve the infrastructure and environment. When creating tourism products with rich cultural connotation, they should pay attention to the participation of tourists to spread the folk custom culture.

## Ⅵ. Conclusions

We need to realize that the development of rural tourism in China has many differences with the one in Spain. So we should take advantage of our unique advantageous conditions to develop and innovate country tourism products with Chinese characteristics, apart from the reference to the experience of Spain. In the process of innovation, the protection of rural traditional culture is emphasized to make the rural tourism condense the modern atmosphere and the traditional Chinese flavor of the countryside.

## ACKNOWLEDGMENT

I would like to express my deepest gratitude to all those who helped me during the writing of the paper. A special acknowledgement should be shown to Professor Ma Liqing , a respectable, responsible and resourceful scholar, from whose lectures I benefited greatly. I shall extend my thanks to Zhang Yingying who had provided me with valuable guidance in every stage of the writing of this thesis. Without her enlightening instruction, impressive kindness and patience, I could not have completed my thesis. I am particularly indebted to Msume who gave me kind encouragement. I am also grateful for the help of Mr. Tian. I also would like to thank all my teachers who have helped me to develop the fundamental and essential academic competence. Finally I wish to give my appreciation to the library assistants who supplied me with reference materials with great values.

## References

[1] Li Lina. The development and enlightenment of rural tourism in Spain[J]. *The Construction of the Old Revolutionary Area*, 2008: 63-64.

[2] Guo Huancheng, and Han Fei, A survey of rural tourism development in China[J]. *Progress in Geography*, 2010, 12: 1597-1605.

[3] Li Chen. Rural tourism in Spain[J]. *Township Enterprises in China*, 2013, 6: 86-87.

[4] Zhang Hongying. The experience of the development of Spanish tourism industry and its enlightenment to China[J]. *Association for Science and Technology Forum (Second Half)*, 2008, 10: 159-160, 121.

[5] Rural tourism development in Valencia, Spain[J]. *Township Enterprises in China*, 2012, 7: 82-83.

[6] Peng Shunsheng. Current situation and development countermeasures of rural tourism in China[J]. *Journal of Yangzhou University (Humanities and Social Sciences)*, 2016, 1: 94-98.

[7] Dai Bin, Zhou Xiaoge, Liang Zhuangping. Comparative study on rural tourism development model between China and foreign countries[J]. *Journal of Jiangxi Science & Technology Normal University*, 2006, 1: 16-18.

[8] José Manuel Cano de Mauvesin Fabaré. *Turismo Cultural:Manueal Del Gesetor de Patrimonio*[M]. Córdoba: Almuzara, 2005.

[9] Ramón de Areces. *50 Años de Turismo*[M]. Madrid: Centro de Estudios, 2002.

[10] Andrés Lorente de las Casas. *Economia y Turismo: Practices*[M]. Adrid: Mc Graw-Hill, 2005.

# An Exploratory Study of Driving Factors of "Asian-ness" Hospitality

Liu Xinru[1*], Nissara Hamloha[2], Tian Sen[3]

**Abstract:** With the rapid development of Asian hospitality industry, top Asian hotel brands plan to deliver Asian hospitality around the world by expanding their brands outside Asia. "Asian-ness" is considered to be the most prominent driving force behind this growth and expansion. This study tried to identify the driving factors of "Asian-ness" hospitality by mixed methods. It was found that facilities are the fundamental requirement for Asian hospitality and people is the driving factor of uniqueness of "Asian-ness". A pyramid of "Asian-ness" hospitality which consists of fundamental requirements, cultural experience and spiritual touch was created.

**Keywords:** "Asian-ness" hospitality; driving factors; Asian cultural values

## Ⅰ. Introduction

The continent of Asia as a whole has been making considerable economic and social progresses and achievements in less than twenty years since the Asian financial crises of 1997. Dadush and Stancil (2010) indicated that by the year of 2050, Asia is going to contribute more than fifty percent of global economy. Asia, traditionally known as an attractive destination, has become a leading source of outbound travel. [1] It was reported that global outbound travel of Asia Pacific had increased 5% in 2015 and the growth will be expected to reach 5% in 2016. [2] At the same time, Asian investors, primarily from China, Hong Kong, Japan and Singapore, represented 43.5% of the cross-border hotel transactions in 2014. Besides investing in western based hotel management companies, Asian-based hotel management companies, such as Shangri-La, Peninsula and Mandarin Oriental, are expanding worldwide. [3] According to the latest release from Shangri-La (2016), there will be a total of 19 exciting new hotels and resorts under development outside Hong Kong, showing company's award-winning Asian style hospitality. [4] The rapid development of

1* Xiamen University of Technology, Xiamen, China; The Hong Kong Polytechnic University, Hong Kong SAR, China. liuxinru@xmut.edu.cn.

2 The Hong Kong Polytechnic University, Hong Kong SAR, China.

3 The Hong Kong Polytechnic University, Hong Kong SAR, China.

Asian hospitality is contributed by the reputation of high quality facility and the uniqueness of excellent service. Compared with western hospitality, which is known for high standard facilities and professional and efficient service, Asian hospitality is more inclined to human relation (Chen & Chon, 2016). [5] This exploratory study is trying to identify the driving factors of "Asian-ness" hospitality through multi-methods approach.

## Ⅱ. Literature Review

*i. Asian cultural values*

There is no doubt that service and culture are fundamentally linked (Shames & Clover, 1994). [6] Asian culture and its values play a crucial role and have a deep root in what Asian hospitality and tourism industry has developed to today's scale and made enormous impact on the growth of global hospitality and tourism industry. Hofstede (2003) defined culture as "a collective phenomenon, shared with people who live or lived within the same social environment, it consists of the unwritten rules of the social game. It is the collective programming of the mind that distinguishes the members of one group or category of people from others" [5]. People are the key factor in culture and value development and retention and "when people are socialized, their thoughts and behaviours are influenced by norms and cultures and formed by a set of values, perceptions, preferences, and behaviours through their families and other key institutions" [6]. There are big differences between eastern culture and western culture where eastern people reflect collectivism and western people represent individualism (Shown in Table 1). Yuan et al. (2011) indicated that "people in the collectivistic culture generally have more hedonic needs (symbolic and experiential needs), whereas people get more utilitarian needs (functional needs) in the individualism culture" [7].

Table 1 Differences between Collectivist and Individualist Societies

| Individualism | Collectivism |
|---|---|
| Everyone is supposed to take care of him or herself and his or her immediate family only | People are born into extended families or clans which protect them in exchange for loyalty |
| "I"—consciousness | "We"—consciousness |
| Right of privacy | Stress on belonging |
| Speaking one's mind is healthy | Harmony should always be maintained |
| Others classified as individuals | Others classified as in-group or out-group |
| Personal opinion expected: one person one vote | Opinions and votes predetermined by in-group |
| Transgression of norms leads to guilt feelings | Transgression of norms leads to shame feelings |
| Languages in which the word "I" is indispensable | Languages in which the word "I" is avoided |
| Purpose of education is learning how to learn | Purpose of education is learning how to do |
| Task prevails over relationship | Relationship prevails over task |

Source: Hofstede (2016).

*A. Confucianism*

In the context of Asian culture, it is indispensable to examine the importance and implication of Confucianism because organizations in Asia develop, operate and improve their businesses on the basis of Confucian values. [8] Different from the Western values, "Confucian values emphasize family and community over the individual, discipline and hierarchy over freedom and equality, and consensus and harmony over diversity and conflict" [9]. Even though Taoism and Buddhism are relatively popular and influential, Confucianism generates much bigger impact and has "become the central gene of society, not as a religion but rather as a mode of thought promoted by institutions at all levels of society" [8].

Confucian values are composed of many virtues and these virtues provide guidance to individual, family, social and business relationships. [8] Out of these many virtues, five virtues are the constant and most prominent ones: benevolence, righteousness, propriety, wisdom and trustworthiness as shown in the Table 2 below.

Table 2 Five Constant Virtues

| Constant Virtue | Philosophical Meaning |
|---|---|
| Benevolence | Love, kindness, friendliness, respect, caring, and helpfulness |
| Righteousness | Being suitable or fit; responsibility and obligation |
| Propriety | Social norms and social values; etiquette and politeness |
| Wisdom | Knowing, rational thinking, ethics, philosophy |
| Trustworthiness | Sincerity, faithfulness, trustworthiness |

Source: Sun et al., 2016.

*B. Benevolence*

Benevolence signifies love, kindness, friendliness, respect, caring and helpfulness and it can be considered as the highest level of human excellence that a person is striving to achieve. Being genuine and sincere are also good qualities of benevolence. Chuang (2005) conducted a quantitative research involving over 480 families and confirmed the importance of benevolence to Asian hospitality. [23]

*C. Righteousness*

Righteousness represents "getting along with others, being reasonable in all dealings, showing reciprocity and altruism, emphasizing mutual profitableness, limiting self-interest". In the case of making business such as Asian hospitality industry, this manifests that the balanced values and benefits should be well taken into considerations between hospitality operators, guests and other parties involved. [8]

*D. Propriety*

Propriety guides and governs social norms, values, etiquette and politeness in all aspects of the society. As pointed out by Sun et al. (2016), "individuals who adhere to propriety will abide by the rules of society, respect local culture, have sound internal managerial systems and responsible images, and will be attracted to other entities that similarly value propriety" [8]. In Asian hospitality, propriety is of great importance and holds a critical position in terms guest services and experiences development and delivery. The basic forms of propriety in Asian countries can start from and be found in hotel staff greetings and grooming based on their cultural origins.

*E. Wisdom*

Wisdom indicates the capability of making distinction between right and wrong behaviours of human being by using and practicing intelligence, judgment and morality. People with wisdom reflect sound knowledge, know-how and skills and aim to pursue excellence in what they are doing and planning.

*F. Trustworthiness*

Trustworthiness contains sincerity, faithfulness and a strong commitment to moral integrity. According to Sun et al. (2016), Zhang et al., emphasized that trustworthiness is the "essence of interpersonal relationships, provides a foundation for social survival, and suggests that adhering individuals will exhibit and be attracted to entities that fulfil their promises in all behaviours and to all stakeholders". This is particularly true to Asian hospitality where mutual faithfulness and trust are the key to successful relationship between hospitality enterprises and guests and crucial to encourage guest patronage and repeated and loyal guests. [8]

*ii. Other relevant cultural values*

Besides, Asian hospitality culture is greatly influenced by other Asian culture such as Yin and Yang dynamic. Yin and Yang, two basic component of universe, are represented by gold, wood, water, fire and earth. Li indicates, for Asian people especially East Asians, "this way of viewing and living in the world is so natural to them that their food, music, arts, sports, medicine, even science and personal creativity are all influenced by this worldview". Another influential and unique culture value for Asian hospitality is Feng Shui, which is perceived as a magical link between man and the landscape. It represents that people share a fate with nature and earth. For Asian hospitality, Feng Shui undoubtedly plays a very important role in hospitality industry including location decision, exterior physical design, interior physical design, marketing and employees etc. [10]

*iii. Asian hospitality service and characteristics*

Asian hospitality is backward from Asian culture in transferring service and shaping people's involvement. It varies from region to region because of different ethnicities, culture, relief, customs, religions as well as languages. [11] Scholars examined Asian hospitality from different angels. By comparing the cultural difference between west and east, Kolesnikov-Jesop (2010) described Asian hospitality involves more cultural elements, emotional connection as well as intangible words. [12] Through investigation from guests, staffs and companies aspects, Chen & Chon (2016) suggested the core values of Asian hospitality include respect, helpfulness, courtesy, sincerity and humility. [5] A successful service has a high yardstick requiring service provider's behaviour to match the customers' expectations all the time "under the conditions of time pressure and inter-customer variability" [13]. Started from guests' perception, Chan and Pang (2015) summarized eight service dimensions of Asian hospitality through observation the interaction between the service providers and customers, including authenticity, caring, control, courtesy, formality, friendliness, personalisation and promptness. These dimensions can be seen as an extension of characteristics of Asian culture. [11]

Based on the basic Asian cultural values, other researchers created a framework showing the relationship between Asian cultural values and characteristics of Asian hospitality. [14] The model can be expounded to 3 main premises. First, Asian values are innate and then honed, making them natural for Asians to apply in business practice especially the hospitality sector. Second, hospitality business in Asia is still an emerging sector with a very bright potential for expansion. Therefore, honing world-class capital in the industry is an advantage, owning to the big population. Lastly, the nature of Asian people with regards to obedience and respect for the elders makes them easier to observe, train, and excel in the service industry.

Asian hospitality nicely fuses unique cultural elements into service while deeply considering interpersonal relationships, and the value of every person, in the work field. It was noted by Wan and Chon (2010) that majority of Asian hospitality brands tend to embody a certain vibe of exoticism, antiquity, and cultural heritage, and personal touch. [15] Suh, Moon, Han and Ham (2015) also noted that while visuals definitely help, intangible factors also have a large bearing in customers' satisfaction in the field of hospitality management. Customers evaluate and leave feedback regarding their experience, guided by all the five senses, and with this, Asian hospitality is best presented by localization. [15]

Furthermore, Chon (2016) emphasized the exceptional characteristic of Asian hospitality which is making intangible service physically available. [16] While it is mostly positive, it also opens challenges to marketers in terms of creativity in developing their products and services, promoting it, and competitively pricing it. [17]

It was defined that "service is any act or performance that one party can offer to another that is essentially intangible and does not result in the ownership of anything" [18]. A correlation has been noted about guests' expectation on the product performance, and their post-consumption evaluation. It has been found that higher levels of performance in turn leads to higher evaluations. The performance is related to interaction between customers and service providers. This experience of a service either tangible or intangible becomes one of the driving factors in the customer's evaluation on the quality of service rendered [19]. Abundant human interaction in hospitality services, especially with the involvement of frontline staffs from a diversified background, also affects the quality of service, resulting in uncontrollable outcomes, and even possible mistakes. [13]

Comparing the 3 frameworks of Asian hospitality service and characteristics, it was found that the first model focused on the nature of interaction between the guests and the service provider while the second framework focused on the nature of Asian people and the its effect to their performance (advantage and disadvantage) in the global arena. Lastly, the third one emphasized the factors that drive Asian hospitality to stand out among other regions in the international market.

## Ⅲ. Research Method

Qualitative research is widely used for understanding a phenomena in various and supplementary ways. [20] As there is no standard feature of "Asian-ness" hospitality, a qualitative approach therefore was employed in this study. In this research, data was collected through three different methods shown as below:

(1) Observations from four Asian hotels, namely Hotel ICON, The Peninsula Hong Kong, Dusit Thani Bangkok and Mandarin Oriental Bangkok;

(2) Primary data analysis through seminars from hospitality professionals, in-depth interviews with hotel guests;

(3) Contents analysis of latest 10 comments of four Asian hotels in TripAdvisor started August 1, 2016.

Data were first labelled and grouped before establishing a formal encoding table. The initial coding table were built by using former literature in Asian-ness hospitality and Asian cultural values. Then, based on Asian culture theory mentioned in the literature review part, the encoding was done according to unique Asian culture and their influence on hospitality industry. Then, a final framework for driving factors of Asian-ness hospitality was developed accordingly.

## Ⅳ. Findings

*i. TripAdvisor comments analysis*

A total of 40 online reviews for 4 Asian hotels from TripAdvisor started from August 1, 2016 were selected. As this study was exploring the driving factors of Asian-ness hospitality, only positive comments were analysed sentence by sentence. After labelling and grouping the comments, total six key attributes and their frequency were generated accordingly shown in Table 3. It was found that the most frequent mentioned factor is hotel facilities such as "High-tech facilities", "Swimming pool", "Fantastic view", "Full amenities", "Cleanness", "Gym", etc. Another frequent mentioned factor is related to people such as "Warmed greeting at arrival", "Sincere staff", "Smiling face", "Feeling of family" and "Remember guest's name" etc. The third factor is service which includes "Attentiveness", "Limousine transfer", "Travel advice" and "Early arrival arrangement". "Food and Beverage", "Cultural elements" and "Atmosphere" are another three factors frequently mentioned by guests. This result confirmed the previous study that the Asian hospitality can be delivered through hardware, atmosphere, service and good food etc. [15] By examining the sub-attributes from another angel, it was found the factor of service can be linked to service provider. Consequently, people is the key factor generated from the comments. In accordance with previous research, human capital, which is greatly influenced by Asian cultures, beliefs, religions and values, is one of the advantage of Asian hospitality. [14]

Table 3 Summary of Positive Comments and Its Frequency Counts

| Key Factors | Attributes | Frequency |
|---|---|---|
| Facilities | High-tech facilities, swimming pool, fantastic view, modern amenities, clean rooms, gym, mini bar, handy phone, special room, cleanness, spa | 64 |
| People (Feeling of home) | Warmed greeting at arrival, sincere staff, smiling face, young staffs, remember guest's name, host-guest interaction, feeling of family, small talk with staffs, meeting GM | 54 |
| Service | Attentiveness, limousine transfer, travel advise, early arrival arrangement, attention to children | 36 |
| Food & Beverage | Huge selection of food, breakfast, themed afternoon tea, local food, fresh food, bar | 31 |
| Cultural elements | Experience local culture, stylish design, historical colonial color, surrounding environment, Thai hospitality, Author's lounge, grooming | 27 |
| Atmosphere | A symbol of luxury and elegant, music, fresh flowers, stylish design, decoration | 21 |

*ii. Hotel mission analysis*

In order to learn the service philosophy of Asian hotels, missions of four Asian hotels were examined accordingly (Shown in Table 4). It was found that these missions are focus on "customer experience" and "people". Taking the example of Shangri-La Hotels and Resorts who is the pioneer in transferring and exporting Asian hospitality to western destinations such as Vancouver, London and Paris, it is always known and remembered for its Asian origins embedded with cultural and service uniqueness. A service from the heart is a vivid reflection of Asian hospitality which starts from caring people. As also emphasized by Mr. Stephen Darling, Regional Vice President that "for loyal Shangri-La guests, the expectation of service style and standards is based on their Asian experience. We must translate that to the North American market through our team" [21].

Table 4 Missions from Four Asian Hotels

| Hotel | Mission |
|---|---|
| Shangri-La | To delight our guests every time by creating engaging experiences straight from our heart |
| Hotel ICON | To train and develop the next generation of elite hotel managers |
| Dusit Thani | Exceeding customers' expectations with each and every experience |
| Mandarin Oriental | To completely delight and satisfy our guests. We are committed to making a difference every day; continually getting better to keep us the best |

*Source*: Shangri-La, 2016; Hotel ICON, 2016; Dusit Thani, 2016; Mandarin Oriental, 2016.

### *iii. Site inspection*

Site inspection from five Asian hotels plus one western hotel was conducted in August 2016. In order to generate the uniqueness of Asian hospitality and explore its driving factors, comprehensive date was collected through interviews, professional seminars as well as observation. It was well noted that Asian-ness existed in many aspects of Asian hospitality business operation and management ranging from hotel design and decoration, staff greeting and grooming, food and beverage presentation to guest service details delivery. The elements were presented and summarized in Table 5 and Table 6.

Table 5 Summary of Observed Elements

| Key Factors | Sub-attribute | Example of Evidence |
|---|---|---|
| People | Sincere greeting; Warmth welcoming; Product knowledge ; Helpfulness; Sincerity; Formality | e.g. Welcome drinks, flowers (Garland), fruits and letter from GM; Personalized and professional travel advice; Appropriate manner showing respects and sincerity etc. |
| Facilities | Luxury facilities; Stylish design | e.g. First class facilities; Spacious room; High-technology in-room amenities; Elegant lobby; Gym facilities; Spa facilities; Swimming pool etc. |
| Cultural elements | Decoration; Design; Customs | e.g. Gable Apax (a part of temple roof) decorated in room; Feng Shui consideration in the interior design and exterior design (Door Gods at the gate of Peninsula); Traditional customs; Thai greeting with traditional Thai drinks and Garland; Author lounge in Mandarin Oriental etc. |
| Food and beverage | Local and traditional cuisine; Variety of food | e.g. Thai restaurant in hotel offering contemporary Thai cuisine with combination of traditional flavour and modern technique; Themed afternoon tea in the Peninsula Hong Kong; Cuisine concierge in Dusit Thani; Huge selection of breakfast and buffet in Hotel ICON etc. |
| Service | Attentiveness | e.g. 3 layers of curtain in Dusit Thani; Floor butler at Mandarin Oriental; Updated notice (Typhoon or Alcoholic drinks policy) presented in-room etc. |
| Atmosphere | Smell; Music; Stylish design; Florist; | e.g. A plenty of flowers used in decoration; Signature smell; Music performance in hotel lobby; |

Table 6 Summary of Professional Seminars

| Key factors | Example of evidence |
| --- | --- |
| People (Families) | e.g. The Peninsula Hong Kong tries its best to engage their staffs through different activities and community service; Dusit Thani tries to build trust between management and staff especially in the difficult period of business; Dusit Thani adapts empowerment strategy; Hotel ICON; Hotel ICON treats people resources as human capital for hotel's development; Mandarin Oriental creates cross cultural training for its staffs etc. |
| Management | e.g. Family owned business requires long term planning; The management team tries to establish a sense of belonging within the organization etc. |
| Innovation | e.g. The Peninsula Hong Kong focuses on technology improvement and facilities upgrade; Hotel ICON has Tomorrow Room for innovative purpose etc. |

First, people is the key for delivery of Asian hospitality. Upon arrival, staff demonstrated to tourists their warm welcome with sincere smile, and welcoming drinks or flowers. They can explain the hotel products and service confidently and proudly. They were helpful and friendly, and they respected the guests at appropriate distance. Although they were shy, sincerity and kindness expressed from the bottom of the heart can easily create an emotional connection with guests. From the management point of view, when asked about the key factor of success, the management all mentioned about the people. The trust between the management team and employees, and the commitment between employees and the hotel are driving factors of Asian hospitality not only in the service delivery aspect but also in the operation and management. This might be influenced by Confucian values which signifies love, kindness, friendliness, respect, caring, responsibility, obligation, sincerity, faithfulness and trustworthiness. "Family" is the most important factor in Asian society which influences the Asian hotel operation greatly.

Second, first class facilities with high-tech amenities and high quality and huge selection of food and beverage are essential for Asian hospitality. For example, the Thai restaurant in Dusit Thani Bangkok combines modern techniques and traditional Thai flavour to create contemporary dishes for guests. All-in-one control pad offered in the Peninsula Hong Kong provides huge convenience for guests. Detail oriented design such as shoes box, third layer curtain can make guests' stay more comfortable. Good facilities and food and beverage are the fundamental expectation for luxury hotel guests. In accordance with previous findings, facilities are the most frequent mentioned factor in the positive comments from TripAdvisor.

In addition, cultural elements were fitted into every single detail in Asian hotels. In terms of tangible aspect, guests can experience local culture showing faith or relief through interior and exterior design and decoration. For example, the suite room in Dusit Thani Bangkok is decorated by a piece of Gable Apax, which is on the corner-top of Thai temple roof; in the gate of the Peninsula Hong Kong, there are two photos of traditional Chinese Door Gods, to keep ghost away and protect the family inside; [22] traditional Asian customs elements are introduced into the hotel staff's uniform as well; welcoming drinks offered in Dusit Thani Bangkok called butterfly pea are traditional Thai drink; moreover, the flowers called Thai Garland presented to the guests upon arrival are a most used item for praying in front of the Buddha's image, monk, Thai Royal Monarchy and elders to show respects to guests. Cultural elements can also be found through intangible aspect such as smell, music etc. This confirmed the previous study related to relationship of culture and hospitality such as Fengshui and hotel development, decoration and operation.

Moreover, Asian hospitality places a strong focus on staff service training and staff enhancement which is well testified through different aspect such as product knowledge, efficiency, attentiveness as well as professions.

## V. Discussion

"Asian-ness" represents the perfect harmony of guest services and exquisite facilities and products. It has been truly felt and reflected from the stay and dining experiences of Hotel ICON, Peninsula Hong Kong, Dusit Thani Bangkok and Mandarin Oriental Bangkok, Asian hospitality is evolving within the "Asian-ness" hospitality pyramid that contains three adjacent fundamental requirements, cultural experience and spiritual touch (see Figure 1). Fundamental requirements are inclusive of hospitality hardware facilities, food and beverage, interior and exterior design and amenities. Cultural experiences represent the cultural elements involved in service, facilities as well as management; while spiritual touch is the highest level in this pyramid being the emotional connection and interaction which are influenced by relief and culture rooted in the history and society. The three levels are internally linked starting from fundamental requirements to cultural experiences and finally to reach spiritual touch. All those are related to the Five Relations and Ten Duties in the *Book of Rites*, which describe the relational behaviours and duties of people correlated the religion, belief and culture of Asian people. Thus, people is the driving factor for the uniqueness of "Asian-ness" hospitality.

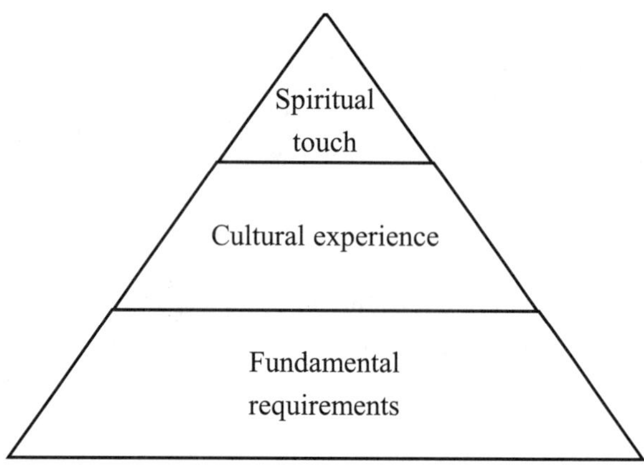


Figure 1 Pyramid of "Asian-ness" Hospitality

The important driving factors of Asian hospitality include impeccable guest services, quality facilities, enriched cultural dimensions, localized food and beverage offerings and the thriving and continuous spirit of innovation. In comparison with the literature review and with the support of the data analysis from this study, the most influential driving factor of "Asian-ness" lies with the factor of people and the people are all involved stakeholders consisting of hospitality operators, developers and owners. People is the core element influencing the whole service experience. Employee are treated as family members where employers gain loyalty from them in return. Asian people, who love stable life, look for long-run relationship, respect elderly people and pursuit harmony, have stronger commitment to hotel and team. The unique and strong beliefs and values such as Confucian rooted in the culture and religions are the markers and differentiators of "Asian-ness" from western hospitality and deeply impact the ways and depth that Asian hospitality services are being generated and delivered. The widely recognized and practiced of Confucian constant key virtues of benevolence, righteousness, propriety, wisdom and trustworthiness contribute to the uniqueness of "Asian-ness". The Yin-Yang dynamics and Feng Shui reveal the special features and impactful forces underlined in Asian hospitality from a cultural point of view.

## Ⅵ. Conclusion and Recommendations

Following the development and maturity of European and American hospitalities in the past decade, Asian hospitality started to develop at a fast pace and strive to lead the way not only in Asia but also more importantly into other non-Asian countries and regions. "Asian-ness" is considered to be the most prominent driving force behind this growth and expansion. Shangri-La Hotels and Resorts, Mandarin Oriental Hotels, Banyan Tree, Peninsula Hotels are among the pioneers to heavily promote and exhibit "Asian-ness" on the global hospitality stage.

"Asian-ness" and Asian hospitality is about being a host to other parts of the world and this requires a continuous focus on meeting and exceeding the needs and expectations of guests, associates and management and feature strong local respect, effective cultural preservation facilitated and supported by sustainable service quality delivery and excellence with Asian cultural and spiritual elements.

With the qualitative interviews and observations of four hotels in Hong Kong and three hotels in Bangkok together with TripAdvisor comments analysis of eight large hotel groups of both Asian hotel companies and western hotel companies, the three levels of fundamental cultural and spiritual requirements, constitute the cornerstones of "Asian-ness" and Asian hospitality with the factor of people of hospitality operators, developers and owners at all levels being the most important driving factor in addition to all the other key factors.

To effectively and efficiently grow and apply "Asian-ness" and Asian hospitality into the rest of the world, it is critical to integrate with local requirements and give serious considerations to distinctive cultural differences like what Shangri-La and Peninsula have been pursuing. Both new and legendary Asian hotel brands must make investments and efforts to "strike a balance between creating home and away, the familiar and the exotic" in order to achieve Asian hospitality brands expansion success operationally and financially.

It is suggested that more studies can be carried out to ascertain how younger generations perceive, react and enhance "Asian-ness" from the perspectives of both an industry professional and a guest. Meanwhile, it will be of good benefit to assess and determine the role played by information technology and how information technology can contribute to the journey of sustainable development of "Asian-ness".

## ACKNOWLEDGMENT

This project is supported by Fujian Social Funding (No. FJ2015JDZ042) Strategic Construct of Fujian Sea Silk Road Cultural Tourism.

## References

[1] Dadush U, Stancil B. The G20 in 2050[J]. *International Economic Bulletin*, 2009.

[2] Berlin ITB. ITB world travel trends report 2015/2016[R]. Berlin: Messe Berlin GmbH, 2015.

[3] Roth H, Fishbin M. *Global Hospitality Insights: Top Thoughts for 2015*[M]. New York: EY, 2015.

[4] Shangri-La Hotels and Resorts. The future of distinctive luxury[EB/OL]. http://www.shangri-la.com/corporate/press-room/future-developments/, 2016.

[5] Hofstede G. *Culture's Consequences: Comparing Values, Behaviors, Institutions and Organizations Across Nations* [M]. London: Sage publications, 2003: 7-12

[6] Glover W G, Shames G W. World-class service[J]. *Hospitality Review*, 1988, 6(2): 6.

[7] Yuan X, Song T H, Kim S Y. Cultural influences on consumer values, needs and consumer loyalty behaviour: East Asian culture versus East European culture [J]. *African Journal of Business Management*, 2011, 5(30): 12184.

[8] Sun Yang, Garrett T C, Kim K M. Do Confucian principles enhance sustainable marketing and customer

equity? [J]. *Journal of Business Research,* 2016, 69(9): 3772-3779.

[9] Inoguchi T, Shin D C. The quality of life in Confucian Asia: from physical welfare to subjective well-being[J]. *Social Indicators Research*, 2009, 92(2): 183-190.

[10] Hobson P J S. Fengshui: its impacts on the Asian hospitality industry[J]. *International Journal of Contemporary Hospitality Management*, 1994, 6(6): 21-26.

[11] Piuchan M, Pang L. Service experience dimensions in Asian hospitality: a case study of hotels in Thailand and Hong Kong [Z]. Asia Pacific CHRIE Conference, Phuket, 2016:15-18.

[12] Kolesenikov-Jessop S. Asian hotel brands make the journey to Europe [EB/OL].http://www.nytimes.com/2010/01/23/business/global/23hotels.html.

[13] Lee Y L, Sparks B. Appraising tourism and hospitality service failure events: a Chinese perspective[J]. *Journal of Hospitality & Tourism Research*, 2007.

[14] Sucher W, Pusiran A K, Dhevabanchachai N, et al. The influence of Asian cultural values in the Asian hospitality services[C]. The 11th APacCHRIE Conference, 2013: 21-24.

[15] Chin D, Pinthong C, Kang Y, et al. What makes Asian hospitality unique? An exploratory analysis, differences in willingness to pay for a restaurant menu price according to hedonic variables [Z]. 14th APacCHRIE Conference, Bangkok, 2016: 24-28.

[16] Chon K. Class notes for Asian paradigm in hospitality management[Z]. Hong Kong Polytechnic University School of Hotel and Tourism Management, 2016.

[17] Reddy A C, Buskirk B D, Kaicker A. Tangibilizing the intangibles: some strategies for services marketing [J]. *Journal of Services Marketing*, 1993, 7(3): 13-17.

[18] Kotler P, Kotler P. *Marketing Management: Analysis, Planning, and Control* [M]. New Jersey: Prentice Hall, 1976.

[19] Grönroos C. A service quality model and its marketing implications [J]. *European Journal of marketing*, 1984, 18(4): 36-44.

[20] Lincoln Y S, Denzin N K. Introduction: entering the field of qualitative research [M]. Denzin N K, Lincoln Y S. *The Handbook of Qualitative Research*, Thousand Oaks, Calif.: Sage Publications, 1994.

[21] Gale D. Shangri-La tigers export Asian hospitality[J]. *Hotels by Marketing & Technology Group*, 2009, 42(1).

[22] Chinese International Travel Service Co., Ltd. Worshipping door gods: a Chinese Spring Festival Custom [EB/OL]. http://www.cits.net/china-travel-guide/worshipping-door-gods-a-chinese-spring-festival-custom.html.

[23] Chuang Yao-Chia. Effects of interaction pattern on family harmony and well-being: test of interpersonal theory, relational-models theory, and Confucian ethics[J]. *Asian Journal of Social Psychology*, 2005, 8(3): 272-291.

# A Research on Leisure and Leisure Consumption

Wu Zumei[1*], Zhao Xiaoning[2]

**Abstract:** The entry to the 21st century opens a new era of leisure. Thus to pursue a healthy and active leisure life is absolutely critical to every one. This paper begins with the nature & definition of leisure based on the related given literature review on leisure. In the thesis spiritual consumption is emphasized as the core of leisure and leisure consumption. Qualitative and quantitative methods are applied in this paper. Such three factors as leisure time, spare disposable income and leisure motivation are considered as the premises of leisure consumption. Then the thesis analyzes the leisure effects on a person's overall development, on a nation as well as on the whole society. Finally on the basis of the current leisure consumption situations in China, this paper puts forward that Chinese government should take some measures to guide high-quality, sustainable and spiritual-oriented leisure consumption.

**Keywords:** leisure; leisure consumption; spiritual leisure; developmental leisure; sustainable leisure

## Ⅰ. Introduction

What is leisure? Let's begin with the definition and interpretations of Chinese expression "休闲". "休", pronounced as "xiu" in Chinese Pinyin means "A person takes a rest leaning on a tree", emphasizing the harmony between nature and human beings. "闲", pronounced as "xian" in Chinese Pinyin, once anciently written as "閒", with " a moon in a door", indicates the mild moonlight pouring upon the courtyard, signifying artistic conception that people enjoy the glorious full moon in a quiet, sweet and marvelous atmosphere.[1] It presents such a beautiful picture which all of people look forward to. Leisure has its special cultural content and distinctive value from Chinese traditional definitions. It expresses a dialectical relationship between labor and relaxation in the course of human being's existence.

1* Sichuan University, Chengdu, China; Hubei University for Nationalities, Enshi, China. 1585395956@qq.com.

2 Sichuan University, Chengdu, China; Southwest University for Nationalities, Chengdu, China.

## Ⅱ. Literature Review

It is until in the industrial society that leisure has its modern sense in the nineteenth century when it was developed in a certain high degree. In the period of more than 100 years some scholars and experts did some researches as to leisure from different perspectives widely and deeply. For its definitions, it is mainly defined from the four most typical perspectives as follows:

*i. From the perspective of time*

In 1862 in Marx's philosophic hand script *The Theory of Surplus Value*, Marx proposed that free time, which belongs to non-labor time when a person could control by himself, should be the main source for the exercise of his talents. [2] In Marx's theoretical system on leisure, he just touched upon leisure item by criticizing the odds and discovering the new world metaphorically. [3] Philosopher Aristotle in ancient Greece named leisure as available time (De Grazia, 1961). In 1899 in Veblen's works he put forward that leisure was the time excluding work time, which new born leisure classes or statuses spent on those valueless creation activities and could spend on product consumption and could act as freely as possible.

In China, Professor Deng Chongqing pointed out that leisure means free time. Furthermore, it is legal time excluding the part of meeting the normal needs time, and in the time of leisure consumption he or she would earn nothing.[4] At the same time he or she will pay more on his or her leisure. Professor Lou Jiajun [5] considered that leisure is the total amount of one's leisure time. Professor Yang Zhenzhi et al. proposed that leisure refer to the all relaxation activities during one's spare time, which includes two aspects: time and activity in fact. [6] This point will not be repeated in the following discussion.

*ii. From the perspective of activity*

Tao Peizhi pointed out that leisure meant "people can achieve the spiritual leisure state through certain leisure activities in their spare/leisure time"[7]. Zhang Guangrui and Song Rui thought that if leisure can be called leisure, it must meet the following two requirements. Firstly, people could choose to engage in some preferred activities in their controllable time freely and willingly. Secondly, those people can gain spiritual satisfaction, self realization and development in engaging those activities. [8]

*iii. From the perspective of the state of existence and internal mind*

Aristotle (De Grazia, 1961 ) labeled leisure as a life state with absence of the necessity of being occupied. Pepoor (1952), a Sweden Catholic philosopher named leisure as a state of thought or spirit in his book *the Basis of Leisure*. He presented three characteristics as follows: Firstly, a state of soul peace and calmness; secondly, a state of meditation; and thirdly, acceptance of the "gift of God"[9]. Among the three characteristics, the state of soul peace and calmness of thought or spirit was considered the essence of leisure, which would be valued most.

John Kelly, a professor at the University of Illinois in America defined leisure should be considered as a process of "being a person", together with the main existence space of individual and social development task to be completed, and the persistent and important life stage of development. Leisure was a kind of freedom that aimed at "existence" and "to be" for oneself and for society. [10] Ma Huidi, the director of China Academy of Art and Chinese Leisure Research Center, discussed leisure in her book named *Leisure: the Beautiful Human Beings' Spirit Home.* She pointed out that "Leisure is a lofty realm of the human spirit; leisure is the result of human introspection and meditation. Leisure is the state of the life form. In general sense, it refers to two aspects: one is to eliminate physical fatigue, the other is spiritual solace. Leisure is a happy state of doing a loved thing".

*iv. From the perspective of all the above aspects*

Jeffrey Goby, the director of health and human development of leisure research department in Pennsylvania State University defined leisure from such four aspects as time, activity, state of existence and state of mind. "Leisure is a relatively free life liberated from external pressure of cultural and physical environment, which can make the individual feel valuable in his delight instinctively, drive actions in the heart of love, and provide a basis for beliefs"(as in e.g. [10]).

Based on the above interpretations, this paper just defines leisure as the follows. Leisure refers to the choice of preferences in people's discretionary non-work time, for leisure and comfort in psychological and mental experience, in order to achieve the purpose of relaxing psychosomatically, thus to promote the comprehensive development freely.

## Ⅲ. Premises of Leisure and Leisure Consumption

Leisure is closely related to consumption. Leisure may result in consumption activities. And consumption activities may include leisure. Of course they also have distinct differences. We think that the main difference is that: leisure values more on state, activities and state of mind, while leisure consumption values more on present implementation ways, process and methods of leisure.

In a narrow sense, Leisure consumption is consumers' behaviors in their spare time, which is aimed at improving consumers' taste and culture, meeting the physical and mental pleasure and satisfaction to a higher level of leisure demand. [11] Leisure consumption is a part of the modern way of the advanced form of consumptions. And leisure consumption is a process of economic activity of leisure products and related services in the leisure time consumption[12]. Free time, redundant money and leisure motivation are the premises of leisure consumption.

*i. Free time: a key point for leisure consumption*

With the rapid development of modern society, the value for cost per unit time is getting higher and higher. Time has become scarce resource for consumers, so that consumers are especially sensitive to rigid time constraints. When it comes to the relationship between labor and leisure, Ma and Yu (2008) thought that "the development history of human beings indicates that work time and leisure time are always a shift in the dialectical relationship". Labor can create value. In reverse, the improvement of labor value in the course of leisure may react on labor productivity. [13] When Marx referred to consumers' spending power, he proposed that "the ability of consumption should be the premise of consumption". Saving work time is equal to the increase in free time, which makes the individual's full development feasible. [14] In China, since 2007 the Chinese government formally has promulgated the "workers paid vacation" system. To this day the number of holidays has already readjusted up to nearly 125 days or so. If the number of holidays is added together, it nearly takes up about one third of a full year. Chinese government has already promulgated its citizen statutory festivals constantly to increase festival days. The intent is to increase people's leisure time. This provides the citizen guaranteed system security in spending leisure time.

*ii. Disposable income: premise for leisure consumption*

In an economic sense, there is a proportional relationship between the actual income and the potential leisure spending power. High income is a vital premise to higher leisure spending power. Here the income security for leisure consumption includes both consumer savings and current income, even the future expected income. Higher current income provides potential leisure consumption. Future expected income guarantees inter temporal consumption & overdraft leisure consumption in advance. One of the key factors for residents' leisure consumption is disposable income per capita of urban households and net income per capita of rural households. In order to illustrate this problem evidently, we just take China as an example. The data issued by the National Bureau of Statistics indicate that there exists upward trend in disposable income per capita of Chinese households ranging from 2006 to 2016 on the whole. According to 2006-2016 statistics of the national economy and social development statistical data issued by the National Bureau of Statistics, [15]-[16] some leisure related economic indexes are presented in Table 1:

Table 1　Chinese Leisure Economic Index: 2006-2016

| Year | Disposable income per capita of Chinese urban household (RMB ¥) | The net income of rural household per capita in China (RMB ¥) | Engel's Coefficient of Chinese Urban households (%) | Engel's Coefficient of Chinese Rural households (%) |
|---|---|---|---|---|
| 2006 | 11,759.5 | 3,587 | 35.8 | 43.0 |
| 2007 | 13,785.8 | 4,140.4 | 36.3 | 43.1 |
| 2008 | 15,780.8 | 4,760.6 | 37.9 | 43.7 |
| 2009 | 17,174.7 | 5,153.2 | 36.5 | 41.0 |

(To be continued)

(Continued Table 1)

| Year | Disposable income per capita of Chinese urban household (RMB ¥) | The net income of rural household per capita in China (RMB ¥) | Engel's Coefficient of Chinese Urban households (%) | Engel's Coefficient of Chinese Rural households (%) |
|---|---|---|---|---|
| 2010 | 19,109.4 | 5,919 | 35.7 | 41.1 |
| 2011 | 21,809.8 | 6,977.3 | 36.3 | 40.4 |
| 2012 | 24,565 | 7,917 | 36.2 | 39.3 |
| 2013 | 26,955 | 8,896 | 35 | 37.7 |
| 2014 | 28,844 | 9,892 | 34.2 | 37.8 |
| 2015 | 31,195 | 11,422 | 34.8 | 37.1 |
| 2016 | 33,616 | 12,363 | 29.3 | 32.2 |

( Source: comprehensively based on the statistics provided by Chinese National Statistics Bureau on the national economy and social development)

First let's talk about the disposable income per capita of Chinese urban households and the net income of rural households per capita in China. According to Table 1 we can find that both the disposable income per capita of urban residents and the net income per capita of rural residents increased year by year despite of income gap between the great disparity of urban and rural residents. What are the reasons? The current prosperity maybe mainly attributes to the continuous & further improvement of market economy, Chinese government's reform-open policy as well as residents' peaceful and satisfactory life and work. Both of the city and countryside in China are now taking on a new look.

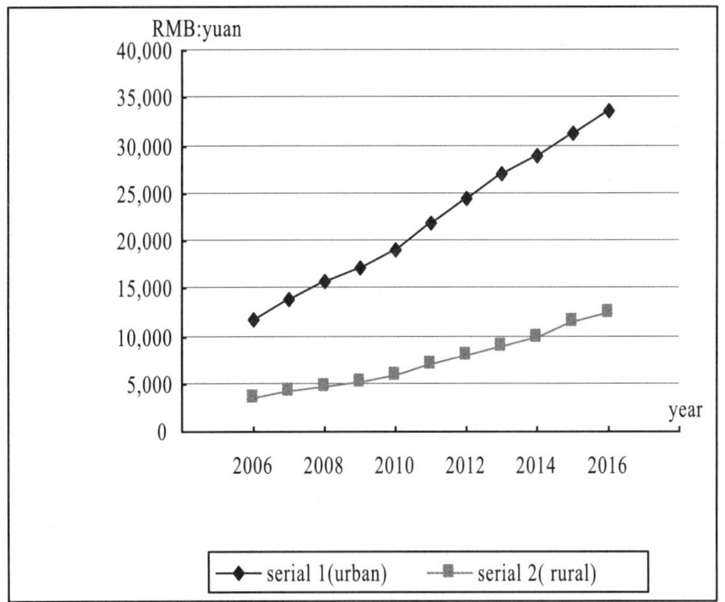


Figure 1 Disposable Income Per Capita of Chinese Urban Households and Net Income Per Capita of Rural Households from 2006 to 2016 in China

( Source: Based on the data on the disposable income per capita of Chinese urban and rural households in Table 1)

Based on the data of the two income columns in Table 1, we can draw Figure 1 as follows. And accordingly, the graphs of the disposable income per capita of urban residents and the net income per capita of rural residents slope upward.

Engel's coefficient is another important indicator to reflect the level of consumption and consumption quality. If the personal disposable income is lower, the Engel's coefficient will be higher, which indicates the lower level of consumption and consumption quality, and vice versa. Still take China as an example, also based on the data of Engel's coefficient column in Table 1, we can draw Figure 2 as follows:

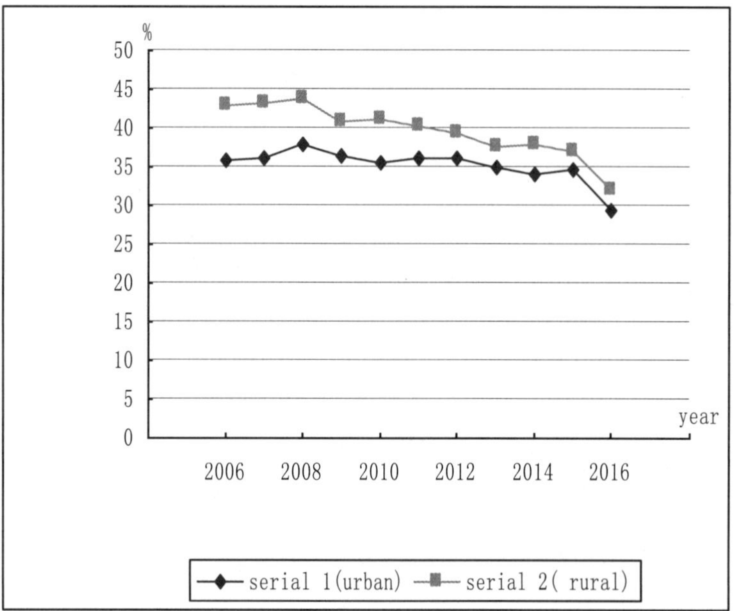


Figure 2 Engel's Coefficient of Urban Households and Rural Households from 2006 to 2016 in China

(Source: based on the data on the Engel's coefficient of urban and rural households in Table 1)

According to Figure 2, it's easy to find that family Engel's coefficients of overall urban and rural residents slope downward constantly, and that the Engel's coefficient of rural residents family is significantly higher than the Engel's coefficient of urban households. Within the recent 11 years from 2006 to 2016, the Engle's coefficient of urban households ranges from 35.8% to 29.3%. According to the standards proposed by the Food and Agriculture Organization of United Nations, more than 59% of Engel's coefficient indicates absolute poverty. 50%-59% of that indicates that the family has enough income to spend on food and clothes. 40%-49% of that indicates fairly well-off. 30%-39% indicates affluence. Less than 30 means utmost affluence. We can see urban residents' living standard has reached utmost affluence. Rural residents family Engel's coefficient ranges from 43.7% to 32.2% which indicates that rural residents' living standard has reached the affluence. Both per capita disposable income of urban households and the per capita net income of rural households have risen steadily. Both the family Engel's coefficients of overall urban and rural residents are generally on the decline. The fact illustrates that residents' life quality has been rising. To some extent, residents' consumption will shift from necessities items to development-oriented consumptions, which provides the possibilities and the basis for upgrading the leisure consumption structure. Of course we can not deny there are still a few exceptions. Maybe some of exceptions occurred because of natural disasters such as the violent 5·12 Wenchuan Earthquake in 2008, heavy snowstorm in south China in the same year and several debris flow in some places of China in recent years, which caused great loss to Chinese economy. On such occasions the whole country had to rescue those affected people in the calamity by providing them food and drinks, which definitely made Engels coefficient rebound a little.

Of course, owing to the improvement of overall citizens' education, health care, pension and the promotion of other social security system as well as factors influenced by all kinds of financial assets in interest rate, people's consumption concept is now changing. People are more willing to spend on immediate consumption instead of putting their money in a bank in the traditional way. With the appearance of the current new financial products, more and more young consumers prefer to choose inter temporal consumption for leisure. They are keenly eager to achieve their demands for their internal psychosomatic relaxation, as long as they have the expected income source. Thus all the above factors for residents' leisure consumption provide leisure consumers with the necessary funds, and especially widen a broad market space for leisure economy development.

*iii. Leisure motivation: desire for leisure consumption*

Leisure motivation refers to the demand for leisure consumption, consumer interest and recreational consumption preferences. If we say the above factors such as "free time" and "high disposable income" just provide a possibility of leisure consumption, it is "leisure desire" that really works. Leisure desire causes consumers to achieve the goal as catalysts by stimulating consumers' recreational motivation. Consumption is divided into basic life consumption and leisure consumption, the former is oriented to survival as the core content of life, the latter belongs to the senior spiritual needs according to Maslow's theory on hierarchy of needs. With the more abundance of human material wealth, people are eager to release psychosomatic press and relax themselves than ever before. Now the pursuit of leisure activity has become the mainstream and trend of modern life.

For leisure consumption, of course we should not attach too much emphasis on material wealth consumption. Therefore, cultural consumption and edification should be paid more attention to ascend the character of human spirit. Marx attached much importance on the taste for spiritual leisure. Leisure consumption in material works only as a carrier. Therefore we must highlight spiritual pursuit, the reasonable essence of Marx's theory on leisure consumption. [17]

A person's preference for leisure consumption depends on the factors mentioned above, such as consumer's disposable time, disposable income as well as the level of education, etc. It determines the diversity of leisure consumption. Guo Lufang thought that leisure could be divided into physical leisure consumption & spiritual leisure consumption, entertainment leisure consumption & developing leisure consumption, non-autonomous leisure consumption & autonomous leisure consumption, passive leisure consumption & positive leisure consumption. [18]

## Ⅳ. Analysis on Leisure and Leisure Consumption Effects

In China, with the increase in residents' income and decline in Engel's coefficient, especially with the promulgation of massive leisure programs by Chinese National Tourism Administration in 2013, we can conclude that domestic leisure consumption will be intensified in China. Leisure consumption will definitely play a vital role in promoting personal development, also social progress together with economic development.

*i. Effects on individuals' all-round development*

As an old English saying goes: "All work and no play makes Jack a dull boy", which emphasizes the importance of leisure activities to human beings. If he had no necessary rest or leisure activities, he would become dull and stupid. Necessary leisure activities would be conducive to the improvement of labor quality by making physical and mental energy restored. Leisure can compensate for labor exhaustion, improve the life quality and inspire the potential for "flow" experience (in Jeffrey Goby's words), and in turn to realize the value of a person. In 1970, the famous "leisure charter" was issued in Brussels, the Belgian capital. In the charter there were such words: "Recreation and entertainment may create the conditions for the compensation of demands contemporary lifestyle to a lot of people. Furthermore, it is by such leisure activities as relaxing the body, engaging in athletics and appreciating art, science and nature. Proper recreation can stimulate a person's sense of responsibility and improve the ability to promote a person's development freely." Those words generalize accurately that recreation and leisure activities are very important to the people in modern society. The performance of leisure consumption is an indicator of a person's lifestyle and taste[19]. Leisure consumption may fully display consumers' ethical nature by satisfying their self realization, showing the freedom of personality and enriching social relationships to achieve its target of promoting ethical value goal of man's all-round development (Tao Peizhi, 2008, as in e.g. [7]). So from the perspective of improving the personal taste, spiritual leisure consumption, conductive leisure consumption and positive leisure consumption should be highly praised of as the main contents of leisure consumption.

*ii. Influences on the progress of the whole society*

Social development refers to the free extension from the freedom of individuals to the whole society, further extension to the social relationship on the basis of personal social ties, which makes personal development agree with social development. As a symbol of a quality of life improvement and leisure consumption, leisure tends to be spirit-oriented and diversified. Leisure consumption plays an important role in the social reproduction. Among them, spirit consumption is the kernel of leisure consumption. The most significant role is that proper leisure can improve the overall quality of the residents, which is beneficial to Chinese socialist spiritual civilization construction. The process of our modernization construction depends largely on the national quality improvement and talent resources development. Leisure consumption and its rationalization problem are not only related to the level of national quality, but also closely related to the process of realizing modernization in China. [20] Leisure consumption should be regarded as one of human consumption behaviors. Marx's consumption theory was obviously different from the decay of leisure class. It was built on the basis of mass consumer culture. And it was born out of the consumption behavior of the leisure class. The leisure consumption pattern has changed the alienation tendency of industrial society, trying to make consumption go back to its authentic meaning, fading the symbolization of phenomenon to achieve the goal of self-improvement and self-regression. [21]

As China is a vast agricultural and population country, leisure consumption as a way of secondary income distribution is conducive to narrow the urban rural income disparity and the gap between the rich and the poor to some extent. Especially with the prosperity of rural leisure consumption, there is no doubt it is feasible to promote social distributive justice so as to promote social harmony and stability through this way.

*iii. Stimulation & promotion on regional economic development*

In Jeffery Goby's book *Leisure and Leisure Service in 21st Century*, he declared that 21st century would be a leisure-oriented era and leisure consumption would be a main source of economic development. In the future leisure consumption will be transformed into job hunting chances. Leisure services will be shifted from standardization and centralization to personalized service.

Firstly, leisure consumption has become a new engine to drive economic growth. As one of the three driving forces (consumption, investment and export) of economic growth, consumption is a dominant factor in Chinese GDP growth. Since Chinese government carried out "October Day" holiday, leisure consumption appeared a big blowout in tourism shopping which was labeled as a "golden week". The amount of merchandise sales on two-day weekends is equivalent to the total amount of the five workdays. Especially on such festivals as May Day, Dragon Boat Festival, Mid Autumn festival, National Day and New Year festival and Spring Festival, the amount of merchandise sales is as two times or more as of that during other times. [22] According to Chinese Social Affairs Ministry survey, nearly 70% of respondents said the total cost of shopping, dining, travel and spending during the holiday seasons was significantly higher than usual. Bound by rigid time limitations, leisure consumption is relatively concentrated in the leisure time of holidays. In this sense, "holiday economy” forces economic growth and expands domestic demand. Now mankind has entered the 21st century, leisure consumption gradually becomes important factors to promote the economy growth. With the era coming of the leisure time, leisure consumption will lead to the economic development of the whole nation.

Secondly, leisure consumption is a new way of promoting employment and stimulating human capital capacity. In terms of promoting employment, the development of the leisure industry has created many new jobs employments. Compared with traditional industry, leisure is mainly a consumption-orientated industry. Personalized service is more demanding. Therefore, leisure services will be characterized from standardization, centralization to personalization. So for leisure industry, market segmentation should be done well in the leisure industry in order to meet the needs of different people’s leisure consumption demands. Leisure consumption is also an important way to stimulate the human capital capacity by providing people more jobs. For many workers (especially for those laid off workers and rural population), the increasing leisure rights means labor rights, to a great extent providing them labor chances means entitling them life rights. To provide them jobs chances is to meet the needs of necessities for their survival.

And thirdly, leisure consumption helps the integrative development of such three industries as agricultural industry, manufacturing industry and service industry. Leisure industry is made up of enterprises and enterprise groups triggered by the leisure demand and engaged in leisure industry by providing leisure related products and services. It covers such industry field related to people’s leisure life, leisure behavior and leisure demand, especially in the tourism, entertainment industry, service industry and cultural industry as the leading economic form and industrial system. [23] Leisure industry has such characteristics as comprehension and diversity, correlation and fusion penetration, etc. As industry carrier, leisure industry can guide and stimulate the reasonable allocation of resources between urban and rural areas. [24]-[25] And it is helpful to adjust industrial structure. Leisure industry is of high alignment and integration with agricultural industry, manufacturing industry and service industry. Leisure consumption will drive agriculture industry, transportation industry and service industry to develop comprehensively. It is subject to the formation of a chain effect and multiplier effect. Take tourism and leisure as an example, tourism involves six elements. The development of tourism industry will drive catering, accommodation, transportation, shopping, entertainment to flourish comprehensively. In regions rich in tourism resources, the development in achieving industrial cluster should be based on leading enterprises, aiming to promote the integration development of the above three industries. [26]-[27]

## Ⅴ. Conclusion

In sum, leisure consumption is an important symbol of human life quality promotion. And it can promote people’s all-round development. [28]-[31] Above all it plays a huge boost and leading role in social economy. Nonetheless, we must be aware that the income gap between urban and rural areas in China is still very big. Such income disparity leads directly to their quite different leisure ways, leisure consumption levels, leisure consumption frequencies, leisure consumption qualities and leisure consumption hierarchies. With the promulgation of Chinese national tourism and leisure programs in 2013, the urgent task at present is to promote the national tourism leisure infrastructure construction and make the plan for national leisure. We hope work-paid vacation system will truly become a reality earlier. At the same time the population engaged in agriculture accounts for the vast majority of Chinese population, thus there is still a long way to go for Chinese government in increasing farmers' and peasants' income and promoting rural leisure consumption. This requires the government to build a long standing mechanism to increase farmers' income, so as to promote rural residents' leisure consumption level and improve the quality of urban residents' leisure consumption.

In theory, on the other hand, we advocate that leisure consumption should be rational, healthy and positive. But in reality there still exist some irrational, unhealthy, non-autonomous leisure consumption behaviors. Unrealistic competitive consumption behaviors, showing off consumption behaviors, and gambling behaviors as well as obscenity tendency of leisure consumption alienation behaviors [32]-[35] can be found commonly. Thus leisure consumption must be directed and regulated to a new type of leisure consumption ethics. We advocate that leisure consumers should seek for internal leisure motivation to enjoy efficient leisure actively so that they can reduce the chances of leisure consumption randomness and imitations of other people (as in e.g. [17]). We propose that spiritual culture should be its kernel in leisure consumption. High quality and high grade developmental leisure should be praised highly of. [36]-[37] Healthy and sustainable leisure consumption would be cherished. Therefore in terms of leisure product designing, kinds of leisure products supply should be enriched through stimulating, even creating the leisure consumption demands to guide the fashion trend of leisure.

## References


[1] Xie Xiuhua. Leisure alienation criticism on industrial society[D]. Changchun: Jilin University, 2008.

[2] Marx C, Engels F. *The Complete Works of Marx and Engels* [M]. Beijing: People's Publishing House, 1974.

[3] Zhang Yonghong. Leisure consumption: based on the theory of Marx's perspective[J]. *Consumer Economy*, 2010, 6: 59 62.

[4] Deng Chongqing. Brief introduction to leisure and leisure consumption[J]. *Reform and Strategy*, 2000, 5: 2-6.

[5] Lou Jiajun. A brief research on leisure [J]. *Journal of Guilin Tourism College*, 2000, 2: 5-9.

[6] Yang Zhenzhi, Zhou Kun. Also talking about leisure city and city leisure [J]. *Tourism Tribune*, 2008, 12: 51-55.

[7] Tao Peizhi. Man's all-round development: the dimension of the leisure consumption ethics[J]. *Journal of Suzhou University (Philosophy and Social Science)*, 2008, 4: 23-26.

[8] Zhang Guangrui, Song Rui. A research on leisure [J]. *Social Scientists*, 2001:18-19.

[9] Gooder T. *Leisure in the History of Human Thoughts*[M]. Sumei Cheng, Huidi Ma, trans. Kunming: Yunnan People's Publishing House, 2000.

[10] Goby J. *Leisure in Your Life* [M]. Zheng Kang, trans, Song Tian, proofread. Kunming: Yunnan People's Publishing House, 2000.

[11] Mou Yan. The macro-analysis on Chinese residents' leisure consumption demand[D]. Shenyang: Liao Ning University, 2011.

[12] Chen Yusong, Wang Yuzhou, Jiang Wenling. Leisure and leisure consumption [J]. *Chinese Business Field*, 2010, 11: 347.

[13] Yu Guangyuan, Ma Huidi. Work and leisure: the 5th dialogue on leisure [J]. *Journal of Luoyang Normal Institute*, June 2009.

[14] Marx C, Engels F. *The Complete Works of Marx and Engels*[M]. Beijing: People's Publishing House, 1980, l: 46.

[15] China News Web. http://finance.sina.com.cn/china/20150118/100314329820.shtml, 2015.

[16] Sina Finance. http://finance.sina.com.cn/roll/2017-07-11/doc-ifyhvyie0979289.shtml, 2017.

[17] Marx C, Engels F. *The Complete Works of Marx and Engels*[M]. Beijing: People's Publishing House, 1972: 26.

[18] Guo Lufang. Chinese leisure consumption structure: empirical analysis on optimization countermeasures [J]. *Journal of Zhejiang University (Humanities and Social Science Edition)*, 2006: 10-12.

[19] Jin Xuefen. The value and implication of leisure in building a person[J]. *Tourism Tribune*, 2012, 9: 99-104.

[20] Pan Jianwei, Zhao Xian, Shi Jianing. A research on influencing factors and countermeasures of residents' leisure consumption[J]. *Journal of Business Research*, 2009: 16 -19.

[21] Ma Huidi. *Leisure Economy to the Humanistic Care*[M]. Beijing: Economic Publishing House, 2004.

[22] Chen Chao, Wang Dan. Holiday leisure consumption and their psychology analysis[J]. *Technology Square*, 2008: 26-27.

[23] Ma Huidi. The 21st century, leisure economy, leisure industry and leisure culture[J]. *Natural Dialectics Research*, 2001, 1: 49 -50.

[24] Yang Guoyong. Leisure consumption: the refraction of era progress [J]. *Economist*, 2002: 62-63.

[25] Guo Liyuan. An exploration on leisure science development in strengthening China through powerful culture [J]. *Journal Nanjing University of Aeronautics and Astronautics (Social Science edition)*, 2016, 6: 69-71.

[26] Wu Sizong, Guo Hai. A research on hedonic/functional attitude of leisure consumption [J]. *Tourism Tribune*, 2010, 3: 55-60.

[27] Xu Doudou, Zhang Qi, The strategic thinking on leisure Fuzhou [J]. *Development Research*, 2009, 3: 40-42.

[28] Pang Xuequan. Several theoretical issues on leisure science research [J]. *Zhejiang Social Science*, 2016(3) :116-119.

[29] Shen Guangsi. A research on the development of Chinese leisure consumption [D]. Chengdu: Sichuan University, 2010.

[30] Song Rui, Jin Zhun. Leisure and sense of subjective happiness: a review on western research[J]. *Hangzhou Normal University (Social Science edition)*, 2015, 12: 112-116.

[31] Zhang Yonghong. An analysis on Marx's leisure consumption theory[J]. *Exploration*, 2010, 2: 154-157.

[32] Ling Xiaoping, Tan Peiwen. Dilemma and choice: leisure and leisure education in the all-around way to build a well off society [J]. *Guangxi Social Science*, 2015, 10: 202-207.

[33] Yang Likun, Reconsideration on scientific leisure[J]. *Social Science Review*, 2015, 2: 46-48.

[34] Yu Guangyuan, Ma Huidi. Leisure and culture: the 2nd dialogue on leisure[J]. *Journal of Luoyang Normal Institute*, 2009(6): 1-5.

[35] Zhang Hui. On leisure alienation[J]. *Lanzhou Tribune*, 2014, 5: 37 -43.

[36] Zhang Jieting, Ma Ji. The artistic conception of leisure science on new holiday system [J]. *Journal of Hefei Industrial University (Social Science Edition)*, 2013(2): 55-57.

[37] Zhang Ye. An investigation into leisure and leisure related concepts from the perspective of Chinese culture[J]. *Tourism Tribune*, 2013, 9: 109-112.

# A Research on the Operational Characteristics of Small and Micro Tourism Enterprises in Lugu Lake

Yang Dan[1*]

**Abstract:** Small and micro enterprises (SMEs) are the basic forces for promoting the development of tourism in tourist destinations. This paper, by taking Lugu Lake in Sichuan as an example, investigates and analyses the operational characteristics of local SMEs through questionnaires and interviews. The results show that two types of tourism management coexist, i.e. the individual entrepreneurship with families as the main body and collective entrepreneurship with village communities as the main body; the spatial distribution of SMEs is uneven, most of which are close to the tourist distribution center and popular tourist spots; with unstandardized operation and management and unsatisfactory business performance of most SMEs, parts of them begin to transfer or close down; with the mature development of tourist destinations, the local SMEs are faced with new development patterns such as external competition and replacement; thus, strong capital will play an important role in the market restructuring of SMEs.

**Keywords:** small and micro enterprises (SMEs); tourism entrepreneurship; entrepreneurial characteristics; Lugu Lake

## Ⅰ. Introduction

The small and micro enterprise is a concept of enterprise scale compared with a large enterprise. Pages (1999) [1] holds that small and micro tourism industry is constituted by accommodation industry, catering industry, souvenir shops, travel agencies, transportation, tourism leasing, tourism organizations and other industries providing tourism services. Most of the domestic scholars define SMEs as enterprises with less than 50 employees and with tourists as the main service targets, including hotels, restaurants, merchandise sales, travel agency services, etc., among which hotels (small inns) account for a comparatively large proportion. [2]

With the miniaturization trend of global enterprises, SMEs begin to take up the main body of the tourism industry, absorbing an annually increasing number of employed

1* China West Normal University, Nanchong, China. 88086505@qq.com.

populations. In the development course of tourism destinations, the development of small and micro tourism enterprises is often regarded as an important benchmark of tourism economy for tourism destinations. Therefore, it is of great reference value to study the development process and characteristics of small and micro tourism enterprises in tourist destinations for judging the comprehensive development of tourism destinations.

## Ⅱ. Literature Review

Rodenburg (1980) [3] researched on small tourism enterprises for the first time. With Bali as an example, he elaborated different social and economic effects of 3 different sizes of tourism enterprises on the development of tourism destinations, i.e. large enterprises, small enterprises and craft tourism. The results show that the emergence and development of small and micro tourism enterprises are affected by many external factors, stakeholders and policy environment. Wang and Krakover (2008) [4] also found that the development of SMEs is also affected by the leadership of the management agencies in tourist destinations and the related impact of stakeholders. Simultaneously, it relies on a series of policy mechanisms, including planning, community development and business support (Bosworth & Farrell, 2011). [5] The higher the degree of tourism entrepreneurship in a community, the higher the degree of social and economic benefits acquired by its residents; it will in turn promotes the sustainable development of tourism (Chiutsi & Mudzengi, 2012). [6]

Although SMEs take up a large proportion in tourism industry, SMEs doesn't get enough attention in tourism research. The research found that small and micro tourism enterprises play a significant role for tourist destinations in driving employment, increasing the competitiveness of the tourist destinations (Johns & Mattson, 2005), [7] economic development, the development of tourist destinations, sustainable tourism, maintaining special ways of life (Shaw & Williams, 2004)[8] and creating social interests (Nilsson et al, 2005). [9] However, most of the researches isolate the macro social environment for the development of small and micro tourism enterprises and fall short of studies on the origin, growth and development of SMEs; thus, the attention paid to the development process, evolutionary reasons and development trends of small and micro tourism enterprises is insufficient.

Lugu Lake is an internationally renowned tourist destination. The tourism researches on Lugu Lake started in the 1990s, which was at the same pace with its tourism development. In the studies of Lugu Lake, the focuses are on social and cultural changes caused by tourism development, scenic environment, economic sustainable development, participation and benefits gained by the community residents. [10] At present, there exists a shortage of researches on different types of tourism entrepreneurship in Lugu Lake.

According to the literature review, this research will integrate tourism entrepreneurship with the study of Lugu Lake. Through the analysis of characteristics and laws of small and micro tourism enterprises, the author reveals the relations between the development of tourist destinations and tourism entrepreneurship of SMEs.

## Ⅲ. Operational Characteristics of Small and Micro Tourism Enterprises

Lugu Lake, located at the junction of Yanyuan County in Sichuan Province and Ninglang County in Yunnan Province, is a tourist destination with multi-ethnic groups gathering together and with Mosuo people as its main minority. Tourism is the absolute dominant industry in this region. Residents' daily lives are closely related to tourism, and the entrepreneurial activities are relying on and centering on tourism industry. In this research, the author conducted a field study in late November to late December 2016, in Lugu Lake. Through the questionnaires and interviews, the author investigates the operational situations of local small and micro tourism enterprises.

*i. Management types*

According to the field study, there are two different management types of small and micro tourism enterprises in Lugu Lake, i.e. individual entrepreneurship with local farmer households as the main body and collective entrepreneurship with village communities as the main body. Individual entrepreneurship with local farmer households as the main body includes Mosuo-style farmyard hotels and other types of small and micro tourism enterprises, which mainly provide services such as boating tour on the lake, home visits, ascending Mountain of Gemu goddess, hiking around Lugu Lake and Buddhist activities.

Collective entrepreneurship with village communities as the main body adopts the method of collective division and cooperation. For example, each household sends a labor force to participate in tourism services every day. They are divided into different groups according to the services, mainly providing services of boating services, horse-leading services, Muosuo bonfire dance performances and singing Lugu Lake love songs for tourists. Collective entrepreneurship with village communities as the main body is mainly due to various disputes and contradictions among community residents caused by individual villagers in the competition for tourists in the initial stage of tourism development. In order to control the vicious competition, villages begin to collectively manage the activities such as boating, horse-leading and evening Mosuo songs and dance performances. Each household in the village sends one person to participate in those activities with the income equally shared by the team members. Tourism entrepreneurship in the form of collectivism helps protect the minimum income level of local villagers the to a certain extent.

*ii. Business types*

Business types of SMEs in Lugu Lake mainly include enterprises of accommodation, catering, bars, entertainment, feet bath, hairdressing and other services that are closely related to tourists' lives; at the same time, businesses concerning drugs, local specialties, tea, accessory, silverwork, subsidiary food, general merchandise and fireworks are also included. Through the field study, the author summarizes a detailed table which shows the proportion of business types (see Table 1).

Table 1 Statistics of SMEs' Business Types of Tourism Entrepreneurship in Lugu Lake, Sichuan Province

| Sequence Number | Type | Amount | Percentage (%) | Sequence Number | Type | Amount | Percentage (%) |
|---|---|---|---|---|---|---|---|
| 1 | Accommodation | 178 | 62.2 | 8 | Silverwork | 2 | 0.7 |
| 2 | Catering | 62 | 21.7 | 9 | Local Specialty | 2 | 0.7 |
| 3 | Subsidiary Food | 18 | 6.3 | 10 | Accessory | 2 | 0.7 |
| 4 | Hairdressing | 7 | 2.4 | 11 | Feet Bath | 1 | 0.3 |
| 5 | Entertainment | 5 | 1.7 | 12 | Tea | 1 | 0.3 |
| 6 | Bar | 3 | 1.0 | 13 | Fireworks | 1 | 0.3 |
| 7 | Drug | 3 | 1.0 | 14 | General Merchandise | 1 | 0.3 |

*iii. Spatial distribution*

From the perspective of spatial distribution, tourism SMEs in Lugu Lake mainly focus on tourism distribution and reception hot spots and lakeside tourism hot spots with infrastructure such as Dazu Village, Wuzhiluo Wharf, Boshu tree, Luowa Village, etc. In general, the hotels, inns and other accommodation facilities services can meet the basic demands of tourists. Living facilities include shopping centers, bars, teahouses, cafes and restaurants; entertainment facilities include dance halls (bonfire party venues), but there are no swimming pools, gyms, cinemas, sports ground and other resort facilities. Business conference facilities mainly include conference halls in hotels, but there are no professional conference centers; the number of shops and shopping products are comparatively small; the grade of roads for transportation is comparatively low; and infrastructures such as toilets in scenic spots are still in need of improvement.

Table 2 "Business Address * Business Type" Cross-Table of Tourism Services SMEs in Lugu Lake Scenic Spot, Sichuan Province

| Business Address | Accommodation | Catering | Bar | Silverwork | Local Specialty | Subsidiary Food | Accessory | Hairdressing | General Merchandise | Drug | Fireworks | Feet Bath | Tea | Entertainment | Total |
|---|---|---|---|---|---|---|---|---|---|---|---|---|---|---|---|
| Lugu Lake Town | 28 | 40 | 0 | 0 | 2 | 17 | 2 | 7 | 1 | 3 | 1 | 1 | 1 | 5 | 108 |
| Dazu Village | 34 | 6 | 2 | 1 | 0 | 1 | 0 | 0 | 0 | 0 | 0 | 0 | 0 | 0 | 44 |
| Dazu Lovers Beach | 3 | 0 | 0 | 0 | 0 | 0 | 0 | 0 | 0 | 0 | 0 | 0 | 0 | 0 | 3 |
| Wakua Lake Bay | 7 | 3 | 0 | 1 | 0 | 0 | 0 | 0 | 0 | 0 | 0 | 0 | 0 | 0 | 11 |
| Zhongwa Village | 0 | 2 | 0 | 0 | 0 | 0 | 0 | 0 | 0 | 0 | 0 | 0 | 0 | 0 | 2 |
| Awa Village | 1 | 0 | 0 | 0 | 0 | 0 | 0 | 0 | 0 | 0 | 0 | 0 | 0 | 0 | 1 |
| Zhao's Bay | 4 | 4 | 0 | 0 | 0 | 0 | 0 | 0 | 0 | 0 | 0 | 0 | 0 | 0 | 8 |
| Goddess Bay | 5 | 0 | 0 | 0 | 0 | 0 | 0 | 0 | 0 | 0 | 0 | 0 | 0 | 0 | 5 |
| Alu Manor | 7 | 3 | 0 | 0 | 0 | 0 | 0 | 0 | 0 | 0 | 0 | 0 | 0 | 0 | 10 |
| Haimen Village | 1 | 0 | 0 | 0 | 0 | 0 | 0 | 0 | 0 | 0 | 0 | 0 | 0 | 0 | 1 |
| Shannan Village | 8 | 0 | 0 | 0 | 0 | 0 | 0 | 0 | 0 | 0 | 0 | 0 | 0 | 0 | 8 |
| Luowa Village | 17 | 0 | 0 | 0 | 0 | 0 | 0 | 0 | 0 | 0 | 0 | 0 | 0 | 0 | 17 |
| Boshu Village | 25 | 0 | 0 | 0 | 0 | 0 | 0 | 0 | 0 | 0 | 0 | 0 | 0 | 0 | 25 |
| Walking Marriages Bridge | 2 | 2 | 0 | 0 | 0 | 0 | 0 | 0 | 0 | 0 | 0 | 0 | 0 | 0 | 4 |
| Wuzhiluo Wharf | 36 | 2 | 1 | 0 | 0 | 0 | 0 | 0 | 0 | 0 | 0 | 0 | 0 | 0 | 39 |
| Total | 178 | 62 | 3 | 2 | 2 | 18 | 2 | 7 | 1 | 3 | 1 | 1 | 1 | 5 | 286 |

*iv. Operation mode*

The 286 small and micro tourism enterprises in Lugu Lake tourist area adopt the operation mode of family workshop, which belongs to self-employment or small-scale employment SMEs with family members or non-family members as employers. For example, family workshops formed by husbands and wives, brothers, sisters and other forms take up a comparatively large proportion in hotels and inns, silverwork production and other enterprises. In the catering industry, most restaurants hire professional chefs from other places and employ local young people as waiters. In order to save operating costs, the average number of employees for each enterprise is 3-4 people. During the peak seasons of tourism, those enterprises will hire local secondary school students as temporary employees to solve the problem of shortage of labor force. At present, owners of small and micro tourism enterprises from other places account for 70% -80%, while the proportion of local owners are declining.

*v. Operation time and space*

Seeing from the whole year, the operation time of small and micro tourism enterprises adapts to the low and peak seasons. In the peak season, the operation time of the enterprises is all-weather 24 hours; however, in the low season, some SMEs' operation time is shortened to half a day; some are even out of business.

In terms of operation space, in addition to the offline operation of stores, many SMEs provide booking links on different travel platforms. In this way, they combine offline operations and online businesses, thus expanding the operation space of SMEs.

*vi. Investment in operation and its management*

From practical surveys and interviews, the author finds that only a small number of newly opened inns invest in renewal and new facilities; other small and micro tourism enterprises don't have new investment but only invest in the basic maintenance of the reception facilities. At the same time, the management of most small and micro tourism enterprises is not standardized, and those without business-related licenses account for 76.2% of the total.

Local SMEs need the acceptance checks from related industries, such as fire control, sanitation and safety industries in the process of handling relevant licenses. The competent department shall accept and check the operation sites and facilities of enterprises and make corresponding suggestions for construction or renewal. At the same time, owners and staffs of enterprises need to meet the requirements of relevant business training and assessment, after which they can acquire corresponding qualifications. As the application procedures are tedious and the requirements are demanding, local shopping-related SMEs such as bars, feet bath and accessory fall short of relevant licenses as showed in Table 3 according to the field study. The proportion of enterprises such as accommodation, catering and entertainment with licenses is less than 30%, which not only reflects the unstandardized management of local tourism SMEs, but also reflects the lack of operation investment.

Table 3 The Situation of Business-related Licenses of Small and Micro Tourism Enterprises in Lugu Lake, Sichuan Province

| Types | Total | Number of Unhandled Licenses | Percentage of Unhandled Licenses (%) | Number of Handled Licenses | Percentage of Handled Licenses (%) |
|---|---|---|---|---|---|
| Bars | 3 | 3 | 100.0 | 0 | 0.0 |
| Feet Bath | 1 | 1 | 100.0 | 0 | 0.0 |
| Accessory | 2 | 2 | 100.0 | 0 | 0.0 |
| Accommodation | 178 | 157 | 88.2 | 21 | 11.8 |
| Entertainment | 5 | 4 | 80.0 | 1 | 20.0 |
| Catering | 62 | 44 | 71.0 | 18 | 29.0 |
| Local Specialty | 2 | 1 | 50.0 | 1 | 50.0 |
| Hairdressing | 7 | 3 | 42.9 | 4 | 57.1 |
| Subsidiary Food | 18 | 3 | 16.7 | 15 | 83.3 |
| Silverwork | 2 | 0 | 0.0 | 2 | 100.0 |
| Tea | 1 | 0 | 0.0 | 1 | 100.0 |
| General Merchandise | 1 | 0 | 0.0 | 1 | 100.0 |
| Drugs | 3 | 0 | 0.0 | 3 | 100.0 |
| Fireworks | 1 | 0 | 0.0 | 1 | 100.0 |

*vii. Operation scale and performance*

As most tourism SMEs do not apply for relevant licenses, the data of their business-related indicators is not reported; the tax department cannot impose business taxes on these enterprises, thus making it difficult to get the indicators reflecting the scales of enterprises such as the annual operating income of local SMEs. At the same time, the survey finds that among the tourism SMEs in Lugu Lake Scenic Area in Sichuan Province, the number of accommodation enterprises is 178 in total, accounting for up to 62.2%, so the number of beds is taken as an alternative indicator for measuring tourism reception scale and capacity. From analysis of the statistical data, among the 178 SMEs, the minimum number of beds is 6 and the largest is 122; the median of beds is 24.00; the average is 29.95; the average reception capacity is less than 30 beds. Among the 178 accommodation enterprises, in terms of the number of reception beds, the top 3 sizes are 18 (8.4%), 20 (7.9%) and 22 (7.3%) respectively. The main reason for the small size of the reception is that the accommodation is provided by the residents by remodeling their own houses; restricted to the limit of construction height, which is 10 meters, the reception volume and the number of rooms are small, so the reception capacity and size are small.

Except for the marketing of tourism SMEs in Sichuan province on Lugu Lake WeChat public account, most of the tourism enterprises in Lugu Lake also have corresponding business reservations on the tourism platform websites such as Ctrip, Qunar, Yilong, etc., but the relevant marketing contents are almost blank. The marketing of those enterprises mainly relies on word of mouth recommendations by guests they once received; active marketing implementation is generally not satisfying.

Through the interviews with enterprises' owners, it can be seen that since 2013, the reception capacity of tourism SMEs in Lugu Lake have been on the wane, with profits and performance continuing to decline. Affected by the less satisfying performance compared with previous years, some enterprises are witnessing some new trends such as out of business and transfer.

## Ⅳ. Conclusions

Through the tourism development course of Lugu Lake tourist area and the investigation and analysis of the entrepreneurial development of SMEs, the research draws the following conclusions:

(1) The emergence and development process of SMEs are basically in accordance with the tourism development cycle of Lugu Lake. After Lugu Lake tourism area entering its mature stage, SMEs at present witness a steady development and local adjustments. Small and micro tourism entrepreneurship includes the individual entrepreneurship with families as the main body and collective entrepreneurship with village communities as the main body. Collective entrepreneurship with village communities as the main body in Lugu Lake is prior to the individual entrepreneurship with famer households as the main body, which protects the minimum living standard and income of each villager, thus narrowing the gap between the rich and the poor to a certain extent.

(2) In terms of geographical space, considering providing services to tourists at the nearest distance, SMEs generally choose their addresses at tourist distribution centers and tourist attractions and reception hot spots, which are easily to be successful. However, in regions far away from the road, lakeside or tourist reception points of the region, small and micro tourism enterprises are scarcely distributed. The distribution of small and micro tourism enterprises as a whole shows a state of imbalance.

(3) The management of most tourism SMEs is not standardized. The majority of the SMEs adopt family-workshop model; without modern enterprise management framework and system, there is a serious shortage of operating investment and the phenomenon of unlicensed illegal business still exists. Although they introduce the Internet technology into the marketing of their enterprises, the marketing effect is unsatisfying. With comparatively low corporate profits and performance, there emerge some new trends such as out of business or transfer.

(4) With the mature development of tourist destinations, the competitive pressure of tourism entrepreneurship is increasing. Entrepreneurs from other places, stepping into tourist destinations, begin to replace the local indigenous residents and become new owners of SMEs. In the process of adjustment and reshuffle of SMEs in tourist destinations, investors and entrepreneurs from other places with capital advantages will be the key forces to promote the transformation and upgrade of local tourism entrepreneurship. In this process, those SMEs with serious products homogenization and less competitiveness will be merged or withered away, which will ultimately give rise to the formation of a new tourism market pattern.

## References

[1] Page S J, Forer P, Lawton G R. Small business development and tourism: Terra incognita? [J]. *Tourism Management,* 1999, 20(4): 435-459.

[2] Yin Shoubing, Liu Yunxia, Zhao Peng. Driving mechanism of small tourism firms in scenic areas: a case study of Xidi Village[J]. *Geographical Research*, 2013, 32(2): 360-368.

[3] Rodenburg E E. The effects of scale in economic development. Tourism in Bali[J]. *Annals of Tourism Research*, 1980, 7(2): 177-196.

[4] Wang Y, Krakover S. Destination marketing: competition, cooperation or coopetition?[J]. *International Journal of Contemporary Hospitality Management*, 2008, 20(2): 126-141.

[5] Bosworth G, Farrell H. Tourism entrepreneurs in Northumberland[J]. *Annals of Tourism Research*, 2011, 38(4): 1474-1494.

[6] Chiutsi S, Mudzengi B K. Community tourism entrepreneurship for sustainable tourism management in southern Africa: lessons from Zimbabwe[J]. *International Journal of Academic Research in Business & Social Sciences*, 2012, 02(08).

[7] Johns N, Mattsson J. Destination development through entrepreneurship: a comparison of two cases[J]. *Tourism Management*, 2005, 26(4): 605-616.

[8] Shaw G, Williams A M. Chapter 7 From lifestyle consumption to lifestyle production: changing patterns of tourism entrepreneurship[M]//*Small Firms in Tourism*, 2004: 99-113.

[9] Nilsson, P Å, Petersen T, Wanhill S. Public support for tourism SMEs in peripheral areas: the Arjeplog project, northern Sweden[J]. *Service Industries Journal*, 2005, 25(4): 579-599.

[10] Guo Ling, Yang Ningdong, Wang Zhizhang. Research on spatial production of ethnic tourism development and ethnic culture: a case study of Lugu Lake, Yanyuan County, Liangshan Yi Autonomous Prefecture of Sichuan Province[J]. *Journal of Southwest University for Nationalities*, 2014(2): 144-149.

# Assessment of Risk Perceptions of Natural Hazards: A Case Study of the Taibai Mountains National Forest Park in China

Wang Xiaofeng[1*], Lü Jinqiao[2], Zeng Tiantian[3]

**Abstract:** In recent years, natural disasters occurred frequently, seriously threatening the sustainable development of regional economy, society and ecological environment. In order to prevent and reduce natural hazards, based on the theories and methods of tourism, geography, psychology and other disciplines, the general rules of natural hazard risk perception of particular individuals in particular area have been revealed in this research. The assessment indicator system of risk perception of natural hazards has been constructed from three aspects of hazard mitigation knowledge, attitudes and behavior; by use of Exponential Model, risk perception exponents of tourists have been set up and calculated quantitatively; taking the representative Taibai Mountains National Forest Park in China as the study area, according to the data of field sampling questionnaire survey, the abilities and differences of tourists' risk perceptions of natural hazards have been assessed systematically. The conclusions have been drawn as follows: the focuses on risk perceptions of tourists are the type and feature of the leading natural hazard, main channels of information disclosure, management of hazard risk, hazard reduction education, facilities and equipment of natural hazard prevention and mitigation, and so on; the differences of tourists' risk perceptions are decided by their seven main demographic characteristics. Finally, countermeasures and suggestions have been proposed from three aspects of tourist activity, safety management of tourist and hazard risk, and macro-control of local government for the study area and the same type regions in the world.

**Keywords:** the Taibai Mountains National Forest Park in China; assessment indicator system; natural hazards; risk perception exponent; the abilities and differences of risk perceptions

1* Shanxi Normal University, Xi'an, China. wangxf@snnu.edu.cn.
2 Shanxi Normal University, Xi'an, China.
3 Shanxi Normal University, Xi'an, China.

## Ⅰ. Introduction

In China, natural disasters such as earthquakes, floods, droughts, landslides, and so on are emerging in an endless stream. They have common characteristics of multiple, frequently happened, widely distributed and great destructiveness. [1] In recent years, some natural disasters had led to great losses in people's lives and properties and the development of local economy and society, such as the Yangtze River Floods in 1998, the Severe Drought in Chongqing and Sichuan in 2006, the Floods in Huai River Basin in 2007, the Snow and Ice Storms in Chinese Southern Areas in 2008, the Violent Earthquake of 8 magnitude in Wenchuan of Sichuan in 2008, 7 magnitude in Ya'an of Sichuan and 6.6 magnitude in Dingxi of Gansu in 2010, and so on. The changes of the climate and natural environment are objective and the natural hazards are inevitable. Therefore, human beings must coexist with these changes and natural hazards, adjust adaptive capacity to achieve development. [2] The primary principle of human adaptation to changes is "draw on the advantages and avoid disadvantages", while the precondition is to perceive the natural changes. The Risk Perceptions of Natural Hazards (RPNH) which is the typical performance of sensing the natural changes has already become the research hotspot in international academic community. [3]-[8] In China, Zhou Qi, Li Jingyi, et al. have done some primary research on measuring the situation of public RPNH through establishing "national disaster perceived ability assessment indicator system"[9]-[14]. The public perception of disaster risk which is the bases of disaster prevention and mitigation has important significance to formulate the disaster-mitigation strategy and improve the capacity of disaster preparedness. However, at present, international research results of RPNH for a special set of people and in specific regions are very few, and need to be enriched and perfected constantly in two aspects of the theory and practice. [15]

The research purpose in this paper is to improve the level of management and ability to cope with the natural hazard risk. Based on tourist questionnaire field investigation, by using assessment indicator system and Exponential Model of RPNH established, from two aspects of ability and difference, the RPNH of tourists with different characteristics in Taibai Mountains National Forest Park in China have been calculated and analysed qualitatively. [16] According to the above, countermeasures and suggestions for tourists, managers of the National Forest Park, local government and regions of the same type in the world have been put forward.

## Ⅱ. Methods

*i. The study area*

The study area is the Taibai Mountains National Forest Park of China, which is located in conjunction area of Taibai County, Mei County of Baoji City and Zhouzhi County of Xi'an City, the dividing crest of two watersheds of Yangtze River and the Yellow River. Its scenery is very charming and changeable with different seasons. "Taibai snow days in June" is one of the eight famous sceneries in Guanzhong Basin. This area mainly includes Taibai Mountain National Forest Park and experimental area of Taibai Mountain Nature Reserve. The regional climate has typical feature of subalpine climate, significant differences from the north and south of China, and distinct vertical variations. The unique natural landscape system consists of the typical mountainous forest eco-system, rich biological diversity, full glacial landforms, clear vertical distribution of forest landscape and the special trapezoidal climatic conditions. With the rapid development of eco-tourism in recent years, the Taibai Mountains Forest Park, Red River Valley Forest Park, Heihe River Forest Park, Green Mountain Forest Park and Ecological Tourism Zone of Taibai Mountain National Nature Reserve have been built in the study area. With a broad prospect for development, this area has become a demonstration area of eco-tourism and representative area of research on the relationship between natural hazards and ecological tourism.

However, the study area is also high incidence zone for natural disasters in China. In recent years, earthquakes, floods, mudslides, landslides and other natural disasters have occurred frequently and brought about great damages to lives and properties of tourists and local residents. [17] At the same time, natural hazards have posed great challenges for the tourism safety, risk management of the National Forest Park, disaster prevention and mitigation of local government, and sustainable development of regional economic, social, ecological environment. Based on the above, selecting Taibai Mountains National Forest Park as the study area, by multidisciplinary approach, this case study will have important significance in theory and practice of raising awareness of natural hazard risks, and improving the abilities of hazard prevention and mitigation. [18]

*ii. Data acquisition*

In the process of designing visitor questionnaire, measurements and metrics have been determined by various methods of Likert Scale (1 equals to totally disagree, 5 equals to totally agree) and Frequency Table, Attitude Scale, etc. Adopt Quotient index formula, the sample capacity of questionnaire is 485. Through tourist field questionnaire investigation, under the probability of 95% and the error range of 0.1, 500 valid questionnaires have been collected. By using two methods of Butler Test of Sphericity and KMO (Kaiser-Meyer-Olkin) statistic analysis, data have been tested for compatibility.

During the data collecting process, domestic and foreign visitors in the Taibai Mountains National Forest Park have been selected as the investigation objects, which have been divided into 3 types: pre-travel, during the travel, post-travel. The content of questionnaire mainly includes three parts: information of visitors, natural hazards and tourists' RPNH. The demographic characteristics of investigation objects mainly include gender, age, occupation, educational background, economic income, family disaster suffering situation, and travel traffic (see Table 1).

Table 1 Demographic Characteristics of Investigation Objects

| Demographic Characteristics | Family Disaster Suffering Situation | | | | Travel Traffic | | | |
|---|---|---|---|---|---|---|---|---|
| | None | Seldom | General | More | Group coach | Bus | Private car | Bicycle |
| Value | 312 | 135 | 46 | 7 | 96 | 211 | 178 | 15 |
| Demographic characteristics | Income monthly | | | | | | | |
| | No income | ≤2,000 | 2,000-3,000 | 3,000-5,000 | 5,000-10,000 | ≥10,000 | | |
| Value | 219 | 54 | 134 | 67 | 21 | 5 | | |
| Demographic characteristics | Educational background | | | | | | | |
| | Junior middle school | Senior middle school | University | Master or above | | | | |
| Value | 38 | 89 | 356 | 16 | | | | |

*iii. Assessment indicator system of PRNH*

There are some influential factors in tourists' PRNH. Further to say, the significant influential factors are the tourists' demographic characteristics, travel behaviors, hazard mitigation knowledge, and so on. [19] In order to obtain the first class indexes, before assessment indicator system of tourists' PRNH had been set up, close visitor interviews in the Taibai Mountain National Forest Park had been conducted through using the semi-structured mode. Based on the interview record sorted, occurrence frequency of 9 items were more than 20%, such as the possibility of collapse, lost and forest fire, the understanding of hazard, safety of transportation tools, the attention of disaster prevention and mitigation, the attitudes to destroy the environment, beyond the bearing capacity, reliability of disaster warning system, travel insurance, coping behavior after the hazard, etc. Finally, the first class indexes of tourists' PRNH have been generalized as hazard mitigation knowledge, attitudes and behaviors. To a greater degree, the second class indexes had been elaborated and made up of 16 ones. The weights of these indexes have been assigned through Delphi Model (see Figure 1).

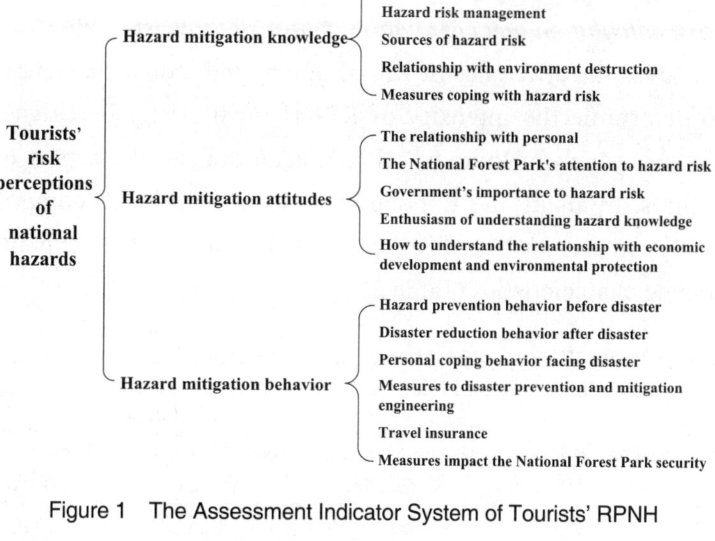


Figure 1 The Assessment Indicator System of Tourists' RPNH

*iv. Exponential model of tourists' PRNH*

Risk perception refers to the individual feeling and understanding of a variety of objective risks existing in the external, and emphasizes the effect of the individual experience gained from the intuitive judgment and subjective feeling to individual perception. [5], [20] Similarly, RPNH is the assessment of natural hazard risk which will happen or not by intuitive judgments and subjective feeling. [18] At present, the Exponential Model is an important method of assessing perception satisfaction. Before quantitative assessment of RPNH abilities of different tourists, Exponential Model of RPNH needs to be established. Based on research results of Zhang Jinhe in 2003, Liu Qing and Du Zhongchao in 2011 and other researchers, [21]-[22] according to tourists' characteristics and regional natural hazards, the exponent equation of RPNH for evaluating ability of RPNH is as follows:

$$G = \sum P_i N_{ij} / \sum N_{ij}$$

Where $G$ is the average value of RPNH intensity of different tourists, that is the exponent of tourists' RPNH; $P_i$ is the score of certain tourists holding in the view of $i$ ($i$=0, 1, 2, 3, 4); $N_{ij}$ represents the number of tourists who hold $i$ kind of views to the problem $j$.

Reference to research results about rural residents perception of mountainous natural disasters in Baiyun Village, Jutou Town of Shaanxi Province in China, [10], [23] $G$ as RPNH intensity is divided into 5 grades: the first grade(value is 4-12) is weak ability of RPNH; the second grade(13-21) is the weaker one; the third grade(22-30) is generally weak one; the fourth grade(31-39) is the stronger one; the 5th grade(40-47) is strong one. The higher exponents of tourists' RPNH are, the stronger ability of their RPNH are, and vice versa.

## Ⅲ. Results and Discussion

*i. Quantitative calculation and correlation analysis of tourists' PRNH*

In order to analyse the difference of RPNH among individual characteristics of tourists, the exponent to determine the intensity of RPNH must firstly be calculated. Based on assessment indicator system of tourists' RPNH, according to the scores of various items in the questionnaires, by using the Exponential Model of RPNH, comprehensive scores of RPNH with different weight have been calculated, that is RPNH exponents of different tourists' demographic characteristics (Table 2).

Table 2 RPNH Exponents from Tourists' Demographic Characteristics

| Demographic Characteristics | | RPNH Exponents | | | |
|---|---|---|---|---|---|
| | | Hazard Mitigation Knowledge | Hazard Mitigation Attitudes | Hazard Mitigation Behaviors | Total |
| Gender | Male | 10.7 | 10.5 | 10.1 | 31.3 |
| | Female | 7.2 | 14.5 | 15.2 | 36.9 |
| Age | ≤14 | 5.65 | 8.35 | 6.85 | 20.85 |
| | 15-24 | 5.8 | 11.5 | 14.5 | 31.8 |
| | 25-44 | 5.9 | 10 | 8.8 | 24.7 |
| | 45-64 | 5.62 | 9.9 | 11.36 | 26.88 |
| | ≥65 | 5.3 | 6.9 | 6.55 | 18.75 |
| Educational background | Junior middle | 5.4 | 8.5 | 11.4 | 25.3 |
| | Senior middle | 6.3 | 7.64 | 11.76 | 25.7 |
| | University | 7.15 | 12.61 | 15 | 34.76 |
| | Master | 8.19 | 11.2 | 14.9 | 34.29 |
| Occupation | Civil servant | 6.03 | 9.02 | 8.1 | 23.15 |
| | Staff | 6.1 | 9.24 | 9.66 | 25 |
| | Worker | 5.92 | 9.64 | 11.2 | 26.76 |
| | Farmer | 5.74 | 10.58 | 14.71 | 31.03 |
| | Student | 6.5 | 11 | 12.8 | 30.3 |
| | Freelancer | 6.02 | 10.22 | 10.3 | 26.54 |
| Monthly income | No income | 9.1 | 14 | 23.17 | 46.27 |
| | ≤2,000 | 8.21 | 13.69 | 17.5 | 39.4 |
| | 2,000-3,000 | 8.24 | 13.3 | 16.1 | 37.64 |
| | 3,000-5,000 | 8.5 | 13.96 | 21.02 | 43.48 |
| | 5,000-10,000 | 9.07 | 14.36 | 25 | 48.43 |
| | ≥10,000 | 8.5 | 12.1 | 16.52 | 37.12 |

(To be continued)

(Continued Table 2)

| Demographic Characteristics | | RPNH Exponents | | | |
|---|---|---|---|---|---|
| | | Hazard Mitigation Knowledge | Hazard Mitigation Attitudes | Hazard Mitigation Behaviors | Total |
| Family disaster suffering situation | No | 8.6 | 13.59 | 16.67 | 38.86 |
| | Seldom | 8.87 | 13.7 | 17.83 | 40.4 |
| | General | 9.2 | 14.37 | 18.1 | 41.67 |
| | More | 9.79 | 14.81 | 21 | 45.6 |
| Travel traffic | Group coach | 8.63 | 13.1 | 16.8 | 38.53 |
| | Bus | 9.11 | 12.19 | 15.42 | 36.72 |
| | Private car | 9.41 | 13.43 | 18.6 | 41.44 |
| | Bicycle | 9.7 | 14.7 | 19.97 | 44.37 |

Through statistical analysis with software tool-SPSS 20.0, it has been shown that there is significant correlation between tourists' demographic characteristics and their RPNH exponents. Along with the differences of gender, age, educational background, occupation, income monthly, family disaster suffering situation and travel traffic, RPNH exponents also have some changes. The results show that the correlation among gender, family disaster suffering situation, occupation and RPNH exponent are the most significant and the next are the educational background, age, monthly income and travel traffic. The correlation coefficients between characteristics and RPNH exponents of tourists have been shown in Table 3.

Table 3 The Correlation Coefficients Between Tourists' Characteristics and Their RPNH Exponents

| The First Class Indexes | Gender | Age | Occupation | Educational Background | Monthly Income | Family Disaster-suffered Situation | Travel Traffic |
|---|---|---|---|---|---|---|---|
| Hazard mitigation knowledge | 0.242** | -0.021 | 0.223** | 0.174 | -0.062 | 0.237** | -0.041 |
| Hazard mitigation attitudes | 0.256* | -0.057 | 0.210*** | 0.155 | -0.074 | 0.221** | -0.029 |
| Hazard mitigation behavior | 0.244** | -0.057 | 0.207*** | 0.079 | -0.043 | 0.218*** | -0.043 |

*** represents the significance of correlation coefficient is 10%; ** represents the significance of correlation coefficient is 5%; * represents the significance of correlation coefficient is 1%.

*ii. Assessments of different indices about tourists' RPNH*

*A. Hazard mitigation knowledge*

In the listed natural disaster types, 76.2% of tourists chose earthquake and landslides, mudslides followed. Because earthquake occurred frequently in China in recent years and affected tourists greatly in the National Forest Park, people paid more attention to learning the knowledge of earthquake disaster prevention. The landslides and mudslides happened along with earthquake, so tourists knew more about these three natural disasters. Tourists knew little about other disasters because the probability of occurrence and the destructiveness of disasters are not as high as earthquake, landslides and mudslides. Tourists often got the information of winds and frost disaster from meteorological station and regarded them as natural disasters rarely. In the process of investigation, tourists thought the main risk encountered in the Taibai Mountains is natural disasters. 76.3% of tourists chose "landslide" and 67.6% of tourists chose "stone rolling" as the major natural disasters more common than other types of disasters in this area, this attributed to its occurring frequency and tourists' familiarity with landslides. Because the geological structure of the National Forest Park is mainly composed of granite, tourists worried about the exposed rocks may lead rolling stones disasters. Main channels that 70% of tourists chose to get disasters knowledge were mass media which include newspapers, television and radio. This proportion is far more than any other channels. The rate of tourists choosing to obtain disaster knowledge based on the methods of disaster reduction education and mobile communication tools was the lowest. The channels by which tourists obtained disaster knowledge are less, but this indicates that they had confidence in the mass media. [24] It can be seen that it is imperative to broaden channels of disaster information and knowledge by use of high-tech and modern communication tools.

*B. Hazard mitigation attitudes*

57.2% of tourists chose item of "basic believe" on the reliability of disaster forecasting system; 55.2% chose "general satisfaction" on the satisfaction of natural disasters information disclosed by government and media; 60.7% chose "general satisfaction" on the satisfaction of hazard mitigation measures made by government; 55.7% chose "general satisfaction" on the satisfaction of hazard mitigation education. These highlights that tourists trust in the ability of social natural hazard mitigation reduction, but the credibility and satisfaction are in the general level. The tourists' attitudes toward hazard mitigation are positive, and they can deeply realize the importance of disaster reduction, and give support and affirmation to disaster prevention and mitigation. However, tourists have higher requirements and expectations to local government on improving the scientificalness and veracity of disasters monitoring and predicting, as well as taking positive and effective measures to improve the ability of social disaster reduction from the perspective of national security.

*C. Hazard mitigation behavior*

71.2% of tourists thought the best disaster prevention propaganda channel was "warning sign", which was followed by the "broadcast in the National Forest Park" and "ticket tips". In the National Forest Park tourists are warned by signs, radio and ticket tips, this may be the most direct way of propaganda. After the tourists ger tickets and enter the National Forest Park, they could receive the propaganda knowledge of hazard mitigation gradually along the visiting process. In the aspect of increasing capital investment, 59.9% of tourists thought more capital should be invested into the emergency rescue equipments, and 55.7% held the view that more money should be invested into the monitoring and forecasting system; in the aspect of improving hazard mitigation education, 65.5% chose the item of "self and mutual rescue"; in the aspect of increasing the emergency rescue facilities, 63.9% chose "emergency shelter"; in the aspect of strengthening infrastructures construction, 74.3% chose "the communication signal coverage". The above describes that most tourists' behaviors of hazard mitigation are positive, more professional, have a certain awareness of self protection and the spirit of team cooperation, able to assist disaster management departments and staffs to carry out the work of disaster prevention and reduction. At the same time, the results of the survey show that the construction of disaster prevention and reduction of the National Forest Park still exist many problems, and need to be strengthened. These provide the basis for taking effective measures to strengthen disaster prevention and mitigation in the National Forest Park.

*iii. Assessments of differences of tourists' RPNH*

The results of tourists' PRNH differences from tourists' gender, age, occupation, educational background, income monthly, family disaster suffering situation and travel traffic. These have been shown respectively in statistical diagram a, b, c, d, e, f, g in Figure 2.

In the aspect of gender, as a whole, RPNH exponents of the females are stronger than the males in natural hazard mitigation attitudes, and the same as in hazard mitigation behaviors. But, the males are stronger than the females in hazard mitigation knowledge. The causes of these differences are: First, the most females prefer humanities such as arts, literary and etc, but the males tend to be more concerned about the natural sciences and have more social activities through which more and comprehensive knowledge could be gained; Second, The characters of the females are more timid sensitive and cautious than the males. In order to ensure their own safety, they often make some preparations for hazard risk in advance. Their hazard mitigation attitudes are stronger than the males.

In the aspect of gender, tourists at 15 to 24 years old have the strongest PRNH, the weakest ones is the tourists at 65 years old or older. The order of tourists' RPNH is coincident from 15 to 24, 45 to 64, 25 to 44, 14 years old or younger and 65 years or older. The reasons are: Firstly, most tourists at 15 to 24 years old have more education opportunities to understand the knowledge about natural disasters in school and to be concerned with current disaster suffering affairs, so as to have higher sensitivity to natural hazards; Secondly, Tourists at 45 to 64 years old are stable in their causes or lives, have certain economic incomes and free time to support their frequent travel, therefore they have higher concern about natural hazards during their travel; Thirdly, tourists at the age of 25 to 44 may be more concerned about their career, family, economic income and haven't more time to travel frequently, so reduce the concern and attention about the natural hazards; Fourthly, most tourists at the age of 14 or below are the students of middle school or primary school who are being educated, because of the influence of age, physical and mental limits, strong ability to accept new knowledge, and pay little attention to social and external environment reflection. When facing natural hazards, they are not courageous, so RPNH abilities are relatively weak; Finally, tourists at the age of 65 or older, although have known or experienced some natural hazards, these activity scopes are relatively smaller, fewer, and conservative, so the abilities of their RPNH are weaker too.

In the face of coming natural hazards, there are also some differences in tourists' RPNH from their different occupations. The stronger is student, farmer, freelancer, worker, staff and civil servant. But there are different levels in three aspects of assessment indicator system of PRNH. The reasons are: students are in the stage of acquiring knowledge and skills, they can receive relatively more comprehensive knowledge about safety education; furthermore, master degree of knowledge of natural hazard reduction decides attitude orientation of the one; in the master degree of knowledge of natural hazard reduction, farmers are less than other occupations, but agricultural production is vulnerable to natural disasters, so through experience, farmers have stronger abilities of RPNH than other occupations in natural hazard mitigation behaviors; freelancers who have widespread types of occupation are easy to obtain more information and knowledge about natural hazards, so they have stronger abilities of RPNH; Workers as a big part of the society members, their attentions to the development of their own and families are greater than those to the social environment and current disaster affairs, and their channels to get information about natural hazards are very narrow so that their abilities of RPNH are not strong; staff always work indoors most of the time, many of them have to work overtime and rarely travel. Although by network and media, they can grasp the relative number of knowledge of hazard mitigation, the perception abilities of hazard mitigation attitudes and behaviors are weaker; civil servants are usually busy with daily administrative affairs, little exposure to the risk of natural hazards and knowledge of hazard mitigation, so their abilities of RPNH are relatively weak.

Statistical diagram d in Figure 3 has shown the results of differences from educational background in tourists' PRNH. Through a comparative analysis of PRNH from the perspective of cultural identity, sequence of RPNH from strong to weak is college or bachelor degree, master degree or above, senior school, junior middle school or the following qualifications. This is mainly because the acquisition level of knowledge and education is a positive correlation with the quantity of hazard mitigation knowledge, the differences of RPNH abilities of tourists between college or bachelor degree, master degree or above is not very different. Meanwhile, these differences also decide tourists' attitudes of RPNH. Therefore, their attitudes to hazard reduction are very clear and strong, and their hazard mitigation behavior is calm and decisive. The lower degree tourists' reflection about hazard risk may be limited by cultural knowledge, so their attitudes and behaviors of hazard mitigation are weaker than the higher degree.

The differences of tourists' RPNH from individual income monthly vary from high to low as follows: ¥5,000-10,000, no income, ¥3,000-5,000, less than ¥2,000, ¥2,000-3,000, more than ¥10,000. The reasons for the differences are: Most visitors who earn ¥5,000-10,000 monthly are high-ranking officers in the enterprises, and have plenty of money and time to travel or contact with the outside world, so they are willing to pay more attention to natural hazard risk, accordingly their hazard mitigation knowledge will be increased, their abilities of RPNH display the highest; The majority of visitors who have no income are students in school, college or university. They are in the stage of being educated, can get comprehensive education and obtain more knowledge on hazard mitigation, and young people usually perform more brave and decisive when facing dangers or risks, therefore they have showed higher abilities of RPNH; Visitors who earn ¥3,000-5,000 and less than ¥2,000 are those have certain career or whose works are not very stable. Visitors whose economic conditions are relatively better will choose a safer way to go out to travel, and have extra time to concern about the external environment they will face, therefore their abilities of RPNH are higher; Those who earn ¥2,000-3,000 monthly are in the development stage of their career. They often spend most of their time on the jobs, and seldom go out and pay less attention to society and hazard risk environment, so they have shown lower RPNH. However, after they pass through this period, their abilities of RPNH will be improved; visitors whose monthly income is more than ¥10,000 tend to overestimate their anti-risk capabilities, and ignore the existence of hazard risks and pay less attention to it, so in fact their abilities of PRNH are the lowest.

To some extent, the results of differences of tourists' PRNH have been caused by family disaster suffering situation. The knowledge, attitudes and behaviors of hazard mitigation are all consistent with the abilities of RPNH, the sequence from weak to strong is no, seldom, general, and more. Analysis of the reason for this difference is: Whether the family experienced natural disaster and the degree of suffering from disasters all belong to the scope of hazard mitigation education. It is usually believed that visitors who suffered more natural disasters have stronger abilities of PRNH. Because they have experiences, and will pay more attention to natural hazard risk than those who have never suffered or suffered a little. So they have got more knowledge of hazard mitigation, more positive attitudes, and will be more experienced and decisive in their behaviors. Among the investigation objects, there are a large proportion of tourists whose families had never or rarely suffered natural disaster, and differences of abilities of RPNH are not very obvious, because of their paying less attention to natural hazard risks.

The differences of tourists' abilities of RPNH from travel traffic vary from strong to weak as follows: by bicycle, by car, by group tour coach and by bus. Young tourists who love travel and adventure prefer riding to the National Forest Park. They have relatively rich experience in the process of cycling tour, and tend to learn more about the natural and social environment of the travel destination, so they would rather master sufficient knowledge of hazard mitigation actively, and also have positive attitudes to hazard mitigation in their daily lives. In addition, riding a bike to travel needs a good physical quality, and has fewer terrain restrictions compared with other travel traffics, so they could get to some natural disasters or risk more easily and directly, and would pay more attention to their own safety. As a result, they have the strongest abilities of RPNH. Tourists who travel by private car with their family members or friends would pay more to the impact on their safety the surroundings have, and would make enough preparation for the trip, so their abilities of RPNH are relatively stronger. Tourists who travel by group coach are weaker in RPNH, for they have strong dependence on travel arrangement made by travel agency. They rarely focus on natural hazards and do not take hazard risks seriously, so they can't act properly and response timely when facing with natural hazard risks; tourists who take bus to the destination are mainly local residents, and many of them are students, so they have more knowledge of hazard mitigation. However, because tourists by bus are usually familiar with the surroundings, they often decrease the emphasis on hazard risks and safety of themselves. As a result, they are the weakest in their abilities of RPNH.

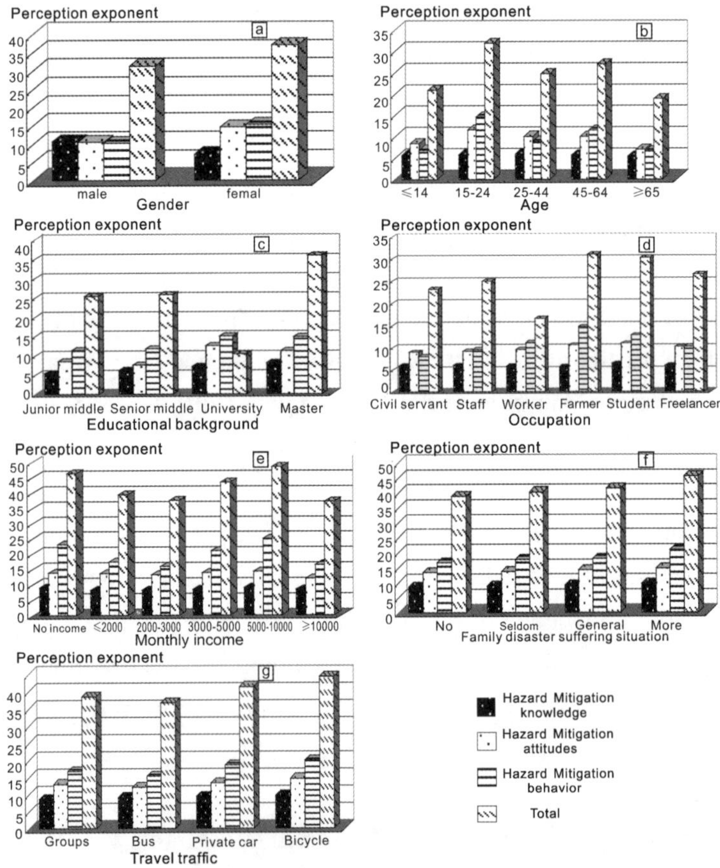


Figure 2 The Differences of RPNH from Tourists' Demographic Characteristics

Notes: (a) gender; (b) age; (c) educational background; (d) occupation; (e) monthly income; (f) family disaster suffering situation; (g) travel traffic

*iv. Discussion*

According to the present situation of natural hazards and distinguishing features and tourism development in China, aiming at the specific study area, assessment indicator system and exponential model of RPNH have been designed and applied. These concrete research contents probably have some differences from the USA, Europe and other developed countries. But, the research direction, contents and methods can be used for reference in management of tourism safety and disaster prevention and reduction.

In this research, under the same conditions of tourist's information acquisition in the Taibai Mountains National Forest Park of China, abilities and differences of tourists' RPNH have been assessed. Regardless of the differences from knowledge, attitudes or behaviors of hazard mitigation, tourists' abilities of RPNH are positively related to the acquisition of information. More contents and channels of information tourists have acquired, more knowledge of hazard mitigation they have. Individual attention and positive attitudes to hazard mitigation also are influenced by the information of social attention, propaganda and correct guidance of natural hazard prevention and reduction. Facing with the risks of natural hazards, tourists' behavior mode is directly decided by timeliness and richness of access to emergency disposal information. Therefore, it is very important to strengthen the channel, content, quantity of information publicity.

There are great differences from tourists' abilities of RPNH between different times and places in the Taibai Mountains National Forest Park. At different travel time, such as pre-travel, during the travel, or post-travel, tourists have different understanding about the disaster-breeding environment in the Park. The longer the tour time, the deeper understanding of the hazard risk environment, the stronger abilities of RPNH. At different tourist attractions in the Park, there are different hazard risks, similarly there are different RPNH. Unfortunately, these researches have not been conducted, and this will be the future research directions.

## Ⅳ. Conclusions

In this research, specific object's perception of a social focus on human sustainable development has been achieved in specific area. From the angle of tourists, taking the Taibai Mountains National Forest Park of China as the study area, according to the field questionnaire investigation data, the assessment indicator system of RPNH has been established; By using Exponential Model of RPNH, tourists' exponents of RPNH have been calculated quantitatively; Furthermore, the abilities and differences of tourists' PRNH have been analysed and assessed systematically.

Finally, the following conclusions have been drawn: The focuses on tourists' PRNH are the type and feature of the leading natural hazards, main channels of information disclosure, risk management of the National Forest Park, social education of hazard reduction, facilities and equipment of natural hazard prevention and mitigation, and so on; the differences of tourists' abilities of RPNH are decided by their different demographic characteristics, such as gender, age, occupation, educational background, income, family natural disaster suffering situation and travel traffic. The National Forest Park and local government should set up different hazard risk reduction preplans and equipments for tourists of different perception type.

In view of research results and conclusions, the recommendations have been put forward from three aspects. From the perspective of tourist activity, we should pay more attention to the importance of natural hazard prevention and reduction. Tourists concerns more about natural hazards in their lives and learn their occurrence mechanism. In response to the government's call, tourists should learn more knowledge and skills, and actively participate in propagandas, lectures, drills, trainings and other public free activities of natural hazard prevention and reduction. In the process of travel, they should actively realize natural hazard risks and make preparation for hazard mitigation; from safety management of tourist and natural hazard risk, the National Forest Park should increase communication channels through a variety of ways of warning signs, tickets, radio broadcast, Internet and others for reminding visitors how to avoid and escape the natural hazard risk, perfecting emergency rescue equipments, setting up refugee passageways and shelters, and cultivating professional rescuers. According to the characteristics of local natural hazard, the National Forest Park also should frequently supply education and training of natural hazard knowledge for visitors so as to improve their awareness and abilities of hazard risk reduction; From macro-control of local government, firstly, the types and characteristics of the natural disasters happened should be investigated and analysed, disaster prevention planning and preplan should also be made. Beyond that, disaster emergency center should be established by local government; [24], [25] secondly, local government should strengthen financial investment in natural hazard prevention and reduction, build and improve the natural hazard warning system. [26] Most of all, by chronically public propagandizing, training and lecturing about natural hazard prevention knowledge for the whole society, the local government should also realize the mission of increasing knowledge, changing attitudes and improving behaviors of all the people toward natural hazard prevention and mitigation. [27]

## ACKNOWLEDGMENT

The authors would like to thank Qi Zhou who provided some information of natural disaster in the Taibai Mountains National Forest Park of China, and 20 undergraduate students who took part in the field questionnaire investigation. This study was kindly supported by the Natural Science Foundation Project of China—"Study on evaluation of tourist risk perception of rainstorm disaster in Qinling Mountains based on Bounded Rationality Model"(No. 41371497) and the Scientific Research Plan Project of Provincial Key Laboratory of Education Department of Shaanxi Province

—"A empirical study on tourist risk perception and risk management of natural hazards in Taibai Mountains Scenic Area"(No. 11JS014).

## References

[1] Ma Zongjin. *Major Natural Disasters of China and It's Reduction Strategies*[M]. Beijing: Science Press, 1994.

[2] An Nan. Coexist with disaster[J]. *Mitigation of China*, 2003(4): 1.

[3] Slovic P. Informing and educating the public about risk[J]. *Risk Analysis*, 1986, 6: 175-184.

[4] Robert A P. Political risk analysis and tourism[J]. *Annals of Tourism Research*, 1997, 24(3): 675-686.

[5] Warmsley D J, Lewis G J. *The Introduction of Behavioral Geography*[M]. Xi'an: Shaanxi People's Press, 1988.

[6] Axlord M, Slovic P. Charactering perception of ecological risk[J]. *Risk Analysis*, 1995, 15(5): 575-588.

[7] Teka O, Vogt J. Social perception of natural risks by local residents in developing countries: the example of the coastal area of Benin[J]. *The Social Science Journal*, 2009, 47(1): 215-224.

[8] Tobin G A, Whiteford L M, Jones E C, et al. The role of individual well-being in risk perception and evacuation for chronic vs. acute natural hazards in Mexico[J]. *Applied Geography*, 2011, 31(2): 700-711.

[9] Li Jingyi, Zhou Qi, Yan Rui. Study on index system for assessment of populace's ability in calamity perception [J]. *Journal of Natural Disasters*, 2002, 11(4): 129-134.

[10] Zhou Qi, Yu Yaochuang. Natural disasters mountainous rural residents perception: Baiyun Village in Taibai Jutou Town of Shaanxi Province[J]. *Journal of Mountain Science*, 2008, 26(5): 571-576.

[11] Yu Qinyuan, Xie Xiaofei. Characteristics of environmental risk perception[J]. *Psychological Science*, 2006, 29(2): 362-365.

[12] Yan Hai, Ge Yi, Li Fengying, et al. A review of the research on psychological measurement paradigm of environmental risk perception[J]. *Journal of Natural Disasters*, 2010, 19(1): 78-83.

[13] Zhang Lansheng, Fang Xiuqi, Ren Guoyu. *Global Change* [M]. Beijing: Higher Education Press, 2003.

[14] Shi Kan, Fan Hongxia, Jia Jianmin, Li Wendong, Song Zhaoli, Gao Jing, et al. Chinese public risk perception and psychological behavior on the information of SARS[J]. *Acta Psychologica Sinica*, 2003, 35(4): 546-554.

[15] Yan Li, Chen Si, Feng Ke. Students' perception of the level of investigation and proposal of mitigation disaster education[J]. *Geological Education of China*, 2007(2): 106-110.

[16] Brooks S, Sutherland C, Scott D, et al. Integrating qualitative methodologies into risk assessment: insights from South Durban[J]. *South African Journal of Science,* 2010, 106(9-10):1-10.

[17] Xi Zhende. Mountainous disasters and countermeasures of disaster reduction in the Qinling-Dabashan Mountains [J]. *Journal of Natural Disasters*, 1994, 3(3): 31-36.

[18] Zhao Ninghong. Advantage and integration of Taibai Mountain Nature Reserve eco-tourism resources[J]. *Forest Science and Technology*, 2009(2): 82-84.

[19] Zhou Xin, Xu Wei, Yuan Yi, Ma Yuling, Qian Xin, Ge Yi. Overview on research methods and application of hazard risk perception[J]. *Journal of catastrophology*, 2012, 27(2): 114-118.

[20] Sun Yue. *Study on the Influence of Turnover Intention on Turnover Risk Perception:Based on the Employees, Investigation on the Knowledge of the High-tech Industry Cluster*[M]. Beijing: China Economic Publishing House, 2012.

[21] Zhang Jinhe. Research on ancient village residents, perceptions of tourism impact: a case of village Yixian-Xidi [J]. *Geography and Geo-Information Science*, 2003, 19(2): 105-109.

[22] Liu Qing, Du Zhongchao, Zhou Qi. Research on the resident's perception difference of the earthquake disaster in Lueyang of Shaanxi Province[J]. *Journal of Xianyang Normal University*, 2011, 26(2): 67-71.

[23] Yu Yaochuang, Zhou Qi. Study on disaster perception for rural residents in western Guanzhong area: a case study of Chencang District of Baoji City[J]. *Normal University of Guizhou (Natural Science)*, 2009, 27(1): 19-23.

[24] Teng Wuxiao. On establishment of disaster prevention plan and emergency management system[J]. *Journal of Natural Disasters*, 2004, 13(3): 1-7.

[25] Gulumian M, Kuempel E D, Kai S. Global challenges in the risk assessment of nanomaterials: relevance to South Africa[J]. *South African Journal of Science*, 2012, 108(108):1-9.

[26] Yang Jun. Discussions on disaster prevention and mitigation and early warning mechanism works[J]. *Disaster Prevention and Mitigation Engineering*, 2003, 23(2): 1-9.

[27] Zhang Xinyong, Bian Xiaohua. Reflections on the disaster prevention education[J]. *Journal of North China Institute of Water Conservancy and Hydropower*, 2008, 24(5): 115-118.

# A Study on Strategies of Sichuan Cultural Tourism Industry Development

Yan Li[1*]

**Abstract:** The rich and distinctive cultural resources are the foundation and prerequisite of cultural tourism industry development. This paper firstly defines cultural tourism, secondly sums up the successful practices of typical cases at home and abroad in regional cultural tourism development, thirdly analyses the problems in the process of Sichuan cultural tourism development, and lastly tentatively proposes the strategies concerned, which are composed of four ways: to fully excavate cultural resources with an integration of culture and tourism, to develop cultural tourism products with a confusion of culture and scientific technology, to produce agglomeration effect of culture industry driven by major cultural tourism projects, to innovate marketing tools so as to manifest the brand effect of cultural tourism.

**Keywords:** cultural tourism industry; strategies; cultural resources; development; Sichuan

## Ⅰ. Defining Cultural Tourism Industry

Cultural tourism industry has been playing a more and more important role in global economy and has already been a key power to accelerate regional economic development. Sichuan government has been valuing it highly and has enacted the policy named Some Advices to Develop Culture Industry listing culture industry as a key field and clarified the detailed orientation and modes. [1] But unfortunately, Sichuan cultural tourism development lagged behind due to the improper exploitation. Therefore, this paper tries to put forward Sichuan cultural tourism development strategies with an integration of Sichuan practices and problems of it.

Different scholars have different understandings towards cultural tourism. Cultural tourism is a supporting system with cultural tourism resources, consisting of three major aspects: cultural aesthetic experience and psychological reaction from the subject of the tourism-tourists; cultural value, landscape value and knowledge discovery value from the

1* Sichuan University, Chengdu, China. 909328352@qq.com.

tourism object-landscapes; practical operation system based on culture creative planning and cultural idea between tourism subject and tourism object. [2] Cultural tourism industry is a coupling of culture and tourism industry and the nature of it is creative industry. [3] Cultural tourism industry is a comprehensive one characterized in experience, creativeness, internationalism and nationality etc. with a carrier of tourism. [4] Cultural tourism industry is a resource to develop tourism market and to allocate historical culture and social culture factors. In a word, the author of this paper considers that the core connotation of cultural tourism industry has two aspects. One is that the tourism activities related to human landscapes reflect human knowledge and wisdoms. The other one is human culture and humanistic spirit. Culture is the soul and motive of tourism. Cultural tourism industry takes shape by exploring cultural resources so as to meet the people's cultural tourism demands.

## Ⅱ. Some Cases at Home and Abroad

Cultural tourism development has a close relationship with regional economy. According to the global economic development history, most developed countries have already made great achievements greatly by developing cultural tourism industry based on their native cultural resources after stepping into 21st century. Therefore, this paper chooses some typical cases from America, France, and China. Their successful cultural tourism development practices will provide a good reference for Sichuan cultural tourism industry development strategies.

*i. Movie and TV culture creativity tourism*

The mode of movie and TV culture creativity tourism means that cultural tourism products are from movie and TV cultural resources and industry, such as theme parks. For example, the famous Universal Studio and Disneyland Park make California very popular landscape attracting so many tourists from the world. Hollywood has already become a well-known business card of American culture industry because it centres on the themes of movies from Universal Film Company, presenting the most wonderful and attractive part for the tourists who can experience it as if they were the actors by using high-tech and creativity. Disneyland originates from cartoon movie and now it has already been the paradise for kids around the world because many vivid cartoon movie figures as Mickey Mouse, Snow-white etc. can have an intimate contact with the tourists, which undoubtedly is a perfect fusion of culture and tourism. Universal Studio and Disneyland Park are the successful world-famous brand with a way of exploring movie and TV cultural tourism resources. Sichuan has a good basis for developing cultural tourism industry. Emei Film Company was founded in 1950s and has produced more than 20 films or TV series, awarded for more than 50 times. Since 1970s, it has made more than 40 films cooperating with foreign film companies from Japan, America, etc. Therefore, referring to Hollywood mode, Sichuan also can make a way to develop movie and TV cultural tourism industry by employing high-tech and cultural tourism resources. For example, it is a good way to build movie and TV culture base, panoramic interaction, etc.

*ii. Art and festival brand cultural tourism*

The mode of art and festival brand cultural tourism means cultural tourism products are formed by building famous festival and celebration brands from art cultural resources. This mode is good to extend cultural tourism industry chain, accelerate related industries and expand regional reputation as well. For example, Provence in the south of France is well known for its lavender. Every year many tourists go for Monton Lemon Festival (in February), Awinion Art Festival (in August) and Provence Lavender Festival. Because of these famous festival brands, Provence has become more and more popular to promote its local cultural tourism industry. Now Provence plays an important role in French tourism. Many artists as Cezanne, Van Gogh, Monet, Picasso, Chagall once came to Provence for their creation and made it an art holy land who greatly improved the popularity of this region in the world. Many tourists travel there by air just for a cup of coffee from Van Gogh café now. Festival tourism has become the leading industry of Provence. In Sichuan, Leshan Dragon Boat Festival and Qingbaijiang Sakura Festival has also become more popular than before.

*iii. Rural cultural tourism*

The rural cultural tourism products are formed by exploring rural cultural resources (natural scenery, folk tradition and customs, etc.) with an orientation of ecological tourism and a tourist destination of countryside. Taiwan's rural cultural tourism has developed very fast. It focuses on an integration of its unique rural tourism cultural resources and new business mode, extending tourism industry chain. It gives priority to market emphasizing tourists' participation and cultural experience, building good service environment, exploring diversified tourism products. For example, Yunlin County of Taiwan is well known for its local drama, which has made the villager merchants acquire good economic benefits. The total revenue from more than 3,000 merchants of several towns almost equals to that of Shaolin Temple scenic spot. [5] Similarly, Sichuan also has a good basis for rural tourism development. For example, Nongke Village and Sansheng Village are very typical. With the fast development of Sichuan traffic, its rural tourism will have great potentials.

To sum up the cases, we comes to the conclusion that the key factors of tourism industry lie in the abundant and distinguished cultural resources. An integration development of culture and tourism is a good path for cultural tourism industry.

## Ⅲ. An Analysis to Some Problems of Sichuan Cultural Tourism Industry Development

*i. Weak awareness of integration of culture and tourism*

Sichuan has a great variety of cultural resources whose economic value hasn't been explored with an integrative development of tourism. Many tourism resources as landmarks and historical sites can't show their cultural connotation well due to a low level of development, which can't meet the market demands of tourism. So the low development of cultural tourism doesn't accord with the abundant cultural resources of Sichuan, which leads to a lack of national and typical cultural tourism projects. So resources superiority can't be converted into industry superiority and market superiority due to a lack of a good integration of industry chain.

*ii. Cultural products with low value-added*

It is the lower development of culture resources that results in cultural products with low value-added. Now the development of Sichuan cultural tourism products is still at an early stage. It mainly remains traditional sightseeing tour instead of driving it into related industries such as food, housing, transportation, travelling, consuming and entertainment. The structure of tourism products is very single, lack of technology and high additional value, which can't meet the tourists' increasing, individualized, diversified and complicate tourism demands.

*iii. Lack of powerful and competitive cultural brands*

In terms of brands building, Sichuan doesn't have famous brands of cultural products at home and abroad with a very low tourism market share. Cultural tourism enterprises are mostly characterized with small scale, low starting point, the total strength mismatching brand positioning.

*iv. Cultural industry development that needs to be more standardized*

On one hand, cultural tourism development can accelerate regional economy to generate new economic growth points. On the other hand, it will lead to some losses of regional cultural resources more or less. It is shown from the research that predatory exploitation is the main problem in cultural resource development, including the ignorance of environmental protection. For example, some places have already been developed into a single function zone of tourism due to the damage of cultural resources.

## Ⅳ. Some Advice on Stratages of Sichuan Cultural Tourism Industry Development

Originally, "strategy" is a term from military science. In this paper it means the method or solution to achieve the goal of Sichuan tourism industry development. So the following four strategies are proposed regarding on an analysis to some problems of Sichuan tourism development.

*i. Deeply digging cultural resources with an integration of culture and tourism*

There should be enough room to integrate culture and tourism because Sichuan has rich cultural resources and a solid tourism basis. By means of existing tourism network and digging cultural resources, it will be effective to extend the tourism industrial chain and optimize tourism industrial structure, convert cultural resources strength into economic strength.

Fully highlighting the theme of historical, regional, revolutionary resources is an effective way. On basis of Sichuan cultural resources, different thematic cultural tourism includes Taoism tourism, Buddhism tourism, poem tourism, Three Kingdoms tourism, red culture tourism, ecological tourism, etc. Chengdu is the origin of Taoism with rich Taoism cultural resources. So the development strategy is to build "Taoism culture tourism destination of the world" so as to expand its influence of Taoism all over China even the world.

The strategy to develop Buddhism tourism is to dig the essence of Buddhism culture with a carrier of Buddhism temples. Sichuan is not only rich in Buddhism culture resources but the center of Zen culture. There are many big or small Buddhism temples in Sichuan. The focus is to show Shu Kingdom's Zen culture and local culture around Emei Mountain and Leshan to make Sichuan a famous Buddhism tourism destination

Poem tourism is characterized with poem culture. Sichuan has had many outstanding poets since ancient times. So the strategy is to fully explore culture resources of famous poets, such as their hometowns, workplaces, poems and paintings. For example, Jiangyou-Li Bai's hometown, Du Fu's Thatched Cottage, Meishan-Chinese poem city, Chengdu-Ba Jin's hometown, etc. should be further built and upgraded. By poem tourism, visitors can appreciate and have a taste of Chinese ancient extraordinary cultural heritages.

To develop Three Kingdoms tourism is to integrate cultural resources of Three Kingdoms to make visitors at home and abroad know its history and development. The statistics show that there are almost total 100 existing heritages related to Three Kingdoms as well as many folk stories, literary quotations and folk arts. [6] The strategy is to innovate Three Kingdoms cultural tourism products. For example, Wuhou Temple can be explored further in some aspects, such as making large music stage of Three Kingdoms or building a video shooting centre, etc.

The strategy of red culture tourism is to dig into the cultural resources of great people and Long March so as to form classic tourism route. The development of red culture tourism resources can make a good education for the teenagers and students on Chinese red revolution history. Moreover, it also can make local regions get a good economic benefit and social benefit. Sichuan is rich in revolutionary relics accounting for around 63%[7] of China, about more than 120, including former residences of marshal, conference sites, historical heritages, important battle field etc.

Then, tourism development of minority cultural resources also should be given more priority. Sichuan has many minorities distributing in west plateau of Sichuan including Ganzi, Aba, Liangshan counties with a majority of Yi and Tibetan nationality. Firstly, it is important to build a vivid image of Sichuan national cultural tourism, which can impress visitors by means of gorgeous tourism slogans. For example, Hainan's tourism slogan is "coconut wind, sea charm". Hangzhou's slogan is "heaven in the sky, Suzhou and Hangzhou in the earth". These slogans help visitors memorize the tourist attractions and promote regional tourism. Secondly, minority regions should emphasize to show and dig local culture so as to build famous cultural brands and establish culture themes. For example, there have been some popular tourism brands as "Jiuzai Heaven", "Oriental Female Kingdom-Luguhu Lake", "Daocheng-the last Shangri-La". Thirdly, minorities regions should attach more importance to tourism planning and strategy, innovating marketing tools, publicizing and sales promotion so as to improve market shares. For example, Ganzi has already become more known and fast-developed tourism region because of its tourism brands "Kangding-hometown of love songs", "Charming Kangba culture", "Chinese Shangri-la tourism centre", etc. Aba also develops its tourism very well because of the famous brand "Jiuzai Valley and Huanglong".

Next, folk culture resources are an important part of tourism development. Folk culture resources mainly cover food, wedding or funerals, festivals, clothing, beliefs, entertainments, etc. Folk culture is a general term of all kinds of customs. Folk tourism development means to explore tourism projects. [8] The strategy of it is all-round, multi-angled and comprehensive including static, experimental and comprehensive modes. Static mode is to make full use of tourism carriers such as folk facilities, folk exhibitions, minority cultural villages, ancient town etc. to meet the tourist's demand of sightseeing. This mode can make tourists know more about folk customs, improve their aesthetic appreciation and promote the protection of traditional folk culture. For example, Chinese Kangba Folk Museum, Xichang Qiong People Stone Tomb Museum, the Torch Festival Museum, Luodai Ancient Town, Pingle Ancient Town etc. are the modes. Experimental mode emphasizes tourist's experiencing local folk customs by participating in folk festivals or other activities from daily life to some important festivals or celebrations. In this modes, experience is the core and essence of tourism from which tourists can fully feel the original flavour of local folk culture. Comprehensive mode is an integration of static, experimental mode and tourism product development. Folk tourism product is very important part of comprehensive mode. The products should stress local folk culture taste and aesthetic quality avoiding vulgarization and low-level repetition. For example, Lijiang is successful in the development of folk tourism products and tourists can buy very special souvenirs with Lijiang culture as scarfs, shawls.

*ii. Developing cultural creative products through the integration of scientific technology and culture*

Because of the keen competition of tourism markets, an innovation of cultural tourism products has already been a unique skill. The idea of creativeness has penetrated into many industries. Creativeness is the fountain to give and promote culture value and the key to innovate new products. It is a good way to reinforce competitiveness of cultural tourism industry by digging the connotation of cultural resources with using high-tech for creativeness. High-tech cultural products can be new elements of cultural tourism industry development. For example, panoramic interactive experience system can be applied into tourism by which tourists can become a captain to drive a "helicopter"to fly over well-known mountains and rivers just by operating remote control level.With a contrast to 3D, 4D movies, this system increases interaction and can make appropriate adjustment according to the tourists' demands. This will be an orientation of tourism in the future.

*iii. Displaying industry accumulative effect with large projects of cultural tourism*

To build big cultural tourism zone and implement all-for-one tourism is a good way to develop cultural tourism. To fully foster compound cultural tourism projects covering culture, experience, entertainment, all-inclusive tourism packages of vacations is important. With cultural tourism as a leading industry, cultural industrial clusters of movie, entertainment, digital culture, international exhibition, creative industry, etc. can be formed and developed. Take cultural tourism complex as an example, firstly it can show the deep culture to strengthen its competitiveness. Then it can increase the guest flow to gather polarity through the integrated development of culture and tourism. The popularity will give great potentials to form cultural clusters.

*iv. Striving to develop Internet plus tourism with an innovation of marketing tools*

Marketing is the last link to realize the value of tourism products. The effective marketing tools will make tourism products into the market smoothly. With the rapid development of Chinese E-business, it is essential to innovate marketing tools, including internet marketing, experience marketing and international marketing. Big data platform should be built for exact marketing. Modern marketing can entitle culture symbols to the brands of products so as to impress consumers. New media have already become more and more common in popularizing tourism brands and exploring tourism markets at home and abroad. American Disneyland is the successful and typical one because of its world-famous brands Mickey Mouse and Mc Donald which are the symbols of American animation or culture.

## V. Conclusion

Culture is the soul and spirit of the region. Culture is a reflection of a national strength. On the one hand, the implementation of China's West Development, the proposals of "One Belt, One Road" and "the Changjiang River Economic Belt" of China are the great opportunities for Sichuan cultural tourism industry. On the other hand, there still existing some limitations in the process of cultural tourism industry for Sichuan, including insufficient investment, incomplete cultural systems and mechanism, incomplete laws and regulations, scarcity of cultural talents, constraints of traditional ideology, etc.

However, as we can see, our president Xi in the 19th CPC National Congress proposed that cultural confidence is so critical to a nation, which should be built and strengthened by many ways, one of which is to develop cultural industry by means of digging into traditional cultural resources. It is important to turn cultural advantages into economic strength by taking different ways, such as innovation of business models, institutional mechanism reform, and introduction of talents, etc.

Therefore, only when Sichuan has enough cultural confidence, could it catch the good opportunities and make full use of the abundant cultural resources so as to make a great leap development for cultural tourism despite of some limitations.

## Acknowledgements

Special thanks to Sichuan University for sponsoring the funding project (SKZX2015-gb16): A Comparative Study between European and Chinese Regional Cultural Resources Industrialization under "One Belt, One Road" Strategy. Also I give my special thanks to my college for its helping me finishing the paper.

## References

[1] Some advices on accelerating Sichuan Cultural industry development[Z]. Official Document from Sichuan Provincial Government, 2012.

[2] Ping Wenyi. *A Theoretical and Empirical Study on Sichuan Cultural Tourism Development*[M]. Chengdu: Sichuan Bashu Press, 2007: 23.

[3] Liu Xiaoli, Xiaonan Zhang, Yu Zhang. A summary of culture tourism industry home and abroad[J]. *Journal of Chinese Business and Trade*, 2010(10): 149-150.

[4] Li Binglei. A study on Guanxi cultural tourism industry development[J]. *Journal of Chinese Market*, 2014(51): 111-113.

[5] Liu Shaofang. *Newspaper of Henan Daily*[N]. 2007-09-12.

[6] Liu Bin. A discussion on Sichuan historical & cultural resources development[J]. *Journal of Chinese Culture Forum,* 2008(8): 182-184.

[7] Zhao Hongchuan. *Chinese Creative Industry Book*[M]. Beijing: Social Science Press, 2008: 268.

[8] Wang Min. A brief discussion of Sichuan folk resources development[J]. *Journal of Culture Research*, 2006(23): 81-82.

# Franchising or Management Contract? An Empirical Analysis of Hotels' International Expansion Strategies

He Xiaorong[1], Hu Qiangsheng[2*]

**Abstract:** Franchising and management contract are important strategic choices for modern hotel industry to achieve rapid worldwide expansion. Based on a survey among the senior management of multinational hotel groups in China Mainland, this paper finds that, as opposed to franchising, management contract is less adopted if a hotel is of larger scale, or the country where the expansion is to occur faces a higher political or economic risk. On the other hand, hotel management contract is more likely to be used for a hotel's international expansion in regions where the education level is higher, international business experience is richer, or hotels are more sparsely located. The finding may provide reference for China's hotel groups' international expansion.

**Keywords:** franchising; management contract; expansion strategy; hotel

## Ⅰ. Introduction

With the service industry's rapid development and its growing contribution to the national economy, lots of researches on the international service industry emerged in the past 30 years, [1-3] which are dominantly about international market entry modes. [4-9] The hotel industry is much studied as an important part of the service industry. Contractor and Kundu found that, non-equity ways, such as franchising and management contract, accounted for 65.5% of international business of the global hotel industry. [8] In North America alone, the proportion of franchising and management contract in the hotel international business is as high as 79%. Still in North America, 41% of the hotels put management contract into practice, while in Europe and Asia, the proportion is 37% and 42% respectively. [8] Therefore, in the tourist hotel management practice, franchising and the management contract are widespread and extremely popular expansion methods of tourist hotels. [10]

China has allowed the entrance of the world's top 10 biggest international hotel

1 Hunan Normal University, Changsha, China.

2* Hunan Normal University, Changsha, China. 345039366@qq.com.

management groups with two major entry modes: franchising and management contract. [11] Marriott Group has been expanding in recent years, at an annual rate of 10 to 20 stores in cities like Shanghai, Dalian and Guangzhou by franchising. [12] Accor group and Marriott Group manage through management contract Peace Hotel and Jing Guang New World Hotel in Beijing, and many other high-end hotels. [13] With the economic globalization, international business is an inevitable choice of Chinese tourism enterprises in the future. [14] Given that there are both similarities and differences between the two entry modes (see Table 1), what factors actually influence tourist hotels' expansion strategies of franchising and management contract? Chekitan investigated the internal determining factors for choosing franchising or management contract on hotel groups' entering international markets. [15] In this study we explore some external factors which influence hotel groups' international expansion strategy choice between franchising and management contract.

This study makes three important contributions. First, it shows that franchising and management contract are the two prevalently acclaimed strategic choices of the large international hotel enterprises (groups) in their transnational operations. Second, the study contributes to determining factors in choosing franchising or management contract for entering international markets, namely, country risk, education level, scale of operation, international experience, and space distribution. Third, the study contributes in empirical methods to verifying the theoretical framework about the choice of hotel's international expansion strategies. [16]

Table 1 Analysis of the Similarities and Differences Between the Franchising and Management Contract

| Business Mode | Capital Concentration | Source of Income | Operating Costs | Claim | Advantage | Administrative Privileges |
|---|---|---|---|---|---|---|
| Franchising | Very low | Brand use fee, the brand continued fees and other service fee | Brand building inputs and the cost of marketing and centralized service | Strong brand strength and the ability of running business, management and service operation | Effective cost expansion and brand output, reducing direct investment and funding risks, franchisees help increase brand awareness and market share | No direct management rights, only the supervision and guidance of the right, lower profits |
| Management contract | Very low | Management fee and other service fee | the cost of marketing and centralized service | Strong hotel management experience and ability | Close control and management of its hotels, reducing investment risk | Management output, direct management rights, higher profit |

Source: Adapted from Li Jinmei (2006).

Following the introduction, the second section presents the hypotheses based on a critical review of literature. The third section describes the study methodology. The fourth section discusses the results and provides conclusions.

## Ⅱ. Literature Review and Hypothesis

Franchising and management contract are both contractual arrangements, which are popular means adopted by hotel groups to enter international markets. Business format franchising was initially applied in the lodging industry and expanded in the United States (US) motel segment in the 1950s. [17] It is a contractual arrangement between the franchisor and the franchisee. On the basis of such arrangement, the franchisor and dozens of franchisees get connected to form a franchising chain or franchising network. [18] It has been widely recognized and accepted that franchising offers a range of advantages including being a less risky way to get into the hotel business, providing worldwide recognition of hotels by foreign travellers and standard services, and producing advantages better than those found in many independent hotels. [19] Even some researchers believe that nothing succeeds like franchising. [20]

Meiseberg supported that franchising imperatives outweigh any generic explanations for chain composition as are studied in previous literatures. [21] A management contract is an arrangement whereby a hotel's owner contracts with a separate company, or an operator, to run a hotel. [22] Some research found that the principal-agent relationship in hotel management contract is flexible and unstable, reflected by the ongoing series of court cases on management contract due to lack of alignment between owners and operators. [23] But the current situation to the top hotel brands is different, such as Four Seasons Hotels & Resorts and Ritz-Carlton, which can generally command longer initial contract terms of the order of 50 years long rather than 10-20 years as usual. [22]

*i. Country risk*

Research on the country risk of multinational corporations' entering mode is well reported in the existing literature. [6, 7, 24] The country risk is of a country's political, economic and legal environment of uncertainty on the stability of enterprises' operation. First of all, we analyse the impact of a country's political and economic risks on the multinational operation strategy used by hotel groups. The traditional transaction cost theory argues that external uncertainty is one of the reasons that businesses choose the form of a hierarchical organization. [25-26] When a high degree of external uncertainty exists, however, the higher the equity ratio and the degree of control of the enterprise, the higher the transaction costs will be. [4-5] Therefore, the transaction cost economics admits that, in the face of high-risk situations, enterprises have a higher demand for the organization form's adaptability and flexibility. [26, 27] When a hotel group enters a potential market at high political or economic risk, it should consider an expansion strategy that adapts to future external changes. At this point, franchising and management contract seem to conform to the requirements of the transaction cost economics; however, the franchising organizational form is the "market", while the form of management contract is a " hierarchical" system. [28] Thus, the franchising should have greater flexibility and adaptability than management contract. Therefore, entering a new market full of uncertainties, franchising compared with a hierarchical forms of organization, is always the hotel enterprises' preference of strategy. We thus put forward the hypothesis (H):

*H1a: the higher political, economic risk which the hotel enterprises face while entering a country, the lower the chance of using the management contract (as opposed to franchising).*

Secondly, in addition to political and economic uncertainty, the hotel enterprises will always encounter a legal risk when entering a new market. Here, the legal risk mainly refers to a country's laws and regulations for the protection of intellectual property, such as trademarks and brands. Generally speaking, the less legal protection of intellectual property rights a country's laws and regulations provide, the more difficult for the agreement to be implemented. However, brand protection for an international hotel chain is very important for international expansion by means of franchising. To a great extent, the brand has become a code of a franchise system, and its indivisible, integrated component. [29] Therefore, lack of legal protection on brands would cause fatal damages to hotel franchising systems. However, management contracts can avoid this kind of legal risks because they do not involve intellectual property transactions but only establish a contractual relationship which tends to be well protected in most countries. Thus we propose the following hypothesis:

*H1b: the higher the legal risk which the hotel enterprises face when entering a country, the smaller the chance of using the management contract strategy (as opposed to franchising).*

*ii. Education level*

Paul L. Ingram's study about US hotel chains' growth in the period of 1896-1980showed that the graduates of Cornell University as a professional manager to join a hotel chain management team have played a positive role in promoting the expansion of the US hotel chain scale (Positively Related). [30] He argued that, professional managers from special hotel schools are able to introduce basic hotel management principles to the hotel chains' management, and help hotel chains to determine the right organizational structure by choosing the correct form of organization to embark on the expansion of networking. Hotel chains use a franchising mode in the process of international expansion, as the franchisor's knowledge (mainly tacit knowledge) and skills need to be transferred. If a country's level of education is low, the potential franchisee's ability of learning in this country can be inevitably weak. According to the view of the transaction cost economics, franchisor hotels may double in cost in the knowledge transfer process. In this situation, the transaction cost theory considers that enterprises, in order to reduce costs, tend to take the form of hierarchical organization to replace the organizational form of the "market" in expansion. [25] Therefore, when hotel companies enter the country with a low level of education, management contract may become the first choice, in order to get better control and supervision of knowledge transfer, and rational use of know-how knowledge such as reservation systems, operating procedures and so on. Here comes the second hypothesis:

*H2: the lower the level of education which the hotel enterprises face when entering a country, the greater the chance of using the management contract strategy (as opposed to franchising).*

*iii. Scale of operation*

Contractor and Kundu found that, in the hotel industry, larger sized hotel enterprises tend to lower the degree of control of their international business models. [8-9] Moreover, the agency theory considers that the "adverse selection" and "moral hazard" problem may increase with the expansion of business scale. Therefore, the larger the enterprise is in scale, the more it will be inclined to choose the form of franchise expansion. [31] Because the franchisee owns the venture and runs the business by himself/herself, he/she strongly expects the business to be successful. [32] The franchisee has claims to his/her shop's surplus profit totally, that is to say, the franchisee's return is directly linked to the shop operating performance, so there is no reason not to work hard, so the problem of moral hazard is solved. [33] Meanwhile a franchisee needs not only huge amount of financial investment in the business, but also sufficient management skills or potentials to gain such skills. When applying for a franchise, only the applicant who is capable and confident with his/her ability in operation and management will be successful, [31] therefore, the problem of adverse selection is solved. In addition, in the franchisee's shop, the franchisee either owns all the equity, or is the largest shareholder. As a result, investment by the franchisee will have to suffer a great loss caused by poor management or the franchise agreement terminating by franchisor because of violating. [34] Therefore, franchising can well reduce the occurrence of "blackmail" behaviour. Compared with management contract, the franchise mode of "market-style" organization is more flexible and adaptable than the hierarchical organization of the management contract model. [16] From the perspective of the agency theory, the larger the enterprise is, the greater agency costs would occur when it chooses to use management contract than franchising. The third hypothesis is therefore:

*H3: the larger the size of the hotel, the less likely for it to use the management contract strategy during the international expansion (as opposed to franchising).*

*iv. International experience*

The transaction cost theory supports that lack of international experience will lead to high organization uncertainty. [25] In the existing research on international experience and international market access models, scholars who focus on the studying of foreign direct investment (FDI) believed that non-equity modes will always be used when an enterprise enters a new market with insufficient international experience, such as exporting, franchising and so on. With experience accumulated, the enterprise will gradually move toward a form with a higher level of control such as joint or wholly-owned ventures. [2, 35] Service management scholars further discovered that service enterprises prefer international expansion through franchise if equipped with international experience. [36] From the conclusions of these studies, we can see that the choice of international expansion mode is linked to the presence or absence of international experience. As for a service-oriented enterprise, if its international experience is limited, franchising is a choice of its international expansion strategy, but it would be difficult to monitor the level of the franchisee' effort. Moreover, it is difficult to assess the operating performance of the franchisee, so it may be more suitable to adopt the management contract. [28] Therefore:

*H4: the less experienced the hotel enterprise is internationally, the more likely for it to use the management contract strategy during the international expansion (as opposed to franchising).*

*vi. Space distribution*

According to the transaction cost theory, dispersed space distribution may produce “internal uncertainty”, as Williamson mentioned, because it will lead to difficulties in the performance evaluation of the employee (agent), and thereby increase the management costs by the way of “hierarchical” management mode. [27] The agency theory also supports this view by arguing that the greater the distance between the principal and agent, the more difficult for the principal to guarantee agents’ working in accordance with the level of effort as required, and the higher the cost will be for the principal’s governance on the behaviour management of the agent. One may observe the opposite in practice, as in some well-known hotel chain groups, where some middle and senior management have very active work ethic, because they reach this position through hard work. Similarly, they are still full of ambition for their future. Therefore, we can assume that in the processes of management contract operation, the motivation of hotel managers’ shirking is not as strong as the agency theory expected. Therefore, the higher degree of concern to new shops, the higher possibility of using the management contract during the expansion of hotels, because the less effort and cost needed for managers in supervision, the more dispersed of new shops in space will be. At this moment, as opposed to the management contract, the franchise way of transferring the residual claiming equity seems more relatively expensive. Therefore, we assume that:

*H5: the more dispersed the hotel enterprise’s new shops are, the larger chance of using the management contract strategy during its international expansion (as opposed to franchising).*

## Ⅲ. Methodology

*i. Method*

This study adopts the Probit model to analyse the factors affecting the selection of hotel enterprises' international expansion strategies. In order to test the hypothesized relationships between the business expansion strategy and country risks and other factors, a regression model between the strategy and various factors is established: Y (hotel enterprises' selection of international expansion strategies, namely franchising or management contract) = F (country risk factors, education level factors, operating scale factors, international experience factors, space distribution factors) +random disturbance term.

Dependent variables of expansion strategies belong to the classification variables. In general, the influencing analysis of dependent variables are discrete variables that always uses Probit model and Logit model. The two models are both effective in econometric analysis; there is no better or worse. [37] This paper selects the Probit model to analyse the influencing factors of hotel enterprises' selection of international expansion strategies. In order to meet the requirements of the model for binary dependent variable, this paper assumes that the international expansion mode of the hotel enterprises come only in two patterns: management contract and franchising, "Management contract" is a pattern whose value is 1. "Franchising" is the other pattern with a value of 0 as a frame of reference.

The specific expression of Probit model is as follows: [38-39]

$$Y* = \alpha + \beta X + \mu \tag{1}$$

and

$$Y=\begin{cases} 1 & Y*>0 \quad \text{management contract} \\ 0 & Y*<0 \quad \text{franchising} \end{cases} \tag{2}$$

In Formula (1), $\mu$ is a disturbance term, subject to the standard normal distribution, thus affecting the hotel enterprise internationalization expansion of the strategy choice of binary discrete selection model, which can be represented as:

$$\begin{aligned} & prob(Y=1|X=x)=prob(Y*>0|x)=prob\{[\mu>(\partial+\beta x)]|x\} \\ & =1-\Phi[-(\alpha+\beta x)] \\ & =\Phi(\alpha+\beta x) \end{aligned} \tag{3}$$

In Formula (3), $\Phi$ is the standard normal cumulative distribution function $Y*$, is a non-observation of the potential variable $Y$, is the actually observed dependent variable $X$, is the influencing factors vector $x$, is an influencing factor. If further refined, we can obtain a hotel corporate international expansion strategy selection Probit model:

$$\begin{aligned} & prob(Y=1|X_i)=\Phi(\alpha_0+\beta_{1n}X_1+\beta_{2n}X_2+\beta_{3n}X_3+\beta_{4n}X_4+\beta_{5n}X_5+\varepsilon_n \\ & =\Phi(\alpha_0+\beta_{11}x_{11}+\beta_{12}x_{12}+\ldots+\beta_{1n}x_{1n}+\beta_{21}x_{21}+\ldots+\beta_{2n}x_{2n}+ \\ & \ldots+\beta_{51}x_{51}+\beta_{52}x_{52}+\ldots+\beta_{5n}x_{5n}+\varepsilon_n) \end{aligned} \tag{4}$$

In Formula (4), $prob(Y=1|X_i)$ is the probability for the hotel companies to choose "management contract" as the international expansion strategy (namely $Y$=1). $X_i$, the independent variable vector, here mainly refers to the country risk, level of education, business scale, international experience and the spatial distribution. $x_{1n}$ represents the $n$-th independent variable under the first argument vector; $\alpha_0$ is a constant, $\beta_{1n}$ represents Probit regression coefficients of the n-th independent variable under the first argument vector, while $\varepsilon_n$ stands for a disturbance, which does not include the influence of the independent variable (its mean values 0, has or does not have the same variance, and it's statistically independent between, and its distribution is normally distributed).

*ii. Measurement*

This paper mainly uses Likert scale tool to measure the country risk, education level and space distribution factors respectively to select "country political risk", "country economic risk", "country legal risk", "regional education level"and "hotel spatial distribution" variable indicators. The two variables of the hotel's scale of operation and the international experience are respectively measured by "the number of hotels the Group has" and "the number of transnational business year". Variables and their definitions are illustrated in Table 2.

Table 2　Variable Definitions

| Variable | Variable Symbol | Definition |
|---|---|---|
| Country political risk | FX1 | 1=Very low 2=Relatively low 3=General 4=Relatively high 5=Very high |
| Country economic risk | FX2 | 1=Very low 2=Relatively low 3=General 4=Relatively high 5=Very high |
| Country legal risk | FX3 | 1=Very low 2=Relatively low 3=General 4=Relatively high 5=Very high |
| Regional education level | JY | 1=Very low 2=Relatively low 3=General 4=Relatively high 5=Very high |
| Hotel operating scale | GM | The number of hotels owned by the Group |
| Hotel International experience | JYAN | The number of years of multinational business |
| Hotel space distribution | FB | 1=Very concentrated 2=More concentrated 3=General 4=More dispersed 5=Very scattered |

*iii. Data*

The study data come mainly from a survey of senior management of some multinational hotel groups in China Mainland.

The survey was conducted from June 7 to July 6 in 2015, at Hilton, Marriott, Accor, Intercontinental, Starwood houses and other foreign brand's high-star hotels in Beijing, Shanghai, Shenzhen, Changsha and Chongqing. The selection of samples was based on the fact that the management contract model of foreign hotel brands in China are basically high-star hotels (four stars and five stars). The questionnaires were distributed to the hotels' deputy general managers and management personnel of higher positions. A total of 150 questionnaires were distributed, and 76 of them were recovered with a recovery rate of 50.66%. 72 questionnaires were assessed as valid, with the effective rate of 94.73%.

## Ⅳ. Results and Discussion

### i. Results

Following the steps of the Probit model, the paper uses Eviews 6.0 software in processing computing model regression coefficients, which can be drawn from the model parameter estimation results (shown in Table 3). Parameter estimates show that the regression results are relatively healthy, the logarithmic likelihood values, and the chi-square test also show that the overall model fits reasonably well.

The model estimates show that the factors of country risk, education level, business scale, international experience and space distribution significantly influence the strategic choice of hotel corporate international expansion. The symbol of the estimated coefficients of the explanatory variables shows a negative correlation between the variables of political risk, economic risk, legal risk, education level, scale of operation contract selection and management contract selection (shown in Table 3).

Table 3 Model Estimation Results

| Explanatory Variables | Estimated Coefficients | Z Statistics |
|---|---|---|
| C | 22.05814 | 5.364429 |
| FX1 | -0.290690 | -3.228054 |
| FX2 | -0.863771 | -4.353365 |
| FX3 | -0.620087 | -2.351734 |
| JY | -6.559470 | -3.592036 |
| GM | -0.081242 | -1.953559 |
| JYAN | 0.062336 | 1.265843 |
| FB | 0.524638 | 3.326102 |
| R2 | 0.854358 | |
| Chi-square test value | 84.08579 | |
| Log-likelihood values | -49.20990 | |
| *P* values | 0.000000 | |
| C | 22.05814 | 5.364429 |

In summary, in the influence factors of risk perception, as opposed to the franchise strategy, the higher the regional political risks and economic risks which the hotel enterprises perceive when entering the new market, the smaller the probability of selecting a management contract; the higher regional legal risk perceived, the smaller the probability of selecting a management contract as well. This shows that the previously proposed H1a and H1b are supported.

In the factors of the regional education level and hotel operators scale, the higher the education level of the hotel where the enterprise is located, the smaller the probability of selecting a management contract; The smaller the operating scale of the hotel enterprise, the greater the probability of selecting a management contract too. This shows that the previously proposed H2 and H3 are also established.

In the hotel international experience and space distribution, the result shows that the more international experience of the hotel enterprise, the greater the probability of selecting a management contract. This finding which is opposite to H4 fails to validate H4. The more dispersed the space distribution of the hotel new stores, the greater the probability of selecting a management contract. This finding is consistent with and therefore supports the establishment of H5. Generally speaking, the lower the perception of political risk, economic risk and legal risk which the hotel enterprises face when entering a region, the more inclined policy makers to choose the strategy of management contract rather than franchising strategy. It also reveals that the regional risk resistance of management contract strategy is poorer, nonetheless, it is more resistant when it comes to franchising strategy.

When the hotel enterprises face lower level of education when entering a region, policy makers are more inclined to choose the strategy of management contract over franchising strategy. When the hotel company's new store in the space distribution of the region shows a more scattered feature, policy makers are more inclined to choose the strategy of management contract rather than franchising strategy. It also reveals that the management contract strategy tends to be applicable to cases with low level of education, while franchising strategy is suitable for the area of the high level of education; Management contract strategy is appropriate for space decentralized management, whereas franchise strategy is fit for the spatial concentration of business.

*ii. Discussion*

This study uses questionnaires and Probit model through the survey of senior managers of transnational hotel groups in China Mainland. Expanding empirical study on the choice of hotel corporate international expansion with five influencing factors, the results of this study have important implications for practitioners.

The study identifies a set of factors that hotel groups should notice and remember as they intend to expand internationally. Franchising and management contract are prevalent and acclaimed strategic choices during multinational operations for the large international hotel management groups. With respect to the franchising, negative relationship between the variables of country risk, education level and scale of operation and management contract selection, and positive relationship between the variables of international experience, space distribution and management contract selection.

The results show that franchising, in international expansion modes, is more likely to survive than management contract, because franchising has a stronger ability to resist risks, in fact, most of the investors are risk averters. [23]

It should be noted that there is a certain deficiency to be improved in future studies. First of all, senior managements of high-star hotels in a foreign hotel brand are this survey's objects, most of whom are very too busy to have time to fill out the questionnaire in time, although the number of valid questionnaires recovered is enough on the statistical significance; however, if there are more effective questionnaires, the results will be more accurate. Secondly, in order to test the associated assumptions, this article tries to apply Probit econometric model. Matching degree and soundness of the model and research purposes, and also more similar studies to test are needed.

In conclusion, this study shows that, facing high country risks, lacking international experience, or operating a large scale or facing high risks, hotel groups' preference is franchising in their transnational expansion strategies. This finding enriches the research about determining factors in choosing franchising and management contract for hotel groups' international expansion. Hopefully, this study will spur further researches on the factors that affect the success or failure of franchising and management contract.

## References


[1] Dunning J, McQueen M. The eclectic theory of multinational production: a case study of the international hotel industry[J]. *Managerial and Decision Economics*, 1981, 2: 197-210.

[2] Terpstra V, Yu Chwo-Ming. Determinants of foreign investment of U.S. advertising agencies[J]. *Journal of International Business Studies*, 1988, 19: 33-46.

[3] Li Jiatao, Guisinger S. The globalization of service multinations in the "Triad" regions: Japan, western Europe and North America[J]. *Journal of International Business Studies*, 1992, 23: 675-696.

[4] Erramilli K M. Entry mode choice in service industries[J]. *International Market Review*, 1990, 7: 50-62.

[5] Erramilli K M. The experience factor in foreign market entry behaviour of service forms[J]. *Journal of the International Business Studies*, 1991, 22: 479-501.

[6] Erramilli K M, Rao C P. Choice of market entry modes by service firms: role of market knowledge[J]. *Management International Review*, 1990, 30: 135-150.

[7] Erramilli K M, Rao C P. Service firms' international entry-mode choice: a modified transaction cost approach[J]. *Journal of Marketing*, 1993, 57: 19-38.

[8] Contractor F J, Kundu S K. Model choice in the world of alliances: analysing organizational forms in the international hotel sector[J]. *Journal of International Business Studies*, 1998a, 29: 325-358.

[9] Contractor F J, Kundu S K. Franchising versus company-run operations: model choice in the global hotel sector[J]. *Journal of International Marketing*, 1998b, 6: 28-53.

[10] Feng Jun. The difference between franchising and other commercial forms[J]. *Business Research*, 2006, 12: 210-213.

[11] Zhou Tongqian. *Hotel Management Strategy*[M]. Beijing: Tsinghua University Press, 2005: 4095.

[12] Li Jinmei, Gao Hong. On the Hotel Group's development during the use of the franchise model[J]. *Journal of Shaoyang College*, 2006, 23: 41-44.

[13] Li Xiuna, Li Tao. Hotel's agent management in the perspective of antitrust[J]. *Tourism Tribune*, 2006, 34: 23-26.

[14] Du Jiang. *China's International Tourism Business*[M]. Beijing: Tourism Education Press, 2006.

[15] Erramilli M K, Agarwal S, Chekitan S D. Choice between non-equity entry modes: an organizational capability perspective[J]. *Journal of International Business Studies*, 2002, 33: 223-242.

[16] Dimou I, Archer S, Chen J. Corporate development of international hotel firms: a transaction cost economics and agency theory approach [J]. *Journal of Marketing Channels*, 2003, 10: 33-53.

[17] Brown J R, Dev C S. The franchisor-franchisee relationship[J]. *The Cornell Hotel and Restaurant Administration Quarterly*, 1997, 38: 30-38.

[18] He Xiaorong, Xu Shaoyang. A study on the performance and its factors of alliance network based on franchising[J]. *Tourism Tribune*, 2009, 24: 54-59.

[19] Cho M. Factors contributing to middle market hotel franchising in Korea: the franchisee perspective[J]. *Tourism Management*, 2004, 25: 547-557.

[20] Murray I. *The Franchising Handbook: The Complete Guide to Choose a Franchise*[M]. London: Kogan Page Ltd., 2006.

[21] Meiseberg B. The prevalence and performance impact of synergies in the plural form[J]. *Managerial and Decision Economics*, 2013, 34: 140-160.

[22] Elana B. Hotel management contract in Europe[J]. *Journal of Retail & Leisure Property*, 2007, 6: 171-179.

[23] Rob V G. Expert attitudes to management contract in the Dutch hotel industry: a DELPHI approach[J]. *Journal of Hospitality and Tourism Management*, 2011, 18: 140-146.

[24] Anderson E, Gatignon H. Modes of foreign entry: a transaction cost approach and propositions[J]. *Journal of International Business Studies*, 1986, 17: 1-26.

[25] Williamson O E. *Markets and Hierarchies: Analysis and Antitrust Implications*[M]. New York: Free Press, 1975.

[26] Williamson O E. *The Economic Institutions of Capitalism*[M]. New York: Free Press, 1985.

[27] Williamson O E. Economic organization: the case for Candor[J]. *Academy of Management Review*, 1996, 21: 48-57.

[28] Dimou I, Chen J, Archer S. The choice between management contract and franchise agreements in the cooperate development of international hotel firms[J]. *Journal of Marketing Channels*, 2003, 10: 33-52.

[29] Liu Fengjun. The essence of franchising and its "cloning" meaning[J]. *Academic Research*, 2001, 29: 22-24.

[30] Paul L I. *The Rise of Hotel Chains in the United States 1896-1980*[M]. New York & London: Garland Publishing Inc., 1996.

[31] Shane S A, Frank H. Franchising: a gateway to cooperative entrepreneurship[J]. *Journal of Business Venturing*, 1996, 11: 325-327.

[32] Brickly J A, Dark F H. The choice of organizational form: the case of franchising[J]. *Journal of Financial Economic*, 1987, 18: 401-420.

[33] Lafontaine F, Shaw K. The dynamics of franchise contracting: evidence from panel data[J]. *Journal of Political Economy*, 199, 107: 1041-1080.

[34] Combs, J G, David J K Jr. Why do firms use franchising entrepreneurial strategy? A meta-analysis[J]. *Journal of Management*, 2003, 29: 443-465.

[35] Agarwal S, Ramaswami S N. Choice of foreign market entry mode: impact of ownership, location and internalization factors[J]. *Journal of International Business Studies*, 1992, 23: 1-28.

[36] Lindquist K F, Laurent L J. Control modes in international service operations: the propensity to Franchise[J]. *Management Science*, 1995, 41: 1238-1250.

[37] Liu Xiuyan, Zhang Yuan, He Xiaohai. Education and the eradication of rural poverty: household survey data based on Shanghai empirical study[J]. *China's Rural Economics*, 2007, 37: 61-68.

[38] Mu Xiangli, Sun Guoxing, Zhang Anlu. Empirical analysis on influential factors of farmers' willingness to agricultural land expropriation[J]. *Chinese Rural Economy*, 2009, 8: 43-52.

[39] Du Xin. Analysis of the influencing factors of rural youth dropouts in China[J]. *Chinese Rural Economy*, 2008, 3: 50-56.

# A Research on Big Data of Tourism Products Based on Internet

Long Rui[1*]

**Abstract:** Based on the development conditions and trends of tourism market and the current hot issues on “big data”, a concept of big data of tourism products is proposed in this paper. Through comparison and analysis of the big data of tourism and the big data of tourism products, the paper explores the respective focuses and specific industrial applications of the two combined with relevant instances. Moreover, it also points out that the research on the big data of tourism products can enable enterprises to improve and optimize their tourism product competitiveness, marketing mode, customer satisfaction, as well as capabilities and means for sorting out and reconstructing the product service process and links. Finally, this paper describes a big data processing method based on the granular computing theory and emphasizes to analyze the constitution and acquisition of the big data of tourism products. The big data of tourism products is divided into 7 classes with 31 subclasses, and the information type of the data falls into static, semi-dynamic and dynamic types.

**Keywords:** big data application; big data of tourism products; granular computing; big data of tourism

The greatest contribution of the Internet is the change of information spreading and communication methods, which fundamentally reduces the cost of information interaction between buyers and sellers. In plain words, the Internet is a data information carrier or channel, and the numerical information loaded on such carrier constitutes the data. By giving unprecedented power to consumers to dominate business, data has contributed in realizing fast and high-frequency information interaction between buyers and sellers and maximizing the values for both sides. [1] Additionally, “data” sparks a big storm in the tourism industry, and numerous institutions and scholars begin to study the applications of big data in the tourism industry.

1* Shanghai Institute of Tourism, Shanghai, China. Longkedan2011@163.com.

## Ⅰ. Origins of Researches on Big Data of Tourism Products

*i. Necessity for a tourism enterprise to apply big data of tourism products*

According to the industrial statistic data, Chinese tourism market is growing at a high speed year by year, wherein, the number of tourists taking self-guided tour grows by up to 30% every year, and the number of tourists enjoying traditional group travel grows by 15% but is now in a decreasing trend. The tourists taking outbound self-guided tour account for a higher proportion, exceeding 70%. The development of self-guided tour will make the customized mode more popular, which is an upgraded version of self-guided tour that can take full account of the demands of tourism consumers with the characters of free travel, deep participation and personalized services.

Obviously, the saying that tourism products rely only on low price and high sales is not adequately established. Customization is not only the demand of a single point, which reflects a problem that the market requires the tourism products to be rich and personalized. If we only consider the transfer from the cost-oriented scale operation to the consumer-oriented customized operation, the tourism enterprises will face big challenges and unforeseeable effects. Due to the relative dependence of tourism products on other product factors, such as transportation, catering, lodging and sightseeing, unrestrained customization lack of reasonable guidance will trap the enterprise in dealing with the repeated resource integration.

So it is one of the problems to be solved promptly that how a tourism enterprise guide can increase the active and reasonable participation of its customer groups to improve its ability to customize tourism products, with its main strategy unchanged. This needs us to start with the data, so as to find an effective solution to constantly help the enterprise promote its product competitiveness from the seemingly unrelated but actually influential massive data.

*ii. Practical significance for all industries (including tourism) to apply big data extensively*

The big data in common sense refers to the application method of the massive data generated in the Internet environment. Many overseas institutions and colleges adopt a broad definition that the big data refers to using mathematical algorithms to mass data for predicting likelihood of an event's occurrence. More specifically, the big data is an information technology and thinking mode to extract the potential values of data by conducting mathematical analysis on various massive data in order to describe current situation, identify problems and predict tendency. The ability of fetching, storage, analysis on massive man-computer interactive data and the corresponding prediction constitute the so called "big data", and the mining and utilization of big data have become a new economic growth point and the source of quality efficiency. [2]

At present, the basic application of big data has penetrated into all walks of life, including the national basic database and information business processing, promoting the information sharing and business collaboration between departments and improving the administration efficiency and service level; the logistics public information service, as the development of modern logistics needs multi-source, massive and space-time data resources; the mining of information value-added products via data comprehensive process, such as Internet of Things, cloud computing, mobile communication, digital earth and other technical supports; the electronic business and enterprise information management, putting more emphasis on the identification, mining and commercial recommendation of the personalized feature information of potential customers. [3]

The typical applications [4] of the big data of tourism are mainly reflected in the following aspects:

Firstly, enhance the capability of precise product launch and cross-boundary integration of digital marketing. For example, periodically and precisely launch products onto the market based on the basic consumption habits and information; rapidly screen, or quickly and steadily increase the target customer groups based on cross-boundary consumer data and information, which seem to be irrelevant to but have inherent relations with each other.

Secondly, improve the capability of data interaction on mobile terminal. For example, enhance the bidirectional functions of client App, such as pushing notifications through App or WeChat to improve the customer adhesion, other than using only mail, email, SMS, website and any other unidirectional means to expand the target customer groups. Gradually analyze the non-confidential personal data of the target customer groups using App for consumption, such as common geographic positions and consumption habits, to improve the precision of targeted screening.

Thirdly, extract the demands of consumers. Continuously improve and perfect products and services upon interactions before purchase decisions, travel notes and photos shared by tourists, as well as final customer satisfaction survey, in order to promote core competitiveness.

Fourthly, monitor traffic in scenic areas and travel destinations.

## Ⅱ. Research Status

### *i. Discrimination of concepts*

The big data of tourism is a combination of tourism and big data, mainly focusing on the general development direction of tourism industry to provide generalized information about the development conditions and trends of the whole industry. Technically, the big data of tourism puts more emphasis on applying the acquisition methods, deduction methods, studying methods and using modes of big data in the tourism industry.

The tourism itself covers massive data of catering, lodging, travelling, sightseeing, shopping and entertainment. The big data of tourism, however, is not only finding the connections in the massive data defined within the boundary of tourism industry, but also counting numbers, analyzing tendencies and conducting regression analysis upon basic models. The big data of tourism is most often based on the tourism industry and extends to the cross-boundary data from other industries related to and interacts with the tourism industry, such as transportation, communication, retail and finance, which are favourable target industries for finding the data links and soft connections. Utilize the available results or trends of big data from other industries to control the market barometer, and find the logical relationship among the loosely-coupled data to facilitate the insight into the condition and trend of the whole industry, for seizing opportunities and making adjustments timely.

The big data of tourism products is not exactly the same as the big data of tourism, except for some correlations and overlaps. Though they have high interoperability at a certain level, they still have obvious differences. Comparing with the big data of tourism products, the big data of tourism is broader, while research on the former is to improve and optimize the tourism product competitiveness, marketing mode, customer satisfaction, as well as capabilities and means for sorting out and reconstructing the product service process and links by gathering, accumulating, sorting out, attempting to associate, adjusting and recreating the association rules and other scientific methods and data processing technologies of the internal and external data related to the tourism products.

In brief, the big data of tourism products not only focuses on the customer demands, but improves the core competitiveness of products and related services by improving the customer satisfaction from all detailed aspects in terms of actual and predictable data, and strengthens the ability for combining, nesting and customizing the tourism products, further promoting the product quality and after-sale service quality to a new level. Through the added values of products, customers will truly enjoy better experience and the profit space of products will be enlarged.

*ii. Status of researches on big data of tourism*

At present, the domestic researches are mainly focusing on the big data of tourism, and a number of institutions, schools, administrative agencies, commercial organizations, large-scale travel agencies and big data specialized service companies are trying to explore their own application methods and application triggering logic for the big data of tourism. According to Li Hong, the big data is the best platform when the tourists are regarded as customers. From consumer portrait to precision marketing and to end consumers, it is to be explored that how the big data are used for serving the tourism, upgrading the big data based public service system of tourism, and utilizing the existing underlying databases to provide the tourists with online intelligent public consulting service. Sun Xiaotian, a senior analyst, points out that the path for capitalizing the big data of tourism lies in utilizing the media big data for self operation, providing to the third parties with the clear and structured contents of big data in the tourism industry, and building a big data platform for providing tourism consulting services, in order to upgrade to a media type think tank.

As indicated by Professor Zhu Puxuan, an enterprise to use the big data for implementing the precision and personalization of service is similar to the big data for diverting the tourist flow for the Potala Palace, which has a great effect. According to Shao Daming, the big data of tourism attaches more importance to the psychological research and analysis of tourists and the experience of tourism products, and therefore, the big data should be truly applied to the experience of tourists to make the tourism organizations aware of the changes of tourism industry and the tourist behaviors, so as to provide targeted products and services. Doctor Chen Xu indicates that the big data can realize the accurate understanding of tourists' demands, realize more precise and targeted marketing service in tourist flow monitoring, public opinion assessment and marketing, to improve the experience of tourists. Moreover, the Golden Palm points out that the big data of tourism will assist the industrial supervision, including destination monitoring, emergency rescue and price guidance; and the big data of tourism will also drive the market forecasting. [5] [6]

Take Beijing as an example, the number of tourists keeps at a high level in Beijing upon the increasing local tourist attractions and increasing nationwide tourism demands. Though the tourism industry operation monitoring and dispatching platform adopted by Beijing can timely monitor the tourist flows of all scenic areas, accompanied by the emergency actions taken upon the camera monitoring information and emergency command systems, the delicacy management of tourism market is still at the stage of on-going monitoring and post-emergency treatment for lacking of advanced tourist flows warning and guiding means due to the absence of data accumulating and big data analyzing systems for digging out the travelling patterns and rules.

Therefore, the Beijing Tourism Consulting Service Centre establishes a scenic area tourist flow analysis system, based on the principle of "conducting multi-dimension analysis of the big data of tourism to provide data support for delicacy management", to portrait the tourism market in multiple lines in Beijing by analyzing the favourite destinations of the overseas tourists and local tourists, in order to dig out the tourist travelling rules and provide data bases for the tourism market management and tourist travelling guides.

Hence, the big data of tourism is applied by the tourism administrations, tourism destinations and scenic areas for overall improving the marketing precision, rationality of resources allocation and guiding the tourists in their travels.

The overseas scholars also pay attention to the applications of big data in the tourism industry, for studying the features and properties of the big data of tourism, as well as the effects of big data on the tourism enterprises. [7] In the research report by Professor Thomas H. Davenport, more than 20 tourism enterprises, including Amadeus, Opera Solutions and Marriott, are fully and pertinently analyzed to point out that the advantages, challenges of the big data of tourism products, as well as the big data of tourism, can assist the tourism enterprises in reorganizing business processes, optimizing profit management, improving distribution capabilities, highly customizing business trips and improving financial capabilities.

*iii. Status of researches on big data of tourism products*

At present, there are no available clear definitions or research outcomes concerning the big data of tourism products. The author, however, finds out the researches on the big data of tourism products by digging out and analyzing the domestic and foreign references on the big data of tourism, including: using the big data to improve the capabilities for customizing the tourism products, control the costs, and make the tours and travels better responding to and concentrating on the demands and preferences by using the big data of tourist satisfaction promotion.

As a kind of special product, the tourism products have relatively special internal data association, and the unpredictability of both internal and external data. Later in this paper, a case concerning the big data of a tourism product is introduced for learning about and understanding in a better way. A tourism product has a period of 5 days, flying from Shanghai to Sanya.

Firstly, the destination, Sanya, lies in the tropical zone with thunderstorms and typhoons prevailing here, where about 4 of 20 typhoons in each year land, mainly during July, August and September. They directly influence Sanya, an island city having less indoor scenic spots to attract the tourists, excepting the outdoor recreational activities. Accordingly, there are many solutions for reducing the adverse affects of the typhoons (tropical cyclones) on the tourists. For example, add one or two days during which indoor activities are arranged in case the typhoon arriving and acting on tourism activities, in consideration of that the historical longest duration subject to the typhoon within the region of Sanya does not exceed 8 hours; the flights avoid arriving or departing within the time influenced by the typhoon; or the tourist product is suspended in selling or operating before or after the known accurate time influenced by the typhoon. Definitely, these ideas are to be adopted based on the market reactions and customer feedbacks. Moreover, the interactions with the customers can be effectively used for adjusting the product policies, by mastering the feedback and preferences of customers during their booking. Don't let any customers feel abrupt or unexpected, but enable them to experience the considerate and full services.

Secondly, the major transportation means is the flights, including the fights of Juneyao Airlines and Spring Airlines every two days, in addition to the daily flights of China Eastern Airlines and China Southern Airlines from Shanghai to Sanya. Preferred and potential airline partners may be selected for a scheduled period according to the big data from the prices of the airlines usually adjusted based on their slack seasons and busy seasons. Objectively, the designer of a tourism product usually attaches more importance to the price factors, but in fact, the on-schedule rates of the carrier and passenger load factor of the fixed routes are important references. A temporary airline with low price at the last route segment depends more on the previous route segment, and has low on-schedule rate due to many uncontrollable factors. In addition, in case of a long flight delay, the rest time will be too short to arrange the scheduled activities for the tourists, who will feel the difference between the actual experience and the promised one, magnifying the defects of products. The considerate feature of products will be improved if a customer's preference for his/her seats is identified as close to the window or aisle.

Thirdly, as for the lodging and catering, also taking the Sanya tour as an example, a vegetarian tourist shall not be catered with animal food; or a tourist allergic to seafood or suffering gout shall be kept away from seafood. Moreover, the wishes of tourists to try some local snacks, e.g. a seafood stall, shall be considered, by providing a good food guide, before arranging the catering. Since such additional services are not cost effective if prepared by using self-owned resources, the cooperation with the food guiding service suppliers will be a good choice to realize the win-win profits with the top-listed restaurants as well as improve the comfort of tourists by providing such considerate service.

As for the procedure for booking a product, the degree and capability for identifying the new users and old members are to be promoted for both Apps and websites. The discrimination between a new and an old member never depends on their IDs and passwords, but depends on the available information about their travelling preferences, favourite food, and favourite hotels. The industrial big data and cross-industrial big data, as well as feedback, are used to refine the product, provide targeted services, expand the exposure of the product and accelerate the receiving of product information. Simplify the booking procedure, keep interacting, and avoid any reworking due to any unexpected pauses or omissions. In addition, the order of a customer shall be effectively confirmed by WeChat, mail or SMS, followed by pushing auxiliary notifications in place corresponding to the tour, including the notifications about the fights and weather immediately before the customer setting out.

Finally, the travelling fatigue of tourists should be mentioned. The sports bracelets are popular with the modern people paying more attention to their life quality, as such devices can be used for monitoring the heart rate, counting step, and recording the deep sleep time. In fact, each bracelet has an SDK (identity) code. The designer of a tourism product may acquire from the bracelet supplier the information about the degree of fatigue, for performing monitoring activities upon the consent of a customer, in order to improve the product from saving physical energy, and provide a reference for the on-site tourist guide or the tourist for monitoring the fatigue strength and avoiding any unnecessary potential risks.

In fact, a tourism product with highly modular design and attaching more importance to the application of data will not merely result in a more quantifiable product with high customization. This paper suggests that the senior executive of a tourism enterprise need to pay attention to the big data of tourism products (e.g. information association, interconnection and interaction), leverage the big data of valuable tourism products to find new profit points, improve the profitability of tourism products and shorten the time for optimizing the tourism products.

## Ⅲ. Prospects of Applying Big Data of Tourism Products

This paper argues that the big data of tourism products has the same characteristics as the big data in common sense, i.e. the four Vs, namely, Volume, Velocity, Variety and Veracity. [9] The general methods and means adopted by other industries for acquiring or accumulating massive data, setting up platforms, building models and analyzing data are also practicable. The tourism products per se do not have strict standards. The big data of tourism products also has special industrial features, highly depending on other industries. Actually, by reasonably utilizing the analysis results of the big data of tourism industry and neighbouring industries, we may use the available data to well prepare for the integration and application of the big data of tourism products.

We may acquire, store, process and deduce from the data of tourism products and the data of relevant factors influencing the tourist experience, to increase the overall value of tourism products and the satisfaction of customers, and then to verify the operations and services of the upstream tourism enterprise according to the market demands.

*i. Method exploration: granular computing*

The granularity plays an important role in the design and implementation of intelligent systems. The granular computing is a "tag" for all theories, methods, techniques and tools related to the granularity and used for solving problems, which is a methodology other than a concrete model or method.

The information granulation aims to create a user-oriented external world based effective concept for simplifying the understanding of physical world and virtual world, and for effectively providing "practical" non-exact solution. As viewed from artificial intelligence, the granular computing is a natural mode for simulating human thinking processes and solving massive complicated problems, to substitute the exact solutions with practically satisfactory approximate solutions so as to simplify the problems and increase the solving efficiency. From the perspective of data analysis and process, the granular computing uses information granules to replace the samples as the basic units for computing by granulating the complicated data, to considerably improve the computing efficiency. The granular computing mainly consists of data granulation, multi-granularity mode discovering and fusion, multi-granularity/cross-granularity reasoning, and other core research contents.

The granular computing is a paradigm for simulating human thinking, so that it is to be analyzed that how each model incorporates the subjectivity of an analyst. The analysis of big data lays emphasis on the relationships between the data, so that the expression abilities are to be compared between the granular constructions (the relationships between granular layers and within the granular layer). The granular computing is based on the big data processing procedure (there are definite corresponding relationships between data acquisition and abstraction, cleaning and integration, presentation and analysis, modelling and explanation). The data granulation is the foundation for the granular computing based on data analysis, and is a process for decomposing the complicated data into information granules according to the given granulation strategies. Various granulation strategies can be adopted according to different data modelling objectives and user demands. As for the granulation of the big data of tourism products, the data acquisition shall be studied at first, including the data contents and sources of data. [10] [11]

*ii. Acquisition and application of big data of tourism products*

As aforesaid, the big data of tourism products is not completely identical to the big data of tourism. The big data of tourism products can be analyzed and used for deducing information to facilitate a tourism enterprise to optimize its products and services. Then, in consideration of the special features of tourism products and the objectives for analyzing the big data of tourism products, it shall be at first judged and identified that which data is within the research category of the big data of tourism products.

According to the most influential definitions in China given by Lin Nanzhi and Tao Hanjun, "as viewed from the tourism destinations, the tourism products refer to all services provided by a tourism operator, upon its tourist attractions, traffic and tourism facilities, to and for satisfying the tourism demands of tourists", and "as viewed from the tourists, the tourism products refer to the experience exchanged by using a certain amount of time, expenditure and energy". [12]

The core of the definition given by Smith S. for the tourism products is that the tourism products are the results from the interaction between a tourism enterprise and tourists, and the final products are the tourism experience provided by the tourism enterprise to the tourists. [13] The view of Smith S. is generally recognized by the foreign scholars, that is, the tourism products are the tourism experience obtained by the tourists.

According to the above definitions, firstly, the tourism products are the tourism experience obtained by the tourists out of their permanent residences; secondly, the tourism enterprises rely on their tourism attractions to provide a series of products and services, including transportation, hotels and scenic areas, to the tourists. Accordingly, the tourism products include the transportation, hotels and tourism attractions.

The tourism transportation has a wide range, including the transportation from the origin to the destination and the transportation between any destinations. For example, for a tourism product from Shanghai to the east coast of America, the major transportation is the flight between Shanghai and New York, and the next transportation from New York to the next tourism destination Boston may be a flight or a bus. As for the major transportation, each airline has its own featured service and distinctive special schedules and prices. The normal rate and on-schedule rate of flights are also very important to the tourism products, for any delays will adversely influence the whole schedule of tourism.

Each tourist may have unique demands for the location and amenities of the hotel. For example, the shopping tourists may select the hotel convenient for travelling, while the vacation tourists may have high requirements for the facilities and equipment of hotel. A tourist who is a VIP of a chain hotel prefers this hotel's brand upon satisfying his/her travelling requirements. Different room prices may be offered by the same hotel. A tourist travelling to an island prefers a sea-view room at the front for better sightseeing, but will pay more than that for other rooms.

The motivation of a tourist is the tourism attractions at a tourism destination. Wu Jinfeng defines the things or phenomena (including natural, economic, social, cultural, political and technical features) at a tourism destination obviously distinguished from the natural, economic, social, cultural, political and technical features of an origin and can produce potential attractions to a tourist from this origin as the tourism attractions. [14] According to Ma Ling, the connotation of tourism attractions can be explained as that, "A tourism attraction is an attractive object for a tourist, having absolute attractive force and relative attractive force. The absolute attractive force originates from a special objective property of a tourism attraction, while the relative attractive force comes from the symbol property, which means that this object constitutes a value identification symbol for a tourist" [15]. This paper suggests that a tourism destination attraction includes the scenic area, cultural and sports activities (concert or competition), festival activities, folk custom and habit, institutional accreditation and logo, and scenery symbolic meaning. [16] Many tourists travel to Taiwan for the purpose of participating in a concert of Jay Chou, or to Tibet just for participating in the traditional Sho Dun Festival in the middle or last ten days of August. The Oriental Pearl Tower and Jiuzhaigou Valley are desirable for the tourists for the former is the symbol of Shanghai, and the later is one of the world heritages.

In addition to the tourism destination attractions, the weather conditions, public traffic conditions, tourism low seasons and peak seasons can also influence the experience of tourists at the tourism destinations.

In general, certain data, which will influence the experience of tourists and the sales of tourism products, can be used for analyzing, to provide intelligent opinions concerning the experience of tourists and the customization of services. Table 1 details and classifies the big data of tourism products.

Table 1 Classification of the Big Data of Tourism Products

| SN | Items | Data Types |
|---|---|---|
| 1 | Airplane | |
| 1.1 | Airline | Static |
| 1.2 | Flight timetable | Semi-dynamic |
| 1.3 | Flight normal rates and on-schedule rate | Semi-dynamic |
| 1.4 | Ticket price | Dynamic |
| 2 | Local Transportation of Destination | |
| 2.1 | Public transportation (subway, bus) | Static |
| 2.2 | Taxi | Static |
| 2.3 | Touring bus | Static |
| 2.4 | Car rental agency | Semi-dynamic |
| 3 | Hotel | |
| 3.1 | Location | Static |
| 3.2 | Hotel amenities | Static |
| 3.3 | Service | Static |
| 3.4 | Hotel brand | Static |
| 3.5 | Room price | Dynamic |
| 4 | Meteorological Data | |
| 4.1 | Origin of trip | Dynamic |
| 4.2 | Destination | Dynamic |
| 5 | Tourism Attraction | |
| 5.1 | Cultural and sports activities | Dynamic |
| 5.2 | Cultural property | Static |
| 5.3 | Peak/low seasons of tourism | Static |
| 5.4 | Natural scenery | Static |
| 5.5 | Scenic area facilities | Semi-dynamic |
| 5.6 | Tourist commodities | Static |
| 5.7 | Institutional accreditation and logo | Static |
| 5.8 | Scenery symbolic meaning | Static |
| 6 | Consumer (Tourist) | |
| 6.1 | Gender | Static |
| 6.2 | Age | Semi-dynamic |
| 6.3 | Occupation | Semi-dynamic |

(To be continued)

(Continued Table 1)

| SN | Items | Data Types |
|---|---|---|
| 6.4 | Consumption history | Dynamic |
| 6.5 | Hobby | Semi-dynamic |
| 6.6 | Fatigue degree | Semi-dynamic |
| 7 | Mass Media | |
| 7.1 | Travelling note | Dynamic |
| 7.2 | Words of mouth | Dynamic |

This paper groups the big data of tourism products into 7 classes with 31 subclasses, and distinguishes the data information type into static, semi-dynamic and dynamic types. The static data is solidified with relative stable structures, which will not change randomly. The semi-dynamic data will change at certain intervals. The dynamic data changes from time to time.

The sources of the big data of tourism products include:

Firstly, the data generated from the activities of and related to the Internet, health, finance, economy and transportation, including the information from Micro Blogs, in forms of letters, images and videos, such as the consumption records, local transportation conditions, tourism destination travelling notes, and words of mouth.

Secondly, the data generated from various computer information systems, in forms of files, databases and multimedia, including logs and other automatically generated information, such as the operation traces of a tourist on an electronic business platform.

Thirdly, the data acquired via various digital devices, experiments and observations, such as the weather information provided by a meteorological system.

As mentioned above, the analysis of big data emphasizes the relationships between the data, and various granulation strategies can be adopted according to different data modelling objectives and user requirements. A tourism enterprise may conduct analysis of the above data based on its granulation strategies.

## Ⅳ. Conclusions and Outlook

This paper clarifies the relations and differences between the big data of tourism and the big data of tourism products, defines the big data of tourism products, and emphasizes the importance of the applications of the big data of tourism products to the tourism enterprises. Emphasis has been put on the feasible application researches on the big data of tourism products in this paper, while it omits the analyses of the big data between the granular layers and granules by combining concrete strategies, which will be further explored by the author. This paper is intended to provide an inspiration for more and further researches on the big data of tourism products based on the operation, management and innovation of tourism enterprises.

## References


[1] Li Wenlian, Xia Jianming. Research status and scientific thinking of big data[J]. *Chinese Journal of Industrial and Commercial Economy*, 2013(5): 83-95.

[2] Li Guojie, Cheng Xueqi. Scientific values of researches on big data[J]. *Bulletin of Chinese Academy of Sciences*, 2012(6): 647-657.

[3] Wang Qinmin. Applications of big data in social and economic development[J]. *Scientia Geographica Sinica*, 2015(5): 691-695.

[4] Fang Wei, Zheng Yu, Xu Jiang. Big data: concepts, techniques and application research overview[J]. *Journal of Nanjing University of Information Science & Technology(Natural Science Edition)*, 2014 (5): 405-419.

[5] Hu Fusheng. Big Data, tourism research and tourism think tank building: 2016 China tourism science annual conference overview[J]. *Tourism Forum*, 2016(5): 92-93.

[6] Pan Haobo. Big data helps promote wisdom tourism [EB/OL]. http://travel.sohu.com/20161128/n474320155.shtml, 2016.

[7] World Travel & Tourism Council. Big data insights for travel & tour[J]. *Future Foundation*, 2016.

[8] Thomas H D. At the big data crossroads: turning towards a smarter travel experience[EB/OL]. http://www.bigdata.amadeus.com/assets/pdf/Amadeus_Big_Data.pdf, 2013.

[9] Gonzalo F. Big data in tourism & hospitality: 4 key components[EB/OL].http://fredericgonzalo.com/en/2013/07/07/big-data-in-tourism-hospitality-4-key-components/, 2013.

[10] Liang Jiye, Qian Yuhua, Li Deyu, Hu Qinghua. Granular computing theory and methods for extracting big data, science[J]. *Scientia Sinica(Informationis)*, 2015(11): 1355-1369.

[11] Xu Ji, et al. Big data processing based on granular computing [J]. *Chinese Journal of Computers*, 2015(8): 1497-1517.

[12] Lin Nanzhi, Tao Hanjun. *Economics of Tourism*[M]. Tianjin: Nankai University Press, 2000.

[13] Smith S L J. The tourism product[J]. *Annals of Tourism Research*, 1994(21): 582-595.

[14] Wu Jinfeng. Distinction of different concepts: tourist attractions and tourism resources, tourism product and tourism experience[J]. *Economic Management*, 2014(8): 126-136.

[15] Ma Ling. Tourism attractions under sociology and construction thereof[J]. *Tourism Tribune*, 2009 (3): 69-74.

[16] Chen Gang. Three forms of tourism attraction symbols and research outlook thereof[J]. *Tourism Science*, 2013(3): 26-36.

# A Research on the Simulation Path of Pro-poor Tourism

Wang Jin[1*]

**Abstract:** This article researches a new analysis method for evaluating and selecting the targeted-poor in pro-poor tourism based on the dynamic simulation in System Dynamics. Firstly, two layers of the targeted-poor are pointed out as the poor village and the poor villager. Then, four subsystems are indicated for screening out the targeted-poor in poverty-stricken area which are subsystems of tourism investment environment and tourism resource from the perspective of the poor village as well as subsystems of personal willingness and family condition from the angle of the poor villagers. Thirdly, causal loop diagram and causal tree of the benefit channels for the poor are analyzed. Lastly, a simulation path are formulated to help the government make strategy on recognizing the accurate poor while implementing pro-poor tourism for alleviating the poor.

**Keywords:** the targeted poor; pro-poor tourism; system dynamics; simulation path; accurate poor reduction

## Ⅰ. Introduction

The purpose of poor reduction lies in the benefits and opportunity for development to the poor. [1] Many studies reveal that the performance of pro-poor tourism (PPT) in most of the poor-stricken area both in China and overseas have been overestimated.[2], [3], [4] Because most of the poor have not been involved in tourism industry and their interest appeal for income increment has not been satisfied.[5] Therefore, it implies uneven benefits in the poor district. As advocated by several researches, an understanding of the targeted-poor for PPT is essential under the background of taking targeted measures to help people lift themselves out of poverty. Based on the above, this article uses the simulation model of system dynamics to analyze the scientific way of screening out the targeted poor in order to enrich theoretical research on PPT, then, providing logic method to PPT organization with effective ways to recognize the poor village where is feasible for developing tourism and the poor who are suitable for attending tourism operation.

1* Chongqing University of Arts and Sciences, Chongqing, China. wangjinecho@foxmail.com.

## Ⅱ. Review on Dynamic Simulation in Tourism Research

*i. Review on foreign researches*

Dynamic simulation (DS) was first put forward by J. W. Forrester, a professor in Massachusetts Institute of Technology. Initially, it was widely used in the research field of manufacturing to assist enterprise and government with making decision on tactic strategy and risk prediction.

Among foreign researches, Nicholas C. Georgantzas(2003) took Cyprus' hotel in Mediterranean as an example to study its value chain and profitability that initially pointed out the term of tourism dynamics which was used for forming series of tourism development strategies for future 40 years of that hotel.[6] Hereafter, the theoretical model of DS could be found in research area of tourism studies. Anthony Dvarskas (2017) illustrated the relationship of variables between sea water quality and ecological capacity by building the causal loop diagram based on the principle of DS in order to illustrate a sustainable dynamic connection between economic model and eco-environment of the coast management. [7]

*ii. Review on China researches*

In recent years, China scholars also realized the significance of DS theory. But few studies connected DS with tourism researches for only fourteen related articles (up to 29th March, 2017) have been indexed in the database of China National Knowledge Infrastructure (CNKI) which is the most popular academic database in China. Though few studies have used DS model in researching China tourism phenomenon, there indicates a creative perspective and effective method to analyze the short-run and long-run performance of tourism industry.[8] As we can see, Wang Miaomiao, Zhang Jinhe and Zhang Xiuling (2010) declared that DS model filled in blanks of dealing with both linear correlation and non-linear correlation in traditional academic area of tourism research.[9] Additionally, Xu Honggang and Bao Jigang (2005) stated the empirical study about applying DS model to tourism planning should abide by the following technical path: Firstly, a reference model must be constructed while the next step is to test the hypothesis and give feedback. Then, an analysis of the model and an empirical study are also necessary.[10] From the perspective of sustainability, Zhang Jiekuan (2011) insisted that subsystems of tourism, population, society, resource and environment are constituents of sustainable tourism. [11] Li Xue, Dong Suocheng, Zhang Guanghai and Jin Xianfeng (2008) substantiated the DS model can be also used to test the tourism competitiveness of a city.[12] They pointed out that tourism development level, tourism influence as well as contribution degree of local tourism must be considered as the first-class indexes when constructing the dynamic simulation model.

## Ⅲ. Methodology

This study aims to explain the simulation path to identify the targeted poor village and the poor family (or individual) by constructing model of DS. The measures of recognizing the poor adopt the principle of subsystem and causal loop diagram which are the main component of DS model. Generally, confirming the problems to build the model indicates the beginning of building the dynamic simulation model. Subsequently, constructing subsystems which display a whole structure of the model are quite necessary for sketching the border of study. Then, level or auxiliary variables included in subsystems should be defined as box variables, rate variables to form systematic structure. Lastly, the causal chain contains positive or negative polarity must be put forward clearly for distinguishing the feedback of the causal loop in the whole system.

## Ⅳ. Conceptual Subsystems

Studies show the most of benefit making from tourism in poor-stricken usually belong to the minority who are investors or outsiders. It implies that the local poor are not out of poverty. According to the essence of PPT, scholars argue that the poor are the target group and beneficiary in PPT. [13] Based on taking target measure in poverty alleviation, this article developed three subsystems to identify whether the poor area have basic condition to develop PPT from the view of village and villager. Finally, three subsystems are designed to explain the path to select the target poor, as Figure 1 shows:

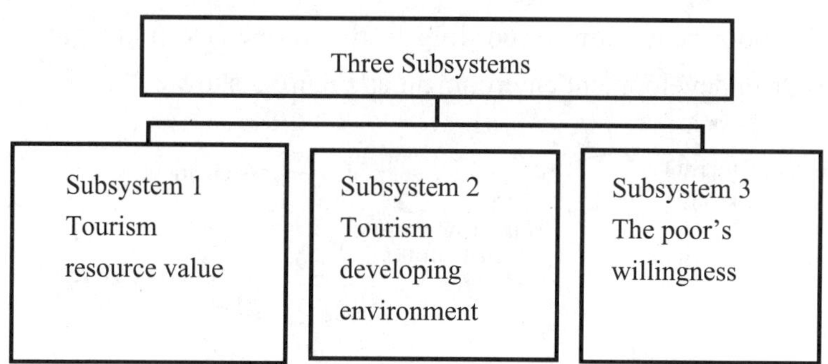


Figure 1 Subsystems of Identifying the Targeted-poor When Developing PPT

*i. Subsystem 1: tourism resource value*

More recently, researchers have documented that PPT are related to many stakeholders, such as local government, tourism investors, the poor as well as non-government organization (NGO). Thus, the evaluation of tourism resource stands for the first important subsystem in recognizing the poor for the value of resource is equivalent of the market prosperity. For this reason, variables and diagram by utilizing causal loop based on DS principles have been pointed out as Figure 2 shows:

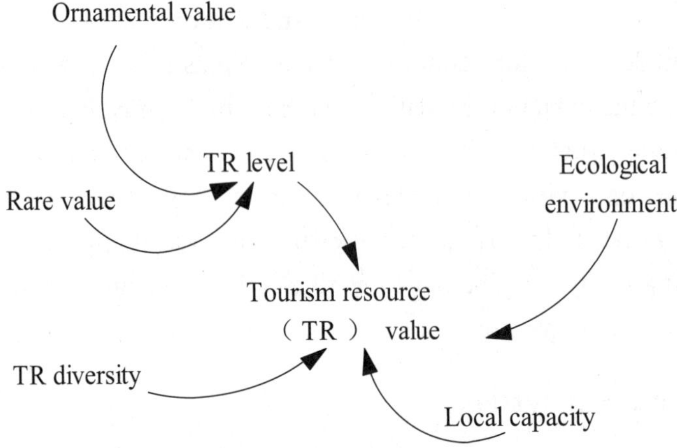


Figure 2 Variables of Tourism Resource Value Subsystem

*ii. Subsystem 2: tourism development environment*

As investment environment of a tourist destination becomes the key consideration to social investors and entrepreneurs, the evaluation of tourism development environment to a poverty-stricken area is the prerequisite to PPT exploration. Many researches confirm the development environment of tourism decides the investment willingness of investors. Some scholars consider that local regional transportation and social economy have closely relationship with poor reduction. According to the above, we point out the variables in subsystem of tourism development environment as Figure 3 shows:

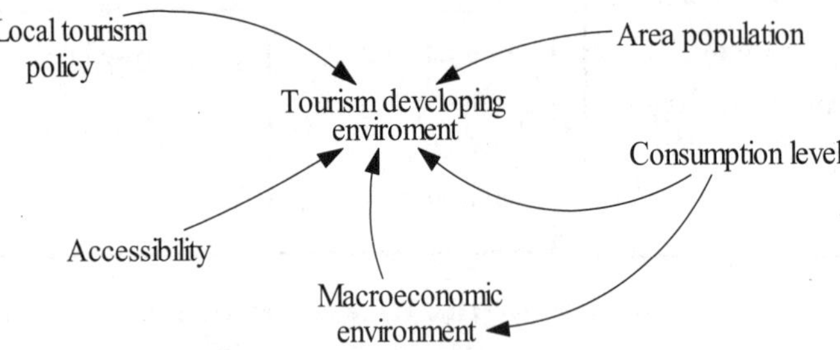


Figure 3 Variables of Tourism Development Environment Subsystem

*iii. Subsystem 3: subsystem of the poor's willingness*

The residents in a poor community account for the target of PPT which means their identification and willingness towards PPT is vital foundation for local tourism exploration. Research shows that residents' perception of getting benefit from economy, society, policy, as well as psychology in local tourism has a positive correlation with community involvement.[14] As the poor are the main beneficiary in PPT while tourism development needs local labors for consideration of cost, both the residents' cultural and social identification effect their willingness to attend PPT, regardless being positive or negative.

Based on previous researches, we proposed variables in subsystem of the poor's willingness as Figure 4 shows:

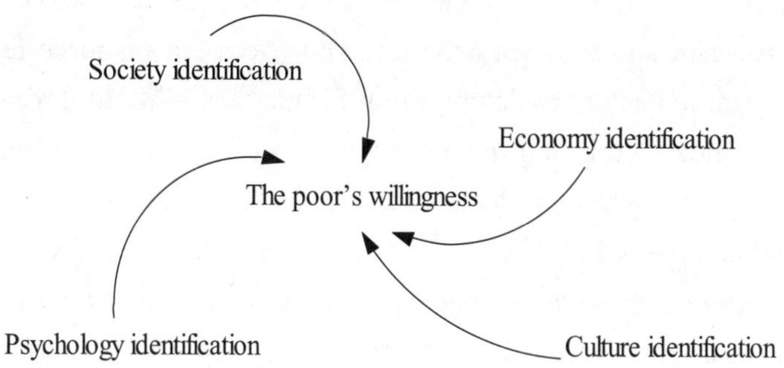


Figure 4 Variables of the Poor's Willingness Subsystem

## V. Simulation Path of PPT Based on Recognition of the Targeted Poor

According to the principles of dynamics system, we take use of Vensim, a software which is usually used to construct simulation model for explaining how to identify the poor who is available for involving in PPT. Based on above three subsystem and their variables, causal chain and polarity should be annotated aiming to perfect the simulation path.

After modified by Vensim, it can be inferred that there are twenty-eight variables in the causal loop model as shown in Figure 5 which include three box variables (A, B, C) to display the subsystems of identifying the targeted-poor and twenty-five auxiliary variables named a1-a11, b1-b7 and c1-c7 respectively to show the causes of box variable A, B and C.

Table 1 Subsystems and Variables

| Variable Subsystem | Box Variables | Auxiliary Variables | Causal Loop |
|---|---|---|---|
| Tourism resource value | A | a1-a11 | — |
| Tourism developing environment | B | b1-b7 | R1 |
| The poor's willingness | C | c1-c7 | R2, R3 |

## VI. Conclusion

According to the theory of system dynamics, a causal chain contains at least two variables which have cause-and-effect relationship with each other. From Figure 4, we can deduce that there are thirty-six causal chains to illustrate how to screen out the accurate poor village and villager. Additionally, three causal loop chains are found in the mode which imply positive correlation on the cause-and-effect variables in forward feedback loop.

*i. Tourism resource value decides feasibility of PPT*

In the subsystem of tourism resource value, there are one box variable (A) and eleven auxiliary variables (a1-a11) among which four variables (a5, a8, a9, a11) can be considered as the first index when evaluating the tourism resource value in a poor-stricken area. Indeed, many scholars argued that both the level and type of tourism resource should be investigated while developing tourism and tourism products.Thus, tourism resource level (a5) and its diversity (a11) are regarded as the basic condition for the feasibility to develop PPT strategy. Furthermore, the essence of tourism development lies on its eco-environment(Chenman, 2011), ecologic environment (a8) and local capacity (a9) also have positive correlation with tourism resource value.

*ii. Tourism developing environment becomes crucial to investors involved in PPT*

Undisputedly, tourism strategy depends on analysis on area environment of tourism development. As mentioned above, one box variable (B) with seven auxiliary variables are included in the second subsystem. From the model, we can see area population (b4) and volume of private cars (b6) are proportional to the value of tourism development environment.

Since investors in PPT also aim for getting profit from tourism industry, the microeconomic environment of the potential tourist market plays a quite vital role in the process of PPT. Except for the variables of local tourism policy (b1), accessibility (b2), area population (b4), consumption level (b5) and macroeconomic environment (b3) account for key factors to recognize whether the accurate poor district is suitable for developing tourism. The first causal loop (R1) we can see in the model can be named as "economy-consumption loop" which comprises of three causal chains as "tourism development environment (B)→+microeconomic environment (b3)→+consumption level (b5)". As microeconomic environment determines consumption level of potential tourist markets, the investigation of micro economy in the cities nearby poor-stricken area plays a key element to identify the economic development value while practicing PPT strategy in the targeted poor village.

*iii. The willingness and perception of the poor on PPT should be surveyed and considered*

Residents' perception has been a hot research perspective both in sociology and anthropology.

In China, under the policy of taking targeted measures to help people lift themselves out of poverty, the poor gradually become the core stakeholder in PPT that signifies the perceptions and attitudes of the poor to the tourism impact their willingness to whether and how to attend PPT. So effective measures should be taken to improve residents' perceptions and attitudes (Lu Song, Zhang Jie, 2009) before carrying out PPT.

In the third subsystem, one box variable (C) with seven auxiliary variables (c1-c7) are presented to explain what do cause the poor's willingness to be involved in PPT.

In addition, result shows there are two causal loops (R2, R3) in subsystem of the poor's willingness. Firstly, R2 reveals the relationship between direct recognition of personal economic benefit and identification to PPT which can be regarded as the loop of "direct economic benefit from tourism (c5)→+economy identification (c1)→+the poor's willingness (C)". Some studies indicate the economic benefit from tourism development has most positive feedback with the residents' identification to tourism (Mostafa, Mastura, Ned & Ghafar, 2017). Moreover, emotional solidarity such as social and psychological benefit can be a key construct to consider when investigating residents' support for local tourism as R3 reveals the four variables (c1-c4) have direct causal effect with each other that the loop is expressed as "economy identification (c1) →+culture identification (c2) →+psychology identification (c3)→+society identification (c4)" which represents multiple factors, except for the economy, influence the poor's involvement in PPT also including social, cultural and psychological effect in the process of interacting with the tourists, local government and tourism investors.

*iv. Limitations and directions for future research*

This study contributes theoretically to the literature of poor reduction through developing tourism in the way of recognizing the poor village and the poor individuals by constructing simulation path which offers insights in understanding the variables and their causal loops while deciding whether and how to implement PPT strategy. However, we caution that the findings may be less generalizable to the empirical analysis because of the limited pages. So taking the poor village as an example to test and modify the theory model could be a direction of future research.

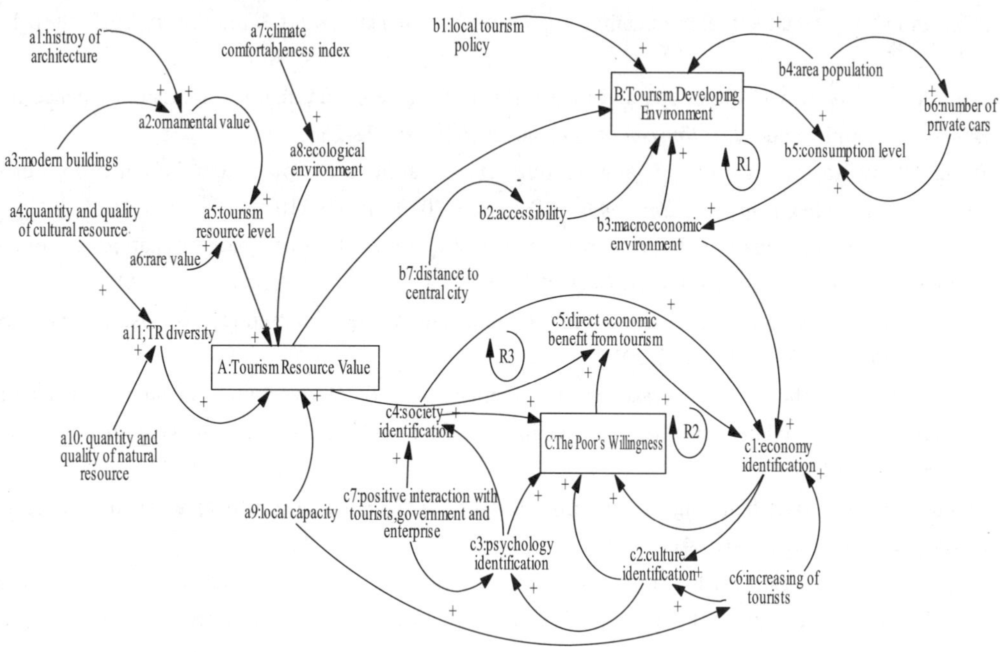


Figure 5 PPT Simulation Path Based on Causal Loop

## ACKNOWLEDGMENT

This research was supported by China Humanities and Social Sciences of the Chinese Ministry of Education, project of The Community Benefit of Ethnic Minority Village in Sichuan from Perspective of Pro-poor Tourism(16YJC630119), project of Development of Sub-tourist Destination Based on Image Defilation Theory (11XJC630015); Project of Chongqing University of Arts and Sciences, Tourism Functional Zone Construction in Western China under the Background of Improvement of Industrial Structure (Z2012LY01).

## References

[1] Zhou Xinhong. Concerning for the basic elements in tourism based poverty elimination[J]. *Tourism Tribune*, 2002(1):17-21.

[2] Bowden J. Pro-poor tourism and the China experience[J]. *Asia Pacific Journal of Tourism Research*, 2005, 10(4): 379-398.

[3] Weinz W, Bolwell D. Reducing poverty through tourism[Z]. International Labor Organization Sectoral Activities Programme Working Paper. Geneva, 2008: 266.

[4] Guo Shn. Industrial chain tracing method for assessing pro-poor tourism impact[J]. *Tourism Tribune*, 2015, 11(30): 31-39.

[5] Deng Xiaohai, Zeng Liang, Luo Mingyi. Study on the accurate identification of tourism poverty alleviation under the background of accurate poverty alleviation[J]. *Ecological Economy*, 2015(4): 94-98.

[6] Nicholas C G. Tourism dynamics: Cyprus' hotel value chain and profitability[J]. *System Dynamics Review*, 2003, 3: 175-212.

[7] Anthony D. Dynamically linking economic models to ecological condition for coastal zone management: application to sustainable tourism planning[J]. *Journal of Environmental Management*, 2017(188): 163-172.

[8] Tsionas E G, Assaf A G. Short-run and long-run performance of international tourism: evidence from Bayesian dynamic models[J]. *Tourism Management*, 2014(42): 22-26.

[9] Wang Miaomiao, Zhang Jinhe, Zhang Xinling. On the application of system dynamics in tourism research[J]. *Yunnan Geographic Environment Research*, 2010(1): 105-110.

[10] Xu Honggang, Bao Jigang. Theory and method of the application of system dynamics in tourism planning[J]. *Economic Geography*, 2003(5): 704-709.

[11] Zhang Jiekuan. Dynamic simulation of sustainable tourism development[J]. *Systems Engineering: Theory & Practice*, 2011, 11: 2012-2017.

[12] Li Xue, Dong Snocheng, Zhang Gnanghai, Jin Xianfeng. A study on dynamic simulation and evaluation of tourism competitiveness in Shandong peninsula urban agglomeration[J]. *Geographical Research*, 2008(6): 1466-1477.

[13] Zhang Zhigang, Xiao Jianhong, Chen Ynfei. Review of overseas on pro-poor tourism[J]. *Resource Development & Market*, 2016(4): 484-488.

[14] Chen Zhiyong, Li Lejing, Li Tianyi. The organizational evolution systematic construction and empowerment significance of Langde Miao's community tourism[J]. *Tourism Tribune*, 2013, 6: 77-86.

# Assessing the Impact of High-Speed Rail on Tourist Attraction Distribution in China

Wu Chuntao[1], He Xiaohe[2], Li Longjie[3], Luo Mingzhi[4*]

**Abstract:** This paper aims to assess the effects of high-speed railway (HSR) construction on tourism industry in China, from a perspective of tourism attraction distribution. In particular, the study selects Beijing-Tianjin-Hebei urban agglomeration and Yangtze River Delta urban agglomeration as study areas, using ArcGIS analysis method to evaluate the operation of Beijing-Shanghai high-speed railway on the distribution of national tourist attractions. The spatial change patterns of the attractions during period 2012-2016 are indicators used to explain the effects. The study results show that HSR has a significant effect on the attraction distribution. On other side, the attractions cluster degree is decided by both of the size of cities along HSR and the distance from attraction to HSR stations.

**Keywords:** urban agglomeration; tourist attraction; spatial distribution; high-speed railway; GIS

## Ⅰ. Introduction

Tourist attraction, the core component of tourist destination, is an important part in tourism industry (Lew, 1987). Constructing, rating and approving national A-level tourism attraction is one the effect methods used by the China National Tourism Administration (CNTA) to improve the quantity and quality of tourist attraction. By the end of 2015, a total of 7,951 scenic area were awarded national A-level tourism attraction. Tourist Attraction Rating Categories is a rating system used by CNTA to determine the quality of the attraction. It is broken up into five categories which are 1A, 2A, 3A, 4A and 5A (4A or 5A attraction is also known as High Level Attraction). The categories are awarded based on, amongst other factors, the importance of the site, transportation, tours as well as issues related to safety, cleanliness and sanitation (Chris et al., 2009). Road level and transportation time to nearby

1 Sichuan University, Chengdu, China.

2 Sichuan University, Chengdu, China.

3 Sichuan University, Chengdu, China.

4* Sichuan University, Chengdu, China. luomingzhi_123@163.com.

airport/port are key elements to value the transportation score.

China has recently built the world largest high-speed passenger rail network and is continuing to expand it rapidly. Certainly, HRS operation can be a tool for tourism destination development by reducing the transportation costs and improving accessibility. However, CNTA does not add HSR sector to Tourist Attraction Rating Categories, the real or potential influence that HSR had on China's tourism industry is unclear, and its impact on tourism industry planning or distributions is still not clear. Therefore, this paper aims to assess the effects of high-speed railway operation on tourism industry in China, from a perspective of tourism attraction distribution. In particular, the study selects Beijing-Tianjin-Hebei urban agglomeration and Yangtze River Delta urban agglomeration as study areas.

This paper includes five sections. After the introduction, is the Section 2, literature review. Section 3 introduces the study area and study method. Section 4 is the calculation results and Section 5 is discussion and conclusion. The study results will give Chinese policy makers and destination planners some useful suggestions, as well as promote transportation-tourism collaborative operation.

## Ⅱ. Literature Review

Researchers have studied the effects of HRS on tourist attraction's aggregation in US, EU and Japan. Sean (2008) argued that HSR can connect the tourist attractions in the southern and northern regions of California, promote the tourism activities, and gather the surrounding tourist attractions together. Masson and Petiot (2009) investigated that if the forthcoming South European HSR lines between Perpignan and Barcelona could make tourism attraction stronger, and found that the resulting increased spatial competition may reinforce the phenomenon of the tourism activities agglomeration around Barcelona to the detriment of Perpignan. Noboru et al. (2011) assessed the socio-economic impact of HRS in Japan. They found that the construction of Tokaido Shinkansen had significantly affected urban functions and tourist landscape, which was reflected by some new tourist attractions appeared nearby the high-speed rail stations (Jiang et al., 2014).

Some researchers have studied the impact of HSR on tourist attraction in China. Such as Wang et al. (2012) found that the influence of HSR are mainly reflected by the elements and structure of tourism destinations. Jiang et al. (2014) said that HSR could reduce travel time, shorten distance between tourists' starting places and destination, but increase the competitiveness bewteen cities or tourist attractions along the railways. While the experiences of US, EU and Japan indicate that HSR construction or operation could change the spatial distribution of tourist attractions, especially led to aggregation of tourist attraction around HSR station. There is no researcher noticed this issue in China.

## Ⅲ. Study Area

This study selects two urban agglomerations to evaluate the influences of Beijing-Shanghai high-speed railway on the location of tourist attraction. One is Beijing-Tianjin-Hebei (BTH) urban agglomeration, another one is Yangtze River Delta (YRD) urban agglomeration.

*i. Beijing-Tianjin-Hebei (BTH) urban agglomeration*

The BTH urban agglomeration includes Beijing City, Tianjin City, and 11 cities in Hebei Province. Beijing and Tianjin are two megacities with population more than 10 million, and Hebei is one of important industrial province in northern China. In 2016, this region has 685 national tourist attractions, and the amount of tourist attractions per capita is 0.000006. Figure 1 shows that the tourism attractions have formed a small-scale agglomeration around Beijing and Tianjin respectively, while the attractions in Hebei Province are more evenly distributed. There is no obvious agglomeration phenomenon of the tourist attraction in the southern in Hebei Province where Beijing-Shanghai high-speed railway passing through.

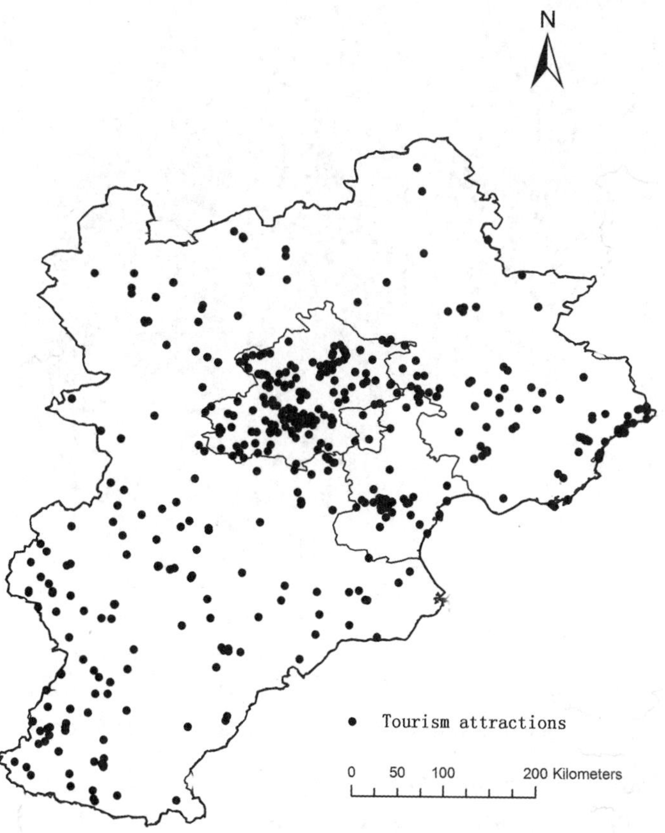


Figure 1 Distribution of Tourist Attractions within Beijing-Tianjin-Hebei Urban Agglomerations in 2016

*ii. Yangtze River Delta (YRD) urban agglomeration*

Figure 2 is the distribution of tourist attractions within the Yangtze River Delta in 2016. The Yangtze River Delta, situated in southern Jiangsu and northern Zhejiang provinces, includes fourteen cities. Shanghai is the main terminus for the delta. Hangzhou is famous for its beautiful scenery around West Lake. By the end of 2016, YRD had 1772 national tourist attractions, and the amount of tourist attractions per capita is 0.000019. Figure 2 shows the distribution of tourist attractions within the Yangtze River Delta in 2016. There is a northwest-southeast convergence tendency in the southern part of Jiangsu Province. The spatial distribution of tourist attractions is consistent with the section of Beijing-Shanghai high-speed railway which runs through Jiangsu Province.

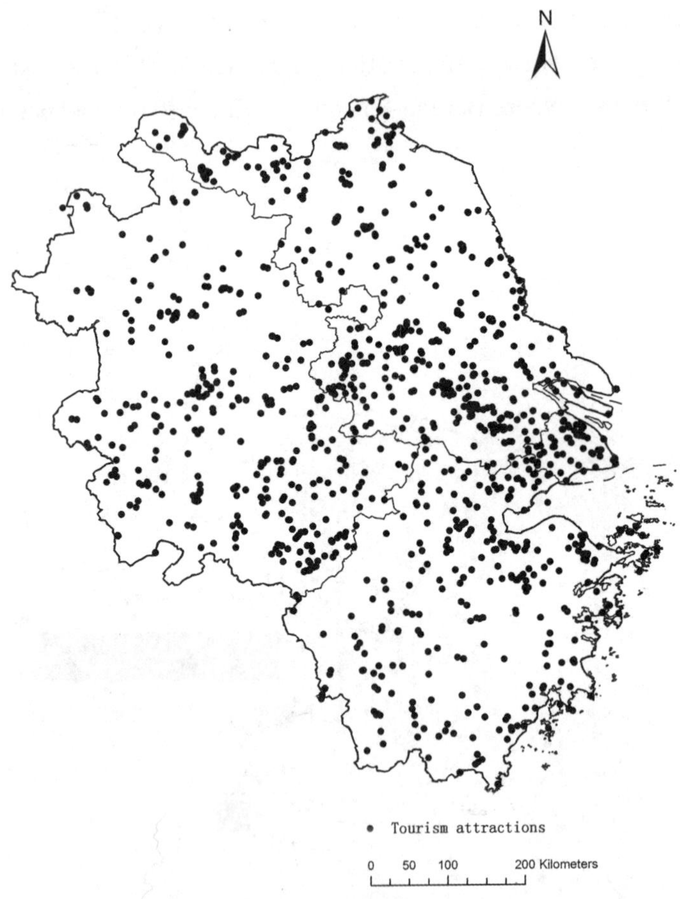


Figure 2 Distribution of Tourist Attractions within the Yangtze River Delta in 2016

*iii. Beijing-Shanghai high-speed railway*

The Beijing-Shanghai high-speed railway is a 1, 318-kilometre long high-speed railway that connects the BTH urban agglomeration with the YRD urban agglomeration. Its construction began on April 18, 2008, and the line commenced operation on June 30,

2011. There are 24 stations on the line (see Figure 3 and Figure 4) which provide a good background to the analysis of the impacts of HRS construction on tourist landscapes.

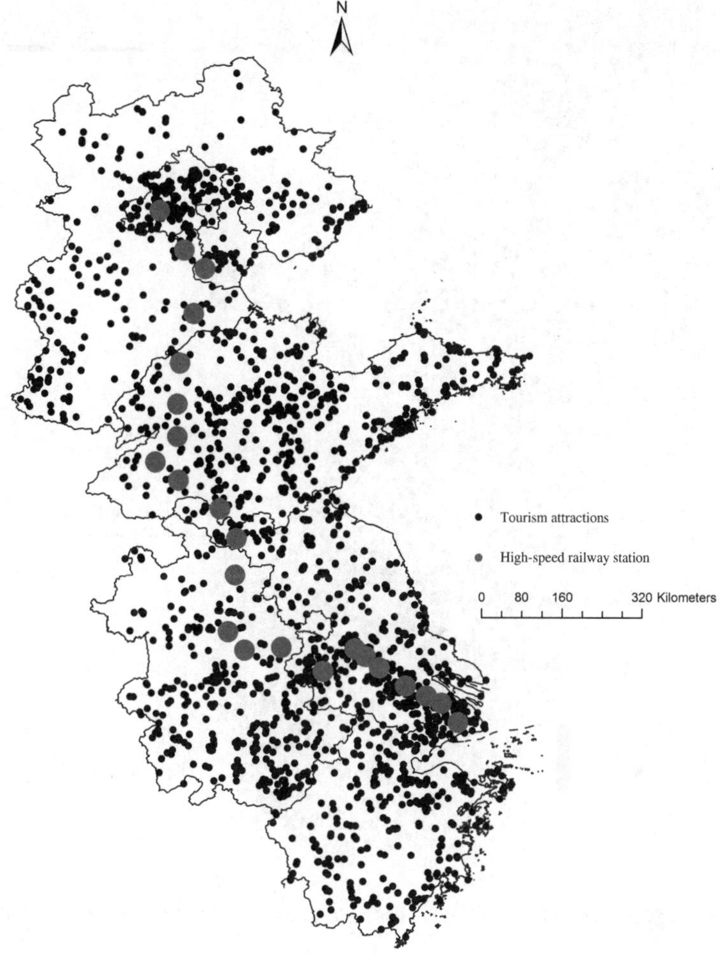


Figure 3 Distribution Structure of Tourist Attractions along Beijing-Shanghai High-Speed Railway in 2012

Figure 4 Distribution Structure of Tourist Attractions along Beijing-Shanghai High-speed Railway in 2016

# Ⅳ. Study Method and Data Source

*i. Data collection*

This study uses two sets of tourism data, tourist attractions and Beijing-Shanghai high-speed railway stations. The tourist attractions in 2012 and 2016 are from the local tourism bureau and China National Tourism Administration (CNTA).The geographical coordinates of tourist attractions and railway stations are collected by author. Using above tourism data, this paper investigates the influence factors of the tourist attractions agglomeration.

*ii. Study Method*

Two-stage spatial analytical approach is employed to clarify tourist attractions agglomeration.

A quantitative research approach with nearest neighbor index through ArcGIS is adopted to analyze the tourist attractions agglomeration along the high-speed railway.

Tourist attractions are abstracted as point, so that the spatial distribution of the elements can be researched objectively. First, calculate the linear distance from one tourist attraction to its nearest attraction (*dmin*). Then consider the set of tourist attraction ($S_i$) and the amount of the tourist attractions (*n*), the average actual distance is calculated as Eq.(1).

$$\overline{d_{min}} = \frac{1}{n} \Sigma_i^1 = 1 d_{min}(s_i) \quad (1)$$

As shown in Eq. (2), the estimate distance (*E*(*dmin*)) can be obtained by the research area (*A*) and the number of tourist attraction (*n*).

$$E(d_{min}) = \frac{1}{2}\sqrt{\frac{A}{n}} \quad (2)$$

The nearest neighbor index(*R*) is the ratio of average actual distance to estimate distance, and expressed as follows:

$$R = \frac{\overline{d_{min}}}{E(d_{min})}$$

The result *R*=1means the high-grade tourist attractions are randomly distributed. *R*>1means the tourist attractions are evenly distributed. *R*<1 means the tourist attractions are agglomeration distributed.

In order to find the positive area of the tourist attractions construction, the high-grade tourist attractions along high-speed rail stations within 50 kilometers are divided into three groups. First group includes the 10 kilometers. Tourist attractions within 10-30 kilometers are classified into the second group. And the third group contains the tourist attractions around the railway station within 30-50 kilometers.

## V. Results

Table 1 shows the density of high-grade tourist attractions of Beijing, Tianjin, Langfang, Ganzhou, Nanjing, Zhenjiang, Danyan, Changzhou, Wuxi, Suzhou, Kunshan and Shanghai.

It can be concluded that the density characteritics of cities are quite different. As the economic and traffic centres, the density of tourist attractions in Beijing, Tianjin, Suzhou and Shanghai is higher than other small cities, which means the amount of tourist attractions is relative to the size and the development level of the cities.

Table 1 Density of High-grade Tourist Attractions in Main Cities of Urban Agglomeration

| | 5A | 4A | 4A-Above | Urban Area/km² | Quantity/Area Ten Thousand km² |
|---|---|---|---|---|---|
| Beijing | 7 | 73 | 80 | 16,410 | 48.75 |
| Tianjin | 2 | 33 | 35 | 11,946 | 29.30 |
| Langfang | 0 | 5 | 5 | 6,500 | 7.69 |
| Cangzhou | 1 | 2 | 3 | 13,419 | 2.24 |
| Nanjing | 2 | 5 | 7 | 6,587 | 10.62 |
| Zhenjiang | 2 | 6 | 8 | 3,843 | 20.82 |
| Danyang | 0 | 0 | 0 | 1,047 | 0 |
| Changzhou | 1 | 5 | 6 | 4,385 | 13.68 |
| Wuxi | 3 | 26 | 29 | 4,628 | 62.66 |
| Suzhou | 6 | 33 | 39 | 8,488 | 45.95 |
| Kunshan | 1 | 3 | 4 | 927 | 43.15 |
| Shanghai | 3 | 51 | 54 | 6,340 | 85.17 |

As shown by Table 2, most of the tourist attractions can be calssified into the second group. However, the quantity of tourist attractions in first group is the lowest. The result indicates that 10-30 kilometers away from railway stations is the best for the construction of tourist attractions.

Table 2 Quantity of High-grade Tourist Attractions of Railway Station Within 50 Kilometers

| Railway Station | 0 km-10 km | 10 km-30 km | 30 km-50 km | 0 km-50 km |
|---|---|---|---|---|
| Beijing South | 10 | 23 | 11 | 44 |
| Tianjin South | 1 | 5 | 1 | 7 |
| Langfang | 3 | 1 | 5 | 9 |
| Cangzhou West | 0 | 0 | 0 | 0 |
| Nanjing South | 3 | 6 | 0 | 9 |
| Zhenjiang South | 10 | 22 | 8 | 40 |
| Danyang North | 1 | 3 | 4 | 8 |
| Changzhou North | 6 | 2 | 1 | 9 |
| Wuxi East | 0 | 8 | 2 | 10 |
| Suzhou North | 0 | 17 | 7 | 24 |
| Kunshan South | 1 | 2 | 1 | 4 |
| Shanghai Hongqiao | 1 | 18 | 9 | 28 |

Table 3 indicates the nearest neighbour index of high-grade tourist attractions are less than 1, which means tourist attractions agglomeration have been formed in the vicinity of the high-speed rail stations. As the transportation hubs of Beijing-Shanghai high-speed railway,

Tianjin south and Nanjing south station aggregate more tourist attractions than other stations.

Table 3 Nearest Neighbor Index of High-grade Tourist Attractions of Railway Station in 50 Kilometers

| | $\overline{d_{min}}$ | $E(d_{min})$ | $R$ |
|---|---|---|---|
| Beijing South | 6.075 | 7.283 | 0.834 |
| Tianjin South | 6.828 | 16.746 | 0.407 |
| Langfang | 8.1 | 18.312 | 0.442 |
| Cangzhou West | 0 | 0 | 0 |
| Nanjing South | 4.233 | 14.767 | 0.287 |
| Zhenjiang South | 7.952 | 8.688 | 0.915 |
| Danyang North | 8.0 | 18.085 | 0.442 |
| Changzhou North | 5.618 | 14.767 | 0.380 |
| Wuxi East | 4.28 | 14.009 | 0.306 |
| Suzhou North | 5.782 | 9.237 | 0.626 |
| Kunshan South | 14.5 | 22.150 | 0.655 |
| Shanghai Hongqiao | 5.168 | 8.376 | 0.617 |

## Ⅵ. Discussion and Conclusions

This study seeks to shed light on the relationship between HSR and tourist attractions. The construction of HSR promotes the tourist attractions agglomeration. And the agglomeration degree of tourist attractions is closely related to the city scale and the distance away HSR.

The overall spatial distribution structure of tourist attractions in China shows a gradually increasing pattern from west to east. The spatial distribution of the tourist attractions is inhomogeneous, especially BTH urban agglomeration and YRD urban agglomeration aggregate most tourist attractions. The distribution in these two urban agglomerations is in coincidence with the Beijing-Hangzhou Grand Canal and Beijing-Shanghai high-speed railway spatially.

The construction of high-speed railway has really generated clustering effect on the distribution of tourist attractions. But the cluster degree of tourist attractions is determined by the size of cities along high-speed railway. The attractions cluster degree in main cities as Bejing, Tianjing, Suzhou, Shanghai is significantly higher than other cities. The tourism attraction in YRD urban agglomeration is also more active than BTH urban agglomeration for the level of cities.

Furthermore, the distance to the railway station is an important factor on the construction of tourist attraction. The distance of 10-30 kilometers to station is benefit to the construction and development of tourist attractions.

This study suggests that transport infrastructure has important impact on the spatial distribution of tourist attractions. Alternatively, the tourism practitioners ought to take the influence of HSR into consideration when planning and building regional tourist attractions.

## ACKNOWLEDGMENT

Support from the Ministry of Education of Humanities and Social Science Project ( No. 17YJAZH090), the Sichuan Social Science Research Program (No.SC17TJ009), and the Sichuan County Economic Development Research Center Project (No.xy2017019) and the Tourism Development Research Center of Sichuan (SCTRC) (No. LYC 18-17) is gratefully acknowledged.

## References

[1] Lew A A. A framework of tourist attraction research[J]. *Annals of Tourism Research*, 1987(14): 553-575.

[2] Chris Ryan, Gu Huimin. *Tourism in China: Destination, Cultures and Communities* [M]. New York & London: Routledge, 2013: 11-37.

[3] Randolph S. California high-speed rail economic benefits and impacts in San Francisco [Z]. San Francisco: Bay Area Council Economic Institute, 2008 (10): 1-44.

[4] Masson S, Petiot R. Can the high speed rail reinforce tourism attractiveness? The case of the high speed rail between Perpignan (France) and Barcelona (Spain) [J]. *Technovation*, 2009(29): 611-617.

[5] Noboru H T. High-speed railway construction in Japan and its socio-economic impact [J]. *Journal of Urban & Regional Planning*, 2011.

[6] Jiang Haibin, Liu Jiangguo, Jiang Jinliang. An analysis of the accessibility of China's tourist attractions under the impact of high-speed railway [J]. *Tourism Tribune*, 2014(29): 58-67.

[7] Wang Degen, Chen Tian, Li Li, Zhang Yun. Enlightenment and research of tourism impact on high-speed rail[J]. *Scientia Geographica Sinica*, 2012(32).

[8] Jin Cheng, Lu Yuqi, Xu Jing. Spatial structure with base of tourist flow scene in Yangtze Delta[J]. *China Population Resources & Environment*, 2009(19): 114-119.

# PART III

# Destination Image and Tourist Behavior

# A Research on the Influence of Consumer Self-brand Consistency on Hotel Brand Attachment: The Moderating Role of Self-motivation

Wang Juan[1], Hu Xiaowen[2*]

**Abstract:** This article draws from the self-concept in consumer research to help explain in hotel industry whether self-motivation plays the role in the process of the influence on self attachment exerted by self-congruity, and how it works. Moreover, this paper discusses the particularity of self-congruity of hotel brand. After postulating relationships among self-congruity, hotel brand attachment and self-motivation, this research first collects data from some hotel customers, and then uses Regression Analysis in SPSS20.0 to verify the research hypothesis. The result are as follows: (1) self-motivation has a significant regulating effect in the process of self-congruity's impact on the hotel brand attachment; (2) the influence factors of the same hotel brand attachment are different due to different self-motivations; (3) the same influence factor has different influence degree of different products because of the regulation of self-motivation; (4) neither actual self-image nor ideal self-image has a positive effect on customers' buying sentiment due to the particular attributes of hotel products.

**Keywords:** self-brand consistency; hotel brand; brand attachment; self-motivation

## Ⅰ. Theoretical Basis and Literature Review

### *i. Self-concept*

The self-concept was first proposed by Harvard psychologist James. In his *Principles of Psychology*, he divided self into two parts: experiential self and pure self. Experiential self is divided into three parts: mental self, material self and social self. It emphasizes that "I" and "belong to me" should not be distinguished, and what are related to "me" in material and spirit are the components of "self". And the pure self emphasizes the subjective initiative "I".

1 Beijing Jiaotong University, Beijing, China.

2* Northwest Minzu University, Lanzhou, China. huxiaowen0620@gmail.com. The two authors contributed equally to this work.

Until 1982, Sirgy systematically summarized the concept of self, and he pointed out that the self-concept is the sum of individual feelings and autognosis, the cognition of one's talent, external, character and personality; It has two important characteristics: firstly, self-concept is subjective cognition, which does not have the attribute to describe the objective state; secondly, its object is the cognition of itself instead of cognition of other external objects. [1] He divided the self-concept into real self, ideal self and social self. On this basis, the theory is enriched and developed.

*ii. Brand personality*

Brand personality can be anthropomorphic as the intrinsic characteristics of a brand, which can be described with human temperament. Jenniffer L. Aaker said the brand personality is —a feature collection of people associated with specific brand users. [2]

Upshaw thought that the essence of brand personality is a link, and the brand show its charm and quality by its personality as well as emotional communication with consumers to expect resonance, so as to form a link between the brand itself and its potential consumers.[3]

Wang Meiling simplified brand personality as a character with a unique personality and behaviour attitude. The definition of brand personality is broad and complex, but in general, it can be considered brand personality as human personality, which can be described and inducted and with certain external performance, more of a symbol. [4]

*iii. Self-motivation*

Swann argues that there are two different motivations in consumer purchasing decisions, which are self-confirmation and self-promotion. Researches on self-confirmation motivations show that individuals are easier to accept the evaluation information consistent with themselves in the process of self-realization. In the self-confirmation, they will deliberately enhance the safety of human-computer interaction, so as to achieve the purpose of interpersonal communication. [5] Bosnjak and Sirgy (2012) suggested that when the self-promotion motivation was stimulated, the role of brand personality would be weakened, and brands with higher degree of self-consistency of consumers can't help consumers and brands to establish emotional ties, thus it was difficult to enhance the role of brand attitude promotion.[6]

*iv. Brand attachment*

Chultz, Kleine and Kerman (1989) and other marketing scholars define brand attachment from the perspective of social awareness and self-concept, with the three dimensions of intergration, individual and temporal orientation. [7] The author stndies the influence of self-brand consistency on brand attachment.

First of all, the research objects of self-brand consistency in recent years are mainly based on the distinction between public social products and private products for personal use, and a more consistent conclusion is obtained, that is, compared to the private products, the brand attachment of public social products is more influenced by the consistency of self-brand. [8] However, there is less attention paid to the products with different division of the right of ownership and use.

Secondly, the effect of self-brand consistency on brand attachment is also widely proved, but the effect of the real-self consistency, ideal self-consistency and social self-consistency of the same consumer on brand attachment is different.

In addition, some scholars found that the self-brand consistency have not always the positive impact, and even consumers have psychological conflict with some high self-brand product. About this issue, Li Yaoqi and Guan Xinhua think the utility of self-brand consistency may be influenced by self-motivation. [9] Similarity does not bring a preference, and it is necessary to consider the influence of self-motivation.

## Ⅱ. Theoretical Model and Questionnaire Design

Product property theory means that the effectiveness of real self-concept and ideal self-concept on brand attachment depends on the brand property. Zinkhan and Hong (1991) showed that the brands used in private places are more influenced by real self-brand consistency than products used in public places by rational self-brand consistency.[10] Therefore, in this conclusion, this study argues that such products with only short-term use right but without ownership rights as hotel brand, is more influenced by the real self-brand consistency, namely, hypothesis one:

*H1: the real self brand consistency is positively correlated with the hotel brand attachment, and the impact utility is stronger.*

*H2: self-motivation has a regulatory role in the influence of self-brand consistency on brand attachment.*

*H3: affected by self-motivation, ideal self-consistency has stronger brand attachment when consumers choose high-star hotel brand.*

*H4: affected by self-conformation, real self-consistency has stronger brand attachment when consumers choose high-star hotel brand.*

*H5: affected by self-promotion, ideal self-consistency has not good brand attachment when consumers choose economy hotel brand.*

*H6: affected by self-conformation, real self-consistency has stronger brand attachment when consumers choose economy hotel brand.*

## Ⅲ. Questionnaire and Data Analysis

After determining the final questionnaire, 200 questionnaires were sent out, and a total of 178 questionnaires were collected, and the valid questionnaires were 143. The investigation period is about 15 days and the effective recovery rate is about 72%.

## Ⅳ. Reliability and Validity Analysis

The reliability test of this questionnaire is conducted mainly through the SPSS20.0, and the Cronbach a coefficient of the questionnaire is analysed. The results are as follows: the Cronbach a coefficient of the questionnaire is 0.908 (larger than 0.7). In addition, the Cronbach a coefficient of each dimension is larger than 0.7, which indicates that the questionnaire has a high reliability, and scales have high consistency and high stability.

The overall validity of the questionnaire was 0.846, which indicates that the questionnaire was suitable for factor analysis.

The first part of the questionnaire mainly involves the following aspects: in order to facilitate the selection and statistics of the sample data, the author remarks the self-consistency difference of the samples less than 1 as high self-consistency, and remarks the attachment degree more than 15 as high attachment. The attachment is equal to the total score of four items of brand attachment dimensions.

The research model takes "self-brand connection" as independent variables and takes "brand loyalty" as the dependent variable, according to the research model of Wang Meiling. The consistency measurement is measured by the difference, with "real self brand personality difference", "ideal self-brand personality difference", "ideal social self-brand personality differences" as independent variables ($X_1$, $X_2$, $X_3$). The real self-discrepancy, ideal self-discrepancy and ideal social-self discrepancy are calculated as follows:

$$X_j=1/5\sum|P_i-S_{ij}|(i=1,2,3,4,5;\ j=1,2,3,4,5)$$

Among them, $P_i$ is the score of consumers for brand personality on the question; $S_{ij}$ is the score of consumers for self-concept on the $i$ question; $X_1$, $X_2$ and $X_3$ are the real self-differences, ideal self-differences, and ideal social self-differences, which are the evaluation of the consumer on self-dimensions. [11]

Simple correlation analysis is used to examine the correlation degree of variables. The calculation of simple correlation coefficient reflects the relationship degrees between variables. In SPSS Statistical Analysis Foundation, Application and Practical Essence edited by Wang Lu and Wang Qin, it is mentioned that the correlation coefficient $|r|=0$ indicates no correlation, and the correlation coefficient $|r|$ between 0 and 0.3 indicates weak correlation, and the correlation coefficient $|r|$ between 0.3 and 0.5 indicates low correlation, and the correlation coefficient $|r|$ between 0.5 and 0.8 indicates significant correlation, and the correlation coefficient $|r|$ about 0.8 indicates high correlation, and the correlation coefficient $|r|$ of 1 indicates complete correlation.

The correlation analysis results of the questionnaire are as follows: most of the correlation coefficient is greater than 0.5, which shows that the correlation is good.

## V. Regression Analysis

After verifying the correlation of the questionnaire, the regression analysis was carried out. In the study on the effect of self-brand consistency on brand attachment, take the difference of real self-consistency ($X_1$), the difference of social self-consistency ($X_2$), the difference of ideal self-consistency ($X_3$) as independent variables, brand attachment level ($Y$) as the dependent variable.

Based on the above data we can create a multivariate equation: $Y = 1.73X_1$-$2.25X_3$. Adjusted $R_2$ is 0.12. Although the $R_2$ is not large, from the sociology, psychology, political science and other disciplines, majority of its interpretation is not more than 0.3, so the model has a better ability to explain. From the results, without considering self-motivation, the real self-brand consistency and hotel brand attachment degree is negatively related, and social self-consistency has little effect on the degree of hotel brand attachment, and ideal self-brand consistency and hotel brand attachment are positive correlation. The assumption of H1 is false.

Then, the concept of self-motivation was introduced, and then to score the self-confirmation and self-promotion through Likert's 5 level in the questionnaire setup and to subtract the two items in the process of questionnaire data statistics. Self-motivation greater than 0 indicates self-motivation, self-motivation equal to 0 indicates no self-motivation intervention, while self-motivation less than 0 indicates self-promotion motivation.

Self-confirmation and self-promotion motivations were introduced in the following two regression models.

Based on the data, we can establish two multivariate equations:

$$Y_1 = -0.82X_1+2.22X_2-2.50X_3;$$

$$Y_2 = -1.6X_1+4.05X_2-3.79X_3;$$

Compared to the first equation, it is not difficult to find that all the coefficient changes, so H2 hypothesis is true. That is, self-motivation has a regulatory role in the influence process of self-brand consistency on brand attachment.

Based on the establishment of this hypothesis, three hypotheses will continue to be tested using regression analysis. So, next, high-star hotels and budget hotels will be tested. In the process of recruiting the questionnaire, I have divided high-star hotels and budget hotels according to the current hotel grading standards, for convenience statistics, three-star and above is regarded as high-star hotel, and below three-star hotel is regarded as economy hotels.

The following two regression models are analysis for the samples of high-star hotel selected.

Based on the above data, we can establish a multivariate equation:

$$Y_1 = -0.07X_1+0.89X_2-1.96X_3;$$

From the analysis of the model, it can be seen that in the regulation of self-promotion motivation, the influence of the self-brand consistency of consumers who choose high star hotel brand on the degree of brand attachment performs as real self-brand consistency is positively related to hotel brand attachment degree, and social self-brand consistency is negatively correlated to hotel brand attachment degree, and ideal self-brand consistency is positively related to the degree of hotel brand attachment. Among them, due to $| 1.96 |>| 0.89 |>| 0.07 |$, the difference coefficient of ideal self-consistency is the largest, so H3 is true. We can establish a multivariate equation:

$$Y_1 = -5.5X_1 - 0.14X_2 - 0.17X_3;$$

In the regulation of self-promotion motivation, the influence of the self-brand consistency of consumers who choose high star hotel brand on the degree of brand attachment performs as realself-brand consistency is positively related to hotel brand attachment degree, and social self-brand consistency is positively correlated to hotel brand attachment degree, and ideal self-brand consistency is positively related to the degree of hotel brand attachment. Among them, due to $|-5.5|>|-0.17|>|-0.14|$, the difference coefficient of real self-consistency is the largest, so H4 is true.

The following two regression models were used to examine the sample selection of economy hotels.

$$Y_1 = -8.79X_1 + 8.21X_2 - 0.48X_3;$$
$$Y_2 = -3.19X_1 + 6.2X_2 - 2.64X_3;$$

Under the regulation role of the self-confirmation and self-promotion motivations, the influence of the self-brand consistency of consumers who choose economic hotel brand on the degree of brand attachment performs as real self-brand consistency is positively related to hotel brand attachment degree, and social self-brand consistency is negatively related to hotel brand attachment degree, and ideal self-brand consistency is positively related to hotel brand attachment degree. Among them, due to $|-8.79|>|8.21|>|-0.48|$, $|6.2|>|-3.19|>|-2.64|$, affected by self-promotion motivation, real self-consistency has a stronger brand attachment when consumers choose the economy hotel brand, while the role of ideal self-consistency in brand attachment is not obvious. So H5 is true.

On the other hand, affected by self-conformation motivation, social self-consistency has a stronger brand attachment when consumers choose the economy hotel brand, so H6 is false.

## Ⅵ. Research Conclusions and Recommendations

This study takes the hotel brand as the object to carry on the empirical research, mainly in order to verify whether the self-brand consistency has a special influence on hotel brand attachment, and whether it is influenced by self-motivation in the action process. Based on this, six hypotheses are put forward to verify, and the results of the demonstration are as follows.

Table 1 Hypothesis Validation

| | |
|---|---|
| H1 | False |
| H2 | True |
| H3 | True |
| H4 | True |
| H5 | True |
| H6 | False |

It can be seen from the research results that self-motivation plays a considerable role in regulating in the influence process of self-brand consistency on hotel brand attachment. For different self-motivation, the influence factors of brand attachment of the same hotel degree are different; under the regulation of the same self-motivation, the same influence factors have different effects on the products at different levels.

## Ⅶ. Theoretical and Practical Significance

*i. Theoretical significance*

First of all, the author selects the hotel brand as the object, as a tourism product with special features, and it is different from products of general social or private ownership, to expand the research field of the influence of self-brand consistency on brand attitudes. Secondly, the author introduces the middle variable of —self-motivation ‖ , and validates the adjustment effect of self-motivation in the process of self-brand consistency's influence on brand attachment, which enriches the results of self-brand consistency research. In addition, how self-motivation adjusts the influence of self-consistency on brand attachment is of great significance to the theory of brand equity management of tourism products.

*ii. Practical significance*

Combined with our results, it can be seen that, as a tourism product with non-ownership transfer but only short-term use, a hotel brand have a greater difference from other generic types of proprietary outright purchases. Although high self-brand consistency has positive effect on the hotel brand attachment, but the brand with high ideal self-consistency does not attract consumers' purchase desire, and the hotel brand with high ideal self-consistency does not necessarily bring high brand attachment. For this phenomenon, in addition to considering the impact of economic income level, it is also necessary to consider the product nature of hotel brand.

## Ⅷ. Research Deficiency and Prospect

In this study, there are still many problems: Firstly, the sample data is insufficient, for the data collection object is mainly concentrated in several hotel lodges in Beijing, lack of collection for their accommodation motivation. There is a big difference between the standard of accommodation for leisure and official business, and the difference between the accommodation at their own expenses and public accommodation will have a great influence on the choice of the hotel brand. The selection and classification of hotel brands are also lack of systematic and rational distribution, so it is uncertain that the results are universally applicable.

Secondly, the measurement dimension of brand attachment is more extensive, but in order to maintain the reliability and validity of the questionnaire, there are a large number of deletions in this paper, and there are few researches on the contract and connection of brand attachment, which can't better reflect the brand loyalty.

Finally, the hotel brand's particularity lacks of more favorable arguments to support the conclusion of this paper, and there is no comparative analysis with other types of brands or other travel products. In the future study, it is necessary to pay attention to the above mentioned problems, to further supplement and demonstrate these findings by quantitative analysis and comparative analysis.

## References

[1] Sirgy, M J. Self-concept in consumer behavior: a critical review[J]. *Journal of Consumer Research*, 1982 (9): 165-180.

[2] Aaker, D A. Measuring brand equity across products and markets[J]. *California Management Review*, 1997 (38): 102-120.

[3] Upshaw L B. *Building Brand Identity: Marketplac*e[M]. New York: John Wiley & Sons, 1995.

[4] Wang Meiling. Research on self-brand connection and brand loyalty based on self-concept[D]. Chengdu: Southwest University of Finance and Economics, 2011: 16-17.

[5] Swann W B, Kwan V S, Polzer J T, et al. Fostering group identification and creativity in diverse groups: the role of individuation and self-verification[J]. *Personality and Social Psychology Bulletin*, 2003 (11): 1396-1406.

[6] Aguirre-Rodriguez A, Bosnjak M, Sirgy M J. Moderators of the self-congruity effect on consumer decision-making: a metaanalysis[J]. *Journal of Business Research*, 2012, 65(8): 1179-1188.

[7] Schultz S S, Kleine R E, Kernan J B. These are a few of my favorite things-toward an explication of attachment as a consumer behavior construct [J]. *Advancesin Consumer Research*, 1989(16): 359-366.

[8] Zinkham G M, Hong J W. Self concept and advertising effectiveness: a conceptual model of congruency, conspicuousness, and response mode[J]. *Advances in Consumer Research*, 1991 (18): 348-354.

[9] Li Yaoqi, Guan Xinhua. From "people-brand" relationship to "people-destination" relationship: the effects of self-destination connection[J]. *Tourism Tribune*, 2015(30): 9.

[10] Zinkham, G M, Hong J W. Self concept and advertising effectiveness: a conceptual model of congruency, conspicuousness, and response mode[J]. *Advances in Consumer Research*, 1991 (18): 348-354.

[11] Wang Meiling. Research on self-brand connection and brand loyalty based on self-concept[D]. Chengdu: Southwest University of Finance and Economics, 2011: 16-17.

# Experience Preference and Recreational Specialization Categories of Rock Climbing Related Tourism Participants in Yangshuo

Hu Jie[1*]

**Abstract:** The theory of recreational specialization can be used to explore the learning process of recreational activities, which is a continuous process of behavior, skill and commitment. Once rock climbing participants show their interests in rock climbing, they will participate in the activities to get more knowledge, skills and experience, and then the specialization of them will move to a high level. This study discusses the characteristics, behaviors and preferences of rock climbing participants on different specialization levels.

This study uses the model of recreational specialization proposed by Scott and Shafer (2001) to measure the depth of specialization, and a structured questionnaire involving three aspects of behavior, skills, and commitment. We interviewed 405 rock climbers in Yangshuo from different countries and regions, and 328 viable questionnaires were compiled. We examined their recreational specialization levels, demographic characteristics, recreation preferences and perception towards rock climbing activities. The results identified four recreational specialization categories: newcomers, amateurs, professionals and devotees. Different groups showed significant differences on their behaviors, skills, knowledge about rock climbing, age, employment, income, preferences on other recreation activities, and expenditure patterns. Therefore, understanding different groups of rock climbing participants and their characteristics and preferences will help managers to maximize visitors' enjoyment and guide the rock climbing-related tourism into a better development in the future.

**Keywords:** rock climbing related tourism; Yangshuo; rock climbing participants; recreational specialization; demographic characteristics; recreation preferences

1* Chengdu Sport Institute, Chengdu, China. 67205692@qq.com.

## Ⅰ. Research Background

Rock climbing has become a recreational activity that is growing rapidly in popularity, especially after officially becoming an Olympic sport, nowadays attracting more and more visitors to different destinations around China. One such premier location is Yangshuo in Guangxi Province. Yangshuo is the best and biggest rock-climbing base in China, having been considered as “The Heaven of Rock Climbing” by both domestic and foreign rock climbing amateurs. A large number of rock climbing amateurs and tourist groups participate in rock climbing activities in Yangshuo as members of the local rock climbing clubs, various tourist groups and outdoor sporting clubs and hotels every year. Rock climbing events in Yangshuo also become one of the favorite activities for climbers and tourists. Todd, from American, has made a documentary about rock climbing in Yangshuo to show it to the world. Rock climbing has made great contributions to the development of local tourism, as well as the economic and social development of the county.

In recent years, an increasing number of indoor and outdoor climbing sites and routes has been developed all around China, and the composition of rock climbing participants is also more complex. Thus, a better understanding of the characteristics and preferences of rock climbing participants in different recreational specialization is significantly important to the development of rock climbing related tourism.

The goal of this paper is to begin the classification of climbing participants by their recreational specialization and participation patterns, analyse their different preferences, and discuss the way of developing rock climbing related tourism better in China.

## Ⅱ. Literature Review

Bryan defined recreation specialization as a continuum from general to professional behavior reflected by preferences on movement or activity places, settings and skills.[1] Many scholars used this definition on application including hunting, fishing, boating, hiking, birdwatching, biking and so on.[2] While exploring the concept of recreational specialization, foreign scholars have measured recreational specialization from behaviour[3] and emotion [4]. McIntyre and Pigram argued recreational specialization process includes three sections: behavior, emotion and cognition.[5] They cited the integration system[6] proposed by Little which includes concepts of environmental cognition, emotion and behavioral responses, and explored the basic concepts of the specialization loop.

Scott and Shafer, however, offered a new conceptual system of recreational specialization[7], which considered recreational specialization to be a continuous process of behavior, skill and commitment. It is different from previous studies. They believed that behavior needed to be evaluated according to people’s involvement in other activities. Skills and experience shouldn’t be confused on experience. People with a strong commitment to the activity are more likely to make it the center of life. The recreational specialization measurement model proposed by Scott and Shafer, including sections of behavior, skill and commitment, has been widely used in the follow-up study of scholars. [8] [9] This study uses this model on measuring recreational specialization of rock climbing participants, hoping to get a in-sight understanding of different climber groups, thus boosting a better development of rock climbing related tourism. Virden and Schreyer argued that the understanding of the level of recreational specialization helps to understand participants' behaviour and attitudes towards resources and other participants.[10] Hollenhorst argued that the information gained from a survey of a climber's specialization level can help managers make better decisions.[11]

## Ⅲ. Research Contents and Methods

*i. Research questions*

(1) Are rock climbing participants different because of their degree of specialization?

(2) What are the basic attributes of rock climbing participants under different recreational specialization categories?

(3) What are the behavioral preferences of different specialization categories of rock climbing participants?

*ii. Research methods*

*A. Research framework*

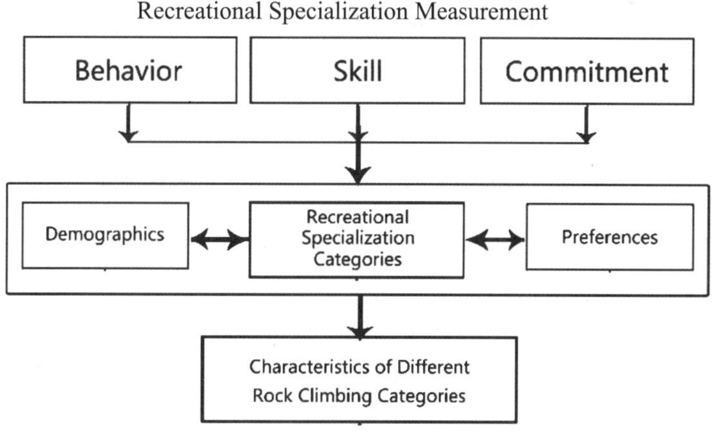


Figure 1 Research Framework

*B. Research instrument*

There are three sections in this survey. The first part is socio-demographic variables, including gender, age, marital status, education, employment and income. The section of specialization was designed according to Scott and Lee's survey. [12] All questions were divided into three sections: behavior, skill and commitment. The third part is about their recreational preferences, including the hobbies they have, if they are willing to give up other hobbies or sacrifice their time on other hobbies to climb, how difficult it is for them to get opportunities and platforms to climb, places they would love to go after rock climbing, places where they communicate with each other, and so on.

Self-administered questionnaire and face-to-face interview were used in data collection. Simple random sampling and cluster sampling were combined. The survey took place in Yangshuo, Guangxi Province during climbing seasons in the year 2016 and 2017. Six of the most popular climbing sites covering routs on all difficulty levels, including the White Cliff, Low Mountain, Wine Bottle, the Egg, Twin Gate Mountain and Leipi Shan, were chosen as the main sites for survey. Altogether 405 climbing participants were asked to complete the questionnaire. 328 viable questionnaires were compiled. 23 persons out of 405 participated in interviews. After the questionnaires were collected, compiled and coded, data files were set up and analyzed through statistical software SPSS 2.30. The analysis includes descriptive statistics, analysis of variance and cluster analysis.

## Ⅳ. Results

This chapter shows the results of analysis used to answer three research questions. The independent variable and its description, and the demographics of participants are described.

*i. Demographic characteristics*

The respondents of this survey were predominately male (73.2%), single (57.9%), between 26 to 35 years old (43.9%), with full-time job (53.7%), graduated from university or college (73.4%). Table 1 contains a simple description of participant demographics including the number of participants that answered each item and the percentage of the population that number represents.

Table 1　Demographic Characteristics of Respondents

| | Number of Participants (N) | Percentage of Sample (%) |
|---|---|---|
| Gender | | |
| Male | 240 | 73.2 |
| Female | 88 | 26.8 |
| Age | | |
| 17 and Under | 4 | 1.2 |
| 18-25 | 90 | 27.4 |
| 26-35 | 144 | 43.9 |
| 36-45 | 73 | 22.3 |
| 46-55 | 17 | 5.2 |

(To be continued)

(Continued Table 1)

| | Number of Participants (N) | Percentage of Sample (%) |
|---|---|---|
| Marital Status | | |
| Single | 190 | 57.9 |
| Married | 120 | 36.6 |
| Divorced | 17 | 5.2 |
| Other | 1 | 0.3 |
| Education | | |
| Primary School | 5 | 1.5 |
| Middle School | 8 | 2.4 |
| High School | 42 | 12.8 |
| University/College | 241 | 73.4 |
| Master | 28 | 8.5 |
| Doctor | 4 | 1.2 |
| Employment | | |
| Student | 62 | 18.9 |
| Full Time | 176 | 53.7 |
| Part Time | 11 | 3.4 |
| Unemployed | 5 | 1.5 |
| Self-employed | 73 | 22.3 |
| Retired | 1 | 0.3 |
| Monthly Income | | |
| Under 1,000 CNY | 62 | 18.9 |
| 1,001-3,000 CNY | 41 | 12.5 |
| 3,001-5,000 CNY | 96 | 29.3 |
| 5,001-10,000 CNY | 71 | 21.6 |
| Above 10,001 CNY | 58 | 17.7 |

*ii. Recreational specialization measurement and recreational specialization categories of rock climbing participants*

*A. Recreational specialization measurement of rock climbing participants*

a. Behaviors of participants

Rock climbing participants sometimes travel to different places in different distances for the activity. In the highest proportion (54.3%), rock-climbing tourists are willing to travel "more than 500km" for the activity. Most climbing tourists are willing to travel more than 100km for climbing (77.2%). A big proportion of climbing tourists climb very frequently. There are 163 of them (49.7%) climbing many times per week, and 82 people (25%) climbing once a week. 79.3% of climbing participants have received various forms of training for climbing. Among these climbers, 23.4% of the participants got targeted training, 46.3% spontaneous targeted training, and 38.7% targeted training with coaches. 19 participants (5.8%) got all three kinds of training.

It is obvious that most climbing participants have consciousness of training and have made great efforts to climb better.

b. Skills of participants

Domestic climbers are now climbing at difficult levels ranging from primary level (below 5.9) to 5.14 c/d. Only a few people in the world have reached 5.15. In this survey, 33.2% participants' average climbing difficulty is 5.10. The number of participants who reach 5.11 is 57 (17.4%). The higher the climbing difficulty level is, the fewer the number of rock-climbing tourists. There are only 8 participants reaching 5.13, and 2 participants reaching 5.14. This is basically consistent with the difficulty level distribution of the majority of rock climbers in China. In all subjects, 62 participants (18.9%) didn't know their climbing level. This is mainly because many domestic climbers only do bouldering in climbing gym, and they didn't have any knowledge about difficulty level, or never paid any attention to their climbing level. The distribution of "the most difficult level they finished" and "average climbing difficulty level" showed a significantly positive correlation between the difficulties. The proportion in the item "the most difficult level you have reached" of 5.11 is 24.4%, of 5.12 is 18.6%, of 5.13 is 10.1% and of 5.14 is 1.2%. It reflects that most climbers' skills are in rising trends.

Most climbing participants (48.2%) engaged in two types of climbing, including sport climbing and bouldering. 25.6% of the participants engaged in three types of climbing, including sport climbing, bouldering and traditional climbing. There are only a few people who engaged in big wall climbing (5.8%) and free solo (1.5%).

259 participants out of 328 had targeted training for climbing, including climbing technology, endurance, arm power, finger power and core strength. 92 of these had all 5 training above. Only 69 participants (21%) never got any targeted training.

c. Commitment of participants

In this survey, only 11 participants (3.4%) did not own any climbing equipment. Among all equipment and related products, the ones owned by individuals from more to less are: climbing shoes (295), climbing harness (282), Carabiners (257), climbing helmet (229), webbing and slings (223), quickdraw (211), climbing ropes (189), ATC or Gri Gri (168), climbing guide books (127), subscriptions to climbing magazines (56), and aid climbing gears (46). In the previous year, 104 participants (31.7%) spent 1,001-3,000 yuan on purchasing climbing equipment, and 99 (30.2%) spent more than 3,000 yuan. Almost half of the climbing participants (47%) also bought membership from climbing gym. Some of them have to climb in the cities where they live due to several factors such as working and study schedule, economy, family and transportation. Some of them got membership because they were hoping to get advice from coaches or training courses in climbing gym. In this survey, 264 participants (80.5%) would love to get targeted training for climbing, 60 participants (18.3%) were not sure if they want it or not, and only 4 participants (1.2%) didn't want it.

*B. Recreation specialization categories of rock climbing participants*

In this survey, clusters analyses were used to discover logical groupings. Hierarchical cluster analysis was used to determine the number of clusters, and K-means cluster analysis discovered 4 logical groups. The resulting four groups of climbing tourism participants have been labelled: cluster 1 with 68 participants, cluster 2 with 116 participants, cluster 3 with 42 participants and cluster 4 with 102 participants. Four categories of climbing participants showed depth of involvement of rock climbing activity. From the first cluster to the fourth cluster, the involvement of participants goes deeper.

Table 2 Result of Cluster Analysis

| | | Cluster 1 | Cluster 2 | Cluster 3 | Cluster 4 | F |
|---|---|---|---|---|---|---|
| Behavior | 1. How far would you like to travel to climb? | -0.98253 | 0.10798 | 0.20042 | 0.44970 | 40.581*** |
| | 2. How often do you climb? | -1.23127 | 0.11758 | 0.41025 | 0.51820 | 80.004*** |
| | 3. How many kinds of training below do you take? | -0.30000 | -0.05894 | -0.44412 | 0.44990 | 13.133*** |
| Skill | 1. Which is the level of the most difficult climb you have ever completed? | -1.33470 | -0.06365 | 0.49726 | 0.75743 | 150.742*** |
| | 2. Which is the average difficulty level of climbs you have successfully attempted? | -1.30133 | -0.04146 | 0.47364 | 0.71968 | 128.398*** |
| | 3. How many kinds of climbing shown below did you participate in? | -0.58309 | -0.24144 | -0.08995 | 0.70034 | 35.124*** |
| | 4. How many kinds of specific training skill do you own? | -0.45618 | -0.23213 | -0.21865 | 0.65815 | 27.618*** |
| Commitment | 1. How many kinds of climbing gear do you own? | -0.95448 | -0.09609 | 0.21751 | 0.65603 | 53.930*** |
| | 2. How much do you spend on climbing gear in the past year? | -1.10555 | 0.13216 | 0.13133 | 0.53266 | 58.430*** |
| | 3. How strongly do you want to be trained? | -0.23330 | 0.47649 | -2.04077 | 0.45396 | 241.586*** |
| | 4. Are (were) you a member in climbing gyms or clubs? | -0.73339 | -0.31844 | 0.34681 | 0.70827 | 50.764*** |
| ***= a significant ≤.001 | | | | | | |

Table 2 describes the percentage of participants by demographic variable across different categories. Determined by the chi-square significance test, the categories did not differ significantly in terms of their gender, marital status, education, and income. However, they did differ significantly in terms of their ages, employments and incomes. From cluster 1 to cluster 4, the average age becomes larger. The proportion of students declines, but the number of freelancers goes up. Participants with high income occupy bigger and bigger proportion.

Table 3 Demographic Characteristics of Respondents by Climbing Categories

| | Newcomer (%) | Amateur (%) | Professional (%) | Devotee (%) | Chi-Square |
|---|---|---|---|---|---|
| Gender | | | | | |
| Male | 72.1 | 73.3 | 59.5 | 79.4 | 6.052 |
| Female | 27.9 | 26.7 | 40.5 | 20.6 | |
| Age | | | | | |
| 17 and Under | 0 | 2.6 | 0 | 1 | |
| 18-25 | 42.6 | 30.2 | 16.7 | 18.6 | 27.241** |
| 26-35 | 35.3 | 48.3 | 47.7 | 43.1 | |
| 36-45 | 19.1 | 16.4 | 23.8 | 30.4 | |
| 46-55 | 2.9 | 2.6 | 11.9 | 6.9 | |
| Marital Status | | | | | |
| Single | 69.1 | 61.2 | 47.6 | 51 | |
| Married | 29.4 | 33.6 | 42.9 | 42.2 | 15.342* |
| Divorced | 1.5 | 5.2 | 7.1 | 6.9 | |
| Other | 0 | 0 | 2.4 | 0 | |
| Education | | | | | |
| Primary School | 1.5 | 0.9 | 0 | 2.9 | |
| Middle School | 2.6 | 2.6 | 2.4 | 2 | |
| High School | 8.8 | 13.8 | 19 | 11.8 | 17.046 |
| University/ College | 80.9 | 72.4 | 73.8 | 69.6 | |
| Master | 5.9 | 10.3 | 4.8 | 9.8 | |
| Doctor | 0 | 0 | 0 | 3.9 | |
| Employment | | | | | |
| Unemployed | 1.5 | 2.6 | 2.4 | 0 | |
| Student | 33.8 | 21.6 | 9.5 | 9.8 | |
| Part Time job | 1.5 | 3.4 | 0 | 5.9 | 40.745*** |
| Full Time job | 54.4 | 54.4 | 66.7 | 48 | |
| Self-employed | 8.8 | 18.1 | 21.4 | 36.3 | |
| Retired | 0 | 0.9 | 0 | 0 | |
| Income (¥) | | | | | |
| Under 1,000 | 33.8 | 19.8 | 11.9 | 10.8 | |
| 1,001-3,000 | 8.8 | 16.4 | 14.3 | 9.8 | 28.074** |
| 3,001-5,000 | 32.4 | 27.6 | 33.3 | 27.5 | |
| 5,001-10,000 | 19.1 | 19.8 | 23.8 | 24.5 | |
| 10,001 and above | 5.9 | 16.4 | 16.7 | 27.5 | |
| | ***= a significant ≤.001<br>**= a significant ≤.01<br>*= a significant ≤.1 | | | | |

Cluster analysis, variance analysis and cross analysis showed that four categories of rock climbing participants have the following characteristics.

a. Newcomers group

Newcomers have the lowest climbing frequency and involvement. Most of them climb one time every half a year or even once a year. They don't want to travel more than 50km to climb. The proportion of people between 18 and 25 years old in this group is highest among 4 groups, occupying 42.6%. 69.1% of newcomers are single, which is the highest portion compared to other groups. Students and full time workers occupy 33.8% and 54.4% in this group. Most of the newcomers took courses from colleges or universities. People's monthly income distributes in two areas: below 1,000 yuan and between 3,001 yuan and 5,000. They don't spent much on climbing equipment. Most of them only have one or two climbing gears, and no membership of climbing gyms. They don't know much about rock climbing, so most of them only experienced one or two types of climbing, and have no idea about their own climbing difficulty level. They are interested in rock climbing to an extent and want to be trained, but obviously still in the initial stage of rock climbing.

b. Amateurs group

This group of climbing participants show their intense interests and enthusiasm for rock climbing. Most of them have steady income and extra time, which help them to climb more frequently and get trained. They are eager to learn more knowledge and skills of rock climbing. The proportion of males with full time job at the age of 26-35 in this cluster was the highest in four clusters (48.3%). Most of them take university or college courses. The distribution of income is relatively average. 27.6% of participants earn 3,000-5,000 yuan every month. Most of participants in this group own more than 8 kinds of climbing equipments. They climb many times per week, start spontaneous training, and hope to get targeted training to improve their skills. They have a clear understanding or the difficulty level of rock climbing, and their climbing ability. Most climbers in this group have reached 5.10. Many of them get membership in climbing gyms, and are willing to travel more than 500 km for rock climbing at the same time. This group represents an emerging force in rock climbing, which is full of unlimited enthusiasm and keen to invest in rock climbing equipments, related products and activities.

c. Professionals group

Rock climbing participants in this category have clear understanding of rock climbing and better climbing skills. Most of them reached 5.11 and 5.12. The distribution of age in this group is obviously different from the first two groups. They are still mainly at the age of 26-35, but the proportion of people at the age of 36-45 goes much bigger. The proportions of married people, high-income people and people who have full time jobs in this group are the highest among four groups. 33.3% of them earn 3,001-5,000 yuan every month, and 23.8% of them earn more than 10,000 yuan every month. They own 9 kinds of climbing equipments in average, and are willing to spend more time, energy and money on rock climbing. 35.7% of them spent more than 3,000 yuan on purchasing climbing gear in the last year. An interesting part is that the number of female respondents is similar with male respondents (40.5%). Among all female respondents, 80.7% of them are at the age of 18-35, and the proportion of female students is 25%, which is much higher than that of male students. Also most of the female climbers are unmarried, so they have more free time and less constrain from family. Maybe these factors made them have better condition to become professionals. But this result of survey which took place in Yangshuo can't show a full image of female climber market in China because of the difference of traveling opportunities and customs between males and females. Through interviews we got to know that a big part of professionals climb in climbing gyms during work days, and go outdoor climbing on weekends and holidays. 64.3% of them have membership in climbing gyms, and usually engage in two types of climbing. They would love to travel more than 500 km, but do not want to take trainings as newcomers and amateurs.

d. Devotees group

Devotees have the highest involvement, great enthusiasm and commitment for rock climbing. The average age of this group is obviously higher than other groups. 30.4% of them are 36-45 years old, which is the highest proportion among four groups. The number of people who have master degree and doctoral degree, and who earn more than 10,000 yuan per month is significantly higher than other clusters. They are well funded, and willing to spent more money and time on rock climbing gears and trips. The number of full time job workers is on average level among four groups, but the proportion of freelancers and self-employed people is the highest. In the investigation, we found that many climbing devotees are willing to change their jobs or move to another place to live in return for more rock climbing opportunities. 74.5% of them climb many times per week to maintain or improve their climbing difficulty level. Some of them even climb almost everyday regardless of bad weather or other bad conditions. A lot of practices will inevitably bring improvement. 31.4% of them had reached 5.11, following by 28.4% of them reaching 5.12, and 26.5% reaching 5.13. Only a few people who reached 5.14 are all in this group. They train a lot on different aspects with different methods, and 99% of them are eager to get professional targeted training.

In all, four groups showed a procession of recreational specialization: (a) a focusing of behaviour, (b) the improvement on gears, knowledge, skills, and social world, (c) a stronger commitment and a tendency of making rock climbing a central life interest, and (d) a close connection or coalesce between rock climbing and their lives.

*C. Rock climbers' specialization categories and other recreational activities*

Among all respondents, people who like several current fashion and popular outdoor activities such as mountain climbing, hiking, cycling, mountain biking, jogging, kayaking, canoeing and paragliding occupy high proportions in newcomers group. Ice climbing and some aquatic sports including scuba diving, snorkeling and surfing are most popular in devotees group. On the whole image, professionals group have the lowest involvement in other recreational activities among four groups.

In this survey, the most popular recreational activities are hiking. 60.4% of the people like it, and the percentage of mountain climbing is 58.8%, jogging 49.4%, cycling and mountain biking 46.6%. Respondents also listed their other hobbies in the item of "other", including yoga, Taiji, skiing, swimming, badminton, archery, windsurfing, skateboarding, football, speleology, and motorcycle trip.

Table 4 Other Hobbies of Respondents

| | Newcomers | Amateurs | Professionals | Devotees | In All | |
|---|---|---|---|---|---|---|
| Mountain climbing | 50<br>73.5% | 68<br>58.6% | 14<br>33.3% | 61<br>59.8% | 193<br>58.8% | 17.383a 0.001 |
| Hiking | 50<br>73.5% | 74<br>63.8% | 15<br>35.7% | 59<br>57.8% | 198<br>60.4% | 16.434a 0.001 |
| Jogging | 42<br>(61.8%) | 56<br>48.3% | 19<br>45.2% | 45<br>44.1% | 162<br>49.4% | 5.647a 0.130 |
| Cycling and mountain biking | 61<br>(59.8%) | 58<br>50% | 12<br>28.6% | 41<br>40.2% | 153<br>46.6% | 13.988a 0.003 |
| Ice climbing | 24<br>35.3% | 33<br>28.4% | 9<br>21.4% | 40<br>39.2% | 106<br>32.3% | 5.565a 0.135 |
| Scuba diving/Snorkeling | 16<br>23.5% | 23<br>19.8% | 9<br>21.4% | 33<br>32.4% | 81<br>24.7% | 4.985a 0.173 |
| Canoeing/Kayaking | 12<br>17.6% | 17<br>14.7% | 4<br>9.5% | 17<br>16.7% | 50<br>15.2% | 1.559a<br>0.669 |
| Paragliding | 11<br>16.2% | 15<br>12.9% | 2<br>4.8% | 12<br>11.8% | 40<br>12.2% | 3.250a 0.355 |
| Surfing | 6<br>8.8% | 11<br>9.5% | 2<br>4.8% | 15<br>14.7% | 34<br>10.4% | 3.759a<br>0.289 |
| Others | 3<br>4.4% | 12<br>10.3% | 7<br>16.7% | 4<br>3.9% | 26<br>7.9% | 8.718a 0.033 |

Newcomers showed that they didn't often go rock climbing partly because they have many other hobbies. In contrast, in amateurs and professionals, there is a clear upward trend to give up other hobbies for rock climbing, which showed a deeper involvement and commitment. Devotees involve themselves the most in rock climbing, but they are less willing to give up other hobbies than professionals.

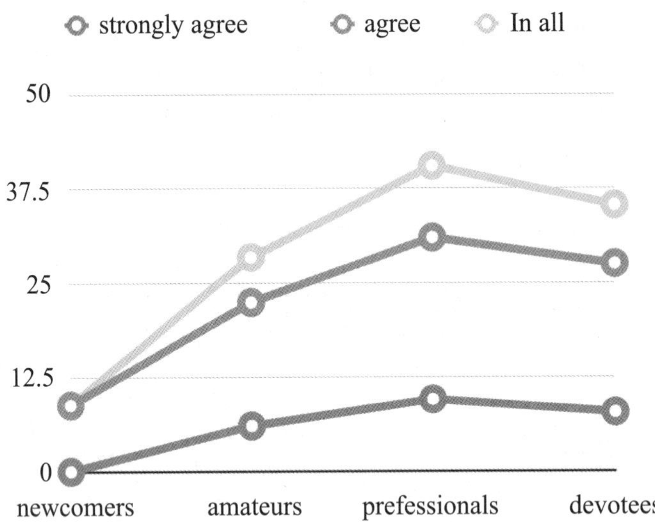


Figure 2 Willingness of Giving up Other Activities for Rock Climbing by Categories

In the item of 'What activity would you like to do after rock climbing?', we found that despite 69.1% of them showed that they would love to rest in their accommodations, there were still many who want to do some other activities. Climbing participants would love to do some other recreational activities. 53.7% of them would love to eat together, and almost half of people would love to have massages except that in newcomers group. 16.5% of all would love to go to cafe shops or bars. There were no obvious differences among four groups at these aspects. Respondents also showed that they would love to stretch themselves, go for a walk, chat with friends, watch TV, enjoy hot spring or do some other sports after rock climbing.

Table 5 Recreation Preferences of Categories

| | Newcomers | Amateurs | Professionals | Devotees | In All | |
|---|---|---|---|---|---|---|
| Relax in bars and cafe shops | 10<br>14.7% | 18<br>15.5% | 8<br>19% | 18<br>17.6% | 54<br>16.5% | 0.536a<br>0.911 |
| Rest in accommodations | 29<br>42.6% | 71<br>61.2% | 24<br>57.1% | 79<br>77.5% | 203<br>61.9% | 21.572a<br>0.000 |
| Have a massage | 29<br>42.6% | 47<br>40.5% | 12<br>28.6% | 51<br>50% | 139<br>42.4% | 5.872a<br>0.118 |
| Eat together | 34<br>50% | 52<br>44.8% | 29<br>69% | 61<br>59.8% | 176<br>53.7% | 9.553a<br>0.023 |
| Do other activities | 0<br>0% | 6<br>5.2% | 1<br>2.4% | 3<br>2.9% | 10<br>3% | 3.976a<br>0.264 |

Rock climbing participants showed a marked propensity to communicate. Only 3 people (0.9%) said that they did not like to communicate with other climbers. The most popular communicating place is climbing site or training gym, which was chosen by 86.9% people, followed by cafe shops and bars with climbing themes (43.9%), accommodation like camping places or hostels (33.2%), and climbing friends' home (29.3%). Only newcomers have lower willingness to communicate in climbing friends' home (10.3%). It may be because they haven't built up their climbing social connections. We also found that bars and cafe shops with climbing themes are quite more popular than regular bars and cafe shops in newcomers group, amateurs group and devotees group, but opposite in professionals group.

Table 6 Communication Places

| | Newcomers | Amateurs | Professionals | Devotees | In All | |
|---|---|---|---|---|---|---|
| Climbing sites or training gyms | 52<br>76.5% | 103<br>88.8% | 35<br>83.3% | 95<br>93.1% | 285<br>86.9% | 10.811a<br>0.013 |
| Cafe shop and bars with climbing themes | 26<br>38.2% | 50<br>43.1% | 17<br>40.5% | 51<br>50% | 144<br>43.9% | 2.657a<br>0.448 |
| Cafe shop and bars without climbing themes | 5<br>7.4% | 10<br>8.6% | 9<br>21.4% | 12<br>11.8% | 36<br>11% | 6.333a<br>0.096 |
| Accommodations like camping place or hostels | 27<br>39.7% | 35<br>30.2% | 11<br>26.2% | 36<br>35.3% | 109<br>33.2% | 2.908a<br>0.406 |
| Climbing friends' home | 7<br>10.3% | 40<br>34.5% | 14<br>33.3% | 35<br>34.3% | 96<br>29.3% | 14.939a<br>0.002 |
| Restaurants | 8<br>11.8% | 15<br>12.9% | 11<br>26.2% | 19<br>18.6% | 53<br>16.2% | 5.440a<br>0.142 |
| Tea houses | 9<br>13.2% | 13<br>11.2% | 4<br>9.5% | 11<br>12.7% | 39<br>11.9% | 0.465a<br>0.927 |
| I don't like communication | 1<br>1.5% | 1<br>0.9% | 0<br>0% | 1<br>1% | 3<br>0.9% | 0.628a<br>0.890 |

Brayan argued that the degree of specialization of individual will bring links to like-minded participants in corresponding levels.[3] The recreational preferences and life styles of rock climbing participants have some intra group similarities and differences between groups.

Most newcomers also like hiking, mountain climbing, cycling and mountain biking, through which these participants get to know about rock climbing. Everybody has limited time, energy and money, so when they develop an interest, they must pay for it at the expense of other interests. At this stage, they have some interests in rock climbing, but they are not very willing to give up other activities for it. Data shows that they also would love to communicate with other climbers, especially in accommodations like camping places and hostels. So these places could be a good platform for newcomers to know more about rock climbing. Promotions, information and activities for rock climbing could be set, and more space for people to communicate may help newcomers to go into higher specialization level.

Amateurs usually have many interests for their leisure life, but also show an obvious willingness to devote themselves more in rock climbing than other activities. They would love to travel for rock climbing, and also love to participate in other outdoor activities. They have very strong desire to communicate with other climbing friends. The proportion of people who would love to communicate in climbing friends' home in this group is the highest. It is easy to see that they have already built links and climbing social world. The liveness of group is relatively high.

Professionals showed the strongest willingness to make rock climbing their most important recreational activity. A lot of them have no other hobbies since they spend almost all their spare time on rock-climbing. After climbing, they are more likely to choose places that are not related to climbing in order to relax, such as restaurants, cafes and bars without climbing themes. It may be because this group of people has already past 'the infatuation period' of rock climbing and gone into 'the stable phase'. They no longer urgently look for a sense of being in a rock climbing community like amateurs, but turn to places and activities that are more closely related to daily life with their relatively stable social world.

Devotees group is the highest liveness, involvement and commitment in four groups. According to data that we collected, devotees have supreme enthusiasm on every section despite they don't want to sacrifice other hobbies for rock-climbing as professionals. Seeking the reasons behind it, it may be because with a lot of climbing experience and great skills, many of them already reached very high level or their limits. At this stage, the progress slows, and further challenges are hard to reach within a short period of time, so they don't give up other hobbies to focus on rock climbing only as professionals, but begin to extend their recreations to other areas to seek stimulation, satisfaction and fulfillment. In addition, there are also some devotees having a more in-depth understanding of rock climbing. They realize that basic ability like power and climbing technology couldn't help them to improve a lot any more, instead they need to pay more attention to rising their psychological and spiritual level. At the same time, along with the complication of rock climbing types and environment, they need to enhance their comprehensive abilities such as observation, judgment and strain capacity, so they start to involve in related fields like ice climbing.

Overall, rock climbing sites and training gyms are the most popular places for climbers to communicate with each other, followed by bars and cafes with climbing themes. Also, massage services are welcomed. Thus, synthesis with different sections that we mentioned above could be considered to use in rock climbing tourism development to meet the demands and needs of rock climbing participants, also bring a better platform for them to communicate, so as to promote the promotion and dissemination of rock climbing.

## Ⅳ. Discussion and Conclusion

Specialization and specialization categories can help to explain different phenomenon of recreational behaviors and climber's characteristics, so as to bring managers better understanding in different attitudes and behavioral patterns of different climbing groups, and a in-depth insight into participants' commitment, participation frequency, skill level, consumption tendency and leisure preferences. These can help managers to manage and improve the rock-climbing site, and ensure the satisfaction of participants by providing better service and products.

In this study we found four categories of climbing participants: newcomers, amateurs, professionals and devotees. They differ from the depth of involvement, knowledge they own about rock climbing, behavioral patterns, skills, commitment and recreational preferences.

More than 70% of the newcomers don't know their climbing difficulty level, and more than 40% only engage in one type of climbing. Recently, bouldering and sport climbing are two of the most popular and promoted types of climbing. Sport climbing mainly takes place on artificial rock climbing wall and outdoor rock in fields, and bouldering are mainly in climbing gym. We found that many respondents mistakenly believed that sport climbing is big wall climbing. This phenomenon has a great relationship with the way of people calling artificial climbing wall as "Big wall". This also reflects that the popularity of climbing related knowledge in our country should be improved, and the content of rock climbing related tourism products should be enriched. At this stage, out door rock climbing activities for newcomers mainly include rock climbing experimental activity and public climbing training courses in fields. In cities, bouldering and sport climbing mainly take place in climbing gyms with more entertainment factors and simple climbing routines. According to the statistics, most of newcomers don't have membership, and rock climbing is only one of their recreational activities. Most of newcomers' climbing is based on curiosity, experience and leisure purpose. Because of the lack of knowledge and skills of rock climbing, their activities were limited in such a highly demanding sport. They could only participate in short climbing activity with a low degree of difficulty. Thus it is hard for them to truly enjoy climbing, which leads to less involvement and frequency in climbing, and they are also sensitive to traveling distance. But 60% of newcomers were willing to get training, and 30% were considering. It is easy to see that most of them do have interest in rock climbing, and are willing to improve their skills, so effective training courses have broad market prospect. It will also help them to get to a higher specialization level, thereby enhancing their involvement and commitment to rock climbing. In addition, we found that supermajority of newcomers like hiking, mountain climbing and cycling. Most of them would rather distribute some time on many hobbies than spending all their time on only one activity like rock climbing. So comprehensive scenic spots with different outdoor activities, for example, outdoor sports parks, may attract this group more. In terms of the design of rock climbing activities, newcomers have their own demands. Scott argued that the sense of achievement is the strongest motivation of rock climbing beginners who don't climb frequently. Thus it is particularly important to design climbing routines that are suitable for beginners. Also it could be a good idea to put more entertainment factors, such as AR technology for interaction, creative climbing holds and games, or giving them different forms of motivation like awards for reaching the top. Attracting them to climb more could be the first step of guiding and developing newcomers' interest in rock climbing.

Amateurs have a better understanding of rock climbing activity and their own climbing abilities than newcomers. They climb more often to raise their climbing difficulty level. Buying membership is one of representations. Their attitude and emotion of climbing had developed from being hesitated and attempting to being interested and enthusiastic. They felt a sense of happiness and fulfillment from their climbing activities, so they are eager to get training and courses to improve themselves efficiently. As a result, they began to sacrifice their time allocated to other recreational activities, while rock climbing had earned a tendency to become their leisure activity center. Amateurs are the fresh blood of rock climbing crowd, and also one of the main forces in the consumer market. They also showed great enthusiasm for the purchase of equipment. On one hand, the reason behind this is that they need more gears for their climbing as they involve in rock climbing. On the other hand, according to researchers' study, Some newcomers or dabblers, for example, hope to make a fashion statement, [5] or because the equipment may help compensate for a lack of skill or knowledge. [1] Likewise, some of them may plunge enthusiastically into a leisure social world, or what Irwin referred to as a "scene", [5] because they are attracted to a perceived lifestyle and identity image. [14] But no matter what the reason is, we can see that amateurs do have great consuming propensity and demands for purchase on membership, outdoor climbing activities, climbing gears and related products and training courses. Thus, reasonable consumption planning and guidance are of great significance. In rock climbing related tourism, they need more information about rock climbing sites, climbing routines and climbing partners. At the same time, rock climbing guides, comprehensive outdoor tourism products, study tour with climbing themes, and organized rock climbing activities in fields may have a great market. In addition, considering their strong demands of learning and communicating, a good atmosphere for climbing, communication activities, experience sharing meeting and movie watching meeting related to rock climbing may meet their needs.

Professionals have accumulated a great deal of experience and knowledge of rock climbing, thus they have better technical skills. People in this group have already made rock climbing their recreation center. Because the high frequency climbing is essential to maintain or raise their difficulty level, they almost sacrifice all their time of other recreational activities for rock climbing. Their attitude and emotion towards rock climbing is relatively smooth and solid. They remain at a relatively high level of consumption, but are clearly more rational than amateurs. They are no longer that eager to improve fast by getting trainings, but maintaining a neutral, uncertain, and wait-and-see attitude towards training courses. One reason may be that most of them have membership, which means they had already knew or tried training courses in climbing gyms. Since there is no advanced, scientific and systematical climbing training in the country, self-training or existing training can't satisfy climbers whose skills are in the middle and high levels. Another reason may be that they do believe training can help them improve, but in this stage, the effect of training doesn't have big advantage comparing to the effect of frequent climbing. Thus, advanced and effective training, abundant climbing style, unique climbing environment and international communicating opportunities may have big market among professionals.

Devotees climb the most frequently and have the most climbing experiences. As their climbing difficulty level goes higher and higher, they gradually got a clear image of their limit in getting bigger progress. Thus most of them began to have spontaneous training and targeted training by coaches. 99% respondents in this group are eager to get trained. At the same time, they understood rock climbing better, and gave more meaning to rock climbing itself. They built a stronger and closer link between rock climbing and their lives. Or even merged them together. They have a deeper and personalized thinking about the relationship between life and climbing. At this stage, some of them regard rock climbing as a kind of life practice and belief, while some of them take climbing as a vertical path to their dreams. They also showed the most active state of consumption trends, including in climbing equipments and related products, membership, and rock climbing related tourism products. They no longer only focus on pursuing higher climbing difficulty level, but are keen to climb in different areas, to try different climbing styles, to develop new climbing routines and areas, and promote rock climbing to others. Devotees have stronger connection to each other, and build up a "circle" with mutual penetration and influence. They are more likely to spread information and cooperate with each other. They also embrace the love and feelings of rock climbing. They could play a leadership role in promotion of rock climbing.

Today, with the rapid development of rock climbing, it is not hard to see that rock climbing related tourism has a great market, and also plays an important role in the development of tourist destination. There is no doubt that the increase number of rock climbers can help to boost economic returns, but in fact, rock climbers' satisfaction may fall as a result of crowding if the number of visitors increases a lot. The space competition may affect the climbers' climbing experience, and noisy crowd may have negative effects on climbing participants. So increasing the total amount only may not be an effectively way to increase income. So, if the goal is to increase economic income in the region, our efforts should be focused on designing and providing corresponding premium and well-directed services and tourism products to different climbing categories based on conditions of scenic spots.

In summary, this study provides empirical support theoretically for research of rock climbing specialization and rock climbing related tourism. At the same time, it brings certain guidance and reference value to managers for their design and management of rock climbing tourism projects.

## References


[1] Bryan H. Leisure value system and recreational specialization: the case of trout fishermen[J]. *Journal of Leisure Research*, 1977: 174-187.

[2] Shuang Panou, Hou Jinxiong. Climber's recreational specialization and preference[J]. *Outdoor Recreation Research*, 2007: 51-74.

[3] Bryan H. Recreation specialization revisited[J]. *Journal of Leisure Research*, 2000: 18-21.

[4] Schroeder S. Identity and specialization as a waterfowl hunter[J]. *Leisure Sciences*, 2013: 218-234.

[5] Mclntyre N, Pigram J J. Recreation specialization reexamined: the case of vehicle base campers[J]. *Leisure Sciences*, 1992: 3-15.

[6] Little B R. Specialization and the varieties of environmental experience: empirical studies within the personality paradigm[M]//S wapner, S Cohen, B Kaplan. *Experiencing the Environment*, 1976: 81-116.

[7] Scott D, Shafer G S. Recreational specialization: a critical look at the construct[J]. *Journal of Leisure Research*, 2001: 319-343.

[8] Lee J H, Scott D. Measuring birding specialization: a confirmatory factor analysis[J]. *Leisure Sciences*, 2004: 245-260.

[9] Miller Z D, Hallo J C, Sharp J L. Birding by ear: a study of recreational specialization and sound scape preference[J]. *Human Dimensions of Wildlife*, 2014: 498-511.

[10] Virden R, Schreyer R. Recreations specialization as an indicator of environmental preferences[J]. *Environment and Behavior*, 1988: 721-739.

[11] Hollenhorst S. What makes a recreation specialist? The case of rock climbing[J]. *Social Science and Natural Resource Recreation Management*, 1990: 81-91.

[12] Scott D, Lee J. An examination of behaviors and attitudes among members of the american birding associations: a follow-up study[R]. Report submitted to the Texas Agricultural Extension Service.

[13] Irwin J. *Scenes: Beverly Hills*[M]. Calif: Sage, 1977.

[14] Haggard L M, Williams D R. Identity affirmation through leisure activities: leisure symbols of the self[J]. *Journal of Leisure Research*, 1992: 1-18.

# Investigating Factors Influencing Customer Recommendation Intention in Theme Restaurants

Liang Xinjian[1], Yin Shimin[2*]

**Abstract:** This study empirically investigates the key attributes affecting customers' satisfaction and recommendation intentions in theme restaurants. A survey was conducted in Chinese ethnic restaurants and logistic regression model was undertaken to analyse the data. This study indicates that decoration, atmospherics, specialties and employees' attitude significantly influence customers' recommendation intentions. The results emphasize that theme restaurant managers should seek effective ways on physical environment and attentive service.

**Keywords:** theme restaurants; word-of-mouth; customer behaviour; recommendation intention; satisfaction

## Ⅰ. Introduction

Theme restaurants have grown rapidly in the past decades. Despite the importance and popularity of theme restaurants in the food service industry, there has been few researches exploring the key attributes affecting consumers recommendation intentions in theme restaurant. Since restaurant services cannot be evaluated before the consumption experience and there are higher risks by purchasing intangible products and services, customers are more dependent on the interpersonal communication, such as positive word-of-mouth and recommendation (Jang, 2011;Jang, 2011). Therefore, understanding customers' recommend behaviour has become more necessary to marketing professionals, [1] and identifying what affects the theme restaurant customers' recommendation intention would be valuable. Based on the previous works, the main purpose of this study is to identify the key attributes affecting customer recommendation intentions.

## Ⅱ. Literature Review and Research Hypotheses

### *i. Recommendation intentions*

Behavioral intention can be defined as the degree to which a person has formulated conscious plans to perform or not perform some specified future behaviour. [2] Previous

1 Chengdu Normal University, Chengdu, China.

2* Anhui University, Anhui, China. yinshimin@outlook.com.

studies found that behavioural intention refers to a customer's anticipation of repeated purchasing, recommendation, and favourable word-of-mouth behaviour in the future. [3, 4] Reference [5]stated that the determinants of favourable post-dining behavioural intentions such as saying positive things about the restaurant, recommending to others, and repeating purchasing could provide practical guidance for restaurant practitioners. Consumers often share opinions, news, and information with others. Since word-of-mouth is the communication between consumers about products or services, in which the sources are considered independent of commercial influence. [6] Word-of-mouth can be positive or negative, restaurateurs and marketers are naturally interested in promoting positive word-of-mouth, such as recommendations to others. Positive word-of-mouth increases the probability of purchase and negative word-of-mouth creates the opposite effect. [7] Therefore, as one type of post-dining behavioural intentions, recommendation intentions can be considered the likelihood of recommending a service provider to others in the future. [8]

*ii. Factors influencing customer satisfaction and recommendation intentions in theme restaurant*

Customers' satisfaction is the result of comparisons between customers' expectations and perceived performance, as well as the predictor of recommendation intention. [5] Prior studies found that customer satisfaction is highly related to recommendation intention. Reference [9]argued that food, atmosphere and fairness of the seating order are key factors related to customer satisfaction. Other studies suggested that the perceived authenticity is positively related to loyalty intentions and can influence consumers' recommendation intentions. [10] Based on the works of service encounter.[11], [12]Reference [13]concluded that the factors influencing the quality of service encounter process in theme restaurant mainly include three parts: customer, personnel and environment. Reference [5] also indicated that food quality, service quality, atmospherics, authenticity and price could be important contributors to customer satisfaction and behavioural intentions.

From the results of the previous studies on dining satisfaction and behavioural intentions (e.g. [5], [10], [14], [15], [16], [17]), food quality, service quality, atmospherics and price fairness are found to be able to directly or indirectly contribute to customers' overall satisfaction and their post-dining behavioural intentions.

Based on these propositions, there are three commonly accepted categories for measuring restaurant experience: food quality, service quality and environment, which influence customer satisfaction and behavioural intentions in theme restaurants.

A. *Environment*

Reference [10] proposed that three key dimensions of the servicescape, the physical setting, service providers and other customers, could influence consumers recommendation intentions. According to [18]'s model, the environment created an emotional response in individuals that elicited either approach or avoidance behaviours. And the decoration and atmospherics are key dimensions for measuring theme restaurant environment (e.g. [19], [20]). Therefore, this study hypothesizes:

*H1: decoration is positively related to the recommendation intention.*

*H2: atmospherics is positively related to the recommendation intention.*

B. *Food quality*

Food plays a vital role in the restaurant experience. Researchers stated that price fairness [21]and food quality including taste, specificity of the food were significant predictors of behavioural intention(e.g.[5], [9], [14]). Based on such considerations, this research hypothesizes:

*H3: price fairness is positively related to the recommendation intention.*

*H4: taste of the food is positively related to the recommendation intention.*

*H5: specificity of the food is positively related to the recommendation intention.*

C. *Service quality*

Earlier studies had examined the dimensions of service quality(e.g.[5], [12], [22], [23], [24], [25]), and the results showed that the employees' attitude and service efficiency influence customer's satisfaction and behavioural intentions in theme restaurants. Thus, this study hypothesizes:

*H6: employees' attitude is positively related to the recommendation intention.*

*H7: service efficiency is positively related to the recommendation intention.*

## Ⅲ. Methodology

*i. Measurement*

To achieve the study's objectives, this study developed a self-administered questionnaire based on the findings of the literature review. The questionnaire was comprised of two sections. The first section was comprised seven attributes that were adapted from previous works. Environment-related attributes included two items: decoration [26] and atmospherics. [19] Food quality-related attributes included three items: price fairness, [21] specificity and taste. [14] Service quality-related attributes included two items: attitude and service efficiency. [13] The seven attributes were abbreviated as follows: Decoration (DEC), atmospherics (ATM), price fairness (PRI), taste (TAS), specificity (SPE), attitude (ATT), efficiency (EFF), and recommendation intention (Y).In this section, respondents were asked to rate the importance of each restaurant attribute. A 5-point Likert scale was utilized to measure the restaurant experience constructs, where 1= not important at all and 5=extremely important. The second section concerned respondents' demographic information, including gender, age group, education level, occupation, family income and dining out cost per month.

*ii. Data collection*

The data for this study was collected from two ethnic restaurants in China. The questionnaires were randomly distributed to customers in each restaurant. A total of 520 questionnaires were collected 511 were used for analysis excluding 9 due to the numerous missing values.

*iii. Analysis*

A logistic regression model was used to analyze the data. All statistical analyses were performed using the SPSS (Statistical Package for the Social Science) program. The function model was estimated by maximum likelihood estimate method. To measure recommendation intention(Y), this study used 0-1 index method, where 1 means willing to recommend and 0 means not willing to recommend.

## Ⅳ. Results and Discussion

*i. Demographics*

Among the 511 valid respondents, there were 263 males (51.4%) and 248 females (48. 6%). For age level, 31 to 40 (30.9%) and 21 to 30 (29.7%) had occupied the greater proportion. For educational level, most of them were college educated (57.9%). For individual monthly income, RMB 2,001-RMB 5,000 (41.0%) had the highest percentage. For the average monthly cost in dining, under RMB 500 (52.0%) had occupied the greater part.

Table 1　The Result of Hosmer-Lemeshow Test

| Step | Chi-square Test | df | Sig. |
|---|---|---|---|
| 1 | 14.369 | 8 | .073 |

*ii. Results*

The regression equation test showed that the Cox & Snell R Square value is 0.088, and the Nagelkerke R Square value is 0.266, ensuring the model statistically significant. The result of Hosmer-Lemeshow test indicated that the p value is 0.073 (see Table 1), exceeding the minimum requirement of 0.05, ensuring adequate good fit of the regression equation. [27]

The results of model parameter estimates was shown in Table 2. Hypothesis 1 predicted a positive relationship between decoration and recommendation intention ($p$=0.006 $p$<0.05). The coefficient is 0.755. Hypothesis 1 was supported. Hypothesis 2 predicted a positive relationship between atmospherics and recommendation intention ($p$=0.000<0.05). The coefficient is 1.545. Hypothesis 2 was also supported. Hypothesis 3, which predicted a relationship between price fairness and recommendation intention was also supported ($p$=0.028<0.05). Hypothesis 4 predicted a positive relationship between taste and recommendation intention ($p$=0.033<0.05). The coefficient is 0.382. Hypothesis 4 was supported. Hypothesis 5 predicted a positive relationship between specificity and recommendation intention ($p$=0.008<0.05). The coefficient is 1.077. Hypothesis 5 was supported. Hypothesis 6 predicted a positive relationship between employees' attitude and recommendation intention ($p$=0.001<0.05). The coefficient is 1.561. Hypothesis 6 was supported. Hypothesis 7 predicted a positive relationship between service efficiency and recommendation intention ($p$=0.030<0.05). The coefficient is 0.934. Hypothesis 7 was supported.

The results of this study indicated that decoration, atmospherics, price fairness, taste, specificity, employees' attitude, service efficiency have positive correlation with the recommendation intention. These findings signified the significance of above factors as determinants of consumers' future behaviour intentions.

Table 2 Model Parameter Estimates

| | B | S.E. | Wald | df | Sig. | Exp(B) |
|---|---|---|---|---|---|---|
| DEC | .755 | .272 | 7.705 | 1 | .006 | 2.128 |
| ATM | 1.545 | .440 | 12.344 | 1 | .000 | 4.687 |
| PRI | -.670 | .304 | 4.849 | 1 | .028 | .512 |
| TAS | .382 | .179 | 4.539 | 1 | .033 | 1.465 |
| SPE | 1.077 | .405 | 7.061 | 1 | .008 | 2.934 |
| ATT | 1.561 | .461 | 11.468 | 1 | .001 | 4.762 |
| EFF | .934 | .430 | 4.716 | 1 | .030 | 2.546 |
| Constant | -13.997 | 3.550 | 15.551 | 1 | .000 | .000 |

## V. Conclusions and Limitations

This study examined the relationships between food, service and environmental concerns and recommendation intention. The results showed that the positive relationship between decoration, atmospherics, price fairness, taste, specificity, employees' attitude, service efficiency and recommendation intention were significant. The results of this study offered several interesting insights. Firstly, authentic environment including design, decoration and atmospherics may increase customers' overall satisfaction with a restaurant experience and their post-dining recommendation intentions. Theme restaurant managers should pay more attention to the physical settings of the restaurant. Secondly, laying stress on the characteristics and specificity of the cuisine can infuse the communication of culture into customers' dining experiences. [28] The restaurateurs should keep updating the features of new meals. Thirdly, employees' attitude and service efficiency are key determinants of service quality. The restaurateurs should improve the employees' satisfaction to obtain their greater attitude to customers.

One main limitation of the study is the data collection, which conducted in two restaurants; a more comprehensive sample across a diverse geography is needed in the future research. Another limitation is the ignorance of consumer perceptions and emotions of authenticity that should be emphasized for future study.

## ACKNOWLEDGMENT

This study is funded by a grant from Centre for Sichuan Cuisine Development (CC12S19) and Centre for Sichuan Tourism Development (LYC16-25) of Sichuan Provincial Department of Education, and Sichuan Tourism Administration (SCTYETP2017L11).

## References

[1] Jeong E, Jang S S. Restaurant experiences triggering positive electronic word-of-mouth (ewom) motivations[J]. *International Journal of Hospitality Management*, 2011, 30(2): 356-366.

[2] Ajzen I, Fishbein M. *Understanding Attitudes and Predicting Social Behavior*[M]. New Jersey: Prentice Hall, 1980: 100.

[3] Warshaw P R, Davis F D. Disentangling behavioral intention and behavioral expectation[J]. *Journal of Experimental Social Psychology*, 1985, 21(3): 213-228.

[4] Jang S, Liu Y, Namkung Y. Effects of authentic atmospherics in ethnic restaurants: investigating chinese restaurants[J]. *International Journal of Contemporary Hospitality Management*, 2011, 23(5): 662-680.

[5] Liu Y, Jang S S. Perceptions of chinese restaurants in the US: what affects customer satisfaction and behavioral intentions?[J]. *International Journal of Hospitality Management*, 2009, 28(3): 38-348.

[6] Litvin S W, Goldsmith R E, Pan B. Electronic word-of-mouth in hospitality and tourism management[J]. *Tourism Management*, 2008, 29(3): 458-468.

[7] Ladhari R, Michaud M. Ewom effects on hotel booking intentions, attitudes, trust, and website perceptions[J]. *International Journal of Hospitality Management*, 2015, 46: 36-45.

[8] Wang Chenya. Investigating antecedents of consumers' recommend intentions and the moderating effect of switching barriers[J]. *The Service Industries Journal*, 2009, 29(9): 1231-1241.

[9] Sulek J M, Hensley R L.The relative importance of food, atmosphere, and fairness of wait: the case of a full-service restaurant[J]. *Cornell Hotel and Restaurant Administration Quarterly*, 2004, 45(3): 235-247.

[10] Wang Chenya, Mattila A S. The impact of servicescape cues on consumer prepurchase authenticity assessment and patronage intentions to ethnic restaurants[J]. *Journal of Hospitality & Tourism Research*, 2015, 39(3): 346-372.

[11] Surprenant C F, Solomon M R. Predictability and personalization in the service encounter[J]. *The Journal of Marketing*, 1987: 86-96.

[12] Berry L L, Carbone L P, Haeckel S H. Managing the total customer experience[J]. *MIT Sloan Management Review*, 2002, 43(3): 85.

[13] Hsieh Tsuifang, Chen Yungkun. Interactive quality control of service encounters in theme restaurants[J]. *Journal of Global Business Issues*, 2009, 3(2): 85.

[14] Namkung Y, Jang S. Does food quality really matter in restaurants? Its impact on customer satisfaction and behavioral intentions[J]. *Journal of Hospitality & Tourism Research*, 2007, 31(3): 387-409.

[15] Saad A S, Conway C. Customer satisfaction in the restaurant industry: an examination of the transaction-specific model[J]. *Journal of Services Marketing*, 2006, 20(1): 3-11.

[16] Ebster C, Guist I. The role of authenticity in ethnic theme restaurants[J]. *Journal of Foodservice Business Research*, 2005, 7(2): 41-52.

[17] Wood N T, Muñoz C L. "No rules, just right" or is it? The role of themed restaurants as cultural

ambassadors[J]. *Tourism & Hospitality Research*, 2007, 7(3/4): 242-255.

[18] Mehrabian A, Russell J A. *An Approach to Environmental Psychology*[M]. Cambridge, Massachusetts: The MIT Press, 1974.

[19] Baker J, Cameron M. The effects of the service environment on affect and consumer perception of waiting time: an integrative review and research propositions[J]. *Journal of the Academy of Marketing Science*, 1996, 24(4): 338-349.

[20] Kim W G, Moon Y J. Customers' cognitive, emotional, and actionable response to the servicescape: a test of the moderating effect of the restaurant type[J]. *International Journal of Hospitality Management*, 2009, 28(1): 144-156.

[21] Xia Lan, Monroe K B, Cox J L. The price is unfair! A conceptual framework of price fairness perceptions[J]. *Journal of Marketing*, 2004, 68(4): 1-15.

[22] Parasuraman A, Zeithaml V A, Berry L L. Servqual: a multiple-item scale for measuring consumer perc[J]. *Journal of Retailing*, 1988, 64(1): 12.

[23] Reuland R, Choudry J, Fagel A. Research in the field of hospitality[J]. *International Journal of Hospitality Management*, 1985, 4(4): 141-146.

[24] Lucas A F. The determinants and effects of slot servicescape satisfaction in a las vegas hotel casino[J]. *UNLV Gaming Research & Review Journal*, 2003, 7(1): 1.

[25] Kanta K N M, Srivalli P. A study on factors influencing service quality in restaurants[J]. *International Journal of Retailing & Rural Business Perspectives*, 2014, 3(2): 938.

[26] Wakefield K L, Blodgett J G. The effect of the servicescape on customers' behavioral intentions in leisure service settings[J]. *Journal of Services Marketing*, 1996, 10(6): 45-61.

[27] Newman A J. Uncovering dimensionality in the servicescape: towards legibility[J]. *The Service Industries Journal*, 2007, 27(1): 15-28.

[28] Su Chengshu. The role of service innovation and customer experience in ethnic restaurants[J]. *The Service Industries Journal*, 2011, 31(3): 425-440.

# Continued Usage Intention of Tourism Mobile Commerce Users Based on Expanded ECM

Wang Sailan[1*]

**Abstract:** In the context of mobile Internet and tourism industry, firstly an initial model of continued usage intention of tourism mobile commerce based on expanded ECM was analyzed through literature review and theoretic analysis. Then the model was testified and modified by structural equations through investigation, analysis and numerical statistics. Finally, the model of continued usage intention of tourism mobile commerce was proposed. It was found the after-use perception of most users significantly affected their continuance, but as an intermediary, satisfaction was decreased significantly. In addition, perceived effects of trust were beyond those of other factors; the perceived risk rarely affected the ongoing intention to use.

**Keywords:** tourism mobile-Internet ECM model mobile commerce; continued usage intention

## Ⅰ. Introduction

The Internet has greatly affected the tourism industry, as it is changing the traditional concept of consumption. In this era, people can search on the Internet for information of the cheapest hotel and ticket, as well as other information of tourism. The Smartphone Usage Survey Report issued by Google and the market research agency IPSOS shows that about 86% of Internet users use smartphones during travel. [1] Mobile-Internet and smartphones have become indispensable tools for numerous tourists on the road. The well-known US Internet statistics company ComScore reported the total sales of online tour products in 2012 in the USA exceeded 100 billion dollars.[2] PhoCusWright, the authority of global tourism industry, also predicted mobile commerce accounted for more than 25% of the total on-line tourism reservation in the US in 2015. At the mobile terminal, this trend would be transformed to a tourism business market worth $ 40 billion. As for China, the potential of the mobile-Internet market is huge. An iResearch report shows the number of smartphone on hand was 0.58 billion in 2013, with a year-on-year growth of 60.3%, and was expected

1* Southwest Minzu University, Chengdu, China. 14795748@qq.com.

to reach 1.13 billion in 2017 (the number of panel computers would exceed 0.1 billion). In terms of mobile applications, the monitoring data in July 2014 showed the overall use time of mobile Apps exceeded 14 billion hours, longer than the service time of PC pages at the same period. These data indicate users stick more to mobile terminal than to PC terminal.[3] Along with the popularization of smartphones and the development of mobile-Internet, it is reasonably believed that the mobile terminal is a new sales channel that impacts the tourism industry.

Despite the explosive development of mobile-Internet, the successful mobile products only account for 1% of all mobile products. Though this figure may be inaccurate, it indicates the high competitive pressure that can be interpreted from the experiences of traditional industries. It was pointed in first step to final success is decided by the users' continuous usage. The cost of new-customer acquisition was 5 times higher than that of old-customer retention. [4] Regarding mobile products and services, the existing products are restricted by severe homogeneity, and the costs of users in searching and comparison are increasingly reduced. Under this background, the will bring about the expected use values. [5] Research on consumer behaviors partially focuses on the intention of continuous use, while research on the decisive factors of consumer retention focuses on two fields of management and marketing. [6] Fornell(1992) [7] and Morgan (1994) [8] studied consumer retention from the perspectives of service management and relationship marketing respectively, and found the major influence factors on consumer retention in traditional enterprises were customer satisfaction and trust. Therefore, the continuous use of users is the key way to promote profit and reduce operating costs. [9] In the field of information products, Bhattacherjee proposed a user continued use behavior model: expectation-confirmation model in the context of IT (ECM-IT), which was proved by many researchers to be very applicable for interpreting the intention in continuous use of information products. Nevertheless, ECM should be expanded according to the specific conditions in any field. Then, the problem is how to expand ECM to be specific to tourism mobile commerce and how to explain the influence factors on user intension in continuous use.

Thus, the objectives of this study are to expand ECM in the scope of tourism mobile commerce, to find out the influence factors on the intension of continuous use, and to investigate whether or not these factors are interactive. This study is of practical and guiding significances for tourism mobile commerce research & development institutions during their targeted technique development, marketing & promotion, and for them to increase user stickiness & retention.

## II. Literature Review

### *i. Technology acceptance model (TAM)*

The TAM proposed in 1986 was extended from the theory of rational behaviors and used to trace how external variables affected the internal belief, user attitude, and use inclination. [10] In TAM, the influence factors of users' acceptance of information technology are briefly summarized into perceived ease of use, perceived usefulness, and attitude to technology. Moreover, TAM builds the logical structures of use intention and actual use behaviors with the above factors. The perceived usefulness and the perceived ease of use are two major concepts in TAM, and they are positively correlated: a system with convenient operation is perceived as more useful by the users. TAM also holds that user attitude will positively affect behavioral intention. When a user who has negative feeling to an information system may still continue to use this disliked system because it improves the working efficiency and reduces cost. In recent decades, some intermediary variables (e.g. perceived enjoyment, perceived security, perceived risk, trust, privacy, and self-efficacy) have been added into TAM to improve the explanatory power and applicable scope.[11], [12], [13] Some famous examples include TAM2 (Venkatesh & Davis, 2000) and the unified theory of acceptance and use of technology (UTAUT; Venkatesh, Morris, Davis et al., 2003). Then a TAM-based IT/IS adoption theory was formulated to predict the continued usage behaviors after acceptance of an information system.

*ii. Expectation confirmation theory (ECT) and ECM-IT*

ECT originating from the field of marketing is widely applied to study customer satisfaction and intention of repurchase. ECT holds that a user first formulates an expectation before buying a product or service, and then forms a perceived performance after accepting and using this product or service. The user then compares the expectation and the perceived performance, which is called confirmation. The confirmation and expectation will impact user satisfaction, which in turn affects the intention of continued usage. A higher satisfaction degree is more likely to induce repurchase, and vice versa.[14] The effectiveness of ECT has been validated in many fields (e.g. automobile sales [15] and camera purchase[16]) with further improvement and extension.

The effectiveness of ECT has been validated many times in the field of traditional product repurchase. Based on ECT and TAM, the ECM-IT was proposed to study the users' continued usage behaviors in an information system.[17] In ECM-IT, a user's intention of continued usage with an information system is determined from three antecedents: satisfaction, confirmation, and perceived usefulness. The confirmation will affect the perceived usefulness and user satisfaction, while the perceived usefulness will affect user satisfaction and willingness of continued usage of the information system.

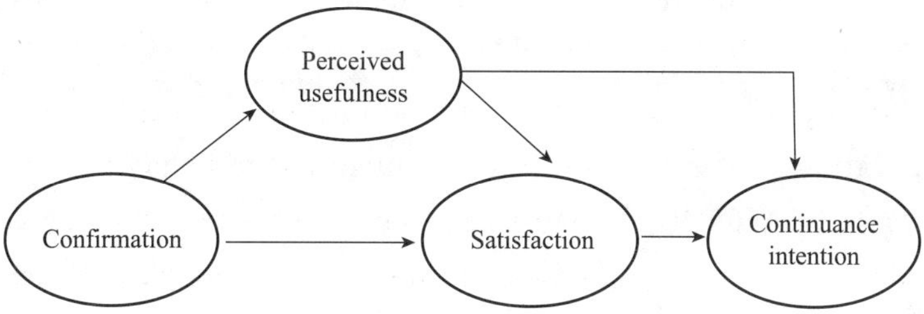


Figure 1 Model for ECM-IT

ECM-IT has been validated extensively despite its short history. For instance, the effectiveness of ECM-IT was validated through E-commerce websites[17] and several information systems (E-negotiation systems[18] and E-learning systems[20]).

Besides simple validation, ECM-IT was also extended for different targets. For instance, researchers investigating the continuous usage intention of mobile network service users integrated the perceived enjoyment and perceived ease of use into ECM-IT.[19] In other studies, the theory of social cognition, perceived fun, and cognitive absorption capacity were also integrated into ECM-IT, which greatly enhanced the explanatory power and applicable scope. In recent years, the continued usage intention has been increasingly studied. A study on mobile services shows that use behavior is directly affected by the perceived fun, perceived ease of use, perceived usefulness, communication effectiveness, perceived service cost, and network externality.[22]

The existing research shows ECM-IT can be expanded by improving and supplementing the perceived usefulness. Tourism mobile commerce is unique in many aspects compared with other mobile applications. For instance, tourism mobile commerce is generally a type of preconsumption, since a tourist has to make judgement and selection based on the acquired information but without any practical experience. Most tourism mobile commerce products are O2O-typed with close offline and online connection. Thus, ECM-IT should be further explored from the aspect of tourism mobile commerce, so as to build a suitable structural model.

## Ⅲ. Model Construction and Questionnaire Design

### *i. Model construction*

In the original ECM-IT, only one factor (perceived usefulness) describes the after-use perception of an information system. ECM-IT has been extended with different targets, and the extended ECM-IT models with higher explanatory power and applicability can better predict the continued usage intention. Some scholars have summarized the impacts of outer factors (e.g. mobile search information system's system quality, information quality and services quality) on perceived usefulness and expectation confirmation; the impacts of personal characters (e.g. self-efficacy) on continuous use intention; the impacts of facilitating conditions on continuous use behavior; relationships among continuous use intention, continuous use behavior and inner factors (e.g. satisfaction, perceived usefulness after use, expectation confirmation).[21] This study focuses on tourism mobile commerce and explores where are other influence factors on user continued usage behaviors in addition to the perceived usefulness. Specifically, a small-size investigation and interview involving 75 users of tourism mobile commerce was conducted. The contents included the extensible factors of ECM-IT studied by other researchers. After sorting, the after-use perceptions cared about by users should include six factors, such as perceived ease of use, perceived enjoyment, and perceived trust. These factors affect the continued usage intention to different degrees. Based on the theory and extension of ECM-IT, the initial structural model constructed here is introduced below.

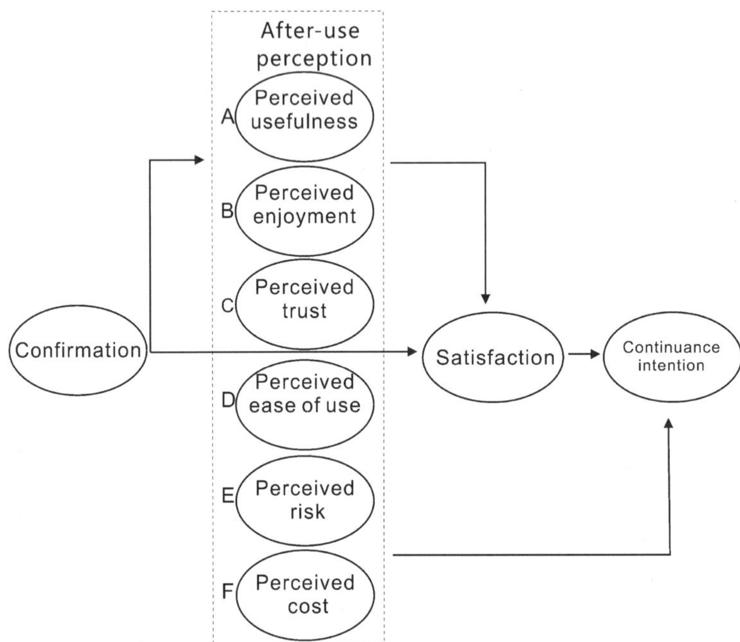


Figure 2 Initial Model for Research

*ii. Design of questionnaire*

The variables involved here include confirmation, perceived usefulness, perceived enjoyment, perceived trust, perceived ease of use, perceived risk, perceived cost, user satisfaction, and continued usage intention. A questionnaire at Likert 5 level was designed and given out in the form of paper through a self-built online investigation website.

These variables were summarized systemically in the existing literatures by measurement methods. According to the specific characteristics of tourism mobile commerce and the individual background of the investigated targets, these methods were modified and improved. Thereby, the preliminary measurement items of the tested variables were established. The measurements of confirmation and ease of use will be elaborated as examples.

Table 1 Gauge of Confirmation

| Please evaluate the after-use perception of this product (tourism mobile commerce) and the before-use expectation | | Disagree ← → Agree | | | | |
|---|---|---|---|---|---|---|
| Confirmation | 1. After use, I find this product better than expected. | 1 | 2 | 3 | 4 | 5 |
| | 2. The application scope of this product is wider than imaged. | 1 | 2 | 3 | 4 | 5 |
| | 3. Didn't expect this product could give so great help during tour. | 1 | 2 | 3 | 4 | 5 |

The questionnaire is shown at http://www.diaochapai.com/survey919699. Since the targets of this investigation are mainly the users of tourism mobile commerce services, most of these user groups are very familiar with the Internet and mobile-Internet. Thus, this investigation was mainly conducted on the Internet, and targeted at college students, employees of private enterprises, workers of state-run institutions, tour pal groups, and tour enthusiasts from all places.

## Ⅳ. Statistical Analysis

*i. Recovery of questionnaire*

To guarantee the accuracy and scientificity of this questionnaire, three experts of this field consulted and collected feedback from some of the subjects. Accordingly, the questions were modified to improve the soundness and scientificity. Because of specialty, the subjects answering this questionnaire were all users of tourism mobile commerce, and mostly were students and white collar workers born in 1980s and 1990s.

A total of 200 paper copies were given out two times, and finally 164 copies were recovered, with a recovery rate of 82%. Totally 162 copies were valid, with a valid rate of 81%. By the end of data collection, totally 284 copies were sent out online, and 246 copies were valid. Therefore, 448 copies were recovered, including 408 valid copies.

*ii. Reliability of measurement and assessment of validity*

Reliability defines the stability and consistency of the measured data, and a higher reliability indicates the scores of different items in the same scale are less erroneous. Reliability was tested via Cronbach $\alpha$ coefficient, and $\alpha>0.7$ indicates high reliability. The data were computed on SPSS and listed in Tables 3 and 4. The $\alpha$ values of all variables are higher than 0.7, which indicates very high reliability of this questionnaire.

Table 2 The Figure of Reliability of Questionnaires (ALPHA)

| Number of tested variables | $\alpha$ |
|---|---|
| 27 | .947 |

Table 3 The Test of Reliability of Latent Variable

| Latent variable | Number of tested variables | *a* |
|---|---|---|
| Confirmation | 3 | .765 |
| Perceived usefulness | 3 | .851 |
| Perceived enjoyment | 3 | .870 |
| Perceived trust | 2 | .701 |
| Perceived cost | 3 | .751 |
| Perceived ease of use | 4 | .856 |
| Perceived risk | 3 | .764 |
| User satisfaction | 3 | .927 |
| Continued usage intention | 3 | .828 |

The validity of continued usage intention means that the measured result reflects the degree of this investigated content. A higher validity indicates the measured results and the investigated content are more consistent, and vice versa. Kaiser-Meyer-Olkin (KMO) test and Bartlett test in the field of factor analysis were used. The results computed on SPSS are listed in Table 4.

Table 4 The Test of KMO & Bbrtlett

| KMO measure with enough samples | | .878 |
|---|---|---|
| Bartlett sophericity test | Approximate Chi-squared | 430.025 |
| | df | 36 |
| | Sig. | .000 |

Generally, KMO is one index of validity test in principal component analysis. KMO>0.9, 0.8-0.9, 0.6-0.7, 0.5-0.6, and <0.5 indicate very high, high, modest, low, and very low suitability for factor analysis, respectively. The validity (KMO value) of this questionnaire is 0.878; KMO<0.7 indicates this questionnaire should be modified. Moreover, sig indicates significant difference.

*iii. Model analysis*

The statistical method structural equation model (SEM) is based on covariance matrix for analysis of between-variable relations and is widely applied into data analysis in social sciences. After acquisition of model parameters, the suitability for data fitting should be assessed. If the model fits the data well, its usability is very high, and the estimated parameters are more significant. In this study, the model was validated on Amos. Usually, the model goodness-of-fit indices are the focus, including ratio of Chi-square value to degrees of freedom ($\chi^2/df$), normed fit index (NFI), incremental fit index (IFI), comparative fit index (CFI), and root mean square error of approximation (RMSEA).

The statistics of goodness-of-fit in the initial model are listed in Table 5.

Table 5 The Goodness-of-Fit of Initial Model

| Index | Value | Evaluation criterion |
|---|---|---|
| $\chi^2/df$ | 2.188 | The smaller the better |
| NFI | .733 | Close to 1 |
| IFI | .835 | Close to 1 |
| RMSEA | .099 | Close to 0 |
| CFI | .832 | Close to 0 |

Clearly, the test results of goodness-of-fit of the initial model are not ideal. The regression weights or the coefficient estimates of the model are listed in Table 7. The CR value provided by Amos is a *Z* statistic and is constituted by the estimated value and its standard deviation. Amos also provides the statistical test concomitant probability *p*, with which, users can test the significance of route coefficient/load coefficient. It is noted that the *p* values of nearly all variables and user satisfaction are large, indicating that 95% confidence levels of their path coefficients are not significantly deviating from 0.

The modification indices (M.I.) provided by Amos indicate the Chi-square value can be reduced by adding a causal path between the variables and the "continued usage intention". From the practical perspective, if tourism users are well affected to the used mobile commerce, they will continue to use next time. On the contrary, if they continue to use mobile commerce, they certainly are satisfied with this product. Thus, from the theoretical and practical perspectives, the variable "user satisfaction" can be deleted, which simplifies the model.

The results from running maximum likelihood on AMOS after the deletion of "user satisfaction" are listed in Table 7.

Table 7 The Goodness-of-Fit of Final Model

| Index | Value | Evaluation criterion |
|---|---|---|
| $\chi^2/df$ | 1.559 | The smaller the better |
| NFI | .924 | Close to 1 |
| IFI | .929 | Close to 1 |
| RMSEA | .068 | Close to 0 |
| CFI | .927 | Close to 0 |

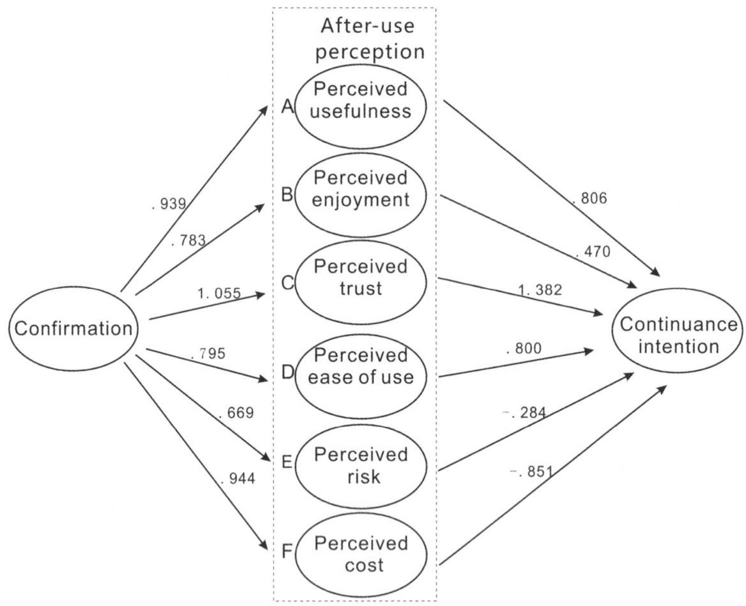


Figure 3　Final Revised Structural Equation Modeling

# Ⅴ. Analysis and Conclusions

The rapid development of smartphones has caused the gradual transition from PC-Internet to Mobile-Internet. The gradual emergence of mobile commerce will be a key in the development of advanced countries. However, relevant research in China focuses on qualitative analysis rather than quantitative analysis, from the commercial application and giant market to the heated discussion in the academia field.

This study referred to the basis of ECM-IT as well as the theory of consumer retention in marketing and management. Thereby, a prediction model of influence factors on the continuous use of tourism mobile commerce was built and validated. The contributions from theory and practice are listed below.

From the theoretical perspective, this study modestly enriches the theoretical research on tourism E-commerce. By targeting at tourism mobile commerce, in addition to the common-sense variable perception usefulness, the expanded model integrated five other variables (e.g. entertainment, trust and ease of use). Analysis and experiments confirm these variables contribute to the intention of continuous use. This study is targeted at tourism mobile commerce, which has not been well studied before. An information system user continued usage behavior model was used, which had been applied extensively in marketing and management, but was rarely used in tourism mobile commerce. The applicable scope of ECM was enriched and the study system of tourism mobile commerce was expanded.

From the practical perspective, the research on continuous usage behaviors is the key factor deciding the survival or failure of a mobile product. The findings in this study can guide the management practice of tourism mobile commerce, and provide practical meanings for research & development institutions. Based on the six influence factors mentioned here, an enterprise in this field can improve its products from the perspectives of research & development, management and maintenance, thereby increasing its market share and profits.

This study has three main conclusions.

First, the modified ECM can effectively explain the continued usage intention of tourism mobile commerce service users. The after-use perceptions will significantly affect the continued usage intention, but the effect of user satisfaction as an intermediary is largely weakened. Thus, this variable is deleted, which will simplify the model. From the perspective of user composition and the characteristics of tourism mobile commerce, on one hand, the after-use perception will directly change their continued usage intention since the users are younger and have their own assertion. On the other hand, owing to the peculiarity of mobile commerce, users are more likely to change their continued usage intention, which indicates lower loyalty.

Second, the after-use perceptions of tourism mobile commerce (including perceived usefulness, perceived enjoyment, perceived trust, perceived ease of use, perceived risk, and perceived cost) are associated with the continued usage intention. In particular, the interpretation degree of perceived trust on continued usage intention exceeds other items. This result indicates users pay high attention to mature products or experienced bands during the selection of tourism mobile commerce products, and the previous successful use will largely enhance the trust of continuous usage.

Third, the difference in the test samples will make the results different. The test sample in this study shows that the largest effect on continued usage intention originates from the perceived risk. This result can be explained as follows: when using tourism mobile commerce connected with financial products, users mostly select famous brands such as Ctrip.com and Tuniu.com, and the user trust largely reduces their expected risks. This fact is consistent with the previous analysis.

Based on these conclusions, three suggestions for development of tourism mobile commerce products are provided.

(1) Based on previous research, user perceived value is dynamic and will gradually be adjusted by user experience. This study also proves user confirmation will affect the after-use value perception. Thus, enterprises should pay attention to the changes of after-use perception for users at different use stages, which will help with management of client relations and reservation of clients.

(2) During the use of tourism mobile commerce products, the continuous usage intention will be affected by many factors. The rate and frequency of these changes are more significant than the traditional products. Thus, the key step for client reservation is the details of user experience, such as how to improve the systemic efficiency and enrich service

contents.

(3) The trust on a product is the most important influence factor on product selection and continuous usage, and with this trust, users will even ignore the potent risks during the usage. This phenomenon reminds large tourism service providers to promote in-time mobile terminal products that match with the traditional products, and also reminds small developers of the importance of creating a brand.

Table 6 The Estimate of Coefficient of Initial Model (Part)

| | | | Estimate | S.E. | C.R. | *P* | Label |
|---|---|---|---|---|---|---|---|
| Perceived enjoyment | - | Confirmation | 1.20 | .19 | 6.45 | *** | par_17 |
| Perceived trust | - | Confirmation | 1.50 | .21 | 7.27 | *** | par_18 |
| Perceived risk | - | Confirmation | 1.13 | .18 | 6.40 | *** | par_19 |
| Perceived ease of use | - | Confirmation | .87 | .17 | 5.03 | *** | par_20 |
| Perceived cost | - | Confirmation | 1.46 | .21 | 7.00 | *** | par_28 |
| Perceived usefulness | - | Confirmation | 1.10 | .21 | 5.31 | *** | par_29 |
| Continued usage intention | - | Perceived enjoyment | -.220 | .19 | -1.16 | .248 | par_21 |
| Continued usage intention | - | Perceived trust | 2.06 | 1.03 | 2.00 | .045 | par_22 |
| Continued usage intention | - | Perceived risk | -.24 | .25 | -.96 | .339 | par_23 |

Table 8 The Estimate of Coefficent of Final Model (Part)

| | | | Estimate | S.E. | C.R. | *P* | Label |
|---|---|---|---|---|---|---|---|
| Perceived enjoyment | - | Confirmation | 1.474 | .24 | 6.15 | *** | par_15 |
| Perceived trust | - | Confirmation | 1.641 | .22 | 7.41 | *** | par_16 |
| Perceived risk | - | Confirmation | 1.217 | .22 | 5.53 | *** | par_20 |
| Perceived ease of use | - | Confirmation | 1.226 | .19 | 6.55 | *** | par_17 |
| Perceived cost | - | Confirmation | 1.354 | .21 | 6.60 | *** | par_18 |
| Perceived usefulness | - | Confirmation | 1.555 | .22 | 7.10 | *** | par_19 |
| Continued usage intention | - | Perceived enjoyment | -.372 | .120 | -3.1 | .002 | par_23 |

## ACKNOWLEDGMENT

I would like to express my heartfelt gratitude to “the Fundamental Research Funds for the Open Research Subject of Tourism Development Research Center of Sichuan (SCTRC)” (No. LYC17-29), which has supported the paper.

## References

[1] 199it.com.Google.http://www.199it.com/archies/138883.html, 2013.

[2] Huxiu. http://www.huxiu.com/article/27451/1.html, 2013.

[3] iResearch. http://report.iresearch.cn/2298.html, 2014.

[4] Parthasarathy M, Bhattacherjee A. Understanding post-adoption behavior in the context of online services[J]. *Information Systems Research*, 1998, 9: 362-379.

[5] Jasperson J, Carter P E, Zmud R W A. Comprehensive conceptualization of post-adoptive behaviors associated with information technology enabled work systems[J]. *MIS Quarterly*, 2005, 29: 525-557.

[6] Liu Jianhua, Zhou Cuicui, Wang Dongchen. A case study on retaining customers on the basis of trust and switching barriers[J]. *Management World*, 2010, 6:131-144.

[7] Fornell C. A national customer satisfaction barometer: the Swedish experience[J]. *Journal of Marketing*, 1992, 56: 6-21.

[8] Morgan R M, Hunt S D. The commitment-trust theory of relationship marketing[J]. *Journal of Marketing*, 1994, 58: 20-38.

[9] Limayem M. How habit limits the predictive power of intention: the case of information systems continuance[J]. *Mis Quarterly*, 2012, 31: 705-737.

[10] Davis F D. A technology acceptance model of empirically testing new end-user information systems: theory and results[D]. Massachusetts: Massachusetts Institute of Technology, 1986:78-80.

[11] Gefen D, Karahanlla E & Straub D W. Trust and TAM in online shopping: an integrated model[J]. *MIS Quarterly*, 2003, 27: 51-90.

[12] Lu June, Yu Chunsheng, Liu Chang, et al. Technology acceptance model for wireless Internet[J]. *Internet Research*, 2003, 13: 206-222.

[13] Venkatesh V, Morris M G, Davis G B, et al. User acceptance of information technology: toward a unified view[J]. *MIS Quarterly*, 2003, 27: 425-476.

[14] Churchill Jr G A, Surprenant C. An investigation into the determinants of customer satisfaction[J]. *Journal of Marketing Research*, 1982, 19: 491-504.

[15] Oliver R L. Cognitive, affective and atribute bases of the satisfaction response[J]. *The Journal of Consumer Research*, 1993, 20: 418-430.

[16] Spreng R A, MacKenzie S B, Olshavsky R W. A reexamination of the determinants of consumer satisfaction[J]. *Journal of Marketing*, 1996, 60: 15-32.

[17] Bhattacherjee A. Understanding information systems continuance: an expectation-confirmation model[J]. *MIS Quarterly*, 2001, 25: 351-370.

[18] Bhattaeherjee A. An empirical analysis of the antecedents of electronic commerce service continuance[J]. *Decision Support Systems*, 2001, 32: 201-214.

[19] Doong Her-Sen, Lai Hsiangchu. Exploring usage continuance of e-negotiation systems: expectation and disconfirmation approach[J]. *Group Decision and Negotiatio*n, 2008, 17: 111-126.

[20] Hayashi A, Chen C, Ryan T, et al. The role of social presence and moderating role of computer self efficacy in predicting the continuance usage of e-learning systems[J]. *Journal of Information Systems Education*, 2004, 15: 139-154.

[21] Thong J Y L, Hong S, Tam K Y. The effects of post-adoption beliefs on the expectation-confirmation model for information technology continuance[J]. *International Journal of Human-Computer Studie*s, 2006, 64: 799-810.

[22] Deng Zhaohua, Lu Yaobin, Zhang Jinlong. Study of individual consumer behaviors in SMS by using TAM and network externality theory[J]. *Chinese Journal of Management*, 2007, 4: 216-221.

[23] Liu Luchuan, Sun Kai. Extending ECM-ISC to mobile search users' continuance usage: a theoretical model[J]. *Library and Information Service*, 2011, 55: 134-148.

# Social Networks in Tourism and Its Utilization

Yang Junting[1*], Cai Jun[2]

**Abstract:** The emergence and development of the Internet has given rise to social media, which is an operating platform for social networks. Nowadays, social networks are formed by different visitors through social media with other visitors, making tourism a social attribute. In order to make better use of social networks in tourism industry, we collect 40 travel blogs and all comments of 10 of them from the travel networks platform. By using content analysis, the paper analyzes the characteristics of information interaction in tourism industry. Finally, it points out the significance of the use of social networks in tourism industry, and puts forward some suggestions for the management of tourism destination.

**Keywords:** social networks; tourist experience; interaction; social behavior; destination marketing

## Ⅰ. Introduction

Over the last decade, increasing attention has been given to network in the tourism industry. The existence of social networks helps visitors obtain information, and have a deeper tourist experience. At the same time, interaction in social networks itself becomes a "spectacle".

In the field of geography, spectacle(landscape) refers to a region or a type of natural scenery, also refers to the creation of artificial forest landscape scenery.While in the field of sociology, spectacle is a social phenomenon expressed through media. It is the result of creation, expression and interpretation of people based on their own world view and their relationship with others.[1]

The word "spectacle" came first from the "spectacle society" theory proposed by French philosopher Guy Erenst Debord. Debord argues that the spectacle is a visible as well as subjective and conscious performance. With the increase of social practice, media-based "spectacle" is produced in large numbers.[2]

1* Beijing Forestry University, Beijing, China. yangjunting2017@163.com.

2 Beijing Forestry University, Beijing, China.

## Ⅱ. The Development and Characteristics of Social Networks

Social media is a type of online interactive media that gives users great space to participate. It is a technology platform that allows people to write, share, evaluate, discuss and communicate with each other. [3] Social media platforms have become a main venue for social interactions nowadays. Social networks bring interpersonal relations in the real world into virtual space, with the help of the development of social media.

The number of Internet users worldwide continues to grow, increasing from 3.2 billion in 2015 to 3.5 billion in 2016, [4] and the global social network users reached 67.4%, [5] nearly 2.359 billion.

The Internet has developed into a huge platform for information exchange. Internet users play not only the role of information receiver, but also the role of information producers and communicators. There are three characteristics of the spread of information in social networks : spread fast, interactivity, and anonymity.

A study by Forrester Research points out that people play seven different roles in social networks:creators, conversationalists, critics, collectors, quoter, joiners and spectators. Now we divide them into only two parts for the convenience of this research: creators who publish photos/videos/articles and influence others by showing their attitude; spectators who are influenced by information which are posted by others on social networks.

## Ⅲ. Social Networks, Great Influence to Tourism

Tourism is one of the industries which has been greatly influenced by social networks on two parts (as shown in Figure 1). In another word, we have come to the social age of tourism.

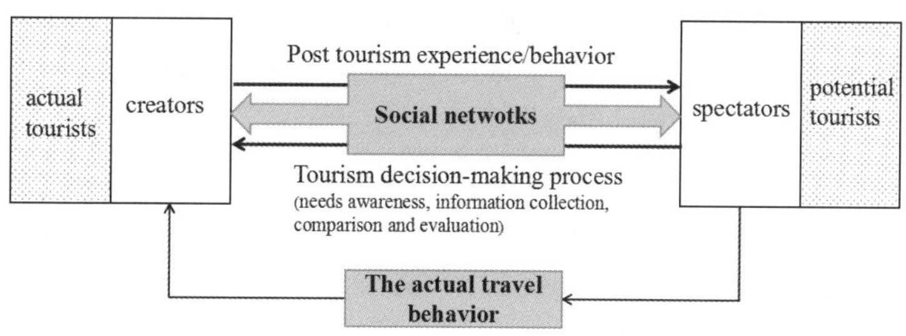


Figure 1 Schematic Diagram of the Social Behavior of Creators and Spectors in Tourism Industry

*i. On the perspective of spectators, usually potential tourists*

While traditional media allow a company to retain control over their marketing message and broadcast it to the consumer, social media have contributed to the development of the prosumer by empowering consumers, allowing them to participate and assess content and share opinions, attitudes and beliefs with one another in relation to that content.[6]

Due to the nature of tourism products, such as invisibility, no-transferability, perishability, post-effect and so on, social networks play an increasingly important role in the decision-making of potential visitors which includes three stages: needs awareness, information collection, comparison and evaluation.[7] Individual travel decision making is affected by social networks through three stages. Travel photos and blogs published by others on social networks may stimulate your travel motivation to some extent. Information and guidelines posted on social networks and public praise are also used for a pre-travel search for destination information. When you can not determine where to go, reading or asking others on social networks may be a good choice.

*ii. On the perspective of creators, usually actual tourists*

The development of WeChat, Micro-blog and other social platforms not only allow visitors to enjoy the natural scenery, cultural landscape, but also give them an interactive social experience.[8]

With the development of Internet, social networks have become an important form to show tourism experiences. Seppo K. Aho proposed that the process of tourism experience can be divided into three stages: before travelling, travelling and after travelling. [9] After travelling, there is a process of sharing travel experience, called “post tourism experience/behavior”, it is also the process of recalling and recreating travel experience.

## Ⅳ. Tourism Information Dissemination on Social Networks

*i. Methodology*

The analysis of social interaction in tourism industry is mainly based on the data from social platforms, and this article uses the content analysis method to deal with information. Content analysis is a research method that specializes in the analysis of communication content which gives objective and quantitative description for the dissemination of the contents. In short, content analysis is to quantify the content of a text according to a certain criterion and make it into structured data.[10]

In order to make better use of social networks in tourism industry, we collected 40 travel blogs and all comments of 10 of them from the travel networks platform of Mafengwo.com randomly to explore the characteristics of tourism information dissemination on social networks. It turns out that interactivity, performativity and personality are three major features of it. The data are analyzed as follows:

Table 1 Information about Content and Authors of 40 Travel Blogs

| | Details | | Quantity | Percentage |
|---|---|---|---|---|
| About authors | Contact information of authors | WeChat/Instagram/Twitter/ QQ/Micro-blog account | 32 | 80% |
| | | E-mail | 18 | 45% |
| | | Telephone number | 3 | 7.5% |
| About blogs | Types of blogs | Travel destination advertising | 4 | 10% |
| | | Personal diary | 28 | 70% |
| | | Both of them | 8 | 20% |
| | Contents of blogs | Blogs with music | 33 | 82.5% |
| | | Blogs with video | 7 | 175% |
| | | The average number of words in blogs | 10,236.1 | — |
| | | The average number of pictures in blogs | 176.8 | — |
| | Attitude toward destination | Positive | 36 | 90% |
| | | Negative | 1 | 2.5% |
| | | Neutral | 3 | 7.5% |

*ii. Interactivity*

Among all comments of 10 blogs collected randomly, we can divide the comments into two parts according to the sender of them. There are many comments posted by spectators (add up to 3,403) as well as comments replies posted by authors(add up to1,044). Communication is the core of tourism social interaction. It could be seen in Figure 2 that the tendency of comments replies was consistent with tendency of comments, tourism information can be shared and exchanged during the reply process.

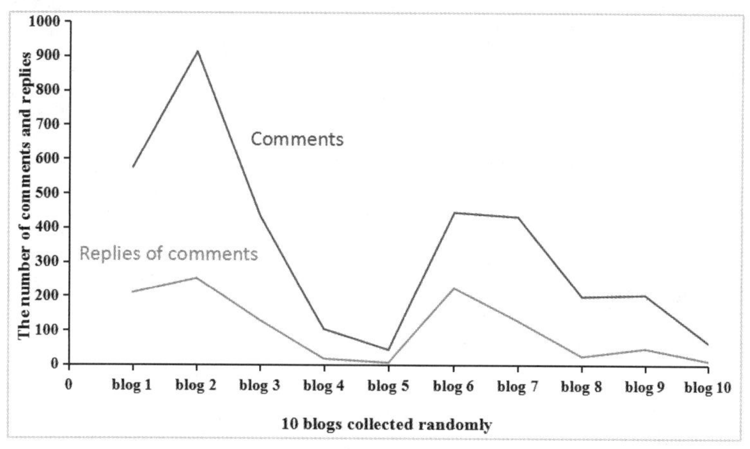


Figure 2 Comments by Spectors and Replies by Authors of 10 Blogs

*iii. Performativity*

Personal social accounts such as Instagram, WeChat and QQ are given by most authors, showing their willingness to "be watched".

We can see from Table 1 that travel experience is based on the text and accompanied by a large number of pictures. The text is used to explain the photos or show the mood, with music forming a wonderful atmosphere. Nearly all authors have a positive attitude toward their travel destination, partly because of the unforgettable travel experience, partly because they want to build a virtuous and bright image of themselves.

Sharing tourist experiences on social media is an act of performance. Tourists' texts should not be viewed merely as instances of "discourse" or "language", but as organic parts of the aesthetic and semiotic aspects of tourism.[11] The development of the user-generated content (UGC) prompting tourist experience is shared on social networks with a strong emotional color and performance factors.[12] Content posted on social networks represents the individual awareness, taste, perspective and insight of visitors, and is the result of a process of performance and recreation.[13]

*iv. Personality*

The biggest difference between social networks and Google is that behind social networks there are real men with different experiences and tastes.[14] When it comes to authors, publishing information on social networks is self-motivated. Most of blogs are personal diary rather than advertisement of destination or tourism industry, making the information on social networks more genuine and believable.

## Ⅴ. Make Use of Social Networks in Tourism Industry

*i. Motivating social behavior in tourism industry*

Social networks were established initially for creating a circle of acquaintances for people with similar fields of interest, [15] now the circle widen to people who have the same interest or concern which named communities.

Nowadays, more and more users take gaining respect and recognition as their main motivations for network sharing.[16] Thus we can know emotional motivation and social interaction are two significant factors affecting the behavior of sharing on social networks in tourism industry. In the value of their own expectations, tourists participate in the tourism virtual community which will form a sense of community identity, and then as an exchange, they will actively participate in community activities and be willing to actively share their own tourism information in the communities.

Tourism industry and enterprises could encourage consumers to publish details of their travel experiences by organizing competition of "find the most beautiful place on XX(destination)", and give prizes and gifts to winners to attract more attention of potential tourists. They can also improve social sharing facilities and improve the tourism social network service system, such as the provision of free wifi on destination, making it more convenient for timely social sharing of tourists.

*ii. Better destination marketing*

Hotel companies are increasingly inclined to adopt social media and make use of social networks. Content published on social networks can provide "real-time" information, which is of great value to destination marketing, [17] and analysis of the information could understand the tourist perception toward specific destination.[18] In addition to textual content, resources such as photos and videos published by visitors are also important analytical data. [19] By studying the spatial and temporal information contained in them, managers can get the "travel digital footprint" which reflects the spatio-temporal distribution of tourist flow.[20]

Using social networks in tourism destination marketing increases the liability and authenticity of marketing, and it may be a good choice for tourism industries to cooperate with "opinion leaders" who are very popular on social media.[21]

By analyzing information on social networks, management of tourism destination can know the preferences of tourists better, which is beneficial to marketing. For example, they can set up a special photo location in symbolic attractions which is popular in blogs or photos posted by tourists. The awesome photos and videos are wonderful marketing materials, which can be used on the advertisement of tourism destinations.

## Ⅵ. Conclusions

The social networks become one of the main channels for tourists to express their tourist experience and give feedback.[22] Because of information on social networks is double-edged, how to make it have a positive influence on tourist's decision-making process is necessary for tourism industry. At the same time, tourism destination needs to use social networks to convert marketing to service and effectively manage the brand reputation of it.

## References

[1] Shao P. Spectacle: media's description and interpretation of the world[J]. *Contemporary Communication*, 2010, 4: 4-7, 12.

[2] Debord G, Wang Z. *Society of the Spectacle*[M]. 2nd ed. Nanjing: Nanjing University Press, 2006.

[3] Kaplan M A, Haenlein M. Users of the world, unite! The challenges and opportunities of social media[J]. *Business Horizons*, 2010, 53(10): 59-68.

[4] The Wuzhen Summit website. http://www.wuzhenwic.org/2016-11/18/c_61834.htm, 2016.

[5] Anonymous. Social network analysis 2016[J]. *China Science and Technology Information*, 2016, 10: 2-3.

[6] Kozinets R V. E-tribalized marketing: the strategic implications of virtual communities of consumption[J]. *European Management Journal*, 1999, 17: 252-264.

[7] Bao Jigang, Chu Yifang. *Tourism Geography*[M]. 3rd ed. Beijing: Higher Education Press, 2012.

[8] Qian J, Law R. The internet plus era of tourism industry changes[J]. *Tourism Tribune*, 2016, 31(6): 2-4.

[9] Aho S K. Towards a general theory of touristic experiences: modelling experience process in tourism[J].

*Tourism Review*, 2007, 56: 33-37.

[10] Tang Liang, Choi S, Morrison A M, et al. The many faces of Macau: a correspondence analysis of the images communicated by online tourism information sources in English and Chinese[J]. *Journal of Vacation Marketing*, 2009, 15(2): 79-94.

[11] Noy C. Pages as stage: a performance approach to visitor books[J]. *Annals of Tourism Research*, 2008, 35(2): 509-528.

[12] Tussyadiah I P, Fesenmaier D R. Mediating tourist experiences: access to places via shared videos[J]. *Annals of Tourism Research*, 2009, 36(1): 24-40.

[13] Li Miao, Xie Yanjun. Blogs as stages: the constructive interpretation of post tourism experience behavior[J]. *Tourism Science*, 2012, 26(6): 21-31, 67.

[14] Xi X. The social age of tourism[J]. *Market Observer*, 2011, 12: 42-43.

[15] Zehrer A, Grabmüller A, Crotts J, et al, Social media marketing in tourism education: insights into the development and value of a social network site for a higher education institution in tourism[J]. *Journal of Vacation Marketing*, 2012, 18: 221-228.

[16] Banyai M, Glover T D. Evaluating research methods on travel blogs[J]. *Journal of Travel Research*, 2012, 51(3): 267-277.

[17] Banyai M. The University of Massachusetts websites. http://scholarworks.umass.edu/cgi/viewcontent.cgi?article=1643&context=ttra, 2011.

[18] Tang J. The Victoria University of Wellington websites. https://core.ac.uk/download/pdf/41340112.pdf, 2015.

[19] Lo I S, McKercher B, Lo A, et al. Tourism and online photography[J]. *Tourism Management*, 2011, 32(4): 725-731.

[20] Fabien G, Josep B, Francesco C, et al. Digital footprinting: uncovering tourists with user-generated content[J]. *Pervasive Computing, IEEE*, 2008, 7(4): 36-43.

[21] Zhang W, Wang X. Tourism blog marketing based on the strength of weak ties[J]. *Tourism Tribune*, 2008, 23(6):10-11.

[22] Leung D, Law R, Lee H A. The perceived destination image of Hong Kong on Ctrip.com[J]. *International Journal of Tourism Research*, 2011, 13( 2): 124-140.

# Sensemaking and Its Significance to Tourist Research

Zhang Jie[1], Dai Guangquan[2*]

**Abstract:** Sensemaking emerged as a distinct topic in the late 1960s, instigated enthusiasm of many academic groups, and resulted in abundant research findings. It is a process through which individuals and groups work to understand issues and events that are ambiguous, novel or confusing. We start from selected definitions, pointing out the recurrent and different themes in definition; then take stock of the methods used in sensemaking; further more, review literature associated with this subject in tourism; finally, outline suggestions for future application of sensemaking in tourist studies.

**Keywords:** sensemaking; definition; tourist experiences; overview; methodology

## Ⅰ. Introduction

Sensemaking—no matter it happens in individual's head or social interaction of organization—is a process. When confronting ambiguous meaning or uncertain outcome, individual seeks to clarify the event and provide order to it. Therefore, the triggers of sensemaking are characteristic of "violating expectation" [1]. Sensemaking, under research for more than forty years, has been prosperous since the publication of Weick's classic work, *Sensemaking in Organizations*. It is rooted in phenomenology, symbolic interactionism and cognitive psychology, and drawn from learning theory and social phenomenology. So, methods used in this subject are vigorous, most of them are qualitative approaches, such as ethnography, case study and so on.

Sensemaking, a central activity in organization, and one that lies at the core of organization, almost has never been used in tourism organization or tourism context. So, we want to examine whether sensemaking is suitable for resolving problems in tourism organization or in tourism context.

This paper is a literature review of sensemaking; we scrutinize the concepts, processes, and research methods of sensemaking. The aims of this review are to distinguish the concept

1 South China University of Technology, Guangzhou, China.

2* South China University of Technology, Guangzhou, China. gqdai@scut.edu.cn.

of sensemaking in different school of research, identify the process of it, and sort out methods used in this subject. And, the contribution of this paper is taking stock of sensemaking, especially definition and research method for the first time.

The structure of the paper is as follows. First, we select and discuss various definitions of sensemaking, and point out the recurrent and different themes across definitions. Second, we take stock of the methods used in sensemaking literature. Third, we review literature associated with sensemaking in tourism field. Finally, we point out the way to moving forward.

## Ⅱ. Definition of Sensemaking

In order to identify relevant research texts included in this review, we first study the frequently cited authors, such as Weick, Gioia, Gephart, Maitlis, Brown, Cornelissen, Balogun, etc. They all have properties of i) being in this field for more than ten years, ii) having stable academic team, iii) having published more than five articles about this topic, so, they have mature thinking about sensemaking.

Sensemaking has always been seen as a notion that is taken for granted, as a "general notion" [1]. Some articles about this subject have been published even without an associated definition. Looking at articles having defined it, we can find the notion has a variety of meanings. While selecting the definition, I give priority to two indicators: reputation of the researcher and citation rate of the research. The table below (Table 1) lists some of those definitions.

Table 1　Selected Definition of Sensemaking

| Author | Definition |
|---|---|
| Gephart (1993) [2] | Sensemaking has been defined as the discursive process of constructing and interpreting the social world. |
| Weick (1995) [3] | Sensemaking is understood as a process that is (1) grounded in identity construction, (2) retrospective, (3) enactive of sensible environment, (4) social, (5) ongoing, (6) focused on and by extracted cues, (7) driven by plausibility rather than accuracy. |
| Maitlis (2005) [4] | Sensemaking occurs in organizations when members confront events, issues, and actions that are somehow surprising or confusing. This happens through the production of accounts—discursive constructions of reality that interpret or explain, —or through the activation of existing accounts. |
| Cornelissen (2012) [5] | Sensemaking refers to processes of meaning construction whereby people interpret events and issues within and outside of their organization that are somehow surprising, complex, or confusing to them. |
| Maitlis (2014) [1] | Sensemaking is a process, prompted by violated expectations, that involves attending to and bracketing cues in the environment, creating intersubjective meaning through cycles of interpretation and action, and thereby enacting a more ordered environment from which further cues can be drawn. |

(To be continued)

(Continued Table 1)

| Author | Definition |
|---|---|
| Brown (2005) [6] | Sensemaking is appropriately regarded as a form of narration, a technical term that refers to those processes of interpretation and meaning production whereby people reflect on and interpret phenomena and produce intersubjective accounts. |
| Gioia (1991) [7] | Sensemaking has to do with meaning construction and reconstruction by the involved parties as they attempted to develop a meaningful framework for understanding the nature of the intended strategic change. |
| Brown (2008) [8] | Sensemaking is a generic phrase that refers to processes of interpretation and meaning production whereby individuals and groups interpret and reflect on phenomena, through processes of sensemaking people enact (create) the social world, constituting it through verbal descriptions which are communicated to and negotiated with others. |
| Balogun (2005) [9] | Sensemaking is primarily a conversational and narrative process involving a variety of communication genre, both spoken and written, and formal and informal.however, more specially, sensemaking involves "conversational and social practices". |
| Varra (2003) [10] | Sensemaking highlights the complex socio-psychological processes through which organizational actors interpret organizational phenomena and thus socially construct or enact their "realities". |
| Hill (1995) [11] | Sensemaking is a "vision" or mental model, which is developed by entrepreneur to cope with these uncertainties of how the environment works. |

*i. Recurrent themes in these definitions*

From Table 1, we can find some recurrent themes among these definitions. They are all subjective, about process and social world, and language can represent sensemaking.

*A. Sensemaking is a process*

Though some researchers argue that the actual process of sensemaking remains relatively vague, [12] we insist that sensemaking is a process. Some scholars view it as a process of metal model development of entrepreneurs, [11] others view it as a "discursive process of constructing and interpreting the social world" [2], or "unfolds as a sequence" [13].

Scholars propose different kinds of phase in the process of sensemaking. Reference [7] suggests four phases in sensemaking and sensegiving of strategical initiation: envisioning, signaling, re-visioning and energizing. Reference [11] admits mental model development process as intuitive models, metaphors, formal models and action. Reference [9] proposes a model which incorporates individual level, intersubjective level and generic level, representing the relation of individual schemata, discourse in groups and culture in society. Reference [3] summarizes the process of sensemaking as: creation process, interpretation process and enactment process.

*B. Sensemaking is subjective*

Most Sensemaking studies, especially case studies, adopt an interpretive approach. It means that individual understanding and action are based on the interpretation of information and events by people experiencing them. [7] In another word, experience is at the root of sensemaking. Experience is subjective, and how significant it will be influenced by a variety of factors.

One more thing should be noticed is that the person doing sensemaking is singular or collective is not sure. Reference [3] describes: when we look at individual behavior in organizations, we are actually seeing two entities: the individual as himself and the individual as representative of his collectivity.

*C. Sensemaking is social*

Even those who emphasize sensemaking takes place within individual would not neglect the nature of sociality in sensemaking. Every sensemaker is affected by social context. Individuals, making sense of their own, are embedded in a sociomaterial context where their thoughts, feelings and behaviors are influenced by "actual, imagined, or implied presence of others" [3]. And people, who are more active, often produce part of the environment they face. [14] That is to say, people are influenced by the social world, which is partly formed by themselves.

*D. Sensemaking is triggered by event violating expectation*

From the beginning, sensemaking is used in crises and changes. [15-17] Scholars in organizations admit that sensemaking occurs when members confront events, issues, and actions that are somehow surprising or confusing. Reference [18] points out that the events, issues, and actions have the nature of "violating expectation". There are two types of violation: something happened unexpected or something expected unhappen.

Besides, scholars from heidegger's phenomenology propose that sensemaking is from awareness of what is absent or concealed, from ruptures to habit that cannot be described as breakdowns in well-established cognitive patterns, or from an exposure to an open, unknowable awareness of future possibility. [19]

*E. Language represents sensemaking*

This is grounded on philosophical hermeneutics, which views language as essence in the world. Reference [2] describes sensemaking as "the verbal intersubjective process of interpreting actions and events". It is easy to see that language plays an important role in sensemaking. Sensemaking literature focused on language has been increased especially during the last two decades, partly resulting from the linguistic turning in the social sciences. [1]

Linguistic factors include discourse, narratives, rhetoric, ropes, and stories, [5, 6, 20, 21] which, in various ways, affect sensemaking efforts. Discursive accounts are produced by sensemakers to organize their thoughts and actions.

*ii. Differences in these definitions*

Despite these recurrent themes, there are obvious differences in definitions.

*A. Essence of sensemaking is different*

Some definitions frame sensemaking as a cognitive process, which is described in terms of developing frameworks, schemata, or mental models in one's head. For example,

Reference [11] describes sensemaking in terms of how people "develop a version or mental model of how the environment works". Reference [22] links sensemaking with situated cognition and describes how the cognitive process of sensemaking connects existing sachems and organizational contexts.

On the contrary, other definitions position sensemaking as a social process that occurs between people, as meaning of negotiated, contested, and mutually co-constructed. This standpoint views sensemaking as the "discursive processes of constructing and interpreting the social world" nowadays. Most of the scholars studying sensemaking follow this perspective.

*B. Sensemaking is studied in different levels*

Reference [23] proposes four levels of sensemaking: the individual level, the intersubjective level, the generic level and the extrasubjective level. Most of the studies are focus on the intersubjective level, generic level, and slippery between those two levels. Studies on extrasubjective level are very scarce. For example, Reference [9] analyzes the sensemaking cycle in individual level, intersubjective level and generic level.

Meanwhile, there are other methods in classifying levels of sensemaking. For example, Reference [24] distinguishes micro-level from macro-level sensemaking, but few scholars follow this method.

*C. The process of sensemaking is different*

Whether sensemaking takes place continuously or in an episodic fashion is an open question. Some researches—grounded in ethnomethodology—assert that sensemaking takes place continuously, without beginning or end. Reference [2] summarizes the ethnomethodological perspective on sensemaking: "The sensemaking practices and the production of social reality are ongoing and continually enacted… there is no time out for sensemaking." On the contrary, others admit that sensemaking is an episodic process, carved out from the "infinite stream of events and inputs that surround any organizational actor"[13]. Within any episode of sensemaking, there is a process of continuous adjustment as sense is made and remade.

*D. The role of action is different*

As mentioned above, a school of scholars adopting philosophical hermeneutics view language as the core of sensemaking and eliminate action in the process of sensemaking, they argue that sensemaking is a discursive process [2]. Meanwhile, another school of scholars adopting social phenomenology admit the role of action in sensemaking. They propose that "cognition lies in the path of action. Action precedes cognition and focuses cognition" [25], action and cognition are thus recursively linked: action serves as fodder for new sensemaking. Reference [13] asserts that action is an integral part of sensemaking, action and language have a recurring cycle in sensemaking process. When action and sense are in sync again, the sensemaking efforts change into a less conscious sensemaking model. [9]

*E. The attitude to interpretation is different*

Many scholars are willing to equate interpretation with sensemaking, Reference [2] defines sensemaking as a discursive process of constructing and interpreting the social world. The others view interpretation as outcome of sensemaking, Reference [3] says, "Sensemaking is about the ways people generate what they interpret." It implies that interpretation is the outcome of sensemaking. Still, others view interpretation as one phase in sensemaking process.

Reference [3] summarizes the differences between sensemaking and interpretation below: Sensemaking is clearly about an activity or process, whereas interpretation can be a process but is just as likely to describe a product. sensemaking is less about discovery than it is about invention. Sensemaking seems to address incipient puzzles at an earlier, more tentative stage than does interpretation. Sensemaking implies a higher level of engagement by the actor.

## Ⅲ. Methodological Analysis

*i. Research method*

Since that sensemaking process has the interactive, emergent, and evolving property, it is a challenge to scholars who endeavored in studying it. These properties imply that sensemaking research needs long-lasting, immersive methods. So, the methods most popularly used are case study, ethnography, longitudinal study and so on. Most of the researches about sensemaking are qualitative ones, for scholars aim at theory construction or theory elaboration.

Case study, no matter single-case study or multiple-cases study, is often used in sensemaking for capturing contextual richness and complexity. [9] While single-case studies are well suited for studying both everyday and extreme examples of sensemaking, multiple-cases study can test and elaborate theory. Reference [4]'s exploration of sensemaking around the same nine issues domains in three symphony orchestras allowed her to identify different forms of organizational sensemaking that varied by issue and organization.

Longitudinal study is another method sensemaking study often uses, for sensemaking is a process of interpretation made and remade. Scholars often indulge in the case study site for a period of time, Reference [5] has kept in touch with people observed for almost two years.

Ethnography is another method often used. Participant observation, immersion in the social context being studied and the "insider-outsider" stance of researcher are all suitable for sensemaking studies. Reference [7] and Reference [9] make theory construction via ethnography.

*ii. Data collection*

Data collection involves first-hand data and second-hand data. While first-hand data is from interviews, diaries of interviewee, observation of meetings, participation observation, second-hand data is from extensive documentary, such as news from media, discipline in organization, archival data, memos, personal notes and so on.

*iii. Data analysis*

A number of methods—including conversation analysis, discourse analysis, [5] narrative analysis, [8] theme analysis, [10] text analysis, [26] content analysis, [2] first-order and second-order analysis [7, 9]—can be used in revealing how participants make sense as time flows.

The method used in macro-level analysis is deconstructive analysis. For example, Reference [6] seeking to understand the BR, deconstructs the BR into understandable units, and connects the power and blame to bankruptcy of Baring Bank, albeit one that is highly convention governed.

The methods used in micro-level analysis are multiple and often under strict steps. Content analysis looks for the themes that made sense and is "talked into existence" and identifies sensemaking differences between actor groups or development in sensemaking over time. Reference [2] uses this method in identifying risks and blames in disaster sensemaking. Discourse analysis investigates what kind of discursive mechanisms and strategies are employed by whom to convey the identified themes. Reference [8] uses Fairclough's discourse analysis in studying impression management and attributed egotism in identity construction. Narrative analysis is used in a research aimed to find the recurrent and different topics in employee' narrative.

## Ⅳ. Sensemaking in Tourism

Almost all the sensemaking literature is studied in a variety of organizations, such as the hospital, transitory organizations, temporal project and so on. It should be noted that sensemking has hardly been used in tourism organization or tourism context.

Fortunately, meaning and sense have increasingly been a subject scholars being interested in. Literature about meaning and sense has seldom been seen in *Annals of Tourism Research* and *Tourism Management*. The study most in concert with sensemaking is Reference [27]'s literature. Drawing upon narratives from travel blog, scholars make sense of how backpacker's travel experience changes into meaningful experience. Other researches connect experience and meaning using phenomenology, [27-29] narrative, [27, 30] quantitative tools, [31, 32] and symbolic interactionism. [33]

These factors are all elements of sensemaking study. For example, Reference [30], using phenomenological method, aims at the relation of meanings of tourist experiences and destination assets, and further proposes a research framework for application of phenomenology on event management. Reference [33] proposes a semiotic framework of tourism as meaning-making practice on account of theory of meaning, cultural geography theory and theory of intertextuality. Researches above are all qualitative ones, otherwise, there is literature using quantitative analysis. For example, Reference [31], using latent dirichlet analysis, mines meaning of the valuable comments provided by visitors, identifies the key dimensions of customer service from a big database. Reference [32], studying tourist' perception and attitudes toward destination, uses canonical variate analysis as a tool in reducing the number of variables needed to be coded in tourist' photograph.

Fortunately, concepts that are closely associated with sensemaking, such as experience, expectation, narrative, qualitative study, have been under research for a long time, or viewed as one of the most significant area in tourism study. All these achievements will soon be used in understanding of sensemaking in tourism.

## V. Ways Out

Tourism, especially extraordinary, once-in-a-lifetime travel, is a rich context to explore ways in which travelers and stakeholders construct meaningful experiences and extract meanings from the experience. Since the experience and meaning attached to it are the core phenomenon in tourism, it is suitable to use sensemaking theory in tourism. Sensemaking can promote tourism study from aspects below:

*i. Exploring and identifying new subjects*

As mentioned above, sensemking has hardly been used in tourism, so there are many subjects that need to be explored or identified. For example, whether tourism organization and tourism context itself has properties different from other organization and context in using sensemaking theory, what kind of factors have influence on different levels of sensemaking, and how to design products from sensemaking perspective, these questions are left to be answered.

*ii. Prompting studies to a higher level*

Since been under research for several decades, some of the related concepts can be incorporated into sensemaking in order to better understand relations between them and prompt the understanding to a higher level or create a new frame.

For example, experience and purchase decision have been under research in tourism for a long time. While sensemaking lends feature of temporality to these concepts, memory should be incorporated into these studies.

*iii. Enriching study methods*

In concert with new tourism turning, [34] qualitative study positions an important role in tourism study. We encourage sensemaking researchers to draw on a wider range of methods to study sensemaking.

Most early sensemaking scholars, aiming at theory construction and theory elaboration, use qualitative methods to investigate different kinds of questions. As the questions we ask about sensemaking become more nuanced and complex, the methods we use should capture that nuance and complexity. So the scholars may incorporate quantitative methods, some of them has made effort on it. Meanwhile, new methods can also facilitate the study of new questions.

## Ⅵ. Conclusions

There has been a burgeoning research in sensemaking. We have known the process and property of it, factors having effect on it. However, scholars use this term differently, and what we have clarified remains a very limited body of work on sensemaking. What we should do is to encourage more work about sensemaking and its connection to tourism organization.

## ACKNOWLEDGMENT

This study is sponsored by National Natural Science Foundation of China, NO.41571132.

## References

[1]] Maitlis S, Christianson M. Sensemaking in organizations: taking stock and moving forward[J]. *The Academy of Management Annals*, 2014, 8(1): 57-125.

[2] Gephart R P. The textual approach: risk and blame in disaster sensemaking[J]. *The Academy of Management Journal*, 1993, 36(6): 1465-514.

[3] Weick K E. S*ensemaking in Organization*[M]. 1st ed. Thousand Oaks: Sage Publications, 1995.

[4] Maitlis S. The social processes of organizational sensemaking[J]. *Academy of Management Journal*, 2005, 48(1): 21-49.

[5] Cornelissen J P. Sensemaking under pressure: the influence of professional roles and social accountability on the creation of sense[J]. *Organization Science*, 2012, 23(1): 118-137.

[6] Brown A D. Making sense of the collapse of Baring Bank [J]. *Human Relations*, 2005, 58(12): 1579-1604.

[7] Gioia D A, Chittipeddi K. Sensemaking and sensegiving in strategic change initiation[J]. *Strategic Management Journal*, 1991, 12(6): 433-48.

[8] Brown A D, Stacey P, Nandhakumar J. Making sense of sensemaking narratives[J]. *Human Relations*, 2008, 61(8): 1035-1062.

[9] Balogun J, Johnson G. From intended strategies to unintended outcomes: the impact of change recipient sensemaking[J]. *Organization Studies*, 2005, 26(11): 1573-1601.

[10] Vaara E. Post-acquisition integration as sensemaking: glimpses of ambiguity, confusion, hypocrisy and politicization[J]. *Journal of Management Studies*, 2003, 40(4): 859-94.

[11] Hill R C, Levenhagen M. Metaphors and mental models: sensemaking and sensegiving in innovative and entrepreneurial activities[J]. *Journal of Management*, 1995, 21(6): 1057-1074.

[12] Sandberg J, Tsoukas H. Making sense of the sensemaking perspective: its constituents, limitations, and opportunities for further development[J]. *Journal of Organizational Behavior*, 2015, 36: S6-32, S1.

[13] Weick K E, Sutcliffe K M, Obstfeld D. Organizing and the process of sensemaking[J]. *Organization Science*, 2005, 16(4): 409-421.

[14] Pondy L R, Mitroff I I. Beyond open systems models of organziation[J]. *Research in Organizational Behavior*, 1979, 1(1): 3-39.

[15] Weick K E. The collapse of sensemaking in organization: the Mann Gulch disaster[J]. *Administrative Science Quarterly*, 1993, 38(4): 628-652.

[16] Gioia D A, Thomas J B, Clark S M, Chittipeddi K. Symbolism and strategic change in academia: the

dynamics of sensemaking and influence[J]. *Organization Science*, 1994, 5(3): 363-383.

[17] Isabella L A. Evolving interpretations as a change unfolds: how managers construe key organizational events[J]. *The Academy of Management Journal*, 1990, 33(1): 7-41.

[18] Cornelissen J P, Mantere S, Vaara E. The contraction of meaning: the combined effect of communication, emotions, and materiality on sensemaking in the Stockwell shooting [J]. *Journal of Management Studies*, 2014, 51(5): 699-736, 2014.

[19] Holt R, Cornelissen J. Sensemaking revisited[J]. *Management Learning*, 2014, 45(5): 525-539.

[20] Brown A D, Colville I, Pye A. Making sense of sensemaking in organization studies[J]. *Organization Studies*, 2015, 36(2): 65-77.

[21] Christensen L T, Cornelissen J. Bridging corporate and organizational communication: review, development and a look to the future[J]. *Management Communication Quarterly*, 2011, 25(3): 383-414.

[22] Elsbach K D, Barr P S, Hargadon A B. Identifying situated cognition in organization[J]. *Organization Science*, 2005, 16(4): 422-433.

[23] Wiley N. The micro-macro problem in social theory[J]. *Sociological Theory*, 1988, 6: 254-261.

[24] Jørgensen L, Jordan S, Mitterhofer H. Sensemaking and discourse analyses in inter-organizational research: a review and suggested advances[J]. *Scandinavian Journal of Managemen*t, 2012, 28(2): 107-120.

[25] Weick K E. Faith, evidence, and action: better guesses in an unknowable world[J]. *Organization Studies*, 2006, 27(11): 1723-1736.

[26] Kjaergaard A, Morsing M, Ravasi D. Mediating identity: a study of media influence on organizational identity construction in a celebrity firm[J]. *Journal of Management Studies*, 2011, 48(3): 514-543.

[27] Bosangit C, Hibbert S, McCabe S. If I was going to die I should at least be having fun: travel blogs, meaning and tourist experience[J]. *Annals of Tourism Research*, 2015: 1-1.

[28] Ziakas V, Boukas N. Extracting meanings of event tourist experiences: a phenomenological exploration of Limassol Carnival[J]. *Journal of Destination Marketing & Management*, 2013, 2(2): 94-107.

[29] Ziakas V, Boukas N. Contextualizing phenomenology in event management research: deciphering the meaning of event experiences[J]. *International Journal of Event and Festival Management*, 2014, 5(1): 56-73.

[30] Xing Xiaoyuan, Chalip L. Marching in the glory: experiences and meanings when working for a sport mega-event[J]. *Journal of Sport Management*, 2009, 23: 210-237.

[31] Guo Yue, Barnes S J, Jia Qiong. Mining meaning from online ratings and reviews: tourist satisfaction analysis using latent dirichlet allocation[J]. *Tourism Management*, 2017, 59: 467-483.

[32] Balomenou N, Garrod B, Georgiadou A. Making sense of tourists' photographs using canonical variate analysis[J]. *Tourism Management*, 2017, 61: 173-179.

[33] Soica S. Tourism as practice of making meaning[J]. *Annals of Tourism Research*, 2016, 61: 96-110.

[34] Tribe J. New tourism research[J]. *Tourism Recreation Research*, 2005, 30(2): 5-8.

# An Analysis of Brand Loyalty of Panda Tourism Using Embeddedness Theory

Li Taohong[1*]

**Abstract:** Based on embeddedness theory of Zukin and Dimaggio, this study builds a research framework which includes brand cognition, brand relation/brand structure, brand loyalty for the purpose of researching the brand loyalty of panda tourism. This study also attempts to gain insights into the internal logic of the brand loyalty of panda tourism by constructing a structural equation model. The results show that brand cognition of panda tourism has the greatest impact on brand loyalty, and the influence coefficient is 0.959. Brand structure of panda tourism has no impact on brand attitudinal loyalty. Brand relationship of panda tourism has impact on brand attitudinal loyalty only, indicating that brand loyalty of panda tourism is mostly reflected in the attitudinal loyalty, while there is less impact on behavioral loyalty. This paper points out that the internal logic of the brand loyalty of panda tourism lays out as brand cognition, brand structure and brand loyalty.

**Keywords:** embeddedness theory; panda tourism; brand loyalty

## Ⅰ. Introduction

China enjoys a world reputation for breeding, protection and wild stocking of giant pandas. As one of the well-known global icons of biodiversity conservation, the giant panda is listed on CITES Appendix I and categorized as Endangered on the Red List of International Union for Conservation of Nature. Setting the giant panda as ecological tourist attraction has become one of the important ways of ecological tourism in China which is widely accepted by people at home and abroad. While there are few research studies examining wildlife tourism in Asia, especially in China which has rich wildlife resources. [17] In particular, there are very few researches on visitors' brand loyalty of panda tourism, it has yet to be empirically analyzed, and the brand potential value of panda tourism has not been fully released for some reasons.

A brand can provide a significant means of differentiation and thus competitive advantage for products and services. [1][2][3] Brand loyalty is a concept based on a relationship

1* Sichuan University, Chengdu, China. 406983418@qq.com.

process, is a cognitive link and an emotional tie between the brand and the consumer, it can be better interpreted as a specific consumer behavior that is necessary for relationship-based marketing exchange activities. [23] The existing researches also point out that strong brand loalty is the culmination of brand building and the formation of brand equity. [23][28]

Granovetter's article on embeddedness asserts that economic phenomena take place in social structures and are shaped by social networks. Tourists' behavior is not entirely defined by macro-environment, their actions are also affected by social relations. When researching the brand loyalty of panda tourism, we should take the social networks into consideration. As a result, this paper attempts to gain insights into the internal logic of the brand loyalty of panda tourism by constructing a research framework which includes brand cognition, brand relation/brand structure, brand loyalty based on embeddedness theory of Zukin and Dimaggio (1990). [27]

## Ⅱ. Research Review

*i. The development course of panda tourism*

The giant panda (Ailuropoda melanoleuca) is a shy and solitary mammal, whose general inhabiting home range is from 3.9 to 6.4 $km^2$. Giant panda is a "living fossil" of ecosystem protection, it is a symbol of wildlife conservation and biological diversity. World Wildlife Fund's "All Time Top 10 Species to See" ranked the giant panda as the top species in the world that people want to see.

The giant panda has a history of more than 3000 years in China. It has been deeply rooted in people's mind that the giant panda is China's national image since the end of the 18th century when the giant panda was recognized by the world. Now, the giant panda is a banner for the world to protect wild animals and giant panda tourism is also developing rapidly. The development course of panda tourism can be generally divided into three stages.

The initial phase (1980s): The development of panda tourism was influenced by both subjective and objective reasons, such as the closed protection policies of the protected areas, political sensitivity, tourism infrastructure, etc. At this stage, the main job was to protect the panda while the development of panda tourism was limited to some extent. The brand potential value of panda tourism had not been fully released.

The wandering stage (late 1980s to the mid-1990s): With China's economy entering the developing period, the domestic tourism infrastructure was gradually improving. At this wandering stage, the main job was to protect the panda and do scientific researches. Panda raising and breeding entered the research stage while the development of panda tourism came to a halt at this stage.

The "panda economy" stage (late 1990s to the 21st century) : At this stage, China's reform and opening up was further deepened, tourism had been vigorously developed and the number of inbound tourists had risen year by year. Panda tourism became popular all over the world, tourists gradually formed a rational brand loyalty of panda tourism. In order to meet the market demand, some panda tourism bases are established, such as Wolong National Nature Reserve, Bifengxia Scenic Area, Chengdu Giant Panda Breeding Research Base and other tourist attractions.

*ii. Brand loyalty*

Earlier than the concept of brand image appeared, Copeland (1923) put forward the concept of brand loyalty. Then there are extensive and in-depth studies of brand loyalty in the academic circles. There are three main points on brand loyalty. They are behavioral brand loyalty, attitudinal loyalty and comprehensive composition.

*A. Behavioral loyalty*

Newman & Werbel (1973) defined loyalty as the repeated purchase of a certain brand and there are only consideration for the brand, no seeking for information that has nothing to do with the brand. Brand loyalty refers to the actual behavior that is repeated over a period of time. As exemplified by Oliver (1997), brand loyalty is a deep commitment to the products and services that are preferred.

Behavioral brand loyalty is the relative weight or frequency of customer purchases. [9] Behavioral brand loyalty theory focuses on the frequency of re-purchase behavior within a timeframe to make up the market share, the possibility of buying. It is defined as consumers' repeat purchasing of a brand, which is revealed through patterns of continued patronage and actual spending behaviors. [17] However, there are differences between re-purchase behavior and loyalty. Re-purchase behavior may be affected by other factors when consumers have no choice but to purchase, furthermore, re-purchase behavior is merely a manifestation of behavior that can not explain its intrinsic substance and can not provide useful information about the factors behind the behavior for the market. While behavioral brand loyalty is based on actual behavior and is easy to identify, and its frequency is easy to track.

*B. Attitudinal loyalty*

Attitudinal researchers investigate commitment to brands and repurchase intentions. [24] Attitudinal loyalty is an attitudinal predisposition consisting of commitment to a brand and intention to repurchase the brand. [22] Attitudinal loyalty emphasizes loyalty as a psychological activity, it is a preference, trust, commitment, or emotional intensity for a certain brand.

Relative to the behavioral loyalty, attitudinal loyalty distinguishes the re-purchase behavior that restricted by objective factors and real loyalty, excludes the random re-purchase behavior by looking into the psychological factors that lay behind the behavior. But there are still shortcomings, although the information can be obtained by asking the customers, sometimes customers themselves may have different understanding of their own minds for attitudinal loyalty which is a psychological activity. Their answers to the questions may differ from their actual attitudes. In addition, there are other factors affecting the attitude and the behavior of customers. For example, customers may have a strong psychological loyalty to the product, but they may consider time, energy and other factors when take actions which may lead to weak behavior loyalty.

*C. Comprehensive composition*

Many re-purchase behavior may be related to opportunities and routines, but has nothing to do with preferences. In this case, it is recommended to use attitudinal loyalty to distinguish between true loyalty and fake loyalty. Repurchase behavior based on fake loyalty may be due to stress, habits or convenience.

Attitudes and behavioral intentions for one or more products or services are all included in the comprehensive composition. To fully understand the reasons for the formation of brand loyalty, Jacoby and Chestnut (1978) added the psychological content to establish the causal relationship net between attitudinal loyalty and behavioral loyalty. They conceptualized brand loyalty as a psychological process function. Customer loyalty is the result of psychological processes and has behavioral manifestations. [8]

Despite the view that brand loyalty is conceptualized broadly and is reflected by both attitudinal and behavioral measures, [4] for further research, attitudinal and behavioral dimensions of brand loyalty should be incorporated. Hence, this research draws on the the conceptual work that both attitudinal and behavioral components should be incorporated. In this paper the embeddedness theory is adopted to empirically link attitudinal and behavioral loyalty to research the brand loyalty of panda tourism, to gain insights into the internal logic of the brand loyalty of panda tourism and to reasonably explain the brand loyalty process of panda tourism.

*iii. Embeddedness theory*

Embeddedness—defined as a set of ongoing social relations—has become a widely used concept since the first time it was used in the seminal work of Karl Polanyi (1957), *The Great Transformation: The Political and Economic Origins of Our Time.* Polanyi's central argument is that nonmarket systems of economic exchange are embedded in society and enmeshed in institutions. [19]

After the work of Polanyi, Pearson (1960) defined embeddedness as a subsystem that related to sociaty and economy. [25] Mark Granovetter (1985) picked up Polanyi's main theme, he "scales down" Polanyi's original concept of embeddedness by switching the focus toward the analytical scale of individual and collective actors in social systems of exchange, rather than the systems themselves.

Many attempts have been made to refine the concept and produce more differentiated understandings of embeddedness by further deconstructing the notion of social embeddedness. Zukin and Dimaggio (1990) distinguished four forms of embeddedness: cognitive, cultural, structural, and political.

Swedberg & Granovetter (1992) divided embeddedness into relational embeddedness and structural embeddedness. Relational embeddedness is developed based on the frequency of past interactions and can be revealed through collaborative activities. [6] Because personal ties may be used to convey information about third parties present within a network, there is reason to think such effects would be at least as strong for the reinitiation of lapsed ties. [14] Relational embeddedness also highlights the strength of a tie that is described as either a strong or weak tie. [14][28] Relational embeddedness is a strong social tie where the social relations have a significant impact on the economic behavior of the involved parties. [7] Researchers have conceptualized relational embeddedness from three perspectives: a direct tie, an asset, and the strength of an interaction.

Structural embeddedness is created in a triadic or more complex structure comprising multiple dyadic relationships. [30] Structural embeddedness provides informational and reputational benefits through the structural position. The focus of analysis is on indirect channels. [25] The structural dimension also emphasizes a monitoring and controlling mechanism represented by norms and sanctions. [6][25]

The recent literature on embeddedness shows that relational embeddedness and structural embeddedness are two different levels for researches. While it is generally considered that structural embeddedness is a more macro perspective for researches and more difficult to grasp.

Following the work of Granovetter (1973, 1985), Zukin and Dimaggio (1990) had developed the embedded theory. From their perspective, culture can influence economic behavior through beliefs and ideas, habitual assumptions or informal normative systems, and thus the limits of economic rationality is setted up. The impact of cognitive factors, structural factors and cultural factors on economic behavior can not be ignored. Zukin and Dimaggio (1990) divided embeddedness into cognitive embeddedness, structural embeddedness, cultural embeddedness and political embeddedness. They are different perspectives for researches. While it is generally considered that cognitive embeddedness is a micro-level perspective, and that structural embeddedness is the mesoscopic perspective, cultural and political embeddedness is a macro perspective. From our perspective, it can be helpful to consider two categories of embeddedness: cognitive embeddedness and structural embeddedness to study the brand loyalty of panda tourism, the relationship between consumer loyalty itself and the consumer.

The recent literature shows that there is a lack of research on loyalty based on the embeddedness theory. Based on the embeddedness theory of Zukin and Dimaggio (1990) and the comprehensive composition theory, this paper employs the concept that the brand loyalty behavior of panda tourism is a kind of social embeddedness to improve our understanding of the brand loyalty of panda tourism. While this kind of social embeddedness is composed of cognitive embeddedness, structural embeddedness and relational embeddedness. The brand loyalty of panda tourism consists of two dimensions: attitudinal loyalty and behavioral loyalty. Thus this paper builds a research framework which includes brand cognition, brand relation/brand structure, brand loyalty for the purpose of researching the brand loyalty of panda tourism.

## Ⅲ. Research Model and Hypotheses

*i. Research model*

Economic activities are embedded in the network of social relations. Similar to that the decision-making behavior of economic actors is influenced by the interaction of members in the social network (Zukin & Dimaggio 1990), brand community's consumer value and brand loyalty of panda tourism can affect consumer's loyalty for the particularity of the structure position of community loyalty. Thus, keeping these conceptual issues in mind, in our paper we adopt the embeddedness theory to empirically link attitudinal and behavioral loyalty to research the brand loyalty of panda tourism, and build a research framework (as shown in Figure 1) to study the internal logic of the brand loyalty of panda tourism.

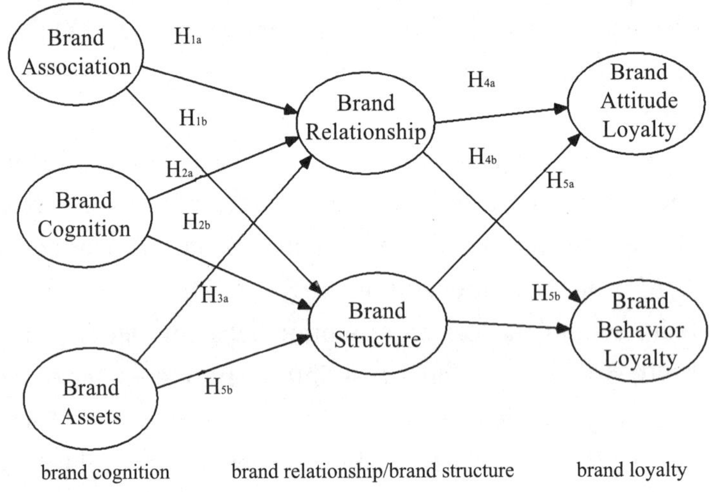


Figure 1 Conceptual Model

*ii. Hypotheses*

*A. Hypothesis on the effect of brand cognition on the brand relationship and brand structure*

Brand loyalty is influenced by the actor's own cognition, and cognition decides actor's behavior. Zukin and Dimaggio(1990) linked cognitive embeddedness to bounded rationality. From this point of view, the research object of cognitive embeddedness is the mental process of the achievement of a variety of economic rational behavior. Keller (1998) pointed out that the source of brand equity is the consumer's brand cognition. [20] David A. Aaker (1991) divided brand cognition into brand awareness and brand image. The former includes brand recall and brand recognition, and the latter includes brand perceived quality and brand association. [8] The recent literature shows that there are two paths for the division of brand cognition dimension. The first one is based on brand association, the other is based on brand assets and brand knowledge perspective. Thus, this paper divides brand cognition into three dimensions: brand association, brand knowledge, brand assets.

Brand relationship is a two-way interaction that shows the consumer's attitude and action to the brand as well as the brand's attitudes and actions to consumer and it consists of trust and satisfaction. This concept personifies brand, defines it as a person with attitudes and behaviors and researches the relationship between the brand and the consumer according to the law of interpersonal relationships. Fournier(1998) put forward the concept of brand relationship quality in which the brand relationship reflects the continuous connecting strength and development capability between consumers and brands. Brand relationship consists of six elements: love and passion, self-connection, interdependence, personal commitment, intimate feelings, brand mate quality.

According to Granovetter (1973), relational embeddedness highlights the strength of a tie that is described as either a strong or weak tie. Compared with the strong tie, the weak tie has a more significant impact on the process of transmission of resources. Hansen (1999) further researched the tie weakness theory and defined the tie weakness as the alienation and inflexibility of the contact. There are many ways to measure the strength of contact in the literature, but the commonly used measurement is the contact frequency and emotional intimacy. Thus, based on the tie weakness theory, this paper measures the brand relationship.

Brand relationship spectrum sketches out a brand portfolio structure defining the essence of the relationship between the role of the brand and the brand itself. The most important issue associated with a brand is the multi-brand, the enterprise should use multi-brand structure rather than a single brand structure. Based on the embeddedness theory, structural embeddedness is the background of contemporary economic exchange in the form of interpersonal relationships (Zukin & Dimaggio 1990). Structural embeddedness can also be viewed as a position which is interconnected by actors. The more the number of actors connected, the closer to the central location of the network structure, the closer to get valuable information from partners of the network. [15] Rowley et al. (2000) verified Gulati's view by measuring the structural embeddedness of the group with network density. Given this, brand structure can be understood as the degree of influence on individual behavior by network structure, contact intensity and spatial distribution of contact. Thus, this paper measures the brand structure.

It has become a consensus in marketing that brand cognition of consumers is the starting point of the formation of brand value. Bhattacharya and Sen (2003), Esch (2006) verified that brand cognition is the basis for the formation of brand relationships, and then the formation of brand loyalty, and further confirmed that brand cognition has a significant impact on brand relations. Research shows that brand awareness has an impact on brand structure.

The following hypotheses have been proposed based on the above analysis.

*H1a: brand association of panda tourism has a positive impact on brand relationship.*

*H1b: brand association of panda tourism has a positive impact on brand structure.*

*H2a: brand cognition of panda tourism has a positive impact on brand relationship.*

*H2b: brand cognition of panda tourism has a positive impact on brand structure.*

*H3a: brand assets of panda tourism has a positive impact on brand relationship.*

*H3b: brand assets of panda tourism has a positive impact on brand structure.*

*B. Hypothesis on the effect of brand relationship on brand loyalty*

Trust and satisfaction are two factors that affect brand relationship. Trust is influenced by risk, credibility and intimacy, satisfaction is a function of initiative and support, and it has a direct impact on loyalty. In the five-star model of brand assets, brand relationship consists of brand awareness, quality awareness, brand association, brand loyalty and other proprietary assets. [8] It further confirms the relationship between brand relationship and brand loyalty.

The following hypotheses have been proposed based on the above analysis.

*H4a: brand relationship of panda tourism has a positive impact on brand attitudinal loyalty.*

*H4b: brand relationship of panda tourism has a positive impact on brand behavior loyalty.*

*C. Hypothesis on the effect of brand structure on brand loyalty*

Brand structure commitment reflects the relationship between consumers and specific brands, it is the desire to maintain a valuable relationship with the consumer in the long-term. The higher the loyalty, the higher the conversion barriers for both sides. Members within the brand structure can not only send a lot of brand information, they can also get a lot of brand information which adds to their loyalty to the brand, and make it more difficult for them to change the brand. Algesheimer et al. (2010) proposed that the richer the brand structure, the better the brand loyalty will be. The following hypotheses have been proposed based on the above analysis.

*H5a: brand structure of panda tourism has a positive impact on brand attitudinal loyalty.*

*H5b: brand structure of panda tourism has a positive impact on brand behavioral loyalty.*

## Ⅳ. Research Methods

*i. Sample and data collection*

This study conducts a questionnaire survey in Bifengxia Scenic Area and Chengdu Giant Panda Breeding Research Base from September 29, 2016 to October 5, 2016. A total of 423 valid questionnaries were collected from 475 questionnaires. The effective sample rate was 89.05%. The structure of the valid sample is shown in Table 1.

Table 1 The Description of Sample

| Sample Characteristics | Feature Distribution | Frequency | Percent (%) |
|---|---|---|---|
| Gender | male | 206 | 48.7 |
| | female | 217 | 51.3 |
| | total | 423 | 100 |
| Age | ≤18 | 9 | 2.1 |
| | 18-35 | 246 | 58.2 |
| | 36-49 | 104 | 24.6 |
| | 50-59 | 23 | 5.4 |
| | ≥60 | 41 | 9.7 |
| | total | 423 | 100 |
| Education | primary and below | 5 | 1.2 |
| | junior high school | 66 | 15.6 |
| | high school | 168 | 39.7 |
| | university (including college) and above | 184 | 43.5 |
| | total | 423 | 100 |
| Career | civil servants | 16 | 3.8 |
| | institutions | 96 | 22.7 |
| | student | 38 | 9 |
| | employees | 123 | 29.1 |
| | retired | 39 | 9.2 |
| | other | 111 | 26.2 |
| | total | 423 | 100 |
| Monthly income | $226 and below | 68 | 16.1 |
| | $227-$527 | 142 | 33.6 |
| | $529-$827 | 122 | 28.8 |
| | $829-$1,137 | 52 | 12.3 |
| | $1,138-$1,508 | 19 | 4.5 |
| | $1,508 and more | 20 | 4.7 |
| | total | 423 | 100 |

(To be continued)

(Continued Table 1)

| Sample Characteristics | Feature Distribution | Frequency | Percent (%) |
|---|---|---|---|
| Year trips | 0 | 1 | 0.2 |
| | 1 | 52 | 12.3 |
| | 2 | 116 | 27.4 |
| | 3 | 107 | 25.3 |
| | 4 times and above | 147 | 34.8 |
| | total | 423 | 100 |
| Per capita consumption | $30 and less | 53 | 12.5 |
| | $31-$60 | 143 | 33.8 |
| | $61-$90 | 111 | 26.2 |
| | $91-$120 | 53 | 12.5 |
| | $120 and above | 63 | 14.9 |
| | Total | 423 | 100 |

*ii. Scale design and measurement*

This model contains seven core variables which are brand association, brand cognition, brand assets, brand relationship, brand structure, brand attitudinal loyalty, brand behavioral loyalty. The questions are based on the 5-point Likert scale, 1 for totally disagree, 2 for relatively disagree, 3 for general, 4 for relatively of consent, 5 for totally consent. In this study, seven demographic variables, such as gender, age, education, occupation, monthly income, annual trips, and per capita consumption are used to control brand loyalty.

*iii. Analytical method*

Structural equation model is the synthesis of the development process of econometric, social measurement and psychological measurement. The estimation of all parameters is determined by the relationship between the observed variables provided in the variance-covariance matrix. The structural equation model gives more general measurement models than the traditional factor analysis structure and it enables the researcher to specifically design the relationship between potential variables. In order to test the hypothesis, the structural equation model is adopted in this study for model contructuring and AMOS20.0 and SPSS19.0 software are adopted in this study for data processing.

## V. Data Analysis and Results

*i. Reliability and validity test*

This study examines internal consistency, combinatorial reliability and other reliability indicators, the test results are shown in Table 2 and Table 3. As can be seen from Table 2, the internal consistency is judged by Cronbach's alpha values, the Cronbach's alpha values for all variables exceed 0.700, indicating that the internal consistency of each variable is very high. The results of the compounding reliability show that the combined confidence coefficients for all variables are above the critical value of 0.700, indicating that the reliability is very good. In addition, as can be seen from Table 2, the factor load of the measured items is greater than 0.500, indicating that these measured items are suitable for measuring the corresponding variables.

Table 3 gives the descriptive statistical results of the variables. The discriminant validity is examined by average variance extraction (AVE), the AVE values for all variables are close to 0.500, especially the AVE value for brand behavioral loyalty is greater than 0.500. Moreover, the CR values for all variables are greater than 0.7000 indicating that the discriminant validity between the variables is strong. The validity of the convergence was tested by confirmatory factor analysis. The results show that the fitting index of the measurement model are $x^2$=2172.646, df=318, $x^2$/df=6.832, GFI=0.716, NFI=0.589, IFI=0.627, CFI=0.624, RMSEA=0.118, indicating that the convergence of each variable is good.

Table 2 The Reliability and Validity of Items

| Items | | Component Matrixa | Cronbachs Alpha |
|---|---|---|---|
| Brand association | BA1 | 0.696 | 0.737 |
| | BA2 | 0.772 | |
| | BA3 | 0.732 | |
| | BA4 | 0.619 | |
| | BA5 | 0.668 | |
| Brand cognition | BC1 | 0.725 | 0.775 |
| | BC2 | 0.774 | |
| | BC3 | 0.745 | |
| | BC4 | 0.697 | |
| | BC5 | 0.693 | |
| Brand assets | BAS1 | 0.735 | 0.831 |
| | BAS2 | 0.817 | |
| | BAS3 | 0.784 | |
| | BAS4 | 0.801 | |
| | BAS5 | 0.725 | |
| Brand relationship | BR1 | 0.751 | 0.753 |
| | BR2 | 0.849 | |
| | BR3 | 0.854 | |

(To be continued)

(Continued Table 2)

| Items | | Component Matrixa | Cronbachs Alpha |
|---|---|---|---|
| Brand structure | BCT1 | 0.783 | 0.768 |
| | BCT2 | 0.883 | |
| | BCT3 | 0.819 | |
| Brand attitude loyalty | AL1 | 0.777 | 0.794 |
| | AL2 | 0.885 | |
| | AL3 | 0.868 | |
| Brand behavior loyalty | BL1 | 0.867 | 0.867 |
| | BL2 | 0.914 | |
| | BL3 | 0.887 | |

Table 3　Convergent Validity of the Construct

| Variables | Item | Standardized Factor Loading | SMC | AVE | CR | Model Fit |
|---|---|---|---|---|---|---|
| Brand association | BA1 | 0.696 | 0.315 | 0.312 | 0.779 | $x^2$=2,172.646, df= 318, $x^2$/df=6.832, GFI=0.716, NFI=0.589, IFI=0.627, CFI=0.624, RMSEA=0.118. |
| | BA2 | 0.772 | 0.433 | | | |
| | BA3 | 0.732 | 0.355 | | | |
| | BA4 | 0.619 | 0.221 | | | |
| | BA5 | 0.668 | 0.235 | | | |
| Brand cognition | BC1 | 0.725 | 0.341 | 0.339 | 0.800 | |
| | BC2 | 0.774 | 0.407 | | | |
| | BC3 | 0.745 | 0.347 | | | |
| | BC4 | 0.697 | 0.311 | | | |
| | BC5 | 0.693 | 0.289 | | | |
| Brand assets | BAS1 | 0.735 | 0.393 | 0.447 | 0.844 | |
| | BAS2 | 0.817 | 0.506 | | | |
| | BAS3 | 0.784 | 0.490 | | | |
| | BAS4 | 0.801 | 0.499 | | | |
| | BAS5 | 0.725 | 0.349 | | | |
| Brand relationship | BR1 | 0.751 | 0.247 | 0.362 | 0.759 | |
| | BR2 | 0.849 | 0.416 | | | |
| | BR3 | 0.854 | 0.423 | | | |
| Brand structure | BCT1 | 0.783 | 0.318 | 0.398 | 0.774 | |
| | BCT2 | 0.883 | 0.488 | | | |
| | BCT3 | 0.819 | 0.387 | | | |

(To be continued)

(Continued Table 3)

| Variables | Item | Standardized Factor Loading | SMC | AVE | CR | Model Fit |
|---|---|---|---|---|---|---|
| Brand attitude loyalty | AL1 | 0.777 | 0.305 | 0.444 | 0.793 | |
| | AL2 | 0.885 | 0.527 | | | |
| | AL3 | 0.868 | 0.499 | | | |
| Brand behavior loyalty | BL1 | 0.867 | 0.511 | 0.570 | 0.847 | |
| | BL2 | 0.914 | 0.631 | | | |
| | BL3 | 0.887 | 0.569 | | | |

*ii. Hypothetical test*

The medieval effect and the regulatory effect of the panda tourism brand loyalty model are tested step by step. The test results (as shown in the Table 4) show that the *p* value of H4b, H5a, H5b are greater than 0.05, indicating that H4b, H5a, H5b are invalid.

Table 4 Results of Hypotheses Tests

| Hypothesis | Estimate | S.E. | C.R. | *p* | Result |
|---|---|---|---|---|---|
| **H1a** | 0.126 | 0.042 | 3.018 | 0.003 | Supported |
| **H2a** | 0.985 | 0.1 | 9.864 | *** | Supported |
| **H3a** | 0.192 | 0.036 | 5.283 | *** | Supported |
| **H1b** | 0.271 | 0.057 | 4.76 | *** | Supported |
| **H2b** | 0.296 | 0.062 | 4.763 | *** | Supported |
| **H3b** | 0.21 | 0.045 | 4.65 | *** | Supported |
| **H4a** | 1.027 | 0.115 | 8.967 | *** | Supported |
| H4b | -0.258 | 0.139 | -1.86 | 0.063 | Not supported |
| H5a | 0.007 | 0.169 | 0.042 | 0.966 | Not supported |
| H5b | 0.248 | 0.232 | 1.068 | 0.285 | Not supported |

Note: Estimate standardized coefficient, *t*-value: C.R. (Critical Ratio), ****p* b.001. ***p* b.01. **p* b.05. Bold in this table indicates that the hypothesis was supported.

*iii. Model modification*

By modifying the model, we find that brand structure of panda tourism has no impact on brand attitudinal loyalty and brand behavioral loyalty which indicating the brand structure variables do not work in the panda brand loyalty model. As a result, the panda brand loyalty model can be simplified as "brand cognition, brand relation, brand loyalty" model (as shown in Figure 2 ). The fitting index of the model are $x^2$=510.106, df=177, $x^2$/df=2.822, GFI=0.900, NFI=0.871, IFI=0.912, CFI=0.911, RMSEA=0.067, indicating that the convergence of each variable is good.

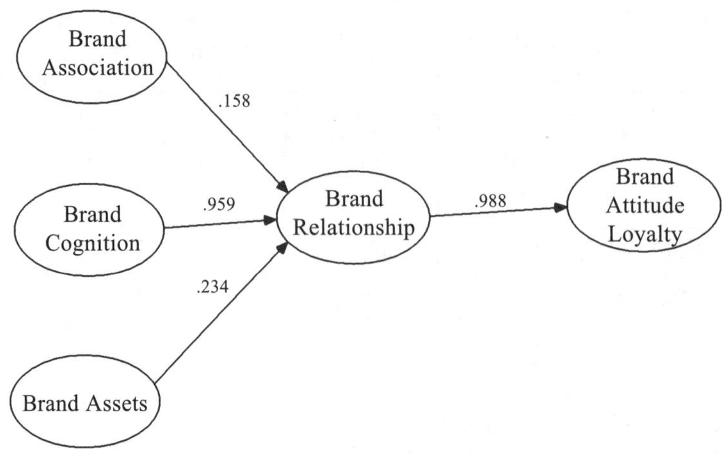


Figure 2 Modifided Model

*iv. Discussion*

(1) Brand cognition of panda tourism has the greatest impact on brand loyalty, the influence coefficient is 0.959. To a certain extent, brand cognition of panda tourism determines the brand loyalty. So that visitors have brand cognition about the brand (panda tourism) may make a difference when evaluating the brand (panda tourism). The more visitors are willingly perceived, the closer it comes to being the norm which, in turn, has greater potential to encourage visitors to continue brand loyalty.

(2) Brand structure of panda tourism has no impact on brand attitudinal loyalty, neither on brand behavioral loyalty indicating that brand structure of panda tourism has no impact on the loyalty model of panda tourism.

(3) Brand relationship of panda tourism has impact on brand attitudinal loyalty only, indicating that brand loyalty of panda tourism is mostly reflected in the attitudinal loyalty, while having less impact on behavioral loyalty. The low re-visit rate of visitors is the embodiment of this phenomenon. Most visitors may tell you that "The giant panda is great, but I will not come next time".

## Ⅵ. Conclusion

This study adds to our understanding of how people respond to the brand (panda tourism). For the first time, it brought together the construct of brand loyalty and the embeddedness theory of Zukin and Dimaggio to examine aspects of the framework for visitors' brand loyalty to the brand (panda tourism). It was found that visitors' brand loyalty to the brand (panda tourism), in particular their brand relationship of panda tourism has impact on brand attitudinal loyalty. Brand loyalty of panda tourism is mostly reflected in the attitudinal loyalty, while having less impact on behavioral loyalty. It also found that brand cognition of panda tourism has the greatest impact on brand loyalty, while brand structure of panda tourism has no impact on brand attitudinal loyalty, neither on brand behavioral loyalty. From this we can conclude that while people with strong brand relationship net of panda tourism might be attached to the brand positively, it can affect their attitudinal loyalty but it may have less impact on behavioral loyalty.

In general, the findings of this study provide both theoretical and managerial implications for maketers to undertake brand promoting of panda tourism. The findings have theoretical implications. Despite most theories of brand loyalty stating that it is worthy of study, very few studies have actually been conducted based on embeddedness theory of Zukin and Dimaggio.

This study also has implications for the framework for psychological response to brand loyalty. The current results somewhat supports the idea that brand relationship of panda tourism is not always related to behavioral loyalty.

## References

[1] Aaker D A. *Managing Brand Equity*[M]. New York: Free Press, 1991.

[2] Aaker D A. *Building Strong Brands*[M]. New York: Free Press, 1996.

[3] Aaker D A, Joachimsthaler E. *Brand Leadership*[M]. New York: Free Press, 2000.

[4] Baldinger A L, Rubinson J. Brand loyalty: the link between attitude and behavior[J]. *Advert Res*, 1996, 36(6): 22-34.

[5] Bonner J M, Kim D, Cavusgil S T. Self-perceived strategic network identity and its effects on market performance in alliance relationships[J]. *Bus. Res.* 2005, 58 (10): 1371-1380.

[6] Bonner J M, Walker O C. Selecting influential business-to-business customers in new product development: relational embeddedness and knowledge heterogeneity considerations[J]. *Journal of Product Innovation Management*, 2004(21): 155-169.

[7] Dayasindhu N. Embeddedness, knowledge transfer, industry cluster and global competitiveness: a case study of the Indian software industry[J]. *Technovation*, 2002(22): 551-560.

[8] Dick A S, Basu K. Customer loyalty towards an integrated framework[J]. *Acad Mark Sci*, 1994, 22(2): 99-113.

[9] Ehrenberg A S C. Repeat-buying: facts, theory and applications[J]. *Empir General Mark Sci*, 2000: 392-770.

[10] Galaskiewicz J. Studying supply chains from a social network perspective[J]. *Supply Chain Management*, 2001 (1): 4-8.

[11] Gardner B B, Levy S J. The product and the brand[J]. *Harvard Business Review*, 1995(33): 33-39.

[12] Granovetter M S. Economic action and social structure: the problem of embeddedness? [J] *Am. J. Sociol*, 1985 (91): 481-510.

[13] Granovetter M. The strength of weak ties[J]. *Am. J. Sociol*, 1973, 78 (6): 1360-1380.

[14] Granovetter M. Economic action and social structrue: the problem of embeddedness[J]. *American Journal of Sociology*, 1985, 91(3): 481-510.

[15] Gulati R, Gargiulo M. Where do interorganizational networks come from? [J]. *Am. J. Sociol.*, 1999, 104 (5): 1439-1493.

[16] Hammond K, East R, Ehrenberg A S C. *Buying More and Buying Longer: Concepts and Applications of*

*Consumer Loyalty*[M]. London: London Business School Press, 1996.

[17] Higginbottom K. *Wildlife Tourism: Impacts, Management and Planning*[M]. Gold Coast: Common Ground Publishing. 2004.

[18] IUCN, 2008. 2008 IUCN Red List of Threatened Species[Z]. IUCN, Glánd, Switzerland. WWW. incnredlist.org (accessed Feb., 2009).

[19] Polanyi K. *The Great Transformation: The Political and Economic Origins of Our Time*[M]. Boston, Mass.: Beacon Press, 1957: 43-68.

[20] Keller K L. Conceptualizing, measuring and managing customer based brand equity[J]. *Journal of Marketing*, 1993(57): 1-22,.

[21] Khoja F, Adams J, Kauffman R. A temporal model of vertical relationships[J]. *Bus. Market*, 2010, 17 (3): 279-307.

[22] Mellens M, Dekimpe M G, Steenkamp J B E M. A review of brand-loyalty measures in marketing[J]. *Tijdschr voor Econ Manage,* 1996, 41(4): 507-533.

[23] Park C W, MacInnis, D J, Priester J. Beyond attitudes: attachment and consumer behavior[J]. *Seoul Journal Business*, 2006, 12(2): 3-35.

[24] Patterson P G, Johnson L W, Spreng R A. Modeling the determinants of customer satisfaction for business-to-business professional services[J]. *Acad Mark Sci*, 1997, 25(1): 4-17.

[25] Pearsons T. *Structure and Process in Modern Societies*[M]. Glencoe, IL: Free Press, 1960.

[26] Rowley T, Behrens D, Krackhardt D. Redundant governance structures: an analysis of structural and relational embeddedness in the steel and semiconductor industries[J]. *Strat Manage*, 2000, 21 (3): 369-386.

[27] Zuki S, DiMaggio P. *Structrures of Capital: The Social Organization of the Economy*[M]. Cambridge: Cambridge University Press. 1990.

[28] Thach E C, Olsen J. The role of service quality in influencing brand attachment at winery visitor center[J]. *Journal of Quality Assurance in Hospitality & Tourism*, 2006, 7(3): 59-77.

[29] Tiwana A. Do bridging ties complement strong ties? An empirical examination of alliance ambidexterity[J]. *Strat. Manage*, 2008, 29 (3): 251-272.

[30] Uzzi B. The sources and consequences of embeddedness for the economic performance of organizations: the network effect[J]. *Am. Sociol. Rev.,* 1996, 61 (4): 674-698.

# Construction of Evaluating Indicator Portfolios on Tourism Destination: A Research Based on the Perspective of Tourists

Ren Yun[1*]

**Abstract:** The study constructs 5 subsystems and 26 specific indicator portfolios for the tourism destination system evaluation from the perspective of tourists. By utilizing the Structural Equation Modeling (SEM), this article proposes a structural model to quantify and test tourists' reviews and judgments on tourism destination, which can improve the scientificalness and accuracy of the study. However, before this, tourism destination evaluation was mainly conducted by the tourism destination itself. In this study, the tourism destination evaluation has been transformed from self-evaluation to tourist-oriented evaluation. It is expected that the research results upon tourism destination system evaluation can contribute to the development and construction of tourism destinations.

**Keywords:** tourist destination system; evaluating; indicator portfolios; Structural Equation Modeling (SEM)

## Ⅰ. Introduction

Tourism destination system refers to an organic unity formed by interacting subsystems of tourism attractions, tourism infrastructure, tourism service, tourism management and related supporting issues on the tourism market needs, following the destination strategy and developing guidance in a certain space (Yun Ren, 2013). Tourism market demand has changed significantly due to the speedy development of tourism sector in recent years. To respond to the tourists demand and improve the development of tourism destination, it is essential to set up a series of indicator portfolios to evaluate the tourism destination. China's State Council indicated in the Suggestions on Accelerating the Development of Tourism Sector promulgated in 2009 that tourist-oriented evaluation mechanisms of tourist destinations need to be established gradually (State Council, 2009). Accordingly, constructing the indicator portfolios of tourism destination system from the perspective of tourists are vital and practical for the development of tourism destinations.

1* Chengdu University of Information Technology, Chengdu, China. 450785331@qq.com.

## Ⅱ. Literature Review

There are abundant researches done on tourism destination evaluation, mainly involving the e-valuation of destination's service quality, the function composition and evaluation of destinations marketing system, the evolution of destination's soft environment, the indicator portfolios of evaluating low-carbon tourism destination, the indicator portfolios of evaluating the image of inbound tourism cities, the evolution of coastal tourism destinations, and the indicator portfolios of evaluating world-class tourism destinations. [1-7] Nevertheless, many of the tourism destination evaluating researches focus on the competitiveness. Crouch & Rithcie (1999, 2000), Dwyer & Kim (2002, 2003) and Kozak & Rimmington (1999) researched on the tourism competitiveness from different angels. [8-12] According to Michael Porter Diamond Model, Jie Li (1999) analyzed the 6 influencing factors and 4 phrases of destination's international tourism competitiveness and summarized the characteristics of different phrases. [13] Yi et al. (2007) adapted and improved Dwyer & Kim's model, and came up with "TDC 5-factor Model". [14] Dong et al. (2009) constructed evaluation indicator portfolios of tourism competitiveness from the perspective of urban agglomeration and inner urban unit. [15]Zhang et al. (2010) suggested the evaluation model and indicator portfolios of sports tourism destinations. [16] Zou et al. (2011) made the evaluation model of urban tourism competitiveness. [17] Xie et al. (2011) applied the "BCG (Boston Consulting Group) Matrix" to analyze the competition of tourism destination markets at provincial level in China. [18]

To summarize, the current research usually focuses on the evaluation of tourism destination's competitiveness, which is referential and useful for the study of tourism destination system evolution. But the current research has done little on the evaluation of tourism destination system, not to mention the evaluation from the perspective of tourist; as a result, it is hard to reflect the tourism market demand and its future trends. Therefore, our study tries to construct the Tourism Destination System Evaluating Indicator Portfolios and quantify tourists' reviews and judgments on tourism destinations, thus, to improve the accuracy and the scientificalness and accuracy of the study. It is expected that the research results upon tourism destination system evaluation can contribute to the development and construction of tourism destinations.

## Ⅲ. Constructing the Evaluating Indicator Portfolios

To construct the evaluating indicator portfolios needs to understand and combine tourism destination's characteristics, by which tourism destinations' development level and capacity can be thoroughly measured and reflected. Based on the current researches and characteristics of tourism destinations, for the convenience of data collection and practical effects of the model, after widely consulting tourism academia, the government, both public and private bodies of the tourism sector and community residents, a total of 5 subsystems and 26 evaluating indicator portfolios relating to tourism resources and products, tourism infrastructure, tourism services, tourism management mechanism and tourism supporting were identified. And the 5 subsystems and 26 evaluating indicator portfolios are constructed based on the perspective of tourists. The development level and capacity of tourism destination are indicated in the 5 subsystems shown in Table 1.

Table 1 Evaluating Indicator Portfolios of Tourism Destination

| Evaluation Subsystems | Indicator Portfolios |
| --- | --- |
| Tourism resources and products | Resources abundance and features (a11) |
| | Products abundance and features (a12) |
| | Rich culture and events (a13) |
| | Unique tourist commodities and souvenirs (a14) |
| Tourism infrastructure | Food specialties (a21) |
| | Unique health and recreational facilities (a22) |
| | Comprehensive set of conference and exhibition facilities (a23) |
| | Unique accommodation (a24) |
| | Convenient transportation (a25) |
| | Unique tourist shopping facilities (a26) |
| | Unique entertainment facilities (a27) |
| | Good water supply and drainage facilities, power supply and tele-communication facilities (a28) |
| Tourism service | Good Service consciousness and attitude (a31) |
| | Convenient tourism information-based service (a32) |
| | High quality guiding and interpretation service (a33) |
| | High quality travel agent service (a34) |
| | Convenient social services (a35) |
| | Friendly degrees of the local residence (a36) |
| Tourism management | Good tourism image (a41) |
| | Brand recognition and reputation (a42) |
| | Good marketing network (a43) |
| | Standardized management (a44) |
| | Resources and environment management (a45) |
| Tourism support | Sophisticated organization guarantee (a51) |
| | Qualified human resources (a52) |
| | Systemic security guarantee (a53) |

## Ⅳ. Validation of the Assessment for the Index System

### *i. Research design*

Based on the above assessment for the index system of the tourism destination, a questionary has been designed for the tourists at home and to Sichuan, whose reliability has been tested by SPSS16.0, and the standardized Cronbach's Alpha is 0.892, which proves its reliability. Meanwhile under 99% confidence level, all the non-standardized coefficients have remarkable statistical significance. It proves the correction model has good structure validity. The questionary consists of two parts. The first is the demographic feature of the tourists, including gender, age, education, occupation, income, tourist source, etc. The second is the five aspects of the assessment system for the tourism destination, including 26 specific indexes. Each test has been quantized by Likert Scale 5, and from 1 to 5, it is not approving, not exactly approving, approving, rather approving and approving a lot.

The questionary was conducted in September, 2012, with 300 copes issued, 273 valid copes received and the rate of valid copes is 91%. The demographic feature of the tourists is as follows:

Table 2 The Demographic Feature of the Tourists

| Project | | Number | Percentage (%) |
|---|---|---|---|
| Gender | Male | 154 | 56.4 |
| | Female | 119 | 43.6 |
| Age | Below 18 | 14 | 5.1 |
| | 18-35 | 173 | 63.4 |
| | 36-50 | 53 | 19.4 |
| | 51-60 | 16 | 5.9 |
| | Above 60 | 17 | 6.2 |
| Education | Below high school | 79 | 28.9 |
| | 3-year college | 73 | 26.7 |
| | Undergraduate | 112 | 41.1 |
| | Postgraduate and above | 9 | 3.3 |
| Monthly income | Below RMB 1,000 | 40 | 14.7 |
| | RMB 1,000-1,999 | 67 | 24.5 |
| | RMB 2,000-2,999 | 48 | 17.6 |
| | RMB 3,000-3,999 | 56 | 20.5 |
| | RMB 4,000-4,999 | 26 | 9.5 |
| | Above RMB 5,000 | 36 | 13.2 |

(To be continued)

(Continued Table 2)

| Project | | Number | Percentage (%) |
|---|---|---|---|
| Occupation | Enterprise personnel | 47 | 17.2 |
| | Civil servant | 12 | 4.4 |
| | Public institution personnel | 28 | 10.3 |
| | Farmer | 8 | 2.9 |
| | Self-employed | 28 | 10.3 |
| | Student | 59 | 21.6 |
| | Army man | 0 | 0 |
| | Retiree | 18 | 6.6 |
| | Freelancer | 44 | 16.1 |
| | Others | 29 | 10.6 |
| Tourist source | Chengdu | 64 | 23.4 |
| | Other regions in Sichuan | 102 | 37.4 |
| | Other provinces | 104 | 38.1 |
| | Abroad | 3 | 1.1 |

Note: N=273, Resource of the data: the questionaire.

*ii. Construction of the mode*

AMOS18.0 for SEM is applied to the construction and analysis of the research in question.

*A. Hypothesis proposed*

a. The effect of the tourism resource and product on the assessment for tourism destination

The tourism resource and product mainly include the type, quantity and degree of the resource, and for the product, it is its type and construction, the featured merchandise, the featured festival activities, tourism town, the route and the resource and ecological protection etc., all of which are of importance to the assessment for the tourism destination.

b. The effect of the tourism facilities on the assessment for tourism destination

The tourism facilities consist of featured food and lodging, traffic convenience, travel service, featured shopping, entertainment facilities, MICE and culture facilities, consulting facilities, facilities for logo and commentary, the washroom and other public service facilities, and all of above are very important to the assessment for the tourism destination.

c. The effect of the tourism service on the assessment for tourism destination

The tourism service includes the administration, residence of the community, proprietors and the awareness, attitude and level of their service. All of the above are important to the assessment for the tourism destination.

d. The effect of the tourism management on the assessment for tourism destination

The tourism management consists of tourism image, brand, management system mechanism, marketing, standardized management, and crisis management, which is crucial to the assessment for the tourism destination.

e. Tourism maintenance

Tourism maintenance includes the organization, policies, talents, security, environment, etc., which is also important to the assessment for the tourism destination.

*B. The mode design and analysis*

Based on the assumptions above, we built the structural equation-model path diagram, as shown in Figure 1. There are 26 observed exogenous variables, and the number of the measurement data is DP 595. The setting condition of the entire model is as follows: (1) There are 26 observed exogenous variables and 5 exogenous latent variables and 1 endogenous latent variable; (2) there are 26 exogenous measurement residuals and 5 endogenous measurement residuals; (3) there are 26 observed exogenous factor load parameters; (4) The first factor load parameters is set to be 1, and a total of six factor load parameters is set to be 1.

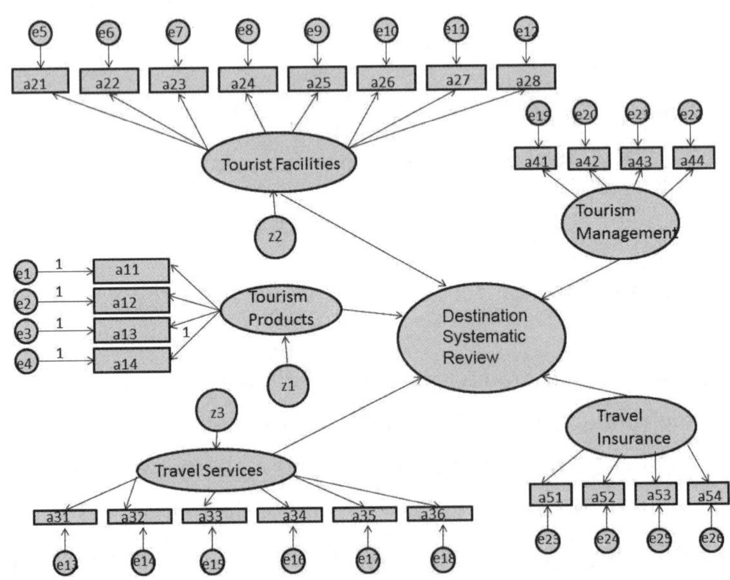


Figure 1 The Hypothetical SEM of the Systematic Assessment for the Tourism Destination

After continual revise of the mode, we have got the optimal SEM for the systematic assessment of the tourism destination (as in Figure 2), and we have also got the direct and indirect effect between each variables in the optimal mode as well as the total effect and path coefficient(as in Table 3, see the end of the article).

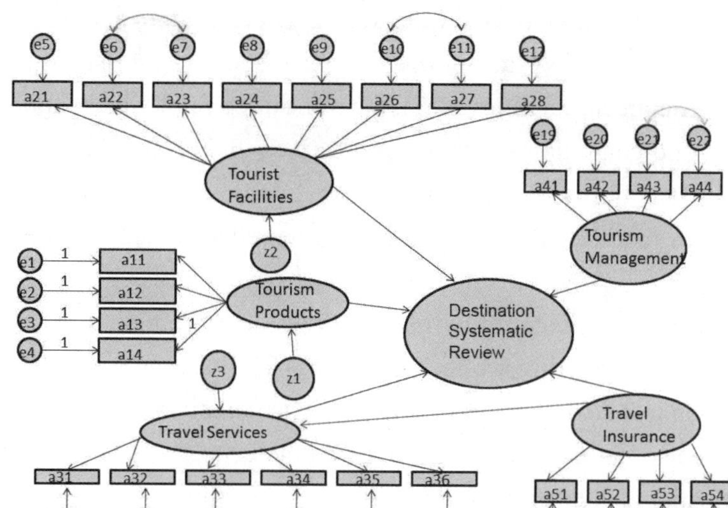


Figure 2 The Optimal SEM of the Systematic Assessment for the Tourism Destination

a. The impacts of tourism resources and products on the systematic evaluation of tourism destination

Suppose the weight coefficient of specific tourism commodity (a14) to tourism resources and products is 1, and then the weight coefficients of specific resources and abundance (a11), the richness and specialty of products (a12), rich cultural and festival activities (a13) to tourism resources and products are respectively 0.728, 0.832 and 0.711. All the values of CR are greater than 2 and it is remarkable under the level of 5%, which indicates that the tourism resources and products can be reflected and evaluated by the above indexes.

The standard path coefficient of tourism resources and products on Systematic Evaluation of Tourism Destination is 0.774, i.e. the direct effect of tourism resources and products on Systematic Evaluation of Tourism Destination is 0.774, which indicates that when other conditions remain unchanged, the potential variable of tourism resources and products will be promoted to one unit, and the whole benefit of the tourism destination will directly be promoted to 0.774 unit.

The indirect effects of specific tourism products (a14), resources features and abundance (a11), the richness and characteristics of products (a12), rich cultural and festival activities (a13) on Systematic Evaluation of Tourism Destination exist. Since the standard path coefficient of tourism resources and products on destination system evaluation is 0.774, the indirect effect of the index on Systematic Evaluation of Tourism Destination is equal to the multiplying of the two coefficients; they are 0.549, 0.564, 0.644 and 0.511.

b. The impacts of tourism facilities on systematic evaluation of tourism destination

In Table 3, suppose the weight coefficient of specific restaurant (a21) is 1, the weight coefficients of specific healthcare facilities (a22), the exhibition facilities (a23), specific commendations (a24), feasible transportation (a25), specific tourism shopping facilities (a26), specific entertainment facilities (a27), the infrastructure of water supply and drainage, electronic supply and communications are respectively 0.577, 0.582, 0.755, 0.741, 0.801, 0.748 and 0.650. The values of CR are larger than 2 and it is remarkable under the level of 5%, which indicates that the tourism facilities can be reflected and evaluated by the above indexes.

The standard path coefficient of tourism facilities on Systematic Evaluation of Tourism Destination is 0.907, i.e. the direct effect of tourism facilities on Systematic Evaluation of Tourism Destination is 0.907, which indicates that when other conditions remain unchanged, the potential variable of tourism facilities will be promoted to 1 unit, and the whole benefit of the tourism destination will directly be promoted to 0.907 unit.

The indirect effects of specific restaurant (a21) is 1, the weight coefficients of specific healthcare facilities (a22), the exhibition facilities (a23), specific commendations (a24), feasible transportation (a25), specific tourism shopping facilities (a26), specific entertainment facilities (a27), the infrastructure of water supply and drainage, electronic supply and communications on Systematic Evaluation of Tourism Destination exist. Since the standard path coefficient of tourism facilities on destination system evaluation is 0.907, the indirect effect of the index on Systematic Evaluation of Tourism Destination is equal to the multiplying of the two coefficients; they are 0.506, 0.524, 0.528, 0.685, 0.672, 0.727, 0.678, 0.589.

c. The impacts of tourism service on systematic evaluation of tourism destination

In Table 3, suppose the weight coefficient of residents' friendliness (a36) to tourism service is 1, the weight coefficient of good service consciousness and attitude (a31), advanced tourism informational service (a32), high qualitative interpretive service (a33), good travel agency service (a34), convenient social service (a35) to tourism service are respectively 0.765, 0.779, 0.857, 0.832, and 0.834. The values of CR are larger than 2 and it is remarkable under the level of 5%, which indicates that the tourism service can be reflected and evaluated by the above indexes.

The standard path coefficient of tourism service on Systematic Evaluation of Tourism Destination is 0.598, i.e. the direct effect of tourism service on Systematic Evaluation of Tourism Destination is 0.598, which indicates that when other conditions remain unchanged, the potential variable of tourism service will be promoted to one unit, and the whole benefit of the tourism destination will directly be promoted to 0.598 unit.

There are indirect impacts of tourism service on Systematic Evaluation of Tourism Destination. The indirect effect of tourism service on Systematic Evaluation of Tourism Destination is equal to the multiply of the two path coefficients, 0.359*0.857=0.308, and the total coefficient is 0.906.

The indirect effects of residents' friendliness (a36) to tourism service is 1, the weight coefficient of good service consciousness and attitude (a31), advanced tourism informational service (a32), high qualitative interpretive service (a33), good travel agency service (a34), convenient social service (a35) on Systematic Evaluation of Tourism Destination exist. Since the standard path coefficient of tourism service on destination system evaluation is 0.5987, the indirect effect of the index on Systematic Evaluation of Tourism Destination is equal to the multiplying of the two path coefficients; they are 0.693, 0.705, 0.776, 0.754, 0.755 and 0.712.

d. The impacts of tourism management on systematic evaluation of tourism destination

In Table 3, suppose the weight coefficient of good image of the destination (a41) to tourism management is 1, the weight coefficient of brand popularity (a42), the sound marketing net (a43), standard management (a44), resources and environmental protection management (a45), to tourism management are respectively 0.818, 0.784, 0.804 and 0.727. The values of CR are larger than 2 and it is remarkable under the level of 5%, which indicates that the tourism service can be reflected and evaluated by the above indexes.

The standard path coefficient of tourism management on Systematic Evaluation of Tourism Destination is 0.967, i.e. the direct effect of tourism management on Systematic Evaluation of Tourism Destination is 0.967, which indicates that when other conditions remain unchanged, the potential variable of tourism management will be promoted to one unit, and the whole benefit of the tourism destination will directly be promoted to 0.967 unit.

The indirect effects of brand popularity (a42), the sound marketing net (a43), standard management (a44), resources and environmental protection management (a45) on Systematic Evaluation of Tourism Destination exist. The indirect effect of the index on Systematic Evaluation of Tourism Destination is equal to the multiplying of the two coefficients, they are 0.794, 0.791, 0.758, 0.778 and 0.703.

e. The impacts of tourism management guarantee system on systematic evaluation of tourism destination

In Table 3, suppose the weight coefficient of scientific and efficient security system (a54) to tourism guarantee system is 1, the weight coefficient of sound organization (a52), high qualitative tourism talents (a53) to tourism management are respectively 0.807 and 0.864. The values of CR are larger than 2 and it is remarkable under the level of 5%, which indicates that the tourism guarantee system can be reflected and evaluated by the above indexes.

The standard path coefficient of tourism guarantee system on tourism destination system is 0.857. The direct effect of tourism guarantee system on Systematic Evaluation of Tourism Destination is 0.857, which indicates that when other conditions remain unchanged, the potential variable of tourism guarantee system will be promoted to 1 unit, and the whole benefit of the tourism destination will directly be promoted to 0.857 unit.

The indirect effects of scientific and efficient security system (a54), sound organization (a52), high qualitative tourism talents (a53) on Systematic Evaluation of Tourism Destination exist. The indirect effect of the index on Systematic Evaluation of Tourism Destination is equal to the multiplying of the two coefficients; they are 0.692, 0.741 and 0.763.

## Ⅴ. Conclusions

(1) Tourism resources and products, tourism facilities, tourism service, tourism management and tourism assurance, these five subsystems and specific evaluation indexes have a close relationship with tourists' evaluation and the development of tourism destination, which indicates that they influence the systematic evaluation of tourists on the tourism destination and its development. By using the Structural Equation Model to prove that Systematic Evaluation of Tourism Destination can use the five subsystems and 26 indexes to reflect and evaluate.

(2) Tourists pay attention to the construction of the destination's five subsystems, but their relevant satisfaction and importance are different. Destination management has the largest impact on tourists' evaluation, and it also has the most important influence on the development of tourism destination. The influence of other factors from big to small are respectively tourism facilities, tourism service, tourism guarantee and tourism attraction, which show that to find the weakness and key links is very crucial to the development of the tourism destination. For instance, whether the tourism guarantee system is sound, and whether the tourism resources and products can appeal to the tourists etc. Tourism management, tourism facilities and the improvement of tourism service are the key factors to promote the development of tourism destination. In order to promote the development of the tourism destination, we must start from the five subsystems and strengthen the construction of the various aspects, therefore, to establish the foundation of the global optimization of the tourism destination.

(3) The paper establishes an evaluation index system based on the tourists-centered comments on the Systematic Evaluation of the Tourism Destination. It breaks through the former evaluation research which is from the view of supply and the tourism destination itself. This evaluation system is scientific and reasonable, and it can be applied to other relevant evaluations of tourism destination.

(4) This paper has a limitation on the research condition and research field of assessment method, questionary design, and index construction. In order to improve and optimize the system and model, we need improve the assessment method, sample capacity and model. In this way, a scientific, reasonable, typical research result can be got.

Table 3 The Direct and Indirect Effect Between Each Variables in the Optimal Mode as Well as the Total Effect and Path Coefficient (Standardized Result)

| | Systematic Assessment of Tourism Destination | Tourism Maintenance | Tourism Resource and Product | Tourism Manage-ment | Tourism Service | Tourism Facilities |
|---|---|---|---|---|---|---|
| Maintenance (direct effect) | .857<br>.857 | | | | | |
| (indirect effect) | | | | | | |
| (total effect) | .857 | | | | | |
| Tourism product(direct effect) | .774<br>.774 | | | | | |
| (indirect effect) | | | | | | |
| (total effect) | .774 | | | | | |
| Tourism management(direct effect) | .967<br>.967 | | | | | |
| (indirect effect) | | | | | | |
| (total effect) | .967 | | | | | |
| Tourism service(direct effect) | .598<br>.598 | .359<br>.359 | | | | |
| (indirect effect) | .308 | | | | | |
| (total effect) | .906 | .359 | | | | |
| Tourism facilities (direct effect) | .907<br>.907 | | | | | |
| (indirect effect) | | | | | | |
| (total effect) | .907 | | | | | |
| a11<br>(direct effect) | | | .728<br>.728 | | | |
| (indirect effect) | .564 | | | | | |
| (total effect) | .564 | | .728 | | | |
| a12<br>(direct effect) | | | .832<br>.832 | | | |
| (indirect effect) | .644 | | | | | |
| (total effect) | .644 | | .832 | | | |
| A13<br>(direct effect) | | | .711<br>.711 | | | |
| (indirect effect) | .551 | | | | | |
| (total effect) | .551 | | .711 | | | |
| a14<br>(direct effect) | | | .709<br>.709 | | | |

(To be continued)

(Continued Table 3)

| | Systematic Assessment of Tourism Destination | Tourism Maintenance | Tourism Resource and Product | Tourism Manage-ment | Tourism Service | Tourism Facilities |
|---|---|---|---|---|---|---|
| (indirect effect) | .549 | | | | | |
| (total effect) | .549 | | .709 | | | |
| A45<br>(direct effect) | | | | .727<br>.727 | | |
| (indirect effect) | .703 | | | | | |
| (total effect) | .703 | | | .727 | | |
| a52<br>(direct effect) | | | .807<br>.807 | | | |
| (indirect effect) | .692 | | | | | |
| (total effect) | .692 | | .807 | | | |
| a53<br>(direct effect) | | | .864<br>.864 | | | |
| (indirect effect) | .741 | | | | | |
| (total effect) | .741 | | .864 | | | |
| a54<br>(direct effect) | | | .889<br>.889 | | | |
| (indirect effect) | .763 | | | | | |
| (total effect) | .763 | | .889 | | | |
| a44<br>(direct effect) | | | | .804<br>.804 | | |
| (indirect effect) | .778 | | | | | |
| (total effect) | .778 | | | .804 | | |
| a43<br>(direct effect) | | | | .784<br>.784 | | |
| (indirect effect) | .758 | | | | | |
| (total effect) | .758 | | | .784 | | |
| a42<br>(direct effect) | | | | .818<br>.818 | | |
| (indirect effect) | .791 | | | | | |
| (total effect) | .791 | | | .818 | | |
| a41<br>(direct effect) | | | | .821<br>.821 | | |
| (indirect effect) | .794 | | | | | |
| (total effect) | .794 | | | .821 | | |

(To be continued)

(Continued Table 3)

| | Systematic Assessment of Tourism Destination | Tourism Maintenance | Tourism Resource and Product | Tourism Management | Tourism Service | Tourism Facilities |
|---|---|---|---|---|---|---|
| a31<br>(direct effect) | | | | | .765<br>.765 | |
| (indirect effect) | .693 | .275 | | | | |
| (total effect) | .693 | .275 | | | .765 | |
| a32<br>(direct effect) | | | | | .779<br>.779 | |
| (indirect effect) | .705 | .280 | | | | |
| (total effect) | .705 | .280 | | | | |
| a33<br>(direct effect) | | | | | .857<br>.857 | |
| (indirect effect) | .776 | .307 | | | | |
| (total effect) | .776 | .307 | | | .857 | |
| a34<br>(direct effect) | | | | | .832<br>.832 | |
| (indirect effect) | .754 | .299 | | | | |
| (total effect) | .754 | .299 | | | .832 | |
| a35<br>(direct effect) | | | | | .834<br>.834 | |
| (indirect effect) | .755 | .299 | | | | |
| (total effect) | .755 | .299 | | | .834 | |
| a36<br>(direct effect) | | | | | .786<br>.786 | |
| (indirect effect) | .712 | .282 | | | | |
| (total effect) | .712 | .282 | | | .786 | |
| a28<br>(direct effect) | | | | | | .650<br>.650 |
| (indirect effect) | .589 | | | | | |
| (total effect) | .589 | | | | | .650 |
| a27<br>(direct effect) | | | | | | .748<br>.748 |
| (indirect effect) | .678 | | | | | |
| (total effect) | .678 | | | | | .748 |
| a26<br>(direct effect) | | | | | | .801<br>.801 |
| (indirect effect) | .727 | | | | | |

(To be continued)

(Continued Table 3)

| | Systematic Assessment of Tourism Destination | Tourism Maintenance | Tourism Resource and Product | Tourism Manage-ment | Tourism Service | Tourism Facilities |
|---|---|---|---|---|---|---|
| (total effect) | .727 | | | | | .801 |
| a25<br>(direct effect) | | | | | | .741<br>.741 |
| (indirect effect) | .672 | | | | | |
| (total effect) | .672 | | | | | .741 |
| a24<br>(direct effect) | | | | | | .755<br>.755 |
| (indirect effect) | .685 | | | | | |
| (total effect) | .685 | | | | | .755 |
| a23<br>(direct effect) | | | | | | .582<br>.582 |
| (indirect effect) | .528 | | | | | |
| (total effect) | .528 | | | | | .582 |
| a22<br>(direct effect) | | | | | | .577<br>.577 |
| (indirect effect) | .524 | | | | | |
| (total effect) | .524 | | | | | .577 |
| a21<br>(direct effect) | | | | | | .558<br>.558 |
| (indirect effect) | .506 | | | | | |
| (total effect) | .506 | | | | | .558 |
| | | | | | | |

## References


[1] Wang Bo, Zheng Honghua. The construction of service quality evaluation model based on eight elements of tourism destination[J]. *Business Studies*, 2007(08):148-153.

[2] Wang Youcheng. The functional formation and evaluation of the marketing system of tourism destination[J]. *Tourism Science*, 2009(02):28-37.

[3] Chen Xuejun. The study of tourism destination's soft environment based on analytic hierarchy process[J]. *Consumption Economy*, 2011 (02): 51-53.

[4] Ma Yong, Yan Qi, Chen Xiaolian. The construction of comprehensive evaluation index system of low carbon tourism destination[J]. *Economic Geography*, 2011(04): 686-689.

[5] Zhao Anzhou, Bai Kai, Wei Haiyan. The study of inbound tourism destination city image evaluation system: Beijing and Shanghai as the case [J]. *Tourism Science*, 2011(01): 54-60.

[6] Kang Yuwei, Chen Yangle. The comprehensive evaluation system of the coastal destination based on tourists perception [J]. *Tourism Forum*, 2012(05): 25-29.

[7] Yang Zhenzhi, Zhang Zhiliang. The substantial development of world class tourism destination from the

prospective of systematic science: Tibet as the case[Z]. The National Social Science Fund, 2012.

[8] Couch R. Tourism, competitiveness and socialprosperity[J]. *Journal of Business Research*, 1999(1): 137-152.

[9] Ritchie J R B, Crouch G I.The competitive destination: a sustainability perspective[J]. *Tourism Management*, 2000(1): 1-7.

[10] Dwyer L, Kim C. Destination competitiveness: a model and determinansts[EB/OL]. Travel & heritage travel association website, 2002.

[11] Dwyer L, Kim C. Destination competitiveness: determinants and indicators [J]. *Current Issues in Tourism*, 2003(5): 369-414.

[12] Kozak M, Rimmington M. Measuring tourist destination competitiveness: conceptual considerations and empirical findings[J]. *Hospitality Management*, 1999(1): 273-283.

[13] Li Jie, Zhao Xiping. On the international tourism competitive power and its evolution[J]. *Social Scientist*, 1999(05): 19-22.

[14] Yi Lirong, Li Chuanzhao. Empirical study on five elements model of tourism destination competitive power[J]. *Journal of Industrial Engineering and Engineering Management*, 2007 (03): 105-110.

[15] Dong Suocheng, Li Xue, Zhang Guanghai, Xianfeng Jin. The comprehensive evaluation system and measure method of city agglomeration[J]. *Tourism Tribune*, 2009(02): 30-36.

[16] Zhang Yunfeng, Chong Cong. The study on the competitive power model and evaluation system of physical tourism destination[J]. *Sport World*, 2009(08): 115-116.

[17] Zhou Tongqian, Qin Yaya, Wang Xiaofang. Competitive power evaluation model of tourism destination cities:comparative study on Beijing and Shanghai[J]. *Tourism Research*, 2011(02): 1-6.

[18] Xie Weiguang, Ma Yunchi. The competitive situation and transference features of provincial level domestic tourism destination city market[J]. *Tourism Research*, 2011(01): 8-13.

# Destination Image, Tourism Policy and Perspective of Internet Public Opinion: A Case Study on Tickets Cancellation of Phoenix Town in Hunan Province

Hu Xiaowen[1*], Ding Yufang[2], Zhang Furong[3]

**Abstract:** As the biggest provider of job opportunities, tourism management has to deal with a wide range of stakeholders as an international industry than many other industries. How to solve the problems existing in the tourism policy reform is significant in tourism management. With the wide penetration of Internet, online comments on reform in tourism have become an emerging source of data to support tourism research. Based on text mining and content analysis, local residents and merchants are the most frequently mentioned stakeholders, while the topic attracting the most attention is the rationality of government management in Phoenix Town. In addition, local government needs to balance the interests of all stakeholders in the tourism policy reform. If the policy reformation is not transparent and reasonable to the public, the negative comments will be posted on the web to show the incredibility of local government. Therefore, balancing all the interests of all stakeholders and reducing the conflicts in tourism policy reform to build good public relations plays a big role in the tourism policy reformation.

**Keywords:** destination image; policy; Internet public opinion; Phoenix Town; content analysis

## Ⅰ. Introduction

Tourism, as the largest industry throughout the world, is highly complex, involving the economic, environmental and social-cultural attributes as well as policy attribute (Richter, 1989). With intense competition worldwide, travel destinations need to consider how to reduce negative impact to enhance competitiveness (Wang & Fesenmaier, 2007). Plenty of evidence reveals that the development of tourist destinations must depend on the management and promotion of local government. Therefore, tourism policies need to be regarded in tourism management. It is important to find out whether local government policy

1* Northwest Minzu University, Lanzhou, China.huxiaowen0620@gmail.com.

2 Northwest Minzu University, Lanzhou, China.

3 Northwest Minzu University, Lanzhou, China.

can improve the local image of the destination or not. The study in the paper will ultimately be helpful to promote the local tourism industry.

Some researchers have realized the importance of this specific study field, and some methods such as questionnaire surveys and interviews have been adopted to collect data to analyze how policy works in destination image management. Although Internet has become a main information source, few studies have focused on mining the data on Internet. However, Internet is an increasingly important information source to identify how the public think of a tourism policy. Therefore, the paper gathers information published on the Internet to identify the relationship between destination image, tourism policy-making and public opinion.

## Ⅱ. Case Background

As of December 2016, there has been 731 million Internet users in China (almost 656 million mobile phone users), equivalent to the total population of Europe. A large number of Chinese people acquire information on the Internet. Chinese people share their opinions on the Internet, and they are affected by the viewpoints published on the Internet. When local governments enact new policies, Chinese people will debate about the rationality of it on the Internet enthusiastically. Therefore, studies of Internet public opinion are the keys to understand what the public really think about the major events in tourism industry, which may provide a reference for the management of tourism industry. Meanwhile, researches of Internet public opinion can also be beneficial for the local government to make good decisions on public relations management and marketing to develop tourism in China.

Phoenix Town is a most famous historic town in China. It is rich in the natural scenery and cultural tourism resource, and attracts visitors from all over the world.

Before April 2013, all the visitors were free to enter it. Later, the local government in Phoenix considered the management should be tightened up, so their solution was to require admission by tickets. The fee was initially charged on April 10th, 2013. However, after the admission by ticket, the number of tourists to Phoenix Town in May, 2013 was sharply down to 50%. 3 years later, on April 10th, 2016, the local government declared that the ticket for Phoenix has been cancelled. The event immediately became a hot topic on the Internet in China.

## Ⅲ. Data Processing

The paper takes the event of tickets cancellation of Phoenix Town in Hunan Province as a case study. 100 web texts are chosen as sample, which consists of 50 official reports, 20 commentaries, and 30 blog posts. The search terms are "Phoenix Town" and "tickets cancellation" in Chinese via Baidu search engine and Sina blogs. These sample articles meet the following requirements:

(1) Immediacy. The online public opinion texts should be published from March 28th,

2016 to April 20th, 2016.

(2) Reliability. The texts should be published on official websites (e.g. Xinhua.net, Tencent, People's net and Sina).

(3) Exclusivity. The selected texts should not be duplicated, and the samples should not include re-posted articles.

(4) Availability. The length of selected texts is over 400 words. Meanwhile, key information should be contained in the text.

The data processing steps are as follows:

First of all, 100 network texts were selected and the data were typed into Microsoft Word.

Secondly, all English abbreviations, numbers and punctuation which had no relation to word frequency analysis were deleted, and then the result was typed in TXT format.

Finally, the software ROST Content Mining was utilized to analyse the texts.

To achieve the research purposes, the paper mainly adopts the methods such as word frequency analysis, social network and semantic analysis, co-word analysis and principal component analysis.

*i. Word frequency analysis*

Firstly, the study segmented the corpus effectively by ROST software. Secondly, it screened and removed all meaningless Chinese words (e.g. "ah", "oh", "what", "how much", "second", etc.). Thirdly, the top 25 high-frequency words of the corpus were identified. Then, the high-frequency words were entered into Excel in order to analyse data. The results are shown in Table 1.

According to Table 1, the author identified the following three categories: (1) There are four typical stakeholder groups related to the event of ticket cancellation. They are government (e.g., "government", 2.61%), local communities (e.g., "local", 1.14%, "merchants", 1.07%), pressure groups(e.g., "old town", 13.89%, "scenic spots", 7.93%, "Phoenix County", 3.44%, and tourists(e.g., "tourists", 6.35%). (2) The public is particularly concerned about the economic development in Phoenix. The high-frequency words are as follows: "ticket checking"(4.12%), "fee"(3.18%), "economy"(2.52%), "development"(1.67%), "Market"(1.18%), "management system of tickets prices"(2.52%), and "business management"(1.55%).These are all technical terms in the economic field. (3) The results reflect the public concern about the tourism management policy of local government. The concern can be manifested in all these words (e.g., "cancellation", "suspension", "management", "three years", "retention") . From April 10, 2013 to April 10, 2016, there was a process of tourism management change. It reflects the public doubt about the change of local government policies.

Table 1 High Frequency Words

| Rank | High Frequency words | | | |
|---|---|---|---|---|
| | News Reports | Comments on Current Events | Blogs | In Total |
| 1 | Old Town 13.75% | Old Town 14.47% | Old Town 13.48% | Old Town 13.89% |
| 2 | Phoenix 13.45% | Phoenix 13.66% | Ticket 12.24% | Phoenix 13.13% |
| 3 | Ticket 9.94% | Ticket 11.84% | Phoenix 12.01% | Ticket 11.08% |
| 4 | Scenic Spots 7.61% | Scenic Spots 8.06% | Scenic Spots 8.23% | Scenic Spots 7.93% |
| 5 | Tourism 7.54% | Tourism 6.23% | Tourism 7.22% | Tourism 7.21% |
| 6 | Tourists 6.15% | Tourists 5.49% | Tourists 7.15% | Tourists 6.35% |
| 7 | Cancellation 4.45% | Cancellation 5.15% | Scenic Spot 3.86% | Cancellation 4.17% |
| 8 | Ticket Checking 4.12% | Scenic Spot 3.37% | Ticket Checking 3.05% | Ticket Checking 3.63% |
| 9 | Phoenix County 4.05% | Ticket Checking 3.2% | Charge Fees 3.01% | Scenic Spot 3.47% |
| 10 | Scenic Spot 3.23% | Charge Fees 3.14% | Cancellation 2.97% | Phoenix County 3.44% |
| 11 | Charge Fees 3.18% | Phoenix County 2.69% | Phoenix County 2.9% | Charge Fees 3.14% |
| 12 | Government 2.57% | Economy 2.52% | Government 2.82% | Government 2.61% |
| 13 | Income 2.1% | Management System of Tickets Prices 2.52% | Economy 2.74% | Economy 2.37% |
| 14 | Economy 2.05% | Government 2.34% | Suspension 2.51% | Suspension 2.14% |
| 15 | Suspension 2% | Income 2% | Income 2.01% | Income 2.06% |
| 16 | Business Management 1.72% | Suspension 1.89% | Management System of Tickets Prices 1.82% | Development 1.64% |
| 17 | Management 1.6% | Business Management 1.7% | Development 1.7% | Business Management 1.5% |
| 18 | Development 1.67% | Development 1.37% | Enclosure 1.74% | Management System of Tickets Prices 1.53% |
| 19 | Enclosure 1.53% | For Free 1.32% | Purchase 1.58% | Management 1.41% |

(To be continued)

(Continued Table 1)

| Rank | High Frequency words | | | |
|---|---|---|---|---|
| | News Reports | Comments on Current Events | Blogs | In Total |
| 20 | Purchase<br>1.3% | Charge<br>1.26% | Charge<br>1.27% | Purchase<br>1.37% |
| 21 | 3 Years<br>1.27% | Purchase<br>1.2% | Merchants<br>1.24% | Enclosure<br>1.36% |
| 22 | Keep<br>1.2% | Local<br>1.2% | Business Management<br>1.12% | 3 Years<br>1.18% |
| 23 | Market<br>1.15% | 3 Years<br>1.14% | Management<br>1.12% | Charge<br>1.15% |
| 24 | Local<br>1.15% | Management<br>1.14% | Guest House<br>1.12% | Local<br>1.14% |
| 25 | Merchants<br>1.24% | Impact<br>1.09% | 3 Years<br>1.04% | Merchant-s<br>1.07% |

*ii. Co-word analysis*

High-frequency words can demonstrate the main field of corpus. In order to acquire more information, a co-word analysis was conducted, which represents the co-occurrence relationship between high-frequency words.

Table 2　High Frequency Co-words

| Rank | Co-words | Frequency |
|---|---|---|
| 1 | Phoenix+Old Town | 571 |
| 2 | Ticket+Old Town | 487 |
| 3 | Phoenix+Ticket | 481 |
| 4 | Phoenix+Scenic Spots | 398 |
| 5 | Scenic Spots+Old Town | 385 |
| 6 | Scenic Spots+Ticket | 383 |
| 7 | Phoenix+Tourists | 368 |
| 8 | Old Town+Tourists | 362 |
| 9 | Ticket+ Tourists | 337 |
| 10 | Phoenix+Travel | 325 |
| 11 | Old Town+ Travel | 305 |
| 12 | Phoenix+Cancellation | 295 |
| 13 | Old Town+Cancellation | 292 |
| 14 | Ticket+Travel | 290 |
| 15 | Ticket+Cancellation | 278 |

(To be continued)

(Continued Table 2)

| Rank | Co-words | Frequency |
|---|---|---|
| 16 | Scenic Spots+ Tourists | 273 |
| 17 | Scenic Spots+Travel | 247 |
| 18 | Travel+Tourists | 240 |
| 19 | Phoenix+Scenic Spot | 237 |
| 20 | Phoenix+Charge a Fee | 228 |
| 21 | Scenic Spot+ Old Town | 227 |
| 22 | Old Town+Charge a Fee | 224 |
| 23 | Scenic Spots+Scenic Spot | 211 |
| 24 | Scenic Spot+Ticket | 209 |
| 25 | Ticket+Charge a Fee | 199 |

It can be observed that the public had a heated discussion of the rationality of ticket management policy of Phoenix. Netizens are concerned about the entire decision-making process, ranging from charging the admission fees to the cancellation of tickets.

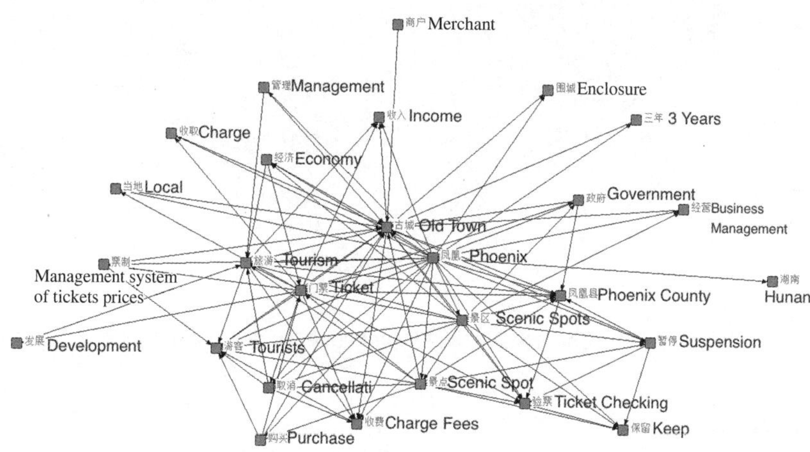


Figure 2 Multidimensional Analysis of High-frequency Key Words Structure

From the multidimensional analysis of the network of the high-frequency co-words, one core layer can be found, which strongly reflects the theme of corpus: the cancellation of tickets for Phoenix. Three years ago, the policy of admission by ticket (148 RMB per person) undermined the interests of tourists and residents. After the implementation of the policy, numerous residents and merchants departed from the old town and the number of tourists reduced by 17%. Meanwhile, some news reported that the local government and t two travel management companies had some conflicts because of the maldistribution of profits(they all profit from selling tickets). We can also find that the travel management agencies in this scenic area (e.g., the scenic spots, Phoenix), the local residents (e.g., local merchants and residents), the public management institutions (e.g., the government) and tourists (e.g., actual tourists and potential tourists) are the closest stakeholders in this event.

According to the second layer, the public (e.g. "income", "economy", "charge for an entrance fee", "cancellation", "suspension", "preservation") doubt the rationality of ticket cancellation. The words such as "development", "management", "economic" and "income" indicate the validity of the government policy implementation. The result shows that local government has lost some of their public trust.

*iii. The principal component analysis of high-frequency keywords network structure*

According to Figure 2, three categories can be identified as follows: (1) Tourism resources management: The public discussed about the relationship between development and protection of tourism goods warmly. (2) Distribution of interests: After ticket cancellation, how to balance the interests of stakeholders becomes a hot topic. (3) Government administration: Some netizens doubt the rationality of local government decision-making process.

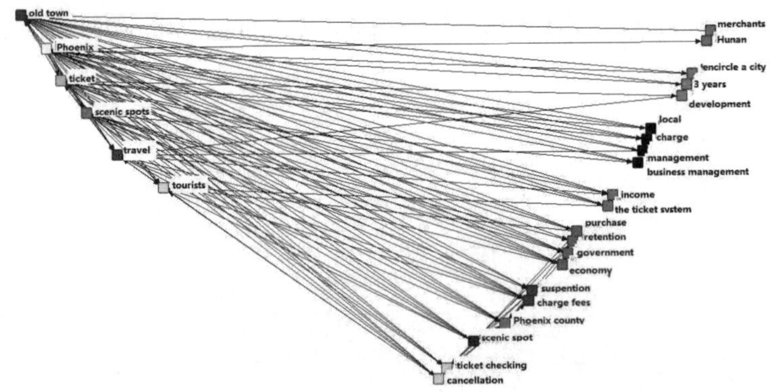


Figure 2 Principal Component Analysis of High-frequency Key Words Network Structure

## Ⅳ. Conclusions

Since 2013, Phoenix, the most famous old town, has been a hot topic in the tourism industry in China due to the incident of entrance fee charging. While on April 10th, 2016, the event of cancellation of tickets makes Phoenix a public hot spot again. From the above research, the following conclusions can be drawn:

Firstly, if the tourist management departments can't ensure open and transparent information during the decision-making, or balance the interests of all stakeholders, the policy would stimulate negative emotions among the public. As a result, the public would not consider Phoenix Town as a desirable tourist attraction to visit because of its disorganized management. Therefore, all the policy changes need to be published after extensive discussions. Meanwhile, the rights of stakeholders should be guaranteed.

Secondly, the government should strengthen the supervision on Internet public opinions in the information age, so that they can respond quickly when a crisis happens online. Moreover, the government needs to guide public opinions on applying the mainstream media to make positive publicity reports to reduce the spread of negative comments.

Thirdly, the local tourism enterprises should make full use of their own social media and other web platforms to improve their public relations timely. These enterprises are always affected directly by online public crisis, so it is necessary for local merchants to communicate with the public in order to reduce negative impact on the image of the tourist destination.

The case study shows that if the local government has insufficient ability to balance the interests of stakeholders, or fails to make the decision-making process reasonable, negative perceptions might go wild on the Internet, because the stakeholders tend to use the Internet as a tool. It will definitely damage the destination image of Phoenix and reduce tourists' demands to visit the place. Therefore, local government needs to reassess the rationality of policy and do research before decision-making to ensure the interests of all stakeholders are balanced.

## ACKNOWLEDGMENT

My deepest gratitude goes first and foremost to Zou Pinjia, my colleague who initially informed me of the good opportunity to communicate with other researchers.

Secondly, I would like to express my heartfelt gratitude to "the Fundamental Research Funds for the Central Universities"( Number 31920170124), which has supported the paper.

## References

[1] Picard M, Wood R E. *Tourism and the State: Ethnic Options and Constructions of Otherness*[M]. Hawaii: University of Hawaii Press, 1997.

[2] WangY, Fesenmaier D. Collaborative destination marketing: a case study of Elkhart County[J]. *Tourism Management*, 2007(28): 863-875.

[3] Pforr C. Tourism policy in the making: an Australian network study[J]. *Annals of Tourism Research*, 2006(33): 187-208.

[4] Li L, Buhalis D. Influential factors of internet users booking online in China's domesday tourism[J]. Beijing: *Journal of China Tourism Research*, 2010(10): 172-2188.

[5] Ayeh J K, Norman A, Law R. Do we believe in TripAdvisor? Examining credibility perceptions and online travelers' attitude toward using user-generated content[J]. *Journal of Travel Research*, 2013(52): 437-452.

[6] Litvin S W, Goldsmith R E, Bing Pan. Electronic word-of-mouth in hospitality and tourism management[J]. *Tourism management*, 2008(29): 458-468.

[7] Mak A H N. Online destination image: Comparing national tourism organisation's and tourists' perspectives[J]. *Tourism Management*, 2017(10): 280-297.

[8] Sun Minghui, Chris R, Pan S.Using Chinese travel blogs to examine perceived destination image the case of New Zealand[J]. *Journal of Travel Research*, 2015(8): 543-555.

[9] Jacquie L, Falkheimer J, Lugo J. Public relations and tourism: critical reflections and a research agenda[J]. *Public Relations Review*, 2007(5): 68-76.

[10] Luo Y. The internet and agenda setting in China: the influence of online public opinion on media coverage and government policy[J]. *International Journal of Communication*, 2014(8): 1289-1312.

# Exploring Brand Image of Tourist Attractions Based on Brand Concept Maps: Taking Jiuzhaigou and Dujiangyan in Sichuan Province as Examples

Zou Pinjia[1*], He Yawen[2]

**Abstract:** Tourist attractions have become increasingly competitive since many attributes from them are roughly similar, which seldom appeal to consumers to visit. Therefore, marketers shifted their focus to brand image shaping so as to identify their unique attributes. To explicitly understand brand image, the paper uses Brand Concept Maps and analyzes brand associations of two famous tourist attractions in Sichuan province. Some useful suggestions for brand strategies of many tourist attractions in China are proposed.

**Keywords:** brand image; brand concept maps; brand association; tourists attractions; Sichuan Province

## Ⅰ. Introduction

Over the past ten years, marketing of popular mass tourism sites has become increasingly competitive.[1] The favorable image of a destination may bring potential competitiveness to the destination. It may be formed by a combination of destination attributes (e.g. attractive landscape, rich and unique culture, safety and various activities).[2], [3] Famous tourist attractions in China also have tended to lay emphasis on attributes of their sites to attract more visitors or enable tourists to stay longer. However, these attributes no long distinguish them from their competitors. Therefore, marketers from these attractions in China have become concerned about branding which is the concept from business because a brand can create a positive identity and image that ties tourists to it emotionally.[4], [5] As a strategic marketing tool that measures the customer perspective on the brand, the concept of customer-based brand equity (CBBE) has been adapted. [6] CBBE can be conceptualized for a destination by brand salience, brand associations, brand resonance and brand loyalty.[7]

However, marketers from enormous tourist attractions in China have tended to focus more on the logo, slogan and promotion instead of brand response from tourists. As a result,

1* Sichuan University, Chengdu, China; Northwest Minzu University, Lanzhon, China. 22183846@qq.com.

2 Sichuan University, Chengdu, China.

products they design and messages they deliver about the tourists attractions still hardly attract tourists or provide them unforgettable experiences. Furthermore, in the academic world, few researches discuss about tourists' brand salience and how they respond to branding from marketers based on brand association.

Thus, the purpose of this study is to examine how consumers perceived the famous tourists attractions by using Brand Concept Maps (BCM), taking Jiuzaigou and Dujiangyan in Sichuan Province of China as examples. The contribution of this study is to offer the support from consumer's perspective when marketer make decisions about brand strategies.

## Ⅱ. Methdology

The BCM method involves the elicitation, mapping, and aggregation stages to provide a technique that is easier to administer and analyze.[8] Comparing with Zaltman's Metaphor Elicitation Technique (ZMET), interviewers need minimal training, and respondents can complete mapping in a relative short time. There are several steps as follows:

Step 1 Elicitation stage: According to open-ended questions (e.g., When you think of brand, what comes to your mind?), data are collected to identify salient associations. The most frequently mentioned brand associations should be selected to form the final set. At least 50% of respondents mentioned will be included in brand associations.

In the section, 30 university students are asked to answer the question: When mention about Jiuzhaigou and Dujiangyan, what comes to your mind? 4 or 5 key words about these two tourist attraction are needed to mention. A total of 50 brand associations of each place are mentioned. 25 key words that most frequently mentioned about brand association of Jiuzhaigou are chosen for mapping stage. They are shown as follows (see Fignre 1):

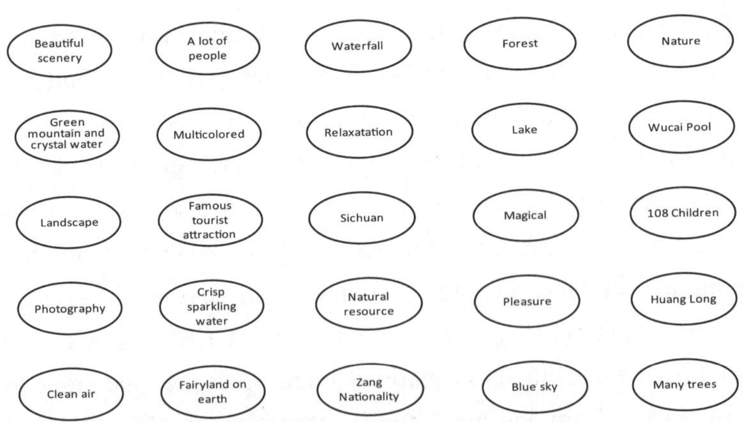


Figure 1 Brand Associations for Jiuzhaigou

Step 2 Mapping stage: Respondents are asked to think about what they associate with brand. Brand associations selected from the first stage will be shown to them to help mapping. By showing the example of BCM, respondents are given instruction of drawing their own maps. It is a requirement that respondents connect brand associations they chose to another by using different types of lines to indicate the strength of connection among associations.

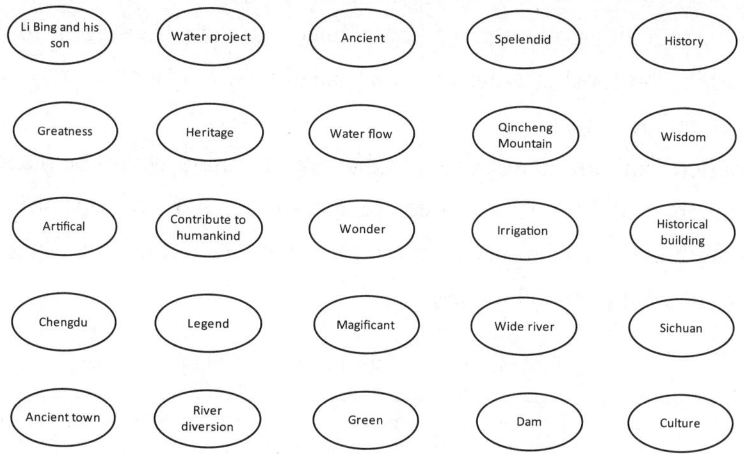


Figure 2 Brand Associations for Dujiangyan

A total of 50 of university students who majored in tourism management participated in the study. Participants were asked to mapping their brand maps in the following questions, "What comes to mind when you think about Jiuzhaigou and Dujiangyan?" To help them with the task, respondents were shown the association from the previous step and could add additional thoughts and feelings. The following step is to explain the nature and purpose of the BCM. Participants were shown a BCM of McDonald's. This example was used to describe the types of associations that might be included on the map, how associations might be linked to the brand. Different types of lines that include single, double and triple lines indicate how strongly an association was connected to the brand or to another association. The more the lines, the stronger the connection. Figure 3 is the example of BCM from one of the students.

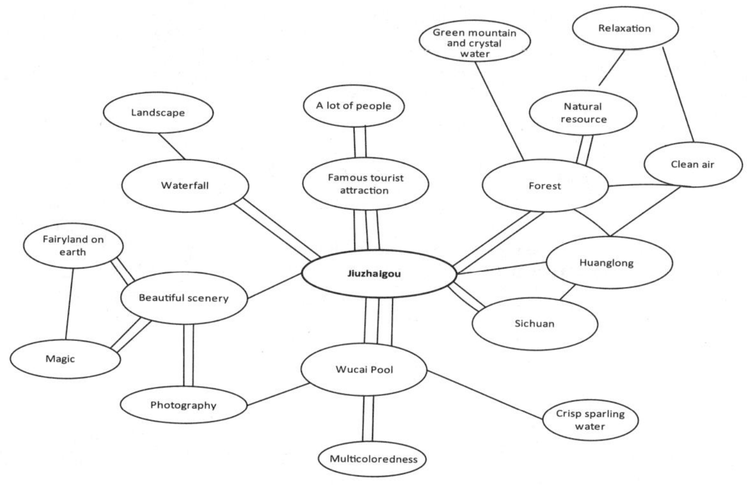


Figure 3 BCM from One Respondent

Step 3 Aggregation stage: Individual BCM is combined into a consensus map based on a set of rules. Frequencies are used to construct a consensus map, revealing the most salient brand associations and their interconnections.

We coded information from each respondent's map in terms of the presence of each of the 25 brand associations, the type of line connecting each association to the brand or to another association, the level at which each association was placed on the map, and which brand association on the map.

In the first step, core brand associations that are identified would be placed on the map. Frequency of mention and number of interconnection are the two types of measurements. At least 50% core brand associations are put on the map. Therefore, we found 12 core brand associations for Jiuzhaigou and Dujiangyan.

Table 1　BCM Mersures for Jiuzhaigou

| Brand Associations | Core Associations | | First-order Associations | |
|---|---|---|---|---|
| | *Frequency of Mention* | *Number of Inter-connection* | *Frequency of First-Order Mention* | *Subordinate Connections* |
| Beautiful scenery | 48 | 48 | 45 | 30 |
| Nature | 45 | 48 | 46 | 38 |
| Green mountain and crystal water | 43 | 45 | 28 | 26 |
| Famous tourist attraction | 43 | 45 | 38 | 30 |
| Sichuan | 40 | 42 | 30 | 32 |
| Magic | 38 | 40 | 40 | 32 |
| Huanglong | 36 | 40 | 28 | 25 |
| Clean air | 34 | 40 | 25 | 24 |
| Waterfall | 34 | 38 | 27 | 20 |
| Lake | 30 | 32 | 24 | 22 |
| Fairyland on earth | 28 | 25 | 22 | 24 |
| Multicoloredness | 28 | 25 | 21 | 26 |

Table 2　BCM Measures for Dujiangyan

| Brand Associations | Core Associations | | First-order Associations | |
|---|---|---|---|---|
| | *Frequency of Mention* | *Number of Inter-connection* | *Frequency of First-Order Mention* | *Subordinate Connections* |
| Water project | 46 | 48 | 42 | 25 |
| Magnificence | 43 | 45 | 35 | 28 |
| Heritage | 45 | 45 | 43 | 30 |

(To be continued)

(Continued Table 2)

| Brand Associations | Core Associations | | First-order Associations | |
|---|---|---|---|---|
| | *Frequency of Mention* | *Number of Inter-connection* | *Frequency of First-Order Mention* | *Subordinate Connections* |
| Wisdom | 45 | 42 | 38 | 30 |
| History | 42 | 40 | 40 | 28 |
| Irrigation | 38 | 35 | 30 | 32 |
| Qincheng Mountain | 35 | 30 | 28 | 25 |
| Splendidness | 34 | 38 | 30 | 25 |
| Wide river | 30 | 28 | 35 | 28 |
| River diversion | 30 | 30 | 20 | 30 |
| Li Bing and his son | 32 | 28 | 25 | 32 |
| Ancient | 30 | 26 | 28 | 28 |

In the second step, we started to build the consensus map by identifying which core brand associations should be linked directly to Jiuzhaigou and Dujiangyan. We selected five core brand associations as first-order associations.

In the third step, the rest of the core brand associations are needed to put on the map. They should be connected to at least one of the first orders. In the fourth step, we added important links between core and non-core brand associations on the map. In the last step, we draw lines including single, double bues and triple to demonstrate the intensity of connections between associations.

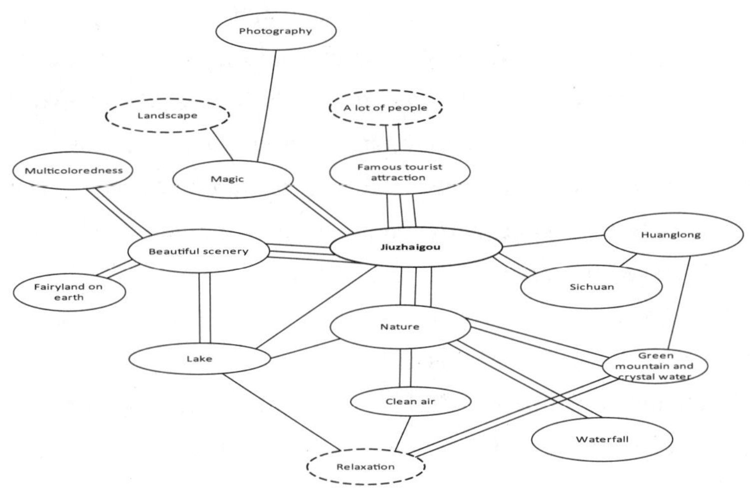


Figure 4 Consensus BCM for Jiuzhaigou

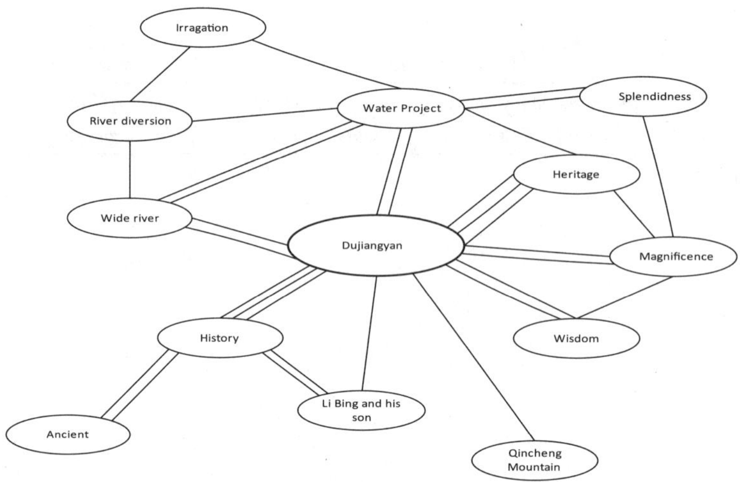


Figure 5 Consensus BCM for Dujiangyan

## Ⅲ. Discussion

Having identified the importance of the network of brand associations held in memory, it is apparent that not all associations are of equal importance. Specially, "the presence of strongly held, favorably evaluated associations that are unique to the brand and imply superiority over other brands are critical to a brand success" [9]. According to the BCM for Jiuzhaigou, there are five key association directly linked to the brand image, which are "beautiful scenery", "nature", "Sichuan", "magical" and "famous tourist attractions". To build and maintain the brand image among tourists, administration of Jiuzhaigou should make sure these associations or other associations connected to them may let tourists resonate. For instance, the image perceived of Jiuzhaigou is "nature". Thus, its branding could emphasize this association when do communication. When the advertisement of this destination shown on different channels, "nature" might be consider as a key theme instead of stressing on many other factors. In addition, when DMO of Jiuzhaigou develops a new tourism product or program, they still need to consider nature to be their focus. For example, based on the unique nature resource, participating in some outdoor activities in Jiuzhaigou is more pleasant experience for tourists.

From what Figure 5 shows, there are six key associations to describe Dujiangyan. "History" and "heritage" can be seen as the strongest connection. One of the first-order associations of Dujiangyan is "heritage". It is essential for management to stress this and deliver the message to people about the significance of heritage which includes our ancestor's great wisdom. What information should be interpreted and how to interpret heritage can be the vital issues for the management. By doing this, the image of tourist attraction or destination can be strengthened and stuck in people's mind.

The core brand associations should be protected from dilution. Nowadays, many tourist attractions tend to design and sell various kind of tourists products to gain more profits from tourists. Therefore, communication with customers may be distracted by a lot of information that does not represent the core image. The messages or the activities from tourist attractions that does inconsistent with the core brand association may destroy the brand, meanwhile, it may lead to confusion to customers or tourists as well and reduce the degree of tourists' experience.

## Ⅳ. Conclusion

By using the BCM method, it presents a picture of how consumers think about brands of famous attractions in China, with a visual format that makes it easy for managers and marketers to see important brand associations and how they are connected in the potential tourist's minds. The paper summarized brand associations of two famous tourism sites, Jiuzhaigou and Dujiangyan. Hence, it is not difficult to see the consumers' responses about the brand of these two places. Through the BCM, the most important brand associations that drive the brand image can be highlighted, which should be the vital concern for marketers and managers preparing brand strategies.

The limitation of this research that involves few samples and inaccurate techniques provides opportunities for further investigation. First, increasing the number and type of the sample could offer more valid results. Second, it would be useful to incorporate procedure into BCM to evaluate the relationship between associations.

## References


[1] Fyall A, Leask A. Destination marketing: future issues-strategic challenges[J]. *Tourism and Hospitality Research*, 2006, 7 (1): 50.

[2] Chi Genqing, Qu Hailin. Examining the structural relationship of destination image, tourist satisfaction and destination loyalty: an integrated approach[J]. *Tourism Management,* 2008, 29: 624-636.

[3] Kim K, Hallab Z, Kim J-N. The moderating effect of travel experience in a destination on the relationship between destination image and the intention to revisit[J]. *Journal of Hospitality Marketing & Management*, 2012, 21: 486-505.

[4] Cai Liping. Cooperative branding for rural destinations[J]. *Annuals of Tourism Research*, 2002, 2(3): 720-742.

[5] Gnoth J, Baloglu S, Ekinci Y, Sirakaya-Turk E. Introduction: Building destination brands[J]. *Tourism Analysis*, 2007, 12: 339-343.

[6] Keller K L. Building customer-based brand equity[J]. *Marketing Management*, 2001, 10(2): 14-19.

[7] Pike S. Consumer-based brand equity for destinations: practical DMO performance measures[J]. *Journal of Travel & Tourism Marketing*, 2007, 22 (1): 51.

[8] John D R, Loken B, Kim K, Monga A B. Brand concept maps: A methodology for identifying brand association networks[J]. *Journal of Marketing Research*, 2006, 43: 549-563.

[9] Keller K L. Conceptualizing, measuring, and managing customer-based brand equity[J]. *Journal of Marketing*, 1993, 57(1):1-22.

# A Study on Influencing Factors of Cultural Heritage Tourism Destination Selection of Youth Groups: Based on TPB Model

Zhou Kun[1*]

**Abstract:** As the main body of today's tourism market, youth groups have a significantly difference from other groups in preference for tourism destinations, especially for the cultural heritage tourism destinations. This phenomenon is due to the different income, education, occupation and consumption habits of youth groups. Based on Theory of Planned Behavior (TPB), the article makes an empirical analysis on the influencing factors of young people's choice of cultural heritage tourism destination by using a questionnaire survey method, which provides theoretical support for the development of cultural heritage tourism destination.

**Keywords:** youth group; cultural heritage; tourism destination; influencing factors; TPB model

## Ⅰ. Introduction

The definition of youth groups vary. The United Nations Educational, Scientific and Cultural Organization (1982) defined 14-34 years old as young people, while the World Health Organization (1992) defined the age group of 14-44 years old. China's National Bureau of Statistics defines the 15-34 years old group for the young population in the census. Wu Yeyu (2002) argues that the current age of Chinese young people should be defined as 16 to 25 years of age, and the definition of youth age can be continually adjusted and modified according to the specific social conditions when it has been changed. [1] Huang Zhijian (2003) proposed that the age of Chinese youth should be 14-30 years old in the 21st century. [2] Based on the content and purpose of this paper, we define the age of young people as 16-30 years old.

Over the past decade (2007-2017), the research on youth groups and tourism problems in China mainly focused on the tourism preference and market development of youth groups in rural tourism, [3]-[5] red tourism[6]-[7] and youth women tourism. [8]-[10] In the literature on

1* Sichuan University, Chengdu, China; Chongqing University of Arts and Sciences, Chongqing, China. zhoukun213@foxmail.com.

youth groups and cultural heritage, some scholars have studied the protection and inheritance of youth groups and intangible cultural heritage, [11] but we have not yet found relevant achievements in the study of youth groups and cultural heritage tourism destinations (Hereinafter referred to as CHTD). In the study of CHTD, domestic academia is relatively concentrated in the protection and development of cultural heritage, especially the resources evaluation of agricultural cultural heritage [12]-[13]and its sustainable development, [14] etc. Foreign scholars focused more on research of cultural heritage tourism, cultural heritage tourism destination, cultural heritage tourism development and management, cultural heritage tourism commentary and authenticity. [15] For instance, Janet Chang (2006) found that young tourists, especially highly educated single youth tourists had a greater interest in the festival itself. [16] Yaniv Poria (2003) used four variables of individual characteristics, including location attributes, consciousness and perception to examine the relationship between tourist perception and their behaviors in the cultural heritage tourism. [17] The study found that there were few articles on the relationship between youth groups and CHTD at home and abroad.

At the most lively age, also with double peak of strength and intelligence, young people have most exuberant needs of learning, healthy living, leisure and entertainment, as well as less shackles of family, career and physical compared to middle-aged people. Young people are one of the main consumers of tourist product, which should not be ignored. However, it is widely believed that the tourism consumption of youth groups is more devoted to the theme parks, landscapes, seaside vacations and other entertainment leisure destinations, while the prominent historic and connotative cultural heritage is more popular among middle-aged tourists. As one of the important cultural tourism products, CHTD looks out of tune with the consumption needs of youth groups, which opens up intangible barriers to market development for it. Therefore, it has great theoretical and practical significance to find out the influencing factors that affect the selection of cultural heritage destinations by young people.

## Ⅱ. Research Models and Assumptions

### *i. TPB Model*

Theory of Planned Behavior (TPB), first proposed by Icek Ajzen, [18] was the successor of Theory of Reasoned Action (TRA). Ajzen added a new concept of self-action "Perceived Behavior Control" to develop TRA into a new behavioral theory research model—Planned Behavior Theory. [19]

Ajzen argues that all factors that may affect behaviors are indirectly influenced by behavioral intentions. And the behavior intention is affected by three related factors, one is derived from the individual for the implementation of a particular behavior held by the "Attitude", the second is derived from the external "Subjective Norm" that affect the individual's behavior, the third is derived from"Perceived Behavioral Control"[20]. Under the influence of the above three factors, an individual forms "Behavior Intention" emerges, and then produces the actual "Behavior". Therefore, TPB model includes five basic elements of Attitude, Subjective Norm, Perceived Behavioral Control, Behavior Intention and Behavior, as shown in Figure 1.

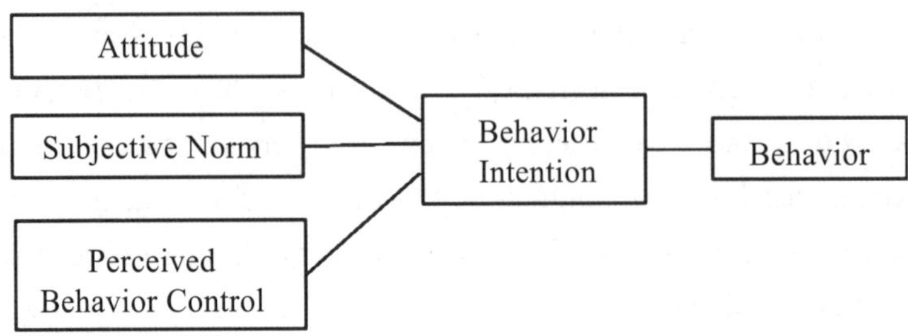


Figure 1 TPB Basic Model

TPB theory has been widely recognized in the scientific research and practical application of selective behaviors, and it has become the mainstream paradigm and classical theory for studying the choice of tourist destinations. [21] Yao Yanhong et al. (2006) constructed the TPB model of tourist destination choice. Their study show that intention, situation and tourism group are the basic influencing factors of tourist destination choice, while the attitude, subjective rule and subjective perception have important influence on intention, with destination image, travel experience, motivation and other nine factors being the most direct impact factors. [22] Song Huilin (2016) used TPB model as a tool to study the influence of demographic characteristics on the outbound tourism destination choice, which shows that the demographic characteristics represented by age, educational level and income plays a significant role in regulating the intentions and choice behaviors of tourism destination [21]. Those above researches lay the foundation for the research hypotheses of this paper.

*ii. Research hypotheses*

The study shows that attitude is the comprehensive understanding of tourism destination which based on the tourists' own qualifications, knowledge, body, occupation and other factors formed by. It's the initial power and basic criteria for selecting the destination. In the tourists' buy behaviors, a certain type of tourist destination, which people give more interest, more positive attitude and better feeling, will have more obvious selection intention as a tourist destination. So, the following assumption is made.

*H1: The attitude of youth groups to CHTD is positively related to the selection intention of CHTD.*

Subjective norm refers to the social pressures individuals perceived when deciding whether or not to take a particular act, that is, the external factors affect individual decisions (such as parents, teachers, friends, spouses, etc.) expect for the behavior of individual decision-making.[23] Visitors choose a type of tourist destination with a certain herd mentality, especially for unfamiliar destinations. So, the following assumption is made.

*H2: the subjective norm of youth group CHTD selection is positively related with CHTD selection intention.*

The perceived behavioral control shows the destination choosing and controlling confidence of visitor, for example, whether the foreseeable factors, like safety, time, and expense, are within their own capacity. The results show that good perceived behavioral control can directly and significantly influence the choice of destination [24]. Therefore, the following assumption is made.

*H3: the perceived behavioral control of cultural tourism of the youth group has a significant influence on the choice of CHTD.*

After gathering information and rational thinking, visitors will generate a tourism destination selection intention to a tourist destination, then form their subjective intention of going or abandoning the tour, which will directly determine their travel behavior. The decision-making capacity of youth groups is strong. Once the selection intention is made, it is highly likely that the intention will be put into practical action. Therefore, the following assumption is made.

*H4: the behavior intention of CHTD choice of youth group determines the choice behavior of the CHTD.*

*iii. Model correction*

In fact, the choice of tourist destination is affected by a variety of factors, such as weather, traffic, tourists body. After the formation of a stronger behavioral intent, visitors may be affected by occasional factors either, which lead to their acceleration or abandon travel behavior. The main reason for advancing or preventing their travels can be summarized as Occasional Events. There includes positive incidental events, for example, the site becoming a well-known film and television drama shooting venue, declaring success of the world cultural heritage, which will play a role in driving tourists. There also includes negative contingencies, such as security incidents, traffic congestion, cultural relics and other unexpected conditions, which will play a role in the inhibition of tourists travel. Young people have a strong ability to collect information, and such incidents can quickly affect their choice behavior. Based on this, the following assumption is proposed.

*H5: occasional events have a significant impact on the selection of CHTD for youth groups.*

Based on the above assumptions, the paper forms the following revised model, as seen in Figure 2.

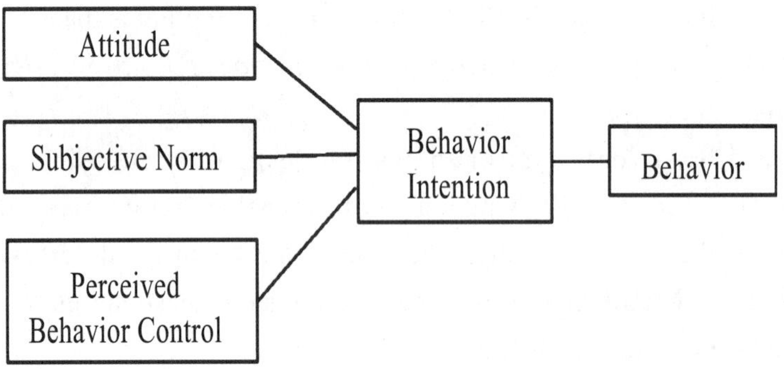


Figure 2 Revised TPB Model for Choosing CHTD of Young People

## Ⅲ. Survey Design and Results

*i. Survey design*

The questionnaire is based on the TPB revised model. For six variables of "attitude", "subjective norm", "perceived behavior control", "behavior intention", "behavior" "occasional events", the questionnaire includes 20 questions, and is revised by a small range of tests. Questionnaire uses the international common Likert five tables, with alternative answers to questions of very disagree, not agree, general, agreed, very agree, followed by 1 to 5. In this paper, we use the network questionnaire survey, for the 16-30-year-old crowd targeted. There are a total of 149 questionnaires being received, with 145 valid questionnaires, and the efficiency 97.3%.

*ii. Reliability and validity analysis*

The Cronbach α is used to detect the questionnaire reliability in the study. According to a general standard, the scale has a considerable degree of reliability when Cronbach $\alpha$ reaches 0.7-0.8, and to be very good reliability when reaches 0.8-0.9. Upon examination, the questionnaire Cronbach $\alpha$ of each variable is over 0.7, and overall reliability is 0.846, showing good reliability. By KMO validity test, it shows that the KMO metric is 0.777, Sig is 0, and each of the six principal components has at least one greater than 0.4, indicating a higher degree of validity. As seen in Table 1.

Table 1 Questionnaire Reliability and Validity

| Variable | Question | Ingredients | | | | | | Cronbach $\alpha$ |
|---|---|---|---|---|---|---|---|---|
| | | 1 | 2 | 3 | 4 | 5 | 6 | |
| Attitude | I think the CHTD is very fun | 0.606 | 0.410 | 0.070 | 0.148 | 0.046 | 0.203 | 0.721 |
| | I am interested in the tourism resources of history, culture, architecture, and village heritage | 0.778 | 0.188 | -0.064 | 0.078 | 0.072 | -0.160 | |
| | Traveling to a CHTD helps to raise my cultural knowledge level | 0.433 | 0.159 | 0.138 | 0.093 | 0.190 | -0.540 | |
| | I have been to the cultural heritage in the past, and I feel good | 0.667 | 0.188 | 0.096 | 0.159 | 0.164 | 0.119 | |
| Subjective Norm | My parents like to travel to cultural heritage | 0.121 | 0.743 | 0.036 | 0.289 | 0.050 | -0.183 | 0.740 |
| | Many of my friends like to visit the CHTD | 0.188 | 0.763 | 0.243 | -0.027 | 0.002 | 0.246 | |
| | Cultural heritage scenic tourism will make people feeling different | 0.336 | 0.217 | -0.028 | 0.682 | 0.053 | 0.076 | |
| | My parents encourage me to travel to CHTD | 0.124 | 0.567 | 0.030 | 0.451 | 0.129 | -0.059 | |
| | Media publicity will make me more inclined to go to CHTD | 0.201 | 0.649 | -0.143 | 0.023 | 0.175 | 0.378 | |
| Perceived Behavior Control | Relatively natural scenic spots, I feel CHTD more secure | 0.070 | 0.055 | -0.084 | 0.570 | 0.262 | 0.403 | 0.712 |
| | Relatively natural scenic spots, I am more familiar with CHTD | 0.282 | 0.212 | 0.133 | 0.670 | 0.058 | 0.293 | |
| | Relatively natural scenic spots, I think the CHTD have more convenient traffic | 0.223 | 0.176 | -0.017 | 0.188 | 0.300 | 0.462 | |
| | Relatively natural scenic spots, people visit CHTD spending less | 0.127 | 0.135 | 0.009 | 0.271 | 0.013 | 0.658 | |
| Behavior Intention | I am willing to travel to CHTD | 0.813 | 0.037 | 0.076 | 0.064 | 0.076 | 0.043 | 0.803 |
| Behavior | If I have the opportunity, I will give priority to CHTD | 0.781 | 0.009 | 0.077 | 0.302 | -0.073 | 0.156 | 0.821 |
| Occasional Events | Weather factors will seriously affect my travel itinerary | 0.111 | -0.059 | 0.767 | 0.390 | -0.079 | -0.035 | 0.705 |
| | Traffic factors will seriously affect my travel itinerary | 0.071 | 0.064 | 0.892 | 0.007 | 0.004 | 0.001 | |
| | Safety factors will seriously affect my travel itinerary | 0.021 | 0.128 | 0.773 | -0.265 | 0.144 | -0.067 | |
| | Declare success of the world cultural heritage and other brands will accelerate my trip | 0.155 | 0.098 | -0.075 | 0.376 | 0.723 | -0.140 | |
| | Famous film and television drama selection will accelerate my trip | 0.049 | 0.083 | 0.131 | -0.055 | 0.889 | 0.173 | |

(To be continued)

(Continued Table 1)

| Variable | Question | Ingredients | | | | | | Cronbach α |
|---|---|---|---|---|---|---|---|---|
| | | 1 | 2 | 3 | 4 | 5 | 6 | |
| KMO | Samples are sufficient to measure the Kaiser-Meyer-Olkin metric | 0.777 | | | | | | |
| Sphericity test of Bartlett | Approximate Chi-Square | 794.187 | | | | | | |
| | df | 190 | | | | | | |
| | Sig. | 0.000 | | | | | | |

*iii. Overall analysis*

The survey shows that a vast majority (68.8%) of respondents interested in historical, cultural, rural heritage and similar types of tourism resources, while most of the respondents (59.7%) are willing to choose CHTD as travel destinations. This result corrects the widely-accepted idea that youth groups prefer natural and themed park tourism destinations to CHTD. The media propaganda has a positive effect on the travel of respondents (48.6%), followed by parental encouragement (37.6%), friend atmosphere (29.5%). Thus, CHTD should pay more attention to media publicity in market development, especially the new media like WeChat, microblogging, micro-film and others. In the occasional events, more than half of the respondents say that the site becoming well-known film and television drama shooting place (56.9%), declare the success of the world cultural heritage (62.4%) and other have a strong influence. Also, traffic (71.6%), weather (49.5%) and safe (71.6%) have a strong impact on tourists' travels, among which traffic and safety factors are most obvious.

*iv. Correlation analysis*

In this paper, we use regression analysis to study the influence factors and its influence of the youth group's choice of CHTD. Before the regression analysis, we need to verify the correlation of each factor. The SPSS20 correlation test shows that attitude, subjective norm, perceived behavior control and occasional events are directly related to behavior intention and behavior. As shown in Table 2.

Table 2 Correlation Analysis of Variables

| Variables | | Behavior Intention | Behavior |
|---|---|---|---|
| Attitude | Pearson Correlation Coefficient | 0.732 | 0.721 |
| | Significant (Bilateral) | 0.001 | 0.003 |
| Subjective Norm | Pearson Correlation Coefficient | 0.428 | 0.478 |
| | Significant (Bilateral) | 0.020 | 0.015 |

(To be continued)

(Continued Table 2)

| | | | |
|---|---|---|---|
| Perceived Behavior Control | Pearson Correlation Coefficient | 0.689 | 0.606 |
| | Significant (Bilateral) | 0.034 | 0.006 |
| occasional events | Pearson Correlation Coefficient | 0.647 | 0.612 |
| | Significant (Bilateral) | 0.013 | 0.016 |

*v. Hypothesis analysis*

(1) Regression analysis of the three variables on travel intention: We use behavior intention as the dependent variable, attitude, subjective norm, perceived behavioral control as independent variables for regression analysis. The results show that the three variables of attitude, subjective norm and perceived behavior control have a certain influence on the tourist travel intention, among which the attitude is most influential to travel intention, while the influence of subjective norm and perceived behavioral control is basically the same, as shown in Table 3. Therefore, the proposed H1, H2, H3 are validated.

Table 3 Regression Analysis of the Three Variables of Travel Intention

| Dependent Variable | Independent Variable | Non-normalized Coefficient | | Standard Coefficient | t | Sig. | $R^2$ | Adjusted $R^2$ | F |
|---|---|---|---|---|---|---|---|---|---|
| | | B | Standard Error | Trial Version | | | | | |
| Behavior Intention | Attitude | 0.481 | 0.469 | 0.190 | 1.026 | 0.000 | 0.353 | 0.328 | 14.175 |
| | Subjective Norm | 2.192 | 0.425 | 0.093 | 5.158 | 0.030 | 0.111 | 0.068 | 2.585 |
| | Perceived Behavior Control | 2.625 | 0.368 | 0.090 | 7.129 | 0.044 | 0.089 | 0.054 | 2.546 |

(2) A regression analysis of travel intention to travel behavior: Taking the behavior as dependent variable, while the behavioral intention as independent variable to do the regression analysis, the result shows that travel intention has a direct and strong impact on travel behavior, as shown in Table 4. H4 is verified to be true.

Table 4 A Regression Analysis of Behavior Intention of Travel Behavior

| Dependent Variable | Independent Variable | Non-normalized Coefficient | | Standard Coefficient | *t* | Sig. | $R^2$ | Adjusted $R^2$ | F |
|---|---|---|---|---|---|---|---|---|---|
| | | B | Standard Error | Trial Version | | | | | |
| Behavior | Behavior Intention | 0.763 | 0.81 | 0.672 | 9.375 | 0.000 | 0.451 | 0.446 | 87.888 |

(3) The impact of occasional events on travel behavior: Taking the behavior as

dependent variable, while the occasional events as independent variable to do the regression analysis, the result shows that occasional events have a direct and strong impact on travel behavior, as shown in Table 5. The H5 hypothesis is verified to be true.

Table 5 A Regression Analysis of Occasional Events of Travel Behavior

| Dependent Variable | Independent Variable | Non-normalized Coefficient | | Standard Coefficient | $t$ | Sig. | $R^2$ | Adjusted $R^2$ | F |
|---|---|---|---|---|---|---|---|---|---|
| | | B | Standard Error | Trial Version | | | | | |
| Behavior | Occasional Events | 2.179 | 0.632 | 0.091 | 3.448 | 0.001 | 0.073 | 0.028 | 1.618 |

## Ⅳ. Conclusions

The study shows that among the multi-factors influencing youth groups' CHTD choices, the attitudes is most significant, followed by the atmosphere of environmental relations and the self-perception of youth groups travelling in CHTD. Occasional events have a clear role in promoting or curbing the travel behavior, and its influence is almost as same as travel intention. Based on the conclusions above, this paper puts forward the following measures to facilitate the development of youth market segments for CHTD.

First, the society should vigorously develop cultural heritage education. On the one hand, through the "Cultural and Natural Heritage Day", "China Tourism Day" and other festivals of publicity, the government imperceptibly to enhance the heritage tourism awareness and favors of youth groups. On the other hand, the government should put museum education, research travel, etc. into the national education system, in order to increase the youth groups', especially children's heritage education. In addition, under the strict protection of cultural heritage at the same time, attracting enterprises and civil society organizations to participate in heritage education through the market approach, can make the seeds of cultural heritage deeply rooted in the hearts of young people.

Second, we should create a heritage tourism social atmosphere. Through the Internet, television, festivals and other different forms, it can form a cultural heritage tourism atmosphere in the whole society. A strong cultural heritage tourism atmosphere is not only conducive to enhance the public awareness of cultural heritage, but also an important driving force to attract the youth groups to visit heritage tourist places.

Third, CHTD should innovative cultural heritage tourism products. In addition to the historical sense of heritage, the core attraction of cultural heritage tourism also could meet the tourists needs in many ways. Around these elements such as novelty, color, dynamic and other which young people prefer, product designers could develop good tourism products which meet the needs of young people, where there will be a great market space. The

Imperial Palace, Zhouzhuang, Lijiang and other cultural heritage sites in China do a good demonstration in this respect.

Fourth, CHTD should pay attention to the impact of accidental factors. On the one hand, doing a positive declaration of key cultural relics protection units, national or world cultural heritage and other destination brands, could format strong brand influence. On the other hand, introducing the film and television drama, Internet, characteristics of festivals to the CHTD, could effectively enhance its visibility and reputation. At the same time, CHTD should pay attention to creating a safe, convenient and comfortable atmosphere of tourist environment.

This paper chooses the TPB model to study the influencing factors of the cultural heritage tourism destination for the young people. However, due to space constraints, as well as the characteristics of the TPB model itself, the studies on internal relationship and mechanism among the impact factors are still inadequate. In the future, we can use the SEM model to focus on how the several influencing factors acting on the selection of young people, in order to deepen and verify the conclusions of this paper continually.

## References

[1] Wu Yeyu. Integration of youth age [J]. *Chinese Youth Research,* 2002 (3): 36-39.

[2] Huang Zhijian. A study on the definition of youth's age[J]. *Chinese Youth Research*, 2003 (11): 31-411.

[3] Wu Jingyu, Huang W. Study on the development strategy of youth group's rural tourism market [J]. *Modern Business*, 2016 (12): 32-33.

[4] Zhong Cheng, Zhu Chuanye, Xiao Xiao, Ma Shuoyan, Zhang Linyun. An empirical study on tourism consumption behavior of young tourists in rural tourism: taking Chengdu city as an example [J].*Resource Development &Market*, 2010, 26(5): 475-475, 480.

[5] Wu Dan. Study on the behavioral characteristics of young tourists in rural tourism [J]. *Green Technology*, 2014 (7): 321-322.

[6] Yang Weihao. A Study on the youth red tourism behavior: a case study of the site of the New Fourth Army in Yan Si [J]. *Journal of Anhui Agricultural Sciences*, 2016 (23):139-141.

[7] Zhang Xue. Study on the demand characteristics and participation intention of young people in red tourism: a case study of Beijing red tourism classic scenic spot [J]. *Special Zone Economy*, 2013 (6): 86-89.

[8] Song Danping, Dang Chunmei, Yuan Xing. Analysis of domestic tourists' consumption behavior of young women[J]. *Products and Quality*, 2011 (8): 44-45.

[9] Shen Yuli, Peng Fenwen. On tourism consumption behavior of young females in Loudi and associated marketing strategies [J]. *Journal of Hunan University of Humanities, Science and Technology*, 2015(4): 114-119.

[10] Xia Wentao. Study on the design of psychological needs of young women's health tourism products[J]. *Economic Theory Research*, 2010 (5): 97-98.

[11] Li Qinxin, Xu Jinde. Reflections on the protection and inheritance of the contemporary youth participation in the intangible cultural heritage [J]. *Literature Education*, 2015 (9): 86-87.

[12] Sun Yehong, Min Qingwen, Cheng Shengkui, Zhong Linsheng, Qi Xiaobo. Study on the tourism

resource characteristics of agricultural heritage[J]. *Tourism Tribune*, 2015, 25(10): 57-62.

[13] Sun Yehong, Cheng Shengkui, Zhong Linsheng, Min Qingwen. Assessment on tourism resources potential for agriculture heritage sites: a case study on Qingtian county in Zhejiang province[J]. *Resources Science*, 2010, 32(6): 1026-1034.

[14] Fan Youmeng, Xie Yanjun. Memory display and gaze: a research on the synergy of protection and utilization about rural cultural heritages[J]. *Tourism Science*, 2015, 29(1): 11-24.

[15] Dong Hao, Zhang Xixi. Research rends of cultural heritage tourism abroad in the last decade: a review of annals of tourism research and tourism management[J]. *Human Geography*, 2012, 27(5): 157-160.

[16] Chang J. Segmenting tourists to aboriginal cultural festivals: An example in the Rukai tribal area, Taiwan[J]. *Tourism Management*, 2006, 27(6): 1224-1234.

[17] Poria Y, Butler R, Airey D. The core of heritage tourism[J]. *Annals of Tourism Research*, 2003, 30(1): 238-254.

[18] Ajzen I. *From Intentions to Actions: A Theory of Planned Behavior*[M]. Berlin: Springer Berlin Heidelberg, 1985: 11-39.

[19] Fishbein M, Ajzen I. Belief, *Attitude, Intention, and Behavior: An Introduction to Theory and Research*[M]. Boston: Addison-Wesley Publishing Company, 1975: 53.

[20] Ajzen I. The theory of planned behavior[J]. *Organizational Behavior and Human Decision Processes*, 1991, 50(2): 179-211.

[21] Song Huilin, Liu Xingyang, Jiang Yiyi. The effects of characteristics of tourists on Chinese outbound tourism destination choice behavior: an empirical study based on TPB model [J]. *Tourism Tribune*, 2016, 31(2): 33-43.

[22] Yao Yanhong, Luo Yan. An analysis of the TPB model of tourists' destination choice[J]. *Tourism Science*, 2006, 20(5): 20-25.

[23] Qi Xin, Liu Jiashu. Study on the influencing factors of entrepreneurial intention of college students based on TPB model [J]. *Journal of Anhui University of Technology (Social Science Edition)*, 2010, 27 (6): 163-165.

[24] Ding Liying. Research of Fuzhou residents to Taiwan tourism intention based on the theory of planned behavior[J]. *Journal of Jilin Normal University (Natural Science Edition)*, 2013, 2(1): 117-119.

# A Study on the Feasibility of Constructing VR Travel Store Business Model

Yu Junfang[1*], Yu Zhu[2]

**Abstract:** The Internet technology revolution triggers significant changes in the traditional business model for travel agency industry. The cross-border joint between the industries and the fragmentation of innovation makes the tourism industry boundary increasingly vague and expanding. This paper follows the supply and demand law of tourism market, and conforms to the tendency of the cooperation and penetration between online and offline travel agencies. With the concepts of "travel plus" and "experiential marketing", this paper innovates the new conception of VR Travel Store Operating Model that was inspired by the existing model of traditional travel agency and Apple Store, and puts forward a specific project plan and profit model, demonstrating its feasibility from facets of economy, techniques and policy. The aim is to enrich the commercial forms of tourism and to explore one more available route for the transformation and upgrading of the tourism.

**Keywords:** experiential marketing; VR Travel Store; new tourism format

## Ⅰ. Introduction

VR (Virtual Reality) is defined as the use of a computer-generated 3D environment—known as a "virtual environment" (VE)—that one can navigate and possibly interact with, resulting in real-time simulation of onc or more of the user's five senses.[1] VR experience can be described by its capacity to provide physical immersion and psychological presence. [2] "Immersion" refers to the extent to which a user is isolated from the real world. In a "fully immersive system" the user is completely encompassed by the VE and has no interaction with the real world, while in a "semi-immersive" or "non-immersive system" (the latter includes contemporary 3D video games) the user retains some contact with the real world. In this paper, VR refers to a virtual environment generated by modern computer high technology, where the users interact with the objects in the virtual world with special input/output devices, gaining the same visual, auditory, and tactile feelings as in real-world, and

1* Hubei Normal University, Huangshi, China. yujf_0103@163.com.
2 Wuhan University, Wuhan, China.

this paper accepts augmented reality (AR)—the projection of computer-generated images onto a real world view[3]—as a type of VR.

VR has already been used commonly in diverse areas including entertainment, design, and simulation training. VR products are gradually introduced into our daily life. In 2015, VR became a top word in the technology industry. By now, the commercial giants have continuously laid out massive amount of capital in virtual reality industry. China Media Consulting released a research report which predicted that the market size of China's virtual reality industry in 2020 will exceed 55 billion yuan.[4] In the past three years, VR companies announced the acquisition of investment almost every day. The VR time is on the way. In fact, VR already has various applications within the tourism sector. The VR Industry Application Investment Statistics[5] and future development trend show that the tourism industry is one of the most important VR directions. At present, the world famous tourist destinations, hotel groups, network booking platforms have joined the major VR technology suppliers in participating in VR tourism content production.

Thomas Cook Group, Qantas Airways and Canada's Destination British Columbia are making VR contents for advertising. Thomas Cook Group has begun to try VR technology since 2015, which hired VR technical staff to shoot 360-degree three-dimensional images in Greece. Besides, those staff also shot the images of the pyramid and six hotels with different styles, as well as the live video of riding motorcycle in the dunes etc. By doing so, they intend to increase their revenue. Australian Tourism Bureau and China VR Industry Storm Technology Group launched a strategic cooperation for the production of the Australian scenic spots VR video. Nowadays, ten branch offices of Thomas Cook in the UK, Germany, Belgium, and other places provide VR experience services. According to Thomas Cook internal data, after providing VR experience services, New York travel project revenue has increased by 190%.

In China, the Home Inn Group provided VR video of "36 self-driving travel lines". Tencent invested 8 million into the hotel booking platform Zanadu to help launch "Travel VR" application and made China's first VR travel video "The Dream". ELong released a number of hotels panoramic videos. More than 4,000 scenic panorama data and image collection have been completed by "Renwoyou", and it produced VR experience discs. VR tourism social platform "A Tour" has more than 500 tourism attraction resources that are well-known in domestic and foreign markets.

There are a lot of equipment providers in VR field, and plenty of VR content producers and platforms who have the VR scenic content. However, there is no VR tourism resource information aggregation platform. Although the huge amounts of VR tourism resources are booming and flourishing, covered with high-tech aura, they are far away from the mass market. As for the consumers, the more information there is, the more confused they are. They are all at sea to find useful tourism resource messages they need.

## Ⅱ. VR Travel Store Brief

Experiential marketing conception considers consumers not only as the buyers who want to meet their needs and benefit from them but also as humans being rational and sensible who want to try different things and experience pleasure.[6] Customers who are sensitive to prices are less tempted to buy unnecessary goods. For this type of customers, making decision to purchase something is not primarily important, but they tend to take part in a promotion related to discount. [7] As asserted by Aronne, Reis & Lobo (2009), experiential marketing is company's way to process and create a whole experience felt by the customers through the most possible and best way provided by the company.

Experience is the core element of experiential marketing, which can create different stimuli such as special areas, atmosphere and new settings. By this way the consumers are expected to respond to these stimuli, becoming active in purchasing goods and getting different feelings like pleasure, entertainment as well as gaining experience. Experiential marketing offers necessary and sufficient information to consumers for purchasing decision and also offers deep tangible experiences. The stimulations through the vision, hearing, touch, taste, and smell may trigger customer's motivations and needs, and encourage them to buy the products to reach the marketing goals.

VR Travel Store is the exact platform which aggregates the resources of the virtual scenic spots, filling the vacancies of VR travel offline marketing channels. It aims to provide an easy and funny way for consumers to get useful travel advice. It is a tourism performance store like Apple Inc., a new way of experiential marketing in tourism.

With the most acceptable and specific offline form, it will catch the market focus, gather more intentional customers to visit, "experience" their desirable products in an amusing way, reduce their decision time, and increase the orders conversion rate. Above all, they are willing to pay a premium for that.

*i. Project market positioning*

VR Travel Store is positioned as "an offline integration platform for virtual tourism products", which focuses on curious, trendy and adventurous consumers who are willing to accept new things. It is neither a traditional travel agency nor an OTA offline entity. It is an independent, self-financing, new format of tourism industry.

*ii. Scope of business*

The business of VR Travel Store includes the publicity, advertising, consultation, pre-experience, reservation and sales of single service and package tour (Table 1). Its main products include: VR tourism project experience, scenic tickets agent, hotel accommodation, specialty traffic reservation and travel itinerary planning and design, which can be described in details as follows:

*A. Provide tourism information consultation*

Tourist destination cities, scenic spots, theme parks even hotels and transportation departments could advertise here. VR travel store is the most comprehensive tourist information hub where customers get quality and targeted travel information covering "eating, housing, transportation, shopping, traveling and entertainment". The clerks are tourist consultants, travel planners and tour guides as well. The immersive video enables the customer to be transported to different destinations that he can gain pre-experience and make a more satisfying and better decision.

*B. Experiencing VR travel*

The consumers who are curious, trendy and adventurous and willing to accept new things can experience the latest VR technology for amusement here, such as sightseeing in scenic spots, checking in the capsule hotel, enjoying a luxury cruise ship, taking a roller coaster, etc. For those who are incapable of outdoor travelling because of money, time or physical condition, but still curious about the world, what they need to do is to step into the store. They can stand on Mount Everest, or walk in the Grand Canyon, travelling around the world right away.

*C. Travel and VR-tech agent*

As the same agency functions as the traditional travel agency, the store provides reservation for transportation, accommodation, scenic ticket and other vocation products. As a platform of VR technology display and promotion, the store could accept the orders of VR equipment purchasing and VR content producing from government departments of tourism destination cities and some related tourism enterprises as well.

Table 1　VR Travel Store Business Scope

| Service Content | Object and Item | Remarks |
|---|---|---|
| Advertise & Advisory | tourist destinations and attractions, scenic spots, theme parks, hotels, traffic, cruise, festival, and events, tradition customs, travel itinerary planning etc. | Free |
| Pre-experience | theme parks, scenic spots, characteristic hotels, cruise, special traffic, festival and events | Pay |
| Reservation & Deal | theme park and scenic spot entrance tickets, traffic tickets, hotel, vocation products; potential VR content provider | Pay |

*iii. Location of value chain*

The value chain is the relationship among the company and its suppliers upstream and downstream. That value chain approach is utilized to analyze the company core competencies to achieve cost reduction and differentiation. The upstream partners of VR travel store cover traditional travel agency, the OTAs, tourism suppliers (amusement parks, scenic area, hotels, airlines, cruise, etc.), and the government departments of tourist destination cities. Its downstream is directly to tourism (potential) customers. VR Travel Store is an innovative terminal of tourism products sales, a new intermediary communicate tourism subjects and objects as well. With the strong sense of immersion and immediacy, VR Travel Store can both make the dream of traveling around the world with low cost come true and set the customer free from the vast numbers of texts, pictures, and even video information, help them develop the optimal travel plan in an efficient method. It will be the indispensable composition of the tourism industry value chain.

## Ⅲ. VR Travel Store Business Model

*i. VR travel store operating model*

The labor division of VR industry mainly includes VR equipment manufacturer, VR content provider, and VR content maker. The vertical division of tourism industry mainly includes tourism suppliers, tourism wholesalers, tourism operators and consumers. The cross-border integration of VR-tech and tourism making the powerful tourism suppliers become providers of VR content. At present, the major hotels, famous scenic spots, and even some destination countries or regions have become the VR content providers, they hire professional VR maker to produce its high quality VR tourism resources. As an offline platform, VR travel store gathers as much as high-quality VR tourism products, makes consumers experience, consulting and generates tourist motives and behaviours. As a VR technology application and promotion company, the store can also be the link among potential content providers, VR content producers and equipment manufacturers. The project has broadened the scope of VR technology application and developed a new tourism business model.

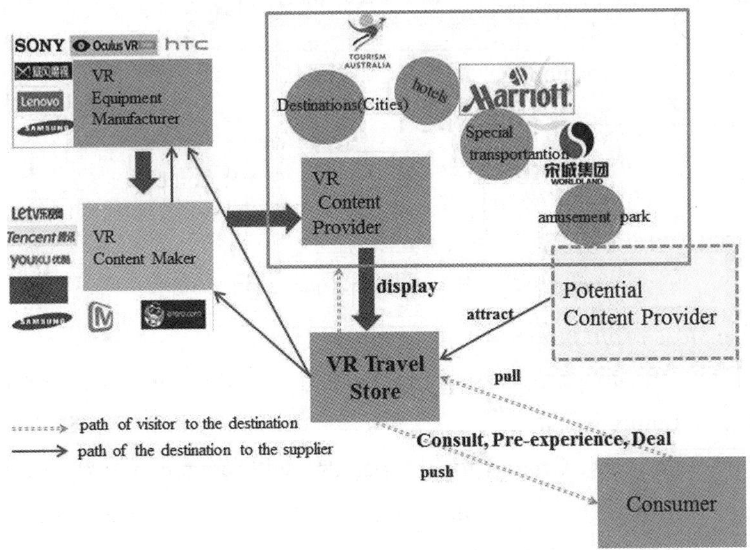


Figure 1 Joint of VR Industry and Tourism Industry

Figure 1 presents the relationships of VR travel store with VR-tech industry and tourism industry. Sony Play Station VR, HTC Vive, Oculus are world's leading VR equipment manufacturers, with their all-in-one machines, external helmets and high quality tourism VR content which provided by destinations and made by professional teams, customers here can enjoy an unprecedented “travel experience”. Attracted and driven by profits, more and more tourist destinations who generate demands for VR resources making will find professional production teams and equipment suppliers through the store.

VR travel store is the upgrading of traditional travel agency and OTA offline store. The introduction of high technologies makes it an important terminal channel in the VR industry chain. It is not only a professional travel consultancy and tour experience service provider, but also a vital place to promote and popularize the VR technology application. It’s not just a travel store, as it were the connection set up between tourism industry and VR industry. VR travel store operating model can be simplified as Figure 2. VR travel store is a trinity of travel agent, VR-tech agent and VR travel experience store where VR tourism resource is concentrated and displayed.

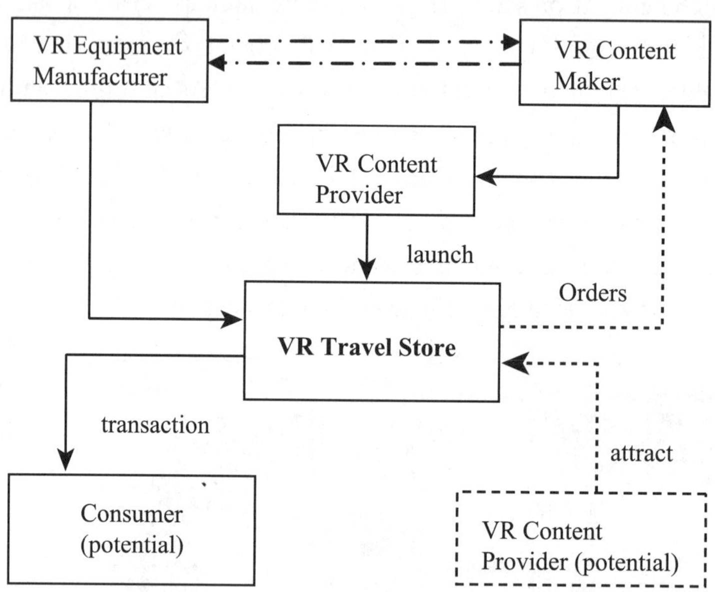


Figure 2　VR Travel Store Operating Model

*ii. VR travel store profit model*

Combined with the above operating model, there are three major profit modules in VR travel store project (Figure 3):

(1) VR tour experience. Charge for the persons who consume VR projects here which constitute one of the main parts of operating income. The variable costs are equipment operating costs and manual guidance costs.

(2) Travel agent and consultation. Charge commission from helping develop travel plans and book hotel rooms, scenic tickets, transportation and other individual or package tour products for those who have the abilities and motivations, but feel confused when faced with

numerous tourism information. The main cost is from travel suppliers.

(3) VR-tech agent. It can also play the role of intermediator between the VR content maker or the VR equipment manufacturer and the tourism suppliers who has not launched VR tourism product yet. Charge commission depends on the number of orders according to certain percentage.

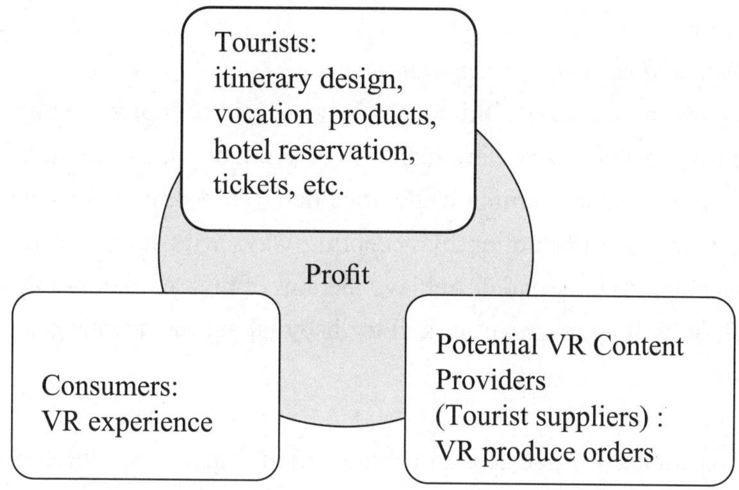


Figure 3 VR Travel Store Profit Model

## Ⅳ. VR Travel Store Implementation

*i. Site selection and decoration*

The site selection of VR Travel Store Project follows the principles of being close to the target market, convenience and eye-catching.

First of all, the overall renovation of the store needs to be simple and stylish, have sense of modern, science and technology. Second, the layout should be reasonable. Experience store is divided into four functional area: entrance & rest area, reception & consultation area, VR experience area and logistics area. The entrance area requires a strong appeal to the guests. In reception and consultation area, there should be professional travel consultants serving consumers with all kinds of tourism needs, and guiding them into the VR tourism experience. This area also should have displaying racks on which neatly place travel journals, scenic information, product leaflets and scenic spots video or other tourism promotional materials. Scientific and reasonable items display in store has positive effect on beautifying the environment, save space, enhancing trust, stimulating sales. Related research shows that the correct use of goods configuration, display skills and the sales can be increased by 10%. Therefore, clear product classification, easily approached brochures, fully displayed stands and creative posters are essential. The equipment facilities should include VR headset equipment, VR resources, computers, telephones, printers, photocopiers, fax machines and other office facilities and so on.

*ii. Specific implementation*

*A. Pre-preparation work*

Store decoration, VR equipment installation, staff recruitment and training. As innovation in tourism industrial, the marketing promotion of VR Travel Store should start early and vigorously. Let as many as consumers understand and look forward to VR Travel Store, produce desire to try.

*B. Advertising and marketing promotion*

The mass consumers usually think that leaning and accepting a high-tech product require more costs, so that many new technology products fail to popularization. High-tech new products' price and learning difficulties deterred potential consumers. Therefore, advertising and marketing promotion by accepting ways with fully considered consumer demand and psychology are essential. Achieve the aim of high market profile and let people know VR travel, be willing to accept it, and try it by taking the advantages of brand effect and brand loyalty.

*C. Soft opening*

VR travel experience for free at soft opening period help increase the consumer flux. Let them truly feel the vivid thrill, amusement and convenient of VR travel, which can stimulate the consumers' curiosity and desire so as to guide them to make purchasing behavior. VR means new changes and development to traditional travel agency. It should aim to improve product value, boost sales, and bring the tourists new and marvelous travel experience.

*iii. Expected performance*

*A. Recent object (1-2 years)*

To occupy and grab market share, recover costs, achieve profitability. Increase awareness in the area where the store is located, then establish and consolidate local tourism market with good reputation, quality service and new technology. The implementation of multi-directional marketing strategy, high-quality and satisfied service will help continue to attract more consumers, and quickly open the market. By the means of innovative publicity, VR tourism will be further promoted. A good long-term relation of cooperation with partners and relevant industries such as the scenic area, hotels, equipment providers etc. should be established. The existing market share should be consolidated and customers' loyalty should be cultivated so as to achieve the absolute dominance in the region.

*B. Medium and long term intent*

Achieve greater victory in VR travel market. To open more stores, expand market share in domestic and overseas, win more users, enrich product lines, and establish broader and deeper industry cooperation. Enhance the competitive advantage of stores. As the leader and demonstration of VR travel store, VR will become the main force of tourism marketing tools, VR technology will change the tourism industry, penetrating into our daily, and making our life better and more fascinating.

## V. Guarantee of Project

Tourism is positioned as a strategic pillar industry in China's national economy. Since 2009, the State Council has issued many relevant policies to support the tourism development and promote tourism investment. From the central to the local government, it shows the unprecedented attention of tourism development. In the context of economic recession, tourism plays an outstanding performance in stimulating domestic demands and heating the global economic. National Tourism Administration research data shows, a total of 4.12 billion people traveled in domestic or outbound in 2015, equivalent to the national population travel nearly three times a year. China's tourism industry contributed 10.1% to the GDP, more than education, banking and automobile industry, of which domestic tourism exceeded 4 billion times, outbound trave 120 million times, tourism income more than 4 trillion RMB. China has entered universal travel era, every citizen's life almost need travel as a necessity. The broad prospects of the tourism market put forward new requirements for the industry development. On the other side, the Ministry of Industry issued the "Virtual Reality Industry Development White Paper 5.0" in 2016, which told the current development of China's virtual reality industry, and put forward the relevant policies, fully affirmed the virtual reality industry from the national level.

In recent years, the development of Internet technology derives a number of new tourism formats such as Online Travel Agency (OTA), which have triggered a major change in the traditional mode of tourism operation. On one hand, OTA seriously impacted the development of traditional travel agencies, made their offline stores have to upgrade by network and information. On the other hand, Ctrip as the representative of the online travel agencies are going to the offline, have built the entity stores layout. Online reception and offline services have become an important model to OTA. It seems that the offline model is still and will always be the indispensable part to the tourism industry.

## VI. Conclusions

Mutual penetration and integration between online and offline is the industry consensus. VR travel store is close to the market, attaching importance to experience atmosphere creation, taking the characteristics of being scientific, interesting, rich into account. It can become the ideal platform for tourism operators and suppliers on which to compete for their tourism products. With the policy support as the basis, the market demand as fundamental and industry trends as the prerequisite, VR Travel Store could be the first choice for entrepreneurs and investors.

## References

[1] Guttentag D A. Virtual reality: applications and implications for tourism[J]. *Tourism Management*, 2010, 31: 637-651.

[2] Gutierrez M, Vexo F, Thalmann D. *Stepping into Virtual Reality*[M]. London: Springer, 2008.

[3] Burdea G C, Coiffet P. *Virtual Reality Technology*[M]. 2nd ed. Hoboken, NJ: Wiley-Interscience, 2003.

[4] The Yiguan analysis website. https://www.analysys.cn/, 2016.

[5] The 36kr. website. http://36kr. com/p/5045252.html, 2016.

[6] Schmitt B. Experiential marketing[J]. *Journal of Marketing Managernent*, 1999, l5: 53-67.

[7] Clow K E, Baack D E. *Integrated Advertising, Promotion, and Marketing Communication*[M]. 6th ed. Global Edition. Pearson Education, 2014.

[8] Aronne C V, Reis M C, Vasconcelos L de. The impact of experiential marketing on the customer's perception of a brand's essence[M]//*XXXlll Encontro da ANPAD*, 2009: 19-23.

[9] Williams A. Fantasy, feeling and fun[J]. *International Journal of Contemporary Hospitality Management*. Tourism and Hospitality Marketing, 2006, l8: 482-495.

[10] Wang Shuchin, Chih Ming, Lin Yiping. Systematic approach for digital marketing strategy through data mining technology[J]. *Journal of Computers*, 2014, 25: 32-51.

[11] The Hotels. Com. Chinese international travel monitor 2016[EB/OL]. https://assets.documentcloud.org/documents/2994781/Hotel.pdf.

[12] eMarketer, website. Most digital travel bookers will use mobile devices [EB/OL]. http://www. emarketer. com/Article/By-2016-Most-Digital-Travel-Bookers-Will-Use-Mobile-Devices/1013248, 2015.

[13] Constanta E. The impact of tourism in enhancing the quality of life[J]. *Review of International Comparative Management*, 2009: 347-351.

# Storytelling Marketing of Chinese Homestays via Social Media

Shao Jun[1], Zhao Yamin[2*], Du Jing[3], Zhang Yujun[4]

**Abstract:** This paper explores the phenomenon of the storytelling marketing of Chinese homestays via social media and the impact on consumers' visiting intentions. Specifically, the research aims at investigating the ways of storytelling shaping brand image and the influence such a story has in terms of inspiring consumers to travel. The contribution of this research lies in linking new forms of media influence to travel as well as in describing the culture of Chinese homestays, which has not been explored enough in previous literature.

**Keywords:** storytelling marketing; homestay; social media

## Ⅰ. Introduction

The homestays in China are playing an important role in the tourism economy. According to the statistics of Meadin Tourism Academy, [1] as of September 2016, there were 42,658 homestays in China Mainland. The number of homestays in Yunnan province ranks first, at 6,466. With the popularity of social media, more and more homestays are using social media for online story-telling marketing. The importance of online images shaped by stories should not be underestimated for homestay operators who are trying to lure tourists with story marketing. Therefore, this paper discusses the phenomenon of the story marketing through social media and the influence of story marketing on the willingness of consumers to visit.

## Ⅱ. Literature Review

*i. The development of storytelling marketing*

Storytelling marketing refers to the marketing mode of using the legend of the events and characters related to enterprises to attract consumers' interest and improve the brand awareness. [2]-[5] Storytelling marketing originates from the story management in enterprise

1 Beijing Forestry University, Beijing, China.
2* Beijing Forestry University, Beijing, China. ymzhao@jianqiao.cn
3 Guizhou Shuitou Qinsen Cultural Tourism Development Co., Ltd. Guiyang, China.
4 Beijing Forestry University, Beijing, China.

management. Specifically speaking, business leaders can use stories to introduce themselves, initiate actions, convey values, promote cooperation, share knowledge, calm rumours, and guide enterprises into the future. [6] The concept of story management is gradually being extended to marketing and story marketing has become a marketing concept. The 2004 bestseller "Purple Cow" pointed out that "commercial success, we have to tell the story of the product itself"[7]. It further elaborated on the principles and steps to be followed in successful storytelling marketing.

Starting with the brand's stakeholders and their actions, closely related to the brand spirit and concept goals, brand story marketing aroused the resonance with the consumers through vivid, interesting and moving expression. [8][9] As distinct from traditional folk tales and literary works, the introduction of stories in a brand is undoubtedly unique in the process of conception and implementation. In a broad sense, brand stories should contain at least the following elements: [8] the narrative frame which is set on the basic story units (motifs); the theme of business advocacy rendering a strong emotional or psychological implied rendering atmosphere; business promotion themes which are used to render strong emotional atmosphere or give psychological cues; story plots which are closely related with enterprise spirit, brand function and consumer interest points; characters or brand spokespersons that deduct the plots. [8]

*ii. The difference between traditional marketing and storytelling marketing*

*A. The shortages of traditional marketing*

Firstly, traditional marketers often misunderstand the audience's awareness of the story. [10] Although companies used to advertise good products directly without storytelling, in the fierce competition for similar products, due to the limitations of ordinary consumers' cognition, many cost-effective products are still defeated. Products with high internal quality are hard to be noticed and easy to be overlooked by potential consumers. Therefore, marketing communication needs to face the audience's cognitive inertia. Only by overcoming the limitations of people's cognitive inertia can the audience understand the information behind the content. [10]

Secondly, the traditional marketing is likely to cause limited communication. People have emotional needs, so brand marketing communication should be able to create emotional significance and symbols for users. [10] In traditional communication, description of the product focused more on promoting the brand itself, not on conveying the meaning of products and brands more vividly and emotionally. [10]

Thirdly, the traditional advertising without storytelling is usually describing factual aspects of a product only. The information provided cannot effectively attract consumers' attention. [10]

*B. The strengths of storytelling marketing*

Firstly, a story can be designed by the vivid, interesting, and tortuous plots, which would overcome people's cognitive inertia so as to achieve effective communication. Consumers are emotional animals, whose behaviours will be led by the emotional value of the story. Storytelling marketing of a brand changes the dull communication to a vivid, lively, interesting way, so it's more attractive to potential consumers. [11][12]

Secondly, a story gives emotional meanings or symbolic values for products or brands, so people's emotional needs are satisfied by story plots [13]. Emotions and symbols are more likely to be resonated by the audience, so the limitations of simple description for products or brands would be get rid of. [14] The humanization of the product shaped by a specific story makes the audience unconsciously accept emotionally.

Thirdly, by storytelling, brands could create a good emotional relationship with the audience. Fournier [15] describes 15 consumer-brand relationship forms, such as arranged marriages, kinships, flings, secret affairs, enslavements, courtships, and others. By the story plots designed related to brands, the interests of consumers were aroused and the awareness to the brand were improved. Storytelling communication is more likely to cause emotional resonance between brands and consumers, comparing with traditional marketing without stories. [16]-[19] The brand-consumer storytelling places an important role in helping consumers seeking for pleasure. [20][21]

## Ⅲ. Methodology

Using three cases of popular homestays in China, which are Blossom Hill Inn in Lijiang, Desti Youth Park in Lijiang, Yunnan Province, and Sweet Cotton Candy in Taiwan, this paper sheds light on how storytelling marketing affects consumers' decision making. These homestays have already started to do marketing with storytelling. Although the performance is far from perfect, there's a lot to be learned from. It is of great significance for the homestay operators.

In order to explore the way in which Blossom Hill Inn and Desti Youth Park in Lijiang became popular by storytelling and how the stories inspired their fans to visit the homestays, a qualitative "netnographic" study [22] using the online postings on social media as well as media interviews of these cases was conducted. Attention was paid only to the contents related to storylines, brand image and influence on others. Regarding Sweet Cotton Candy in Taiwan, both field study and participant observation on its postings in WeChat circle were conducted. The data has been collected and is currently analysed.

## Ⅳ. Results and Discussion

*i. Case studies of three Chinese homestays*

*A. Blossom Hill Inn*

The authors learned about this homestay by a number of well-known traveller stars' blogs. These traveller stars described their own thoughts and feelings in this homestay, showing accommodation experience and environment to readers directly. Such story marketing belongs to the category of consumers' story marketing, so the success of the Blossom Hill Inn also has some useful reference.

Figure 1　Blossom Hill Inn in Douban

Source: https://www.douban.com/people/54300888/.

The web page of Blossom Hill Inn in Douban was shown in Figure 1. It showed the mission of the homestay: "Blossom Hill Inn share beauty and joy in the senior private inn. An inn out of the fantasy, a house grows out of the flowers, a place measured by heart, an utopia that all the people yearn for. Not only are we the center of the destination, but we are the destination; not only for you to dig the stories of mountains or rivers, but we are the stories".

As a homestay for high-end market, Blossom Hill Inn not only created a beautiful mood for visitors in its own brand interpretation, but also attracted the attention of tourists through the promotions of many well-known tourists. Consumers actively engaged in discussions in the relevant sites and forums. In addition, *Blossom Hill Inn* also regularly participated in public welfare activities, causing a lot of attention within the industry, creating a positive brand image, and forming a good reputation.

*B. Desti Youth Park*

Desti Youth Park's owner is Zhang Jinpeng, a well-known Chinese traveller star, the author of a book entitled *Backpack for Ten Years*. Because of its operator's popularity in the industry, Desti Youth Park triggered a lot of discussion at the beginning of its opening. Zhang Jinpeng launched a microblogging topic "I want to build a hostel" on Weibo, telling the whole process of the establishment of the homestay in a live broadcast. He also used the Weibo article "What Does Hostel of 'Bigger than Bigger' Like?" to introduce the location, decorating, layout, and exciting activities of homestays. By quoting tourists, his Weibo showed the "free" and "happy" life atmosphere of the homestay. With the help of pictures, visitors could virtually experience and feel the pleasure of living in it.

In addition to Zhang Jinpeng's personal marketing, the official blog of Desti Youth Park also updated and reposted the visitor's stories in real time, the interaction between colleagues, difficulties and successes during the establishment of the homestay, promotional activities, and sweet stories with customers and so on.

Figure 2 Desti Youth Park in Sina Weibo

Source: https://weibo.com/desti0888.

Desti Youth Park emerged in the major Lijiang recommended homestays list after only running less than a year. Besides Zhang Jinpeng's personal influence, he also had told a "good story" for the homestay. Desti Youth Park's marketing clearly identified its target customer groups. The followers of Zhang's personal microblog and the homestay's microblog are those who are born during 1980s to 1990s concerning about the backpack travel and experience. The message could be directly conveyed to this target groups via social media. By telling the story of the growth of the brand and the operator's personal story, Desti Youth Park quickly built its brand reputation.

In summary, the success of Desti Youth Park illustrates the following steps of storytelling marketing: First, identify the target groups and tell the story to them. Then, provide brand operators and consumer stories, which could be shared by tourists in their social circle, making tourists the best ambassadors to promote the homestay.

*C. Sweet Cotton Candy in Taiwan*

The authors visited Sweet Cotton Candy in 2014, which is located in Hualien City, Taiwan Province. It is the "Legitimate Homestay" approved by Hualien County, which is also identified as the "Hospitality Homestay" by the tourism bureau. One of the authors booked this homestay through the booking.com website in May 2014. Then the host contacted the author via WeChat APP, which is popular among Chinese people. Through the host's WeChat circle of friends, the authors could see the story shaped by the homestay.

This is a homestay without a lot of decorations, the homestay owner couple have worked in the service industry for many years. They insisted on being careful, considerate and attentive to welcome every guest who comes to Hualien, and let their guests deeply feel what they want to convey is the happiness of a family. On the first floor, the walls were plastered with postcards from lodgers who liked the homestay. The rooms were simple, but it can be seen that the owner is very attentive. The pink soft tone creates a soft comfort, which makes people feel good. Guests get up in the morning and come to the top floor to enjoy the grandeur of the central mountains. The white clouds that float across the mountain every day are as soft as the Sweet Cotton Candy. Guests could enjoy the sweetness of Hualien from this homestay.

Through the host's "narrative" story at Wechat with a large number of pictures rendering, this homestay accurately convey a "hope every visitor has a happy experience" brand concept to guests. In addition, the owner of the homestay cited the visitors' comments on booking.com, so that visitors can have a sense of trust in the homestay and be sure that they would have a good experience after checking in.

With product service as the starting point, Sweet Cotton Candy launched the story marketing and cooperated with the consumer's experience story to correctly shape its brand image of "warmth", "happiness" and "original ecology". This image is consistent with the overall image of Hualien tourism, which has added value to customers seeking the original ecology and good life, and is willing to pay for it.

Figure 3 Sweet Cotton Candy in Booking

Source: https://www.booking.com/814df4344d54e07ce.

However, we believe that this storytelling marketing of Sweet Cotton Candy has many shortcomings: In terms of story spread channel, the host chose WeChat circles of friend, which means that the tourists can only see the story once they become WeChat friends with the host after booking. This limits the spread of the story before booking and puts the storytelling marketing in a passive position.

Based on the analysis of the above three homestay cases, the following conclusions are drawn:

(1) Regardless of the type of story marketing, consumer stories, operator stories, brand growth stories and other types of story marketing, each homestay has its own specific theme, and the plots are based on the interpretation of the theme.

(2) A homestay should be able to accurately identify social media usage habits in target market and choose social media channels.

(3) The story should be able to reflect the characteristics of home stay facility, advantages, service quality, etc. When necessary, in addition to texts, pictures should be provided to intuitively show the homestay's accommodation and living environment, let visitors to obtain relevant information effectively.

(4) Stories of other customers have a great impact on consumer decisions. Consumers are easily attracted by the warm and beautiful travel stories described by customers, so hosts should pay close attention to the customers' evaluation after their trips.

(5) Visitors are also interested in the story of operators and the foundation of the brands.

If the operators are well known in social media, or has some talent, or has the common interest with the tourists, visitors will have a favourable impression of the operators, which will result in the desire to spend in the homestay.

(6) Homestay operators should pay attention to real-time interaction with consumers, and provide courteous, warm, thoughtful and effective online services to provide consumers with a good pre-purchase experience.

(7) The personalization of products and services can make a homestay stand out from the homogenization of this industry. Unique products can quickly attract consumers' attention.

Table 1 The Themes of Three Homestays' Stories

| Homestays | Story Themes | Atmosphere |
|---|---|---|
| Blossom Hill Inn | an inn out of the fantasy | freedom, misty |
| Desti Youth Park | a youthtel of bigger than bigger | freedom, happiness |
| Sweet Cotton Candy | another sweetness of Hualien | cosy, happiness |

*ii. In-depth interview with homestay operators and consumers*

From the above case studies, this research investigated how a story-telling marketing influences consumers' purchase intention, and summarized the experience of the story marketing of homestays, which provides background information for the in-depth interview. Next, interviews were conducted with the homestay operators and consumers respectively. The purpose is to find out more features of story marketing, which is useful to design a questionnaire survey in future.

According to the purpose of the interview, five interviewees from the homestay operators and consumers were selected. Among them, two interviewees are homestay owners who have rich experience in homestay operation. Not only do they have a good understanding of the homestay consumers, but also they have made a lot of efforts in story marketing. The other three interviewees are consumers, who have many experience in staying at homestays, and have a certain understanding of the development of the homestay industry.

Based on the interview, this study preliminarily learned the behavioural characteristics of homestay guests during their trip, and summarized as follows:

(1) When making accommodation decisions before the trip, quiet, neatness, and traffic are the main factors which tourists consider most. In addition, the interview also found that some tourists have considerable attention to the comfort of both the bathroom and the bed in the room.

(2) Consumers mainly use social media to search information for homestays. With

the development of online travel agents (OTA), as well as the popularity of tourism guide websites, tourists get the information they need mostly through online channels especially travel guides, and tourist reviews in OTA websites. In addition, the offline channels for consumers to know about homestays are mainly recommendation by friends and relatives, which have a great impact on consumers' decision-making.

(3) Young people are the main market for homestay, with medium-level income and well education. They not only enjoy the process of interacting with others during the journey, but also pay attention to the cultural experience, and be willing to be evolved in the local community. Living in homestays has become the best experience in their journey.

(4) Homestay customers mainly travel with friends, lovers, or by individual. Due to the restrictions on accommodation conditions, most homestays are unable to provide a suitable environment comparing with the standard hotels, so the majority of the guests are mainly the young tourists who concern more on the emotional experience than physical conditions.

(5) Tourists who have booked their homes through WeChat and Weibo will consult with the homestay operators before their trips. Operators' opinions and suggestions will have a certain impact on the tourists' travel plans.

According to the interviews with homestay operators, this study summarized information about homestay storytelling marketing as follows.

(1) Operators usually arrange a dedicated staff to manage the room reservation system based on the personnel allocation.

(2) At present, homestays are mainly publish information via online travel websites for consumers to book. In addition, considering the diversified reservation channels, Weibo and WeChat have also become their booking channels.

(3) The interviewees are all willing to share, so they are more or less engaged in story marketing, communicating with potential consumers in the form of "telling stories".

(4) The interviewees said that in their opinions, the story of a homestay has a certain influence on the consumers, and the guests will actively learn about the homestay with the host during their stay.

(5) In the process of story marketing, the operators found stories told in the perspective of consumers more attractive to consumers. Stories telling by the consumer perspective could establish the word of mouth among consumers, because consumers will feel the story is very objective, then believe the information is more credible.

(6) When telling stories from the angle of the operators, if the operators have a certain reputation, the story also have certain influence to consumers. In addition, some well-known figures in the circle of tourists and other tourist professionals also have an influence on tourists.

From consumers' point of view, it can be concluded that:

(1) The brand and reputation of the hotel have a greater impact on the purchasing

decision of the consumer, which is reflected on the feedback of the visitors who have visited. Consumers are more willing to choose homestays having good reputation by friends or online evaluation.

(2) The channels for consumers to know the information about homestays are mainly online recommendation and recommendation of friends. Online recommendation is mainly from travel blogs.

(3) The interviewee said they would pay attention to the stories of homestays. These stories were mainly from the popular travel blogs and the recommendation by online opinion leaders, or WeChat and Weibo homepages operated by homestays. They claimed that whether there is a story in homestays will have a certain impact on their purchasing decisions.

(4) If as homestay is to adopt the story marketing, the interviewees said that it will be more attractive telling a story from the perspectives of corporate culture or consumers.

(5) Interviewees confirmed that if they had a good experience in a homestay, after their travelling, they would spread the story of the homestay through WeChat, Weibo and other travel blog websites.

## V. Conclusions

This research finds empirical evidence for homestay storytelling marketing. First, regardless of the storyline types, such as operator story, consumer story, or brand growth story, each homestay has its own specific theme which story interpretations are based on. Second, all stories are able to reflect the features, advantages, service quality and other aspects of homestays, so that consumers could get useful information from the story. Third, customer stories in homestays have a great influence on other consumers' decision-making as they are very attracted to the sweet and beautiful travel stories posted by consumers. In addition, homestay consumers are also very interested in the stories of operators, especially those enjoy high exposure profiles in social media. Also, consumers would appreciate those operators who are talented, or have common interests with them, and then would be stirred the desire to visit the homestays.

This paper presents the storytelling marketing of homestays via Chinese social media, focusing on how they told stories with their consumers and what inspired the audience to travel. Therefore, the paper will contribute to a broader understanding of story-induced homestay travel in an increasingly networked world. This research suggests the following marketing strategies of homestay stories.

(1) Finding a definite target market and telling one story at one time.

According to the case analysis and interviews, this research found that a definite target in the market can help the homestays to save much energy, comparing with the mass marketing strategy. Clear market positioning can help homestay marketing. Although stories could be told from different angles, these stories need to be around a theme. In this way, the unified image of a homestay can be shaped, and the brand value of a homestay is accurately expressed. If a brand tells different stories, consumers may lose faith in them, which will also cause the confusion of brand positioning.

"One story at one time" does not mean that there is only one story version, but that each story should keep a consistent theme. The design of the story conveys the core value of the brand, which is reflected in the theme of the story. The lack of a theme in story marketing can easily be drowned out in thousands of messages and ignored by audience. The attraction of the homestay is that each marketing is centered on the motif, giving the brand an impressive image in the eyes of consumers.

(2) Making use of the social media and controlling the right of information dissemination.

First, the target customers' favored new media channels should be identified. Weibo, WeChat, BBS forum are the common platforms people use to search for the information of homestays. Energy could be saved if homestays put their information on these platforms. Secondly, the rhythm of story marketing needs to be identified. Since the audience is concentrate in the young groups and the attention of these people generally do not remain too long, so the story of the arrangement should be compacted and intuitive, which is acceptable by the audience. Besides, the story marketing should avoid strong commercial atmosphere. The process for audience to accept the value of the brand is subtle. It will be easy to cause the antipathy if the brand's concept is straightforward to the audience. Finally, the story should be able to cause the conversation among consumers, so that they have more opportunities to participate in the discussion. It can also be spread by the power of opinion leaders to gain a wider reputation. People's herd behavior would be aroused and then the homestays get a better publicity effect.

(3) Creating a local atmosphere and inspiring visitors to explore.

This study suggests that the local cultural atmosphere should be set up in story marketing, based on the finding that the most important reason for consumers to choose a homestay is to integrate into local life and contact local culture. The plots deduction should inspire the potential guests' emotional resonance and then make them to explore more in the destination. In addition, as the pursuits of individuality and novelty are also important reasons for tourists to visit a homestay, the personalized decoration style of a homestay should not be ignored in story marketing. During the guests' stay in the homestay, hosts should let them experience the local authentic service face to face. In addition to the in-room experience such as tasting local specialties, the hosts could provide the services such as tour guides and instructors in nature hikes and bike excursions to nearby areas, food and drink tastings, and events available for guests to take part in.

This research also suggests the following design strategies for homestays in terms of the stories.

(1) Sticking to the basic principle: authenticity and integrity.

The design of the story should avoid exaggeration or absolute fiction, which could lead to excessive expectations of consumers. If consumers' field experience is far from their expected value, it is not conducive to the establishment and dissemination of brand reputation. In addition, the integrity of the story does not mean a story must have the six elements of the narration: the cause, the process, the result, the time, the place and the character/characters, but means that the story can contain and convey the brand's core value. [23] It can be a description, or a sentence.

(2) Using diversified ways to make stories interesting.

Consumers also pay attention to the enjoyment of the story. They are interested not only in the story itself, but also in helping to spread it. The form of story should be diversified, which can be either traditional words or dictation, or pictures, video, music, etc. In China, different social media platforms offer different forms of story communication. For example, a piece of music could be embedded within a travel blog in Mafengwo.com. Using pictures and music matching the storyline, it could not only attract people's interest in reading stories online, but also spread and share the story easily.

(3) Leaving some room for imagination.

Shankar et al. [4] believes that the story ought to leave some room for imagination by the audience, letting them build their own stories, so as to maximize the power of the story. In the same way, the brand story narration should give consumers space for imagination. Consumers use brand stories to explain their consumption and even the meaning of life. They identify with the values of the story, imagining they enter the story, and become a part of the story.

In summary, this study explores the impact of story marketing on the brand image of homestays, which not only can be used by homestay practitioners, some conclusions can also be helpful for story marketing of other industries. This research would also provide valuable literature reference in the field of tourism marketing.

## Ⅵ. Limitation and Future Study

There are some shortcomings of this study because of the limitations of the investigation: (1) the limitations of the sampling. Generalizations about the results of this research are usually not able to be made due to the small samples chosen and random sampling method. (2) The in-depth interview was conducted via the internet, so it was impossible to know whether the interviewees were comfortable and not distracted by other things. In the future, quantitative research methods such as experiment method and questionnaire survey can be carried out to investigate storytelling marketing. The power of user-generated content will exceed the content generated by the brand and the importance of online reviews of travel experiences is increasing. As a response to this trend, future study should pay attention to the co-creation of storytelling between brands and consumers.

## ACKNOWLEDGMENT

We acknowledge the Fundamental Research Funds for the Central Universities (NO.2015ZCQ-YL-04) for supporting this research.

## References

[1] Meadin Tourism Academy. The evaluation report on the development of Chinese homestays in September 2016[EB/OL]. Retrieved March 3rd, 2017 from: http://res.meadin.com/IndustryReport/134697_1.shtml.

[2] Dan P, Allen D. Communicating experiences: a narrative approach to creating service brand image[J]. *Journal of Advertising*, 1997, 26(4): 49-62.

[3] Li J & Hu H. Story marketing on the Internet[J]. *News World*, 08: 282-283.

[4] Shankar A, Elliott R, Goulding C. Understanding consumption: contributions from a narrative perspective[J]. *Journal of Marketing Management*, 2001, 17(17): 429-453.

[5] Stern A. Interactive fiction: the story is just beginning[J]. *IEEE Expert*, 1998, 13(6).

[6] Denning S. *Leader's Guide to Storytelling*[M]. Wiley & Sons, 2010.

[7] Godin S. *Purple Cow: Transform Your Business by Being Remarkable*[M]. Penguin General UK, 2003.

[8] Su, Y. Brand story marketing model and its components[J]. *Journal of Chongqing University of Science and Technology (Social Science Edition)*, 2013, 04: 119-121. (in Chinese)

[9] Padgett D, Allen D. Communicating experiences: A narrative approach to creating service brand image[J]. *Journal of Advertising*, 1997, 26:49-62.

[10] Sun, Y. How to use story marketing communication?[J] *Sales and Marketing (Management Version)*, 2009, 06: 41-43. (in Chinese)

[11] Escalas J E, Stern B B. Sympathy and empathy: Emotional responses to advertising dramas[J]. *Journal of Consumer Research*, 2003, 29(4): 566-578.

[12] Holt D B. How brands become icons[J]. *Journal of Advertising Research, 2004,* 45(2): 282-283.

[13] Wachtman E, Johnson S. Discover your persuasive story[J]. *Marketing Management, 2009,* January/February: *29-34.*

[14] Woodside A G, Sood S, \Miller K E. When consumers and brands talk: storytelling theory and research in psychology and marketing[J]. *Psychology & Marketing*, 2008, 25(2): 97-145.

[15] Fournier S. Consumers and their brands: Developing relationship theory in consumer research[J]. *Journal of Consumer Research*, 1998, 24(4): 343-374.

[16] Arnould E J, Wallendorf M. Market-orientated ethnography: interpretation building and marketing strategy formulation[J]. *Journal of Marketing Research*, 1994, 31(4): 484-503.

[17] McKee R. Storytelling that moves people: A conversation with screenwriting coach, Robert McKee[J]. *Harvard Business Review*, 2003, 81(6): 51-55.

[18] Schank R C. *Tell Me a Story: A New Look at Real and Artificial Memory*[M]. Cambridge, U.K.: Cambridge University Press, 1990.

[19] Zaltman G. *How Customers Think*[M]. Boston: Harvard Business School Press, 2003.

[20] Bagozzi R, Nataraajan R. The year 2000: Looking forward[J]. *Psychology & Marketing*, 2000, 17: 1-11.

[21] Nataraajan R, Bagozzi R. The year 2000: Looking back[J]. *Psychology & Marketing*, 2000, 16: 631-642.

[22] Kozinets R V. The Field behind the Screen: Using Netnography for Marketing Research in Online Communities[J]. *Journal of Marketing Research*, 2002, 39 (1): 61-72.

[23] Vincent L. *Legendary brands: unleashing the power of storytelling to create a winning marketing strategy*[M]. Dearborn Trade Publishing, 2002.